TWENTIETH-CENTURY BRITAIN

TWENTIETH-CENTURY BRITAIN:

ECONOMIC, SOCIAL AND CULTURAL CHANGE

Edited by

Paul Johnson

LONGMAN
LONDON AND NEW YORK

Longman Group Limited
Longman House, Burnt Mill,
Harlow, Essex CM20 2JE
and Associated Companies throughout the world

*Published in the United States of America
by Longman Publishing, New York*

First published 1994

ISBN 0 582 22817 4 PPR

British Library Cataloguing-in-Publication Data

A catalogue record for this book is
available from the British Library

Library of Congress Cataloging-in-Publication Data

Twentieth-century Britain : economic, social, and cultural change /
  edited by Paul Johnson
    p.   cm.
  Includes bibliographical references and index.
  ISBN 0-582-22817-4 (pbk.)
  1. Great Britain–History–20th century.   I. Johnson, Paul, 1956–.
DA566.T84   1994
941.082–dc20   93-46674
                                                         CIP

Set by 7 in 10.5/12.5 Baskerville
Produced by Longman Singapore Publishers (Pte) Ltd.
Printed in Singapore

Contents

List of Illustrations

List of Figures

List of Tables

Acknowledgements

The publishers would like to thank the following for their permission to reproduce illustrative material: Newcastle upon Tyne City Libraries & Arts for plate 1.1; London Borough of Hackney, © LSE Housing, for plate 1.2; © Museum in Docklands Project for plate 2.1; the British Library of Political & Economic Science for plate 2.2 (col. misc. 519); Ford Motor Company Limited for plates 3.1 and 3.2; BEAMISH, The North of England Open Air Museum, County Durham for plate 4.1; Merseyside Record Office for plate 5.1; © Museum of London for plates 5.2, 6.1, 6.2 and 8.2; © the Board of Trustees of the Victoria & Albert Museum and Theatre Museum for plate 7.1; The Illustrated London News Picture Library for plate 7.2; © The Scout Association for plate 8.1; Imperial War Museum for plate 9.1; © The Estate of Mrs J.C. Robinson (the Museum of London) for plate 10.1; EMI Music Archives for plate 11.1; © The British Library for plates 12.1 and 14.1; the National Museum of Labour History (the Hulton Deutsch Collection Limited) for plate 12.1; © Mail Newspapers Plc (Solo Syndication and Literary Agency Limited) for plate 13.1; Punch for plates 13.2, 17.1, 21.2; © BBC for plate 15.1; Lumière Pictures Limited for plate 15.2; © Popperfoto for plates 16.1, 16.2, 26.1 and 26.2; Barnaby's Picture Library for plate 18.1; the Electricity Association for plate 18.2; Saatchi & Saatchi Advertising for plate 19.1; © the *Sun* (the British Library) for plate 20.1; *Evening Standard*/Solo Syndication and Literary Agency Limited (the Centre for the Study of Cartoons and Caracature, University of Kent at Canterbury) for plate 20.2; the Controller of Her Majesty's Stationery Office and the Syndics of Cambridge University Library for plate 21.1 (from the Ministry of Education Pamphlet No. 9, *The New Secondary Education*, 1947); © *Woman's Own* (the British Library) for plates 22.1 and 22.2; Charlie Phillips and Lawrence & Wishart Ltd for plates 23.1 and 23.2 (from *Notting Hill in the Sixties*, London, 1991); the Open University for plate 24.1; © Mark Simmons 1993 for plate 24.2; © Greenpeace/Hodson for plate 25.1; © CND/Udo Hoffmann for plate 25.2; the Controller of Her Majesty's Stationery Office for plate 27.1; the Liverpool Record Office, Local History Department, for plate 27.2.

The publishers would also like to thank the copyright holders of the following tables and figures for permission to reproduce their material: Cambridge University Press and Dr C.H. Feinstein for table 12.1 from C.H. Feinstein, *Statistical Tables of National Income, Expenditure and Output of the United Kingdom, 1855–1965* (1972); Central Statistical Office for table 20.5 from *Social Trends* 23; Blackwell Publishers for table 22.1 from Jane Lewis, *Women in Britain since 1945* (1992); Liverpool University Press for figure 2.1 from S.B. Saul, *Studies in British Overseas Trade 1870–1914* (1960); Nicholas Barr for figure 18.4 from *LSE Quarterly* vol. 4 (1988); Blackwell Publishers for figure 22.1 from H. Joshi (ed.), *The Changing Population of Britain* (1989); the Controller of Her Majesty's Stationery Office for figure 22.2 which is Crown copyright.

1 Introduction: Britain, 1900–1990

Paul Johnson

More than ninety years of almost continuous economic growth have made Britain today a much wealthier, more comfortable place to live than it was in 1900. Despite the manifest achievements of the Victorian age – the majestic engineering of the railway builders, the economic pre-eminence of industrialists and financiers, the global dominance of an imperial navy – daily life for most of Victoria's subjects was, by modern standards, pretty grim. If sick they could resort to a multitude of patent medicines (such as Dr John Collis Browne's opiate-based 'chlorodyne') but until the development of sulphonamide drugs in the 1930s and penicillin during the Second World War, doctors could do little to cure illness other than recommend rest and a good diet. If lucky enough to live into old age – and barely half of twenty year olds in 1900 could expect to survive to the age of sixty-five – they faced the prospect of dependence on a semi-punitive Poor Law. If young they also faced the prospect of poverty. Research by the pioneering social investigator Seebohm Rowntree in 1899 indicated that many, perhaps most, working-class families endured a period of below-subsistence income when children were young.[1] And the majority of healthy adults experienced a life of hard and heavy manual labour, whether in the primary (agriculture and mining) and manufacturing sectors in which 60 per cent of the workforce was employed, or in homes untouched by the labour saving amenities taken for granted today: fridges, washing machines, electric lights, central heating.

Without doubt there have been enormous improvements in average living standards since 1900 yet the economic history of Britain in the twentieth century is often presented as a history of failure, the period when Britain was transformed from being 'the workshop of the world' to 'the sick man of Europe'. In 1900 London was the world's capital city three times over – in political terms as the fulcrum of the British Empire, in commercial terms as the centre of banking and finance with sterling the dominant international currency, and in industrial terms as the largest port in the largest trading nation in the world. Today the Empire lives on only in the imagination of incurable romantics or political extremists, sterling rests on a par with the

Greek drachma and the Portuguese escudo in the order of economic weakness, and substantial contraction of the industrial sector in the 1980s and early 1990s has left Britain incapable of achieving a balance on its trading account even in the depths of a recession.

These divergent interpretations of twentieth-century history – of simultaneous improvement and decline – present something of a puzzle. Neither is obviously untrue, yet individually they are both inadequate and misleading. The historical record is too complex, too diverse, to be neatly pigeon-holed as success or failure. Judgements made depend upon the subject of study, on the method of analysis, on the criteria adopted for assessment, and on the ideological beliefs and preconceptions of different historians and social scientists. This chapter provides a survey of some of the more significant economic, social and cultural changes that have occurred in twentieth-century Britain in order to highlight reasons for the differing assessments made of this period of modern British history.

Economic Change, 1900–90

To assess the performance of the British economy since 1900 we first have to decide what level of economic activity we wish to examine and what criteria we wish to adopt to determine adequacy or inadequacy. A purely macro-economic approach uses aggregate measures of economic output, usually gross domestic product (GDP) per capita, to determine the average value or level of goods and services available for the population to use or consume. The faster GDP per capita increases, the faster is the rate of economic growth in society. As Table 1.1 shows, by this measure the country, and so the average Briton, had a real income 3.3 times greater in 1989 than in 1913, which represents a compound annual growth rate of just under 1.6 per cent. This is a very creditable performance if compared with the hey-day of the Victorian period when, despite Britain's unchallenged dominance of the international economy, GDP per capita grew at only 1 per cent per annum. But comparison of British data in Table 1.1 with that for other countries shows Britain in a less favourable light. Although twentieth-century performance has been good in relation to Britain's own past it has been poor relative to other major industrialized nations. Which is the more valid, or illuminating, comparison?

This depends on the extent to which countries are similarly endowed with economic resources. An assessment of the US and UK economies in 1900, for instance, does not compare like with like. The US was a large, sparsely-populated country with enormous reserves of land and raw materials, while the UK was densely populated, heavily urbanized, and dependent on imports for both a large part of her food supply and for many raw materials other than coal. The potential in America for further economic growth through the exploitation of natural resource endowments was clearly much greater than in

Table 1.1. Economic growth, 1870–1989

	GDP per capita ($ in 1985 relative prices)					
	1870	**1890**	**1913**	**1950**	**1973**	**1989**
UK	2,610	3,383	4,024	5,651	10,063	13,468
USA	2,247	3,101	4,854	8,611	14,103	18,317
France	1,571	1,955	2,734	4,149	10,323	13,837
Germany	1,300	1,660	2,606	3,339	10,110	13,989
Japan	618	842	1,114	1,563	9,237	15,101

	Growth of GDP per capita (% per annum)			
	1870–1913	**1913–50**	**1950–73**	**1973–89**
UK	1.0	0.8	2.5	1.8
USA	1.8	1.6	2.2	1.6
France	1.3	1.1	4.0	1.8
Germany	1.6	0.7	4.9	2.1
Japan	1.4	0.9	8.0	3.1

Source: A. Maddison, *Dynamic Forces in Capitalist Development* (Oxford, 1991) pp. 6–7, 49.

the UK, so it is not obvious that we should expect their growth rates to be similar in the early twentieth century. Among European countries with broadly similar resource endowments the natural constraints on growth were much more similar, so comparison of relative economic achievement is more illuminating. It should be pointed out, however, that the contribution of physical factor endowments to national economic performance has declined over time as transport costs have fallen. Today Britain's extensive coal reserves are of practically no economic consequence as it is cheaper to import coal mined in Australia. Cheap transport and the internationalization of commodity markets now result in nearly all countries facing the same raw material prices.

Nevertheless, British economic performance does appear to be lacklustre when compared to her European competitors, even in the 1950s and 1960s when the country achieved its highest ever rate of recorded economic growth. The slower growth in Britain after the Second World War was not the result of resources standing idly by – the economy was working flat out and unemployment dipped to trivial levels of 1–2 per cent in the 1950s. The difference between Britain and other European countries was that Britain did not enjoy the same improvements in the efficiency of resource utilization – in other words, its rate of productivity growth was slower. Many explanations have been proposed for this relatively poor twentieth-century productivity performance. Overcommitment to old-fashioned industries, an overvalued exchange rate, the lack of tariff protection, the power of organized labour, a shortage of capital, or of scientists, or of entrepreneurs are among the hypotheses discussed in the following chapters. But none of these explanations seems adequate; there are too many historical counter-examples of countries or industries or firms which have faced similar barriers to success but which have succeeded nonetheless.

The difficulty of determining the roots of economic success or failure derives in part from our lack of understanding of the way in which complex economies work. In the 1950s and 1960s most economists believed that theoretical models based on the ideas of the British economist J.M. Keynes (discussed in Chapter 11) gave them real insight into the working of the macro-economic machine. In fact they even used a hydraulic model of the economy in which coloured water was pumped around perspex tubes to show how the system worked and how economic 'errors' such as inflation could be easily corrected (see Chapter 18). The advent of inflation together with high levels of unemployment in the 1970s – an impossibility in a simple Keynesian economy – demonstrated that existing macro-economic models were inadequate. An alternative economic faith – monetarism – was tried in the early 1980s, but this also failed. The scourge of inflation was supposed to be eradicated by strict control of the money supply; once price stability was regained, confidence, investment and economic growth would all return. In practice inflation took a path quite independent of the amount of money in the economy, and investment fluctuated without reference to the inflation rate. In the 1990s macro-economics is in a sorry state. Sophisticated computer models of the economy have replaced the coloured water and perspex tubes, but these models repeatedly fail to predict the course of the economy for even twelve months ahead. Reading the signs in the tea leaves might be almost as good.

Even comparative explanations of modern macro-economic performance seem rather barren. Careful models have been constructed to show why the performance of similar economies should converge, why the laggards should catch up with the leaders. Yet the long-run historical record of Britain, and the shorter-run history of the relative economic performance of countries in the European Community, give little support to the concepts of convergence and catch-up. Over the twentieth century Britain has fallen down the international league table of economic performance. In 1890 British GDP per capita was the highest in Europe and still exceeded that of the US. By 1913 America had pulled ahead but average income levels in Britain far exceeded those in the rest of Europe. By 1989 Britain still lagged behind the US but now came behind not only France and Germany but also Denmark, Finland, Norway, Sweden and Switzerland in a European ranking of average income per capita.

Macro-economic performance has clearly been poor by international standards, but whether it could have been improved substantially still remains an open question, as the chapters below show.

If instead of looking at macro-economic performance we examine the growth record of separate parts of the economy we see a different and more varied picture. Some sectors have experienced devastating long-term decline which has imposed substantial adjustment costs on both workers and owners of capital. In 1900 over a million men worked in the mining industry and employment was expanding; by 1993 only 40,000 remained in the industry, and they faced uncertain job prospects. Shipbuilding, steelmaking, cotton-spinning – the other late Victorian 'staple industries' – all endured a similar demise as Britain lost her comparative advantage in these sectors first to North America and Europe, then to Japan, and then to Korea and other newly industrialized nations.

Yet some 'traditional' sectors have maintained a significant presence in the British economy by undergoing enormous internal change. This is best demonstrated by the case of agriculture which is now a highly mechanized, highly capitalized and very efficient industry. The proportion of the workforce engaged in agriculture, forestry and fishing has dwindled from the already low level of 13 per cent in 1901 to just 2 per cent in 1991, yet labour productivity and output per acre have increased so much that the country produces an excess of a wide range of foodstuffs. European Community agricultural policy now encourages farmers to leave land fallow and restricts output with production quotas in order artificially to reduce productivity. Though European food mountains are in part a consequence of the bizarre incentive structure of the Common Agricultural Policy, they also demonstrate how far twentieth-century mechanization, technology and organizational change have been able to boost farming productivity.

The counterpart to the decline of the staple industries has been the absolute and relative expansion of the service sector, which by 1971 accounted for 54 per cent of the workforce, compared with 39 per cent in 1901. This increase in the number of white collar jobs over the last ninety years has created unprecedented opportunities for upward occupational mobility as many people from blue collar families have themselves moved into white collar employment. Not only are wages on average higher in white collar than blue collar work, but employment conditions (hours of work, holidays, sick-pay entitlements) are better and job-security greater. Even in blue collar work in the manufacturing sector, in engineering for instance, there have been profound changes in the nature of employment. Many of the old craft skills needed to use lathe or metal press have been replaced by new skills in the operation of numerically-controlled machine tools. The design work formerly carried out by draughtsman and pattern-maker can now be done with CAD software and a microcomputer. People with old skills who have been unable or unwilling to retrain have suffered from these changes in the nature of work, but for younger labour market entrants there have been many opportunities for high earnings. Yet the economic rewards for particular skills in specific sectors have not evolved along any simple linear path. As we will show below, the experience of each worker in the labour market has depended crucially on the luck of being born at the right time.

A third way to view economic change since 1900 is from the perspective of individuals and their living standards. Although the economy overall has been sluggish, and although some sectors have contracted, Table 1.2 shows that average living standards have improved substantially. In 1914, the average weekly earnings of a semi-skilled manual worker were around £1 6s 8d (£1.33), whereas in 1978 the equivalent sum was £73.60 and in 1991, £235. There has, of course, been an enormous degree of price inflation over the intervening years – a retail price index standing at 100 in 1914 had risen to 3,302 by 1991. If the 1914 income figure is converted into 1991 prices, it stands at £44 compared with the actual 1991 figure of £235 – in other words, average real earnings for male manual workers have risen more than five-fold over the course of the twentieth century, and practically no full-time workers now have real earnings as low as the *average* in 1914; even juveniles had average earnings of around £100 per week in 1991. The final column of Table 1.2 shows that this increase in average real incomes for manual workers has been more or less continual, even during the depressed interwar years.[2]

Table 1.2. Average earnings for an adult male semi-skilled manual worker

	Average weekly wage				Average annual wage (£)	Retail Price Index 1913 = 100	Average annual wage in 1913 prices (£)
	£	s	d	£ p			
1913–14	1	6	8	1.33	69	100	69
1922–24	2	8	5	2.42	126	174	72
1935–36	2	11	6	2.58	134	142	94
1955–56	9	0	5	9.02	469	11	51
1960	11	3	5	11.17	581	331	76
1970	24	15	9	24.79	1,289	485	266
1978		–		73.60	3,827	1,324	289
1991		–		235.00	12,220	3,302	370

Note: The currency in the UK was decimalized in 1971, from which date the pound has been divided into 100 new pence (p). Before 1971 each pound was divided into shillings (s) and pence (d). There were twenty shillings to the pound and twelve pence to the shilling (and so 240 pence to the pound). The first column of the table gives average weekly earnings in pre-decimal denominations, the second column gives the decimal equivalent.

Sources: G. Routh, *Occupation and Pay in Great Britain 1906–1979* (London, 1980) pp. 120–1; Central Statistical Office, *Retail Prices 1914–1990* (London, 1991) Tables 1, 84; Department of Employment, *New Earnings Survey, 1991* (London, 1991) Part A, Table 15.

Average income figures can be very misleading if the underlying distribution of income changes over time – an increase in average income can be consistent with the rich getting richer and the poor getting poorer. However, a comparison of average real earnings in low skill/low pay occupations shows a similar picture to the average for all male earnings – for instance, a five-fold increase between 1914 and 1991 in real incomes for agricultural labourers. The same is true for people who have been reliant on public welfare payments owing to sickness, disability, unemployment or old age. Although substantial changes in the administrative structure of the social welfare system since the Edwardian period mean that not all types of benefit have followed an identical path, there is nevertheless a long-run consistency in their value relative to real earnings. Atkinson has noted:

> there has been a tendency over the century for benefits to rise at least as fast as average net earnings. Those on benefits have shared in rising national prosperity. In the case of the unemployed, National Insurance benefit has declined relative to net average earnings since the mid-1980s, but it is still the case that in April 1989 it represented 22% of net earnings for a person at the average for *manual workers* (not *all* workers), or virtually the same as in 1948 – and also in 1911 when unemployment insurance was introduced. In the case of the retirement pension, there has been a distinct improvement over the century.[3]

Some households, of course, continue to have very low incomes; a single pensioner wholly dependent on the state pension in 1991 had a weekly income of only £52, and in 1987 25 per cent of pensioner households, 58 per cent of single parent households and 59 per cent of unemployed households had incomes less than half of average household disposable income. The point is not that welfare benefits are generous (they clearly are not), but that even the low paid and welfare recipients have benefited from the twentieth-century increase in real income.

Since 1913, when she ranked second only to the United States among the industrialized nations in terms of average income per capita, Britain has been slowly but consistently slipping down the international league table of economic well-being. Yet even so the real living standards of the population have increased substantially as is shown by measures of rising life expectancy, rising levels of education and falling hours of work, as well as by the more narrowly economic criteria of income and wealth. Whether Britain has performed below her economic potential in the twentieth century, and if so for what reason or reasons, remains a matter of speculation for economists and historians alike. But one thing is clear – few Britons would wish to forego the material benefits of a century of almost continuous economic growth.

In focus: Why it Pays to be Born at the Right Time

The long-run improvement over the twentieth century in real incomes does not necessarily mean that economic conditions have improved steadily for each successive generation. Within the general trend there has been considerable short-term variation, and comparatively brief economic downturns in the economy as a whole or in particular sectors can have significant long-run effects on the economic life-histories of certain groups. This is the case because initial job choice and training tends to lock people in to a type of employment from which it is often difficult to move later in life. The fortune of birth, therefore, is as much a question of when someone is born as the type of family they are born into.

We can see this by examining the early employment experiences of four different generations (or birth cohorts) of boys and girls born in 1900, 1925, 1950 and 1975. The majority of the 1900 birth cohort left elementary school at the age of 14, just at the beginning of the First World War. The enlistment of millions of men in the armed forces (two million had volunteered by 1916, and over five million served in the army over the entire 1914–18 period) created a great demand for civilian labour. In the years before the war youth unemployment had been perceived as a serious social problem, but by 1915 there was work for all who wanted it, and new opportunities for girls to avoid domestic service by taking jobs in manufacturing or the service sector (see Chapter 9). By their late teens, however, the generation of 1900 faced less bright prospects. At 18 men were conscripted into the army to fight in the closing but very bloody stages of the war. Demobilization in 1919 saw women being replaced by ex-soldiers in many of the less traditional employments they had entered during the war, but when the postwar boom ended abruptly in 1921, many men of the generation of 1900 faced unemployment just as they were about to start earning full adult wages (usually paid from the age of twenty-one). For those who were lucky enough to remain fully employed during the 1920s and 1930s, this was a time of rising living standards, but most manual workers, even those employed in highly successful companies such as Morris Motors at Cowley, faced repeated periods of unemployment or short-time working. In many respects, therefore, the birth cohort of 1900 was an unlucky generation, with limited prospects of building a good career as young adults.

Not so those born in 1925. Early teenage experiences were remarkably similar to those of the 1900 birth cohort – leaving school in the first year of a war, entering a youth labour market that offered plenty of choice and fairly high wages for both boys and girls (though rationing restricted spending opportunities), service in the armed forces for men aged eighteen. But postwar employment opportunities were very different from those of 1918. Although many young women left employment after the war to raise families (see Chapter 22), there was no marked contraction of female job opportunities, partly because the postwar boom this time lasted for more

Why it Pays to be Born at the Right Time (continued)

than two decades rather than just two years. For the generation of 1925, the peak earning years from their early twenties to their mid forties coincided with the most sustained period of full employment and rapid economic growth in modern British history.

The two postwar generations have also had diverse experiences. The birth cohort of 1950 began to leave school at the age of fifteen and entered a still buoyant labour market, though the rapid expansion of higher education in the early 1960s meant that a growing number of (mainly middle-class) children stayed on at school to the age of eighteen, took 'A' levels and entered university at a time when the interests of the young seemed to dominate. The year 1968 saw student protests in Grosvenor Square against the Vietnam War, the opening on the London stage of the musical *Hair* with its celebration of sex, drugs and nudity, and the first birthday of the BBC's youth radio station, Radio 1 (see Chapter 26). The generation of 1975, by contrast, began to leave school (at a minimum age of sixteen) in 1991 into a thoroughly depressed labour market in which many young people found no alternative to low-quality youth training schemes followed by unemployment. In just twenty-five years the golden aura of youth had become tarnished.

Social and Cultural Change

Although the benefits of twentieth-century economic growth are readily apparent and unlikely to be willingly sacrificed, many of the accompanying social and cultural changes have been judged less positively. A nostalgia for 'the good old days' – when family values reigned, when neighbours would always do a good turn for each other, when you could leave your front door unlocked, when policemen and teachers were respected and children were obedient – runs deeply through modern society. Perhaps this is not surprising in a country in which institutionalized nostalgia in the form of the tourist industry is a major employer and one of the biggest earners of foreign currency. It reflects a longing for some lost Arcadia in which the competitive pressures of the modern world are absent and where gentler, more communal, values live on. But the good old days were less rosy for many of those who experienced them than for those who now imagine them.

British society in 1900 was sharply divided along class and gender lines. Women were, in a quite unambiguous sense, second-class citizens since it was not until 1918 that they could vote in parliamentary elections. Although the majority of adult male manual workers did have the vote by the late nineteenth century, they were expected to be spectators to a parliamentary game pursued by a Tory and Liberal elite. The embryonic Labour Party was formed in 1900 (until 1906 operating under the name of the Labour

Representation Committee) and the 1906 General Election saw thirty Labour MPs elected, but they were reliant on their sponsoring trade unions and socialist societies for financial support. It was not until 1911 that the cosy amateurism of affluent backbenchers was disturbed by the payment of a salary to MPs.

Although belief in self-help as the path to social and economic preferment was deeply entrenched in Victorian society, in the labour movement as much as in the middle class, in practice the opportunities for social mobility in Britain in 1900 were strictly circumscribed. Few working-class children managed to continue their education beyond the age of fourteen, and although there was an expansion in the number of grammar school scholarships available in the interwar years, it was middle-class children who took most advantage of the opportunity to stay on at school, just as it has been middle-class children who have benefited most from the expansion of higher education since the early 1960s. Educational achievement has been a potent force for social and occupational mobility in twentieth-century Britain, particularly since the Second World War, but the children of manual workers have never managed to gain their fair shares in an expanding educational system.

The class and gender-structured status quo was certainly not meekly accepted by everyone in Edwardian Britain. Militant suffragettes and moderate suffragists campaigned not only for the political enfranchisement of women but for an opening-up of female employment opportunities beyond the 'traditional' sectors of domestic service, textiles and clothing, for improved maternity and infant welfare services, for better education and information about birth control, and for a decent 'family wage'. Socialist societies argued for an equalization of income and wealth, and in 1918 the Labour Party committed itself to the ideal of public ownership of the means of production, distribution and exchange. Most trade unions, however, concerned themselves with the more mundane affairs of raising the wages and preserving the jobs of their members. There was never any popular challenge to the legitimacy of the elected government, not even during the upsurge of industrial militancy just before the First World War or during the short-lived General Strike of 1926.

No doubt the relatively high living standard in Britain and the prospect of economic improvement even within a class-structured society contributed to the political tranquillity. Rising real incomes gave people the means to participate in new forms of leisure and recreation, and a shortening of the average working week (from 54 hours before the First World War to 48 hours by 1920 and 40 hours by the mid 1960s) gave them the opportunity. The Edwardian music hall and the 1930s Odeon and Gaumont cinemas were contemporary dream worlds where the harsher realities of life could be laughed at or forgotten. The interwar cinemas marked a decisive democratization of popular culture, since the (mainly American) films were watched by an audience drawn from across the social classes. In the 1950s television broadcasting began to bring entertainment directly into the home, and the rapid spread of TV ownership (by 1963, 82 per cent of households possessed a TV) has contributed further to the creation of a common culture. The TV set is as much a necessity in an aristocratic mansion as in a council flat, and programmes are as likely to feature labourers as lords.

The role of economic improvement in lessening class differentials in Britain should not be overstated; statistical measures of the distribution of income indicate that it is no more equally spread today than it was in the late 1940s. However the overall increase in the average level of income has greatly enhanced the ability of working-class households to purchase non-essentials. In the 1880s about half of working-class income was spent on foodstuffs. By the 1930s this had fallen to around 40 per cent, and by the mid 1980s it was no more than 25 per cent even in low-income households. The nutritional status of the population improved at the same time as expenditure on clothing, entertainment, consumer durables, transport and holidays increased. In addition, technological advances and productivity improvements have substantially reduced the real cost of many of these items, further increasing their availability. In 1935, for instance, a Hotpoint electric kettle cost £1 6s 6d, or about half the weekly income of a semi-skilled manual worker, whereas in 1991 a typical kettle (much better designed and made than the 1935 version) cost little more than 5 per cent of a weekly wage. The temporary interruption in the early 1970s of electrical power and petrol supplies by a series of strikes by mining, electricity and oil company employees provided a very inconvenient reminder of how dependent we have become on twentieth-century consumer durables.

Life without these modern conveniences is hard and uncomfortable, but consumerism has involved costs as well as benefits. Growing concern in the 1980s with the health of the environment has seen cars viewed as polluters and roads as despoilers of the environment. This is a far cry from 1958 when the opening of Britain's first stretch of motorway (eight miles of the Preston bypass, now part of the M6) heralded a new age of motoring for the masses. Even then, however, some of the costs of widespread car ownership and use were becoming apparent; 1958 also saw the first parking meters introduced in London in an attempt to ration scarce parking places.

Television has also been blamed for a host of social evils – killing the art of conversation, making children idle and unhealthy, promoting violence and sexual promiscuity, undermining traditional family activities and thereby leading to the fragmentation of family life. The evidence is ambiguous. Certainly TV has had a tremendous impact on patterns of recreation since the 1950s, but it is as easy to point to positive as to negative outcomes. It has made people better informed, created as many opportunities for conversation as it has destroyed and provided a focal point within the home for family entertainment. Television programmes discuss sexual activity more openly today than thirty years ago, but so do clergymen, politicians, teachers, journalists, actors, advertisers and members of the Women's Institute. Television reflects and follows social and cultural trends as much as it directs them.

Other doubts about social and cultural changes relate less to the physical artifacts of twentieth-century life than to the nature of interpersonal relationships. Since 1900 family structures have changed and, according to recent pronouncements by some government ministers, family values are in decline. Rates of divorce and the proportion of children born to single or unmarried parents have risen sharply since the early 1970s, but it is not clear how this has affected the nurturing role of the family. There is no evidence that children are less loved or cared for today than they were at the beginning of the century. In fact the fall in average family size since the late nineteenth century may have increased the amount of parental attention received by each child while improvements in housing conditions have created more comfortable domestic environments. Families continue to be the primary providers of care, as they always have been. As the population has aged over the twentieth century (fewer than 5 per cent of Britons were aged over sixty-five in 1901, compared with over 15 per cent in 1985), additional responsibilities have been assumed for the care of elderly relatives. It has been estimated that in 1987 the value of this informal care for the elderly and

Plate 1.1. Sandgate, Newcastle in 1897. The physical conditions of life in overcrowded city slums were poor, but residents often had a strong sense of community. The street was an extension of the home – a place for neighbours to chat and children to play.

disabled was six times greater than all public provision by the personal social services. The fact that family structures are changing cannot be taken to imply that family values are in decline.

A second lament is that social life has become less cohesive over the twentieth century as traditional communities have been weakened by urbanization, geographical mobility, slum-clearance and rehousing schemes, immigration, and by a retreat into selfish individualism. It must be remembered, of course, that by the beginning of the twentieth century Britain was no longer some rural idyll; almost 20 per cent of people lived in Greater London and a further 20 per cent in the six next largest conurbations. But much of the perceived change in community life has occurred within these urban areas. In an influential study of family and community life in east London after the Second World War, Michael Young and Peter Willmott recorded the destabilizing effect of suburban rehousing schemes on a tight-knit working-class community in which mothers lived close to their married daughters, where neighbours provided extensive informal support for each other, and in which the local corner-shop or pub served as community centre, advice bureau and labour exchange rolled into one.[4] This is a world that flourishes now only in the TV soap operas of *Coronation Street* and *EastEnders*. There is some doubt as to how representative and 'traditional' was

Plate 1.2. Tower Blocks in the London borough of Hackney. Housing designers in the 1960s aimed to build 'streets in the sky'; instead they produced vertical slums. Many 1960s tower blocks in Hackney and elsewhere have now been demolished.

the stable East End community investigated by Young and Willmott since other historical studies have found very high rates of residential mobility in working-class areas. But if we accept that the nature of community life has changed over the last century, we need to consider why these changes have come about.

Again economic growth is important. Higher incomes, cheaper transport and suburban development have greatly reduced the need for employees to cluster within walking distance of their place of work. Modern neighbourhoods tend, therefore, to be occupationally much more diverse (and so more resilient to economic change) than in the past. Where single employers continue to dominate a town or village, as in some coal mining areas, the communal solidarity generated by common workplace experiences and loyalties is seldom sufficient to overcome the problem of economic homogeneity if the primary place of employment closes down.

Other concomitants of economic growth such as improvements in the housing stock and smaller families have reduced the propensity for adult children to reside with parents, and larger more comfortable homes have lessened the need for recreation to be taken in the street or pub. Relative affluence has allowed people more time and space for their social life, and they appear to have chosen less rather than more communal interaction. Middle-class nostalgia for the idealized simplicity of old-fashioned communities now finds an outlet in the summer migration to villages in Tuscany and Provence – a physical and spiritual retreat from the modern – but few appear to be prepared to forego the benefits of modernity for fifty-two weeks of the year.

Changes in the structure of community relationships in the twentieth century are frequently associated with instances of civil unrest. Urban riots in the early 1980s, notably in Brixton, Toxteth and Bristol, marked a low-point in social harmony, an outpouring of disaffection compounded by racial tension and economic disadvantage. It has to be remembered, however, that outbursts of popular protest are not just a phenomenon of the late twentieth century. In 1886 unemployed dockers marched to Trafalgar Square and then went on a window-smashing rampage down Oxford Street and in the Edwardian period the East End of London was marked by a simmering tension between the indigenous population and Jewish immigrants which occasionally spilled over into violence. But the moments of high profile violence in labour relations or race relations are exceptional. Critics of immigration, for instance, have been quick to appeal to images of violent social conflict; more balanced reflection might instead emphasize the extent to which immigrants from Europe, the Caribbean, the Indian subcontinent and East Africa have enormously enriched the cultural life of the country. Immigrant groups have also been some of the most determined upholders of what are often seen as 'traditional' community values. For instance, the country's largest annual street festival, the Notting Hill Carnival, is a celebration of black community life.

It is also commonly asserted that the modern world has become a more individualistic, more selfish place than the old. Assessment of this change has been ambiguous. The dynamic individualism of entrepreneurs was much lauded in the 1980s, most famously by Prime Minister Margaret Thatcher, though as Chapter 19 shows, the economic achievements of this period are uncertain. At the same time the seamy side of individualism, whether the money-grabbing of City fraudsters or the bag-snatching of high-street muggers, was recognized as a growing social problem. The number of indictable offences reported to the police has risen inexorably since the beginning of the century, though this may reflect both an increased opportunity to commit crime as people have accumulated more valuable possessions, and a rising propensity to report crimes (itself linked to more widespread property insurance). Most crime today is committed by juvenile and young adult males, and this leads to frequent rhetorical denunciations in the media of 'the younger generation' and of the failings of their parents and teachers. Yet the same was true at the turn of the century; the establishment of the Boy Scouts in 1907 was a deliberate response to a perceived problem of juvenile waywardness and delinquency in Edwardian Britain. Furthermore the alleged drift towards individualism and anti-social behaviour in the 1980s should be set against the upsurge of charitable endeavour demonstrated by Live Aid and Comic Relief, and the widespread and active support for welfare, civil liberty and environmental pressure groups. An overall assessment of twentieth-century developments in personal and community relationships, as with most other aspects of social and cultural change, depends crucially on which elements are included in the analysis. For every deterioration it is possible to find an improvement, for every benefit a cost.

In focus: Success and Failure in Housing Policy

A good example of simultaneous improvement and deterioration in twentieth-century social conditions can be found in the study of housing policy. Official involvement in housing dates back to a mid Victorian concern with slum properties as breeding grounds for epidemic disease, vice and lawlessness. Local authorities were given powers to clear and rebuild slum areas, and to establish minimum criteria for the size, density and sanitation of new buildings. These powers, in conjunction with rising real incomes and public investment in the urban infrastructure, led to a rapid improvement in housing conditions in Edwardian Britain. Particularly important was the extension of piped water supply to the majority of urban dwellings between the 1880s and 1914; in Manchester, for instance, all but 2 per cent of dwellings had water closets by 1913, compared to little more than a quarter in 1899. Physical improvements in the housing stock have continued through the twentieth century. By 1951, for instance, 62 per cent of homes had a fixed bath or shower, and this had risen to 88 per cent by 1971 and 98 per cent by 1986.

Nevertheless, slum conditions persisted. In 1911 almost a third of the population of Newcastle and Sunderland, and over half that of Glasgow,

Success and Failure in Housing Policy (continued)

lived in overcrowded conditions. The regional variations were enormous, however. Blackburn, Bristol and Leicester had fewer than one in twenty people living in overcrowded accommodation. Overcrowding arose from a shortage of affordable housing for rent (people of all classes rented their homes in Edwardian Britain, and only 10 per cent of homes were owner-occupied), something which could not be resolved by market mechanisms without a rise in real incomes and an increase in the supply of rentable homes. However a series of rent strikes in 1915 in protest at the wartime inflation of rental levels led the government to fix the rents of cheaper properties at their August 1914 level. Although it was originally intended that rent control would cease at the end of the war, it has continued in some form ever since. The effect has been to reduce the return on capital invested in rental housing, and so further to restrict supply. Partly because of this government-induced contraction of supply, partly as a continuation of slum clearance schemes, and partly as a transient attempt to meet wartime pledges to provide 'homes fit for heroes', subsidized public housing became an increasingly important part of the rental sector, accounting for 11 per cent of all homes by 1938, compared with 54 per cent in the private rental sector. By this date owner-occupied homes constituted around a third of the total. Rebuilding after the Second World War further increased the size of the public sector; between 1951 and 1981 council housing increased from 17 to 35 per cent of the total, private rented housing fell from 52 to 12 per cent, and owner-occupied housing increased from a third to over half, reaching two-thirds of the total housing stock by 1988.

Although the growing scale of public intervention in the housing market has greatly reduced the number of physically substandard properties and ensured that even the poorest of tenants can enjoy a decent level of amenities in their homes, it has also created new housing problems. The suburban council estates of the interwar period often lacked the social amenities – shops, clubs, churches, pubs – which were needed to construct a sense of community among the new residents, and the daily reliance on public transport for travel to work imposed additional costs that poorer tenants could ill afford. The attempt in the 1950s and 1960s to provide more inner-city accommodation at necessarily higher housing densities led councils to build flats rather than houses, and often to build more than six storeys high. By the mid 1960s over half of all local authority construction was of flats or maisonettes, and half of these were high-rise. The planners were intent on social engineering – building socially diverse 'streets in the sky' – but they failed to take account either of the residents' preferences for their own front door, or of the allocation policies of councils who increasingly were driven to create socially homogeneous council estates by the use of socio-economic criteria to allocate scarce housing places. Too often it was slums in the sky that were created, and following the collapse of the 23-storey system-build Ronan Point in Newham in 1968 after a gas explosion, and the

Success and Failure in Housing Policy (continued)

increasing cost of strengthening and repair in similar high-rise blocks, some of the worst examples of 1960s high-rise design have now been demolished. Elsewhere the combination of inappropriate planning, the disadvantaged socio-economic status of many tenants, and sharp reductions in maintenance expenditure through the 1980s, have created socially dysfunctional estates which have disconcerting similarities to the slums of the Victorian period. This seems scant reward for a century of intense public sector involvement and investment. Although legislation and direct provision of housing has encouraged and enforced an improvement in the physical structure and quality of new houses, it has also created significant new social problems in ghettoized 'problem estates', and has so distorted the housing market as to almost eliminate private rented accommodation, thereby restricting the choice of tenants when much of the aim had been to increase the range of housing options open to people.

Conclusion

For judgement to be made of any economic, social or cultural change – whether it has been good or bad, fast or slow, expected or unanticipated, desired or resented – necessarily requires that there be some fixed point of comparison against which the new conditions can be assessed. This chapter has shown in outline, and the subsequent chapters demonstrate in more detail, how difficult it is to find, and then to stick to, relevant bench-marks against which the social and economic developments of Britain in the twentieth century can be measured. International comparisons may mislead because so many aspects of the social and economic system differ between countries, even when they have similar levels of GDP per capita, or similar natural resource endowments, or similar industrial structures. Comparisons with earlier or later periods in a country's own history may be rendered irrelevant by historically specific events – wars or depression, for instance. And comparison of actual achievement with some hypothetical 'best practice' performance requires enormous faith in the ability of the investigator to construct and apply a meaningful counterfactual model.

Of course historians and social scientists continually resort to one or more of these forms of comparison when they assess past economic and social trends, but in doing so they make deliberate choices about what to compare, and how to compare it. These are not neutral choices; they are a strong force in determining where praise or blame is directed, and whether the final assessment is positive or negative. There is seldom a 'right' answer because the historical evidence is usually patchy and often ambiguous. The chapters which follow offer a guide both to this historical evidence and to the interpretations placed on it, and readers are encouraged to draw conclusions for themselves.

Many people, especially those with a political cause to justify, have attempted to interpret recent history to suit their own ends. These appeals to historical certainty should be rejected. Though we may have to place our future in the hands of politicians, we should not allow them to appropriate our past.

Bibliographical Note

The most comprehensive single-volume economic history of Britain in the twentieth century is Sidney Pollard's *The Development of the British Economy 1914–1990* (London, 1992). Michael Dintenfass, *The Decline of Industrial Britain 1870–1980* (London, 1992) provides a more sketchy, long-run survey. A more quantitative treatment is provided in R. Floud and D. McCloskey (eds), *The Economic History of Britain since 1700* (Cambridge, 1994). Volume 2 covers the period from the 1860s up to the Second World War, Volume 3 deals with the years since 1939. There are also many good essays on this postwar period in N.F.R. Crafts and N. Woodward (eds), *The British Economy since 1945* (Oxford, 1991). A good, sociologically-slanted, account of social developments in the twentieth century is A.H. Halsey, *Change in British Society* (Oxford, 1986). Three separate studies which present a broader coverage of twentieth-century social history are: José Harris, *Private Lives, Public Spirit. A Social History of Britain 1870–1914* (Oxford, 1993); J. Stevenson, *British Society 1914–45* (Harmondsworth, 1984); A. Marwick, *British Society since 1945* (Harmondsworth, 1982). Although the essays in F.M.L. Thompson (ed.), *The Cambridge Social History of Britain 1750–1950* (3 vols, Cambridge, 1991) cover a longer period, they provide an excellent survey of the state of research in British social history up to the late 1980s.

Notes

1. B.S. Rowntree, *Poverty. A Study of Town Life* (London, 1901).

2. Note, however, that this increase in real *earnings* is proportionately greater than the rise in real per capita dollar *income* reported in Table 1.1. The difference is accounted for by an extension in coverage and increase in the rate of income tax since the Edwardian period, and by a fall over time in the real purchasing power of sterling relative to the US dollar.

3. A.B. Atkinson, 'A national minimum? A history of ambiguity in the determination of benefit scales in Britain' in T. and D. Wilson (eds), *The State and Social Welfare* (London, 1991) pp. 121–42.

4. M. Young and P. Willmott, *Family and Kinship in East London* (Harmondsworth, 1962).

PART ONE: 1900–1914

2 Britain in the World Economy

Maurice Kirby

Britain's International Economic Role in the Late Nineteenth Century

On the eve of the First World War Britain, by virtue of its status as the world's greatest trading nation, occupied the pivotal position in the international economy. More deeply penetrated by foreign trade than any other contemporary economy, and providing through the financial institutions of the City of London sophisticated commercial and lending services, the British economy had played a critical role in promoting international economic stability and hence the expansion of world trade. This was especially the case in the quarter-century before 1890. In this period British overseas lending to areas of recent settlement possessing immense advantages in the production of primary foodstuffs and raw materials had precipitated the growth of international trade in such products. Since the bulk of British lending was concentrated on internal transportation improvements – in railways and dock and harbour facilities – the flow of capital redounded to the advantage of both debtor and creditor alike. Borrowing countries received a powerful external stimulus to their economic development, whilst for Britain the import of cheap foodstuffs proved invaluable in sustaining the domestic standard of living via rising real incomes for the vast majority of the population.

Foreign lending went hand in hand with Britain's commitment to free trade, a policy which had been laid down in the 1840s and consummated in the repeal of the Corn Laws in 1846. In this latter respect it is possible to argue that the expansion of food imports after 1870, in severely depressing wheat prices, led to the sacrifice of Britain's cereal farmers on the altar of free trade. But, as it has also been argued, the close economic relationship between Britain and her principal overseas suppliers meant that foreign lending was tantamount to investing in the primary sector of the British economy itself.[1]

Not only that, foreign lending acted to prevent, or limit, the transmission of economic recession from one part of the international economy to another. The working of this mechanism was wholly dependent upon Britain's dominant position in the world economy and it was a profound source of international economic stability at a time when the world was still divided into separate areas of multilateral settlement linked only through Britain.

Britain's International Economic Role, 1890–1914

After 1890 the pattern of world trade evolved into a truly integrated international economy with a corresponding pattern of trading accounts settled multilaterally. As industrialization proceeded in Europe, the US, and later Japan, demand for primary products, not least from the British Empire, increased dramatically. Although the industrializing countries increased their sales of manufactured goods to the primary producers, mainly at the expense of British exporters, the balances of their merchandise trade moved into deficit, most notably with India and Australia, and to a lesser extent with Ceylon, Malaya and British West Africa. European visible trade deficits, however, were financed by surpluses with Britain and with a surplus on invisible trade with the US. The latter covered its European and Indian deficits by payments surpluses with Britain and Canada. For Britain, the net results of these commercial relationships were visible trade deficits with the US and Continental Europe, and also with a number of its own imperial territories – Canada, New Zealand, South Africa, East Africa, Ceylon and Malaya. These were offset by impressive surpluses with West Africa, Australia and, in particular, India.

The pivotal role of Britain in underpinning this worldwide multilateral trading system in the period down to 1914 can be illustrated by the development of international monetary relations. The quarter-century before the First World War witnessed the triumph of the Gold Standard as the institutional basis for settling inter-country indebtedness. In theory, gold outflows and inflows in response to deficits and surpluses on the balance of payments resulted in internal price movements – either deflation or inflation – which would eventually produce external equilibrium. In reality, the operation of the international Gold Standard was based far more on the role of sterling. As one authority has observed, 'sterling operated as an international currency on equal terms with gold'[2] with the latter being transferred between countries as a residual balancing item. To fulfil this role of sustaining international liquidity there were two essential prerequisites – first that sterling should be in liberal supply, and second that it should be a currency of unshakeable strength. In the decades before 1914 these conditions were fulfilled admirably as a result of the structure of Britain's balance of payments.

Table 2.1. Balance of payments and export of capital in the UK, 1891–1913 (£m)

Year (annual average for 5-year period)	Net imports (a)	Exports of UK products (b)	Balance of commodity trade (c)=(b)–(a)	Income from services (d)	Income from interest and dividends (e)	Balance on current account (f)=(c)+(d)+(e)	Accumulating balance abroad (g)
1891–95	357.1	226.8	–130.3	88.4	94.0	52.0	2,195
1896–1900	413.3	252.7	–160.6	100.7	100.2	40.3	2,397
1901–05	471.5	296.9	–174.6	110.6	112.9	49.0	2,642
1906–10	539.6	397.5	–142.1	136.5	151.4	145.8	3,371
1911–13	623.2	488.9	–134.3	152.6	187.9	206.1	3,990

Notes: (1) All columns save final are annual averages. Final column (g) represents total in final year, in each quinquennium. (2) All figures in £m and in current prices. (3) Income from services includes shipping credits, insurance, banking, emigrant funds, tourist spending, profits from foreign trade, etc. Columns (d) and (e) represent net figures. (4) Bullion transfers and ship sales not included.

Source: A.H. Imlah, *Economic Elements in the Pax Britannica*, (Oxford, 1958) pp. 37–8, 70–5, 94–8.

As Table 2.1 indicates, the fact that the current account balance was in surplus throughout the period posed a potentially serious adjustment problem elsewhere in the international economy in the form of deflationary pressure in response to the external drain of gold. That this did not occur can be attributed directly to the sustained outflow of capital from the British economy, as reflected in the final column of the table. Thus, the prevailing theory of the gold standard, with its focus firmly on differential processes of inflation and deflation between surplus and deficit countries, neglected the key role of British capital exports in sustaining world liquidity. Deficit countries were thereby able to avoid deflation at the same time as the receipt of British capital aided internal economic development.

In a fundamental sense, the complement to British capital exports in stabilizing the international economy was the country's ongoing commitment to free trade. In the first instance, open access to the British domestic market facilitated debt servicing on the part of borrowing countries via their exports to Britain. Equally important was the contribution of free trade to the smooth working of the multilateral payments network. By exporting manufactured and other goods to Britain, industrial Europe and the US were able to cover their deficits with primary producing countries. In this respect Britain's visible trade deficit, in reducing competitive pressures in overseas markets, played a vital role in restraining international economic rivalries. As one observer of Britain's overseas trading pattern has pointed out, in the absence of free access to the British home market 'both industrial Europe and the United States would have been forced either greatly to adapt their internal economies and seek new sources of supply – for example, develop and extend their own colonies and active spheres of influence – or intensify world competition in manufactured goods. Probably the growth of world trade would have slackened and international friction would have increased'.[3]

The return to the British economy from its role as lynch-pin of the international economy is well reflected in columns (d) and (e) of Table 2.1. The former, setting out income from internationally traded services – dominated by the financial institutions of the City of London – had been in surplus since the end of the Napoleonic wars. On the eve of the First World War, it had grown in magnitude sufficient to more than outweigh the deficit on visible trade. An even greater return was obtained from the interest and dividend income emanating from Britain's overseas assets, valued at £4 billion in 1914. Indeed, the point has been made that invisible income under this heading provided the resources to maintain Britain's ongoing commitment to foreign lending.

Plate 2.1. Ships unloading, 1905. The London docks were at the hub of Britain's international trade network in the Edwardian period.

Emergent Weaknesses in Britain's International Economic Position

It was the sustained expansion of the international economy from the 1870s onwards which prompted the economist J.M. Keynes to characterize the prewar decades as 'an extraordinary episode in the economic progress of man', an age of commercial expansion grounded in multilateralism, and based upon an economic 'Pax Britannica'.[4] Writing in the aftermath of the First World War, and deeply perturbed at the implications for international economic instability of the peace settlement inflicted on the Central Powers, Keynes was concerned not only to acknowledge Britain's stabilizing role before 1914, but also to emphasize the sheer fragility of international commercial relationships which had yet to be disrupted by a catastrophic world war. This perspective of a finely balanced international economy is validated by emergent weaknesses in the structure of multilateralism, compounded by the erosion of Britain's international economic hegemony. For example, the growth of world demand for primary products after 1890 meant that British overseas investment could potentially no longer fulfil its former stabilizing function. If recession were to occur simultaneously in the major industrial countries, the volume of British lending, though considerable, would in all probability be insufficient to prevent the depression from spreading to the primary producing countries to the detriment of British exports of manufactures. Furthermore, the US was already emerging as a major force in the international economy before 1914. With rising exports of manufactured goods and virtual self-sufficiency in many traded commodities, the US moved into balance-of-payments surplus with Canada, Australia and Argentina, countries which had required only marginal multilateral settlement of their accounts before 1890. Moreover, as American food exports to Britain began to decline after 1900, the latter, obliged to seek alternative supplies, moved into increasing deficit with Canada and Argentina. This served to reduce the bilateral deficit with the US, but since Britain continued to import large quantities of American manufactures, a balance-of-payments adjustment was required.

The evolving pattern of international commodity trade meant that Britain was increasingly dependent upon a trading surplus in its bilateral settlements with India for sustaining balance of payments stability. It has been estimated that in the final years before the First World War the favourable Indian balance was sufficient to finance more than two-thirds of Britain's total deficits. The balance of payments situation *vis-à-vis* industrial Europe, China and Japan was improving (in the European case because of rising coal exports), but this was largely offset by deteriorating balances with Canada and Argentina after 1900, and in the immediate prewar years with Australia and Brazil. As Figure 2.1 reveals, India was, indeed, the jewel in Britain's imperial crown, enjoying trading surpluses with precisely those areas where Britain was most heavily in deficit. A significant proportion of Indian exports was admitted duty free to industrial Europe and up to 50 per cent to the US. The critical implication of

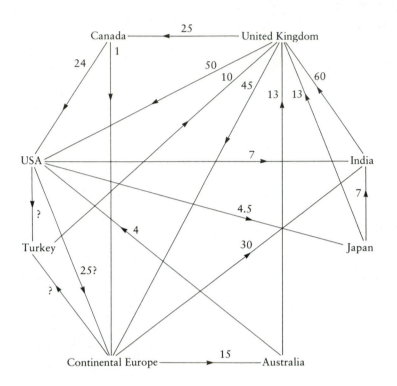

Figure 2.1.   World patterns of multilateral settlement, 1910 (£m). *Note:* The arrows point to the country of each pair having a surplus with the other, indicating therefore the direction of the flow of settlement. Thus the United Kingdom had a surplus of £60m in trade and payments with India. *Source:* S.B. Saul, *Studies in British Overseas Trade 1870–1914* (Liverpool, 1960) p. 58.

this was that as long as the Indian market remained open to British manufacturers, Indian exports, in an increasingly protectionist world, would indirectly overcome foreign tariff barriers for the British economy. Britain's international economic position on the eve of the war thus rested on insecure foundations. In the home market the import penetration of manufactured goods continued to make the inroads that had begun well before 1900. The bilateral trade deficit with the US alone, amounting to £82 million in 1913, heralded the emergence of a 'dollar gap' in the network of international payments which was to be a source of weakness for Britain in later years. The growing economic dependence on India was one consequence of this before 1914.

Direct evidence of contemporary awareness of the threats to Britain's international economic hegemony is provided by the emergence of a tariff reform campaign after 1880. Protectionist sentiments were expressed first by the 'Fair Trade' movement in the early 1880s and were later combined most

Plate 2.2. Tariff reform poster: 'The Dumping Ground'. Derogatory national stereotypes were used extensively by the Tariff Reform League in their campaign for protection against manufactured imports from America and Germany.

spectacularly with the concept of Imperial Preference by the Liberal Unionist politician Joseph Chamberlain in the period 1903–6. In pressing the case for a British general tariff, Chamberlain's motives were complex. In the first instance, protection would facilitate closer commercial integration within the Empire. In return for tariff preferences on their primary product exports to the metropolitan market, Canada, Australia and New Zealand would offer their own preferences on British manufactures. Export markets for British industry would thus be guaranteed within the Empire, and although the domestic cost of living might rise, this would be offset by greater security of employment for British workers. A further consideration for Chamberlain and his supporters was their perception of Britain's increasing vulnerability as a world power. In the words of Chamberlain himself, 'a great empire' whose economic base was founded on 'jam and pickles' and interest from foreign loans was not only at the mercy of every cyclical disruption in the world economic order but also highly vulnerable to the mounting political and military challenge of competing countries such as Germany whose considerable industrial structures were themselves buttressed by tariffs. A British 'imperial *Zollverein*' would mitigate this threat to the balance of power, all the more so if the imperial tariff structure were used as 'a retaliatory battering ram' to enter protected markets in industrial Europe and the US.[5]

As a practical means of resolving the mounting challenges to Britain's international economic hegemony the concept of an imperial customs union was deeply flawed if only because it conflicted directly with the 'cosmopolitan capitalism' of the City of London and also with the market interests of a number of key exporting industries. It is true that tariffs and preferences were supported strongly by Chamberlain's fellow industrialists in the metal-working trades of the West Midlands, hard hit by German and American competition in the home market. But they had little appeal for Britain's cotton manufacturers, colliery owners and shipbuilders, many of whom were confronted by rapidly expanding export markets in the decade before 1914 – the very years which, ironically, coincided with the mounting of Chamberlain's campaign. In its imperial guise, moreover, the tariff reform programme was based upon an increasingly outdated view of the role of the British Empire in the international economy. Imperial preferences may have been an attractive policy to Canada and New Zealand – countries which continued to export the great bulk of their foodstuffs to the British market – but they could be of little interest to those imperial territories with increasingly complex trading links outside the Empire. Ironically, this applied with great force to India and, most of all, to Britain itself. In 1913 the Empire was very far from being a self-sufficient economic community. Britain obtained only one-fifth of its net imports from the Empire and this proportion had remained remarkably stable after 1880 despite a dramatic territorial expansion in imperial possessions. What the tariff reformers failed to perceive, therefore, was that the Empire made its contribution to British prosperity as 'an open dynamic system integrated into the main current of the international economy'.[6]

In the event, Chamberlain's campaign failed to convince a majority of the electorate. The Liberal Party, espousing traditional free trade principles won a landslide victory in the General Election of 1906, having focused popular attention on the cost-of-living implications of protectionism. The Conservative Party, moreover, was far from united in its support for Chamberlain, with the established landed elite reacting adversely both to his radical political past and status as a provincial manufacturer.

For liberal economists favouring the virtues of free trade from the standpoint of international comparative advantage, there can be few justifications for protectionism. In the British case it can be argued plausibly that the enactment of Chamberlain's programme would have resulted in unfortunate consequences for the structure of British industry. In 1907, for example, the old-established staple trades of textiles, coal mining, iron and steel and general engineering accounted for approximately 50 per cent of net industrial output and employed 25 per cent of the working population. Most were heavily dependent upon an increasingly narrow range of export markets located mainly within the British Empire, South America and Asia; and textiles, iron and steel and coal mining alone contributed over 70 per cent of the country's export earnings. Imperial tariff preferences could only have reinforced this industrial 'overcommitment' to the detriment of progressive structural change and productivity advance. In terms of the structure and quality of demand for their products, protectionism would have tied the staple export trades ever more closely to slowly growing markets with relatively low real income levels.

In order to illustrate the distinctive market orientation of British industry in the generation before 1914 the cotton textile and locomotive building industries can serve as complementary case studies, the former because of its status as the exemplar of Britain's export trade in manufactures and the latter because of the close links between its market penetration and the pattern of British overseas lending.

In focus: British Industry and World Markets

Cotton Textiles

The cotton textile industry had been heavily export oriented throughout the nineteenth century and continued to be so down to the outbreak of the First World War. Indeed, in the prewar decade the industry had added considerably to its productive capacity in order to cope with a burgeoning export demand. Taking the more extended period from 1889 to 1913 the total value of piece-goods exports rose by 92 per cent, with market-specific increases ranging from 54 per cent to China, 89 per cent to India and 205 per cent to Egypt. The Indian and Chinese markets alone absorbed 46 per

British Industry and World Markets (continued)

cent of the value of British piece-goods exports in 1889, a figure which had fallen only marginally to 43 per cent by 1913. These figures are a testament to the industry's continuing international competitive advantage in low-income markets, an achievement which was all the more remarkable in view of the onset of low wage competition after 1900 in India, China and Japan in Asia, and Brazil and Mexico in Latin America. That this competition was resisted successfully can be ascribed in part to the British industry's long-standing access to external economies of scale, and a persistently high level of capacity utilization, both of which were complemented by the inherited skills of an experienced labour force. Of more immediate relevance as a response to foreign competition, however, was the increasing use after 1900 of inferior quality cotton which was entirely compatible both with the existing technology and a continued presence in low-income markets. As two acute observers of the industry have pointed out, 'This production strategy of the degradation of product quality was particularly viable for cloth to be worn in warmer climates and also opened up new possibilities for the types of goods that could be made affordable to low-income but fashion-conscious customers'.[7] It is the very success of the industry in sustaining competitive advantage before 1914 which serves to undermine allegations of entrepreneurial lethargy and incompetence. As the following chapter indicates, such allegations are firmly rooted in the historiography of British economic history, with the most recent contribution focusing critical attention on the failure of industrialists in general, and cotton entrepreneurs in particular, to innovate in order to overcome inherited institutional barriers to technical and organizational progress.[8] The point to be made in the present context, however, is that having industrialized first, Britain's comparative advantage in world trade lay in the products of the established staple industries, whilst Germany and the US developed manufacturing capability in sectors consistent with the 'second industrial revolution' with its focus on electrical power and capital intensity in the production process. It is true that the possession of comparative advantage provides no insight into the relative technological or economic efficiency of production in different countries and to that extent it may well be consistent with entrepreneurial failure. It is important to note, however, that a substantial part of the case for declining standards of entrepreneurship in the later Victorian and Edwardian periods is based upon the market collapse of Britain's staple industries between the wars, prompted in part by a decisive shift in the roots of competitive advantage across the divide of the First World War.

Locomotive Building

The locomotive building industry provides further insights into the market position confronting Britain's pre-1914 export trades. The industry owed its

British Industry and World Markets (continued)

foundation in the 1820s to Britain's pioneering role in innovating the steam railway. By 1850 there were approximately 20 specialist builders, although by that time the industry was undergoing profound structural change as a result of the decision of several of the major railway companies to develop their own building capacity in company workshops. Increasingly, in the second half of the nineteenth century, the specialist builders were treated as a reserve source of supply by the home railways with the result that their attention was focused increasingly on export markets. Their very success in generating overseas sales was reflected in the industry's status in 1900 as the second largest of the UK engineering trades after the textile machinery manufacturers. The price that was paid for this success, however, was a high one. The industry's markets were truly global, embracing the British Empire and Dominions, and supplemented by significant sales after 1880 to South America. The long-term consequences of this market structure were graphically portrayed in a PEP report on the industry in 1951 which drew attention to the historic problem of design proliferation in response to the availability of different fuels, the quality of water, climate, gradients, and track curvature. In the South American market alone locomotives had been built for six different gauges, from 3ft to 5ft 6ins.[9] If overseas orders had been for large, standardized runs of locomotives the adverse effects of differing physical conditions (not to mention the idiosyncrasies of consulting engineers) would have been mitigated. In practice, however, overseas sales were invariably made in small batches of five, or fewer, locomotives. Unable to depend upon a stable home market, unlike their German and American counterparts, British firms failed to achieve scale economies. Specialization for particular markets made some contribution to standardization, but in general terms the wide market range, in combination with small orders and divergent engineering specifications, rendered the British industry susceptible to predatory foreign competition for the few large overseas orders that became available. It is difficult to refute the claim that this market fragmentation was both a cause and effect of the pattern of British overseas lending where, as noted above, a considerable proportion of available capital exports was directed to primary producing countries in order to develop transport infrastructures. Orders for British railway equipment are readily understandable in this context, especially from within the Empire and those countries, such as Argentina, which possessed close commercial links with the London capital market. Insofar as these sources of overseas demand existed it is hardly a criticism of British locomotive builders that they sought to meet them, but it is certainly possible that their very success in capturing the lion's share of foreign contracts served to retard the development of more advanced industrial sectors in the home economy. On the eve of the First World War Britain certainly possessed substantial capacity in the heavy sectors of the engineering industry, but the development of the

British Industry and World Markets (continued)

industry as a whole was incomplete. Advanced machinery in the lighter trades, notably in the critical area of machine tools, had to be imported from abroad, mainly from the US and Germany, thus raising the costs of those firms which utilized engineering goods in their production processes.

Interpretations of British Industry and Economic Decline

That Britain's pre-1914 industrial structure was biased in favour of a narrow range of staple export industries catering for relatively low-income markets has led some historians to conclude that the economy was 'overcommitted', with too high a proportion of its resources located in sectors which were technologically static and possessed a low or negative growth potential. The market and commodity composition of exports helped to retard the development of such modern sectors as road vehicles, advanced chemical products, electrical engineering and scientific instruments. These industries were the 'wave of the future' and their slow development before 1914 was to render Britain highly vulnerable to changes in the international economy after 1918. It is this fact of apparent structural rigidity, together with problems of technical modernization, which has given rise to a considerable historiography based on the premise that the roots of Britain's relative decline as an industrial and trading nation in the twentieth century are firmly located in the later Victorian and Edwardian periods. Such an interpretation appears all the more valid in view of the statistical trends indicated in Tables 2.2 and 2.3 pointing to a slackening in the rate of growth of the pre-1914 economy and, Britain's international economic role notwithstanding, a declining share of the world market for manufactured goods in the post-1880 decades.

Table 2.2. Comparative annual growth rates (%) of real GDP, 1880–1913

	United Kingdom	Germany	US
1880–90	2.2	2.9	4.1
1890–1900	2.1	3.4	3.8
1900–13	1.5	3.0	3.9

Source: Sidney Pollard, *Britain's Prime and Britain's Decline: The British Economy 1870–1914* (London, 1989) Table 1.4, p.5.

Table 2.3. Comparative shares (%) in world manufactured exports, 1880–1913

	United Kingdom	Germany	US
1880	41.4	19.3	2.8
1890	40.7	20.1	4.6
1899	32.5	22.2	11.2
1913	29.9	26.4	12.6

Source. Pollard, *Britain's Prime and Britain's Decline*, Table 1.17, p. 15.

In explaining the onset of economic and industrial retardation historians have constructed an array of competing, sometimes complementary hypotheses, most of them grounded in academic objectivity, but with some notable and passionate polemics. In the 1960s the established 'declinist' literature[10] was greatly enlivened by the debut of the 'entrepreneurial failure' school which laid the blame for retardation on the shoulders of British industrialists. Confronted by the rise of foreign competition from the 1870s onwards entrepreneurs failed to rise to the challenge and their lethargy was well reflected in organizational and technical inertia, combined with inferior sales and marketing strategies. These deficiencies were themselves the result of a misplaced belief in the inherent superiority of British industry both in terms of products and processes. They were also a reflection of the onset of 'third generation' decline following the demise of the dynamic cohorts of innovators who had propelled Britain's early industrialization before 1840. There can be few historians today who subscribe to the thesis of entrepreneurial failure in view of the weight of evidence which has been unearthed of dynamic entrepreneurship and the supposed 'rationality' of decision making on the part of British businessmen in a range of industrial and commercial sectors.[11]

Such evidence is also inconsistent with the thesis of cultural atrophy advanced more recently by Martin Wiener. Bearing some similarities to the 'entrepreneurial failure' school, Wiener's interpretation of the causes of economic decline is also grounded substantially in the pre-1914 entrepreneurial environment.[12] For Wiener, British society, from the later nineteenth century onwards, has never come to terms with the values of 'industrialism' despite its evident desire to enjoy the fruits of economic growth. Ingrained cultural norms which have served to retard technological change and productivity advance were established in the latter half of the nineteenth century. During this period key elements in the middle and upper stratas of British society reacted adversely to the growing political power of the newly emergent manufacturing class by creating a social and intellectual climate inimical to industrial advance. By the end of the century the 'industrial spirit' which had produced rapid economic advance before 1850 had declined to the extent that there was little evidence of the earlier adulation of industrial pioneers of the calibre of George and Robert Stephenson and I.K. Brunel. On the contrary, industrial society was perceived increasingly in subjective terms as being synonymous with 'dark Satanic mills' and the despoliation of 'England's green and pleasant land'. In a situation where hostility to economic growth was pervasive, being reflected in a broad spectrum of cultural expression, men of business reacted to the new social climate by accommodating themselves to it. Successful industrialists whose forebears had challenged the power of landed society now chose the path of assimilation: public school education followed by classical studies at the ancient universities were the chosen routes for their sons, complemented wherever possible by the acquisition of a country estate.

In general terms the scholarly response to the Wiener thesis has been to acknowledge the elegance and polemical force of his exposition, but with profound reservations on his selective use of evidence.[13] Particular criticism has been directed at Wiener's failure to define the notion of an 'industrial spirit', let alone its origins, an omission compounded by an apparent ignorance of the lack of respect accorded to merchants and men of business long predating the onset of industrialization. Equally significant is Wiener's assumption that all-pervasive cultural values are positively correlated with an economy-wide process of decline. As critics of the original 'entrepreneurial failure' thesis pointed out, there may have been a weakening of competitive advantage in some British industries before 1914, but the historic performance of the business sector as a whole was not marked by persistent failure. It is this very fact of uneven business performance which is viewed as a convincing challenge to the assumption of a uniformly hostile cultural climate.

The most recent contributions to the debate on the pre-1914 origins of Britain's relative economic decline have been more firmly based than a number of earlier hypotheses. Their common theme is well described under the collective designation of 'the new institutional pessimism'.[14] One critical aspect of the relevant literature, focusing on the disintegrated structure of British industry, is highlighted in the following chapter. Another variant, based on the alleged bias of the capital market, is more appropriately reviewed here insofar as it derives its validity from Britain's distinctive international economic role before 1914. It has already been suggested that capital exports served to retard structural change in the engineering industry. The capital bias argument, however, complements this perspective with the accusation that City financial institutions, ignorant of the condition and needs of British industry in its domestic setting, were irrationally biased in favour of large foreign capital issues. The cumulative effect was to produce a scarcity of capital resources at home leading to low industrial investment and productivity advance and the culpable neglect of advanced sectors such as electricity generation and motor vehicles.

A difficulty with this argument is that it tends to ignore the methods by which industry in general raised finance in Britain before 1914. The typical firm was small scale, organized in the form of a partnership or private limited company, and securing its financial requirements through a combination of bank overdrafts, mortgages and trade credit, with the lion's share being derived from retained profits. The investing public, moreover, did not ignore domestic industry. Between 1860 and 1910 the number of investors in domestic joint-stock companies other than railways and utilities grew tenfold to 500,000, and their interests embraced new as well as established industrial sectors, a fact confirmed by the £4 million placed at the disposal of motor vehicle manufacturers in the period to 1914. Even if it is accepted that overseas lending served to reinforce 'overcommitment' in Britain's industrial structure this does not mean that investors were acting irrationally. The great attraction of foreign investments lay in their security, combined with high or moderate yields. These properties were all the more attractive at a time when returns on traditional domestic investments such as land and consols were declining. In any event, the foregoing discussion of Britain's international economic role underlines the fact that a reduced volume of capital exports would have entailed not only a different British economy, but also an international economy which was more susceptible to instability and far less oriented towards multilateralism in trade and payments. The volume of trade in primary foodstuffs and raw materials would have been lower, leading to more restricted markets for Britain's staple exports. British farmers might have been better off, but at the expense of consumers as a whole who would have experienced lower real income growth.

Conclusion

In surveying Britain's evolving position in the world economy before 1914 it is difficult to disagree with Sidney Pollard that the domestic economy, despite emergent 'signs of weakness', was 'fundamentally sound'. In the prewar generation the contribution of the staple export industries was slowly declining as a proportion of overseas earnings and national income. That the economy was responding successfully to changing market circumstances is confirmed by the rise of the service sector, both domestic and international, complemented by the consumption-led growth of mass production industries such as soap, chocolates, tobacco, newspapers, pharmaceuticals and drugs, and ready-made clothing and footwear. As Pollard concludes,

> In the years to 1913 the British economy was not only still the most productive in Europe, but also flexible and possessing hidden reserves at least the equal of any other. Nowhere had it lost contact with the best, or made irremediable mistakes. More significant still in this context was its ability to install and operate successfully a whole range of industries hitherto hardly known in Britain or dependent on Germany, as soon as war-time needs made this imperative.[15]

In this latter respect it was the rapid development of the chemical, optical glassware, aircraft and motor vehicle industries in the period 1915–18 which provided firm evidence of the economy's latent capacity for scientific, technical and industrial progress. But although the First World War gave rise to some favourable micro-economic adjustments in Britain's industrial structure, its overall impact in relation to the country's international economic role was profoundly destabilizing. By intensifying the pressure of foreign competition on the staple export industries, the war and the peace settlement which followed accelerated the need for structural change and, at the same time, placed major impediments, both psychological and material, in the way of this process. Equally significant was the war's legacy of disrupted trade patterns, protectionism, and international financial rivalries. The baleful consequences of these developments for the British economy are the subject of Chapters 9 and 10.

Bibliographical Note

Readers interested in Britain's international economic role before 1914 should consult S.B. Saul, *Studies in British Overseas Trade 1870–1914* (Liverpool, 1960) and M.W. Kirby, *The Decline of British Economic Power since 1870* (London, 1981) ch. 1. The growth of the international economy is analysed with clarity in A.G. Kenwood and A.L. Lougheed, *The Growth of the International Economy, 1820–1980* (London, 1981). Excellent surveys of the condition of British industry in general and the staple export trades in particular (both of them highlighting the fact of uneven performance) are to be found in D.H. Aldcroft (ed.), *The Development of British Industry and Foreign Competition, 1875–1914* (London, 1968) and Sidney Pollard, *Britain's Prime and Britain's Decline: The British Economy, 1870–1914* (London, 1989). An invaluable long-run perspective is provided in Michael Dintenfass, *The Decline of Industrial Britain 1870–1980* (London, 1992). The key contributions to the debate on Britain's relative economic decline are as follows: for the entrepreneurial failure school see D.H. Aldcroft, 'The entrepreneur and the British economy, 1870–1914', *Economic History Review*, 2nd ser., vol. XVII (1964), pp. 113–34 and D.S. Landes, *The Unbound Prometheus: Technological Change and Industrial Development in Western Europe from 1750 to the Present* (Cambridge, 1971); for the counter-argument focusing on the 'rationality' of entrepreneurs, see D.N. McCloskey and L. Sandberg, 'From damnation to redemption: judgements on the late Victorian entrepreneur', *Explorations in Economic History*, 2nd ser., vol. IX (1971), pp. 89–108. The 'new institutional pessimism' is well represented in Mancur Olson, *The Rise and Decline of Nations: Economic Growth, Stagflation and Social Rigidities* (New Haven, 1982), Bernard Elbaum and William Lazonick (eds), *The Decline of the British Economy* (Oxford, 1986), and W.P. Kennedy, *Industrial Structure, Capital Markets and the Origins of British Economic Decline* (New York, 1987). For commentary and critique see M.W. Kirby, 'Institutional rigidities and economic decline: reflections on the British experience', *Economic History Review*, vol. XLV (1992), pp. 637–60 and R.C. Michie, *The London and New York Stock Exchanges 1850–1914* (London, 1987). The cultural case for industrial decline is stated elegantly in Martin Wiener, *English Culture and the Decline of the Industrial Spirit 1850–1980* (Cambridge, 1981, 2nd edn, Harmondsworth, 1985). For an effective riposte see the essays in B. Collins and K. Robbins (eds), *British Culture and Economic Decline* (London, 1990).

Notes

1. A.K. Cairncross, *Home and Foreign Investment, 1870–1913* (Cambridge, 1953) pp. 2, 225, 232–3.

2. W.M. Scammell, 'The working of the gold standard', *Yorkshire Bulletin of Economic and Social Research*, vol. 17 (1965), p. 33.

3. S.B. Saul, *Studies in British Overseas Trade 1870–1914* (Liverpool, 1960) p. 63.

4. J.M. Keynes, *The Economic Consequences of the Peace* (New York, 1920) pp. 10–11.

5. M.W. Kirby, *The Decline of British Economic Power since 1870* (London, 1981) p. 23.

6. François Crouzet, 'Trade and Empire: the British experience from the establishment of free trade until the First World War', in Barrie M. Ratcliffe (ed.), *Great Britain and Her World 1750–1914* (Manchester, 1975) p. 227.

7. William Mass and William Lazonick, 'The British cotton industry and international competitive advantage: the state of the debates', *Business History*, vol. 32 (1990), p. 29.

8. M.W. Kirby, 'Institutional rigidities and economic decline: reflections on the British experience', *Economic History Review*, vol. XLV (1992), pp. 637–60.

9. Political and Economic Planning (PEP), *Locomotives: A Report on the Industry* (London, 1951) pp. 51–2.

10. For a brief review of this literature see Kirby, *Decline*, pp. 4–7.

11. See, for example, L.G. Sandberg, 'The entrepreneur and technological change', in R. Floud and D.N. McCloskey, *The Economic History of Britain since 1700, Volume 2 1860 to the 1970s* (Cambridge, 1981) pp. 99–120; Sidney Pollard, *Britain's Prime and Britain's Decline: The British Economy, 1870–1914* (London, 1989) pp. 18–57.

12. Martin Wiener, *English Culture and the Decline of the Industrial Spirit, 1850–1980* (Cambridge, 1981, 2nd edn, Harmondsworth, 1985).

13. See, for example, the essays in B. Collins and K. Robbins (eds), *British Culture and Economic Decline* (London, 1990).

14. See, for example, Mancur Olson, *The Rise and Decline of Nations: Economic Growth, Stagflation and Social Rigidities* (New Haven, 1982); Bernard Elbaum and William Lazonick (eds), *The Decline of the British Economy* (Oxford, 1986); G. Ingham, *Capitalism Divided? The City and Industry in British Social Development* (London, 1984); W.P. Kennedy, *Industrial Structure, Capital Markets and the Origins of British Economic Decline* (New York, 1987).

15. Pollard, *Britain's Prime*, p. 271.

3 Regions and Industries in Britain

Clive Lee

The Victorian Economy

The two or three decades prior to the First World War saw the culmination of the achievements of the first generation of modern industrialization and the beginnings of the second generation. In Britain, as the economy most closely associated with the former, the apogee of established industrialization was more marked than the appearance of the new. Here manufactures like textiles, mining, shipbuilding and mechanical engineering reached the peak of their importance in the national economy, often marked by the achievement of their highest level of employment. In both textiles and clothing manufacture employment reached its highest level ever at the 1911 Census of Population while mining, stimulated by the war, reached its peak in 1921. Domestic service, another major source of employment in the Victorian economy, reached its peak on the eve of the First World War. As these great industries reached the height of their importance, there appeared the precursors of industries more characteristic of the twentieth century in the emergence of electricity as a form of energy, in the development of new types of engineering and chemical manufacture, and the appearance of new industries like motor car production. These changes in the composition of production brought related changes in the process of manufacture itself, in the relative needs for labour and capital and, since many industries were geographically concentrated, in the structures of regional economies.

Recent estimates suggest that the British economy grew at an annual average rate of just under 2 per cent during the half century before the First World War, although this modest achievement was losing impetus during the first decade of the new century (see Table 2.2). As usual, economic growth was marked by structural change in the composition of output. The share contributed by manufacturing, by transport and communications, and commerce increased substantially, as more modestly did the relative shares of mining, utilities and the professions. The main relative decline was experienced by agriculture whose share of GDP fell from 18.4 per cent in 1856 to only 6.4 per cent in 1913. Such growth in output may be achieved by increasing labour and capital inputs, and by productivity gains through their more efficient use. Between 1856 and 1913 the growth in GDP was achieved by a combination of these factor inputs and productivity with an average annual contribution of a little over 40 per cent from increased labour and about 30 per cent each from increases in capital and from productivity gain.[1]

The most obvious change in the Victorian economy was the great increase in the labour force, from 9.37 million in 1851 to 18.28 million in 1911, although reductions in working hours meant that the actual increase in the labour input was less than these figures would suggest. But this does not reflect the sum of new jobs created because there was a substantial outflow of workers from the land as agricultural employment fell from its peak of two million in the mid nineteenth century, releasing 600,000 jobs by the First World War. All other sectors of the economy benefited, especially the service industries, with very large increases in employment in transport, domestic service and distributive trades. Although Britain had a notoriously low investment ratio (of investment to national income), and a very high propensity to export capital in the late nineteenth century, there were increases in capital inputs for production. Manufacturing, transport/communications and professional/public services were the principal beneficiaries. The structure of the national economy in 1913 reflects the relative size of these productive sectors.

Table 3.1. Sector shares in the UK, 1913

	Output	Labour	Capital
Agriculture/Forestry/Fishing	6.4	11.5	6.2
Mining/Quarrying	6.4	6.5	2.1
Manufacturing	26.6	32.1	18.5
Construction	2.9	4.9	0.6
Gas/Water/Electricity	1.9	0.6	4.8
Transport/Communications	10.5	7.8	23.4
Commerce	27.2	28.5	9.8
Public/Professional Services	10.2	8.1	11.1
Dwellings	7.9		23.5
Total	100	100	100

Source: R.C.O. Matthews, C.H. Feinstein and J.C. Odling-Smee, *British Economic Growth 1856–1973* (Oxford 1982) pp. 222–3.

The Structure of Production

The productive process exhibited a range of specializations from a relatively heavy use of capital relative to labour, termed capital intensity, at one extreme to a relatively heavy dependence on labour, or labour intensity, at the other. The principal example of the former was undoubtedly the railway industry which also contained many of the largest businesses in Edwardian Britain. In 1904 the combined market value of twenty-two railway companies accounted for 71.7 per cent of the total worth of the fifty largest companies in the economy. They also had a relatively high capital/labour ratio, close to £1,500 per employee in many companies on the eve of the First World War. In sharp contrast, some famous manufacturers, like the shipbuilding and armaments combines of Sir W.G. Armstrong Whitworth and Vickers Sons and Maxim, and steel and engineering firms like Guest Keen and Nettlefold, John Brown, Cammell Laird and William Beardmore utilized modest capital/labour ratios between £182 and £664 per employee.

The labour intensity of major manufacturing firms at this time reflects the importance of this type of production structure. Coal mining remained heavily reliant on manual labour as only 6 per cent of coal was cut mechanically in 1913. Employment in this industry increased from 382,000 in 1851 to 1.2 million by 1911, reflecting rising demand for coal and a need to compensate for the reduction in hours worked. It also reflected the development of larger and deeper mines which required extensive work in providing ventilation shafts, lifts, and increasingly complex underground transport systems, so that the proportion of workers actually at the coal face declined. Equally labour intensive and characteristic of the Victorian era was domestic service. This industry reached a peak of 1.7 million workers on the eve of the war, from less than one million in 1851, 1.4 million of whom were female semi-skilled employees. Domestic service was the principal source of employment for women before 1914, and the increase in the industry reflected both the growth of middle-class incomes in Victorian Britain and the availability of cheap labour. The first two decades of the twentieth century witnessed a critical change in domestic service as middle-class attitudes towards the employment of servants reflected dissatisfaction with the living-in system, so that the maid was replaced by the charlady, a daily visitor rather than a member of the household. Falling birth rates which reduced the demand for domestic help, and alternative employment for women which increased labour costs, undermined domestic service in the twentieth century so that employment declined between the wars and collapsed after 1945.

Since much of industry was oriented towards using labour in greater amounts than capital, it is not surprising that the element of skill in production depended on high quality manual craftsmen. Shipbuilding was typical. At the beginning of the twentieth century Britain held 60 per cent of the world market, although the market share was falling quite rapidly under pressure of competition from rivals protected by tariffs. Since the demand for shipping was erratic, most firms sought to avoid high overhead costs which could be crippling in a recession. The majority of shipbuilding firms were small scale enterprises operating a highly labour intensive mode of production. The machine tools which were developed for use in this industry in the late nineteenth century were supplementary to the work of skilled craftsmen, and had to be sufficiently versatile to produce a variety of components. The fact that many yards specialized in particular types of vessel and were willing to build ships to order enhanced this requirement. Mechanization increased the productivity of skilled men, and did not deskill the workforce or replace men. At the turn of the century 60 per cent of shipyard workers were classified as skilled. Where there was substitution of labour by machines, it took the form of the replacement of semi-skilled and unskilled men by mobile cranes in handling ship plates.

The form of production which evolved in this industry was necessitated by small scale production units, a diversified product, and manual skilled labour. The proliferation of specialized skills as vessels became more sophisticated and thus needed the attention of electricians, engineers, plumbers, and painters, increased the specialization of function within the labour force. Demarcation disputes were common in determining the allocation of tasks between the various trades. But the craft unions provided both training and organization of the labour force and acted as a quality control mechanism. The scale of activity, and the concentration of shipbuilding in heavily concentrated pockets of activity, allowed these specialized workers to move from yard to yard providing, in sequence, their particular contribution to the construction process.

The peculiar structure of the shipbuilding industry which had evolved by the end of the nineteenth century enabled expansion and diversification of production within the established framework of labour intensive methods, and the industry was able, in this way, to retain its world market leadership into the middle of the twentieth century. In some other branches of manufacture this type of structure was less enduringly successful; steel is a familiar example. In this industry the British share of world production fell from 43 per cent in 1870 to 10 per cent by 1913 as its share of world exports fell from 75 to 33 per cent and the share of imports in home consumption rose sharply. In part, this reflected the international trade environment in which competitors enjoyed the protection of tariffs while British manufacturers were exposed by the government's adherence to free trade. This closed the major expanding world markets to British firms and subjected them to the effects of dumping in their domestic market. The limits thus imposed on the markets for British steel acted as a severe constraint on the introduction of new mass production technology and confirmed the fragmented and small scale productive structure. By the turn of the century oligopolistic competition and mergers in the United States created a single massive firm while in the smaller British market a dozen companies manufactured ship plate and a further dozen supplied the sheet steel and tinplate industries while a third group manufactured rails.

The failure to expand capacity imposed by market constraints deprived the industry of the necessary incentive to invest in new plant and to replace old technologies. Further, the atomistic competitive environment precluded any kind of coordinated response by firms in the market, and this tied them all into suboptimal strategies. Not surprisingly, the productivity performance was less than impressive. The enduring small scale of production also inhibited the development of more complex managerial structures or the introduction of technical training.

The combination of commercial policy and a traditionally fragmented industrial structure did not provide an environment conducive to modernization at the beginning of the twentieth century. Consequently investment remained very modest in much of British industry and productivity increase, which determines per capita growth, was poor. For much of British industry the present century has constituted an enduring struggle to sustain the traditional structures or to adjust, usually reluctantly, to new methods. One obvious manifestation of this in recent times has been the improvement of productivity by means of shedding excess labour. But the Victorian era also provided harbingers of that change, most spectacularly through the reduction in the agricultural labour force. Two particular forms of mechanization, both imported from the United States, were effective. The reaper/binder version of the reaping machine saved two to three worker-days compared to traditional methods, while the threshing machine increased a labourer's output by a factor of four or five. These two innovations together are sufficient to explain half the loss in employment in Victorian farming.

In focus: British and American Motor Car Production

The motor industry, which became such a dominant feature of twentieth-century economic development and social change, had its origins in the two decades before the First World War. France was soon established as the leading European producer, a dominance which was retained until the 1930s, but was quickly overtaken by the United States as the leading manufacturer in the world. By 1913 American firms occupied the top twelve positions in annual production and the leading British manufacturer, Wolseley, lay in twenty-first position. But there was a substantial increase in British production in the decade before the war and a great and ephemeral boom in firms and models. By 1913, 198 different makes of British motor car had appeared and 103 of them had already been discontinued.

The links with the bicycle industry were manifest as several such firms moved into motor production in the early years of the century, including Star and Sunbeam in Wolverhampton and Swift, Rover and Singer in Coventry. Other firms had antecedents in other branches of engineering, like the Wolseley Sheep Shearing Machine Company in Birmingham. The original concentration of production in the West Midlands, London and

British and American Motor Car Production (continued)

Glasgow reflected the critical combination of engineering firms with skilled labour, and the proximity of component suppliers. But engineering firms elsewhere also explored the possibilities of motor car production, including Armstrong Whitworth, the shipbuilding and armaments combine based on Tyneside, which made cars between 1906 and 1912. Competition also came from the giant American firm, Ford, which introduced the Model T in Britain in 1908. In 1911 Ford opened a plant in Manchester, initially to assemble kits shipped from the company headquarters in Detroit, but manufacturing commenced in the following year and Ford opened the first British mechanized assembly line in 1914.

By 1914 Ford was established as by far the greatest manufacturer of motor vehicles in the world, and this reflected the revolutionary production methods which the company pioneered and which, in time, spread through the industry. As the first mass producer of motor vehicles, Ford combined the use of standardized interchangeable parts with an assembly line production, thus cutting unit costs by the scale of production. Large volume production required close synchronization of the assembly process. In 1912 Ford's new factory at Highland Park, Detroit introduced an endless belt to transport foundry sand to the moulders. In 1913 the magneto assembly line was reorganized. As in the foundry, manufacturing operations were performed on a moving product but a variety of operations were required in assembling magnetos. The job was now divided into separate tasks for 29 men rather than one man alone undertaking all the tasks. This change reduced the assembly time from 20 to 13 minutes of manpower input. Further refinements the following year reduced the assembly line to 14 men and the magneto assembly time to five minutes. In 1914 the moving assembly line was adopted for chassis and engines, cutting the time from 840 to 93 man-minutes and from 594 to 238 man-minutes respectively. Costs and prices were cut, work became semi-skilled and employee acceptance of the changes was ensured by substantial pay increases.[2]

These sensational gains in productivity were stimulated by the problems of mass production which required the organization of thousands of workers and components into coordinated activity. The use of a large amount of expensive machinery further encouraged managerial control. Having tried spies on the shop-floor and profit sharing inducements to control the effort of workers, Ford used the speed of the moving assembly line to control the flow of production.

British production increased in the Edwardian period, albeit less dramatically, but the central aspects of the Fordist system were not borrowed although American machinery was imported and adopted. The principal difference lay in the fact that while American firms were essentially assemblers of components, their British counterparts manufactured the entire vehicle. The metalworking tradition enabled British workers to fulfil a

British and American Motor Car Production (continued)

variety of tasks, but meant that management faced highly complex organizational problems which necessitated workers retaining substantial control over their efforts. The system adopted to try to induce effort from workers was the piece rate payment scheme which had been increasingly used in the engineering industry since the 1890s. The basis for this system lay in the expectation that the worker would drive production forward by seeking to ensure he maintained an acceptable level of income. The desire to earn bonuses was intended to drive the system and extend the workers' concerns to include plant maintenance, parts delivery and efficiency in general since they all affected the bonus level. Under this system labour

Plate 3.1. US car production: Highland Park plant *c.* 1913. The world's first mechanized production line in Detroit produced Model 'T' Fords at prices no-one else could match.

British and American Motor Car Production (continued)

retained the power to slow down production, but at a cost in lost income. Historians have argued that this limitation on management control in the British industry restricted scope for change.[3]

    There are other explanations for the British production system. The market was too small to sustain a very large volume of production, and skilled labour was too abundant and cheap to warrant a shift to semi-skilled labour combined with expensive machinery. British firms had little difficulty in raising capital, and high dividend payments eased entry into the industry and created potential excess capacity.

Plate 3.2. UK car production: Trafford Park plant *c.* 1914. Ford's assembly plant in Manchester did not achieve US levels of productivity. The manufacturing process still involved extensive use of skilled labour and strict job demarcation.

British and American Motor Car Production (continued)

Before 1914 the British motor industry performed reasonably, achieving lower productivity levels than Ford but higher than many other American producers. In the decade before 1913 British producers cut production time from 3,000 – 5,000 man-hours to 1,000 – 3,000. Ford at the latter date required 200 man-hours per vehicle. Not surprisingly Ford undersold competitors in the British market, offering the Model T at £135 while few other cars sold for under £250. By 1914 the British motor industry had established an organizational framework which was characterized by reliance on craft skills, short production runs, and a diversity of models. In all crucial respects it was the antithesis of the American system.

Regional Economic Structures

British industry had evolved a distinctive structure by the beginning of the present century. One aspect of that which had considerable influence later was the high level of regional concentration of many activities. In part this reflected the constraints of location which obviously determined where coal mines and shipyards were sited. Other industries were drawn to them, like iron and steel manufacture and engineering as well as transport and distributive trades. There emerged in the course of the nineteenth century a number of clearly defined regional types – mining, textiles, and engineering orientations being prominent – which combined several of the major industrial sectors in close integration. The resultant regional structures carried a heavy reliance on these integrated industries. In extreme cases a locality could be dominated by a single activity. By 1911 mining accounted for 33 per cent of employment in Glamorgan and Monmouth, 29.1 per cent in County Durham, and over 20 per cent in Derbyshire and the Central and Fife regions of Scotland. Textiles accounted for 29.8 per cent of employment in Tayside, 26.1 per cent in Lancashire and 21.2 per cent in the West Riding, and 25.5 per cent in the Borders. Many industrial areas had a variety of such industries. The East Midlands, Yorkshire and Humberside and the North West all encompassed textiles, mining, clothing and engineering, while steel manufacture, shipbuilding and engineering were found in central Scotland and northern England.

Historians have identified and debated the regional problem in the context of interwar unemployment levels. But the origins of these regional variations in prosperity lie in earlier industrialization, in the concentrations established in the Victorian period. The potential problem was apparent then in differential levels of unemployment. Recent estimates of unemployment rates in a variety of trades – including skilled engineers, carpenters, iron founders,

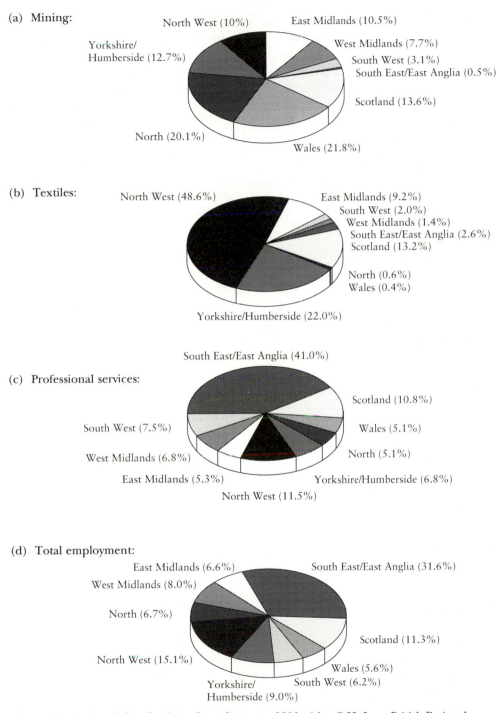

Figure 3.1. Regional distribution of employment, 1911. *After:* C.H. Lee, *British Regional Employment Statistics 1841–1971* (Cambridge, 1979).

and shipyard workers – suggest that before the First World War as well as after it the unemployment rates were higher in the industrial areas of northern England and central Scotland than they were further south. Unemployment among skilled engineers averaged 12.1 per cent in the United Kingdom in April 1909. But the rate was less than 10 per cent in the south and west of England and far higher elsewhere; reaching 19.4 per cent in Tyne and Wear, 17.8 per cent on Clydeside and 15 per cent in West Yorkshire. This kind of

Figure 3.2. Great Britain and Ireland: standard regions

disparity appears to have been prevalent through much of the second half of the nineteenth century. Estimates of regional per capita incomes for the 1860s and 1880s also suggest that the industrial regions fared rather badly. Wales and the North lagged well behind the rest of Britain while the South East was far above the average, by almost 50 per cent in 1879–80. All measures confirm that principal disparity, between the South East and the rest of the country.[4]

This region, and especially the Greater London area at its heart, was an industrial centre, but it did not include much of the classic Victorian industries: steelmaking, mining or textiles. Engineering tended to be oriented less towards locomotives or textile machinery than instruments and the newer forms of electrical engineering. But this region was far less reliant on industry and far more structured towards services than the rest of the economy. The majority of domestic servants were found here, a reflection of relative wealth, while the international financial services of the City were an important element in the structure of this region. By 1911 the South East had 52.3 per cent of its total employment engaged in the service industries, compared to a national average of 41.4 per cent. While the region accounted for 28.7 per cent of the national population its share in certain services was far higher, close to 40 per cent in banking and finance and the professions, and even higher in domestic service. Furthermore, much of the increase in employment in Britain from 1851 to 1911 had been channelled into the South East. High activity rates, for women as well as men, low unemployment, a substantial component of high-income employment, a structural diversity, and a disproportionately large share of consumer oriented activities like printing and publishing, instrument engineering, food processing, and the newer branches of chemical manufacture explain both the Victorian prosperity of the South East and its greater success in avoiding the interwar depression than most other regions. The basis for both regional prosperity and recession experienced between the wars was set before 1914.

In focus: Industrialization in Tyne and Wear

By the beginning of the twentieth century, industrialization in Britain had established a distinctive and specialized set of regional economic structures. The inherent viability of those structures was to be tested severely in the interwar recession with devastating effects in areas like Tyne and Wear.

This area, set in the heart of the North East of England, provides an example of one of the classic forms of early industrialization based, from the eighteenth century, on coal mining and shipbuilding, to which were added in the course of the nineteenth century iron and steel manufacture, engineering and a network of railways. Crucially these various industrial activities were closely bound together as a single integrated structure. Local ironworks took almost a quarter of the increase in coal output of the North

Industrialization in Tyne and Wear (continued)

East in the second half of the nineteenth century, while railways, steamships, local industry and domestic consumption were important consumers. The growth of coal exports stimulated the improvement of the navigation of the Tyne and by the 1890s some 5.6 million tonnes of coal passed annually through the Tyne Dock at South Shields, a scale of activity without parallel elsewhere. The expansion of trade stimulated shipbuilding. Iron-hulled colliers, oil tankers, refrigerated ships, liners and warships were all built on the Tyne. Output for the merchant fleet reached a peak in 1906 at just over one million tonnes. The Tyne shipbuilders had a strong professional interest on both sides of the Russo-Japanese War of 1905, and Admiralty contracts were prized by the largest yards, such as Armstrong Whitworth at Elswick and Palmer's yard at Jarrow.[5]

In turn, the shipyards took coal and iron from the region's producers. In 1905 the five companies which constituted the North East Platemakers Association sold 72 per cent of their 489 million tonnes output within the North East. The Consett Iron Company had reached an output of 147 million tonnes of ship plate annually, most of which was sold locally. The company's annual bill from the North Eastern Railway, for delivering plate to the shipyards and bringing iron ore from the docks, reached £150,000. In its turn the railway company derived a third of its income from mineral traffic.

The close links between these industries in demand for each other's products and services were reinforced by ownership and integrated production. The Palmer family business included coal and iron ore mining, iron manufacture and shipbuilding, thus encompassing the entire production process. Armstrong Whitworth's yard included engineering, a steel works, and ordnance departments as well as shipbuilding. The Consett Iron Company owned ten collieries capable of an annual output of one million tonnes in the 1890s. Elsewhere in the North East, Furnace Withy of Hartlepool extended production from shipbuilding to include coal mining and iron and steel production, in the process becoming the South Durham Steel and Iron Company in 1898. On the Tyne, Swan Hunter absorbed two smaller yards and amalgamated with Wigham Richardson in the 1900s to achieve the scale of operation required to tender successfully to build the *Mauritania*, the largest ship ever seen on the river at the time of its launch in 1906.

Clearly the high degree of integration between the industries of the North East rendered them vulnerable to recession. An equally serious weakness in the economic composition of the area lay in the fact that the fruits of industrialization were not widely dispersed. While substantial fortunes were made by shipbuilders and coal owners, and shared through charitable bequests to hospitals, churches and educational institutions, for many in the region the standard of living remained at a low level. One

Industrialization in Tyne and Wear (continued)

characteristic of this was the proportion of owner-occupied housing which
reached only 17 per cent in Gateshead in 1885 and 27.3 per cent in
Sunderland in 1900. By 1911, a third of the population of these two towns
lived in overcrowded conditions, and 60 per cent lived in three rooms or
less. The ratio of wages to rent on Tyneside reached only 1.2 to 1.4 by the
early twentieth century.

Poor housing was linked to poor amenities. In Newcastle and Gateshead
together in 1898 only 6.3 per cent of houses had gas cookers, although this
did rise to 59.5 per cent by 1913. While over 80 per cent of the houses in
Newcastle and Sunderland had water closets by that date, in Gateshead the
proportion was only 18.9 per cent. Poor housing conditions engendered
disease. In 1913 the average male death rate stood at 20 per cent above the
national average in Gateshead. Even worse, it was 21 per cent above in
Hartlepool, 28 per cent above in Sunderland and 34 per cent above in
South Shields. In 1912–13 Tyneside was 30 per cent above the national
average for tuberculosis, a complaint usually associated with overcrowding,
undernourishment, large families and high infant mortality.

Conditions in the pit villages were no better, even though much of the
housing was provided free by the colliery companies. Fresh water supplies
and adequate drainage were exceptional; the ash pit and ash closet were far
more common. Free housing did not make a significant improvement to
living standards because it was provided instead of wages, so that the money
wage in the northern coalfield was lower than in other mining areas where
housing was not provided.

From an economic perspective, the significance of poor living standards,
housing, and health lies in the inability of incomes to provide sufficient
demand to generate the multiplier and stabilizing effects of consumer
spending. Family incomes were also restricted by the severely limited
working opportunities for women, a characteristic of all mining areas.
Consequently the level of service sector employment, usually associated with
personal affluence via personal, financial and professional services or
community provision of health and education, was very low in the North
East. In 1911 the ratio of service sector employment per thousand
population averaged 186 in Great Britain, while the respective ratios for
County Durham and Northumberland were 119 and 157. Had the ratio been
increased to the national average in these counties, total employment in
County Durham would have increased by 7 per cent and that in
Northumberland by over 17.5 per cent. The region thus combined the
instability of a highly interrelated, and export oriented, industrial structure
with the weakness of low consumer spending. The fragility of this was
realized in the economic decline and enduring poverty which has
characterized the area throughout the twentieth century.

Hypotheses and Interpretations

The performance of the Victorian economy has long been debated by historians, many of whom have sought to explain the modest growth rates achieved in the late nineteenth century and the declining contribution to productivity of mining and manufacturing. In the 1960s historians attempted to explain this in terms of the lost impetus of the industrial revolution and a fall in entrepreneurial zeal within the business community. Illustrative examples of poor industrial management, often defined in terms of a failure to adopt the latest machinery, were countered by examples of new and profitable ventures. Attempts in the 1970s to measure the effects of business strategies raised important issues both of definition and competence without resolving the essential dilemma. But the enduring debate has clarified the principal issues and recent work has been of a far more consensual nature, providing a variety of theses which are complementary to each other as partial answers to the main questions.

The institutionalist explanation, which gained support in the 1980s, argued that organizational structures and practices were essential determinants of the way in which industries functioned and the extent of their responsiveness to changed circumstances.[6] British industrial decline was explained in terms of rigid institutional structures which obstructed efforts towards economic renovation. Such historians set themselves against the neoclassical explanations which relied, they claimed, on an unquestioning belief in market forces. In practice, the difference between these theses is far less dramatic, both recognizing a similar phenomenon under different labels as 'market imperfection' or 'institutional rigidity'. Both recognized the significance of the enduring predominance of the family firm in British industry as a potent barrier against the development of corporate capitalism as in Germany and the United States, characterized by oligopoly, managerial hierarchies, vertical integration, and a much larger scale of operation.

Lazonick's exploration of the British and American cotton industries lies firmly in this institutionalist tradition, as the different technologies adopted are explained in terms of organizational structures. While American manufacturers were quick to adopt ring spinning, a technology which used better quality cotton but less skilled labour, their British counterparts remained loyal to the mule which could handle lower quality cotton but required skilled operatives. Lancashire producers were thus able to cut costs in the late nineteenth century by resorting to cheaper cotton yarn, a strategy supported by the workforce since it endorsed the craft status of the machine minders. Central to this interpretation is the belief that employers ceded control of the shop-floor to organized craft unions which protected levels of pay and working conditions in return for a commitment to high levels of output. In effect, the workers also undertook to provide training and, since much of industry was heavily localized, created regional pools of trained labour allowing economies of scale through the spreading of fixed costs over a larger output. Such a system minimized fixed costs for manufacturers, enabled them to offset the risks of trade depression onto the workforce through redundancy, and protected them from the need to obtain outside capital or develop managerial structures. While these strategies enabled much of British industry, like cotton textiles, to retain a competitive advantage before 1914 they were, in the longer term, extremely risky.[7]

The institutionalists retained a critical attitude towards entrepreneurial performance arguing that, although many businessmen acted rationally in terms of the economic environment in which they operated, essential action to change that environment was lacking. They did not, however, indicate how that Olympian task might have been accomplished. Others, content to make judgements within the context of Victorian society, have in some cases concluded that investment in new technology would have been ineffective and thus a foolish strategy. The steel industry has been described in such terms. In the two decades before the First World War, British steel exports slumped while imports soared to reach two million tonnes of iron and steel by 1913. Given that American and German manufacturers were by this time far more technologically efficient than their British counterparts, and that the rising cost of importing ore from Spain together with the slow growth in demand meant the industry was not particularly profitable, reluctance to invest was a rational strategy.[8]

All these explanations depict the inherent weaknesses of British industry in terms of small scale production, fragmented control and low investment, but sustained by craft skills. This strategy could be justified in the context of the pre-1914 world market structure. Few of these recent explanations blame the quality of entrepreneurship for the performance of industry.

Another important element in determining the context of Victorian industry which has received attention recently has been the role of the state. There is general agreement that the steel industry had little chance of competitive success while it was, uniquely amongst its competitors, exposed to the rigours of free trade. Other aspects of government intervention inhibited economic performance. Victorian legislation imposed social obligations on the railway companies by making them provide services which were not profitable. Customer lobbying prevented restructuring through amalgamation in the railway industry for half a century before it was eventually achieved in the 1920s. Government legislation also prevented railways from increasing their rates to cover the additional costs incurred in running more frequent services to a higher level of punctuality, with deleterious effects on productivity. A similar ambivalence characterized the administration of public monopolies such as the General Post Office which was instructed both to achieve profitability and to provide a social service which included deliveries to remote areas, an aspect of the operation which was certain to lose money. Government legislation hindered the growth of electricity supply since the activities of each power company were restricted to the area under the control of a single local authority. Since the growth of the AC system depended on serving a large area from a central power station to achieve maximum efficiency, the provision of cheap electricity was delayed in Britain. The legislation gave control of electricity development to local authorities which, as the principal owners of gas supplies, had a vested interest in slowing development. The same was true of tramway electrification since the 1870 Act gave local authorities the right to lease tramway services to private companies and to purchase them at scrap value after twenty-one years. As contracts expired the companies ran down their capital commitments so that electrification of the tramways in Britain lagged twenty years behind the United States and Western Europe.

While the problems of industrial change have continued to attract the attention of historians during recent decades, the regional dimensions of such changes have received very limited consideration. The 'regional problem' has usually been perceived as a phenomenon of the interwar years, manifest in the substantial disparity in unemployment rates between different parts of the country. Curiously, this problem does not appear to have been attributed a historical dimension in explanations, other than as a manifestation of industrial decline. The regional problem which emerged in the interwar years was, of course, inherent in the economic structure which evolved in Victorian industrialization. One of the advantages claimed for the Victorian type of industrial structure was the concentration of specialized workers in close proximity to shipyards in the North East, textile workers in northern England and the Midlands, and coal miners in South Wales, central Scotland, and the north. Their vulnerability to unemployment through fluctuations in export markets is very obvious. It is also clear that distinctive regional structures were distinguished by considerable differences in income and wealth. In particular the industrial regions were considerably poorer than the South East. Clearly an orientation towards finance, the professions, government and a wide range of personal services generated greater affluence and greater stability than Victorian industry.

The problem of early twentieth-century industry is often approached as a supply side dilemma, concentrating on organizations, dynamism, entrepreneurship and technical innovation, while the regional dimension is a descriptive variant on the same theme. One recent explanation of the success of Scottish industry in the nineteenth century compared to its weakness in the twentieth century was based on the possession and loss of a regional supply side advantage in the form of cheap labour, which was eroded by national wage bargaining. But there is another aspect to the problem, that of demand, variations in which are reflected in unemployment and income. The disadvantage of low Scottish wages before 1914 was the limit they placed on effective demand in Scotland for consumer goods and services, as indeed was true of Tyneside and other industrial areas of Britain. This was a crucial weakness in determining the poor development of consumer industries and services in Scotland and elsewhere.

There is considerable scope for exploration of the links between regional structure and industrial performance. Much of the work on the latter in recent years has been consensual in contributing to a generally accepted pattern of change in which, while individual agents are seen to have acted rationally and reasonably, the weight of historically evolved structures became a source of debility from which the economy is still not free. The regional dimension confirms this and is a critical part of the structural rigidity. From the vantage point of late twentieth-century industrialization, the early developments of the present era, manifest in the development of machine tools, interchangeable parts and mass production can be clearly identified in the second half of the nineteenth-century. But they cannot be identified very clearly in Victorian Britain where production seems closer in type and spirit to eighteenth-century proto-industrialization than its successors.

Bibliographical Note

The enduring interest in industrial decline ensures that this is the best served aspect of the material covered in this chapter. The fullest exposition of the institutional thesis is found in the study of the British and American cotton textile industries by William Lazonick, *Competitive Advantage on the Shop Floor* (Cambridge, Mass., 1990). Other industries are treated in the essays edited by Bernard Elbaum and William Lazonick (eds), *The Decline of the British Economy* (Oxford, 1986), and the motor industry is analysed by Wayne Lewchuk, *American Technology and the British Vehicle Industry* (Cambridge, 1987). Peter Pagnamenta and Richard Overy, *All Our Working Lives* (London, 1984) provide a host of pertinent illustrations in the book based on a series of television scripts dealing with major industries. Regional variations have received much less attention; the principal texts are confined to the twentieth century. A general summary of fairly recent work is found in C.H. Lee, *The British Economy since 1700: a Macroeconomic Perspective* (Cambridge, 1986). This book remains the most recently published survey, while the volume by R.C.O. Matthews, C.H. Feinstein and J.C. Odling-Smee, *British Economic Growth 1856–1973* (Oxford, 1982) is the most recent study of the quantitative dimensions of long-term change. Most of these books have extensive bibliographies.

Notes

1. R.C.O. Matthews, C.H. Feinstein and J.C. Odling-Smee, *British Economic Growth, 1856–1973* (Oxford, 1982) pp. 210, 228–9.

2. J.P. Bardou, J.J. Chanaron, P. Fridenson and J.M. Laux, *The Automobile Revolution: The Impact of an Industry* (North Carolina, 1982) pp. 61–74.

3. Wayne Lewchuk, *American Technology and the British Vehicle Industry* (Cambridge, 1987) p. 112ff.

4. Humphrey R. Southall, 'The origins of the depressed areas: unemployment, growth and regional economic structure in Britain before 1914', *Economic History Review*, 2nd ser., XLI (1988), pp. 246–53; C.H. Lee, *The British Economy since 1700: a Macroeconomic Perspective* (Cambridge, 1986) p. 131.

5. N. McCord and D.J. Rowe, 'Industrialization and urban growth in north-east England', *International Review of Social History*, XXII (1977), pp. 34–8; D.J. Rowe, 'The North East' in F.M.L. Thompson (ed.), *The Cambridge Social History of Britain 1750–1950, Volume 1 Regions and Communities* (Cambridge, 1990).

6. Bernard Elbaum and William Lazonick, 'An institutional perspective on British decline' in Bernard Elbaum and William Lazonick (eds), *The Decline of the British Economy* (Oxford, 1986).

7. William Lazonick, *Competitive Advantage on the Shop Floor* (Cambridge, Mass., 1990) pp. 136–7, 301.

8. R.C. Allen, 'International competition in iron and steel 1850–1913', *Journal of Economic History*, 39 (1979), p. 913.

4 Edwardian Britain: Empire, Income and Political Discontent

Peter Wardley

Introduction

The performance of the British economy in the decade-and-a-half before 1914 appeared problematic to contemporaries and the consequences of pessimistic perceptions were far-reaching. Negative perceptions of economic performance had a direct bearing on the articulation of political ideologies and beliefs. Although the economy continued to grow it appeared that a climacteric, or break in trend, had occurred around 1900 when productivity growth slowed, halted or even fell. In other words, it appeared that the application of additional productive inputs, labour and capital, yielded output at the level of productivity achieved before the turn of the century but without further efficiency gains. A pessimistic reading of the evidence suggested that productivity had fallen and this was seen by many as a cause of increased emigration and the wave of labour disputes which swept the economy in the last five years before the First World War.

Recently economic historians have re-examined the structure and performance of the British economy during the Edwardian period to suggest that a more sophisticated explanation is required. However, Edwardians, individually and collectively, acted according to their perceptions of change and a convincing explanation of their behaviour will require consideration of their opinions as well as a historical assessment of their objective conditions. Furthermore, economic and social conditions varied geographically and change occurred at the regional and local level at varying rates. Within the United Kingdom there were large regional differences in employment structures and variations in income levels (see Chapter 3); the discrepancy between average household income represented by the extremes of the South East of England and the South West of Ireland was politically as well as economically significant. An acceptance of the importance of perceptions in determining behaviour also requires an appreciation of the relativity of individual judgement; this was clearly demonstrated, in Britain and Ireland, by political positions adopted over the 'Irish Question'.

Imperialism, Nationalism and the Economy

The Edwardian period saw the creation or transformation of a multitude of institutions, and several comfortable assumptions held by the British about their place in the world were confronted. Accommodation of change was not always easy, particularly where vested interest was contested, and sometimes change was opposed vigorously. Manifestations of social and political discord prompted, and gave added urgency to, the development of statistical analysis in the social sciences. The great debates of the day – relative economic performance, national efficiency, tariff reform, Ireland, female suffrage, unemployment, the economic impact of trade unions, the distribution of wealth and income – generated from politicians a demand for information which the agencies of the state sought to address. Although developments in applied social research made available systematic information concerning the economy and society, most contemporaries drew mainly on their own experiences to assess their world. In such assessments, perceptions of change, including perceptions of alterations in rates of change, were important determinants of attitudes and behaviour for all members of society.

Uneven economic development had an important role in most of the major political concerns of the day, including imperialism, nationalism, and labour relations. The British Empire, largely a recent creation of the late Victorian period, posed several problems for a country whose politicians had expressed for three generations a strong commitment to free trade. No one quite knew what the British Empire was for, but the alternatives of giving it up or attempting to create a truly multicultural commonwealth were unthinkable for the statesmen who dominated domestic politics. Constitutions and powers of self-government had been granted to the four Australian colonies (1850), New Zealand (1852), the Cape Colony (1853) and the dominion of Canada (1867). These territories, which had been largely settled by UK emigrants, were formally recognized within the Empire as self-governing Dominions in 1907. By contrast, the aspirations of Irish nationalists within the United Kingdom, and Indian nationalists within the British Empire, remained unfulfilled.

Imperial defence was expensive and contentious, provoking disputes between Britain and the dominion and colonial administrations, but it was inextricably related to naval strategies designed to secure long-distance ocean shipping which served Britain, and the bulk of the burden fell on the British taxpayer. There was some logic in the position adopted by the colonial administrators; at the end of the Edwardian period over 40 per cent of world merchant shipping was British-registered and over 60 per cent of the world's tonnage was constructed in British shipyards. Moreover, the battleships which augmented the British fleet provided wages and profits which accrued, respectively, to British workers and capitalists. The Empire, which contained within it territories that represented the full range of economic development, was obviously important for the British economy, providing food and raw materials, markets, investment opportunities and destinations for migrants. However, the United States was also a major trading partner and destination for capital and emigrants; and Europe, including Germany, provided important markets for British industrial products. An additional aspect of the Empire, or more specifically India, was that it provided the balancing item in the international financial settlements system which sustained liquidity essential for the expansion of world trade and economic growth (see Chapter 2).

Nationalism posed many related problems. Within Britain, nationalist ideologies defined the major issues which divided the Conservative and Unionist Party from the Liberal Party after Gladstone's conversion to Home Rule for Ireland in 1885 had acted as the catalyst for political realignment on both sides of the Irish Sea. Political debates, outside as well as at Westminster, were rarely conducted during the thirty years before 1914 without consideration of an Irish dimension. Within the British Isles, the Liberal Party's adherence to Gladstone's proposals resulted in internal schism and, subsequently, an alliance between Liberal Unionists and the Conservative and Unionist Party. As a consequence both of this political realignment and of electoral successes in Ireland, the nationalist Irish Parliamentary Party came to occupy a pivotal position in the House of Commons which, along with Labour Party support, maintained the Liberal Party in government between 1905 and 1916. This support for a minority administration gave both parliamentary groups an opportunity to influence Liberal governments beyond their absolute numbers. In Ireland, these developments led to a further polarization of unionist and nationalist positions which exacerbated cultural distance and eventually prevented political dialogue.

Nationalist ideology posed other difficulties which impinged upon the British. Throughout the Victorian period Britain benefited from the liberal international economic regime which permitted largely unfettered movement of labour and capital, goods and services. In particular, the City of London had prospered, providing financial, trading and transportation services to a world market. By 1900, however, many British businessmen believed that markets in advanced industrial countries, particularly the United States and Germany, were restricted by protectionist tariffs, or import duties, designed to foster import substitution and the expansion of manufacturing output. These perceptions led to demands for a 'Fair Trade' policy rather than a 'Free Trade' stance in the face of foreign protectionist policies (see Chapter 2).

Nationalist ambitions held by those outside the Empire were also important. The territorial ambitions of the major European powers in the period after 1885, prompted in part by Britain's example and nationalistic in intent, resulted in Africa, apart from Abyssinia, being carved up into European colonies. The consolidation of British colonies also contributed to the assertion of Afrikaner nationalism which resisted British imperialist ambitions in the First and Second Boer Wars of 1881 and 1899–1902. The German Kaiser's telegram of support to the Boer government in 1896 was of little consequence except that it indicated the reality of nationalist rivalry among the great powers. In these circumstances the potential consequences of Britain's diplomatic isolation were recognized and the Foreign Office sought international agreements which would contribute to international security. Although Britain's first treaty for half a century was with Japan in 1902, and designed to counter the threat of joint naval action by the French and Russians, the threat to the balance of power within Europe posed by the German-Habsburg alliance encouraged cooperation amongst these four powers. Nationalist attitudes in Britain and Germany resulted in the naval race which followed the construction of the battleship *HMS Dreadnought*. The immediate cause of the First World War was the assassination of the heir to the Austro-Hungarian throne in Sarajevo, the final spark of a series of Balkan episodes which threatened European peace in the Edwardian period. This provoked a cascade of ultimatums which resulted in Britain's unsuccessful demand that Germany should recognize Belgian neutrality. However, the First World War was also the outcome of the long-standing imperialist rivalries of the great powers.

The Political Economy of Empire

Economists and economic historians have long debated the consequences of British overseas investment and the impact of the institutional structures which served the financial sector have also proved controversial. For example, the extent to which the direction of funds abroad contributed to neglect of potentially profitable domestic opportunities has been disputed. However, it is a common feature of such cost-benefit analysis to curtail the final reckoning on the eve of war and only consider peacetime earnings until 1914. If overseas empire and capital accumulation abroad are regarded as a combined investment *and* insurance policy, then the final reckoning should be taken in 1919.

When the European economies were challenged by the demands of modern warfare, the British government was not only able to secure strategic raw materials but it also utilized privately accumulated financial assets to acquire resources in the world's markets. This resulted in a more flexible response than would have been the result of a neo-Bismarckian strategy of directing capital to increase prewar investment in domestic blast-furnaces and factories. The potential purchasing power of British overseas investment, which was at least four times greater than that of Germany, was enormous. In the event, and by contrast with the Second World War, it was necessary to liquidate only a quarter of these assets before 1919. Furthermore, the blockade imposed by the Royal Navy not only prevented the importation of strategic materials into Germany but it also reduced competition by removing German products from the international goods market – to Britain's advantage.

Britain gained much during the long peace of international economic expansion and in the First World War the strategic value of both Empire and overseas investment was immense. However, the benefits of Empire and overseas investment accrued differentially within Edwardian society. It appeared to contemporaries that the far from equal distribution of income was becoming more skewed and the flow of incomes from overseas assets was differentially augmenting the fortunes of the wealthy; one estimate held that 1 per cent of the population owned 65 per cent of the wealth. Proposals made by the Liberal government to fund defence and social welfare schemes by taxes on income and wealth provoked political controversy. The extent to which British society was dominated by a plutocratic elite was indicated by the rejection of the 'People's Budget' by the House of Lords in 1909. Economic expansion, partially stimulated by capital exports, in countries which were more democratic, offered higher standards of living, and where English was spoken, enhanced the attractiveness of emigration for British citizens.

Living Standards and the Domestic Economy

In 1900 the inhabitants of the United Kingdom enjoyed an average income per capita which exceeded that experienced by the nationals of any other European country. In this context British economic performance cannot be judged to have failed. Only the inhabitants of the United States and Australia were better-off than the British by this index of economic well-being. Therefore, a pessimistic judgement must rest on an assessment of British economic performance relative to *either* a pair of economies which were exceptionally well endowed with natural resources *or* a theoretical British economy blessed by a more efficient but hypothetical productive structure. Such a verdict is not as compelling a story as is often assumed.

Evidence of continued material progress was available to contemporaries in the officially compiled demographic statistics; the population of the United Kingdom increased from 41.5 million in 1901 to 45.3 million in 1911. The vital statistics of the period provided additional demographic testimony of increased material well-being as there were significant falls in the death rate, birth rate and infant mortality rate.

However, the migration statistics offered a more ambiguous picture, being uncertain in nature and open to a variety of interpretations. No official UK migration statistics were compiled, but port authorities were required to record the entry and exit of passengers. In the period 1900–14 recorded passenger movement between the UK and extra-European ports reveals that 7.5 million passengers left the UK, 4 million entered the UK, indicating a net

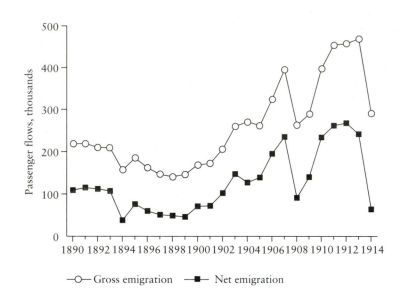

Figure 4.1. UK emigration, 1890–1914. *Source:* see text.

outflow of 3.5 million; for UK citizens the data are 4.5 million leaving, 2.2 million entering and a net outflow of 2.3 million. Although somewhat overstated by these statistics, emigration from the UK was a characteristic and significant feature of the Edwardian period. North America was the most important destination for departing UK citizens, with the majority migrating to the United States until 1910, when Canada became the most popular single destination.

The decision to migrate is also difficult to interpret. The most common motive was a perception of opportunities for increased material well-being overseas, although the would-be migrant may have taken a long-run view which looked to the life chances of his or her children rather than to more immediate gains. However, as the potential emigrant required sufficient resources to relocate, the poorest members of society, who had most to gain, were prevented from taking this option by their lack of financial resources. In making the decision the emigrant would consider conditions in potential destinations relative to those at home; here migrants often relied on news provided by family members, friends and newspaper reports which informed their decision.

The evidence of the Edwardian migration statistics suggests that an increasing number of UK citizens came to the conclusion that a better future could be found overseas. Figure 4.1 shows gross and net passenger movements of UK citizens between UK ports and extra-European ports,1 the most useful indicator of annual emigration available. There is a sharp contrast between the last decade of the nineteenth century, which saw emigration on a downward trend, and the first decade of the twentieth century, when a much more rapid upward trend emerged that was only halted by the outbreak of war in 1914.

Emigrants may have been influenced by an impression that living standards in Britain had reached a plateau and their decision may have had some substance. Information on the consumption of foodstuffs, including drink, suggests little evidence of either progress or retrogression in the Edwardian period. A substantial portion of the British diet was imported and consumption per head for a vast range of foodstuffs can be estimated. This evidence, taken with information on domestic agricultural production and contemporary household surveys, suggests that diets, and therefore calorific and nutritional intake, changed little between the last decade of the nineteenth century and 1914. Of much greater significance, particularly for the working class, was the persistent discrepancy between the dietary composition of better fed males and less well fed females and children. Additional evidence that the British diet changed little for many in the working class in the Edwardian period is found in reports on the physical condition of volunteers who joined the Army in the Boer War and First World War.

However, more generally, changes in the commercial distribution of goods which had begun in the Victorian period were maintained; chain stores with multiple outlets, such as Liptons, Home & Colonial, Boots and W.H. Smith & Son, grew throughout the Edwardian era. The Co-operative movement also continued to expand; its local retailing societies prospered and the Co-operative Wholesale Society, its manufacturing sector, was one of Edwardian Britain's largest industrial employers. These tendencies contributed to a standardization of product and improvement in quality which was reflected in the mass production of goods ranging from beer to biscuits, and cigarettes to clothes. Similarly, improved technology, in the form of faster ocean transit and more effective meat storage, allowed the importation of frozen meats which altered patterns of food consumption. In the face of this and other evidence of prosperity, a relatively affluent urban worker probably found the decision to emigrate far from easy.

Earnings, the Cost of Living and Real Earnings

However, the view that the rate of increase in living standards slowed or even stagnated during the Edwardian period was not only commonly held but it also received the support of expert opinion. Many commentators, including advisers to the British Cabinet,[2] concluded that this ceiling on workers' aspirations was a cause of the widespread industrial conflict evident in the years between 1908 and 1914. One of the most influential statisticians of this period was A.L. Bowley, whose work informed both contemporary debate and subsequent historical opinion. Bowley's conviction that the economic statistics produced by state agencies were inadequate, and therefore unable to inform the policy debates of the Edwardian period, led him to campaign for more effective official collection of representative labour market data. His own pioneering time series indices for prices and wages rates appeared in contemporary reports and were later consolidated in his *Wages and Income in the United Kingdom since 1860* published in 1937. Although Bowley expressed a preference for the term 'Quotient' rather than 'Real Wages', stressing 'the numerous qualifications with which it must be used', he knew, even as he wrote, that this caveat would be ignored.

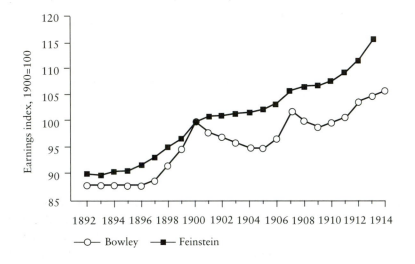

Figure 4.2. Earnings, 1892–1914. *Source:* See text.

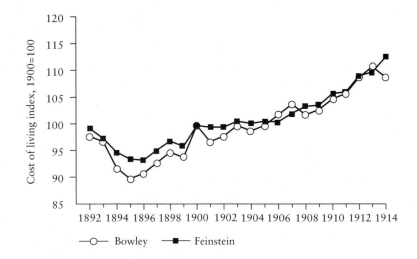

Figure 4.3. Cost of living, 1892–1914. *Source:* See text.

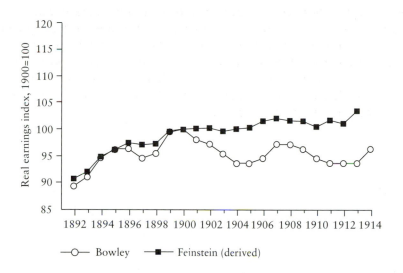

Figure 4.4. Real earnings, 1892–1914. *Source:* See text.

Bowley's series for the Edwardian period are presented here as graphs: earnings in Figure 4.2; the cost of living in Figure 4.3; and, real earnings in Figure 4.4.[3] Two aspects of these graphs are designed to provide an impression of change as it might have appeared to an Edwardian; first, a perspective from the beginning of the twentieth century is obtained by making 1900 the base year for each index; and, secondly, each series starts in 1892 to give an impression of trends at the end of the Victorian period.

The impression gained from Bowley's series can be described as follows. Figure 4.2 shows that after a period of stability in the early 1890s earnings rose in the late 1890s to a peak in 1900. During the Edwardian period earnings fell away until a recovery in trade resulted in a peak in 1907; the subsequent downturn lasted until 1910, after which recovery continued until 1914, when the earnings series reached its maximum value. Figure 4.3 depicts Bowley's cost of living series which fell from 1892 to 1895; thereafter his cost of living exhibited a persistent long-run upward trend for the next twenty years. The combination of these two series provides an indication of the purchasing power of wage earners during this period and is presented in Figure 4.4. Real earnings trended upward to a peak in 1899, after which they fell until 1904; a recovery in real earnings to 1908 failed to recoup all the ground lost after 1900 and the subsequent slow downward trend was only interrupted by a minor recovery in 1914. The implication of Bowley's story was that real earnings had peaked at the very end of Victoria's reign and had either ceased to grow or fallen in the first decade-and-a-half of the twentieth century.

Until two of its facets were recognized, Bowley's work remained a standard, and largely unquestioned, reference point for investigations of the Edwardian labour market. Gourvish identified, first, the all-pervasive influence of Bowley's data upon the historiography of the period; and, secondly, provided a critique of Bowley's work which, while recognizing its seminal importance, indicated several methodological difficulties which beset his statistical series.[4]

Some of the problematic aspects of Bowley's data have now been addressed in a series of articles and essays by Feinstein;[5] who, incidentally, had concluded previously that improvement to Bowley's data was unlikely.[6] Feinstein's new estimates for earnings and the cost of living and a derived real earnings series are also presented in Figures 4.2, 4.3 and 4.4; where they can be compared with Bowley's original series. Taking first money earnings, as in Figure 4.2, Feinstein's data suggests that the post-1895 upward trend continued after 1900, rising significantly until 1914, and the cyclical pattern was less marked than Bowley had suggested. Figure 4.3 demonstrates the robust nature of Bowley's original cost of living series which corresponds closely to the reworked series provided by Feinstein.[7] The full significance of Feinstein's reappraisal appears in Figure 4.4, where the real earnings series presents a much more optimistic story than that told by Bowley. Feinstein's series suggests that real earnings rose to 1900 but, by contrast with Bowley, these gains were at least retained if not marginally improved upon in the next decade-and-a-half to 1914.

This reassessment is important because it changes our perspectives on other aspects of this period; for example, explanations of the industrial discontent after 1909 which rest upon Bowley's story require reconsideration. It seems unlikely that individual workers were under the impression that their incomes had fallen by the end of the Edwardian period, though there might have been a widely held perception that living standards in general had fallen. It would appear more likely that labour militancy had its causes in the perceptions of specific groups of workers who believed that their incomes were declining relative to other groups who were becoming more prosperous. Two pieces of evidence can be offered to indicate that relative incomes were changing. First, the number of white collar or salaried workers increased significantly during this period; and, secondly, a number of Feinstein's earnings series for specific groups of workers, which were significant elements of Bowley's study, indicate slower growth than the new aggregate earnings series over the period. This suggests that the wave of labour discontent after 1910 was not caused by a general mood of dissatisfaction; rather, it was rooted in particular circumstances and specific industries.

The World of Work, Labour Relations and Industrial Discontent

In Britain the transition of industrial production from workshop to factory was a slow process and one which continued throughout the Victorian era despite the application of the popular term 'Industrial Revolution' to the half century before 1840. Although some industries, particularly cotton spinning and weaving, were renowned by the middle of the nineteenth century for factory production, other industries, including branches of the textile trades, persisted with putting-out and workshop production and did not adopt this form of organization until much later in the century. By 1900, however, factory production had diffused across the industrial sector to become the prevalent, though by no means the only, form of organization. The other sectors of the economy also contained a variety of organizational forms which ranged from the agricultural small holding to the large landed estate, and the solicitor's office to the stations, workshops and footplates of the Midland Railway Company, Britain's largest company.

The lengthy and slow process of industrialization, which was associated with the gradual diffusion of factory production, contributed not only to the slow growth of productivity in the industrial sector but also to the low labour productivity of the industrial sector relative to other sectors within the British economy. These characteristic features of British industrialization, taken with the accommodation of expansionary periods in the business cycle through increased employment of labour by industrial enterprises, played important roles in determining the nature of the labour market in 1900.

The extended and uneven pattern of industrial development in the United Kingdom was also associated with the evolution of two types of trade union: the craft union, which attempted to control many aspects of more skilled occupations, including entry to the job; and the general union, which provided an organization for unskilled workers and general labourers. Both types of trade union, however, committed by far the largest portion of their expenditure to welfare functions, including insurance provisions against sickness, accidents, old age, death and unemployment, and devoted relatively little to political activity. Table 4.1 reveals the growth of trade union membership from 1.5 million in 1893 to 4.1 million in 1914; it also reveals the increased propensity for workers to join trade unions as reflected in the index of trade union density, the ratio of actual to potential trade union members in the workforce, which increased sharply after 1910.

British trade unions exhibited two other characteristics at the beginning of the twentieth century. On the one hand, trade unions wished to maintain their autonomy and independence, which limited their scope for joint action. But, on the other hand, they also recognized interests which they shared with other labour unions that ensured collective reactions to common problems, and to legal difficulties in particular. The position of trade unions which had been established in the 1870s, by legislation and judicial decisions, was challenged in a series of legal judgements at the beginning of the twentieth century. However, labour legislation passed before 1914 confirmed the status of trade unions and removed the impediments to their activities which had been revealed in the courts. In 1906 the Trades Disputes Act effectively reversed the Taff Vale Judgement of 1901, offering trade unions protection from civil actions, and the Trade Union Act of 1913 reversed the Osborne Judgement of 1909, which had effectively outlawed political levies on behalf of the Labour Party. Trade unions also lobbied for the enactment of labour legislation. In the case of the 1908 Coal Mines Act, which limited the miner's working day to

Table 4.1. Trade union statistics of the UK, 1893–1913

	1	2	3	4	5
Year	Potential union membership (m)	Total union membership (m)	Union density (2):(1) (%)	Number of disputes	Number of workers directly affected (000s)
1893	14.947	1.559	10.4	615	594
1894	15.092	1.530	10.1	929	257
1895	15.236	1.504	9.9	745	207
1896	15.370	1.608	10.5	926	148
1897	15.524	1.731	11.2	864	167
1898	15.668	1.752	11.2	711	201
1899	15.812	1.911	12.1	719	138
1900	15.957	2.022	12.7	648	135
1901	16.101	2.025	12.6	642	111
1902	16.267	2.013	12.4	442	117
1903	16.433	1.994	12.1	387	94
1904	16.599	1.967	11.9	355	56
1905	16.765	1.997	11.9	358	68
1906	16.932	2.210	13.1	486	158
1907	17.098	2.513	14.7	601	101
1908	17.264	2.485	14.4	399	224
1909	17.430	2.477	14.2	436	170
1910	17.596	2.565	14.6	531	385
1911	17.762	3.139	17.7	903	831
1912	17.841	3.416	19.1	857	1233
1913	17.920	4.135	23.1	1497	516

Sources: Columns 1–2, G.S. Bain and F. Elsheikh, *Union Growth and the Business Cycle* (Oxford, 1976) p. 134; columns 4–10, A.L. Bowley, *An Elementary Manual of Statistics* (London, 3rd edn, 1923) p. 163.

eight hours, political pressure obtained an extension of the supervisory role of the state at the workplace which had its origins in the various Factories Acts and the Mines Regulation Act of the Victorian period. Less successful, though indicative of changed circumstances and attitudes, was the response to high rates of unemployment in 1908 and 1909 which saw the introduction of a Right to Work Bill. This issue faded from the political agenda with the

6	7	8	9	10
Number of workers indirectly affected (000s)	Aggregate number of days lost by disputes (m)	Number of disputes settled		
		In favour of workers (%)	In favour of employers (%)	Compromise or indefinite (%)
40	30.5	40	34	26
68	9.5	35	36	29
56	5.7	35	37	28
50	3.8	41	33	26
63	10.4	38	36	26
53	15.3	33	32	35
42	2.5	32	35	33
53	3.2	31	34	35
68	4.1	25	44	31
140	3.5	24	47	29
23	2.3	23	48	29
31	1.5	17	51	32
26	2.5	20	46	34
60	3.0	31	37	32
47	2.2	32	41	27
72	10.8	20	44	36
131	2.8	18	46	36
130	9.9	25	37	38
131	10.3	25	32	43
230	40.9	27.5	30.5	42
173	11.6	29	25	46

restoration of high levels of employment after 1910, to reappear in the 1920s.

The expansion of employment in the mining, industrial, utilities and communications sectors, here most notably railways, was associated with a tendency for firm size to increase. Well established by the 1880s, this tendency was accelerated by consolidation which occurred in many sectors including railways, banking and industrial enterprise. The management structures which emerged in many of these companies were often relatively weak and underdeveloped. In these circumstances, employers found that worker organization could bring advantages, since strong unions effectively took some of the shop-floor management decisions about training and work allocation. But strong unions could also involve costs: the successful organization of a strike by a trade union, combined with a demonstration of solidarity on the part of the workforce, placed a limit to management discretion over the setting of wages and conditions of work.

Table 4.1 provides contemporary evidence collected to ascertain the state of industrial relations. Two of these annual series are plotted in Figure 4.5 to indicate a long-run perspective on labour disputes in the United Kingdom between 1893 and 1913: the number of disputes which resulted in lost time; and, the number of days lost, in millions, due to the direct and indirect

Plate 4.1. Durham miners, 1908, on their way to the annual gala. In the early twentieth century trade unions did more than just negotiate over pay and conditions of work. Many unions paid welfare benefits to members and organized social events. One the largest of these was the annual Durham miners' gala, a combination of picnic, fair and political meeting.

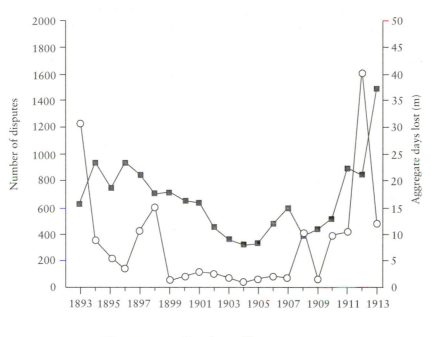

Figure 4.5. Labour disputes, 1893–1913. *Source:* Table 4.1.

consequences of lock-outs and strikes. These series are indicative of general tendencies in the labour market, though their shortcomings were recognized by the Board of Trade officials who constructed them.

The number of labour disputes fell throughout the decade after 1896 and it was only after 1910 that a rising trend emerged. In the case of the number of days lost each year a similar story could be told about a more volatile indicator; between 1899 and 1907 there was an era of industrial peace which contrasted sharply with the periods before and after. This picture is confirmed by an examination of the numbers of days lost relative to the number of potential trade union members, an indication of the total workforce. Between 1901 and 1910 the average number of days lost due to disputes was 0.25 days per worker, or one half of the average over the full twenty-one year period and, by contrast, 2 days and 2.3 days were lost per worker in 1893 and 1912 respectively.

Columns 8–10 of table 4.1 provides a further indicator of industrial relations which is suggestive of changes in the labour market: the nature of settlements achieved after a labour dispute. Unlike the earlier period, the years 1901 to 1909 saw the largest portion of disputes settled in favour of employers; by further contrast, a compromise or indefinite outcome was the most likely result of an industrial dispute between 1910 and 1914. Overall, these series confirm an increase in industrial militancy at the end of the Edwardian period.

A closer examination of the statistics reveals, as contemporaries were well aware, the significant contribution to these data of disputes at the coal mines in 1893 and 1912. Other important disputes included: engineering in 1897–98, shipbuilding and cotton spinning in 1908, and the docks and railways in 1911. This evidence reveals a system of industrial relations which was relatively successful, as indicated by these data, until rising prices provoked workers who increasingly looked to trade unions and more militant collective action to increase their earnings commensurately.

Overall, as average real earnings did not fall, it is probable these actions were motivated by a desire either to maintain existing living standards or to increase levels of consumption. This suggests that workers reacted to static or more slowly growing levels of income with behaviour that sought to maintain the increases in living standards which occurred in the last decade of the Victorian period. Furthermore, workers may have attempted to maintain relative income levels which had been established before 1910, sometimes unsuccessfully. The contemporary retardation of productivity growth apparent in some sections of the extractive and manufacturing sectors was a serious barrier to these objectives and the resulting discontent produced disputes. While this was a major problem in some of the important export industries, it boded ill for the future of the coal industry in particular, as the experiences of the 1920s were to prove.

In focus: Irish Economic Development, Home Rule and Ulster Unionism

---

The last major domestic political event before the outbreak of the First World War was the passage of the Home Rule Act which legislated for the devolution of limited powers to a parliament in Dublin. Implementation of the Act was suspended until the end of the war but subsequent events, including the Easter Rising by the Irish Republican Brotherhood in 1916, the ensuing polarization of Irish opinion, and the Anglo-Irish war rendered the Act a dead letter. In 1920, one hundred and twenty years after the Act of Union of Britain and Ireland had achieved royal assent, the government of Ireland Act divided Ireland into two parts, each with its own parliament. This reactivation of the Home Rule Act failed to reflect the political shift which had occurred among Irish nationalists in the intervening period. The following year, while six northern counties remained part of the United Kingdom, twenty-six southern counties gained dominion status within the British Empire as the Irish Free State. The events which resulted in this settlement were propelled by two contending nationalist ambitions on the part of inhabitants of Ireland: a nationalism which favoured the creation of a separate Irish political entity and a nationalism which identified with the British crown and maintenance of the United Kingdom. Furthermore, although there was support for political union in the southern counties of Ireland, the majority of Ireland's unionists lived in Ulster.

Irish Economic Development, Home Rule and Ulster Unionism (continued)

However, although these contending nationalist aspirations provided the initial dynamics of the 'Irish Question' in the half-century before 1921, the importance of economic factors should not be neglected. Relative economic development and relative levels of average income, within the United Kingdom and within Ireland itself, provided important considerations which contributed to the process that resulted in political bifurcation. Moreover, despite its underdevelopment relative to Britain, there is evidence that Ireland, particularly in Dublin and Ulster, exhibited features which were similar to those of the British labour market described above. In Ireland, however, these features were too weakly developed to counter the structural divisions caused by the cultural differences and uneven development which divided the North and South.

Nineteenth-century Ireland, which had a predominantly agrarian economy, was the poorest of the four constituent countries which comprised the United Kingdom; Ireland alone experienced a fall in population, a trend which persisted until the First World War. Industrial development in Ireland occurred very unevenly, reflecting to some extent the limited endowment of appropriate natural resources, particularly coal which was imported from Britain. Dublin, the major administrative centre, was a relatively underdeveloped industrial centre which processed the agricultural produce of its rural hinterland. Ulster, the northern province, had Ireland's highest average per capita income and produced the bulk of Ireland's manufactured goods though labour productivity in its industrial sector was low relative to Britain. Belfast, Ireland's largest city and Ulster's industrial centre, depended heavily upon three industries which were oriented towards the export trades: linen manufacture, engineering, and shipbuilding.[8] In the second half of the nineteenth century, Ulster prospered under the stimulus of external demand as world trade expanded. Although American markets were significant, British and Empire markets provided the most important outlets for the linen factories and Belfast shipyards.

However, this pattern of uneven economic development within Ireland reflected a long standing division which was cultural, political and religious in nature. This split was clearly indicated by the 1911 census of Ireland:

	Protestant	Catholic	Total
Ulster	891,000	691,000	1,582,000
Three southern provinces	250,000	2,550,000	2,800,000
Ireland	1,141,000	3,241,000	4,382,000

Irish Economic Development, Home Rule and Ulster Unionism (continued)

In the South, where the population was predominantly Roman Catholic, especially in the rural areas where peasant farming dominated, the landowning class, which included many Protestants, was socially isolated and experienced a decline in its political influence. In part, this was the result of resistance which had its roots in a rejection of rule from Westminster which predated the consequences of the failure of potato crops in the late 1840s. However, the two dramatic consequences of the Potato Famine, death and emigration, left a lasting and bitter resentment in the Irish countryside. It was also a consequence of measures introduced subsequently by successive governments to increase the security and independence of the peasant farmer in the hope of defusing rural discontent. In the last quarter of the nineteenth century the hegemony of the Anglo-Irish was finally undercut by the development of effective political organizations by Irish farmers.

In the North, and by contrast, there was a substantial Protestant community which had its origins in sixteenth and seventeenth-century English and Scottish settlement, though it had been augmented by more recent migration from Britain. More importantly, this community incorporated members of all social classes and included owners of large agricultural estates and factories, tenant farmers and factory workers. Furthermore, the members of this community perceived acutely their collective identity which was defined by their assessment of the cultural superiority of the Protestant over the Catholic and loyalty to the British crown.

In the last instance, however, the loyalty of Ulstermen was pledged to the British crown only in as far as it secured the Protestant supremacy in Ulster. The Orange Orders, which commemorated the triumph of William III, the Protestant Prince of Orange, over Roman Catholic James II in 1690, provided the embodiment of the Ulster Protestant identity; they also counted among their ranks two-thirds of the Protestant males in the province. Whenever Ulster Protestants feared that Irish nationalist demands might result in legislation which would devolve political power to an Irish parliament in Dublin their reaction was political mobilization around slogans which asserted 'Home Rule is Rome Rule' and 'No Popery, No Surrender'. This was the response to each of the Home Rule Bills of 1886, 1893 and 1912; and, on each occasion new political associations were established in Ulster to coordinate rejection and resistance to the proposals.[9]

The Ulster unionists reacted to the Home Rule Act of 1914 with plans to take unilateral political action which they recognized could result in civil war; the opposition of the Ulster Volunteer Force was not to be dismissed lightly as it had obtained 24,600 rifles and 3 million rounds of ammunition. It was also clear from the reaction of the officer class of the British Army, in an incident remembered as the Curragh Mutiny, that there was much sympathy among the British elite for this stance. Negotiations on the implementation of Home Rule continued through the summer until the outbreak of the First World War when the issue was shelved.

Irish Economic Development, Home Rule and Ulster Unionism (continued)

Three prominent aspects of Ulster's economic structure reflected uneven economic development in Ireland. First, the labour market in Ireland was segmented by a regional and sectarian divide. In 1907 James Larkin's attempt to organize a united non-sectarian labour movement, built around the Independent Labour Party and the National Union of Dock Labourers, foundered in the face of sectarian reaction and riots in Belfast. The entry restrictions of craft unions had long combined with loyalty to Orange sentiment to exclude Catholics from skilled jobs in the shipyards but a particularly violent incident saw 'Fenians' and 'Home Rulers' expelled from their place of work in 1912. By contrast, Dublin shared with the rest of the United Kingdom the strike wave of 1911–13 which culminated in thirty labour disputes in the summer of 1913, many of which saw confrontations between nationalist employers and socialist republican workers. This period of labour militancy ended with the defeat of the Irish Transport and General Workers' Union, founded in 1908 and organized by Larkin and James Connolly, after a four-month lock-out by the Dublin United Tramways Company, in January 1914.[10]

Second, the Ulster business community provided a centre for Protestant reaction. The Ulster businessmen, who defined themselves, amongst other things, in terms of their determination, business-capacity, and courage,[11] were capable organizers who played an active role in the mobilization of resistance to the Home Rule Act passed in 1914. Furthermore, the economic institutions of Ulster, and notably the Belfast Bank which held the account of the Ulster Defence Council and provided the finance which secured the arms landed at Larne in 1914,[12] played an active and partisan role as civil war loomed in Ireland.

Third, the resolve of Ulster's Orange organizations was fortified by their economic analysis of the consequences of Home Rule. In addition to a conviction that a government of Ireland located in Dublin would be incompetent, and a fear that preferential treatment for Catholic interests would discriminate against those of Protestants, there was apprehension about the objectives of nationalist economic policy. From its inception in 1905, Sinn Féin ('Ourselves Alone') had indicated an intention to introduce protectionist measures in order to foster industrialization of the South. For Ulster industrialists, who feared retaliatory economic measures by British governments, there was a much more immediate threat; tariffs introduced in Ireland which discriminated against British products could jeopardize Ulster's export markets throughout the British Empire.[13]

After partition, conditions were far removed from any which had been predicted or desired by political parties, north or south of the new border. During the depressed interwar years Northern Ireland experienced rates of unemployment higher than the average for the United Kingdom and this pattern has persisted until the present day. In the South economic policies

Irish Economic Development, Home Rule and Ulster Unionism (continued)

differed from those which might have been expected and there was no attempt to introduce the protectionist policies advocated by Sinn Féin before the First World War. By contrast the boycott of Belfast goods in 1920–22 and the Anglo-Irish trade war of 1932–38 were nationalistic in inspiration, the latter prompting an autarkic anti-British policy which achieved little or nothing by way of economic development. The final irony of the interwar period was the significant role played by the financiers among Dublin's Protestant bourgeoisie in determining an orthodox fiscal policy far removed from that envisaged before the Home Rule Act was passed.

Historical Interpretations

The first fifteen years of the twentieth century, sometimes conveniently but inaccurately labelled the Edwardian era,[14] have been depicted by some historians as a particularly important period in British history. For most contemporaries a stark contrast was provided by their perceptions of the domestic tranquillity and international stability which had characterized the second half of Victoria's reign. Ensor, a leading historian of the period who drew extensively on his personal experience, remarked on 'the seething and teeming of the pre-war period, its immense ferment and its restless fertility'.[15]

The result of this turmoil was to establish trends and patterns of economic, social and political change that transformed both domestic and international circumstances. Although some of these tendencies were established before 1900, and many were to require up to fifty years or more to come to maturity, the consequences of these changes were to reverberate for the rest of the century. Furthermore, if the First World War, which may have accelerated the rate at which these conditions were transformed, is seen as a symptom of international and domestic conditions, this suggestion only emphasizes further the pivotal nature of the Edwardian period.

In the face of domestic and international circumstances the *laissez-faire* state of the Victorian era was viewed increasingly as inappropriate. In part, dissatisfaction with the liberal ideal stemmed from a perception that the British economy was performing badly relative to the United States and Germany; the burdens of imperial defence and social welfare would weigh less heavily on an efficient Britain. Attempts to recast liberal philosophy to accommodate a reconciliation of individual liberty and state intervention, for example, L.T. Hobhouse's *Liberalism* (1911), indicate the shift of ground which had occurred since Herbert Spencer's *The Man versus the State* (1884). Hobhouse, however, remained convinced that the state should act only to secure conditions which would allow individuals to prosper. Many trade unionists and Labour Party members also viewed extensions of state intervention with suspicion and were deeply distrustful of proposals which called for comprehensive nationalization of the means of production. Despite the many difficulties which faced citizens of the United Kingdom between 1900 and 1914, the ideological inheritance of Victorian liberalism was not jettisoned easily, even by those who objectively stood to gain most.

The year Ensor's book first went to press, 1936, also saw the publication of Dangerfield's *The Strange Death of Liberal England, 1910–1914* which mourned the demise of an all-embracing ideology rather than the passing of a political party. Dangerfield has had his critics, who have suggested that his thesis underestimated the degree of continuity with the late Victorian period or overstated the degree of change in the subsequent period, but the continuing engagement by historians with his contention is testament to an abiding interest in the period immediately before the First World War.

Bibliographical Note

A survey of the causes and consequences of the protracted and relatively slow process of industrialization in the United Kingdom appears in C.H. Lee, *The British Economy since 1700: a Macroeconomic Perspective* (Cambridge, 1986). The recent recognition by economic historians of the relative importance of the service sector, one of Lee's major themes, can be discerned in a comparison of the first and second editions of volume two of R. Floud and D.N. McCloskey (eds), *The Economic History of Britain since 1700* (Cambridge, 1981, 1994). The significance of slow and uneven economic development for the history of labour, industrial relations and class formation is demonstrated in P. Joyce, 'Work', in F.M.L. Thompson (ed.), *The Cambridge Social History of Britain 1750–1950, Volume 2 People and their Environment* (Cambridge, 1990) pp. 131–94; accompanying chapters consider aspects of consumption: M.J. Daunton, 'Housing', pp. 195–250 and D.J. Oddy, 'Food, drink, and nutrition', pp. 251–78. Trade unions, the major concern of labour history until attention switched to the workplace, can still be discovered in Henry Pelling, *A History of British Trade Unions* (Harmondsworth, 3rd edn, 1976).

A.L. Bowley and G.H. Wood collected contemporary wage and price series; a quarter of a century later these were restated in A.L. Bowley, *Wages and Income in the United Kingdom since 1860* (Cambridge, 1937). The extent to which economic historians had relied upon Bowley's data and the problematic nature of his series were identified in T.R. Gourvish, 'The standard of living, 1890–1914', in A. O'Day (ed.), *The Edwardian Age: Conflict and Stability, 1900–1914*, (London, 1979) pp. 13–34; this volume also includes complementary historiographic survey chapters which consider Edwardian society and politics. A detailed reassessment of earnings between 1880 and 1913 appears in C.H. Feinstein, 'New estimates of average earnings in the United Kingdom, 1880–1913', *Economic History Review*, 2nd ser. vol. XLIII, no. 4 (1990), pp. 595–632; this also provides a survey of historical sources and recent journal literature.

R.C.K. Ensor, *England 1870–1914* (Oxford, 1936) remains a highly useful overview of economic, social and political developments during this period. J.J. Lee, *Ireland 1912–1985: Politics and Society* (Cambridge, 1989) and L. Kennedy and P. Ollerenshaw (eds), *An Economic History of Ulster 1820–1939* (Manchester, 1985) outline, respectively, the Irish dimension and the development of the Ulster economy.

Notes

1. B.R. Mitchell and P. Deane, *Abstract of British Historical Statistics* (Cambridge, 1962) pp. 47–50.

2. G.R. Askwith, 'The present unrest in the labour world', draft paper, 25 July 1911, CAB 37/107/70; cited by T.R. Gourvish, 'The standard of living, 1890–1914', in Alan O'Day (ed.), *The Edwardian Age: Conflict and Stability, 1900–1914* (London, 1979) pp. 13–34.

3. A.L. Bowley, *Wages and Income in the United Kingdom since 1860* (Cambridge, 1937) pp. 6, 30, 121.

4. Gourvish, 'The standard of living, 1890–1914'.

5. C.H. Feinstein, 'What really happened to real wages?: trends in wages, prices, and productivity in the United Kingdom, 1880–1913', *Economic History Review*, 2nd ser., vol. XLIII (1990), pp. 329–55; *ibid*, 'New estimates of average earnings in the United Kingdom, 1880–1913', *Economic History Review*, 2nd ser., vol. XLIII, no. 4, (1990), pp. 595–632; *ibid*, 'Variety and volatility: some aspects of the labour market in Britain, 1880–1913', in Colin Holmes and Alan Booth (eds), *Economy and Society: European Industrialisation and its Social Consequences: Essays Presented to Sidney Pollard* (Leicester, 1991) pp. 154–74.

6. C.H. Feinstein, *National Income, Expenditure and Output of the United Kingdom, 1855–1965* (Cambridge, 1972) p. 14.

7. C.H. Feinstein, 'A new look at the cost of living 1870–1914', in James Foreman-Peck (ed.), *New Perspectives on the Late Victorian Economy: Essays in Quantitative Economic History 1860–1914* (Cambridge, 1991) pp. 151–79.

8. R.C.K. Ensor, *England 1870–1914* (Oxford, 1936) p. 452; R. Kee, *The Bold Fenian Men* (London, 1976) p. 99; P. Ollerenshaw, 'Industry, 1820–1914' in L. Kennedy and P. Ollerenshaw (eds), *An Economic History of Ulster 1820–1939* (Manchester, 1985) pp. 62–108.

9. J.J. Lee, *Ireland 1912–1985. Politics and Society* (Cambridge, 1989).

10. Henry Patterson, *Class Conflict and Sectarianism: The Protestant Working Class and the Belfast Labour Movement 1868–1920* (Belfast, 1980) pp. xiv, 41, 66, 89; R.F. Foster, *Modern Ireland 1600–1972* (London, 1988) pp. 388–9; 442–3.

11. Lee, *Ireland*, p. 4.

12. P. Ollerenshaw, *Banking in Nineteenth Century Ireland: the Belfast Banks, 1825–1914* (Manchester, 1987).

13. P. Ollerenshaw, 'Businessmen in Northern Ireland and the Imperial connection, 1886–1939', in Keith Jeffrey (ed.) *Ireland and the Empire* (Manchester, 1994).

14. The heads of state of Britain and Ireland during this period were Victoria (1837–1901); Edward VII (1901–10); and George V (1910–36).

15. Ensor, *England 1870–1914*, p. 557.

5 Poverty and Social Reforms

E.P. Hennock

'The question of poverty is that of death, disease, winter or of any other natural phenomenon. I do not know how either is to stop.' (Thackeray, 1848) Like these other natural phenomena its challenge was to the compassion of the more fortunate. Later in the nineteenth century such a view was no longer the dominant one. In the 1880s many educated people worried about the 'problem of poverty in the midst of plenty'. To them it was a problem, not merely a fact of nature, because they believed that their society had discovered the means of progress. In view of the undoubted 'progress of the working classes' monitored and celebrated in publications of the 1860s, they asked themselves what was the significance of the residue of great poverty that still existed? By the end of the decade few people believed that it endangered their civilization, but whether the means of progress had been adequately understood so that all that remained was to pursue or commend them with greater determination was a much debated issue.

National Efficiency

To these two concerns, for the suffering of the poor and for the encouragement of progress, educated people at the beginning of the twentieth century added a further reason for taking poverty seriously. The military set-backs of the Boer War (1899–1902) had been deeply disillusioning. They focused attention in the first place on questions of military and governmental efficiency, but the publicity given to the number of recruits rejected as unfit for military service focused attention also on the fitness of the nation for its imperial task. There were two reasons why these figures should have been regarded as a serious indicator of malaise.

The first was that Britain had become a nation of town-dwellers. By 1901, 77 per cent of the population of England and Wales lived in towns. Urban life had always been unhealthy and had been unfavourably contrasted with country life. True, the national death rate had seen an encouraging decline since the mid 1870s, which meant that towns were no longer the devourers of population that they had once been. But how fit were those who survived to grow up in the urban environment? Was a 'town-bred population' capable of being an 'imperial race'?

Military efficiency in a world of competing empires was not the only issue. It was a Quaker pacifist, Seebohm Rowntree, who found roughly 30 per cent of the population of York to be in poverty and claimed in 1901 that this was typical of urban England as a whole. He made a point of demonstrating the connection between poverty and physical deterioration, and went so far as to calculate a 'poverty line' in terms of income insufficient for bare physical efficiency. His discovery that every labourer with a normal-sized family of three children passed through a period of probably ten years when he and his family would be underfed had implications both for the fitness of the next generation and for the efficiency of the present labour-force, as he was at pains to point out. 'The stress and keenness of international competition', to use Rowntree's own phrase, was to raise poverty – a poverty that could result in a nation unfit to retain its share of the world market – into a matter of urgent national interest. The humanitarians had acquired an argument calculated to appeal to national self-interest and therefore capable of giving rise to political action.[1]

What that action should be was much in dispute. For there was a further change that had come over the population of the country. The decline in the death rate had been followed by a decline in the birth rate, but not as in past times mainly through restricted opportunities to marry. It was less the number of families that declined than the number of children born to the family. All this might have been welcomed as indicating a diminution of suffering and hardship, were it not for the fact that the decline in the birth rate and in family size was greatest in professional and middle-class families and not found at all among the unskilled working class, the labouring poor. We now know that family limitation would spread gradually throughout society, but at the beginning of the century it looked as if the poorest were outbreeding the well-to-do. This rang alarm bells. The smaller stature of working men compared with gentlemen was a matter of common observation. Furthermore eugenicists were pioneering the study of the inheritance of mental characteristics and, as is often the case with a new science, were claiming far more for their subject than later more careful investigations would bear out. If all sorts of socially undesirable traits – both mental and physical – that were found among the poor were inherited, then the prospect of progressive deterioration stared the nation in the face.

The government responded to this literature of doom in 1904 by the appointment of the Inter-departmental Committee on Physical Deterioration. The Committee's historical importance derives not from the boldness of its proposals for action, for these could hardly have been less bold. It derives from the fact that it disposed of the issue of progressive deterioration. It decided that the 'abundant signs of physical defect' were due not to nature but to nurture, and this determined the direction of future reforms to improve the fitness of the nation; not, as the eugenicists demanded, by altering the relative fertility of the good and the bad stocks in the community, but by accepting the proposals that emanated from the medical officers of health. Nurture was partly a matter of food, partly of the environment, and the crucial period of life was that of childhood. Among the fifty-three rather disparate recommendations of the committee, thirty were concerned with children or their mothers. On the other hand, unlike Rowntree, the committee took no interest in either the level or the regularity of working-class income.[2]

What mattered about the report was not the rather mealy-mouthed proposals but the direction in which these pointed. The Education (Provision of Meals) Act, 1906, which granted permission to levy a compulsory rate rather than relying on charity for the provision of school meals, and the Education (Administrative Provisions) Act, 1907, which introduced regular medical inspection of school children (not merely the measurement of height and weight), went well beyond what had been envisaged in the report. But even this was a mere beginning. Not until 1914 were local authorities actually obliged to provide school meals, while the medical inspection of school children merely emphasized the need to provide treatment. However, by 1914

Plate 5.1. This very early photograph shows Liverpool's underfed scholars. The 'abundant signs of physical defect' found by the Interdepartmental Committee on Physical Deterioration in 1904 could be seen among urban working-class children. They were shorter and thinner than their middle-class peers, a direct consequence of inferior nutrition.

school clinics were widespread, if not universal, and financial arrangements with hospitals were not uncommon. These measures together with the many provisions contained in the Children's Act (1908), the licensing of midwives (1902) and the personal health services for mothers and infants described in Chapter 6 are the clearest instances of the new priorities. But considerations of national efficiency were to play a significant part in many of the other social reforms of the period.

Nothing reveals more clearly than the introduction of old age pensions in 1908 that concern for national efficiency, however significant in many cases, is not the key to all the social reforms of the Edwardian era. Except for education, old age pensions cost the taxpayer more than any of the other social reforms. By 1914 they cost £12.5 million, all spent on those over seventy and contributing nothing towards economic or military efficiency. This indicates that other considerations were also at stake. We shall look at the introduction of old age pensions in detail, for it is the key to much else that was to follow.

In focus: The Introduction of Old Age Pensions

The aged poor had always been its responsibility, but in the 1870s and 1880s the deterrent nature of the Poor Law – originally intended to apply only to the able-bodied – had been extended to the aged and infirm. This attack on the expectations of the poor to be supported by the community after they had ceased to be able to support themselves provides the background to the movement for state pensions.

It lent a special significance to a set of figures collected for the first time in 1890 and subsequently refined, which divided the recipients of poor relief over the age of sixty into five-year age groups. The percentage of the population aged sixty-five and over who were on poor relief, when compared to that of the adult population under sixty was about 30 per cent compared to 3 per cent. This revealed the numerical importance of the 'aged deserving poor', those who had kept themselves from being dependent on relief until advancing age and infirmity forced them into dependence on the Poor Law, an institution designed to deter loafers, which was quite inappropriate for decent old people.

The figures suggested that a policy of systematic deterrence was neither just nor realistic compared with an acceptance of old age pauperism as a fact of life. They sparked off a debate over the way to treat the aged poor which led to the appointment of a Royal Commission (1893–95). In this debate the advocates of pensions, Charles Booth, Joseph Chamberlain and many others, emerge as advocates of a deterrent Poor Law. Pensions were intended to reinforce deterrent Poor Law policies by removing a large category for whom deterrence seemed highly unsuitable. The majority report of the Royal Commission rejected all proposals for old age pensions and recommended easier out-relief for the aged deserving poor. For those who

The Introduction of Old Age Pensions (continued)

needed institutional care they recommended privileged non-deterrent treatment within the workhouse. This was a defeat not merely for the advocates of old age pensions, but equally for the advocates of general deterrence. Between 1895 and 1900 the Local Government Board circulars recommended this policy to the local Poor Law authorities and thereby signalled the official abandonment of the strict policy favoured since 1870. Thus the first result of the publication of the figures was the reassertion of traditional policies in the face of the innovators; both the rigid innovators who believed that a policy of general deterrence was feasible, and the flexible ones who hoped to make a policy of deterrence feasible by offering pensions outside the Poor Law.

But proposals for old age pensions could not be so lightly dismissed, for the figures of 1890–92 also held a message for the working-class electorate and for any politician who wished to obtain its support. They revealed that a significant proportion of working-class voters, men whose way of life was far removed from that of the habitual paupers, lived under the threat of ultimate degradation. These men were capable of organizing and delivering political support, and once they understood the message, they could be mobilized in favour of a pensions policy designed to save them from the pauper taint.

Joseph Chamberlain was the first major politician to understand this. His various proposals from 1891 onwards for state subsidies to underwrite old age pension savings schemes, including those to be organized by the working-class thrift societies, were part of his bid for the vote of the organized working class; i.e. that element of the working class organized in Friendly Societies, in trade unions, and similar institutions. He failed, but not, as is often suggested, because he was opposed by the Friendly Society movement. His scheme was destroyed by the opposition of the Treasury ministers in the Cabinet. The Friendly Societies dashed Chamberlain's hopes, not by anything they did to oppose him, but by their lack of positive and effective support. Their lack of enthusiasm for his proposals came from a distrust of the control over their institutions that was likely to follow such a partnership with the state. Since working-class thrift institutions were valued first and foremost for the independence from patronizing superior authority that they offered, this went to the heart of the matter.

Nothing but effective political pressure would ever have induced any government to impose the necessary taxation. That pressure was mobilized by the National Committee of Organised Labour for Old Age Pensions, founded in 1898. The launching of a broad-based pension campaign owed something to the encouragement derived from the introduction of old age pensions in New Zealand in the same year. But the programme was not borrowed from abroad; it was provided by Charles Booth, who had first proposed universal tax-financed pensions in 1891.

The Introduction of Old Age Pensions (continued)

There were two reasons why Booth's proposals appealed to the leaders of organized labour. Unlike Chamberlain's proposals for helping voluntary contributors to regular savings schemes, Booth's would have provided for the very poor. The National Committee of Organised Labour for Old Age Pensions was evidence that the message of the Poor Law figures had struck home in the privileged world of organized labour with its strong status consciousness. The figures of aged pauperism suggested a common identity between a group of the really poor and those in employment and relative comfort. Such an identification did not and does not always occur. Around 1900 organized labour moved into the politics of poverty along a limited number of routes where identification with the really poor was easy. Among these the politics of old age and of unemployment were the most important.

Moreover Booth's proposals had a special appeal for organized labour. His scheme carried no threat to the independence of working-class thrift institutions. The pension was to be a bonus added unconditionally to whatever income there was from other sources. It involved no means test and no subsidies. It was this which made his proposals attractive to organized labour.

The obvious objection to universal pensions was their cost. 'Proposals which could never have been recommended by a government to Parliament' was how the Chancellor of the Exchequer described them in 1899. It was a measure of how remote the leaders of organized labour (including the fledgling Labour Party) were at that time from considerations of governmental responsibility that the cost did not prevent them from committing themselves to universal pensions, to an even more generous version of Booth's proposals, demanding pensions for all at the age of sixty.

Nor did any such considerations prevent the National Committee from becoming a remarkably effective pressure group. By 1901 the support of the TUC and the Co-operative Movement had been won; by 1904 that of the Labour Party. The National Conference of Friendly Societies did not go so far, but in 1902 they declared themselves in favour of non-contributory pensions at least for the poor, if thrifty and deserving; in other words for their own members when in need.

During the course of the 1906 General Election a substantial body of MPs, both Liberal and Labour, were returned to Parliament pledged to old age pensions. It was the skilful deployment of backbench pressure in the House of Commons that induced Asquith, the Chancellor, in April 1907 to commit the government to a Pensions Bill in the following session, and to set £4 million aside for the purpose.

To take the wind out of the National Committee's sails, pensions would have to be non-contributory. Moreover the report of the Select Committee on the Aged Deserving Poor (1900) had made it clear that such people could not be left to the good will of the Poor Law Guardians. The rest depended on calculations of financial expediency. The money immediately

The Introduction of Old Age Pensions (continued)

available was under £7 million. That required a harsh means test and at the last moment even caused the qualifying age to be set at seventy, not at sixty-five, which the figures had identified as the crucial age for old age pauperism.

That decision made nonsense of the original intention of saving the aged deserving poor from the indignity of the Poor Law. Furthermore in an attempt to identify the deserving the Bill actually disqualified anyone recently dependent on the Poor Law. This disqualification combined with an unrealistically high pensions age was so blatantly at odds with the alleged object of the policy that Parliament insisted that it should lapse after two years. Only in 1911 was the vast body of paupers over seventy on out-relief able to opt out of the Poor Law (95 per cent of them) and obtain old age pensions instead. The Act of 1908 clearly failed in its alleged objective to save the deserving elderly poor from the Poor Law. But when regarded as a political expedient, a government ducking out under pressure by means of a legislative gesture, the Act makes sense. Its inadequacy was frankly admitted, excused on financial grounds and accompanied by a pledge that provisions would be improved when more money became available.

For anyone over seventy not disqualified by nationality, character or previous conduct, whose income was £21 per annum or less, i.e. just over 8s a week, the pension was 5s a week. It was reduced on a sliding scale to nothing for those with an income of around 12s a week. The maximum weekly income of pensioners was thus around 13s a week; the minimum 5s. To maintain physical health it was estimated at the time that an old age pensioner would have to spend 4s 7d a week plus rent. The 1908 Act did not rule out the possibility of modest amounts of earnings or savings, but the pension on its own was not intended to suffice without some family support. The figures thus provide no basis for any sharp contrast between community support and family support for the elderly. They make it clear that what was expected was a combination of both.

The case for pensions rested on the identification of a respectable section of the working class in distress for reasons beyond their control. For such people the deterrent Poor Law with its social stigma appeared inappropriate, and it proved possible to mobilize a combination of working-class and humanitarian opinion in support of a more honourable form of support. Pensions owed their political prominence to pressure group politics operating both outside and inside Parliament. The important decision in favour of tax-financed pensions rather than subsidized contributory ones was also imposed on the government by outside pressure. The detailed provisions were determined by the government mainly with an eye to the limited amount of finance that it had made available. For that reason the provisions fell short of what had been widely demanded.

Consequences of the Old Age Pensions Act

The 1908 Act marks the beginning, not the termination of a process of reform. Since the poor law disqualification was only temporary and since the costing of the original proposals was wildly out, pensions soon required large additional finance. Moreover the introduction of tax-financed benefits saddled the government with a most expensive precedent when it was forced to consider the equally deserving claims of other groups. The decision to pay pensions only at the age of seventy had after all left the aged and infirm below that age still unprovided for. Moreover all that could be said on behalf of the elderly could be and was equally well said on behalf of the unemployed.

Lloyd George had become Chancellor of the Exchequer in 1908. Presenting his first budget in April 1909 he boldly announced a new solution to each of these problems.

(1) He repudiated Asquith's promise to lower the general pensions age. He proposed instead to do what had been done in Germany, to combine long-term disablement benefit with short-term sickness benefit, and thereby to make pensions below seventy depend not on age but on inability to work. This was to target benefits on those in genuine need.

(2) The underfunding of the existing pension scheme, as well as the need for naval rearmament, was to be financed by a new 'super-tax' laid on the very rich and by higher tax rates on the so-called unearned income of the rentier class.

(3) Most important of all, for additional groups of the deserving poor he repudiated the precedent of tax-financed benefits. He proposed instead to introduce a system of compulsory contributions to guard against the consequences of breakdown in health, as the Germans had done, and to apply the same principle to the consequences of cyclical unemployment.

Health Insurance

The constitutional crisis caused by the rejection of the Budget by the House of Lords, followed by two general elections in 1910, caused the new social policy to be delayed until 1911. Part I of the National Insurance Act (1911) dealt with Health Insurance. It imposed compulsory contributions on all manual workers and most other employees earning £160 per annum or less.

Contributions of 4d per week (3d for women) were withheld from the worker's wage packet by employers, who themselves contributed 3d. There was a state subsidy of roughly 2d per week. Sickness benefit of 10s (7s 6d for women) was paid for a maximum of 26 weeks, and was followed, if necessary, by disablement benefit of 5s. In addition the contributors but not their dependants were entitled to medical treatment. This distinction clearly indicates that the purpose of Health Insurance was to prevent the poverty that would follow from the worker's illness and consequent inability to earn. It was a measure directed against poverty, and against illness only insofar as it was necessary to restore the wage-earners in the household to health.

The administration of cash benefits was left to the existing Friendly Societies and any other societies approved for the purpose, such as the specially established subsidiaries of insurance companies. The exceptional cases who were unable to join any Approved Society had their benefits administered on a less favourable basis by the Post Office. Medical treatment was provided by doctors belonging to the scheme, and paid according to the number of insured persons on their list, as was to be the case in the National Health Service after 1948. There was some provision for the treatment of tuberculosis in sanatoria, but hospitals were not incorporated in the scheme.

Compulsory Health Insurance significantly increased the number of those able to see a doctor, and consequently increased doctors' incomes. It also enabled doctors in working-class areas to emancipate themselves from direct employment by Friendly Societies on the harsh terms that had reflected the competition of doctors for patients at the lower end of the social spectrum. Under Health Insurance doctors were answerable to local Health Committees on which the medical profession was strongly represented, while their rates of pay showed a marked improvement over the past. This is an instance of a general truth, that the development of social services benefited those providing the service at least as much as those for whom it was intended.

Unemployment

The regular workmen, thrown out of a job by the operation of the trade-cycle which had by now been identified as a recurrent feature of the economy, were the other prominent group of the deserving poor. In the aftermath of the slump of 1903–5, Parliament passed the Unemployed Workmen's Act (1905) which established distress committees to organize public relief works for the temporarily unemployed outside the deterrent aegis of the Poor Law. Much of the money was expected to be raised by voluntary appeals as in the past; the commitment of public funds was strictly limited and totally inadequate. The Act was temporary and due to expire in 1908. To have turned this half-hearted gesture into a set of provisions adequate for the needs of the unemployed in the next down-turn of the trade cycle would have required massive central government subsidies in support of the rates, particularly in the poorer industrial areas. It would also have required appropriate institutions at both local and central government levels for monitoring levels of unemployment. The Labour Party's Unemployed Workmen's Bill (1907), drafted in consultation with the trade union movement, contained just such proposals so as to provide work or maintenance for all workers registered as unemployed.

The government opposed the measure but had no policy of its own, apart from waiting for the outcome of a Royal Commission. When the Labour Bill (often known as the Right-to-Work Bill) was reintroduced in 1908 at a time of rising unemployment, it attracted enough support to give notice to the government that they would have to produce their own policy.

Government policy differed significantly from that of the Labour Party. It drew on the ideas of William Beveridge, who had concluded after investigation that, instead of benefiting the regular workmen for whom they had been intended, public relief works merely attracted the large army of under-employed casual workers who comprised a permanent component of the labour force. Beveridge considered that under-employment led to the deterioration of the labour force and constituted a serious form of economic inefficiency. He regarded it as the result of defective organization of information in the labour-market, and therefore advocated the establishment of a national network of labour exchanges. If properly worked, he believed, these could become the instruments by which casual labour, with its casual and irregular way of life, would be replaced by regularly employed workers able to lead a life of respectability and to swell the ranks of organized labour. The unemployment of the regular workmen during times of slump was best dealt with by compulsory unemployment insurance. Beveridge strongly condemned the public relief works that had been at the centre of the 1905 Unemployed Workmen's Act as well as of the Labour Party's Bill.[3]

These policies produced the 1909 Labour Exchanges Act, which was intended to reduce unemployment by placing as many men in posts as possible, while also providing the administrative structures for the compulsory unemployment insurance that was introduced in the 1911 National Insurance Act. This was limited to seven trades in which workers were particularly exposed to unemployment during slumps rather than to such alternative strategies as short-time working. It required equal contributions from both workers and employers and added a state subsidy of a further one-third. This entitled the unemployed worker to 7s a week for a maximum of 15 weeks in the year, at the rate of one week's benefit for five weeks' contributions. This strict limitation underlines the fact that the insurance was aimed at temporary cyclical fluctuations. It was not intended to deal with long-term unemployment, and this was to cause many problems in the different circumstances of structural unemployment after the First World War (see Chapter 12).

Although the Liberal government had no interest in public relief works for the unemployed, it showed itself receptive to the idea of counter-cyclical public works schemes. This was at the centre of the policy for the unemployed proposed by the Webbs in 1909 in the minority report of the Royal Commission on the Poor Laws. It played no such central role in government policy, but 1909 saw the establishment of a fund under the control of a central Development Commission for such purposes of national investment as road building, afforestation and harbour-works. In theory this investment could have been scheduled so as to counteract the effect of the trade-cycle, and some lip-service was paid to this policy. In practice no machinery was ever created that would have enabled such an 'unemployment policy' to be carried through. In dealing with the problem of the unemployed the Liberal government concentrated not on counter-cyclical investment but on labour exchanges and insurance.

Sweated Trades

The year 1909 was one of the few occasions when Parliament was prepared to intervene in the wage contract. The Trade Boards Act targeted a few occupations, the so-called sweated trades. It was in the first instance limited to only four: ready-made and wholesale bespoke tailoring, paper and cardboard box making, chain-making and the finishing and mending of machine-made lace. Another four had been added by 1914: sugar confectionery, shirtmaking, hollow-ware, cotton and linen embroidery in Ireland. The occupations were considered pathological, not only on account of their exceptionally low pay and long hours, but because the circumstances of their workers – mostly women working at home – impeded self-help through trade union organization. Regional boards set up for these occupations consisted of an

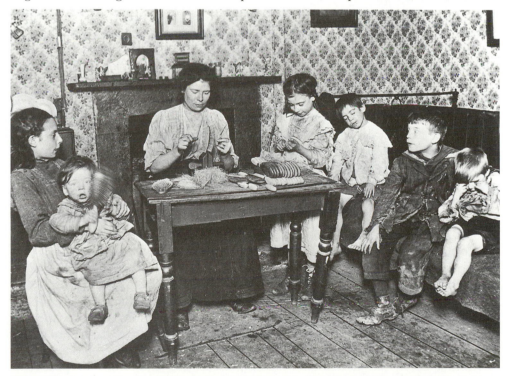

Plate 5.2.   Family of brushmakers, *c.* 1900. Very low rates of pay in the sweated trades forced mothers to use the labour of their children in an attempt to earn an adequate income.

equal number of representatives of workers and employers with an outside chairman. They were empowered to fix wages that all firms would be compelled to pay. The system of workers' representation was an encouragement of trade union organization, and the action of the boards was much like compulsory arbitration. The Trade Boards Act indicates that collective bargaining, though far from universal, had become accepted as a norm. The resultant rates of pay differed between the various occupations; they were genuine products of bargaining. Significantly enough there was no attempt to lay down a generally applicable minimum wage based on considerations of health. Nor was all low-paid work regulated by trade boards; a wide variety of other domestic employments such as the making of brushes, artificial flowers, and domestic decorations remained unregulated and exploitative.

There is evidence to suggest that the momentum of social reform was far from exhausted in 1914 when the outbreak of war cut across the preoccupations of peacetime. Overshadowed though they were by the Ulster problem, the social reform preoccupations included rural wages, rural housing and poor law reform.

Interpretations and Debates

The social reforms of this period began to attract the attention of historians in the 1960s, who regarded them as the origin of the 'welfare state', the phrase used to describe the social provisions introduced after the Second World War. This is indicated in the titles of pioneering surveys, such as Maurice Bruce's *The Coming of the Welfare State* (1961) and Bentley Gilbert's *The Evolution of National Insurance. The Origins of the Welfare State in Great Britain* (1966). The prominent role accorded to National Insurance by the postwar Labour government had drawn attention to the Act of 1911, and historians were quick to note the link provided by Beveridge's role on both occasions that he had drawn to their attention in his autobiography of 1953. The expansion of the school meals service during the Second World War and its retention as a regular feature of state provision focused attention similarly on the 1906 Education (Provision of Meals) Act. Like the Act of 1911 it was presented as the 'origin' of an important feature of the welfare state. But above all it was the erroneous belief that the postwar welfare state had emancipated the needy citizen from dependence on the Poor Law, or National Assistance as it was then called, i.e. that the citizens' rights to benefits had replaced discretionary hand-outs, that endowed the earlier reforms (designed to remove specific groups from the Poor Law and provide them with alternative state-guaranteed sources of income) with a special historical status.

At first there was a tendency to emphasize the similarities to post-1945 provisions but a sense of contrast soon began to intrude. Compulsory insurance in 1911 was remarkably limited compared with the universalism and subsistence principle proclaimed in the 1940s, while after 1918 unemployment insurance quickly became inappropriate to the economic situation and the policies that were then pursued. Over a time-span that included the interwar years the history of school meals was discovered to be one of regression rather than progress. Above all it became apparent that the principles of the Poor Law exerted a strong influence even over such breaches with the past as the introduction of old age pensions. But whether the stress was on similarities or differences, the history of Edwardian social reform was dominated by the categories of the post-1945 welfare state.

There have been two principal explanations for the innovations that are the subject of this chapter. Taking their cue from the Edwardian preoccupation with national efficiency, historians have interpreted them as part of the process of modernization. They have emphasized the shift in the priorities of government, parliament and public in response to anxieties generated by international rivalry. This preoccupation with the efficiency of the human resources of the nation can equally well be interpreted in Marxist terms as the use of the state to safeguard the reproduction of capital. That would have been required by what Marxist historians regard as capitalism's inherent contradictions. In the first place, because the owners of capital were able to deprive labour of its rightful share in the benefits of production, wages were inadequate to cover the costs of the necessary reproduction of labour power. That required the state to step in, if a deterioration of the labour force relative to that of other nations was to be avoided. Secondly, international rivalry in the period of 'monopoly capitalism' and imperialism led to militaristic preoccupations. Much of this is little more than a difference of language. Whether in its Marxist or its 'Realpolitik' form, the emphasis of this explanation falls on the ability of those in power to determine the priorities of reform and to innovate in the light of their perception of the 'national (or capitalist) interest'.

That is what historians deny who adopt the other explanation. They regard the social reforms as the response to political pressure from below. They see this pressure generated by organized labour, operating with marked success through the political processes which resulted from the widening of the franchise and the restructuring of the system of representation in 1884–85. The interpretation of the coming of Old Age Pensions given in this chapter runs largely along those lines. Within such a framework there is ample scope for disagreement on details, e.g. on the actual role of the Labour Party, on the importance of socialist politics outside the Labour Party, on the relation between Labour and Radical Liberals anxious to demonstrate their own responsiveness to the aspirations of the working-class electorate, and on the ability of the government to redefine policy even when it could not avoid the priorities imposed on it. Whether reforms were taken up by government because of actual pressure or in order to forestall the conversion of the electorate to 'socialism' is another matter on which the evidence has been differently interpreted. Among such differences one should not lose sight, however, of the common emphasis on social reform as the consequence of democratic mobilization.

These two interpretations are not incompatible. Apart from the briefest of interpretative essays all treatments of the subject refer to both, while differing in the degree of emphasis placed on each. This is in part because the art of political reform, as of all politics, lies in persuading people with different priorities to agree to the same course of action. The 1911 National Insurance Act could and did appeal to both preoccupations. That is less obvious with old age pensions and this in turn underlines an important point about the democratic electorate. Its demands were not unacceptable, because they were not revolutionary. They were based not on a radical rejection of the existing order but on a widely shared morality. It was because organized labour could appeal to that morality that it obtained the political leverage without which it would have been isolated. The influential minority whose response to poverty sprang from compassion could therefore cooperate with the new democratic forces, just as they could appeal to the national self-interest with considerations of efficiency.

That brings us to the final point, which also focuses on morality. As historians of this period have become less interested in seeking the origins of the post-1945 welfare state, they have increasingly become drawn to it by an interest in what is often called social control. That is a phrase with several meanings and has been used in this context sometimes to describe the disciplining of the working class in general, sometimes the curtailing of the independence of the organized working class.

The relief of poverty is always an act of power. The giver is always able to attach conditions to the provision of help. In this sense all societies attempt to impose acceptable behaviour through the relief of poverty. A period, such as this, in which there were important innovations in the relief of poverty, saw new and different forms of behaviour being demanded in return. In this context the question to be posed is not 'Was this a form of social control?', but rather 'What form did social control now take?'

A moralistic approach to the poor had long been common. Not only was their disorderly life held responsible for their poverty, but moralizing conditions had usually been attached to its relief. In this period there is a recurrent emphasis on the importance of regularity and foresight. There is no doubt that the new policies and provisions were deliberately intended to discipline the habits of the wage-earning population. To what extent they also undermined the independence of the organized working class or were intended to do so is a matter of some dispute.

There is therefore a moral dimension to this subject, both in the sense that reforms tended to focus on 'deserving' groups, and in the sense that the new provisions were intended to train the population in habits of morality, a morality that was considered essential for the functioning of an industrial society.

Bibliographical Note

Useful textbooks for the period covered by this book are P.M. Thane, *The Foundations of the Welfare State* (London, 1982) and D. Vincent, *Poor Citizens. The State and the Poor in Twentieth Century Britain* (London, 1991). The former pays attention to international comparisons; the latter is particularly valuable for looking at the process also from the perspective of the poor themselves. Vincent is impressed by the destruction of old forms of working-class participation and control. J.R. Hay, *The Origins of the Liberal Welfare Reforms 1906–1914* (London, 1975) is a slim, thoughtful introduction.

B. Gilbert, *The Evolution of National Insurance in Great Britain. The Origins of the Welfare State* (London, 1966, out of print) is authoritative on Health Insurance and provides a survey of the subject as a whole. J. Harris, *Unemployment and Politics. A Study in English Social Policy 1886–1914* (Oxford, 1972) is authoritative and detailed; her *William Beveridge* (Oxford, 1977) is also valuable. E.P. Hennock, *British Social Reform and German Precedents. The Case of Social Insurance 1880–1914* (Oxford, 1987) treats the subject from the perspective of the German influence. It emphasizes the importance of democratic pressure, is useful on old age pensions and includes policy on compensation for industrial accidents. See Gilbert (above), and B. Semmell, *Imperialism and Social Reform* (London, 1960) for the efficiency emphasis. See J. Morris, *Women Workers and the Sweated Trades: the Origins of Minimum Wages Legislation* (London, 1986) on trade boards and M. Freeden, *The New Liberalism* (Oxford, 1978) on the intellectual changes. A. Briggs, *Seebohm Rowntree* (London, 1961) is useful, not least for the plans of 1912–14.

Notes

1. B.S. Rowntree, *Poverty, a Study of Town Life* (London, 1901).

2. *Report, Interdepartmental Committee on Physical Deterioration*, British Parliamentary Papers, 1904, Cd.2175 XXXII.

3. W.H. Beveridge, *Unemployment, a Problem of Industry* (London, 1909).

6 The Social, Economic and Political Status of Women

Pat Thane

The years before the First World War were a period in which women projected themselves decisively onto the political scene, and when their social and demographic, but to a much lesser extent economic, statuses began to change.

Birth and Death

Table 6.1 shows that a majority of the British population was female in 1900, as it had been since at least the beginning of reliable census taking in 1841. This was due to the higher survival rates of females especially in infancy and in very late age groups, together with the higher rate of male migration overseas. This majority was perpetuated rather than caused by the loss of male lives during the First World War.

Table 6.1. Male and female population in Britain, 1901–31 (000s)

	Males	**Females**
1901	17,752	18,934
1911	19,775	21,112
1921	20,446	22,368
1931	21,486	23,345

Source. C.H. Feinstein, *Statistical Tables of National Income, Expenditure and Output of the United Kingdom, 1855–1965* (Cambridge, 1972) T120–21.

If one set of events more than any in history has transformed women's lives it must be the fall in the birth rate and the spread of modern practices of birth control which can be detected from the later nineteenth century. New parents in the 1900s had only half as many children as their parents. Their own children had only two-thirds as many children as they had. At the end of the nineteenth century family size was very diverse; no single size category between 0 and 17 children contained more than 10 per cent of all families. By the mid 1920s there was a decisive clustering around the two-child norm. Also important was the trend towards concentration of childbirth into the earlier years of marriage. Already at the end of the nineteenth century upper and upper-middle-class women were completing their families by the time they reached their mid thirties. By the 1930s this had spread to all social classes. The fall in fertility was evident in all classes from the later nineteenth century but moved fastest among some middle-class groups. In the early years of the twentieth century the wives of such professional men as barristers, surgeons and bank officials were giving birth to an average of around 3.5 children; the wives of miners, the most fertile group, averaged 7.36. In textile districts, where wives frequently worked in the factory after marriage, fertility was closer to middle-class levels. As with other aspects of demographic change, fertility patterns were converging across social classes by the 1930s.

Table 6.2. Children born to parents marrying 1886–91 and surviving to 1911*

Social class	Children born	Children surviving	Percentage surviving
Upper and middle	340	286	84.1
Skilled	491	388	79.0
Unskilled	558	421	75.4
Textile workers	441	334	75.7
Miners	655	486	74.2
Agricultural labourers	545	457	83.9

* Per 100 families by Registrar General's social classification.

Source: Michael Anderson 'The social implications of demographic change' in F.M.L. Thompson (ed.), *The Cambridge Social History of Britain 1750–1950. Volume 2* (Cambridge, 1990) p. 43.

The proportion of children surviving to adulthood also rose from the early years of the twentieth century as an historic decline in infant mortality became evident. The proportion of males in England and Wales dying in the first year of life fell from 17 per cent in 1891 to 9 per cent in 1921; among females, from 15 per cent to 7 per cent. The decline occurred in all social classes, though a marked social class differential remained (see Table 6.2). Among mothers, deaths in childbirth did not show a significant decline until the later

1930s when the development of sulphonamide drugs made possible the control of puerperal infection. Maternal death occurred in around five births in every thousand between the beginning of the century and the 1920s, but it was below four in every thousand in the later 1930s.

More widespread and strongly correlated with social class was long-term ill-health resulting from inadequate care or advice before or after childbirth. An extension of midwifery and maternity and infant welfare services from the Midwives Act 1902 to the Maternity and Child Welfare Act 1918 (partly in response to agitation by women) brought some improvements especially in the interwar years, though these were locally uneven since their implementation was at the discretion of local authorities. Before 1914 expansion of such services was more notable in the voluntary than in the statutory sector, providing clinics, health visitors, district nurses and other services for poor families. Their impact on infant and maternal health and survival remains uncertain and controversial. Public funding for such services was stimulated by the discovery of the poor standards of health of recruits to the services during the First World War, which was attributed to poor diet and medical care throughout their lives, and also by the need to replace the members of the population who were killed in the trenches.[1]

As part of their campaign for improved maternity services the Women's Co-operative Guild (the largest working class women's organization of the period) collected and published in 1915 accounts of their members' experiences of maternity. The following was typical both in the circumstances described and in the author's determination to take responsibility for improving her own life as best she could:

> I was married at the age of 22 and by the time I had reached my thirty-second birthday was the mother of seven children, and I am sure you will pardon me if I take the credit for bringing up such a family without loss of even one, seeing that it entailed such a great amount of suffering to myself.
>
> During pregnancy I suffered much. When at the end of ten years I was almost a mental and physical wreck, I determined that this state of things should not go on any longer and if there was no natural means of prevention, then, of course artificial means must be employed, which were successful and I am happy to say that from that time I have been able to take pretty good care of myself, but I often shudder to think what might have been the result if things had been allowed to go on as they were. Two days after childbirth I invariably sat up in bed knitting stockings and doing general repairs for my family. My husband at that time was earning 30s. per week and out of that amount claimed 6s.6d as pocket money, and when I tell you that through all my difficulties there were no debts contracted on my part, you will be able to form some idea of what women are, in some cases, called upon to endure.[2]

Paid Work

The above account suggests something of the burden of unpaid work in the home for a woman whose husband earned a fairly average manual wage. It was an important campaigning point of women in the labour movement at this time that such domestic labour should be defined and socially valued as 'work'. They argued that labour in the home was as hard as paid labour outside the home, as essential to the economy and as socially valuable.

It is difficult to arrive at exact statistics of the numbers of women in paid employment. Part-time and casual work has long been a feature of the female labour market in Britain and in this period much work of this kind was not recorded in the censuses or in other official sources. Of women aged 15–34, 77 per cent were shown as being in paid employment in the census of 1901. In the age group 35–44 the percentage was only 13, and 11 per cent among those aged 45–59. This provides us with minimum numbers of women in paid work. Overwhelmingly these women were working class. The figures suggest that women were most likely to be active in the paid labour market before and in the early years of marriage, when children were young and it was a struggle to make ends meet. Many of them withdrew from the double burden of paid and unpaid work when their children grew old enough to earn. Probably more were doing so by the beginning of the twentieth century than for much of the preceding century. However given the irregularity of income of almost all male manual workers, including the most skilled – due, for example, to seasonality of demand or the effects of the weather on such occupations as construction or shipbuilding – few working-class women were able to withdraw entirely from contributing to household resources. Taking in lodgers, dressmaking and childminding were among the host of means women had long used to bolster family living standards, as was attention to careful housewifery.

Some women were the chief income earner in the family. In 1901 one woman in eight was widowed, often with children to support. An unknown number (statistics are not available) were deserted by their husbands. Single women might support elderly parents, and married women sick or unemployed husbands. The largest single paid female occupation was domestic service, which employed 11.1 per cent of the entire female population of England and Wales in 1911. The nature of women's employment and also expectations as to whether they would work after marriage varied from place to place. In the Staffordshire Potteries married women who did not contribute to the family income were regarded as 'lazy'. The rhythm of work with frequent breaks in production, the tradition of self-imposed work routines and the fact that workers lived close to the workplace eased the integration of domestic and paid labour.

In the Leicester hosiery industry it was taken for granted that married women would work. It was also common in East London with its mixed economy of small scale production of everything from clothing to jam, and had long been so in the Lancashire textile districts. In the weaving town of

Preston, for example, the wives of relatively skilled and supervisory workers were employed in weaving in significant numbers though it cannot have been necessary to keep their families from starvation. It did however give them independence, companionship, the capacity to save and to improve their family's lives.

Cotton weaving was one of the few occupations in which women could be paid equal rates with men. Even so, there was a clear gender division of labour throughout the workforce. Most tasks were defined, not always rationally, as appropriate only for one or other sex, and employers could not easily substitute female for male labour except in abnormal conditions such as wartime. However notions of appropriateness varied from place to place: for example, women were employed in printing in Scotland but not in England.

The range of female work opportunities, career prospects, and wages was less than that of males. However women did work at a variety of levels of skill and pay. Though most of the work available to them was defined as unskilled some tasks recognized as highly skilled were open to a minority, for example the painting of pottery in the Staffordshire Potteries. Though it appears from aggregate average wage rates that women only earned about half of male wages, it has to be remembered that the female average was pulled down by the very young age of a high proportion of the female labour force. Even within a single industry such as cotton textiles, female (and male) wage rates could vary from town to town. Female workers in some occupations, such as textiles, would earn more than men in other occupations, such as agriculture.

White collar Work

There was a marked expansion of respectable 'white blouse' occupations for women in the expanding public and service sectors: as teachers, nurses, typists, telephonists, or behind the counters of department stores. Their career prospects were generally more restricted than those of men in comparable occupations, as was their pay. Even in teaching, where men and women might be thought to perform identical duties, female salaries were lower. Nevertheless there was normally an oversupply of females suitably qualified for such occupations (indeed often overqualified), in need of an income and/or in search of independence. They came from skilled working class backgrounds and had benefited from the expansion of secondary education which started in the later nineteenth century, or from the large swathes of the middle class who could afford to educate their daughters but not to support them in idleness.

The number of female clerks had increased four-fold between 1861 and 1911 to 149,215, 20 per cent of the clerical workforce. The technological innovations which transformed the Dickensian counting house into the modern office offered a new range of skilled if subordinate jobs to women. The telephone, telegraphy, the typewriter, dictating and adding machines, new methods of filing and retrieving data, were operated mainly by women. They appropriated or were assigned such work where it was new or without a male

Plate 6.1. Female telephonists in a GPO telephone exchange. New technology created service-sector employment opportunities for women in areas which had no tradition of male employment. These new forms of 'women's work' had relatively low rates of pay and few promotion prospects.

tradition and where it could be routinized and separated from a career ladder. They gained from its expansion during a period in which the supply of suitably educated women with limited alternative prospects greatly outstripped that of suitably qualified men. This gave women in such occupations a certain bargaining power; although they were rarely unionized, many of them used their experience and skills to bargain individually for higher pay and status. They could not achieve equal prospects with men but more women than before at this level of society were able to achieve for themselves a degree of independence and access to leisure and cultural activities.

The Professions

The same desire for independence was evident among women higher in the social order (as the range and vigour of their public activity in the later nineteenth century suggests it had long been). Though some families still sought to confine their daughters to domesticity, others encouraged them to seek education and wider horizons, if not perhaps quite as wide as those offered to their sons. More women acquired a serious education at private secondary, teacher training and university levels, mainly but not always in arts subjects. Sixty-nine were studying science degree courses at University College London in 1909–10, 31 per cent of all science students. Of all students at UCL, 35 per cent were female over the period 1908–13, a fall from 45 per cent in 1903–8.[3]

Teaching in these same institutions was the most easily accessible career, though there are strong signs that women wanted training and access to a wider range of careers and took advantage of it when available. But as Table 6.3 shows, such opportunities opened up only slowly. By 1911, women made up only 6 per cent of the higher professions, a proportion which had risen only to 8 per cent by 1951.

Table 6.3. Female occupations according to the census of 1901

Schoolteachers	172,000
Sick nurses	64,000
Female artists	3,700
Actresses	6,400
Musicians	22,600
Physicians and surgeons	212
Dentists	140
Architects	6
Accountants	2
Vets	3
Barristers, solicitors, engineers, surveyors	0

Unpaid Work for Middle and Upper-Class Women

Better-off women also worked in the home. Of course they had the help of servants, but a surprising number of middle-class homes did not employ living-in servants if there were women of the family able to run the household, though they might employ cleaners, laundresses and others who came in by the day. Above the level of the poor, servant-keeping seems to have been determined as much by need as by status. Relatively poor artisan households containing children or other dependants and no adult female other than the mother could, and did, employ workhouse girls for little more than their board. In consequence the experience of being a servant varied immensely depending upon the social status and the personality of the employer. There are signs that the rapid decline in the servant population at the beginning of the First World War owed as much to the desire of employers to be rid of an often intrusive presence as of women to escape an often demeaning occupation.

The stereotype of the more or less functionless Edwardian middle-class housewife (as of her Victorian predecessor) can be based on, at most, a narrow stratum. The management of a complex household, amid the dirt and pollution of a late Victorian town or city, with minimal assistance from domestic technology, was no trivial matter; though more widespread application of gas and electricity in the home was easing certain domestic tasks for those able to afford them, it also raised the standards expected of housewifery. Indeed given the centrality of purposeful work to Victorian and Edwardian socialization, deeply rooted in the religious conviction and practice which remained the norm, it should not be surprising that idleness was not prized by most of even the comfortably off. Hence many women who were too wealthy to be consumed by household tasks or had time to spare from them sought other forms of fulfilling activity.

It was barely acceptable for upper and upper-middle-class women to work for payment before marriage, and not at all thereafter. Voluntary action-philanthropy – the active promotion of 'causes' – provided the main alternative; for example, running the voluntary maternity clinics mentioned earlier. Philanthropy in particular was not the easy, lightly undertaken, patronage of the Lady Bountiful that it is sometimes made to appear. To work, often unwelcomed, in inner-city slums required courage and resilience for respectably brought up women, as did speaking on a public platform. Though unpaid, women often saw philanthropic work as a long-term commitment which they approached as professionals. Indeed in so doing they were laying the foundations of many of the professional social service occupations that developed for women and men in the twentieth century. It was estimated that at the end of the nineteenth century around 500,000 women worked continuously and semi-professionally in voluntary activities, and many others were more marginally involved.[4]

Women and Protest

Such encounters with appalling social conditions led some women, from the later nineteenth century, to seek a wider public role, including the vote, on the grounds that men in power had manifestly failed to bring about changes for which there was a crying need. Some channelled their activities into local government where female ratepayers had had the vote since 1869. By 1900 there were one million female local government electors. In 1907 they were enabled to stand for town and county councils; forty-eight had successfully done so by 1914, 320 by 1919–20. Women ratepayers had been able to vote in elections for Poor Law Guardians since 1834, but no woman had tested their right to run for office until 1875. By 1914 there were 1,546 female Guardians, 2,039 by 1919–20. From 1870 women could vote and stand for school boards and about 270 were serving on these boards in 1900. The boards were abolished in 1902, but the storm of protest from women at this removal of one of their public roles led the government hastily to rule that at least two women should be co-opted to every local education committee; 679 were co-opted by 1914. From 1895 women were elected to rural and urban district councils. Some women, and men, believed that activities of this kind – local and closely involved with social services – lay more suitably with the 'female sphere' than

Plate 6.2. 'What a woman may be and yet not have the vote': suffragette poster. The indefensible inequality of the pre-1918 electoral system provided a focus for the women's movement, but the campaign for gender equality extended beyond politics into a wide range of legal, employment and welfare issues.

did involvement in national politics. To others, however, such involvement made women's exclusion from the national vote even more absurd.

Although women lacked the vote in parliamentary elections the major political parties came to depend upon them as canvassers, organizers, campaigners; often speaking for their parties on the same platform as men who actively denied them the vote. Large numbers of women were members of support groups for the major political parties, such as the Women's Liberal Federation, the Conservative Primrose League, and the Women's Labour League after the formation of the Labour Party in 1906. In none of these organizations were women mere mouthpieces for men. By the early 1900s it was rare for any serious political cause to be promoted without substantial involvement of women. When, for example, the Liberal Free Trade Union was founded in 1903 to fight Tariff Reform it had an active women's association, sending female speakers around the country.

In other ways, too, women did not readily submit to inequality. We have seen women as individuals negotiating to improve their conditions in white collar occupations. Women are often seen as having been reluctant to join trade unions – they constituted only 7.8 per cent of all trade unionists in 1900. However their membership rates were not lower than among men in comparable low paid, low skilled occupations. They were high in Britain compared with most other countries and followed a similar pattern of growth to male membership, more than doubling in numbers between 1906 and 1914 to 357,956, and shooting up to 1,086,000 by 1918. By this time they constituted 17 per cent of all trade unionists, and 19.9 per cent of all recorded full-time female workers were unionized. Nor is there any sign that women were less willing than men to engage in industrial action in various forms, indeed women often brought to strikes and marches a vivacity and sense of the ridiculous not normally prevalent in the labour movement. This was often because they were very young. Young jute workers paraded the streets of Dundee during disputes in the 1900s, singing, dancing, dressing up to mock their employers in front of their peers, publicly to subvert their authority.[5]

In a variety of ways women, often with male support as well as sometimes fierce male opposition, challenged gender inequalities. A critique of the existing marriage legislation as embodying inequality runs through the period, reflected even in such respectable places as the letters pages of the *Daily Telegraph*. The Royal Commission on Marriage and Divorce of 1912 largely accepted the proposals put forward most clearly by the Women's Co-operative Guild that women should be enabled to obtain divorce on equal grounds with men, that the cost of divorce proceedings should be reduced in order to open them to poorer people, and that female judges and lawyers should be appointed. The war delayed implementation, but the divorce law was liberalized on these grounds in 1923 and 1937 and in 1918 women were enabled to enter the legal profession and to become JPs.

Most women did not engage actively in protest, but there is evidence of widespread support for protest. In 1901, 23,359 women cotton textile workers signed a suffrage petition. That *Votes for Women*, the weekly newspaper of the militant suffragist Women's Social and Political Union (WSPU) had 160,000 readers at its peak, and such major advertisers as Dunhill cigarettes, the Express Dairy and the major London department stores continued to advertise in it even in 1914, when the militants were widely regarded as crazy, suggests no minority phenomenon. The big London stores dressed their windows in WSPU colours at the peak of the demonstrations, which also suggests that they did not believe that their customers were alienated by the militancy, though it is reasonable to assume that many were indifferent.

The demand for the national vote reached a peak between 1903 and 1914. It should already be clear that this was not women's only 'cause', though it provided a focus for protest about a range of gender inequalities. The vote was seen as an essential means to bring about further changes. Mrs Pankhurst's WSPU was established in 1903 and became steadily more militant, goaded by increasingly harsh treatment by the authorities. The public militancy of the WSPU was complemented by the quieter lobbying of the moderate suffragists of the National Union of Women's Suffrage Societies (NUWSS), which continued the steady pressure upon politicians and the insertion of women into an indispensable role in public life that has already been described. A major triumph for this tactic was the admission of women to town and county councils in 1907. This at last admitted women to elected bodies which had major financial responsibilities outside the 'caring' sphere. Once this had been conceded the argument against women voting at national level was thin indeed and it was increasingly evident that it could not long be resisted. The war probably delayed the concession of the vote. Throughout it, though with an initial lull, the NUWSS kept up the demand for the vote, which in 1918 (Representation of the People Act) was given to women over thirty who were householders, wives of householders, occupants of property worth £5 annually or graduates of British universities. For all the tension between the wings of the suffrage movement and between their protagonists among historians, they are best seen as complementary, the tactics of each assisting achievement of the vote.

In focus: Women Printers in Edwardian Edinburgh

A number of women in Edwardian Scotland were employed in the printing and paper trades which were thriving due to the expansion of demand for books and periodicals. Their employment was at a variety of levels but a number were in what was regarded as highly respectable skilled work; in particular in bookbinding, which was also a skilled trade for women in England, and in printing, which was not. At the beginning of the twentieth century there were only about 300 female compositors in England, in a few progressive firms, and about 800 in Edinburgh. In Scottish printing women followed their fathers into the trade, though men and women did not do identical jobs. Women had entered Edinburgh printing in the course of a

Women Printers in Edwardian Edinburgh (continued)

strike by male compositors in 1872–73. Employers decided to take on 'girls of good education' as apprentices. When the men returned they did not object, but taught the women the trade and began to put their own daughters into it. Their own jobs were not threatened and the practice of apprenticing women spread elsewhere in Scotland.

The women were paid at half the rate of men – a maximum of 16s compared with 32s, after training. Part of the argument for lower pay was that women did not serve a full apprenticeship and learned only the more routinized tasks in the trade. This was so, though there is no evidence that women could not or would not learn the trade in full. Also it was assumed that they would cease to work on marriage and so there were few experienced older women qualifying for higher rates. The fact that they gave up on marriage was used to justify their abbreviated apprenticeship. Some women would have liked to stay on after marriage, but their husbands 'would not allow them to'. Some men were doing the same restricted job as women yet being paid more than the women (though less than fully trained men). The work was more highly skilled and better paid than that available to almost any other female manual workers though the pay was still less than for men in comparable jobs. Other reasons stated for the relatively low female wage were the general level of women's wages in the economy and the assumption that a man required a wage sufficient to keep a family whereas a woman did not, regardless of the likelihood that many men were unmarried or their families grown and that women might contribute to an impoverished household. It was also asserted that women 'make more mistakes' and 'they are always going off for sickness of some kind, or their mother is ill'; statements that were rarely substantiated.

As trade became more unstable in the 1900s male workers became more resentful of the women and battled with the employers over their presence. Employers asserted that women were ideally suited to certain routinized jobs, for example the feint line ruling in exercise books 'was simple enough work to be given to girls'. However they could not praise women's skills too much lest they ask for more pay. The unions admitted that the women worked competently, but they argued, not unjustifiably, that women were being used to undercut their wages, and that the work was bad for the health of potential mothers.

By 1909 there were 850 female compositors in Edinburgh and about 1,000 male ones. The introduction of new technology in the form of Monotype composing machines threatened male skills. The machines consisted of a keyboard like a typewriter, to which in other occupations female dexterity was said to be ideally suited. It was clean work, quite divorced from the casting of hot metal. Initially men disdained the new machines until it became evident that much new work was going to women.

Women Printers in Edwardian Edinburgh (continued)

In 1909 the Edinburgh printers struck, demanding that no more girl apprentices should be hired for six years and that all new Monotype keyboards should be given to men. They won. No existing female compositor lost her job, but no new ones were recruited, the six-year limit passing unnoticed in the midst of the war. Of the 800 women working in 1910 about three-quarters had left through marriage or retirement by the late 1920s. About 200 stayed on, some as late as the 1950s, but they were the last female compositors in Scotland; no new women were recruited.

The women themselves were divided on the issue. About half agreed with the men. Their threat to join the strike if the male demand was not met led to the speedy settlement in the men's favour. They did not feel personally threatened and they were working alongside their fathers, brothers, and male friends. Workplace relationships appear to have been friendly and they had no means of knowing that the ban would outlast six years. They found it natural to support male fears of the loss of breadwinning jobs. Half of the women disagreed, though they recognized the conflicting but real priorities of men and women. Their petition to the masters read:

> While recognising that the men have had a real grievance in that some firms have employed an unfair proportion of young girls at apprentice wages, or nearly so, we women regard it as a great injustice that one of the main skilled industries in Edinburgh should be closed against them.

It took courage to say so much in the face of abuse. The decision against them was made at talks at which no women were present and it decided the gender composition of the trade for the remainder of the twentieth century.

Why were women so easily marginalized from an occupation from which many of them obviously drew satisfaction? Firstly, as in many other occupations, they were young, facing more experienced men who were often their own older relatives. The employers rather disliked employing older married women whom they regarded as insufficiently docile. Employers and trade unionists were men of similar age and had developed a shared culture of negotiation in which women, who were not invited to join the union, did not share. After the strike of 1909 the diminishing number of female compositors were invited to join the union. Their membership and commitment soon reached levels comparable with those of the men. As one woman said to an interviewer much later: 'Oh! I loved my work. I'd have worked weekends if they'd have let me'. And another: 'I'd go back to-morrow but they don't take women now'. Male and female workers were caught in conflicts of interest and culture that could not easily be resolved.[6]

Debates and Interpretations

It has been suggested that the most important and lasting change and improvement in women's lives in this period was the historically unprecedented fall in the birth rate and in norms of family size. The facts are clear enough but the reasons continue to elude historians and demographers (see Anderson, cited in bibliography). Although modern birth control techniques were available, they, or even knowledge about them, were difficult to obtain and not widespread (see R. Soloway, *Birth Control and the Population Question in England 1877–1930* (Chapel Hill, 1982). The most common techniques appear to have been the age-old ones of *coitus interruptus* or abstinence. In *Prosperity and Parenthood* (London, 1954), the decline in fertility was explained by J. Banks in terms of the middle classes coming under increasing financial pressure in the later nineteenth century which led them to restrict family size, a practice which other classes later emulated. However there is no evidence for widespread financial pressure of this kind; the decline was simultaneous among many social groups whose material circumstances differed from one another and within each group, and if emulation did occur to some degree it requires explanation since one social group does not copy the practices of another without good cause. It may also be suggested that although overt feminism was not widespread, more women than ever before were acquiring a sense that they could exert some control over their lives (like the member of the Women's Co-operative Guild quoted earlier) and that freedom from repeated pregnancy and the physical and material problems which could result was a more immediate objective for some of them than the vote. More men as well as women may have realized that smaller family size would improve family living standards. And both may have been influenced by the realization that the infant mortality rate was falling and that more of the babies born had a chance of survival, though the dramatic fall in the infant mortality rate followed rather than preceded the beginning of the fall in the birth rate. Probably these and other factors combined to bring about this fundamental change.

How many women were in the paid labour force is a topic about which we do not have adequate facts. This is because our main source of information is the census, but women often did not record their paid work in the census return, particularly if it was part-time or casual. This was because they, or the census enumerator, did not regard their paid rather than their unpaid domestic work as their *primary* occupation; or because they changed casual jobs frequently; or because they happened not to be in paid employment at the time of the census. Others, such as farmers' or shopkeepers' wives, might not be recorded as employed even though they played a large and essential role in working on the farm or in the shop. The deficiencies of the census in this respect have been made particularly evident through the use of oral history (e.g. Roberts in the bibliography) which reveals a greater extent and variety of women's work than does the census. Consequently census figures have to be treated as *minimum* numbers of women in paid work. In particular it is difficult to trace the history of women's part-time work, though it has evidently long been important in Britain, as it still is.

This chapter has indicated a high degree of gender inequality in the workplace, in politics and in society more generally. A central problem is how we explain it. Was it simply the natural outcome of the biological differences between men and women, especially in a period of high fertility, which disabled many women from public activity for long periods of their lives? We have to remember, though, that levels both of non-marriage and of infertility were significantly higher than in the late twentieth century, and that many women could, if they chose, delegate child care to servants. Was it simply rational that in the workplace women merited lesser pay and career opportunities because most willingly gave up work on marriage, were very young and less experienced than male workers? We have seen evidence, however, that some women wished to remain at work after marriage and that others, for instance in cotton textiles, did so without evident harm to their families or themselves. Furthermore there is no sign of the lesser capacity of females in any of the occupations in which both men and women worked, such as schoolteaching. Or should we just ascribe it to enduring male prejudice of the sort described by Brian Harrison in *Separate Spheres: the Opposition to Women's Suffrage in England* (London, 1978)?

Women of this period, especially in the middle and upper classes, are often portrayed as dependent and housebound, leading severely constrained lives in a 'private sphere' separate from a 'public sphere' inhabited largely by men. Yet this chapter has suggested how many women in all classes were active outside the home, in 'public', in paid or voluntary work, in pressure groups and in active campaigns to extend the 'public space' open to women. Nevertheless such campaigns were necessary because the range of activities open to women was throughout the period more restricted than that available to men. How useful is the concept of 'separate spheres' for analysing the differences between male and female life chances?

A related issue is that the experience of women in relation to men at this and other times tends to be interpreted either in optimistic or pessimistic terms. The stress is either upon the elements of gender inequality which endure or upon changes leading in the direction of greater equality. It is a version of the 'is the bottle half-full or half-empty?' conundrum. Which approach is the more helpful for this period? Or do both have a certain truth? Or is a more important point that we cannot generalize about 'women' and both approaches can be applied simultaneously to different women or to different aspects of the lives of many women?

An important question is why at this period of history – though beginning earlier, in the mid nineteenth century – there began a critique of gender inequality and campaigns to rectify it which have been sustained to the present, though they have been more prominent at some times than at others. Like the fall in the birth rate, this is another historical turning point of great importance. Why did it come about? It is sometimes argued that industrialization worsened the condition and opportunities of females relative to males, for instance as regards power within the household or in the range of work opportunities open to them. But there is little clear evidence for this. Industrialization changed the *forms* which gender inequality took in certain respects, but not necessarily its *degree*. More probably this should be seen as a period of rapid social change which enabled more people readily to imagine possibilities for further change and to believe that they could be achieved. In this respect many women behaved like many under-privileged working men of the period; the pre-1914 suffragette militancy was paralleled by unusual levels of trade unions militancy. Also there were more independent, educated middle-class women than ever before and increasing numbers of independent-minded working-class women able and willing to promote 'The Cause'.

The question is often raised as to whether women could have achieved greater equality through greater militancy, or whether the militancy of the suffragettes retarded attainment of the vote and other changes by creating so much opposition. It is obviously difficult to know, though we should not allow the publicity gained by the suffragettes to lead us to underestimate the importance and effectiveness of the parallel quieter campaigning and lobbying of the suffragists, as described by Sandra Stanley Holton (see bibliography).

We also should not avoid the question of what was meant by 'equality'. The term encapsulated a wide range of goals: sometimes single-issue and specific, such as equal rights to property; or broader claims to equal opportunities with men on all fronts for those women who chose to exercise them; or claims, rather, for equal respect and value to be given to the different aspirations and qualities of women. Feminism and aspirations for greater gender equality were no simpler before 1918 than in the late twentieth century.

It is sometimes thought that women received the vote as a reward for their efforts in the First World War rather than – or even despite – their pressure for it before the war. As Holton shows, the pressure was sustained during the war by the non-militants, though not by the militant suffragettes. It seems clear that the Liberal government was very close to giving way to the women's pressure by the beginning of the war and the war may have delayed action. More broadly the war is often thought to have transformed women's opportunities on a number of fronts. Such a view must however be severely qualified, especially in respect of working-class women, but this issue is dealt with in Chapter 9.

Bibliographical Note

The chapter by Michael Anderson 'The social implications of demographic change' in F.M.L. Thompson (ed.), *The Cambridge Social History of Britain 1750–1950. Volume 2* (Cambridge, 1990), is the clearest and most accessible survey of the demography of the period. On efforts to improve the health and survival of infants and mothers and the debate as to whether such improvements as there were – in particular the significant fall in infant mortality – were due to voluntary or statutory efforts or to improved living and/or environmental standards, see the items listed in Footnote 1.

On paid and unpaid work the essays in the collection edited by Angela John, *Unequal Opportunities. Women's Employment in England 1800–1918* (Oxford, 1986) provide studies of a good selection of manual and non-manual occupations together with useful references to further work. Elizabeth Roberts' *Women's Work, 1850–1950* (Basingstoke, 1988) succinctly surveys mainly manual employment. Her *A Woman's Place. An Oral History of Women in Lancashire 1890–1940* (Oxford, 1984) complements this vividly by surveying the lives in and out of the home of Lancashire women in their own words.

Patricia Hollis, *Ladies Elect* (Oxford, 1987) surveys an important dimension of women's 'public' activity in local government which has often been forgotten. Sandra Holton's *Feminism and Suffragism* (Cambridge, 1986) is an up-to-date study of the more familiar territory of the campaign for the national vote. This does justice to the role of the moderate suffragists and to the importance of the continuing campaign during the war. A good complementary study is Jill Liddington and Jill Norris, *One Hand Tied Behind Us* (London, 1978) which vividly examines support for the suffrage among female textile workers in the North of England. José Harris, *Private Lives, Public Spirit. A Social History of Britain 1870–1914* (Oxford, 1993) is an up-to-date survey which discusses most of the issues raised in this chapter and places them in the wider context.

Notes

1. D. Dwork, *War is Good for Babies and Other Young People* (London, 1987); J. Lewis, *The Politics of Motherhood* (London, 1980); J.M. Winter, *The Great War and the British People* (London, 1986).

2. M. Llewellyn Davies (ed.), *Maternity. Letters from Working Women* (1915, reprinted 1978, London) pp. 60–1.

3. These statistics are taken from the PhD research of Julie Stevenson of Thames Valley University. I am grateful to her for allowing me to use them.

4. F. Prochaska, *Women and Philanthropy in Victorian England* (Oxford, 1980) contains much of relevance to this period.

5. Eleanor Gordon, *Women and Labour in Scotland* (Oxford, 1991).

6. Based on Sian Reynolds, 'Women in the printing and paper trades in Edwardian Edinburgh' in E. Gordon and E. Breitenbach (eds), *The World is Ill-Divided. Women's Work in Scotland in the Nineteenth and Twentieth Centuries* (Edinburgh, 1990) pp. 49–69.

7 Sport and Recreation

Tony Mason

Recreation and Class

The Working Class

Sport and recreation demand time, money and energy. For most people in Britain in the fourteen years before the First World War work was the dominating experience of their lives. Most men and women were working-class: 'they worked with their hands, were employees and not employers, and, in comparison with the latter, were poor and lacked material goods ...'.[1] Three-quarters of the population were in this position. Working hours were long. Some skilled engineering workers organized in trade unions had negotiated a fifty-four hour week in the early 1870s. In 1890 those in the North East obtained a twelve o'clock finish on Saturdays. Textile workers had long had their working hours fixed by Parliament and an Act of 1901 stipulated that their working week should also stop at twelve on Saturdays. But many other workers were less fortunate. Agricultural labourers worked six, sometimes seven days a week and very long hours during certain seasons of the year such as harvest time. Many shopworkers were still putting in an eighty or ninety hour week at the beginning of the century although some did win a half day holiday in 1911. Workers in the notorious sweated trades, those in casual employment, and domestic servants, many of them women, had neither fifty-four hour weeks nor Saturday afternoons off. The years before 1914 were not ones in which the amount of spare time for most workers increased much.

There seems to be general agreement that many working-class families were better off and had more disposable income after the necessaries of life had been met than ever before. Real wages rose by a third between 1875 and 1900 although there may have been some decline after that and up to the war (see the discussion in Chapter 4). But our knowledge of how this extra income was spent and how much of it might have gone on sport and recreation remains incomplete. However, more bicycles, newspapers and pianos were being bought and more holidays taken. There was also a decline in the proportion of income spent on drink. Nonetheless expenditure on alcohol was still over half that spent on other leisure goods and services in 1914 and consumption of beer per head of the population remained close to record levels between 1895 and 1904 before gradually falling back.

Working-class families still spent three-quarters of their income on food and housing. Nor should we neglect the widespread poverty which was as endemic in Edwardian as it had been in Victorian Britain. Historians seem to agree that the calculations of Charles Booth for the early 1890s in London and Seebohm Rowntree for 1899 in York – that 30.7 per cent and 27.84 per cent, respectively of the populations of those cities lived in poverty – were accurate. Studies of the budgets of working-class families show that for the bottom third there was rarely anything left over for spending on recreation. It is salutary to recall that expenditure on leisure apart from alcohol was scarcely possible at all for a third of the working class; that about half were able to participate fairly fully, and the remainder only intermittently.

Participation in recreation and sport was also related to gender and to the stage of the life cycle. Most working-class children went to elementary school until they were thirteen. Poverty forced many to take casual jobs or help at home. But few would be completely deprived of the chance to play in the streets or to watch the free shows of the itinerant entertainers or go to the fair, both continued features of urban and rural Britain alike. Boys probably had more opportunities for enjoyment than girls. Excursions and holidays would be available for the better-off, often provided by old institutions like chapels, churches and their Sunday schools and new ones like the Boy Scouts.

But it was young workers who were best placed to take advantage of the growing variety of things to do when they were not at work. Regular employment meant money in the pocket which could be spent, in the towns at least, on theatre, music hall, cinema and fish and chip shop especially on Saturday night. If money was particularly tight then seeing the sights might have had to be sufficient. Young wage earners of both sexes shared these leisure opportunities but women were probably more restricted than men and would almost certainly have earned less.

It was not usually marriage that put an end to these regular outings but the coming of children. Working-class couples with young families had little time, energy, or spare cash for sport or recreation outside the home. This was especially true of the women with their responsibilities for managing the home and looking after the children. Young married men sometimes found it difficult to give up pleasures like the pub or a bet on the horses and disputes over male spending on leisure must have been one of the most common sources of conflict within working-class households. On the other hand M.E. Loane visited numerous working-class households in her job as a London district nurse and found many couples satisfied by a shared domesticity.[2] This was encouraged by the increasing comfort of working-class houses and the growing interest in and opportunity for reading. Sixty per cent of the population were within reach of a public library by 1914. Once the children had grown up and taken jobs then the family economic position could improve. Expeditions into the commercial leisure world might be possible. But before 1914 working-class life was essentially insecure. Prosperity was often temporary. Booms gave way to slumps which often meant short-time working or unemployment. Many jobs were casual or seasonal. In such circumstances, expenditure on recreation was probably the first to go.

The Leisure Class

At the other end of the social spectrum the leisure class did not have to worry about money and its members certainly did not have to work for it. Gladstone had called British landowners the leisure class. By 1900 the traditionally landed elite had been joined by the new plutocrats of financial and industrial wealth to make up a leisure class of some four thousand families. With no work and all the chores done by an army of servants conspicuous leisure and year-round enjoyment provided a reason for living. Of course some of the men had intellectually demanding hobbies like botany, history and politics – still unpaid and amateur until the Parliament Act of 1911 brought in payment of MPs – some were patrons of the Arts, or leading lights in the Jockey Club or the M.C.C. and some still devoted time to business, but large numbers lived a life devoted to enjoyment. This could involve the traditional country pastimes of hunting, shooting and fishing and the breeding, owning and betting on of racehorses. Many of the younger, male generation found solace in travel and being on the loose in London where a life of sexual and social pleasure could place a strain on bank balances and constitutions. New and expensive hobbies like motoring and old and expensive ones like sailing had many adherents. The upper classes, led in 1900 by the Prince of Wales, were seen at their most playful during the 'Season' – that spell of balls, parties, theatre trips and sporting events which distinguished the southern English summer. Shooting at Bisley, horse-racing at Ascot and Epsom, croquet and tennis at Hurlingham, the Eton and Harrow cricket match at Lords, rowing at Henley and yachting at Cowes; these were the places to be if you were somebody. Not that the Season did not have an even more important social purpose. It was the top people's marriage market. Young debutantes 'came out' and under the close supervision of their mothers had about three 'Seasons' to arrange a satisfactory marriage. This display of leisured wealth was beginning to provoke criticism in the years before 1914.

The Middle Class

The middle class were a much larger and more heterogeneous group than the leisure class. Leading metropolitan professionals such as lawyers and clerics were close in lifestyle and values to the plutocracy. At the other end of the scale, large numbers of clerks, elementary school teachers and shopkeepers struggled to separate themselves from the workers. In many small towns, small businessmen and high street traders ran local chapels, clubs and the town council. The home and the suburb were the centres for much middle-class recreation. This was particularly notable in sport where older cricket and rugby clubs were increasingly being joined by even more exclusive golf and tennis clubs. The big social advantage of these latter two sports was that men and women could play both either together or separately. The suburb was also the site for a platoon of clubs and societies often closely connected with religion. Churches and chapels were not only spiritual centres but recreational centres where members of opposite sex could meet in approved circumstances. Voluntary and philanthropic work was an important part of the recreational life of many middle-class women. The suburbs symbolized fresh air and the outdoor life. Gardening was a growing preoccupation and cycling continued to be popular both as a way of discovering the countryside and for sexual and social reasons. In many towns and villages it was the middle class who ran and largely peopled the clubs and societies with their concerts, lectures, outings and tea parties.

It would be wrong to imply that the classes and the masses did not share some recreational interests. Sports like horse-racing, for example, were appreciated by rich and poor. But the rich sat on the grandstand and never mixed with the poor out on the course. Nor did they have any contact with those larger numbers of working-class men and women who placed their illegal bets in street, corner shop or workplace but never went near a racecourse. Indeed the Street Betting Act of 1906 emphasizing the illegality of off-course betting was stigmatized as one of the most blatant examples of class legislation, penalizing the small working-class punter who could not obtain credit but not the better-off one who could still bet with his bookmaker on account. Similarly the music hall was one of the most popular and commercially successful entertainments in Edwardian Britain which increasingly attracted members of every social class but there was a world of difference between those who paid for the best seats and the inhabitants of pit or gallery.

Music Hall

A Manchester journalist in 1893 speculated on the reasons for the success of music hall.[3]

> Well then, in the first place, the programme asks no thought of the spectator. He receives amusement without any effort from himself. Next, it furnishes variety, everything by turns and nothing long. This is an age of bits. Thirdly, the hall gives a comfortable seat at a low price, and discards 'early' doors and the 'packer'. Anyone can eat, drink, smoke or walk about

in a roomy promenade without interference. Fourthly, for witnessing the entertainment it is not necessary to be there at the beginning, nor stay until the end, two privileges beyond the reach of the theatre-goer.

The music halls had their origins in the entertainments of the public house. Back room get-togethers evolved into singing saloon concerts. The more successful ones began to expand their premises and pay the performers. By the 1850s publican entrepreneurs had made the music halls into a distinct institution. Drink was still sold in the auditorium but it was the entertainment that the audience paid to see. By 1870 London had thirty-one large music halls and many more smaller halls gradually to be squeezed by safety and building regulations or due to a failure to have their drinks licences renewed. The scale and commercialization of the bigger halls correspondingly increased. By 1910 London had sixty-three large halls while numbers in the rest of the country had fallen to 254. As the halls got larger and more opulent – the new Palace of Varieties built in Manchester in 1891 had 3,000 seats – ownership became concentrated in nationwide chains. In 1899, for example, the Moss Empires of Edward Moss had a capital of £1 million. He was knighted in 1906 and in 1910 his chain merged with the theatre circuit of Oswald Stoll. At its peak this chain owned and ran thirty-three music halls. The smaller halls and pub concert rooms were not completely eliminated: there were still close to 400 in Manchester in 1891. But the music hall had become big entertainment business offering an evening out to all classes. The Manchester Palace, for example, charged one and two guineas for its boxes, 5s for the best seats, 1s 6d for the pit and 1s for the gallery in the 1890s. This price segregation meant that the different classes neither sat together nor shared entrances and exits but they were all in the same building and each saw something of the other 'in action'.

What did this audience pay to see? Long before 1900 the performers had become professionalized and the leading lights were national stars. The turns system allowed the top acts to appear in London at up to four different halls every night. Most of them also went on provincial tours thereby contributing to the construction of a national taste in entertainment. A single evening's show at one of the larger halls would include a wide range of turns or acts. When Marie Lloyd made her debut at Charles Morton's Palace in London in 1898 she shared the bill with, among others, a Banjo sketch artiste, an American Biograph which showed a pillow fight in reverse, a performance of extracts from Mendelssohn's *A Midsummer Night's Dream,* and a troop of boomerang throwers. Acrobats and jugglers were also a regular feature although there was a clear trend away from material that owed its origin to the circus and towards the comic or dramatic sketch with its links to the more traditional theatre.

The core of the entertainment was the comic song and the choruses in which the audience usually joined. Going to the music hall was not a merely passive experience although as the halls got grander the entertainment

Plate 7.1.   A cover from a music hall programme. Marie Lloyd was one of the major stars of the Edwardian music hall, with fans drawn from across the social spectrum.

became more respectable and the participation more restrained. But one shouldn't take this too far. It is difficult for the historian to capture what a performance was like. With humour, parody and innuendo so much depends on the way it's done, the tone, gestures and facial expressions. Marie Lloyd was a star with fans among all social classes and was a mistress of the sly wink, meaningful gesture and double meaning. Her song, 'A little of what yer fancy does yer good' depended for its full impact on her interpretation of it as did another of her favourites, 'Every little movement has a meaning of its own'. That there was an upmarket shift in tone seems clear enough; partly under the threat from moral reform groups and the need to obtain licences from magistrate or local authority; partly because the new owners with their elegant, stylish and safe variety theatres aimed at a more affluent and respectable clientele. As a leading proprietor, with sixteen halls, MacNaghten, wrote in 1903, 'the old music hall is in the transition stage from the singing-room to the new vaudeville variety theatre. The MacNaghten Vaudeville Circuit will provide theatres to which a man may bring his wife'. But at the Leicester Pavilion those who had gallery seats still consumed fish and chips and pigs' trotters during the performance.

Historical Interpretations of Music Hall

One way of looking at the music hall is as the epitome of the 'Good Old Days' when we may not have had much money but we did see life. The 'people' laughed and cried but, like the sturdy and self-reliant people they were, they not only enjoyed it but even shared this enjoyment with their betters.[4] This is the romantic version which BBC television used to offer in its series *The Good Old Days*. A variant of this is the notion of the halls as expressing the 'soul' of the people with the essential, and superior, British quality of being able to laugh at one's self. More radical critics would scoff at such feebleness. They would point out that music hall may have begun as an expression of the people's culture but well before 1900 it had become part of the entertainment industry with songs and sketches written and performed by professionals before an increasingly passive audience. This was not *of* the people but put on *for* them by big business. The audience may have been still largely composed of the working class but they were merely passive consumers of something they had never made. Some critics might go further and suggest that music hall was specifically designed to remove any earlier radical cutting edge which it may have had leaving, in the words of Stedman Jones, a 'culture of consolation'[5] which helped to reconcile the workers to their lot in a society which gave them no power nor even fair shares. Music hall was certainly not radical. But the idea of a culture of consolation seems too dismissive. There was, after all, disagreement amongst society's leaders about whether music hall was a good thing or not. Moreover it was not only the working man, his lifestyle and values who was ridiculed in song and sketch, but also authority figures from the middle and upper-class worlds: the policeman, the vicar, the landlord, the employer and the snob. Music hall not only celebrated but reflected the conflicts and contradictions of real life both between social classes and within them. It was a way of having a good time on the Marie Lloyd principle of a little of what you fancy does you good, and it was available, for many of the music hall crowd, every week. The catch phrases, jokes and songs in particular formed a second language for all classes. Moreover its headquarters was London, and as Jeremy Crump has underlined, far from being centres of local cultural expression, the provincial halls were yet another institution through which 'national standards of performance and national imagery' permeated the country.[6] Music hall was a 'powerful integrative force in English society'.

Football

Football as an organized, seasonal spectacle grew dramatically after the Football Association accepted professionalism in 1885. One measure of this growth is the rise in entries for and attendances at the final match of the Football Association's knock-out cup competition. The year professionalism was legalized 116 clubs entered and 12,500 saw the final played at the Oval cricket ground between Blackburn Rovers and the Scottish amateurs, Queen's Park. By 1901, 220 clubs entered the competition and 110,820 went to the final between Sheffield United and Tottenham Hotspur at the Crystal Palace. Even this huge crowd was exceeded in 1913 when 120,081 saw Aston Villa and Sunderland compete for a trophy which had attracted 455 other clubs. A professional league was formed in England in 1888, a second division being added in 1892, and Scotland had two divisions of its own and a knock-out cup. Professional football began in the urban settings of the Midlands, North of England, and Central Scotland. The headquarters of the Football League was at Preston. There were more clubs and players per head of the population north of the Trent. But it was never only a regional game. The FA's offices were in London which reflected both its origins and a growing popularity in the South. Another sign of this was the formation of the Southern League, which itself had two divisions, in 1894. Tottenham Hotspur became the first southern club to win the cup in 1901; the League was not won by southerners until Arsenal's victory in 1931. Professional football was popular nationwide and reading the results in the newspapers provided a useful geography lesson to many elementary schoolboys. Only four towns with populations exceeding 100,000 had no professional league clubs in 1911 – Birkenhead, Gateshead, Halifax and South Shields. In all there were about 158 professional clubs in England and Wales in 1914, perhaps another thirty in Scotland and many more semi-professional ones. Nowhere outside football grounds did such large crowds of mainly working men regularly gather through a season which lasted from the end of August until the beginning of April.

Professional football was a business. Most clubs were limited liability companies run by a board of directors who were usually local businessmen or professionals – accountants, doctors, journalists, solicitors, schoolteachers with publicans and brewers often involved. But if it was a business it was business of a special kind. The directors received no payments. In England, dividends to shareholders were limited to 5 per cent. The home team, while banking the bulk of the gate receipts, paid a small proportion of receipts to the visitors. Profits, if any, tended to be ploughed back. The directors, like the fans, wanted a winning team. To be a director obviously brought prestige and it might bring building or catering contracts but directors were utility maximizers rather than profit maximizers. The directors ran the club, usually

Plate 7.2. The FA Cup final in 1901. 110,820 people gathered at the Crystal Palace to watch this match between Sheffield United and Tottenham Hotspur – some of them climbing nearby trees and roofs to get a glimpse. Despite the enormous numbers and minimal policing, crowd disturbances at football matches were rare.

selecting the team although a trainer was employed to look after the players. Of course if things went badly on the field then the directors could face public criticism.

There were signs that responsibility for playing matters was being transferred to the club secretary, a paid officer, who could be dismissed if the team did not play well. George Ramsay at Aston Villa and Tom Watson, first at Sunderland and then at Liverpool, were prototypes of the modern football manager.

In some ways the players were like music hall stars: but nothing like so well paid. The maximum wage was £4 a week but many players did not receive it. For those who did it was good money, being double the earnings of skilled workers and much more than labourers could hope for. It was an insecure job, a short career often cut shorter by injury or loss of form. Nor could players move freely from club to club. But life for most workers was also insecure. Professional football seemed an attractive job to many young men, providing, as well as money, enjoyment, fame and an attractive lifestyle. Not all were successful and many who were frittered away their good fortune. But others were more prudent. Bob Crompton of Blackburn Rovers kept up his trade as a plumber and later ran a successful business. He was the first professional to captain England in 1904, and one of the first to drive a motor car. Well before 1914 footballers were local and national celebrities.

In focus: The Football Crowd

Football matches are like a story. They have a beginning, a middle and an end. And the audience is the crowd. Without the crowd the football match would not have attracted so much attention. And if the music hall audience could be thought of as participating in the evening's performance how much more involved was the football crowd. Most matches were won by home teams and it was widely believed that crowds could influence the outcome. By 1911–12 the average attendance at matches in the English first division was 16,775. FA Cup ties were an even bigger attraction. Every Saturday and public holiday throughout the season a full programme of matches was held. It was a largely male, largely working-class crowd, most of whom paid sixpence to get in. Most stood on open terraces. It usually cost more for shelter and more still for a seat. Only the better off – the lower middle or more middle-class patrons who probably bought a season ticket – could afford to sit in the grandstand. The tram and the railway meant that spectators could travel some distance to matches. Aston Villa, in Birmingham, recruited many of their fans from the nearby Black Country. But few could afford to travel to away matches. Cup ties or local derbies between traditional rivals might be exceptions to the rule. Crowds were exciting but also frightening. The roars of triumph, especially following a home team goal, or of disappointment, of expectation and apprehension

The Football Crowd (continued)

could often be heard miles away. The crushing and swaying as men spilled down the steep terraces could be terrible both to behold and take part in. There were occasional accidents: in retrospect it seems surprising there were so few. In 1902 a wooden stand behind one of the goals at Ibrox Park, Glasgow, collapsed during the international match between Scotland and England; twenty-six men fell forty feet to their deaths and five hundred people were injured. Crowd disturbances were not uncommon. A riot at the end of the replayed Scottish Cup Final in 1909 seems to have been caused because the crowd expected extra time before a third match. But in both Belfast and Glasgow religious sectarianism sometimes led to fighting between the rival supporters. Watching football was an emotional experience. Loyalties and passions ran high. In a football crowd individuals might do and say things they would not do elsewhere. Referees, visiting players and occasionally visiting supporters might be targets. Overcrowding could also produce problems. But most crowds were orderly enough and policing was minimal. It is difficult not to agree with Nicholas Fishwick that, at least before 1950, there was no sign of that dissident subculture which later in the century was to do so much to discredit the game.[7]

Professionals and Amateurs

Professional football had its critics. Amateur ideals of sportsmanship and fair play, they alleged, were neglected. As C.B. Fry's *Fry's Magazine of Sport* characterized them in 1913, crowds were fanatical, irrational and rowdy. 'A magnificently fought out game ending in a goalless draw will leave the crowd sullen and morose; they will wend their way home from the ground with blacklooks, cursing the bad luck of the home side. An undeserved victory for the home team will leave no regrets ... There is no sportsmanship in a football crowd ... Partisanship has dulled its idea of sport and warped its moral sense.' A common criticism was that spectators should be playing instead of watching. This ignored the fact that not everyone could play due to age, lack of ability, or a shortage of pitches and also that many of those who watched had played or still did so. Football *was* a game of players and their numbers were rising. Beneath the spectacular tip of professionalism was a large participatory iceberg. There were probably 750,000 registered players in England alone in 1914, members of 12,000 clubs. Not all would play every week. But especially in areas like Glasgow, north east England, Birmingham, Yorkshire, Lancashire and London, football subcultures flourished buttressed by the improvements in transport we noted earlier and the coverage provided by local newspapers. By 1914 organized schoolboy football was a vigorous part of elementary school life. Games periods were only first recognized as an official part of the curriculum in 1906 and football was allowed under the Board of Education's Physical Training Syllabus in 1909. Local football clubs were patronized by churches, chapels and employers. In Sheffield in 1914, 150 clubs were linked to religious bodies. Many clubs were based on pubs or even streets and democratically run by working men. There was unorganized football aplenty played in streets and parks by boys, youths and men. It was not always to the liking of local residents and street football could lead to prosecutions. What is clear is that football was played as well as watched and certainly much more than critics were prepared to acknowledge.

It was in these years that sport in general and football in particular became a significant British cultural export. It often accompanied investment and trade not only in the countries of formal Empire but also in Europe and Latin America. It was less a manifestation of cultural imperialism than a reflection of the fact of British power and the status and influence which went with it. British engineers, sales representatives, teachers, clerks and manual workers took their games far afield aided by employers and entrepreneurs like Sir Thomas Lipton, for example, who gave a cup for competition between Argentina and Uruguay in 1902 thus initiating what has become the most often played international football match. British communities in cities like Buenos Aires established their own schools with sport a prominent part of the curriculum. British football teams, both amateur and professional, not only went on spring and summer tours to Europe but regularly crossed the South Atlantic to Latin America. Southampton did it first in 1904 and the leading amateurs, Corinthians, had been to Brazil three times by 1914. A combined England side including both amateurs and professionals had embarrassingly easy victories over Austria, Hungary and Bohemia in 1908. British professionals took coaching positions abroad. The first two Olympic football tournaments, in 1908 and 1912, were won by Britain. In football at least, British supremacy was unchallenged.

The People's Game?

Football was largely a male world, played and watched by working and lower middle-class boys, youths and men, mainly in the age range fourteen to fifty. Few women were involved. Indeed it could be argued that football encouraged men to spend time away from home and away from women. It was enjoyable and an opportunity for talk and friendship with mates. Working men often had important positions in junior football but were rarely in the offices where power was wielded. Professional clubs, the FA, the Football League, the County Football Associations, were mostly in the hands of middle-class men. There were working-class shareholders of professional clubs in both England and Scotland, but they only held a small number of shares. In such circumstances shareholding was an extension of being a fan. Football was not controlled by the people. On the other hand football supporters gave a loyalty and commitment to the game which looks unique when compared to other forms of working-class leisure and consumption. Football may have taken the place of religion for some in terms of collective commitment, ritual and identity. Support of the local club probably developed a sense of belonging to towns and cities which had become not simply large but complicated and stratified. International matches between England and Scotland, played annually since 1872, became for the Scots not simply the opportunity to defeat their more powerful neighbour but to celebrate Scottish identity. It was in the first decade of the twentieth century, especially in those alternate years when the match was played in England and large numbers of Scots travelled south to support their team that a national tradition was born, 'part of a sturdy subculture of symbols, slogans, heroes and myths which sustains an apolitical, inverted, but palpable subnationalism which combines a strong identity of being Scottish with a very weak national project'.[8]

Football and Social Control

There were always contemporaries both on the right and left of politics prepared to say that a range of pleasures, including football, kept the workers out of mischief. An example was the Conservative politician F.E. Smith, later Lord Birkenhead. In 1911 he saw the importance of football:

> What would the devotees of athletics do if their present amusements were abolished? The policeman, the police magistrate, the social worker, the minister of religion, the public schoolmaster ... would each, in the sphere of his own duties, contemplate such a prospect with dismay ... The poorer classes in this country have not got the tastes which superior people or a Royal Commission would choose for them and were cricket and football abolished, it would bring upon the masses nothing but misery, depression, sloth, indiscipline, and disorder.[9]

It is one thing for historians to point out that individuals recommended the use of football to keep the workers happy. It is quite another to be able to demonstrate that that was the role it actually performed in pre-1914 Britain. For one thing while not denying its popularity, many working men were untouched by it. If newspapers gave it wide coverage it was in part because they recognized that there was a significant public interest although they were also contributing to its importance. As for employers, many of them enjoyed it for the same reasons as some of their workers did. It might also provide positive publicity that was good for business and industrial relations. It seems doubtful that interest in football kept working men from more serious matters, such as joining trade unions or taking an active interest in politics. There are numerous examples of workers combining an interest both in their local football team and the Labour Party. It is also likely that football would not have been as popular as it was if more recreational choices had been available to working-class males. Finally it needs to be remembered that powerful people in society differed about how far football was socially beneficial. Many were hostile to it and F.E. Smith was partly arguing against them in the article quoted at the beginning of this section.

Historical Interpretations of Sport and Recreation

Contemporaries talked a good deal about the problem of leisure by which they meant the problem of leisure for young wage earners of both sexes and adult working-class males. Theirs was a louder debate than among historians. In 1912 King George V attended the first Music Hall Royal Command Performance. Two years later, he went to his first FA Cup Final. The implication was that both music hall and football had become accepted features of the British way of life. But doubts were still expressed that recreation ought to be for improvement, for things like education and politics and not squandered on frivolous amusement. Ross McKibbin has tried to bridge the gap between what people actually did in their spare time and its value. He has pointed out that working-class hobbies might have involved the cultivation of some of the qualities demanded by their detractors. He makes four points. First, that they were activities freely chosen, practised in free time and often talked about at work. Second, that the approach to them was not random or disorganized. It required regular application and physical or intellectual discipline. Thirdly the pursuit demanded knowledge and sustained interest. Finally, that interest was usually accompanied by the creation or discharge of some kind of mental and physical tension.[10] Commitment to a particular sport such as football could involve all or some of these qualities. We have already emphasized that football was not simply the escapism of the petty consumer. It involved loyalties to club and community. Many contemporaries noted the knowledge which some young men had about the game. Some could probably have taken a degree in it. At the least they were certainly informed observers. It would be imprudent to characterize the whole of the football crowd in this way but we should be wary of the facile generalization, especially where recreation and its meaning are concerned.

Recreation was not necessarily collective. It was, in part at least, based on individual choice. It could be and often was pursued alone, privately in the home or outside. It is true that the choice for working men was limited by time, money and energy. And in that sense an argument could be mounted that recreation was a formidable competitor to politics. And also that, as we noted earlier, football might not have been as popular as it was if the choice of recreational opportunity had been wider. It must also be emphasized that for working-class women, recreation was constrained by convention as well as the obstacles their menfolk had to face. Moreover, most working-class leisure was probably not spent in the commercial world but in the streets, markets, parks and at home, before the First World War.

Middle-class people had more choice. We need to know more about how they exercised it. We also need to know more about gender differences in recreation in general, and within the middle class in particular. By 1914 sport and music hall, along with advertising, the popular press, and the cinema were all contributing to the formation of a national popular culture cutting across lines of class. A century before, popular culture seemed to be inextricably linked with class conflict. By 1914 the waters were muddier.

Bibliographical Note

Most of the pioneer works on this subject have been influenced by Marxist notions of class and the structural imperatives of capitalism. G. Stedman Jones offered the clearest example of the method in his lament for the independent artisan world of nineteenth century London lost in a changing industrial urban and technological complex. His essay (see Footnote 5) together with some words of warning about the use of 'social control' in leisure studies was reprinted in his *Languages of Class* (Cambridge, 1983). Two influential studies on the place of leisure in Victorian society were those of Hugh Cunningham and Peter Bailey. Cunningham, *Leisure in the Industrial Revolution* (London, 1980) was designed to show that the impact of the industrial revolution on leisure was not as negative as had once been thought. His essay in John Benson's collection, *The Working Class in England 1875–1914* (London, 1985) remains the best introduction to recreation in the lives of workers. See also his 'Leisure and culture' in F.M.L. Thompson (ed.), *Cambridge Social History of Britain 1750–1950, Volume 2 People and their Environment* (Cambridge, 1990). Peter Bailey, *Leisure and Class in Victorian England* (London, 1978) examined the failure of rational recreation to eliminate more popular pastimes. It was reprinted with a new introduction in 1987. Two essays by Ross McKibbin have argued that the recreation of male workers should be seen as more of an individual response to the world in which they found themselves. Both can be found in Ross McKibbin, *The Ideologies of Class* (Oxford, 1991).

Detailed studies of music hall can be found in Peter Bailey (ed.), *Music Hall: the Business of Pleasure* (Milton Keynes, 1986), J.S. Bratton (ed.), *Music Hall: Performance and Style* (Milton Keynes, 1986) and D. Russell, *Popular Music in England 1814–1914. A Social History* (Manchester, 1987). For the history of football and other participatory and spectator sports see Richard Holt, *Sport and the British. A Modern History* (Oxford, 1989) and Wray Vamplew, *Pay Up and Play the Game. Professional Sport in Britain, 1875–1914* (Cambridge, 1988).

Notes

1. Elizabeth Roberts, *A Women's Place. An Oral History of Working-Class Women 1890–1940* (Oxford, 1985).

2. M.E. Loane, *An Englishman's Castle* (London, 1909).

3. Quoted by Bob Dickinson, 'In the audience', *Oral History* 11, 1, Spring 1983.

4. I am very conscious throughout this section of my debt to Peter Bailey (ed.), *Music Hall: The Business of Pleasure* (Milton Keynes, 1986) and especially his own introduction and the essays by Jeremy Crump and Dogmar Höher.

5. G. Stedman Jones, 'Working-class culture and working-class politics in London, 1870–1900' *Journal of Social History* (1974) reprinted in his *Languages of Class* (Cambridge, 1983) pp. 179–238.

6. Jeremy Crump in Bailey, *Music Hall.*

7. Nicholas Fishwick, *English Football and Society 1910–1950* (Manchester, 1989).

8. Quoted by Richard Holt, *Sport and the British. A Modern History* (Oxford, 1989) p. 259.

9. Quoted by Tony Mason, *Association Football and English Society 1863–1915* (Brighton, 1980) pp. 226–7.

10. Ross McKibbin, 'Work and hobbies in Britain 1880–1950' in J.M. Winter (ed.), *The Working Class in Modern British History* (London, 1983) p. 129.

8 Nationality and Ethnicity

David Feldman

A Multinational State

What is nationality? The answer, in part, is a subject for legal historians. The law determines who can and cannot claim British nationality. For centuries, for most people, this status has rested on being born within the Crown's Dominions. In other words, nationality has been determined by birthplace. Until the 1981 Nationality Act ancestry was irrelevant to the nationality of a person born within the United Kingdom. In this respect, Britain differs from states such as Germany in which nationality is derived not from territory but from membership of an historic people. But the doctrine of personal allegiance to the Crown brought the citizens of the UK together within a wider imperial nationality. In 1914 when the King declared war on Germany, he did so on behalf of colonies, dominions and the Indian Empire as well. These facets of British nationality were restated at the end of our period in the British Nationality and Status of Aliens Act of 1914.

But nationality also exists in another sense: it is a matter of how historical actors see themselves. The nation can provide answers to questions such as 'where do I come from?' 'where do I belong?' 'to whom do I owe allegiance'? In this sense, the nation is a cultural creation as well as a legal one. It is in Benedict Anderson's helpful phrase, an 'imagined community'.[1] As such, it can be 'imagined' in different ways.

The difficulties and ambiguities in applying the concept of nationality to the United Kingdom highlight these subjective aspects of the term. Both demographically and politically England has dominated the United Kingdom. In 1900 its population accounted for roughly three-quarters of the whole. London was the capital of both England and the UK. Historically many English people have spoken or written of England when they have also referred to the other constituent parts of Britain. Famously, an early edition of the Encyclopaedia Britannica included the entry 'Wales: see under England'.

But notwithstanding English dominance, the United Kingdom is a multinational state. It contains differences of culture, language and religion which carry associations with other, subordinate national units. In Wales, for example, at the turn of the century, over half of the population were Welsh-language speakers. In Ireland, unlike the remainder of the UK, the majority of the population was Catholic. In Scotland, notwithstanding the lack of a linguistic or religious issue to act as a focus, the late nineteenth and early twentieth centuries witnessed a revival of a national consciousness. This was evinced in phenomena as diverse as the middle-class fashion for sporting highland dress on Sundays and the emergence of a distinct Scottish Football Association. At a legal level this was not a problem since English, Irish, Scots and Welsh alike were subjects of the Crown. However, any subjective concept of nationality which has sought to encompass the whole of the UK has been forced to accommodate or oppose this heterogeneity.

The UK in 1900 was a multinational state in a second sense – its population included a portion of immigrants. The largest group were the Irish although, strictly speaking, in view of the Union, the Irish who settled elsewhere in the UK were not immigrants. In 1901 there were 426,565 Irish-born in England and Wales and 205,064 in Scotland, where they respectively comprised 1 per cent and 3.7 per cent of the population. There were major concentrations of Irish in urban Lancashire, London and Glasgow as well as in garrison towns such as York and boom towns such as Cardiff with a voracious appetite for labour.

Since the 1860s, however, the migration of Irish to other parts of the British Isles had been in decline. At the turn of the century it was the immigration of East European Jews that was increasing and drew public attention. Over 120,000 Jews settled in England between 1880 and 1914, and roughly the same number remained for anything between a few days and few years *en route* to the United States. About one half of these immigrants settled in London. Other centres of concentration were Leeds, Manchester, Liverpool, Glasgow and Birmingham.

At a legal level, then, the UK contained a single nationality, its people united by their common status under the Crown. But the demographic, religious and cultural composition of the state, as well as its imperial role, fostered different ideas of nationality. Among the Celtic subordinate nationalities, there were movements, most significantly in Ireland, which sought to reshape or even break the Union. With regard to immigrants, many perceived them as an unwelcome and unassimilable element and this gave rise to the Aliens Act of 1905 which restricted the number of foreigners able to settle in the country. Finally, as the nation's imperial power was challenged by other nations, the empire became increasingly prominent in cultural and political invocations of national identity and interest.

The Crisis of the Union

In 1900 all parts of the UK elected representatives to Westminster but there was also an element of administrative devolution. In the case of Scotland, there was a Secretary of State who was a member of the Cabinet and, among other responsibilities, answered for public health, the Poor Law, roads, bridges and fisheries. In Ireland, the administration was presided over by the Chief Secretary for Ireland who was also a member of the Cabinet in London. In 1912, however, the Liberal government introduced a bill to Parliament that would extend this practice of devolution decisively by allowing home rule in Ireland. Home rule was not independence; under the Liberal bill Irish MPs would continue to sit at Westminster but there would be an Irish legislative assembly and this would be empowered to raise revenue through taxation. Home rule, it was hoped, would give expression to Irish nationality and reconcile Ireland to the Union. But by 1914 not only the future status of Ireland was uncertain but the future of the United Kingdom as well. When the Prime Minister, H.H. Asquith, had introduced the Home Rule Bill, he anticipated it would be 'only the first step in a larger and more comprehensive policy'.[2] Home rule for Scotland and even Wales were future possibilities. Winston Churchill went so far as to propose parliaments for the English regions.

Irish home rule revealed the contested nature of nationality. According to its Liberal supporters, home rule signified a preparedness to entertain pluralism within the UK and an idea of nationality that accommodated diversity. John Morley entertained the hope that a reshaped Irish government would 'leave room for an independent and spontaneous growth of Irish civilisation along its own lines.' Writing in *The Times* James Bryce claimed that 'the opinion of each of the nationalities surviving in our islands is worth regarding'. In the case of Wales and Scotland, distinct national feelings were not incompatible 'with attachment to the greater nationality of the United Kingdom' and there was no opposition between them. In the case of Ireland, however, the historic injustices meted out by England meant that it was only through a new constitutional arrangement that Irish grievances could be reconciled with the sovereign parliament of the UK and be contained within the British nation.[3]

But how many nations were there in Ireland, one or two? Religion was a central element in Irish nationalism. But among the nine counties of Ulster, four counties contained clear majorities of Scots-Protestant descent and in two other counties, though just in the minority, this group was numerous. From the 1890s Irish nationalism was infused increasingly with cultural as well as political goals. The Gaelic Athletic Association and the Gaelic League rejected anglicization and promoted programmes aimed to preserve and develop Irish national identity. Ulster Protestants wanted no part of this Catholic, Gaelic national identity. They proclaimed their right to remain British subjects. On 28 September 1912 nearly a quarter of a million Protestant men pledged in the Solemn League and Covenant to resist home rule by any means. The

Ulster Volunteers, established in January 1913 to carry to action this threat of force, soon enrolled 100,000 members. By their own lights, these men were loyal rebels; their loyalty, they claimed, was to the Crown not Parliament.

English opponents of home rule took the view that the UK contained a single British nationality. According to Andrew Bonar Law, the leader of the Conservative Party, the claims of Ireland were merely those of a region within the UK and if this was the case then the claims of another region – Ulster – should be considered as well. It was unthinkable, he told the House of Commons, 'that any Prime Minister could give orders to shoot down men whose only crime is that they refuse to be driven out of our community and deprived of the privilege of British citizenship'. Bonar Law appeared to be offering support to the Ulster rebels. The Unionist intellectual A.V. Dicey claimed 'we only are entitled to the name of Nationalists'. From this standpoint, in 1913 he urged 'it is the duty of Unionists, and indeed of all patriots, to make sure that the Home Rule Bill does not pass into law'.[4] In March 1914 this cry was realized when the mutiny of British officers at the Curragh seemed to show that the Liberal government was incapable of facing down the Ulster rebels. Only the outbreak of war in August averted a constitutional crisis. But the controversy and conflict which surrounded the future of the Union offers a vivid demonstration that ideas dealing with national identity were intellectual and cultural creations and by no means commanded agreement.

Democracy and Empire

In these years the Conservative Party and imperial-minded pressure groups *claimed* a monopoly on patriotism. But the association of the Conservative Party with patriotism should not be seen as inevitable or self-evident. In 1878, for example, when Disraeli had threatened war with Russia in defence of the nation's imperial interests he was opposed by a wide-ranging peace movement which placed a different interpretation on patriotism and the nation's interests. Imperialism and militarism were seen as alien growths which, by exalting the armed forces, threatened, in the words of one newspaper 'the constitutional traditions of the English race'.

The development of Tory, imperial patriotism in the early twentieth century was a response to two developments of fundamental importance. First, there was the mass electorate. By 1910 this had grown to approximately 6 million and its empowerment created a strategic dilemma for Conservative politicians. Not surprisingly, some advocated a popular Toryism; an appeal to the enfranchised masses. After 1901, in the face of a series of by-election defeats, these innovators gained in influence. Their analysis seemed to be confirmed and their influence was further swollen by the Liberal Party's massive victory in the General Election of 1906 and by the emergence of the Labour Party.

The second vital development was the growing evidence of Britain's relative economic decline. Portents of relative decline began to register in public debate. In 1896 E.E. Williams published his bestseller *Made in Germany*. In 1902 Frederick Mackenzie's *The American Invaders* similarly decried the loss of markets at home and abroad to foreign competitors. The changing balance of power had a military as well as an economic dimension. The growing wealth and technological sophistication of other industrial powers made them naval as well as economic rivals. In 1883 the Royal Navy possessed thirty-eight battleships, only two fewer than the rest of the entire world. By 1897, however, this gap of two had increased to thirty-four. But seapower was essential to Britain's economic and imperial health. Not only did British industry and commerce rely on access to overseas markets but the British people relied on imports for a large and increasing part of their food.

These two influences were brought sharply into focus by the Boer War. In 1899 the campaign against the Boer republics began disastrously. In the course of the 'Black Week', between 9 and 15 December, the British Expeditionary Force suffered three shattering defeats. But at last, on 18 May 1900, information reached London which signalled a turning point in the war: the siege of the British garrison at Mafeking had been relieved. In response, boisterous street celebrations erupted the length and breadth of Britain. The jubilant crowds lent credence to Conservatives who believed that the cause of empire offered them one way of appealing to the working-class electorate. The activities of rowdies who broke up peace meetings, the surge in recruitment to the regular army and to the Volunteers could also support a similar interpretation. The Conservative landslide victory in the Election of 1900 appeared to translate these currents of opinion into votes and seats in Parliament.

But the Boer War was important in a further sense. The setbacks of the 'Black Week' had been traumatic. Even the drawn-out process of victory, two years of guerilla warfare, gave sufficient cause for alarm. By the end of the war in 1902, Britain had put 450,000 men into the field to defeat two republics with a combined population of no more than 60,000. Worse still, as many as one-third of the men who had presented themselves as recruits in the war had had to be rejected on account of their poor physical condition. On one side, then, some Conservative politicians and supporters had begun to see their electoral future secured by an imperially oriented working class. On the other, there was wide agreement that the poor physical health of the urban masses might lay at risk the imperial future.

The years following the Boer War were notable for the profusion of patriotic leagues – pressure groups – which strove to respond to these dual political and imperial imperatives. The first of these organizations, the Navy League, in fact, was founded as early as 1895. Several more followed in the early years of the next decade: the National Service League in 1902, the Tariff Reform League and the British Brothers League the following year, and between 1907 and 1909 a number of less significant organizations, the Union

Defence League, the Imperial Maritime League, and the Anti-Socialist League, were created. The advent of a cheap, national, mass circulation daily press influenced the tone of the expanding democracy and its pressure groups. In 1900 the *Daily Mail*, after only four years of existence, was selling 700,000 copies daily at a halfpenny each – whereas *The Times* retailed at 3d. It was soon joined by competitors such as the *Express*, the *Sketch* and the *Mirror*. This 'yellow press' was notable for its veneration of monarchy and empire, its anti-radicalism and its raucous distrust of foreigners.

By the turn of the century the Navy League had identified the German naval challenge as the main threat to the nation's imperial future. In 1913, under the influence of the naval race and periodic international crises membership had grown to 125,000. By mobilizing popular support and a press campaign, the League aimed to put pressure on governments to increase the naval budget and to pursue an enlarged programme of battleship construction. The League appealed to its potential constituency as patriots: 'Sink your party feelings for a day; be neither Conservatives nor Liberals but something greater and better, be ENGLISHMEN'.[5]

The National Service League was established in 1901. It was one facet of the immediate reaction to the trauma of the Boer War and, in particular, to its revelation of the empire's limited military resources. NSL's programme called for all schoolchildren, girls as well as boys to undergo a compulsory programme of military and physical training, followed by stints of between two months and two years for adults between fifteen and twenty-two. The training would relieve the army and navy from the burden of home defence and release them for imperial tasks. But, additionally, it would improve national physique, induce habits of order and discipline and a heightened sense of patriotic duty.

The NSL's growing popularity paralleled that of the Navy League. By 1912 it had enrolled just under 100,000 full members as well as 219,000 adherents – a different class of supporter who were required to pay a subscription of just 1d. Like the Navy League, the NSL claimed to be above party politics and devoted to the national cause. But it is undeniable that these groups saw the national cause and that of the Conservatives as flowing in the same direction. At different times the NSL claimed the allegiance of 105 to 177 Members of Parliament but only three were ever Liberals. Similarly, in 1910 when the Navy League published its list of eighty-three candidates it considered 'sound' on naval issues all but six were Conservatives.

The prognoses of these organizations, their suspicion of foreigners and their vision of social unity at home gave a set of common characteristics to these patriotic leagues. It was the Tariff Reform League which, for a few years, brought these themes together in a coherent programme. The introduction of duties levied on foreign imports, combined with a system of preferences for imperial goods, could be made to promise many things; the revival of Britain's economic supremacy, lower unemployment, a barrier to the spread of socialism among the working classes, the consolidation of imperial bonds, and the provision of revenue essential to meet the costs of social reform and naval defence.

The revival of protectionism was precipitated by a speech made by the Colonial Secretary, Joseph Chamberlain, at Birmingham on 15 May 1903 in which he announced his conversion to the cause. The first meeting of the Tariff Reform League took place at a London hotel on 27 July 1903. As with the other Leagues, success depended upon the TRL extending its appeal beyond the propertied classes. Accordingly, in April 1904 it formed the Trade Union Tariff Reform Association which by 1907 had fifty-four branches. Joseph Chamberlain claimed to 'represent Labour ... which thinks not of itself as a class, opposed to any other class in the community, but as responsible for the obligations of the country and the Empire to which it belongs'. The historical destiny of the working class was not as an antagonist to capital but was akin to an estate within the nation. In return, tariff reformers would protect working men from the unemployment and reduced wages caused by cheap foreign imports. The TRL's propaganda appealed to fair play and patriotic disdain for 'the foreigner' and 'Herr Dumper', who flooded British markets while protecting their own.[6]

Chamberlain and the TRL engaged in a battle to capture the Conservative Party and by 1908 they had succeeded admirably. The further fortunes of the TRL followed the contours of party conflict. Thus after the Budget of 1909 in which Lloyd George managed both to sustain free trade and to finance increased naval expenditure and social reform, the future of the Conservatives appeared to hinge on the alternative fiscal strategy encased in tariff reform. In 1909, therefore, the income and propaganda output of the TRL soared. In that year the nation's life was enriched by over 53 million pamphlets, leaflets and posters advocating tariff reform. But after the two Liberal election victories in 1910, the Conservative leadership began to distance itself from protectionism. Tariffs were now seen as an obstacle to regaining power and contributions to the TRL dwindled.

These pressure groups had a dual impact. First, patriotism became more associated than it had been before both with imperialism and with a campaign to strengthen Britain economically and militarily against foreign rivals. Second, the leagues promoted the idea that the Liberal Party could not be trusted to defend the nation's interests. At one level, then, these groups were calling for national unity but as a matter of political reality they were divisive.

Children, Lads and Militarism

These Leagues were not isolated attempts to build a patriotic and imperial consensus in the face of external competition and social division at home. The same motivations informed the new youth movements of the late nineteenth and early twentieth centuries: the Boy Scouts, the Boys Brigade, the Church

Lads Brigade, the British Girl's Patriotic League. Baden Powell, the hero of Mafeking and the founder of the Boy Scouts, wrote in his 1909 manual *Scouting for Boys*:

> Remember, whether rich or poor, from castle or from slum, you are all Britons first, and you've got to keep Britain up against outside enemies, you have to stand shoulder to shoulder to do it. If you are doing harm to yourselves you are doing harm to your country. You must sink your differences.[7]

The Boys Brigade was the first of these organizations, established in Scotland in 1883 by William Alexander Smith. By 1899 the Brigade was 35,148 strong but its expansion was ultimately disrupted by the creation of the Boy Scouts. Smith's notion was to provide moral discipline and recreation for working-class lads in the years between leaving Sunday School and joining the YMCA. His conception of the form this should take was shaped by his

Plate 8.1 A Scout camp. Healthy outdoor pursuits, militaristic discipline, and a heavy dose of patriotism were the hallmark of the Boy Scouts

background as a Sunday School teacher and as a member of the 1st Lanarkshire Rifle Volunteers. Recruits to the Boys Brigade were provided with a weekly routine of drill, bible class and club room. The Church Lads' Brigade, established in 1891, was an Anglican competitor to the Boys Brigade and by 1908 it had a membership of 70,000. Like the Boys Brigade, the CLB was designed as a bridge between Sunday School and adult membership of a temperance society.

Whereas these two organizations straddled the ground between Christian discipline and patriotic sentiment, the creation of the Boy Scouts in 1907 signified a decisive shift from the former to the latter. Baden Powell was influenced by fashionable fears of moral and physical deterioration. The Scout movement was fashionable also in its rejection of urban industrial values. The source of deterioration was the city; the cure would be found in healthy outdoor pursuits. This modishness helps to explain why a converted army training manual, *Scouting for Boys*, became a huge commercial success and the basis of a youth movement. The book was sold in six fortnightly parts at 4d each and included twenty-eight 'camp yarns' on topics such as camp life, tracking, endurance, chivalry, woodcraft and patriotism. By 1913 there were 150,000 Boy Scouts but since there was a high turnover of members the movement reached many more.

Youth movements captured only a fraction of the nation's young but, in theory at least, the classroom caught them all. At all levels, from the slumland elementary school to the nation's public schools, the empire took on growing significance. In 1895 Rev. J.E.C. Welldon, the headmaster of Harrow, told a meeting of the Royal Colonial Institute that the role of the public schools was to mould the coming generation of imperial administrators. Indeed, these schools often provided the empire's school teachers, missionaries, professionals and technicians as well. The habits of authority and the ethic of service promoted by these schools was mixed with militarism. By the start of the century the country's public schools could boast 110 army cadet corps.

If public schools were designed to produce imperial leaders, elementary schools were to provide a mass of loyal as well as obedient subjects. From 1878 the history and geography curricula were infused with imperial knowledge. The significance of the colonies was also impressed on schoolchildren on Empire Day which was first widely observed in 1904. Classrooms were decorated with the flags of the Dominions, teachers used maps to illustrate the extent of Britain's possessions and children sang patriotic songs and sometimes enacted plays or pageants on a suitable theme.

The rise in militarism also registered in the large number of men who had some sort of military experience. Michael Blanch has estimated that between 1881 and 1898, 600,000 men enlisted in the regular army, a further 656,000 joined the militia – a part-time army for home defence – and 797,000 joined the Volunteers – a force that was both part-time and unpaid. He calculates that in 1899, 22.4 per cent of the male population of the United Kingdom between the ages of seventeen and forty had had previous military experience. This, he suggests, was a powerful influence educating the working class into nationalism.[8] Indeed, recruitment to the Volunteers increased during the Boer War and this rise was sustained thereafter.

Spectacle and Consumption

Ever since 1876, when Queen Victoria had been installed by Disraeli as Empress of India, the monarchy had been presented as the focal point of an empire, not merely of a United Kingdom. Colonial premiers and troops flocked to London for the Queen's jubilee parade in 1897. The occasion became a celebration of the expansion of the British Empire. The old queen was cheered through six miles of London's streets. It had not always been so. Victoria's coronation had been unrehearsed and, predictably, botched. As recently as 1872 Gladstone had complained 'the Queen is invisible, the Prince of Wales is not respected'. By 1900, however, indifference and ambivalence had given way to popular veneration and alongside this change another had taken place; the Crown had become firmly identified with empire. In 1902 Edward VII was the first British monarch to be crowned emperor of India and ruler 'of the British Dominions beyond the seas'.[9]

The progress of mass consumption helped to promote this imperial conception of national identity. The great celebrations of imperial monarchy were moments for the proliferation of royal ephemera. Firms catering for the growing mass market such as Cadbury, Rowntree and Oxo used images of royal events to advertise their products. But in normal times as well, the marketing of tea, tobacco, chocolate and soap used the imperial connection to sell consumer goods. The advent of cheap photography and the picture postcard also brought images of empire to a mass audience: photographs of weird natives, heroic generals and brave missionaries were retailed at corner shops in every town.

The theatre, the music hall and the new medium of cinema were also suffused with representations of empire and monarchy. In 1897, to celebrate and exploit the Diamond Jubilee, the Alhambra music hall in Leicester Square, London, presented an elaborate sketch, entitled 'Victoria and Merrie England'. Its local competitor 'The Empire' presented 'Our Empire' in 1895 and again in 1899 and 'Our Crown' to mark the coronation of 1902. The emphasis in music hall representations of empire shifted at this time. The idea that British rule symbolized freedom and liberty for slaves all over the globe gave way in the late nineteenth century to an emphasis on imperial grandeur and indignation at the threatening pretensions of other nations.

Moving pictures, of coronations, royal funerals and the colonial troops at each, brought monarchy and empire to a mass audience in new and tantalizing ways. These were shown not only in cinemas but also in music halls whose 'bioscope' or 'viagraph' portrayed recent events. Newsreels offered a positive impression of the Boer War and, more creatively, battles were staged and filmed on Hampstead Heath and in a garden near Bolton. Outside of the music halls, theatres promoted imperial, military and naval spectacles to draw in the crowds. Plays with titles such as 'Wake up England', 'Nation in Arms' and 'A Plea for the Navy' transmitted the messages of the patriotic leagues. The conventions of melodrama, which depicted the world as the site of a Herculean conflict between good and evil, were easily adapted to imperial and racial themes, 'in which white heroes and heroines could triumph over black barbarism'.[10]

Countervailing Currents

The Conservative Party and right-wing leagues, however, did not possess a monopoly on patriotism in these years. We have already noticed the way in which the Liberal Party presented Irish home rule as something that would strengthen the Union rather than break it. More generally, Conservative invocations of patriotism, national identity and interest were contested by their political opponents.

During the Boer War, opponents of the war argued that it was not being fought for British interests, let alone patriotic ones. In *The Psychology of Jingoism*, published in 1901, the radical pro-Boer J.A. Hobson berated the false patriotism of the war party: 'the businessmen who mostly direct modern politics require a screen, they find it in the interests of the country, patriotism. Behind this screen they work, seeking private gain'. Indeed, opponents of the war habitually portrayed it as a conflict fought on behalf of Jewish financial interests in South Africa. Thus the war's opponents vindicated their own love of country and presented the jingos as the dupes of cosmopolitan forces.

The Boer War was a moment when imperial patriotism was dominant. But this was a rare moment. In fact the development of right-wing patriotic ideology is more associated with political failure than success so far as the Conservative Party was concerned. The Liberal Party emerged as the governing party after its massive victory in 1906 and its more slender successes in 1910. It did so not by abandoning the ground of patriotism but by arguing upon it. In 1904 Lloyd George presented a rebuttal of the argument for tariff reform in a speech at Bristol which was published under the title 'Patriotism and Free Trade'. He concluded with the following peroration:

Do you know there are two kinds of patriotism. I have discovered it especially in the last five years. There is a kind of patriotism that swells with ostentation when it thinks of an empire of 400,000,000 that can, in three years, conquer a little community of herdsmen, the population of Bristol. That is one type of patriotism ... I'll tell you when I feel the truer patriotism. It is when I contemplate the spectacle of this little island in the sea, one-thirtieth part of the United States of America, standing against

Continents armed at all points with the most systematically devised tariffs, standing alone armed only with the weapon of freedom, and yet beating them all on land and sea.[11]

This was the patriotism of free trade and liberty which had been the hallmark of nineteenth-century radicalism.

In 1910 the Conservative attempt to reject Lloyd George's budget in the House of Lords, and to replace it with their own fiscal policy of tariffs was presented by the Chancellor of the Exchequer as an insidious and dangerous 'attack upon the freedom, the liberties and the privileges of the people of these islands'. Thus the patriotism of tariff reform was countered by another version which identified the nation's traditions and interests with hard-won liberties – in this case the right of the House of Commons to determine taxation – rather than with empire. Indeed, the image of John Bull was pressed into service by Liberals as well as Conservatives in the early twentieth century. In the 1906 General Election the Conservatives used posters in which the party protected John Bull and the Colonies from a gang of Liberal thugs. But the Liberals themselves portrayed John Bull as a judge at the head of a Royal Commission on Conservative mismanagement of the war.

We can discover similar counter-currents at a cultural level too. Adoration of healthy rusticity, the location of authentic national identity in the countryside, away from the corruption of urban life, was not the sole prerogative of movements such as the Boy Scouts. The revival of English folk music in the early twentieth century that was led by Cecil Sharp had a powerful influence on many radicals and socialists. Sharp himself joined the Fabian Society in December 1900 and his team of morris dancers appeared at Fabian functions. Newspapers such as *The Clarion* and *Labour Leader* extolled the virtues of 'merrie England' and national aesthetics. The suffragist and socialist Mary Neal, who from 1905 was active in the folk song and dance revival in London, wrote as follows:

This revival of our English folk music is ... part of a great national revival, a going back from the town to the country, a reaction against all that is demoralising in city life. It is a reawakening of that part of our national consciousness which makes for wholeness, saneness and healthy merriment.[12]

In focus: Jewish Immigration

At the start of the twentieth century, immigrants intending to settle in the United Kingdom were able to do so without any restriction. This had been the case since 1826. Under this relaxed system, between 1880 and 1900 the number of East European Jews in England and Wales increased nearly six-fold from 14,468 to 82,844. By the end of 1905, however, new and effective legislation was introduced to reduce drastically the level of immigration.

At the turn of the century it was the immigrants' impact on the housing market in the East End of London, where roughly one half of them settled, which aroused the greatest public concern. The period was one of rapidly advancing rents in London. Between 1880 and 1900 rents rose by between 10 per cent and 12 per cent over the capital as whole but in the eastern boroughs the increase was 25 per cent. The borough of Stepney was most severely affected; here rents increased by an average of 25 per cent in the 1890s alone. This cannot be attributed solely to the impact of immigration but undoubtedly it was one contributory factor.

Immigration restriction was advocated by enthusiasts of empire and others drawn to the modish pursuit of 'efficiency'. In view of the poor physical condition of the working class, revealed during the Boer War, the immigration of thousands of Russian Jews, who were portrayed as physically weak, willing to work for a pittance, and prepared to live in slum conditions became an issue of grave concern. Writing in *Nineteenth Century and After* in September 1903, H. Hamilton Fyffe detailed his alarm at the influx of aliens 'who teach us nothing, who bring no wealth or spending power into the country ...':

> Is it not clear that this continual inflow already hampers us in the great fight we have to wage against ignorance and inefficiency with all their hateful brood, and that its hampering effect must increase in a more and more rapid ratio so long as we let it go on?

The influx of these immigrants could only advance the decay of national intelligence and physique.

Supporters of an immigration act aligned their project with other measures designed to adjust to a world in which Britain's industrial, commercial and naval pre-eminence increasingly was open to question. Just as tariff reformers unfavourably compared Britain's policy of free trade with the protectionism of her competitors, so too the practice of allowing unlimited immigration was contrasted with the restrictive laws enforced by Germany and the United States. Indeed, tariff reformers tried to mobilize working-class support by exploiting the similarities between the two causes: by presenting the two issues as variants upon the single evil of unfair 'dumping' – of cheap goods and destitute 'aliens' – by 'the foreigner'.

Jewish Immigration (continued)

Supporters of an immigration act were able to mobilize a popular movement in their support. In particular, the issue was promoted by Conservative politicians who were eager to win support among the labourers, skilled workers, shopkeepers and tradesmen of East London, and who sought to use the appeal of empire to this end. This first became apparent in the General Election of 1892. But around 1900 the populist and imperial rhetoric of these Conservatives meshed with the sharpened hostility to immigration among the native population of East London caused by rapidly increasing rents. The campaign for statutory restriction of immigration was organized by the British Brothers League which gathered popular support through petitions, parades and public meetings in East London between 1901 and 1905.

By examining the sources of support for the BBL we can explore how ideas of patriotism and nationality took shape and meaning in a specific social context. The BBL blamed Jewish immigrants for the housing crisis in the East End. The immigrants, it was said, were 'displacing' the native population. 'Displacement' was portrayed, in part, as a physical process in which the native population was forced out of the district by rising rents. But it meant more than this, for along with this movement of population, it was said, went the decline of community. According to James William Johnson, a Stepney labourer and chairman of the BBL executive:

> This great influx is driving us out of hearth and home ... Some of us have been born here, others of us have come into it when quite young children, have been brought up here, educated here; some of us have old associations here of such a nature that we feel it a hardship to be compelled to be parted from.[13]

Moreover, the newcomers' habits, the way they overcrowded their houses, were seen as an affront to a peculiarly British respectability. National identity was thus connected to daily life.

This emphasis on hearth and home established the ground upon which landlords, shopkeepers, skilled and casual workers were able to come together and protest against unfettered immigration. It also enabled some Conservative politicians to draw powerful connections between housing and the nation, the East End and the empire. At the first of the great demonstrations organized by the BBL, William Evans Gordon, the Conservative MP for Stepney, described the meeting as one of 'the English people of East London ... of all classes, of all creeds, of all shades of political opinion'.[14] He drew his audience into a community which included both

Plate 8.2. A Jewish printer/publisher in East London. There was tension between Jewish immigrants and native East Enders in this period, but there was also considerable integration. The signs in the window suggest that customers came from the English and Yiddish speaking communities.

Jewish Immigration (continued)

property owners and the propertyless, and members of all political parties: the question was presented as one of home and country – which they all possessed.

The Conservative Party's declining fortunes led ministers to attend to this expression of popular opinion. Between the General Election of 1900 and May 1903 the government lost eight by-elections. In these circumstances, the Conservatives' electoral dominance in the East End of London could seem a prize worth retaining. Immigration restriction became a matter of practical politics. A Royal Commission, weighted in the restrictionists' favour, was appointed to investigate the problem of 'alien immigration'. Predictably enough, its report called for legislation to stem the flow of undesirable foreigners and in 1905, at the second attempt, an Aliens Bill duly passed into law. As well as barring criminals, the insane and anyone likely to become a charge on the rates through disease or infirmity, the Aliens Act of 1905 required immigrants to demonstrate that they were able to support themselves and their dependants 'decently'. The Prime Minister, A.J. Balfour, speaking in the House of Commons asserted: 'we have the right to keep out everybody who does not add to the strength of the community.' Both literally and rhetorically, then, the anti-alien agitation had managed to exclude Jewish immigrants from the national community.[15]

But even in this case, in which a patriotic league achieved a rare legislative triumph, the version of patriotism and national identity articulated by imperial and populist Conservatives was contested. The opponents of the Aliens Act claimed it was a departure from national traditions. One Liberal MP condemned the machinery of immigration restriction as 'unworthy of the reputation of a humane and free people, and it did violence to the strong and hereditary sympathy of the people of this country in regard to the poor and oppressed of every land'.

Historical Interpretations

To what extent did imperial patriotism command a consensus in these years? The debate on this question can be traced back to dismayed radical intellectuals such as J.A. Hobson and Charles Masterman at the start of the century as they contemplated the 'mob passion' of the jingo crowd. They ascribed this to the malign influence of the yellow press and the music hall. The latter, in particular, was seen by Hobson as a 'potent educator' which through its songs and recitations promoted 'crude notions upon morals and politics'. Love of one's own nation had thus become hatred of another and the result was working-class participation in the celebrations of Mafeking night and the absence of working-class opposition to the war in South Africa.

In the 1960s and 1970s, the growth of labour history and of social history generated a different view. In particular, Henry Pelling, in an essay published in 1968, and then Richard Price, in a book-length study of working-class attitudes to the Boer War, set out to argue that there was little evidence to adduce working-class enthusiasm for empire. These historians contributed to a widely held interpretation of working-class culture: namely, that it was concerned with what was immediate to everyday experience and that all forms of idealism, whether socialist or patriotic in inspiration, were alien to it. Indeed, far from being a working-class phenomenon, Price suggests that jingoism was an expression of the status anxieties of the lower-middle class.[16]

Pelling and Price reinterpret the weakness of opposition to the Boer War and reassess anything which appears to demonstrate working-class enthusiasm for it. Pelling draws attention to the fact that the leaders of organized labour did oppose the war and Price attributes the weakness of extra-parliamentary opposition to the war to institutional factors rather than working-class attitudes: he cites the tactical failures of the anti-war organizations, the divisions in Liberal ranks, and the absence of a figure such as Gladstone to act as a figurehead for opposition. Similarly, both historians ascribe the result of the 'khaki' Election of 1900 to the weak and divided state of the Liberal Party. Indeed, the key characteristic of the Election, Price argues, was 'voter apathy': 1.3 million fewer votes were cast than in the previous election of 1895.

Both Price and Pelling draw a distinction between the composition and actions of the crowds on Mafeking night, celebrating British pluck and a victory against the odds, and the disruptive groups which broke up anti-war meetings and attacked the homes and businesses of individual 'pro-Boers'. Whereas the former did contain a large working-class component, the latter, which contained the real jingo element, did not and were largely composed of middle-class men, often leading local figures in the Conservative Party, and youths. Both historians also point out that recruitment to the army in the early months of the war was disproportionately from the non-working-class sections of the population. Working-class recruitment followed a different pattern and peaked just before the end of the war in January 1902. This pattern broadly coincides with the rising level of unemployment in these years. The army was a traditional resort for the unskilled and unemployed, and recruitment during the Boer War, Price suggests, was no exception.

Some of these conclusions have since been questioned. Using the years 1881–98 as a basis for judgement, Michael Blanch has estimated that the war years generated 72,476 extra working-class recruits to the army above the 128,015 which might have been expected in view of the rising trend of unemployment. Moreover, the number of working-class recruits under-estimates those who presented themselves: many were rejected on medical grounds and recruiting officers from Volunteer regiments had a preference for men who could ride and shoot. It is also possible to question whether anti-war attitudes were, in fact, anti-imperial. Miles Taylor has shown that radical opponents of the war such as Hobson and J.L. Hammond, did not oppose all manifestations of British imperial might. Rather, they opposed that imperialism which was mercenary in origin and devoid of morality and restraint.[17]

But apart from these particular points, in the 1980s historians such as Hugh Cunningham and John Mackenzie developed a wide-ranging alternative interpretation. It was no coincidence that this emerged at a time when the Falklands War and a period of Conservative dominance had revived interest in the history of patriotism and national identity. In a pioneering article published in 1981 Hugh Cunningham argued that from the 1870s 'the ruling class sought in patriotism a means of defusing the consciousness of the working class' and that it cannot be argued that 'the ability of working-class people to interpret patriotism in their own way immunized them in any thorough-going way from the virus of right-wing patriotism'. The fullest version of this argument has been presented by John Mackenzie. In his book *Propaganda and Empire: the Manipulation of British Public Opinion, 1880–1960* he argues that a new type of patriotism came into being in the late Victorian era. This focused on Britain's unique imperial mission and was 'propagated by every organ of British life in the period' and that it had the capacity 'to create some semblance of unity across class and party lines'.[18] He identifies the elements of this ideology as militarism, devotion to royalty, identification and worship of national heroes and racial ideas associated with social Darwinism.

Mackenzie and his collaborators have demonstrated that these were important elements in British culture in the early twentieth century.[19] The question remains, however, whether they constituted the dominant influence which they claim for them. The profound crisis over Ireland with which this period ends must, at the least, qualify the idea that empire, national identity and patriotism were points of consensus. Not only was the home rule crisis a point of sharp political division, it also indicated widely divergent ideas concerning national identity in the UK. It might be suggested that in a multinational state such as the UK, a growing sensitivity to issues of national identity could as easily generate fragmentation as consolidation.

But aside from problems within the Union, what of the significance of imperial patriotism? The idea that there was a consensus around empire rests on the assumption that socialization and propaganda had their desired effect. But there is evidence to prompt scepticism on this point. For instance, it was not until 1916 that the government officially supported Empire Day. In the decade before the First World War its observance was patchy. In 1906 it was most likely to be honoured in the middle-class suburbs of London, in cathedral cities and in southern coastal towns; in short, in the strongholds of propertied Conservatism. By contrast, it made little impact that year in the industrial North West, and in the whole of Scotland it was observed in only sixty-one schools, twenty-seven of which were in the most English of Scottish cities – Edinburgh. Participation in organizations such as the Boy Scouts was restricted to the children of families who could afford the uniform and regular subscriptions. Where there was participation it could be for reasons other than those intended by the founders and leaders of an organization. One colonel in the Volunteers thought the men who joined were not motivated by high patriotism but were attracted by the show, the dress and the camp.

However, neither the old school of interpretation which plays down the significance of working-class patriotism, or the new one which emphasizes the significance of imperial patriotism give due weight to the existence of competing versions of patriotism in this period. It is too often assumed that associations of patriotism with liberty had fallen away by the start of the twentieth century. But as the work of Ann Summers, Miles Taylor and the present author suggests, this was not the case. Ann Summers points out that the Volunteers represented a patriotic voluntarism in British society that was at odds with the collectivism of the Leagues. Hugh Cunningham, the pre-eminent historian of the force, suggests, 'it is not too much to say that it was the Volunteers who made conscription politically impossible in pre-war Britain'. Indeed, it is notable that in 1914 even the NSL did not call for the introduction of conscription. A French observer was amazed at the process of British recruitment: 'The root idea was that a man should enlist just as he might join the Salvation Army, by virtue of a certain working of his mind, a new connection, a perception of good and evil, justice and injustice, awakened in him by this active and well organised campaign'.[20] But it is important to realize that the war was presented as a defensive and liberal war: as a fight for the rights of small nations in the face of German militarism. The cause was perfectly consistent with the precepts of liberal patriotism.

To the extent that the nation was a cultural creation it could be created in different ways. National identity and patriotic duty frequently have been invoked in highly emotive terms. But we would be mistaken to regard patriotism only as a primordial force whose particular content is of little interest. On the contrary, historians have learned to attend to what people have meant when they called themselves patriots or invoked the nation's interests. It is, in part, the changing content of patriotism which gives it its history. Moreover, in the context of the UK it is important to see that men and women might adopt more than one patriotism. When the Liberal intellectual James Bryce observed that an Englishman had 'but one patriotism because England and the United Kingdom are to him practically the same thing' he implied that others may have more than one patriotism and that this, so far as he saw the matter, was not a problem. Because, at a legal level, nationality did not depend on cultural or racial criteria, merely on being a subject of the Crown, it was possible for men and women to sustain their Celtic national identities within the UK. As Linda Colley has pointed out, England did not suppress these other loyalties so much as superimpose itself upon them.[21] In the case of Ireland, above all, this did not provide a stable solution but even here it is notable that Irishmen, as well as Englishmen, Scotsmen and

Welshmen, rushed to the colours in 1914. This consideration of national identity as a plural identity should also prompt us to assess how significant any version of patriotism was when measured against the pull of other collectivities such as class. The fierce industrial unrest of the prewar years serves to remind us that the nation is only one community among several within which people might place themselves.

It is the response to war in 1914 and the human toll of that war which gives particular significance to the history of patriotism and national identity in the early years of the twentieth century. Between August 1914 and the end of that year over one million men voluntarily presented themselves for military service. A further 1.4 million chose to join the army before conscription was introduced in 1916 and, over the war as a whole, British volunteers easily outnumbered conscripts. Vast sections of the populace identified the cause of the government and of the army as their cause and acted spontaneously to show this. The community which united the people and their governors was the nation. Political leaders and propagandists invoked the nation's interests and ideals to justify the slaughter and sacrifice of human life in war. The people responded loyally because they saw themselves as a part of this same nation. They did so at the same time as the values invested in this community remained the subject of disagreement, and its territorial limits and constitutional realization were the cause of strife.

Bibliographical Note

On English identity see R. Colls and P. Dodd, *Englishness: Politics and Culture, 1880–1920* (Beckenham, 1986). On Ireland see the relevant chapters in R.F. Foster, *Modern Ireland 1660–1972* (London, 1988) and F.S.L. Lyons, *Culture and Anarchy in Ireland 1890–1939* (Oxford, 1979). On Scotland, C. Harvie, *Scotland and Nationalism: Scottish Politics and Society, 1707–1977* (London, 1994) presents a lively survey. For Wales the best starting point is K.O. Morgan, *Rebirth of a Nation: Wales 1880–1980* (Oxford, 1981). The patriotic leagues are best covered in F. Coetzee, *For Party or Country? Nationalism and the Dilemmas of Popular Conservatism* (New York, 1990). The impact of empire on popular consciousness is discussed in J. Mackenzie, *Imperialism and Propaganda: The Manipulation of British Public Opinion* (Manchester, 1986). For a more sceptical view of its impact see R. Price, *An Imperial War and the British Working Class* (London, 1972). A general survey of immigration is provided by C. Holmes, *John Bull's Island: Immigration and British Society, 1870–1971* (Basingstoke, 1988). On Irish immigrants consult S. Fielding, *Class and Ethnicity: Irish Catholics in England, 1870–1939* (Buckingham, 1993). On Jewish immigrants see L. Gartner, *The Jewish Immigrant in England, 1870–1914* (London, 2nd edn, 1973) and D. Feldman, *Englishmen and Jews: Social Relations and Political Culture, 1840–1914* (London, 1994). Finally, R. Samuel (ed.), *Patriotism and the Making and Unmaking of British National Identities* (3 vols, London, 1989) is an uneven but essential collection of essays on the subject.

Notes

1. B. Anderson, *Imagined Communities: Reflections on the Origin and Spread of Nationalism* (London, 1983).

2. A. O'Day, 'Irish Home Rule and Liberalism' in A. O'Day (ed.), *The Edwardian Age: Conflict and Stability* (London, 1979) p. 114.

3. *Ibid*, p. 118; D.G. Boyce, 'The marginal Britons: the Irish', in R. Colls and P. Dodd (eds), *Englishness: Politics and Culture, 1880–1920* (Beckenham, 1986) p. 236.

4. R. Blake, *The Unknown Prime Minister: The Life and Times of Andrew Bonar Law, 1859–1923* (London, 1955) p. 127; Boyce, 'The Marginal Britons', p. 234; A.V. Dicey, *A Fool's Paradise* (London, 1913) p. vi.

5. A. Summers, 'The character of Edwardian nationalism: three patriotic leagues', in A.J. Nicholls and P. Kennedy (eds) *Nationalist and Racialist Movements in Britain and Germany before 1914* (London, 1981) p. 77.

6. B. Semmel, *Imperialism and Social Reform* (London, 1960) pp. 93–4, 117.

7. J. Springhall, *Youth, Empire and Society: British Youth Movements 1883–1940* (London, 1976) p. 42.

8. M. Blanch, 'British society and the War' in P. Warwick (ed.), *The War in South Africa* (Harlow, 1980) pp. 214–5.

9. D. Cannadine, 'The context, performance and meaning of ritual: the British monarchy and the invention of tradition, c.1820–1977', in E.J. Hobsbawm and T. Ranger (eds), *The Invention of Tradition* (Cambridge, 1983) pp. 120–34.

10. J. Mackenzie, *Propaganda and Empire: The Manipulation of British Public Opinion* (Manchester, 1984) p. 45.

11. D. Lloyd George, *Patriotism and Free Trade* (London, 1904) p. 12.

12. V. Gammon, 'Folk song collecting in Sussex and Surrey', *History Workshop Journal*, Autumn 1980, p. 80.

13. *Royal Commission on Alien Immigration*, PP 1903 vol. IX, q.8,558.

14. *East London Observer*, 18 January 1902, p. 2.

15. *Parliamentary Debates*, 4th ser., vol. CXLV, column 804.

16. R. Price, *An Imperial War and the British Working Class* (London, 1972); H. Pelling, 'British labour and British imperialism', in R. Price (ed.), *Popular Politics and Society in Late-Victorian Britain* (London, 2nd edn, 1979) pp. 82–100; R. Price, 'Society, status and jingoism: the social origins of lower-middle-class patriotism, 1870–1900', in G. Crossick (ed.), *The Lower Middle Class* (London, 1976) pp. 89–112.

17. Blanch, 'British Society and the War', pp. 225–9; B. Porter, *Critics of Empire: British Radical Attitudes to Colonialism in Africa* (London, 1968) pp. 179–80; M. Taylor, 'Imperium et libertas? Rethinking the radical critique of imperialism during the nineteenth century', *Journal of Imperial and Commonwealth History*, January 1991, pp. 14–16.

18. H. Cunningham, 'The language of patriotism, 1750–1914', *History Workshop Journal,* Autumn 1981, p. 27; Mackenzie, *Propaganda and Empire,* p. 2.

19. For example, J. Mackenzie (ed.), *Imperialism and Popular Culture* (Manchester, 1981), and J. Mangan, *Making Imperial Mentalities: Socialisation and British Imperialism* (Manchester, 1990).

20. M. Taylor, 'John Bull and the iconography of public opinion in England c. 1712–1929', *Past and Present,* February 1992; D. Feldman, *Englishmen and Jews: Social Relations and Political Culture, 1870–1914* (London, 1994); A. Summers, 'Militarism in Britain before the First World War', *History Workshop Journal,* Autumn 1976, p. 117; H. Cunningham *The Volunteer Force: a Social and Political History, 1859–1908* (London, 1975) p. 130.

21. L. Colley, 'Britishness and otherness', *Journal of British Studies,* October 1992, p. 327.

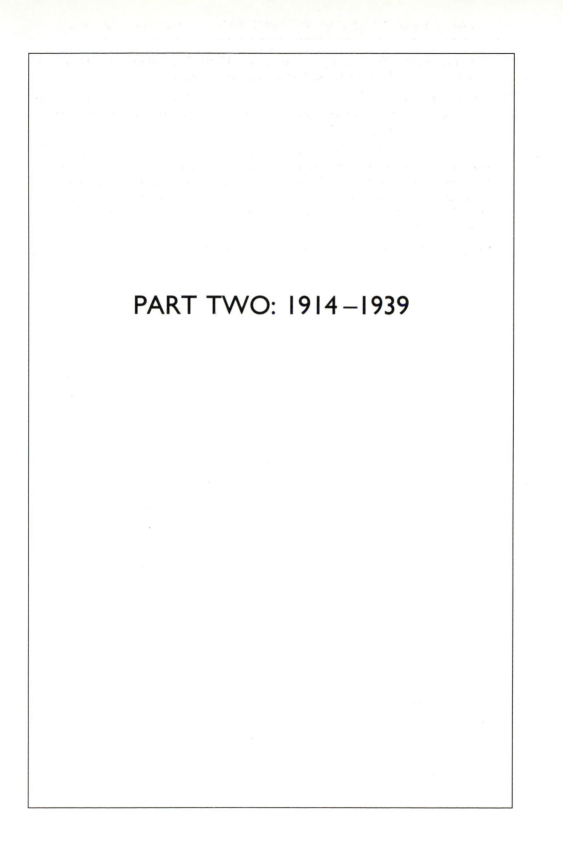

PART TWO: 1914–1939

9 The First World War and its Aftermath

Jon Lawrence

Society at War

When Britain went to war in August 1914 there were few people who had any comprehension of the conflict that was about to be unleashed. Popular opinion held that 'it would all be over by Christmas', but even less sanguine observers generally accepted that advanced western societies could not long sustain the economic and social strains of war. In fact, the war was to last more than four years, and claim the lives of over nine million combatants. British casualties totalled nearly two-and-a-half million, including over 700,000 killed.

At the beginning of the war, however, British strategy envisaged only a limited Continental commitment, and minimal interference with the normal channels of civilian life. Sizeable detachments of the army (the British Expeditionary Force) would be sent to support the French and Belgian forces, but Britain's primary contribution would be to blockade German ports, and to bank-roll the war effort of her Continental allies. When politicians reluctantly agreed to demands from Lord Kitchener (the newly appointed Secretary of War) for the raising of a large volunteer army in August 1914 they did so convinced that the war would be over before the new units could be trained and equipped. With her armies intact, and her navy pre-eminent, it was assumed that Britain would then be able to impose a lasting peace settlement on friend and foe alike. This strategy has aptly been characterized as one of 'Business as Usual' (after the slogan popularized early in the war when many feared a collapse of economic confidence). It was a strategy which assumed that victory depended on preserving Britain's economic strength, and especially her overseas trade and capital, rather than developing a domestic war machine. But if 'free trade' lay at the heart of British strategic thinking, this was not because the government was obsessively non-interventionist. On the contrary, it acted quickly to smooth mobilization by assuming overall control of the railways, and showed few qualms about commandeering transport vehicles and cart-horses *en masse* for the Front. Similarly the government intervened swiftly to restore stability to the money markets, for instance through the moratorium on prewar debts, whilst it also made bulk purchases of vital foreign raw materials and foodstuffs to guarantee supplies.

As the conflict dragged on into 1915, and the 'war of attrition' succeeded the 'war of manoeuvre' on the Western Front, Britain's strategy of husbanding her economic and military resources began to disintegrate. The naval blockade had clearly failed to paralyse the German war effort, and Britain's allies were becoming dissatisfied at their disproportionate losses on the battlefield. Little by little the government abandoned the central tenets of a 'free trade war'. As British forces became ever more embroiled in the fighting both in France and in the Near East, so pressure grew on domestic munitions industries. Press outcries over a series of so-called 'shell scandals' led many to question the adequacy of traditional procurement methods at the War Office, and resulted in the government assuming the power to control most aspects of armaments production under DORA (the Defence of the Realm Act). This was first enacted in August 1914 and repeatedly strengthened thereafter. It allowed government departments to requisition raw materials, finished product, whole factories, in fact just about anything. At the same time Lloyd George persuaded leading trade unionists to agree to an industrial truce and the relaxation of 'restrictive practices' in the essential war industries (the 'Treasury Agreements'). In May the government consolidated these measures by creating a Ministry of Munitions with Lloyd George at its head. Besides tightening its control on existing munitions industries (notably through the legal sanctions of the Munitions of War Act, 1915), the new ministry quickly set about building massive new National Factories across the country in order to accelerate the production of ammunition, armaments, and other war material. The Ministry, based at Whitehall Gardens, played a key role in the coordination of production for the British and Allied war effort. By the end of the war its head office alone employed more than 20,000 officials administering a vast bureaucracy with powers to set price and profit levels, to determine workplace conditions, to intervene in industrial relations, but above all to shape the pattern of supply and production to the finest detail. Britain was taking the first faltering steps towards the development of a war economy.

By October 1916, when hopes of a 'knock-out blow' on the Somme were already fading, approximately 340,000 workers (4 per cent of the total industrial workforce) were employed directly in government factories. A further 1,700,000 were employed in the so-called 'Controlled Establishments' (mostly engineering factories), where the Ministry of Munitions exerted detailed control over all aspects of production and labour discipline under the Munitions of War Act and DORA (see Table 9.1). Altogether nearly half of the industrial workforce was employed on war work of various kinds by October 1916, a figure which rose to over 60 per cent at its peak in July 1918. Even outside the controlled industries the state had considerable influence over production, primarily through its monopoly control of many raw materials. By the end of the war the government controlled the supply of hides and leather, wool, oils and fats, and key foodstuffs such as meat, sugar, cereals, cheese and margarine. By regulating the release of these commodities the government was able to adjust the balance between production for military and civilian needs.

Table 9.1. Estimates of the changing character and composition of the industrial workforce in Britain, 1914–18 (000s)

Date	Industrial workforce (excl. govt workers)		Workers employed in govt factories			Total industrial workforce (M&F)	Industrial workers employed in 'controlled ests' Total (M&F)[a] %		Industrial workers engaged on govt contracts Total (M&F) %	
	Male	Female	Male	Female	%					
July 1914	6,160	2,180	76	2	1	**8,418**	–		–	
Oct 1914[b]	5,500	2,040	110	4	1	**7,654**	–		–	
Oct. 1915[b]	5,350	2,330	160	8	2	**7,848**	–		2,778	35
Oct. 1916	5,100	2,580	223	119	4	**8,022**	1,714	26	3,850	48
Oct. 1917	4,950	2,710	254	216	6	**8,130**	1,993	30	4,553	56
July 1918	4,860	2,740	257	225	6	**8,082**	–		4,930	61

Notes: All figures are estimates derived from Board of Trade surveys covering firms employing approximately 60 per cent of the industrial workforce and have been rounded to the nearest 10,000.
(a) It should be noted that employment figures for Controlled Establishments exclude the mining industry and government factories.
(b) Estimated figures for workers engaged in government factories based on returns from Woolwich Arsenal and general information from *The History of the Ministry of Munitions,* vol. viii, pt 2.

Sources: PRO, SUPP5/1051 'Statement of employees'; Board of Trade, *Report on the State of Employment in the United Kingdom in October 1914* (PP1914-16 Cd.7703 XXI); Board of Trade, *State of Employment Reports,* Oct. 1915 – July 1918 (unpubl. BLPES, London) discussed in P. Dewey, 'Military recruiting and the British labour force during the First World War', *Historical Journal* (1984).

It is difficult to identify any clear turning point in the development of the British war effort. There was no sudden conversion to the need to organize for 'total war'. The formation of a Coalition government in May 1915 and the succession of Lloyd George to the premiership in December 1916 were watersheds in political rhetoric rather than practical policy. Instead, government strategy developed piecemeal throughout the war; shaped more by short-term factors – 'the pressure of events' – than by any broader vision of how to organize for 'total war'. In some fields, notably industrial relations and housing, the government intervened early in the war in order to head off disputes which could damage war production (hence the zealous work of the Munitions Tribunals under the Munitions of War Act, or the introduction of rent control in December 1915 when tenant militancy threatened to spark widespread industrial unrest). In other fields such as retail price control, food rationing, taxation, and even military conscription the government acted much more slowly, less because it was wedded to liberal principle than because it feared the political consequences of precipitate action. The labour movement was deeply suspicious of military conscription, fearing that it would pave the way for the introduction of industrial conscription as had happened in France where many munitions workers were conscripts subject to military discipline. The government finally abandoned voluntary enlistment early in 1916 (though not before more than two million had already enlisted), but plans for a general conscription of labour were never implemented – indeed as fears of industrial unrest mounted in 1917 the government actually weakened controls on labour by abolishing the leaving certificate system which restricted the movement of workers in controlled factories.

The government also had strong grounds for acting cautiously on rationing, since in the early years of the war it was widely believed that rigid controls on consumption might actually undermine civilian morale. Significantly, even in 1917 the government considered it politically impossible to ration bread supplies lest such a 'panic' measure should reinforce rumours that the German U-boat campaign against merchant shipping was bringing Britain to the brink of starvation. Instead the government allowed bakers to adulterate their flour, and spent vast sums subsidizing the price of a standard 'Government loaf'.

The approach to fiscal policy was similarly cautious. Early wartime budgets introduced only modest increases to taxation, despite the massive increase in government expenditure necessitated by war. As the war dragged on so fiscal policy was gradually tightened, but politicians remained fearful about the political consequences of heavy taxation. As a result they readily embraced the formula that 'sound finance' demanded only that taxation be raised sufficiently to meet the likely post-war charges on the government's massive wartime borrowing. According to a Treasury estimate in 1922, taxation covered just 10.7 per cent of the total cost of the war, leaving the remainder to be found from borrowing, primarily in the form of government war bonds sold to domestic investors. (Even so maximum tax rates still rose from 12.5 to 52 per cent during the war.) As many critics have commented, this strategy, which saw the National Debt rise from £650 million in 1914 to £7,435 million in 1919, was highly inflationary, especially during the immediate postwar period when debt-holders stimulated a major private spending boom.

Perhaps ironically, this gradualist approach to the demands of 'total war' may have been one of the great strengths of the British war effort. For one thing it meant that many of the new administrative structures set up during the war remained surprisingly flexible and adaptive. For instance the Ministry of Munitions constantly updated its procedures to control profits and guarantee quality, while the Ministry of National Service continually amended its definitions of 'essential war workers' in response to the changing balance between military and industrial needs. The flexibility of administrative structures was even more important when it came to the crucial political question of determining how scarce resources should be distributed between different sections of the civilian population. Here the state made great use of *ad hoc* local committees similar to the Pension, Labour Exchange and National Insurance committees established to administer prewar Liberal legislation. Politicians, businessmen, trade unionists and other prominent citizens were brought together to oversee the operation of wartime emergency legislation at the local level. Government legislation was given a human (though not always a humane) face. Certainly this pluralist, locally negotiated approach to the waging of war proved much more effective than the centrally directed policies characteristic of Germany after the introduction of the Hindenburg Plan in 1916.

Political pluralism was by no means the only factor helping Britain to contain the social tensions thrown up by war. Britain's superior access to material resources was also crucial since, unlike Germany, she could draw upon the resources of a massive global empire, and could rely upon the economic cooperation of long established trading partners such as the United States and Argentina. During the dark years of 1916–18 it was these international trading links which sustained the Allied war effort – and in this respect at least it could be argued that Britain continued to fight a free trade war, albeit one increasingly financed by American credit rather than British capital and domestic borrowing. Indeed the German U-boat campaign against Allied and neutral shipping sprang directly from the recognition that Britain's ability to draw resources from across the globe provided the key to victory in a protracted 'war of attrition'.

Living Standards on the 'Home Front'

Britain had other material advantages over her enemies. In particular the prewar strength of her staple export industries such as coal, textiles and shipbuilding meant that once initial concerns about preserving a healthy balance of payments had been abandoned, Britain had considerable industrial capacity that could be diverted to war production without squeezing domestic consumption. Indeed one of the great strengths of the British war economy was that the massive expansion of the munitions industries did not undermine employment in essential civilian industries such as foodstuffs or clothing. As late as July 1918 total employment in the food and drink industry had fallen by just 14 per cent since the beginning of the war (compared with nearly 50 per cent in Germany) thanks mainly to the massive influx of new workers to replace men enlisted into the armed forces. Remarkably this overall stability was achieved in the absence of a truly coordinated labour policy. There were no controls on the movement of labour outside the munitions industries – where the leaving certificate system gave employers' considerable control over workers' mobility until its abolition in 1917. In the end the balance between civilian and military production appears to have been sustained by two factors. Firstly, the government used its control of raw materials to ensure that essential domestic industries were not forced to close (although shortages did force many onto short-time in 1917–18). Secondly, the relative buoyancy of consumer demand helped to sustain production, and even to cover increased wages. Although these did not generally keep pace with the movement of prices, they shadowed wage rates in the war industries much more closely than in Germany (see Table 9.2). Even compositors and bricklayers fared better than many non-manual workers such as teachers and clerks who often had no increases in salary during the war.

Table 9.2. The movement of retail prices and nominal weekly wage rates for selected occupations, 1914-20 (indexed at July 1914=100)

Date	Board of Trade Cost of Living Index	Engineering		Woollen/ Worsted	Compositors	Railways	Brick- layers	Bricklayers' labourers
		craft	labourers					
Jul. 1914	100	100	100	100	100	100	100	100
Jan. 1915	118	–	–	–	–	–	–	–
Jul. 1915	132	110	–	115	100	110	102	103
Jan. 1916	145	–	–	–	–	–	–	–
Jul. 1916	161	111	–	126	105	120	108	115
Jan. 1917	187	–	–	–	–	–	–	–
Jul. 1917	204	134	154	144	120	155	122	134
Jan. 1918	206	–	–	–	–	–	–	–
Jul. 1918	210	173	213	164	156	195	157	185
Jan. 1919	230	–	–	–	–	–	–	–
Jul. 1919	209	199	255	196	196	225	185	224
Jan. 1920	236	–	–	–	–	–	–	–
Jul. 1920	258	231	309	239	246	280	235	300
Jan. 1921	278	–	–	–	–	–	–	–
Jul. 1921	219	–	–	–	–	–	–	–

Note. Wage data refer to time rates for a normal week and to average piece rates, they do not necessarily reflect movements in average *earnings* (see text). Cost of living data refer to a fixed basket of consumables deemed to represent a typical prewar 'working-class' budget – they do not therefore take account of wartime changes in consumption patterns.

Source. A.L. Bowley, *Prices and Wages in the United Kingdom, 1914–1920* (London, 1921) pp. 35, 105.

It would be wrong to suggest that the war did not bring real hardship on the 'Home Front'. Although there is no definitive measure of wartime inflation, it is clear that the cost of living rose dramatically for all social groups between 1914 and 1918. According to the Board of Trade index (which was based on prewar working-class consumption patterns) prices had more than doubled by the end of the war, with the steepest increases occurring in the first six months of the war, during the second half of 1916 and after the armistice (see Table 9.2). Manual wage rates rose more slowly in almost all industries until at least 1917. There were, however, compensating factors which softened the impact of inflation. Firstly, it is clear that consumers adjusted their consumption patterns during the war to take account of differential price movements, although estimates of the extent of this dietary substitution vary greatly. Secondly, disposable income was boosted for most working families by wartime rent controls which pegged their housing costs at August 1914 levels. In addition, full employment and heavy overtime greatly increased the earning potential of many workers. The war also greatly increased the fluidity of the labour market, so that many workers were able to transfer to better paid occupations; this was particularly true for young women for whom war work often provided an attractive alternative to low-paid domestic service. Finally, flat rate 'War Bonuses' undoubtedly helped to reduce income differentials between 'skilled' and 'unskilled' workers in many trades (e.g. engineering and bricklaying, Table 9.2), although Alastair Reid has convincingly argued that national wage rate data exaggerate the gains of the 'unskilled'. Indeed, he suggests that in some industries such as shipbuilding and iron and steel, differentials actually *widened* during the war as craft workers took advantage of informal shop-floor bonus schemes, generous piece rates and heavy overtime.[1]

On the debit side, it is clear that many families were thrown into poverty by the loss of a principal breadwinner to the armed forces. The 'Separation Allowances' paid to servicemen's dependants continually lagged behind inflation, and caused real hardship in families with no means of securing supplementary earnings. Similarly families dependent on fixed incomes – primarily sections of the established middle class – found their standard of living greatly diminished during the war. This was also true for the large numbers of non-manual workers whose salaries remained pegged at 1914 levels throughout the war (although it should be stressed that postwar salary rises re-established prewar income differentials between manual and non-manual labour).

It would therefore be foolish to try and generalize about civilian well-being on the basis of wage and price data. For workers previously condemned to the chronic poverty of casual employment the war probably did represent 'The Great Release' – as Robert Roberts recalled the First World War in his recollections of *The Classic Slum*.[2] For others, however, the war brought unknown material hardship, exacerbated not only by endless queuing for food and fuel, but also by the common fear for kith and kin at the Front.

The success of British mobilization for war was not that it preserved prewar domestic living standards; it did not, and could not. Rather, it was that mobilization was never pursued so ruthlessly that the well-being of the civilian population was sacrificed to military and industrial requirements. At times the *ad hoc* nature of government policy threatened to starve the military of manpower or munitions; but ironically it also played its part in sustaining morale on the 'Home Front', especially through the difficult months of 1917 or the shock of the short-lived German breakthrough of Spring 1918. In contrast, Germany under the Hindenburg Plan developed a much more powerful military-industrial complex, but in doing so it distorted the domestic economy in ways which placed unendurable strains upon the civilian population.

In focus: The War and Women Workers

Between July 1914 and July 1918 the industrial workforce in Britain fell by just 4 per cent (336,000) despite the enlistment of approximately 2.8 million men from industrial occupations (see Table 9.1). It is often assumed that the vast majority of these new recruits to industry were women workers, especially the wives of servicemen at the Front. In fact, however, women accounted for only 31 per cent of the workers brought into industry – the remainder, some 1,700,000 according to Board of Trade estimates, were male workers sucked in from non-industrial occupations such as shop-work, transport and the service sector, drawn out of retirement, or drawn from the prewar reservoir of casual and unemployed workers.[3] Despite the dominant image of women workers pouring into the vital war industries, more women were in fact drawn into non-industrial sectors. By July 1918 nearly 430,000 women had found jobs in finance and commerce, 200,000 in national and local government, 100,000 in transport, and 110,000 in the service sector. That said, the 700,000 women who took up work in Britain's metal, chemical and munitions factories clearly played a vital part in the war effort.

Where did these new women workers come from? Despite the dominant view portrayed by wartime propaganda, many were not new recruits to paid employment. Probably between 400,000 and 600,000 had in fact transferred from occupations not covered by official statistics, most notably domestic service. Perhaps a further 300,000 would have been girls leaving school, many of whom chose war work in preference to more traditional occupations such as domestic service. Indeed according to one estimate only 34 per cent of 'new' women workers would have been adult women not in paid employment in July 1914.[4] Probably few of these would have been women who had *never* worked for wages. Moreover, it is also now generally acknowledged that even in the engineering industry women workers made only limited inroads into traditional male occupations, despite government encouragement of 'dilution'. And where women were employed on former male tasks they generally received only a limited training, often on mass

Plate 9.1. 'For King and Country': female munition workers in the First World War. Government propaganda emphasized the important role of women in munitions production, but even more new jobs for women were created in commerce, government and the service sector.

The War and Women Workers (continued)

production processes which bore little resemblance to peacetime production methods. They were not acquiring skills that would allow them to compete equally with male craftsmen after the war.

In any case, the female 'dilutee' was an exception. Most new women workers found themselves working on processes which had already been defined as women's work before the war including shell-filling, basic machining, and various finishing processes. In all, the wartime challenge to customary notions of the gendered division of labour was much more modest than is often imagined. Deborah Thom has suggested that many women accepted the official ideology that their employment was purely temporary: that they were doing their bit 'for the duration', especially in dangerous occupations like shell-filling.[5] It also seems likely that many would have accepted that employers had prior obligations to employees who had enlisted, and to ex-servicemen disabled in the war. But if many of the 600,000 women workers who left paid employment between November 1918 and April 1920 did so voluntarily, probably as many did so because the work they had been doing simply disappeared after the Armistice as the government opted for a rapid wind-down of the war economy. Here the limited nature of wartime 'substitution' (women workers directly replacing men on a one-for-one basis) was clearly crucial. Even so, Board of Trade figures suggest that approximately half of the 'new' women workers taken on during the war were still employed as late as April 1920 (excluding 150,000 attributable to natural population growth, but including ex-domestic servants). A year later, with the economy in deep recession and unemployment at historically high levels, this was no longer true. According to the 1921 census, only in commercial occupations did women now show any permanent gains on prewar employment levels. There are therefore strong grounds for suspecting that whilst the pressure to remove women from the labour market during the boom of 1919 may have been exaggerated, there was a very real 'comb-out' during the slump of 1920–21 as employers chose to shed women workers rather than men.

Demobilization and Reconstruction

At the Armistice in November 1918 Britain faced the serious problem of how to demobilize over five million servicemen and reabsorb them into civilian life. Equally pressing was the problem of what would happen to approximately five million workers currently employed on government war work – 500,000 of them working directly for the state in National Factories (Table 9.1). The government had been developing plans for demobilization and the restoration of 'normal' economic conditions since early 1917. It was decided to push for a rapid 'decontrol' of industry. War production was to be wound up as quickly as possible, even if this caused considerable short-term unemployment. At the same time military demobilization was to proceed more slowly so as not to flood the domestic labour market.

Perhaps surprisingly there was a broad consensus around the need to free the economy from state regulation. Even the trade unions raised only limited objections, since most were anxious to see an end to state intervention in industrial relations. 'Decontrol' only met with serious resistance where there had been strong *prewar* pressure for greater state intervention. For instance, there were concerted campaigns for the nationalization of the railways and the coal industry (historic Radical and Labour objectives), but little opposition to the suspension of state controls over the rest of industry. Conservatives clamoured for the retention of wartime import controls for similarly historical reasons, and were partially satisfied by the maintenance of the wartime McKenna duties on luxury imports and the protection of certain strategic industries.

Fearful that economic dislocation would spark serious social unrest, the government quickly decided that unemployed munition workers and ex-servicemen should be supported by state payments similar to wartime 'separation allowances'. The resulting 'Out-of-work Donation' was introduced in November 1918, and was quickly extended to cover all workers laid off during the transition to peace, not just former war-workers. Though designed as a temporary solution to a specific social problem, the Out-of-work Donation was important because it enshrined two principles previously denied in peacetime legislation: firstly, that benefit scales should vary to take account of a claimant's dependants; and secondly, that benefits should be universal, i.e. paid to all, irrespective of individual means or previous financial contributions.

Signs of serious unrest within the army during January 1919 prompted the government to accelerate military demobilization. Only 260,000 men had been demobilized by the end of December 1918, but by the end of February 1.7 million had been demobilized, and by the end of May the figure had reached 2.8 million. Unemployment reached a peak in April 1919 with approximately 1.1 million out of work – nearly 400,000 of them ex-servicemen. Mindful of events on the Continent, many became fearful that Britain was on the brink of social revolution. Though greatly exaggerated, these fears were widely held throughout 1919 because of heightened industrial unrest and sporadic urban disturbances.

It was against this backdrop of social upheaval and widespread disorder that the government was expected to introduce its policies for 'social reconstruction'. Government committees had been devising bold schemes of social reform throughout the later years of the war, and at the General Election of November 1918 the pledge to build a 'Land fit for heroes' had been embraced by all parties. However, there were also powerful forces ranged against the prospect of sweeping social reform. Not the least of these was the Treasury. Politically strengthened by the importance of war finance, the

Treasury was now determined that the reorganization of the nation's massive war debt should not be jeopardized by new expenditure commitments. Although many of the Treasury's injunctions to 'sound finance' were initially ignored because of the fear that deflation and retrenchment would exacerbate postwar social unrest, the Treasury orthodoxy of balanced budgets and restoration of the Gold Standard was nonetheless enshrined soon after the Armistice.

Initially the influence of the Treasury orthodoxy was felt mainly in the scaling down of the more ambitious wartime schemes for social reform. Wartime plans for the introduction of universal secondary education evaporated. Instead the Fisher Act of 1918 confined itself to introducing a standard school-leaving age (14), new Continuation Schools for day-release teaching, and increased funding for scholarships and teachers' salaries. Wartime plans for a comprehensive system of public health provision also fared badly in the new climate. Although a new Ministry of Health was established in 1918, its powers were strictly limited and public health remained a haphazard arena of public, charitable and commercial provision. The Addison Housing Act of 1919 came closer to realizing the aims of reconstruction; in theory it committed the Treasury to reimburse local authorities for all building costs above a penny rate. However, the Act proved a failure partly because no attempt was made to limit spiralling building costs or to direct the activities of private builders towards public housing schemes, and partly because it appeared to offer a blank cheque to local councils.

It is often suggested that between 1918 and 1921 noble plans for postwar reconstruction were betrayed by a government dominated by 'hard-faced men who look as if they had done well out of the war' (as Stanley Baldwin is said to have described the MPs returned in 1918). There is much in this assessment, but it tends to overlook the fact that many on the Left were also deeply sceptical about state-centred welfare schemes. The voluntary hospitals had as many friends among trade unionists and local Labour politicians as among health professionals; while local Labour Party campaigns to transform Poor Law administration should also be seen as part of the Left's post-war emphasis on local rather than national strategies. The traditional view also tends to underestimate the extent to which the Government intervened to offset the effects of rapid decontrol and demobilization. For instance, regulations restricting Out-of-work Donation benefits were relaxed during 1919 as workers threatened to exhaust their entitlement, although from November 1919 the Donation was paid only to ex-servicemen (reflecting the state's determination that they should not be forced onto the Poor Law). In addition Rent Restriction Acts in 1919 and 1920 greatly extended the scope of rent control whilst sanctioning only modest increases in the level of rents, thereby consolidating the redistribution of income from landlord to tenant first sanctioned by emergency wartime legislation. Perhaps most important of all, however, was the government's decision to unpeg the sterling-dollar exchange rate and come off the Gold Standard in March 1919. In effect the government was pledging itself to maintain a lax monetary policy despite the rapid escalation of inflation during the postwar boom. In a sense inflation was tolerated as the price that had to be paid to blunt social unrest and to secure the smooth reabsorption of millions of displaced servicemen and munitions workers into a growing labour force.

The postwar boom lasted from approximately April 1919 to May 1920. Its origins lay partly in the sudden release of pent-up demand within the economy – both from industrial restocking and deferred consumption – and partly in the inflationary pressure of rapidly rising real wages. As such the boom was unsustainable. Much of the increased demand (including that from war-torn European states) was purely temporary, while there is also evidence that British industry was becoming seriously uncompetitive as employers failed to achieve gains in productivity to offset higher wage costs and the widespread adoption of the eight-hour day during 1919. Both demand and supply factors therefore contributed to the postwar cycle of boom and slump – as did government monetary policy which, having maintained a lax regime throughout the inflation of 1919–20, became increasingly severe as the economy lurched into slump during 1920–21.

By late 1920 economic recession was further undermining the cause of social reform, although not before a number of important measures had reached the statute books, including not only the education, housing and rent measures already discussed, but also the Unemployment Insurance Act of August 1920. This legislation was intended to extend the limited prewar insurance scheme to cover all industrial workers (excluding agriculture, domestic service, the railways and public service). As unemployment mounted during 1921, the government came under strong pressure (especially from the labour movement) to extend the scheme – both by recognizing the needs of dependants (as wartime allowances and the Out-of-Work Donation had done), and by providing extended (or 'uncovenanted') benefits to workers who had exhausted their entitlements under the insurance scheme. The government conceded on both points, partly because it assumed that the unemployment crisis would be temporary, and partly because it shared Labour's misgivings about the moral and political implications of condemning large numbers of workers and their families to the indignity of the Poor Law (especially since many were known to be ex-servicemen).

These concessions to the unemployed were all the more remarkable because they were made at a time when the government was under great pressure to impose major cuts in state expenditure. Indeed it was during 1921 that the so-called 'Anti-waste' movement was at its height – especially in the Conservative heartlands of the South East where it secured a number of notable by-election victories against government candidates fighting on a platform of retrenchment and reduced taxation. Hence the decision, in August 1921, to appoint an independent committee of prominent businessmen under the chairmanship of Sir Eric Geddes to examine the scope for cuts in government expenditure. Its report, produced early in the new year, underlined the eclipse of the postwar vision of social reconstruction, and significant cuts were eventually introduced in education, public health and defence spending. Historians have therefore suggested that in 1922 the vision of a 'Land fit for heroes' was finally sacrificed in the name of lower taxation for the middle classes. This view has much to recommend it, but we should not forget that much social legislation survived the 'Geddes Axe' of 1922, including the massively extended system of unemployment support. Indeed one might even argue that improvements in social services such as health and education were sacrificed as much to maintain transfer payments to the unemployed as to restore the living standards of the middle classes.

The Legacy of War

Historians are deeply divided about the long-term impact of the First World War on British society. For some the war marks a fundamental disjuncture in British social, political and economic development. For others it marks little more than a blip in prewar trends of development: accelerating change in one field, retarding it in another. Historians also disagree about whether the legacy of the war should be characterized as essentially positive or negative. As is often the case, each camp can point to substantial evidence which supports its interpretation of the war. This reflects the uneven, *ad hoc* nature of wartime developments. As we have seen, in some sectors change was rapid and dramatic, in others it was incremental and strictly limited. Moreover, the complex processes of negotiation and contestation which shaped wartime change continued after the war as different groups sought to influence the nature of the postwar settlement. In this respect much of the legacy of the war was indeterminate, constructed more through political struggles than through 'objective' processes of social and economic change. As a result we cannot talk in sweeping terms about 'the impact of the war' – there cannot be a single, definitive story. The war affected all aspects of British life, but its effects were anything but uniform. For instance, a broad range of factors (cultural, legal, demographic and economic) combined to limit the impact of the war on women's employment patterns. In contrast, the psychological strains of mass bereavement had profound effects on British cultural life from the popularization of spiritualism to the iconoclastic modernism of the avant-garde arts.

In the remainder of this discussion I wish to look in greater detail at the way that historians have understood the impact of the war on two key aspects of British life: economic development and social policy. The discussion of the economic legacy of the First World War has understandably been dominated by the spectre of mass unemployment between the wars. Historians have advanced many conflicting explanations for interwar unemployment, but they tend to stress three main causes: structural maladjustment, demand-deficiency and labour market rigidities. Structural explanations suggest that prewar growth patterns and the demands of the war economy distorted the 'natural' adjustment of the British economy by boosting nineteenth-century staple industries such as coal, textiles, iron and steel and heavy engineering.[6] The short-lived postwar boom compounded this problem, leaving Britain's basic industries unable to adapt to the subsequent collapse of traditional markets, and therefore forced to shed workers *en masse*. Moreover, it is argued, the newer consumer industries, though dynamic, proved slow to absorb the unemployed because their development had been seriously retarded in earlier years, and because they were geographically remote from areas of high unemployment. In contrast, historians influenced by Keynesian economics place the collapse of the staple industries in a wider context, arguing that it transmitted shock-waves throughout the economy undermining aggregate demand and thereby retarding growth in *all* sectors.[7] Again the dislocation caused by war is acknowledged, but greater emphasis is placed on the failures of postwar economic policy – especially the deflationary monetary policies adopted from 1920 as a prelude to the restoration of the Gold Standard at prewar rates of exchange (see Chapter 10). Historians who emphasize labour market rigidities also focus on the postwar period. For some the crucial period is 1919–20, when strong trade unions were able to win major reductions in the hours of labour and boost real wages without any commensurate increase in labour productivity. As a result, it is argued, British industry suffered a rapid fall in competitiveness which exacerbated the effects of the subsequent slump.[8] For others it is 1921, when the government responded to the crisis of mass unemployment by greatly extending the scope of social welfare payments. This, it is argued, placed artificial constraints on wage reductions and reduced the incentive for workers to find employment. Not surprisingly this argument has been widely criticized, both for its political insensitivity and for its complete failure to think historically about the experience of unemployment between the wars.[9]

Few historians would give exclusive weight to any one of these explanations of interwar unemployment. And although it would be wrong to suggest that there is an emerging consensus on the question, there *is* a growing emphasis on the critical nature of political decisions taken during the crisis period of 1918–20, including the lax monetary policy of 1919 (which both fuelled inflation and created the conditions for a significant fall in labour productivity), the tightened monetary policy from 1920 (which aggravated the postwar slump), and the decision to accept responsibility for state support of the unemployed (if not for solving unemployment).

Perhaps even more than unemployment, the field of social policy has suffered from the tendency to seek definitive interpretations of the impact of war. Most historians agree that the First World War presents a dismal story of hopes dashed – especially in contrast to the achievements of 'reconstruction' after the People's War of 1939–45. Disagreements focus mainly on the chronology of failure, and on the relative weight to be ascribed to administrative, political and economic causes. Some writers trace the roots of failure back to the war itself; stressing either the administrative weakness of the Ministry of Reconstruction and its allies, or the fact that the decision to fund the war primarily through borrowing rather than taxation condemned postwar governments to servicing a massive debt – making it hard to finance new social spending from a still relatively narrow tax base.[10] Others focus on the growing ascendancy of the Treasury in government circles by late 1918, or on the weak reforming credentials of the 1918 Parliament and the frailty of its would-be reforming ministries.[11] Yet others take the reforming claims of the Lloyd George Coalition government more seriously and insist that the frustration of 'social reconstruction' should be attributed directly to the fiscal and political consequences of the slump of 1920–22. Finally, there are historians who accept this chronology but insist that the retrenchment programme of 1922 represented a much more strategic response aimed at placating the demands of middle-class Britain.[12]

This emphasis on the failure of social reform is understandable given the grand rhetoric of a 'Land fit for heroes' which accompanied the 1918 Election, but it has tended to obscure the stark contrasts between the limited achievements in the fields of education and public health, and the dramatic innovations in housing policy and unemployment provision. As a result there has often been a failure to stress the extent to which developments in one field of social policy had major implications for other policy fields. For instance, the continuation of rent control after the war undermined the prospects for renewed private building of working-class housing and meant that public housing could no longer be limited to 'social housing' for the very poor. Similarly by breaching the actuarial principles of unemployment insurance during the crisis of 1920–22, government policy increased the pressure on politically less sensitive forms of social expenditure in health and education. In both cases we see the essentially *ad hoc* nature of postwar social policy. Like the wartime coalitions, Lloyd George's government was responding to short-term crises rather than working out some master plan for social reconstruction. But just because social reforms may often have been shaped by short-term pragmatism, and may even have been conceded grudgingly, we should not underestimate their cumulative effects. The period 1914–21 saw a wholesale transformation in state-societal relations in Britain, which is perhaps best epitomized by the contrast between government responses to the prospect of mass unemployment in 1914 and 1918. At the beginning of the war the government was content to rely on private charity (the Prince of Wales Relief Fund) to relieve distress. By 1918 few doubted that the government would have to provide a guaranteed minimum payment to all unemployed workers and ex-servicemen and their families (the Out-of-work Donation). It was this which subsequently became the blue-print for interwar social payments rather than either the relief fund of 1914, or the limited, flat rate insurance scheme introduced by Lloyd George in 1911. Once made, the commitment to the principle of 'work or maintenance' could not be unmade.

At most politicians could chip away at the rights of politically more marginal groups such as married women, unmarried mothers and single men. As a result the absolute destitution which had haunted the poor of Edwardian Britain was banished, though deprivation certainly continued to blight urban Britain throughout the interwar period.

Bibliographical Note

The outstanding general history of Britain during the war is Trevor Wilson, *The Myriad Faces of War: Britain and the Great War, 1914–1918* (Cambridge, 1986). It presents a more nuanced picture than Arthur Marwick's *The Deluge: British Society and the First World War* (London, 1965). Jay Winter, *The Great War and the British People* (London, 1986) presents an essentially 'optimistic' view of the impact of the war on civilian health and living standards – challenged by Linda Bryder in 'The First World War: healthy or hungry?', *History Workshop Journal* (1987). Richard Wall and Jay Winter (eds), *The Upheaval of War: Family, Work and Welfare in Europe, 1914–18* (Cambridge, 1986) contains many important essays including Thom on women's work and Reid on wage differentials. An equally valuable collection is Kathleen Burk (ed.), *War and the State: the Transformation of British Government, 1914–1919* (London, 1982) which includes French on 'Business as Usual', Wrigley on the Ministry of Munitions and Burk on the growing strength of the Treasury during the war. On the centrality of global economic power to the British and Allied victory see Avner Offer, *The First World War: an Agrarian Interpretation* (Oxford, 1989); on its demise as a result of war see Kathleen Burk, *Britain, America and the Sinews of Power, 1914–1918* (London, 1985), and A.S. Milward, *The Economic Effects of the World Wars on Britain* (Basingstoke, 2nd edn. 1984). John Turner's recent *British Politics and the Great War: Coalition and Conflict, 1915–1918* (London, 1992) offers an exhaustive study of wartime politics and an interesting analysis of the war's impact on political allegiance. For almost a lone voice defending the reforming credentials of the postwar Coalition see Kenneth O. Morgan, *Consensus and Disunity: the Lloyd George Coalition Government, 1918–1922* (Oxford, 1979). Key works attacking the Coalition's record include P. Abrams, 'The failure of social reform, 1918–1920' *Past and Present* (1963) and P.B. Johnson, *Land Fit for Heroes: the Planning of British Reconstruction, 1916–1919* (Chicago, 1968). Finally two useful historical pamphlets on the period are Anne Crowther, *Social Policy in Britain, 1914–1939* (Basingstoke, 1988) and Rex Pope, *War and Society in Britain, 1899–1948* (London, 1991).

Notes

1. A Reid, 'The impact of the First World War on British workers' in R. Wall and J. Winter (eds), *The Upheaval of War: Family, Work and Welfare in Europe, 1914–1918* (Cambridge, 1986).

2. R. Roberts, *The Classic Slum: Salford Life in the First Quarter of the Century* (Manchester, 1971) ch. 9.

3. One must also allow for the likely natural growth of the male workforce between these dates, early school-leaving and delayed retirement among older workers.

4. N.B. Dearle, *Labour Cost of the World War to Great Britain, 1914–1922* (New Haven, Conn., 1940) pp. 66–8.

5. D. Thom, 'Women and work in wartime Britain' in Wall and Winter (eds), *The Upheaval of War*.

6. For example H.W. Richardson, 'Over-commitment in Britain before 1930', *Oxford Economic Papers* 17 (1965).

7. For example R.C.O. Matthews, 'Why has Britain had full employment since the war?', *Economic Journal* 78 (1968).

8. J.R. Dowie, '1919–20 is in need of attention', *Economic History Review* (1975); S.N. Broadberry, *The British Economy between the Wars: a Macroeconomic Survey* (Oxford, 1986) chs 8 and 9.

9. D.K. Benjamin and L.A. Kochin, 'Searching for an explanation of unemployment in inter-war Britain', *Journal of Political Economy* 87 (1979); criticized in M. Collins, 'Unemployment in inter-war Britain: still searching for an explanation', *Journal of Political Economy* 90 (1982).

10. P.B. Johnson, *Land Fit for Heroes: the Planning of British Reconstruction, 1916–1919* (Chicago, 1968); G.C. Peden, *British Economic and Social Policy: Lloyd George to Margaret Thatcher* (London, 1985).

11. M. Short, 'The politics of taxation: budget-making in Britain, 1917–1931' (Univ. of Cambridge PhD, 1985); P. Abrams, 'The failure of social reform, 1918–20', *Past and Present* 24 (1963).

12. K.O. Morgan, *Consensus and Disunity: the Lloyd George Coalition Government, 1918–1922* (Oxford, 1979); R. McKibbin, *The Ideologies of Class: Social Relations in Britain, 1880–1950* (Oxford, 1990) ch. 9.

10 The Onset of Depression

Dudley Baines

The effects of the First World War on British industry and trade were described in Chapter 9. The long-run effects of the war on the international economy were serious and particularly so for Britain. In 1918 Britain was still dependent on trade which amounted to some 25 per cent of GNP, but the great British export 'staples' – coal, cotton, engineering, shipbuilding – would never regain the prosperity of the years before the First World War. There was an even more serious problem, however. Because Britain's trading position was weaker she was no longer able to dominate the international economy in which the United States was now the most important player. The different motives and actions of the United States exacerbated international economic problems and ultimately contributed to the breakdown of the international economy in the 1930s.

The International Economy

Some of the postwar changes in the international economy were essentially political. For example, one effect of the Russian Revolution was to destroy the country's ability to trade. Since Russia had been the world's largest wheat exporter in 1913, this was of no small consequence. The other major political problem was economic nationalism – the counterpart of the political nationalism enshrined in the Treaty of Versailles. Many new countries were created in Europe, the biggest changes coming as a result of the break-up of the Austro-Hungarian Empire. Its 'successor states' like Hungary and Poland were very nationalistic and erected tariff barriers in order to favour their own nationals. Obviously, this adversely affected international trade and directly or indirectly British exports.

Another key difference in the postwar international economy was the growth of industrial production outside Europe and North America. When primary producing countries such as India were cut off from industrial supplies during the war they began to make some for themselves. At the end of the war they raised tariffs to protect their new 'infant industries' from imports. 'Import substitution' was a serious problem for Britain because before the war most of her exports had been aimed at the primary producing countries where Britain dominated the market. In 1913 British exports of cotton textiles to India were about 10 per cent of all British commodity trade. The importance of India to the British economy before the First World War was explained in Chapter 2. British exports to India had been far greater than British imports from her (i.e. Britain had an export surplus with India). This allowed Britain to purchase imports from the United States and Germany, (i.e. Britain had an import surplus with them).

The United States' Trade Surplus

The most important problem for the international economy was the growth of the American export surplus. This came about because Germany and Britain were unable to meet the demand for their exports during the war and many of their markets were taken over by the United States. At the same time Britain and France needed to import great quantities of materials from the US. This meant that the US, which had long been the largest economy in the world, had, because of the war, become the biggest player in the international economy with a large surplus of exports over imports. By the 1920s, the United States produced nearly a half of the world's industrial output, nearly always at prices which Britain and the other European countries could not match. In addition, the United States had high tariffs but this was not the reason that countries found it difficult to export to her (see the example of the Model T Ford below). The dominance of the United States' economy was not 'caused' by the war, but the war brought it forward and the international economy needed to adjust very fast. As we will see, this was something that it could not do.

The problem of the American trade surplus was magnified by the very high levels of international debt, both private and between governments. During the war the European countries had financed most of their imports by borrowing. The United States had been the biggest lender and, hence, was now the biggest creditor. Germany had not been able to borrow abroad during the war but she was saddled with 'reparations' which were, in effect, war debts which Germany had to repay to the Allies. (Reparations were doubly attractive, especially to the French, because they weakened Germany economically.) To repay the debts and reparations, countries had to obtain foreign exchange which meant they needed to run an export surplus. But, as we have seen, most countries had trade deficits with the United States which was the dominant economy. Hence, it was effectively impossible for the debt to be repaid. The debt problem was part of an even bigger problem. There was little political cooperation in the interwar period. Recriminations over debts and reparations made it impossible to negotiate solutions to the serious problems that beset the international economy. Hence a crisis was inevitable.

In focus: The Model T Ford

The famous Model T Ford was built in Britain at Trafford Park in Manchester in the early 1920s. It cost about £160 and was at the time probably the best value vehicle in Britain. The same car sold in the US for $270 which at the then current exchange rate was about £60. The American tariff was 33 per cent. These data demonstrate two things. Firstly, the difficulty that the British experienced when attempting to sell in the US was not because of American tariffs but rather the vastly lower costs of American industry. Secondly, the British motor industry could only survive if it was protected from American imports. In the interwar period, the American motor industry was so powerful that every country either bought American vehicles or gave its motor industry heavy protection. This was the same kind of international economic dominance as had been enjoyed by British cotton textiles in the nineteenth century.

Summary

The main problem of the international economy in the 1920s was the decline of the British trade surplus. Because the trade surplus declined, Britain could no longer remain the major provider of international investment as it had been before the war when Britain owned 40 per cent of overseas investment. After the war the demand for overseas loans was if anything greater than before, but the loans could only come from the United States. Yet borrowing from the United States was not the same as borrowing from Britain had been before 1913. Before 1913, Britain had been a huge importer of primary products and also of industrial goods. The debtor countries could repay the loans by selling in the British market. In other words, the debts were easily recycled. After the war, the debts could not be recycled. The United States was the cheapest producer of most foodstuffs and most manufactures. It was difficult to repay American loans and many countries, notably Germany, became increasingly indebted to the United States. Many of the loans were short term. If there was a financial collapse in the United States, the loans would be recalled from Europe which would precipitate a financial collapse there. This happened in 1931.

British Economic Performance, 1919–29

The history of the British economy in the 1920s is relatively simple. After a postwar boom Britain suffered the fastest economic collapse in her history. This collapse showed that the old export 'staples' of the British economy would never regain their prewar dominance. Hence, sustained recovery, if it was to occur, required that the British economy be restructured. The history of the 1920s is a history of this often very painful restructuring. The share of GNP that was traded fell from about 25 per cent in 1919 to only 16 per cent by 1938 (a much lower percentage than in the 1990s), yet by 1929 the economy was already stronger than it had been in 1919. In 1929 the economy was hit by a second international depression but, as we will see, Britain was less affected by that depression than most other countries. The main problem for the British economy was the postwar collapse of 1920–21, not the second depression of 1929–32.

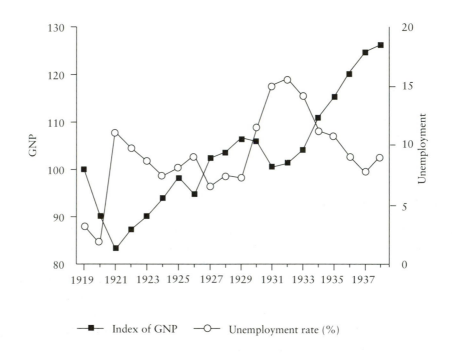

Figure 10.1. Output and unemployment in Britain, 1919–38. *Source:* C.H. Feinstein, *Statistical Tables of National Income, Expenditure and Output of the UK, 1855–1965* (Cambridge, 1972) T22, T126.

The basic contours of British economic performance may be seen in Figure 10.1. The postwar boom of 1919–20 was quite a strong one. This was because consumption had been restricted in nearly all countries during the war. Once the war was over there was a backlog of consumer demand and a backlog of demand for raw materials (restocking). Demand in many countries was fuelled by government borrowing. This led to full order books for the British export industries in 1919–20 and to full employment. But, as we have seen, the prospects for international trade were rather bleak. The boom was followed by the most rapid economic collapse in British history. Industrial output fell by 10 per cent in just over a year. The depression was rooted in the export industries. These so-called 'staple' industries (coal, iron and steel, mechanical engineering, shipbuilding and textiles) lost 1.1 million of their 4.5 million workers (Table 10.1). These losses were never made up before the Second World War.

Table 10.1. Changes in employment in coal mining, iron and steel, mechanical engineering, shipbuilding and textiles, 1920–38 (000s)

Number employed in 1920	**4,510**
Change 1920–21	–1,107
Change 1921–29	+52
Change 1929–32	–713
Change 1932–38	+408
Total change, 1920–38	**–1,360**

Source: Feinstein, Statistical Tables, T129.

The British Export Industries

The British export industries remained in trouble in the 1920s. This was for two reasons. Firstly, and as we have seen, the international economy was much weaker than it had been before the war. Trade only recovered its 1913 level in 1925 and then grew more slowly than before the war. If we think of international trade as a pie, the problem was that the pie was too small. The second reason for the problems of the British export industries was that they were less competitive than before the war. In other words, not only was the pie smaller but the British slice was proportionally smaller again.

Cotton Textiles

Lancashire had totally dominated the world market in cotton textiles before the First World War. She was the cheapest producer of all but the lowest quality cottons. The British dominance had been based on high-grade technology plus a highly trained labour force. Before the war, this was an unbeatable combination so that countries either bought British cottons or, if they did not, their industries had to be protected. After the war the cotton masters invested heavily in new machinery – and in some cases new mills – to take advantage of the expected postwar boom. Unfortunately, the cotton masters – in common with nearly all British entrepreneurs – had misinterpreted the signals. They did not see that the postwar boom was temporary and thought that prewar conditions would return. Machinery prices were very high, leaving the industry 'overcapitalized' and carrying large debts.

In fact, two things had happened to the industry during the war. More countries began to produce for themselves and to protect their markets, and Lancashire's lead was eroded as other countries acquired new technology, much of it made in Britain. This meant, for example, that countries with low wages (like Japan) were now able to compete with Lancashire in world markets. The bigger problem for Lancashire, however, was import substitution. By 1938, the total world trade in cotton textiles was only two-thirds of the exports from Lancashire alone in 1913. And she now had some dangerous competitors. Lancashire could still do quite well at the quality end of the market but that was not enough. It was (just) possible for Lancashire to become more 'efficient' but the relative efficiency of the Lancashire industry was largely irrelevant. There was just not enough trade. The industry had no choice but to contract; in 1937 the output of cotton yarn was only two-thirds of its 1913 level. This explains the industry's high unemployment, the short-time working and the low wage levels.

Shipbuilding

The reasons for the success of the British shipbuilding industry in the nineteenth century were rather similar to those of the cotton textile industry. It too had high quality and low prices before the war and dominated world exports. Clydeside alone built a third of all the world's ships in 1913. The main contrast with cotton was that the bulk of its output was not exported. This was because the bulk of the world's merchant fleet was British owned. After the war, the British share of international trade declined as new countries, including the United States and Japan, built up large merchant fleets. Even if the shipping companies in these countries had wanted to buy British ships, their governments would not have allowed them to do so. It is, of course, well known that the British shipbuilding companies were rather conservative in the interwar period. They were well behind the Norwegians and the Dutch in the design and construction of motor vessels and they did not build many oil tankers. But the demand for these types of vessel was small, enough for the Dutch and Norwegian industry but not for the much larger British industry. The British industry depended on the demand for basic cargo ships. It was not allowed to compete in a large part of the market because of protectionism, and where it was allowed to compete the demand for new ships was depressed because of the low level of international trade in the 1920s and 1930s. The industry had no option but drastically to contract with devastating results for communities like the Tyneside town of Jarrow which had been totally dependent on the industry.

Coal mining

The coal industry was the third of the great 'staples' to be economically devastated by the war. But here the problems were compounded by serious inefficiencies and inappropriate organization in the industry to a far greater extent than was the case in cotton and shipbuilding. Again, exports collapsed, and home demand was affected by the more efficient use of coal (electric versus steam power, for example). The coal problem was exacerbated in 1919 because coal was still largely mined by the picks and shovels of Britain's 1.1 million miners. Machine cutting and mechanical conveying were far less developed than in Germany, not to say in the United States. Coal was a labour intensive industry in Britain partly because the British mines were small and partly because there were literally hundreds of financially weak owners. Hence, the coal problem was of a different order to the cotton textile or the shipbuilding problem. The demand for coal fell which meant the closure of pits, and the remaining demand could be mined by far fewer workers. A drastic decline in the number of miners was inevitable.

We know, of course, that labour relations in coal mining in this period were not of the best. Two-thirds of all days lost in strikes in the interwar period were in coal mining. Despite the industry's weak competitive position the unions were very strong. At one point they forced the government to give a subsidy to prevent wage cuts, but in the long run the prognosis was hopeless. Unless the miners could persuade the government to give permanent and massive subsidies to the industry, which, of course, they could not, the coal mining industry would have to lose about a third of its workers, roughly 400,000 people.

Regional Problems: the Location of Industry

Chapter 3 showed that the export industries were geographically very concentrated. The main industrial areas were Clydeside (shipbuilding and engineering), Tyneside (shipbuilding), Lancashire (cotton textiles and engineering) and, of course, the export coal fields in South Wales and the North East of England. It was the high degree of industrial concentration that leaves the most enduring image of the interwar period – the phenomenon of the depressed area. The depressed areas had high levels of unemployment, low levels of participation – especially by women – and they usually suffered disproportionately from other social problems (see Chapter 12). Infant mortality tended to be high, for example.

The great industrial areas of Greater London and the East and West Midlands were far more prosperous. Because of this prosperity, they were called 'inner Britain' in contrast with 'outer Britain' which was the depressed North and West. Throughout the interwar period 'inner Britain' was able to attract a range of 'newer' industries and services which depended on the home market rather than on exports. Hence, the reason for the existence of the depressed areas was fundamentally a question about the location of industry. The most important single characteristic of a depressed area was that it was dependent on a narrow range of industries. The prosperous areas had a much wider range of industries and services. Why was this? Why were the newer industries not located in the old export regions?

It is easy to explain the location of the 'staple' industries. There was usually some unique feature about the region which conferred an 'absolute advantage' on the industries located within it – the local availability of coal fuel was one. But a whole range of industries, including the newer industries of the interwar period, could be located almost anywhere. London and the Midlands did not confer an absolute advantage. The main reasons for the location of, say, the manufacture of electric irons would be: proximity to markets, a labour force with appropriate skills, proximity to components manufacturers and proximity to specialized services – e.g. legal services, advertising. These would be most abundant in areas where similar industries already existed. It was the 'comparative advantage' that mattered. Long before the First World War London held a comparative advantage over the export regions. For example, even when Clydeside was the most important shipbuilding centre in the world it was not creating employment as fast as London. Between 1841 and 1911 the number of jobs on Clydeside grew by 180 per cent compared with 302 per cent in Greater London. In other words, even in the nineteenth century Clydeside was only expanding in those industries that had to be located on Clydeside. In other industries and in services the pull of London was too great. Hence, Clydeside had little to fall back on when shipbuilding and engineering declined.

Regional income differentials did not narrow in the interwar period. Why was this? Simple neo-classical economics would suggest that workers would move from low to high income regions and that new firms would locate in depressed areas to take advantage of low wages, industrial sites etc. (There was some policy to make it easy for industries to locate in the depressed areas in the 1930s but it was not very effective.)

It is important to realize that wages were not relatively low in the depressed regions. Coal miners and shipbuilders had relatively high incomes. The reason that the regions were poor was that they had low *participation*; unemployment was high among prime age males and – because the regions had little new industry – there were few jobs for women. In fact, out of all the British regions in the interwar period only London and the Midlands had any increase in employment. In other words *all* the net increase in jobs occurred in the South East and Midlands. The key point is that the labour market was not tight anywhere in the country; there were few vacancies in London and the Midlands. Hence, employers could obtain all the labour they wanted in the 'South', where their comparative advantage lay, without having to pay high wages. There were, it is true, disadvantages in having a factory in, say, Central London but these were easily solved by a move to the suburbs. (A classic example is the move of part of the furniture industry from Shoreditch in Central London to Edmonton in the northern suburbs about seven miles away.) The relocation of industry *within* the conurbations was only possible because of the introduction of the motor lorry. The motor lorry made it possible to locate industries in cheap locations in the South and the Midlands and to distribute the products throughout the country. There was no need to manufacture the products in the North.

Government Policy

After the war the government was willing to intervene rather more in the economy than in the years before the First World War but only to a limited extent. Government policy had two strains. The first was to help the export industries via the resurrection of the international economy. The cornerstone of this policy was to return to the Gold Standard (fixed exchange rates) as soon as possible. The argument was that only the Gold Standard would guarantee stability in the international economy which would create a framework for the regeneration of the staple industries. The intention was to return to the Gold Standard at the same exchange rate as before the war. Because the pound had floated downwards this policy implied that the economy would have to be deflated to bring costs (prices and wages) into line with the new exchange rate. The budget had to be strictly balanced or if possible should be in surplus. Hence, there would have been no finance available for a policy of industrial regeneration even if the government had been in favour of such a policy. And, of course, an exchange rate that was too high would make it even more difficult for the British export industries by making exports more expensive and by necessitating continued high interest rates. (On the other hand, a lower exchange rate would not have gone very far towards solving the problems of the British export industries.) The second policy was directly aimed at industry. The government did realize that the staple industries could not regain their prewar dominance. Hence, they encouraged 'rationalization' – closing down some plants and concentrating production. 'Rationalization' would make industry more profitable and more 'efficient'. (It would decrease competition, however.) Of course, rationalisation did nothing for employment in the export industries.

What the government would not do, however, was to intervene directly. As we have said, the main reason was that it was unwilling to spend significant sums of money for industrial regeneration. To be exact, it was totally unwilling to borrow money to help industry and was committed to running a balanced budget. At the time the budget was dominated by only two items – unemployment benefit and the interest on the National Debt. Government debt was a real worry. The government had financed the war by borrowing abroad and by issuing 'Treasury Bills'. Borrowing through Treasury Bills had risen to unprecedented levels during the war and the Treasury believed that people would only be willing to hold additional government debt if offered exceptionally high rates of interest. Obviously, this made government borrowing very problematic. If the government borrowed to help industry, interest rates would rise with implications for the National Debt. There was to be no subsidy for lame ducks and no help for the newer industries either.

The Decision to Return to the Gold Standard at $4.86
In the immediate aftermath of the war most currencies including sterling floated, but in 1925 the British government decided to fix the exchange rate.

It also decided to fix it at a rate of $4.86 to the pound, which was the prewar parity. Keynes argued at the time that the parity was a mistake and most of the later commentators have agreed with him. The exchange rate may have been as much as 10 per cent too high. In other words, British exports became 10 per cent more expensive and imports about 10 per cent cheaper. An exchange rate of $4.86 meant that the economy would have to be deflated. Government expenditure would have to be strictly controlled and interest rates kept high. The exchange rate of $4.86 was not compatible with full employment.

Why did the government (supported by the Bank of England) follow such an apparently disastrous policy? We must remember that their thinking was dominated by the need for a *fixed* exchange rate, to be achieved by fixing the currency to gold as it had been before the First World War. The actual parity was hardly considered. The argument for fixed exchange rates in the 1920s seemed overwhelming. The international economy before the war when the Gold Standard operated was very stable. After the war it was very unstable. It was believed that if the Gold Standard could be resurrected trade would grow and with it the British economy. Other countries would fix their exchange rates once Britain had done so. It was up to Britain to give a lead just as she had done in the past when she was the dominant player in the international economy.

There was a related argument in favour of a resurrected Gold Standard. After the war there had been serious currency instability in many countries, and some had runaway inflation. For example, in the German hyperinflation of 1923 prices rose by a million million times in not much more than two years. Obviously, if exchange rates could be fixed, runaway inflation would be impossible. Hence, one argument in favour of the Gold Standard was that it was 'knave proof' – it stopped governments spending more than they earned in taxes because to do so would be inflationary and, hence, would threaten the exchange rate. This was a powerful argument against social expenditure by left-wing governments. Populist governments may have preferred inflation to unemployment, but in the main, the central bankers were able to convince them that inflation and an unstable currency would be disastrous.

With hindsight we can see that there are several problems with these arguments. The first is that they put the cart before the horse. The Gold Standard had worked because of *non-monetary* factors, such as the high demand for imports in the dominant economy which was Britain. The Gold Standard was not the cause of prewar stability, so resurrecting the Gold Standard could not solve the deep-rooted problems of the postwar international economy. A second problem is that the obsession with the Gold Standard misidentified the cause of Britain's economic problems. By the mid 1920s many of the once famous British exports were less competitive than they had been and many markets had been lost. Hence, even if the international economy had regained its prewar prosperity – which it did not – the problems of the British economy would not have been solved. It would have been better to support the more dynamic sectors of the economy which at that time depended mainly on the home market.

There was little argument about the actual exchange rate. This was largely because when Britain had announced in 1919 that she intended to return to the Gold Standard 'as soon as practicable' it was assumed that it would be at $4.86. Overseas central banks held sterling as part of their reserves and they effectively assumed that Britain would return at the old rate. If Britain had returned to gold at a lower rate it would have destroyed her credibility as a first rate financial power. There was a feeling that $4.86 might be a little high since the pound had normally floated below $4.86 but this was not thought too serious since it was believed that prices and wages would fall within Britain to compensate, thus leaving the average person no worse off in real terms. The problem with this argument was that the days when wages went up and down readily had long gone. The burden would fall only on the export industries which would suffer even more unemployment.

The argument over whether Britain should have devalued, or technically not revalued, in 1925 is in the main only an intellectual exercise. In the first place, Britain could not have devalued against the Empire currencies. Nor do we know what the reaction of the other European countries would have been. They might have returned to the Gold Standard at an even lower parity. We can say, however, that it would be naive to think that the problems of the British export industries could have been solved by a 'devaluation' of 10 per cent.

The 1920s: a Successful Transition?

Despite the terrible problems of the export industries, the 1920s were not a disastrous decade for the British economy. The growth rate was respectable by British standards and far higher than in the Edwardian period (say, 1900–13) which is commonly supposed to have been the heyday of the British export industries – coal, cotton, shipbuilding, engineering etc. The growth rate in GNP per head in that period was 0.4 per cent compared with about 1.5 per cent in the supposedly depressed 1920s. The reason for the paradox is probably that the great export industries were not quite as productive as their success in the international economy made them appear. Hence, when the economy began to rely less on the export staples in the 1920s this meant the beginning of a shift towards the high productivity industries that we associate with the twentieth century – motor vehicles, consumer durables and electric power. These industries depended on the home market, not on exports. In 1913, Britain traded about 27 per cent of her GNP. By 1929 this had fallen to only 22 per cent – a partial shift away from exports that was not a moment too soon for the British economy. Hence, the problems that we observe – for example, the very high unemployment in the export industries – were a sign that the economy *was* adjusting to the new circumstances of the 1920s rather than that it was failing to adjust.

The World Depression of the Early 1930s

The weakness of the international economy led to a disastrous collapse in the early 1930s – the most serious slump to date. All countries suffered although not all to the same degree. Typical features of the depression included a massive fall in prices, high levels of unemployment and the collapse of thousands of banks. What we have to explain is how the depression spread so quickly around the world and why it was so protracted.

There were three centres of the economic crisis; the United States, Germany and the primary producing countries. It turns out, however, that the depression in Germany was partly a *consequence* of the depression in the United States. And the United States was, of course, the most important primary producing country with about a quarter of the labour force in agriculture.

We have seen that the structure of international trade, international debts and exchange rate problems made it inevitable that a depression in the United States would very quickly spread to the rest of the world. The United States fell into depression in 1929 and the economy declined continuously until 1933. By 1933 real GNP had fallen by 29 per cent and industrial output by 50 per cent. At that time about a third of the population either had no job or worked very short-time. The Great Depression was a shattering experience for the majority of the American population which has remained important in political consciousness to this day.

In the United States the depression was signalled by a massive collapse of share prices on Wall Street – the New York Stock Exchange. The excesses of the speculative mania on Wall Street which led to the Crash were not the only cause of the depression in the United States, however. Agriculture had been seriously depressed for some time. The mass production companies that produced the industrial products of the 1920s were running out of markets because wages were not rising while productivity was rising. In other words, by the late 1920s, people were not being paid enough to buy enough motor cars, suburban houses and consumer durables – the products that had sustained the boom. Finally, the Federal Reserve Board – in effect, the Central Bank – made a disastrous policy miscalculation in 1931–32. It raised interest rates and made money scarce when it should have made money easier. As a direct result, a large proportion of the banks in the US were bankrupted and many people lost their life savings.

The American depression spread throughout the world in several ways. The first was through trade. Falling incomes in the United States meant that Americans bought fewer imports. American imports were another country's exports. The second country then faced a balance of payments deficit because exports fell and imports did not. In fact, the immediate reaction of most governments to the depression was to increase tariffs. The most notorious example was the American Hawley-Smoot tariff of 1930 which raised duties to unprecedented levels in a market which, as we have seen, was already very difficult to penetrate. The Hawley-Smoot tariff led to immediate retaliation.

The upshot of the tariff wars was that international trade contracted even faster.

At the same time there was a collapse of world food prices. There had been severe overproduction of food in the 1920s. The capacity of the world to produce food was outstripping the world's ability to consume it. For example, the introduction of the tractor into grain farming increased the number of acres that could be devoted to grain because horses were no longer needed. In turn this released the acreage that had been needed to provide food for the horses. At the same time, population growth in the industrial countries was slowing down but *per capita* consumption of food was not rising.

The increase in supply relative to demand for food had two effects. The price of foodstuffs was declining and large quantities of unsold stocks were building up. Naturally, stocks had to be financed. Dealers (and sometimes governments) had borrowed to buy the food which they could not sell. The crisis came in 1929. Following the Wall Street Crash and the subsequent banking crises the loans which had financed the stocks were called in. Merchants had no option but to dump the food on the world market for what it could fetch. The world price of wheat and other foodgrains fell by about two-thirds in three years. At the same time the industrial countries reduced their imports of industrial raw materials. (As we have seen, demand for industrial products was falling.) Hence, the price of, for example, rubber, cotton and nickel also collapsed.

In focus: The Nature of a Financial Crisis, 1931

In a financial crisis people are unwilling to lend their money and prefer to hold cash (in economists' jargon, their 'liquidity preference' rises). They withdraw the money they have lent to banks. To cover the withdrawals of cash, the banks have to recall their loans. It is normal for banks to create credit by lending more than the value of the cash that was originally deposited. If the ratio of cash to loans is 1 to 4, that means that the original bank will have to recall £4,000 of loans for each £1,000 that was originally deposited. Some of these loans will have found their way into another bank forcing that bank to recall its loans. (Only £1,000 for each £1,000 deposit, however, because these deposits are not cash.) Hence, the crisis spreads rapidly unless the central bank creates money to cover the withdrawals. This was difficult under the rules of the Gold Standard.

In principle, there is no difference if the banks are situated in different countries except that the withdrawals are in foreign currency. Hence, there is an exchange rate risk because the central bank in the foreign country has to provide the foreign exchange demanded by the people who are withdrawing money from the banks. Under the Gold Standard, the central bank had to provide it at a fixed rate. If the run continued the central bank

The Nature of a Financial Crisis, 1931 (continued)

would run out of reserves. It then either had to introduce exchange control or devalue the currency – i.e. it had to leave the Gold Standard. Of course, if either was anticipated the rate of withdrawals would increase and exchange control (as in Germany) or devaluation (as in the UK) would become inevitable.

In 1931 the central banks in Europe were heavily indebted, mainly to American banks, which meant that a run on the American banks would precipitate a run on the European ones. The first sign of the crisis came in May 1931 when the *Kreditanstalt*, the largest bank in Austria, was declared bankrupt. There was a run on the Austrian currency. The Austrian government, anxious to remain on the Gold Standard, requested a loan from several countries including France. The French government chose to use its power to grant the loan to weaken Germany. Germany was proposing a customs union with Austria and the German navy was beginning to build some 'pocket battleships'. The French price for their agreement to the loan was that both cease. By the time this was agreed it was too late, and the Austrian government had introduced exchange control, thus trapping some assets in Austria. (This was but one example of the enormous political mistrust which made it impossible to negotiate a way out of the economic crisis – i.e. political mistrust made the crisis inevitable.)

Attention now turned to Germany which was already in the depths of depression. Germany was the world's largest debtor and there were massive withdrawals of deposits mainly by American and French banks. This put the German banks under enormous pressure and they began to collapse. And, of course, the Reichsbank lost all its reserves as it changed reichsmarks into dollars, French francs and gold. Again the overseas loans were too little and too late. They had no option but to introduce exchange control in July, immobilizing more funds in Germany.

The Economic and Political Crisis in Britain, 1931

The events of the early summer of 1931 placed the British Government and the Bank of England in an invidious position. Obviously, people who had assets frozen in Austria and Germany would have to withdraw their holdings in London banks. In an ordinary year sterling would have looked quite strong, but 1931 was no ordinary year. Britain was not a debtor overall, as was Germany, but the country was in financial difficulties. Britain had gone back to the Gold Standard at an overvalued rate in 1925 which made her currency more vulnerable than, say the French franc, which had deliberately been

Plate 10.1. The Bank of England. This satirical cartoon by Heath Robinson presents a jaundiced view of the dangers to the economy of an easy money policy.

undervalued. Britain had also made huge overseas investments in the primary producing countries, such as Australia and Argentina. Because the prices of primary products had fallen so much these investments were of only low value in 1931. Hence, Britain's short-term debts could not easily be covered. The problem was well known, not least because a government report in July had obligingly pointed out the extent of Britain's short-term debts (in other words, the financial system was very 'illiquid'). Increasingly funds were withdrawn from London and a run on the pound began.

A Labour government had been in office in Britain since 1929 but did not have a parliamentary majority and relied on Liberal support. It was not a radical government and in normal years would have been quite well regarded by international bankers. For example, Labour policy was to stay on the Gold Standard. There was a problem in a depression, however, because the budget was deeply in deficit.

A deficit of £120,000,000 (3 per cent of GNP) was predicted. (In 1931, a balanced budget was the sign of 'good housekeeping', which showed that a government was in charge of the situation.) The problem was that the government was determined to defend the pound which meant that there had to be an overseas loan. The overseas bankers, not unreasonably in the circumstances, asked the government to confirm that the Conservative opposition would support its economic policy. Unwittingly, this gave the Conservatives the means to defeat the government. Their price was that the budget deficit be cut. This was a price that the government could not pay – as the Conservatives well knew. Forty per cent of the budget deficit was directly due to unemployment payments to which the Labour Party was ideologically committed. Most of the rest was the interest on the national debt which was inviolate.

The Labour government was impaled on the horns of a dilemma. They could not choose between two equally unacceptable policies. If they obtained the loan they would have to cut unemployment benefit. If they did not obtain the loan they would have to leave the Gold Standard. It neatly solved the dilemma by resigning, and was replaced by a so-called 'National government' with the same prime minister and chancellor (Ramsay MacDonald and Phillip Snowden). Almost immediately, the new government went off the Gold Standard. Within three months the pound had fallen by nearly 30 per cent against the French franc and the dollar. The National government also cut public expenditure – including a cut of 10 per cent in unemployment benefits.

This was a very painful episode which led to great recriminations, particularly in Labour Party circles. There is an important point to make, however. Britain was forced off gold but the government had done the right thing for the wrong reasons. Firstly, Britain went off gold before the banks collapsed. Once the pound fell it became a desirable rather than an undesirable currency. Foreign exchange that had been lost in the summer flowed back into London. More generally, Britain had managed to disentangle herself from the Gold Standard at a time when staying on it was making recovery impossible. Going off gold was the foundation for Britain's early recovery from the international depression (see Chapter 11).

There is a more general and more profound issue. The Gold Standard was destroyed in 1931 leading to a period of great problems for international trade. But most countries *did* recover from the depression, some very strongly. Obviously, the Gold Standard of the late 1920s could not have saved the international economy from its most serious crisis ever. But, as we will see in the next chapter, recovery could not come while bankers and governments were ideologically committed to the Gold Standard. This means that the destruction of the Gold Standard in the summer of 1931 was not only inevitable but desirable.

Debates and Interpretations

Labour Costs, the Postwar Boom and Industrial Performance

There has been some controversy about the effect of the post 1919–20 boom on the British economy in the 1920s. Dowie argued that it had serious effects on economic performance.[1] The boom was fuelled by pent-up demand, a large budget deficit and rather lax monetary conditions. Not surprisingly, there was a wage and price explosion. The unions lost some of the gains in money wages in the subsequent slump (1920–21) but not all. In addition, the working hours of some seven million people were permanently reduced, typically from fifty-four to forty-seven hours per week. According to Dowie, hourly wages in British industry in July 1922 when conditions had stabilized were 66 per cent higher than four years earlier. This was more than the increase in product prices and more than any possible increase in productivity. Since, as we have seen, the existing exchange rate could not be altered, Britain's manufacturing costs had increased more than those of her competitors. In addition, wages rose relative to profits which reduced investment and, in turn, the long-run growth of British industry.

Dowie's argument is persuasive but it is unlikely to be sufficient. Even if wage costs had not risen in 1919–20, the competitiveness of the British export industries would still have been in question.[2] Lazonick has shown that many of the staple industries had a weak industrial structure – they were rarely vertically integrated, for example.[3] And Hannah's work on the development of the business corporation demonstrates that even in those industries that did have a modern industrial structure – motor vehicles and chemicals, for example – management performance was weak.[4] In other words, even if labour costs had not risen as far as they did in 1919–20, a great deal of British industry would still have been facing severe problems. Similarly, it is equally unrealistic to argue that British industry was severely handicapped by an inappropriate exchange rate, as we will see.

The British Economy and the Exchange Rate, 1925–31

The effect of the sterling exchange rate on the economy after 1925 has attracted controversy. Most observers concur that the pound was overvalued but they differ over the extent to which a lower exchange rate could have benefited the British economy. The question concerns the *elasticities*. For example, if the pound rises, the price of British exports rises when priced in foreign currency, and normally we would expect less to be sold. Conversely, the price of imports to a Briton falls when priced in pounds and normally more would be sold. The elasticities measure *how much more or less* would be bought. Moggridge estimated that the price elasticity of demand for British exports and imports was 1.5 and 0.5, respectively.[5] Exports were worth £801 million and exports £1,137 in 1924 and the surplus on invisibles was £409 million. These elasticities imply that if the exchange rate had been $4.40, the balance of payments would have benefited by about £70 million. This could have assisted the economy in many ways – overseas lending could have been increased or overseas debts reduced, for example. Alternatively, it would have allowed domestic output to increase by £70 million and hence employment. To calculate the effect on employment we need to know the size of the employment multiplier. It has been estimated that this was about 1.5. A 10 per cent lower parity would have meant about 300,000 fewer unemployed. Actual unemployment in 1928 was about 1.5 million, so on these assumptions, the effect of an overvalued pound on employment would have been limited. The calculation includes only first order effects, however. For example, as Hatton points out, a stronger export performance would have made it possible for the government to have adopted a slightly more expansionary monetary and fiscal policy. Under these circumstances the employment gain would have been closer to 500,000.[6]

Naturally, these calculations are very sensitive to the assumptions used. An export price elasticity of 1.5 in the late 1920s may seem rather high if the British export industries were not very efficient and if their products were not very desirable. If the export elasticity was 1.0, the employment gain from a 10 per cent devaluation (including Hatton's revisions) would not have been much more than 300,000. Alternatively, the pound may not have been overvalued by as much as 10 per cent in 1925 – after all the British export performance was not better before 1925 when the pound floated below $4.86 than it was after 1925. If this was the case the employment cost of a $4.86 pound was less than 500–300,000 – i.e. only a small part of the unemployment.[7]

It is important to remember that these calculations tell us only the advantages of a lower exchange rate. It does not mean that there was any realistic possibility that Britain would adopt a lower rate. Britain could not have devalued against many of her trading partners and in any case the government was committed to returning to the Gold Standard with a clear expectation that the rate would be $4.86.

Bibliographical Note

The best introductory book on the international economy in the period is A.G. Kenwood and A.L. Lougheed, *The Growth of the International Economy, 1820–1990* (London, 3rd edn, 1992). J. Foreman-Peck, *A History of the World Economy. International economic relations since 1850* (Hassocks, 2nd edn, 1993) is more sophisticated.

There are many good books about the British economy in the 1920s. D.H. Aldcroft, *The British Economy. Volume 1, The Years of Turmoil, 1920–1951* (Hassocks, 1986) is a very clear simple account. R. Floud and D. McCloskey (eds), *The Economic History of Britain since 1700*, Volume 2 (Cambridge, 1994) is the most up to date textbook.

Monetary policy is covered in detail in D.E. Moggridge, *British Monetary Policy. The Norman Conquest of $4.86* (Cambridge, 1972).

Notes

1. J. Dowie, '1919–20 is in need of attention', *Economic History Review*, 2nd ser., vol. 28 (1975).

2. S. Broadberry, 'The impact of the world wars on the long term performance of the British Economy', *Oxford Review of Economic Policy* (1988).

3. W. Lazonick, 'Competition, specialization and industrial decline', *Journal of Economic History* 41 (1981).

4. L. Hannah, *The Rise of the Corporate Economy* (Cambridge, 1977).

5. D.E. Moggridge, *British Monetary Policy. The Norman Conquest of $4.86* (Cambridge, 1972) pp. 246–50.

6. T. Hatton, 'The outlines of a Keynesian solution', in S. Glynn and A. Booth (eds), *The Road to Full Employment* (London, 1987) pp. 84–5.

7. N.H. Dimsdale, 'British monetary policy and the exchange rate, 1920–38', *Oxford Economic Papers (Supplement)* (1981).

11 Recovery from Depression

Dudley Baines

The causes of the international depression of the early 1930s were discussed in Chapter 10. It hit Britain in 1929. The problems suffered in Britain were similar (although not identical, as we will see) to the problems suffered by the other industrial countries – a large fall in the prices of commodities, a fall in industrial output and rapidly rising unemployment.

How Serious was the Depression in Britain?

People often think of the 'Thirties' in Britain as a wasted decade dominated by the problem of unemployment. The most enduring images, for example, are the man on the Wigan street corner and the marchers of the Jarrow Crusade. Obviously, on the evidence of unemployment the depression in Britain must have been severe. The export industries were experiencing difficulties in 1929 and unemployment, at about 1.5 million, was already high. By 1932, at the bottom of the depression, it had risen to 3.4 million, or 17 per cent of the labour force (see Table 12.1).

In recent years, however, economists and historians have been able to create far better data about the economy in the 1930s than were available at the time. Data in Figure 11.1 show that output and employment fell less in the 1929–32 depression in Britain than in most other countries. Industrial output fell by 9 per cent compared with about a half in Germany and the United States, for example. These data imply that although unemployment was high in Britain it must have been even higher elsewhere. In Germany, the number of unemployed was at least six and possibly eight million – proportionally double the British rate. The recovery from the depression was also relatively fast in Britain. GNP regained its 1929 level by 1934. The United States regained its 1929 output in 1937 – only to fall again. France did not recover until after the Second World War.

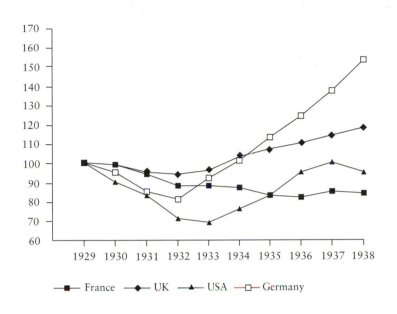

Figure 11.1. Index of real GNP, 1929–38 (1929 = 100)

The depression came to Britain through the external account – trade and overseas investments. Most British overseas investment was in the primary producing countries and they were very vulnerable to the price falls. This was an important factor in the 1931 financial crisis, as we have seen in Chapter 10. The main problem, however, was the collapse of international trade which left the British export industries no option but to cut output. Nearly a half (713,000 out of 1.9 million) of the rise in unemployment between 1929 and 1932 was in iron and steel, coal, shipbuilding, cotton textiles and mechanical engineering. Employment losses were larger in the export industries and the regions where the export industries were located (South Wales, Lancashire, the North East of England and Central Scotland). Note that the decline in the export industries did not collapse the rest of the economy. This means that some powerful countervailing force must have kept many domestic industries reasonably profitable.

Why was the Depression Mild?

There were two main reasons for the relative mildness of the depression in Britain: Britain was the world's largest importer of food and raw materials; and there was no financial collapse. The causes and consequences of the sharp fall in the international price of food and raw materials were discussed in Chapter

10. When the price of imported food fell in Britain, the real income of consumers rose, and this released purchasing power for industrial goods which helped investment. Naturally, low food (and raw material) prices depended on the British government being willing to allow duty free imports but free trade was an article of faith for the Labour government and there could be no general tariffs before Labour's demise in 1931. New tariffs were not imposed until 1932 when the economy was beginning to turn around and even then they did not seriously increase the price of food. British trade policy in the depression was in marked contrast to the policy of the other industrial countries where the most common reaction to the fall in import prices was immediately to increase tariffs.

The fall in import prices had a profound effect on the British economy. Low import prices in Britain were low export prices in the primary producing countries. Hence, the market for British exports fell and in turn this led to unemployment in the British export industries. Yet the real income of the majority of the population actually rose. The total amount paid in wages and salaries seems to have fallen by about 10 per cent between 1929 and 1932 but this was the same as the fall in prices, so total consumption must have remained about the same (the usually accepted estimate is that consumption rose marginally by 2 per cent).[1] The greatest losses were suffered by the newly unemployed and by the rich (since profits fell sharply), but the standard of living of the 19 million or so workers who did not lose their jobs must have risen. This meant that demand held up and businesses that did not depend on exports could continue moderately to prosper.

The second reason for the mildness of the depression in Britain was that there was no financial collapse. In contrast to many other countries where the financial institutions, including the high street banks, closed, the British banks were never put under serious pressure from failing domestic business. The main threat to financial stability came from overseas, particularly during the international banking crisis of the summer of 1931 (see Chapter 10). There was a run on the pound but the run stopped when the Bank of England took the pound off the Gold Standard, allowing the exchange rate to fall to a level which made it attractive to hold sterling again. This crucial decision had very important implications for interest rates and money supply which will be discussed below. These financial decisions also had important political implications. Because the depression in Britain was mild there was no majority for a radical solution. In many countries the economic and social problems were so great that people turned to radical governments that promised to intervene in the economy to promote recovery. Some of the radical governments preserved democracy as Roosevelt did in the USA. In Germany, however, the depression led to Hitler and fascism.

The Recovery

The depression in Britain bottomed out by the autumn of 1932 and output recovered its 1929 level by 1934. Historians and economists have offered several explanations of the recovery, many of which have been related to changes in government policy. It is important to remember, however, that we do not *need* an exogenous explanation of the recovery. The financial system was intact, the terms of trade moved in Britain's favour and consumption was unaffected. The recovery would come irrespective of government policy as long as the government did not do anything to prevent it.

There has nevertheless been great scholarly interest in government policy of the period in recent years, particularly over the issue of whether Britain would have recovered more quickly from the depression if the government had followed the prescriptions of John Maynard Keynes. Keynes' *General Theory* is often taken as a turning point in the history of economic policy. An implication of Keynes' work was that governments could intervene in the economy to maintain employment. But British governments did not do so; the budget was balanced between 1932 and 1937.

The story of economic policy in this period has sometimes been told as the history of a conservative and hidebound Treasury which was resisting attempts by 'progressive' economists to introduce more radical economic policies. It is important to distinguish between the theoretical issues involved – what the government *should* have done, and what the government *could* do or was likely to do. No country recovered from the depression because Keynesian economic policies were introduced. The countries that did recover through government spending – Japan and Germany – did so because of rearmament, not via consumption as Keynes proposed. Even in the United States, where in 1932 a Federal government was elected that was committed to intervention in the economy (the 'New Deal' programme), Keynesian policies were not understood and government spending was strictly limited before the onset of rearmament in the late 1930s.

It is not surprising that it took so long for fiscal policy to be accepted. The *General Theory* was not published until 1936. But even if it had been published earlier there would have been serious obstacles to putting an expansionary fiscal policy into effect. Fiscal policy would have required the government to accept responsibility for the management of the economy, something which had never been done in peacetime and not properly in wartime. In the early 1930s, economic management was often confused with economic control, as in the USSR. Moreover, there was no agreement either among economists or in the business community about what the government should do, except that the majority of both groups had always thought that intervention would be disastrous. Most important, economic management would have required profound changes in the political power of government and the way that it did its day-to-day business.

The Bank of England and the Treasury had a more sophisticated approach to monetary policy than to fiscal policy. It was accepted that, if possible, interest rates should be low to stimulate recovery. There has been some controversy about the effect of the fall in interest rates in Britain. Today's monetarists would argue that falling interest rates were a *sufficient* cause of recovery – investment would automatically have risen as interest rates fell. There is evidence, however, that businessmen were also expecting profits to rise at the same time. We have seen that money wages did not fall by very much in the depression, but mainly because the unions were weak, wages did not rise very much in the recovery. This meant that profits were minimal in 1929–32, but rising from 1932; hence, businessmen increased their investment.

In focus: Keynes and 'The General Theory'

The most famous economist in this period was John Maynard Keynes, born in 1883 and died in 1946. His first job was at the India Office where he suggested a reform of the Indian currency – which was carried out. He was an important member of the British delegation to the Versailles Peace Conference but resigned because he opposed the imposition of reparations on Germany. Having resigned as a civil servant, he then attempted to influence government policy through books and journalism (the collected edition of his works comprises thirty volumes). For example, he was at the famous dinner with the Chancellor in 1925 when the decision to return to the Gold Standard was taken (he opposed it). At the same time he was teaching economics at Cambridge and was Bursar of King's College. He (reputedly) made two fortunes and lost one in currency speculation. He was a notable patron of the arts and in effect the creator of the Arts Council. In the Second World War he was the most important government economic official and led the British delegation to the Bretton Woods conference in 1944. He made many contributions to the development of economic theory but his most important theoretical contribution was to show that the labour market could be in equilibrium without the economy reaching full employment. Before Keynes, economists had believed that markets always cleared since prices would move up or down to ensure that supply always equalled demand. In theory, this would mean that, in the long run, unemployment could not exist. It was obvious that unemployment did exist in the long run but it was explained by institutions – e.g. because trade unions held wages above the level that cleared the market. Similarly, it was also believed that the price of money (i.e. interest rates) would ensure that what people were trying to save would always equal what businessmen were trying to invest. If both the labour market and money market cleared automatically then there was little role for government in the economy except to make the market function more perfectly. This implied that the government's budget should always be balanced since the government could not spend taxpayers' money more efficiently than the taxpayers could themselves.

Keynes and 'The General Theory' (continued)

Keynes' views took some time to work out but were most clearly stated in the *General Theory of Employment, Interest and Money* which was published in 1936. The book contained many important innovations, including a new and radically different theory of how interest rates were determined. But politically the most important assertion was that the economy might be in equilibrium when it did not have full employment – i.e. there was no automatic tendency for the labour market to clear. If this was true, it was clearly the government's duty to intervene in the economy to reduce unemployment, something which it had never done. According to Keynes, the government could do this by increasing its spending above its receipts – i.e. run a budget deficit. Keynes' argument was helped by the calculation of the 'multiplier' relationship by one of his students, Richard Kahn, in 1931. The multiplier showed that national income would increase by more than the increase in government spending.

Opposition to an unbalanced budget was fierce, both before and after the *General Theory*. Some of these objections were well thought out. For example, the Treasury had problems financing (paying interest on) the National Debt and argued that a budget deficit would further increase borrowing, thereby raising interest rates and delaying recovery. This seemed a good reason for the Treasury to be sceptical but, curiously, when interest rates fell in the early 1930s, making the National Debt easier to finance, the Treasury did not cease to object to an unbalanced budget. In practice, the balanced budget was a policy *objective* rather than a policy *instrument*, and the main argument for balancing the budget was that it *prevented* the government intervening in the economy.

It took a long time for Keynes' views to be accepted. At first Keynes attempted to convince the Treasury mandarins. When that failed he turned to his fellow economists since the Treasury could not be persuaded while economists were divided among themselves. The *General Theory* was written for this professional audience; it is very theoretical with few references to economic policy *per se* and largely impenetrable to the general reader. By the late 1930s, however, Keynes and his students were beginning to have an effect on the intellectual climate and on economic policy. How large the change of heart actually was among the economic establishment is difficult to determine since the need to manage rearmament and war completely changed economic circumstances. The problem became one of too much demand – an 'inflationary gap' – not too little (see Chapter 16). But what Keynes and his supporters had done was to force governments to think in macro-economic terms. The 'Keynesian Revolution' marks the beginnings of government intervention, of the profession of economics and of economic management by government.

Recovery and the International Economy

The crisis of 1931 was a turning point for the international economy. The Gold Standard collapsed, to be replaced by currency blocs and exchange control, and there were further rises in tariffs and, increasingly, quotas. At the same time government intervention in the economies of many countries increased, particularly where there were military objectives. These less flexible trading arrangements meant that international trade could not grow as fast as world output. The level of world trade was still below its 1929 level in 1939 when the domestic output of most countries was much higher. In consequence it was not possible for Britain to recover through increased exports, but this did not mean that Britain could afford to ignore the rest of the world.

Because Britain was less depressed than most countries and was recovering faster, her economy had to be partly insulated from the rest of the world. If, for example, the economy had kept the old exchange rate, Britain would have suffered serious balance of payments crises leading to runs on the currency because she was recovering relatively fast. If Britain had not left the Gold Standard in 1931 and floated the pound, the Bank would have had to supply gold or foreign currency to anyone who had pounds to sell. To persuade people not to sell pounds the government would have had to offer high rates of interest on sterling assets. In other words, low interest rates and monetary expansion were incompatible with Britain remaining on gold – recovery depended on devaluation. It is also possible that if Britain had stayed on the Gold Standard, public expenditure would have had to be cut (public expenditure cuts were minimal in Britain, although there were a few well-known examples in 1931). This scenario is what happened in France. France did not devalue the franc until 1936, and in consequence the government was forced to maintain high interest rates and cut expenditure. As a result, the French, on average, were still poorer in 1939 than they had been in 1929.

We might doubt, however, whether the British government had an economic policy, particularly in the crucial early stages of the recovery. What seems to have happened is that it did the right thing for the wrong reasons. As we have said, it was a precondition of recovery that Britain left the Gold Standard, but Britain did not leave it in order to aid recovery but because the run on the pound gave the Bank of England no choice (see Chapter 10). It was predicted in Cabinet that leaving gold would be an economic disaster, although in practice, once Britain had left the Gold Standard in September 1931, foreign currency flowed into Britain making it possible for interest rates to fall. Far from welcoming this the Treasury was afraid that falling interest rates would be inflationary – a bad thing in the economic orthodoxy of the time. The Treasury then realized that falling interest rates would reduce payments on the National Debt, something they had been trying to engineer since the end of the war. It was only after several months had passed that the Treasury saw low interest rates as a way out of the depression. The answer to the question 'Did government intervention cause the recovery?' should be clear – it didn't. But we must be careful. It is also clear that the government did not make any disastrous policy mistakes, as happened in several other countries.

The Introduction of Tariffs

Some industries were protected by tariffs in the 1920s but the move to general protection in 1932 was a major turning point in the development of the British economy which had pursued a free trade policy since the middle of the nineteenth century. Free trade policy no longer seemed sensible in the 1930s. A large proportion of world trade was not competitive but was dependent on prior bilateral negotiations between two countries. Britain was the only large country with a relatively open market and it was argued that an open market put Britain at a massive disadvantage in trade negotiations because she had nothing to offer a protectionist country. Her negotiators would be 'walking naked into the conference chamber'.

It was also thought that protection would reduce unemployment by replacing some imports with home production. It is not clear, however, that protection did increase output and reduce unemployment. Companies that were in direct competition with imports – e.g. some of the steel firms – benefited, of course, but that meant that the rest of the economy had to pay more for steel which they needed as an input. The rest of the economy lost income and employment. Moreover, in the case of steel the government gave the industry a tariff (ultimately of 50 per cent) on condition that the industry was modernized, but once the industry was protected from foreign competition there was no pressure to modernize, and the industry did not do so. Whether the costs of protection to the economy as a whole outweighed the benefits is a difficult technical question but the most careful analysis to date suggests that the costs of tariffs did exceed the benefits and on balance hindered recovery.[2]

The introduction of general tariffs in 1932 was followed by an attempt to negotiate an Empire trading bloc. This idea was first mooted in the early twentieth century (see Chapter 2). The expectation was that the Empire countries – particularly Australia and Canada – would be willing to exchange privileged access into their markets for British manufactures in return for privileged access to the British market for their food and raw materials (they would either face no tariffs or tariffs that were lower than those faced by non-Empire countries). There was a famous conference at Ottawa in 1932 but it proved difficult to negotiate an Empire trading bloc because of an underlying conflict of national economic interests. The Empire countries were anxious to reduce their dependence on food and raw material exports and to build up their own manufacturing, so they wanted *protection from British exports*.

Recovery and the Domestic Economy

As every political historian knows, rearmament came very late in Britain. It was not a significant part of the economy until 1938, when 9 per cent of GNP was spent on armaments (three years later this was 55 per cent). There was a second depression in the international economy in 1938 which Britain avoided partly because of the rearmament spending. But this is really another story because the British economy was well out of the depression by then. Britain managed to recover from the 1929–32 depression without rearmament, which was not true of many other countries.

We can use the history of housing in the 1930s to show the forces that were making the British economy grow. There was a housing boom, with three million dwellings built in the 1930s, which was the fastest ever rate of construction up to that time. Two-thirds of the houses were for owner occupiers. The demand for houses was high in the 1930s for several distinct reasons. First, the population contained a high proportion of young adults who came from the large working-class families of the Edwardian period, so the rate of family formation was high. Secondly, the wartime housing shortage had not been made up in the 1920s, partly because rents were controlled, and building houses for rent in the 1920s was unprofitable. In the 1930s, rent control was progressively abolished which allowed rents to rise and made it profitable, once again, to build houses to rent. There were also some important technical changes which affected supply – i.e. they made houses cheaper. One was the growth of the motor vehicle which made it possible to build houses outside the city centres where land was cheap. Technical change was also reducing the price of materials such as bricks, tiles and prefabricated windows and doors. For instance, bricks were now made in huge brickworks as at Peterborough (in Northamptonshire) and Stewartby (in Bedfordshire).

Table 11.1. The cost of buying *the same* 3 bedroom house in a London suburb

	1928	1936	1990
Cost to buy	£600	£450	£100,000
Deposit	£300	£50	£10,000
Balance to Finance	£300	£400	£90,000
Interest Rate (%)	6	4.5	11
Repayment Period (yrs)	15	25	25
Percentage of a (male) secondary schoolteacher's annual salary needed to repay the mortgage			
	10%	8%	43%

We should note, however, that demographic change, the growth of suburbs and the technical changes did not become important just in 1932 when the housing boom began. They cannot therefore have been a *cause* of recovery. The end of rent control did coincide with the housing boom, and we may say that it was a cause, but only a third of the new houses built were rented. What caused the boom in the two-thirds that were sold? This is easy to see from Table 11.1. Most people depended on credit to purchase houses, and builders also depended on credit to construct them. When interest rates fell in 1932, building society interest rates did not follow the market down. They fell only from 6 per cent to 4.5 per cent when the bank rate remained at 2 per cent. Not surprisingly, the building societies were full of funds. They began to lend on easier terms than they ever had before and this reduced the weekly cost of buying the houses. It is hardly surprising that there was a house-building boom. But low interest rates (and cheap labour) were a consequence of the depression. In other words, it is incorrect, in the main, to say that the housing boom caused the recovery.

Unemployment

The complex causes of unemployment in the 1930s are discussed in Chapter 12. Here we will consider only one question – why unemployment remained high through the 1930s. If the 1929–32 depression was mild and the recovery rapid, why did 2.2 million people remain unemployed in 1938? Table 11.2 shows why this was so. There were 3.4 million unemployed in 1932 and the vigorous recovery meant that 2.6 million jobs (mainly in quite different industries) had been created by 1938. Unfortunately, the number of people looking for work rose by 1.4 million. We know that the exceptionally large numbers of young adults in the population in the interwar period increased the demand for houses – they were the survivors of the big Edwardian families. For the same reasons the number of people searching for work was exceptionally high.

Table 11.2. Employment and unemployment, 1929–38

	LF	E	UE	UE%	UE (R)%
1929	21.0	19.5	1.5	7.3%	10.4%
1932	22.2	18.8	3.4	15.6%	22.1%
1938	23.6	21.4	2.2	9.3%	12.9%

Notes: LF – Labour Force (m); E – Numbers in employment (m); UE – Number unemployed (m); UE% – Percentage of labour force unemployed; UE(R)% – Percentage of insured labour force unemployed.

After: C.H. Feinstein, *Statistical Tables of National Income, Expenditure and Output of the United Kingdom, 1855–1965* (Cambridge, 1972) T126.

We explored the reasons for the existence of 'depressed areas' with very high levels of unemployment in Chapter 10. The main conclusion was that there were not enough jobs in the prosperous regions to reduce unemployment in the depressed regions. The persistence of regional unemployment was not, in the main, because labour was immobile. National unemployment levels were higher in the 1930s than in the 1920s. Hence, it was less likely that the regional unemployment problem could be solved.

The depression in Britain was very serious for a great many people although not for the majority. The main effect was to *redistribute* income – from the unemployed to the employed. Think about the effect of the changes in the terms of trade which – because of the international depression – improved between 1929 and 1932 by 10 per cent (exports paid for 10 per cent more imports). Hence, the cost of living fell, which, in the main, protected the standard of living of those who did not lose their jobs. But because fewer goods could be exported about two million more people became unemployed, many of whom had little chance of getting their jobs back. At the same time most of the population were doing reasonably well. It was the unfairness that made the 1930s so difficult to bear. In these respects the 1930s had some features in common with the 1980s and early 1990s.

Debates and Interpretations

'New Industries' and Recovery from the Depression

It has been argued that 'structural change' was the *cause* of the recovery in the 1930s because the old export staple industries with low growth prospects were being replaced by 'new' and more productive consumer industries, such as motor vehicles, which sold their products in the home market. This view has been associated with H.W. Richardson who popularized the idea that the British economy had been 'overcommitted' to the old export staples until the 1930s when the development of new technologies had moved the economy onto a new and higher growth path.[3]

Richardson's argument has been subject to serious criticism, initially by Dowie.[4] He pointed out that the argument depends on two things being true: the main source of growth in the 1930s would have to be the 'new', that is 'non-staple', industries; and the growth rate in the 1930s would have to be higher than in the 1920s. In the first place, some of the fast growing industries in the recovery that Richardson identified, such as the motor industry, were not 'new' at all but had grown out of an 'old' industry – i.e. mechanical engineering in the case of motor vehicles. (And in what sense was building 'new'?) What Richardson had done was to define the growing industries as 'new'. Moreover, the 'new' industries were still not important enough to dominate the economy. Hence, recovery must have depended on 'old' industries unless it can be proven that the 'new' industries were a 'development bloc' of high productivity industries which were connected to each other but not to the 'old' industries like steel and engineering. Obviously, this was not the case.

But most important, if recovery was *caused* by structural changes in the economy, those changes would have to have been particularly rapid in the 1930s. Growth between 1932 and 1938 was very fast but this was because the period started with a depression. If we compare 1924 with 1929 and 1929 with 1937, which were years of comparable unemployment rates, we find that there was no difference in growth rates in the two periods. The economy seems to have been modernizing in the 1920s at roughly the same rate as it was in the 1930s. In other words, Richardson failed to establish that there was an increase in the *trend* growth in the 1930s on which his argument depended.

Plate 11.1. Testing radios at the Gramophone Company, Hayes, in the 1930s. New consumer goods industries such as radio manufacture were stimulated by the rise in real earnings and hire-purchase. The location of these industries near the growing consumer markets of the South and Midlands did little to ease the economic problems of the depressed regions.

The Real Wage Debate

The debate about the causes of unemployment in 1929–32 has been a fundamental one. The main reason for this interest is, of course, the light that can be shed on controversies about *current* government policy. This was shown very clearly by the different contributions to a study of the depression commissioned by the Bank of England.[5] Capie *et al.* argued that the course of the depression followed the course of real wages. Real wages rose from 1929 to 1932 and then fell. This is not surprising because prices fell in the depression, and if money wages did not fall in line, the real wage would rise. If the price of products fell more than wages, businesses would go bankrupt. (Foreign prices fell by more than British ones which explains why the problem was more serious in the export industries.) Hence, the reaction to rising real wages was to dismiss workers, i.e. relatively high wages caused the unemployment. According to Capie *et al.*, after 1932, when prices increased, real wages were declining (or possibly static). Hence, profits rose leading to higher investment, falling unemployment, and economic recovery.

Unfortunately, we do not have a good series which shows the actual prices of British manufactures. This is not the same as the Retail Price Index, of course, since the latter includes imports. Hence, there has been room for disagreement on the course of wage costs. Dimsdale, by using a different series was able to argue that real wages were high until 1933–34 and began to fall too late to have been the cause of the turnaround in the economy. Hence, demand factors must have been important.[6] The implication is that if the main cause of unemployment was demand deficiency then the government may be blamed for not expanding the economy. If, on the other hand, the problem was that wages were too high relative to profits then government policy was correct. It would be fair to say, however, that most economists at the moment would favour a real wage explanation.

Would Keynesian Policy have Pulled Britain out of the Depression of the 1930s?

Latter day Keynesian economists and historians have not been inhibited by the passage of time from castigating the government for failing to stimulate demand in the 1930s. A recent recalculation of the 'constant-employment' budget by Middleton has shown that it was in surplus and therefore deflationary for every year from 1929–30 until 1936–37. The first important deficit was only in 1938–39 when rearmament was making a substantial contribution to economic growth.[7] (The device of a 'constant-employment' budget has to be used because, in a depression, tax revenues tend to fall faster than a government can reduce its expenditure. We would *expect*, therefore, that the budget would be in deficit. The 'constant-employment' budget recalculates the budget to take account of this tendency.)

As was pointed out above, the contribution to economic recovery of a budget deficit depends on the nature of the problem. A deficit budget to stimulate demand would only have solved the problem of demand deficiency in Britain, and could not solve that part of the problem caused by high British costs, nor could it increase demand for British exports in other countries. Even if the policy was correctly targeted, the effect of a budget deficit on output would depend on some technical considerations, including the size of the multiplier. The usual estimate is that the multiplier in the 1930s was between 1.25 and 1.5; hence, an increase in government spending of £100 million would increase output by £125–150 million and employment by about 350,000–400,000.[8] To put these figures into perspective, £100 million was about 2.25 per cent of GNP. To reduce unemployment from more than 3 million to less than 1 million (assuming, implausibly, that unemployment was all caused by demand deficiency) would have required the government to increase its expenditure by about £600 million. As a consequence of the rise in employment, tax revenues would have increased by about £300 million so the deficit would have been about £300 million, or about 7 per cent of GNP.

The success of an increase in public expenditure of this magnitude depends on its effect on two other variables – the balance of payments and interest rates. As we have seen, Britain was a more open economy than most others in the 1930s. At the same time most other countries were more depressed than Britain. If the British government had increased demand unilaterally, the balance of payments would have worsened probably to the extent of £30 for each £100 of government expenditure. Additional expenditure of £600 million would imply an increase in the balance of payments deficit of about £180 million or 4 per cent of GNP, an unsustainable amount and one that would have precipitated a balance of payments crisis. The other problem would have been the effect on interest rates. It is possible that even a modest budget deficit would have been difficult to finance – i.e. it would have required an increase in interest rates to encourage people to lend money to the government particularly if, as suggested above, there was an exchange rate risk. The question then would be how dependent was the recovery on low interest rates. This is controversial, but we do know, for example, that the housing boom which may have been responsible for a third of the new employment in the 1930s did depend on low interest rates to a considerable extent.

The question of the effectiveness of an expansionary fiscal policy is purely a theoretical one, of course. The *General Theory* was not written until Britain had recovered from the depression, but even if it had been, and even if the government had been converted to a large (planned) budget deficit, the success of 'Keynesian' policy would have been limited. Unemployment was high, but not all of the unemployment was 'Keynesian' – i.e. was caused by a lack of demand. A budget deficit could not have eradicated unemployment, and as we have seen, the costs of 'going for growth', as in the late 1980s, might have been very high.

Bibliographical Note

The best book on the international depression remains C. Kindleberger, *The World in Depression, 1929–1939* (London, 1973) but the argument is very compressed and it should be read only in conjunction with either G. Kenwood and A.L. Lougheed, *The Growth of the International Economy, 1820–1990* (London, 3rd edn, 1992) or J. Foreman-Peck, *A History of the World Economy. International Economic Relations since 1850* (Hassocks, 2nd edn, 1993). The latter is more sophisticated.

For the British economy in the 1930s, D.H. Aldcroft, *The British Economy. Volume 1, The Years of Turmoil, 1920–1951* (Hassocks, 1986) is a very clear, simple account while S. Glynn and J. Oxborrow, *Interwar Britain: a Social and Economic History* (London, 1976) also covers some of the social aspects of interwar unemployment. R. Floud and D. McCloskey (eds), *The Economic History of Britain since 1700, Volume II* (Cambridge, 1994) is the most up to date textbook. S. Glynn and A. Booth (eds), *The Road to Full Employment* (London, 1987) contains many useful thumb-nail sketches on different aspects of the economy in the period, including chapters by Capie on unemployment, and two by Hatton and Peden on Keynes. The best analysis of the 1930s depression and the recovery remains Bank of England, Panel of Academic Consultants, *The U.K. economy in the 1930s* (London, 1984). It is perfect if the reader has good economics, but is otherwise best avoided.

Two recent articles in *Refresh* are very useful. R. Middleton, 'The rise and fall of the managed economy', *Refresh*, 5 (1987), and B. Eichengreen, 'Unemployment in Inter-War Britain,' *Refresh*, 8 (1989).

Notes

1. Calculated from C.H. Feinstein, *Statistical Tables of National Income, Expenditure and Output of the UK., 1855–1965* (Cambridge, 1972) T55, T126.

2. F. Capie, *Depression and Protectionism in Britain between the Wars* (London, 1983).

3. H.W. Richardson, 'The basis of economic recovery in the 1930s', *Economic History Review*, vol. 15 (1962). The argument is developed at length in his *Economic Recovery in Britain, 1932–39* (London, 1967).

4. J. Dowie, 'Growth in the inter-war period: some more arithmetic', *Economic History Review*, vol. 21 (1968).

5. For example G.D.N. Worswick, 'The recovery in Britain in the 1930s and M. Beenstock, F. Capie and B. Griffiths, 'Economic recovery in the U.K. in the 1930s', *Bank of England Panel Paper,* no. 23 (1984).

6. N. Dimsdale, 'Employment and the real wage in the inter-war period', *National Institute Economic Review*, vol. 110 (1984).

7. R. Middleton, 'The constant employment budget and British budgetary policy, 1929–33', *Economic History Review*, vol. 34 (1981); M. Thomas 'Re-armament and economic recovery in the late 1930s', *Economic History Review*, vol. 36 (1983).

8. See T. Hatton, 'The outlines of a Keynesian solution' in S. Glynn and A. Booth (eds), *The Road to Full Employment* (London, 1987) pp. 82–94. pp. 89–90; W.R. Garside and T. Hatton, 'Keynesian policy and British unemployment problems in the 1930s', *Economic History Review*, vol. 38 (1985).

12 Unemployment and the Dole in Interwar Britain

Bernard Harris

For many people, the most powerful image of the 1920s and 1930s is still that of the dole queue. For eighteen years between 1921 and 1938 the official unemployment total never fell below one million, and the unofficial total was significantly higher. The social effects of unemployment were marked on the faces of unemployed people and their families and reported in a wide range of fictional, and documentary sources. The memory of these years helped to lay the foundations for the Labour Party's election victory of 1945 and it continues to play an important part in debates about the rise of mass unemployment in our own period. For all these reasons, the history of interwar unemployment remains one of the central topics of twentieth-century British economic and social history.

This chapter seeks to provide a general introduction to the social history of unemployment in the interwar period. The first section examines the numbers of people who were unemployed, the age, sex and social class of those who were most at risk, and the occupations and areas in which unemployment was greatest. Section 2 discusses the services which central and local government provided in order to protect unemployed people and their families against the consequences of being out of work. Section 3 discusses the efforts made by the voluntary sector to alleviate unemployment, and Section 4 examines the efforts made by unemployed people themselves to influence relief policy. Sections 5 and 6 discuss the impact of unemployment on the health and welfare of unemployed people and their families in the light of recent historiographical debates.

The Nature and Extent of Interwar Unemployment

Before we can examine the basic characteristics of Britain's interwar unemployment problem, we need to consider the sources from which most of the statistical information is derived. The most important sources of unemployment statistics were the official returns published by the Ministry of Labour in its monthly *Gazette*. These statistics recorded the total number of unemployed insured workers who registered for work at the employment exchanges. However, the statistics themselves need to be treated with a certain amount of care. In the first place, they represent the prevailing definition of unemployment, and may underestimate (or overestimate) the total number of people who might have been regarded as unemployed if other definitions had been applied. Secondly, the statistics were strongly influenced by changes in the unemployment insurance system which meant that people were more or less likely to register for work at the employment exchanges. Thirdly, the insurance system itself did not include all groups of workers, and the official unemployment statistics did not include uninsured workers who were also out of work. In 1972, Charles Feinstein estimated that the total number of unemployed workers would have been approximately 20 per cent greater if these workers had been included (see Table 12.1).

With these comments in mind, we can now proceed to sketch in the basic pattern of unemployment in the interwar period. As we can see from Table 12.1, the years between 1921 and 1938 were characterized both by an increase in the total volume of employment and by the persistence of high levels of unemployment. The total size of the employed workforce rose from 15.9 million in 1921 to 19.2 million in 1938. However the total number of people who were unemployed remained above one million throughout the whole of this period. The official unemployment statistics show that the number of people who registered for work at the employment exchanges fell from 1.8 million in 1921 to 1.1 million in 1927, before rising to 2.8 million in 1932 and falling to 1.5 million in 1937. Unemployment rose again in 1938 and only began to turn decisively downwards after the outbreak of the Second World War.

These figures provide only the basic outline of Britain's unemployment problem during the interwar years. In order to understand the impact of unemployment more fully, we need to examine its incidence by sex, age, class, occupation and region. One of the most important characteristics of unemployment was that the risk of unemployment did not affect all sections of the population equally. Men were more likely to be unemployed than women (although comparison is rendered difficult by changes in the unemployment insurance regulations), and older men were more likely to be unemployed than younger men. The risk of unemployment rose sharply between the ages of eighteen and twenty-four and among men over the age of fifty-five. In November 1932, 32 per cent of insured men aged sixty to sixty-four were registered as out-of-work.

The incidence of unemployment also varied according to social class. At the time of the 1931 census, workers in social classes I–IV (professionals and semi-professionals; employers and managers; clerical workers; foremen and supervisors) accounted for 25.07 per cent of the total workforce but only 8.34 per cent of the unemployed workforce. By contrast, workers in social classes

Table 12.1. British unemployment statistics, 1921–38

	Employed workforce	Insured workers		Total workers	
		Number unemployed	Unemployment rate	Number unemployed	Unemployment rate
	(1000s)	(1000s)	(%)	(1000s)	(%)
1921	15,879	1,840	17.0	2,212	12.2
1922	15,847	1,588	14.3	1,909	10.8
1923	16,068	1,304	11.7	1,567	8.9
1924	16,332	1,168	10.3	1,404	7.9
1925	16,531	1,297	11.3	1,559	8.6
1926	16,529	1,463	12.5	1,759	9.6
1927	17,060	1,142	9.7	1,373	7.4
1928	17,123	1,278	10.8	1,536	8.2
1929	17,392	1,250	10.4	1,503	8.0
1930	17,016	1,979	16.1	2,379	12.3
1931	16,554	2,705	21.3	3,252	16.4
1932	16,644	2,828	22.1	3,400	17.0
1933	17,018	2,567	19.9	3,087	15.4
1934	17,550	2,170	16.7	2,609	12.9
1935	17,890	2,027	15.5	2,437	12.0
1936	18,513	1,749	13.1	2,100	10.2
1937	19,196	1,482	10.8	1,776	8.5
1938	19,243	1,800	12.9	2,164	10.1

Notes: The figures in Column 1 represent Charles Feinstein's estimate of the total employed workforce. The figures in Columns 2 and 3 are derived from the Ministry of Labour's official unemployment returns. The figures in Columns 4 and 5 represent Feinstein's estimates of the incidence of unemployment among the workforce as a whole. Although not all workers were covered by the unemployment insurance scheme, the incidence of unemployment tended to be higher among those workers who were covered. Consequently Feinstein's figures show a higher incidence of unemployment but a lower unemployment rate than the official statistics.

Source: C.H. Feinstein, *Statistical Tables of National Income, Expenditure and Output of the United Kingdom, 1855–1965* (Cambridge, 1972) T128.

V–VII (skilled, semi-skilled and unskilled manual workers) accounted for 74.33 per cent of the total workforce and 91.66 per cent of the unemployed workforce. The incidence of unemployment among the first group of workers varied from 1.31 per cent in social class II (employers and managers) to 5.06 per cent in social class III (clerical workers). By contrast, the incidence of unemployment in social classes V–VII varied from 11.9 per cent among skilled and semi-skilled workers to 20.51 per cent of unskilled workers.

In addition to these figures, we can also examine the way in which unemployment varied across different industries and in different regions. For most of the interwar period, unemployment rates were at their highest in the old staple industries, which had provided the basis of Britain's industrial wealth in the nineteenth century, and at their lowest in the 'new' industries which had begun to develop after the end of the First World War. The average rate of unemployment in industries such as coal mining, shipbuilding and cotton-textiles exceeded 30 per cent during the first half of the 1930s, whereas unemployment rates in the newer industries, such as chemicals and electrical engineering, were well below 20 per cent. These differences were also reflected in regional unemployment rates. In 1932 the average rate of unemployment in the 'old' industrial regions of Wales, Scotland and the North of England was twice the level of unemployment rates in the 'new' industrial regions of the Midlands and South East.

One of the most important characteristics of unemployment was the length of time for which people remained out of work. During the interwar years many observers regarded the expansion of long-term unemployment as one of the most serious of all the social problems which unemployment raised. In 1944 Sir William Beveridge calculated that the percentage of unemployed workers who had been out of work for more than twelve months had risen from 4.7 per cent in September 1929 to 25 per cent in August 1936, and although recent scholars have criticized the details of Beveridge's analysis, his basic point still stands. In 1987 Nicholas Crafts calculated that the 'average interrupted spell length' of each unemployed worker (in other words, the length of time for which the average unemployment benefit claimant had been out of work) rose from 22.3 weeks in September 1929 to 40.2 weeks seven years later. The average interrupted spell lengths of unemployed workers in the depressed regions of Scotland and Wales were 58.34 weeks and 64.63 weeks respectively.[1]

Unemployment Relief Measures

Although interwar governments were well aware of the problems caused by unemployment, they possessed a very limited range of measures with which to deal with it. Most politicians adhered to the so-called 'Treasury view', which held that any attempt to intervene in the economy to boost the demand for labour would simply be counterproductive. Consequently, the government devoted most of its efforts to the administration of various forms of welfare provision which were designed to mitigate the social consequences of unemployment until economic conditions improved. The most important form of welfare service for the unemployed was the unemployment benefit system, but unemployed workers and their families also relied heavily on the Poor Law, the municipal welfare services, private charities, and more informal systems of family and community support.

The unemployment insurance system was introduced under Part II of the National Insurance Act of 1911. The original scheme was limited to approximately 2.25 million workers in a small number of specially-selected industries, and it made no provision either for the relief of long-term unemployment or for the relief of dependants. However the scheme was extended in 1920 and 1921, and by the end of 1921 it provided insurance against both short and long-term unemployment for approximately 11 million workers and their families. The expansion of the unemployment insurance scheme imposed a much greater burden on the 'Insurance Fund', and the government introduced a number of measures to restrict access to it. The most important restrictions were the 'genuinely-seeking-work test', which required the majority of claimants to prove that they were actively seeking work, and the means test, which was applied to all claims for long-term benefit between 1922 and 1924 and 1925 and 1928.

The government introduced a number of further changes to the unemployment insurance system at the beginning of the 1930s. In 1931 the newly formed National Government decided to impose a ten per cent cut on all benefit rates, and to introduce a new form of benefit, known as 'transitional payments', for all those who had been unemployed for more than six months. The introduction of the transitional payments scheme caused considerable hardship, because applicants for a transitional payment had to submit to a household means test, which meant that their entitlement to benefit was judged not only on the basis of their own income, but on that of other members of their family as well. The government restored the ten per cent cut in benefits in 1934, and the transitional payments scheme was replaced by unemployment assistance, but the household means test continued to play a central role in the administration of unemployment relief throughout the 1930s.

The second major form of state aid for the unemployed was the Poor Law. Historians have tended to pay comparatively little attention to the history of the Poor Law after 1914, but it continued to play a major role, particularly in the most depressed areas. The average number of unemployed workers claiming poor relief during the 1920s was rarely less than 100,000, and it reached a peak of 420,000 during the 1926 General Strike. The vast majority of these claimants were insured workers who had either exhausted their entitlement to unemployment benefit or who needed to have their benefit payments 'topped up', but between 10 and 20 per cent of claimants were not covered by the insurance scheme at all. The total number of people, including dependants, who relied on the Poor Law during periods of unemployment ranged between 200,000 and 1.5 million.

The government made a number of important changes to the administration of the Poor Law at the end of the 1920s, and poor relief was renamed public assistance, but the newly-formed Public Assistance Committees continued to play an important role in the support of unemployed people and their families. In addition to administering the transitional payments scheme, the Committees also dispensed other forms of relief to both insured and uninsured workers. In March 1934, the Public Assistance Committees were providing relief to 153,000 unemployed wage-earners, 96,000 of whom were also covered by the insurance scheme. It was only after the implementation of the 1934 Unemployment Act and the Unemployment Insurance (Agriculture) Act of 1936 that the Poor Law ceased to play any significant role in the provision of unemployment relief.

In addition to the provision of various forms of cash benefit, the government also provided a limited range of benefits through the municipal welfare services, including the maternity and child welfare service and the school meals service. The maternity and child welfare service was established at the end of the First World War, although similar services had been provided by voluntary agencies since 1907. In 1918 the government said that every local authority should endeavour to provide a maternity and child welfare centre and a health visiting service. By the 1930s the majority of local authorities were providing milk and other forms of nutritional supplementation for mothers and infants up to the age of one year, and many also provided milk for children up to the age of three. However, the level of provision varied considerably from area to area, and the service was often least well-developed in areas of greatest need. The main reason for this was that poorer areas found it more difficult to raise the money necessary to support welfare initiatives, but some Medical Officers of Health also objected to nutritional supplementation on ideological grounds.

The government also provided a limited amount of nutritional supplementation through the school meals service. This service was launched in 1906 in response to fears about possible 'physical deterioration' (see Chapter 5), and by 1914 more than 130 local education authorities were providing meals and over 420,000 children were receiving them. However, during the interwar years the government generally sought to discourage local authorities from incurring 'excessive' expenditure, and the number of children receiving meals rarely went above 200,000. During the first half of the 1930s, the Board of Education said that free meals should only be offered to children who were both poor and malnourished, and it was only later that these restrictions were relaxed. However the 1930s did see a considerable expansion in the number of children receiving free or subsidized milk. By the end of the decade virtually all local education authorities were providing milk and the number of children taking milk at school, which had been around 500,000 in 1929, stood at 2.63 million on the eve of the Second World War.

Voluntary Responses to Unemployment

Historians of social policy in the twentieth century have tended to devote most of their attention to the role played by the state in the provision of welfare services, but the voluntary sector continued to play an important role throughout this period. During the 1920s and 1930s voluntary organizations played a very important part in highlighting the social consequences of unemployment and in seeking to improve the condition of the unemployed. Their motives were often extremely complex, but their efforts provide an index of the extent to which unemployment pricked the social conscience of the nation and inspired it to help the unemployed in the interwar period.

The most obvious form of voluntary assistance was the cash appeal. During the 1920s and 1930s voluntary organizations launched a host of financial appeals to help unemployed people and their families. The majority of these appeals were locally-based, but there were also some notable national appeals. For example, in 1928 the Lord Mayors of London, Cardiff and Newcastle launched an appeal, with the active support of the national government, for the relief of women and children in the distressed mining areas of Durham and Northumberland and South Wales. The appeal funds were augmented by money from towns and villages in prosperous areas which had 'adopted' coal mining communities, and in November 1928 the government agreed to swell the coffers still further by 'donating' a pound for every pound raised by voluntary subscriptions.

In addition to these cash appeals, the voluntary sector was also involved in a campaign to establish educational 'settlements' and unemployed clubs in different parts of the country. Many of these initiatives were sponsored by the National Council of Social Service, often acting in conjunction with members of the Society of Friends, or Quakers. Between 1927 and 1939 the Society of Friends helped to establish nine educational settlements and 488 clubs and play centres in the mining villages of South Wales, and well over a thousand unemployed clubs were established in the country as a whole. The Society of Friends was also involved in a number of voluntary employment schemes, including a national allotment society, two 'subsistence production schemes', and a number of public works initiatives.

The reaction of unemployed people and their political representatives to these ventures was mixed. The unemployed clubs (or voluntary occupational centres) clearly provided a useful service to the men and women who chose to join them, but many unemployed workers believed that they were little more than a crude attempt at 'social control'. George Orwell thought that the clubs had 'a nasty YMCA atmosphere' about them, and Wal Hannington claimed that they were designed 'to deflect [the unemployed] ... from the course of struggle, lure them from the influence of militant organisations ... and ... guide them into a state of complacency'. However this view was not shared by all the unemployed, as an unemployed miner in the Rhondda valley pointed out in 1934:

We "Adopt" a South Wales Town

ONLY those who know South Wales can measure in their minds the full misery and piteousness of the plight into which so large a part of its population has fallen. Before the War 250,000 men and boys earned a fair livelihood by work in the collieries. The mining villages which occur at intervals up the narrow, deep valleys that corrugate the country sheltered a million people or more, thriving, intelligent, proud of their homes. The children were well clothed and sufficiently fed. Nothing could make the villages beautiful nor the hills above them from which trees had long since disappeared anything but bleak and bare. But the men and women, the boys and girls, supplied the charm which their surroundings lacked. They were bright-eyed, pleasant-featured; they sang divinely; they flocked to classes and lectures as well as to concerts. An air of prosperity was about them and in their homes.

This fortunate state continued until about 1921. Whether its break-up was due to our hasty return to the gold standard, which made it impossible for many of the foreigners buying coal from South Wales to buy it any longer, it is of small avail now to discuss. What we have to do is to find remedies or palliatives for the appalling unemployment which has dropped like a blight upon South Wales, not to choose this moment for fixing responsibility here or there. Between 1924 and 1926, before the Coal Strike, 40,000 colliery workers were turned off. During the last two and a half years nearly 50,000 more have lost their jobs. On the colliery owners' books at this moment there are 162,000 names in place of the quarter of a million employed not long ago.

Translate that statement into more vivid terms and what do we find its meaning to be? Allowing for the boys and unmarried men, it means that in 70,000 homes there is not enough to eat. It means that from most of those homes the children, if there are children, must go to school hungry. It means that as clothes wear out they cannot be replaced, that boots no longer serve to keep the wet out, that self-respect sinks in those who know they look shabbier every day. Large numbers of the miners who hang about wretchedly because " no man hath hired them " are not even getting unemployment benefit. The South Wales Miners Federation has taken a census among 50,000 of its members who are idle in certain districts: as many as 10,000 receive nothing from the State Insurance fund. They must rely on parish relief and on what is sent by kindly folk who feel for their distress.

Since the spring warnings have been heard from time to time of the increasing need for help, and help has been given. The Lord Mayor of London started a fund which has raised £100,000. The Daily Mail has started a fund and has raised a large sum of money to provide Christmas hampers. Other efforts have been made. But the misery is unabated, the piteousness of cold and hunger with disease close behind them is more poignant now that winter is here. " Save us or we perish " is the unuttered cry from those seventy thousand homes, and the Rural Deans of South Wales, pleading for those who are not able to plead for themselves, have appealed for aid in a new form. Taking a hint from the " adoption " by certain British towns of certain places in France and Belgium ravaged by the War, the Rural Deans ask if parishes in other parts of the country will not " adopt " parishes in South Wales. Not parishes alone may help in this way. Any society, any institution, any group of men and women, " with hearts at leisure from themselves to soothe and sympathize,"

can choose some particular place and do their best to lessen the unhappiness in it.

The plan is excellent. We are all readier to relieve special cases rather than general. If we can take a personal interest in those who receive our gifts, if we know just what is being done with our money, we are stimulated to give more than we should in the usual conditions. Very many, it is certain, are willing to do what they can if the opportunity is put in their way. We propose to put it in the way of those who read the *Spectator*. We ask them to " adopt " the town of Aberdare in South Wales. All the money they entrust to us will be at once applied to the relief of the most painful need. All the clothes they send will be instantly distributed among those who most require them. We shall tell them every week where their gifts go and how they diminish the suffering caused by this unexampled disaster.

Aberdare has been chosen at the request of the South Wales Miners Federation. It is a small town of some 50,000 inhabitants (the population was larger before the catastrophe befell Coal); and close on *half the insured workers living in it are unemployed*. The exact figure is 46 per cent.; there are only half-a-dozen places worse than this in the whole of the afflicted area, and Aberdare is worse off than most of these, seeing that a great many of its workers have been out of work through no fault of their own since 1921. The slump began there before it became general. When the coal trade is depressed everything suffers. As the writer of some striking articles on South Wales in the *Times* a few months ago put it, " when the pits are closed there is nothing to live for."

Face to face with a national crisis of this extent, we are bound every one of us to make what effort we can to soften the blows it inflicts on those of our fellow-subjects who are in the centre of the storm. These times are testing-times; they bid us show whether we do in truth feel that we are all members one of another, whether our talk of the solidarity of all classes and all sections of our British population is genuine or not. It was genuine during the War. What we must remember is that we are at war still, and with a more dangerous enemy that any arrayed against us fourteen years ago. If we display the same good comradeship now as we displayed then, the consequences may be far more lasting. We ask without hesitation, therefore, and with certainty that the response will be generous. Let us make sure that no one in Aberdare goes without a Christmas dinner, that no child reproaches

Santa Claus for not bringing a present, that the New Year comes in more brightly and hopefully for the help which we can give.

The *Spectator* opens the fund with a gift of £50. That will provide 400 food parcels for hungry families or 20●

Plate 12.1. 'Adopting a South Wales town'. The depth and duration of the unemployment problem prompted a wide range of philanthropic responses. *The Spectator*, a conservative weekly newspaper, appealed to its well-heeled readers to help unemployed Welsh miners.

In the beginning ... many people [thought] ... that the clubs were dope on the one hand and injurious to industry on the other, but neither is right. The clubs are really helpful. Where a man cannot afford to repair a chair, or boots, etc., at the clubs leather is supplied at cost price, tools are at his disposal, and friends ready to help him do the job.[2]

Unemployment and the Labour Movement

In contrast to the work of the voluntary organizations, the response of the labour movement and of unemployed workers themselves to unemployment has received a great deal of attention. However, although the image of the Hunger Marchers has left a powerful imprint on the popular memory of the 1930s, historians have disagreed over their actual impact. In 1982 Peter Kingsford wrote that 'the persistent protest, against all odds, of these ill-fed, ill-clad, ill-housed heroes – and heroines – of depression offers a sharp contrast with those shabby decades'. However other historians have tended to play down the impact of the Hunger Marchers, preferring instead to emphasize the relative passivity of the unemployed and their apparent unwillingness – in contrast to workers in other countries – to engage in political 'extremism'.[3]

Before we discuss the history of unemployed protest, it is necessary to look first at the part played by the official labour movement. It is well-known that the position of the Labour Party was strengthened enormously by the First World War, and in 1924 Labour formed its first minority government. However, in spite of this progress, Labour was able to make little impact on the problem of unemployment during the interwar years. There were two principal reasons for this failure. The first was that the Labour Party was unable to develop an independent economic policy, and it was therefore obliged to accept the largely passive role advocated by the Treasury. The second was that the party itself was fundamentally divided over the decision to reduce unemployment benefit rates in 1931, and this meant that it was confined to the political wilderness – at least in national terms – for the rest of the decade.

In the absence of effective parliamentary leadership, the responsibility for organizing protests against unemployment fell largely to extra-parliamentary bodies, of which the most important was the National Unemployed Workers Movement, whose leader, Wal Hannington, wrote a series of damning indictments of the government's policy on unemployment during the second half of the 1930s. Many historians have argued that the NUWM's effectiveness was blunted by its association with the Communist Party, but it organized a succession of marches and demonstrations against government policy, and these helped to ensure that unemployment remained at the forefront of national debate. The movement also set up a network of advice centres which

Plate 12.2. The unemployed lie down in Oxford Street, 1939. Unemployment touched 3.4 million in 1932 and there were still over 1.3 million people without work on the eve of the Second World War. Yet protests and hunger marches by the unemployed were muted even during the depths of the depression, and by 1939 they were little more than token activities.

informed workers of their benefit entitlements and helped them to obtain more generous payments.

Historians have been sharply divided in their assessment of the work of the NUWM. Some historians have argued that the movement's failure to launch a revolutionary campaign against capitalist society was symptomatic of its political impotence, but others argue that the NUWM displayed a realistic awareness of the limits of political possibility, and that it succeeded in winning a series of important concessions on questions of relief policy.[4] From this standpoint, the movement achieved its greatest triumph in the winter of 1934/35, when the government sought to impose uniform relief scales on the long-term unemployed. A series of demonstrations took place in all parts of the country, and the government was forced to delay the introduction of the new scales for a further eighteen months. This episode suggests that the maintenance of political stability during the interwar years rested on a rather more fragile basis than some historians have been inclined to suggest.

The Impact of Unemployment

Readers of this chapter in the 1990s may well be accustomed to the idea of mass unemployment as a normal feature of economic and social life, but many observers in the 1920s and 1930s regarded the high unemployment of their period as a new and rather frightening development. Their anxieties were reflected in a wide range of social investigations into the causes of poverty, the nature and consequences of unemployment and the condition of what Fenner Brockway called 'Hungry England'. These investigations did much to bring the plight of the unemployed to the attention of a wider contemporary audience, and they exercised a powerful influence on the campaign for social reconstruction which developed further during the Second World War.

For many contemporaries, the most obvious consequence of unemployment was poverty, but it is important to realize that unemployment did not necessarily lead to a loss of income. Many employees experienced low or intermittent wages, and for such people unemployment benefit might have the double advantage of being more substantial and more dependable than the income they derived from work. However, the majority of unemployed workers did suffer a drop in income, and the income they received often fell below the level which contemporary investigators regarded as necessary for the maintenance of basic needs. Under such circumstances, unemployed workers relied very heavily on their savings, on the money which they could borrow from their relatives and friends, on casual work, and, on occasion, from petty crime.

The close association between unemployment and poverty was reflected in a wide range of contemporary publications. Virtually all the interwar poverty surveys revealed that unemployment was a (if not the) major cause of poverty, and that the poverty experienced by unemployed workers was particularly severe. For example, in 1936 Seebohm Rowntree found that 86.4 per cent of the unemployed families in York were living below the poverty line, and that whilst unemployment accounted for 28 per cent of all the poverty in the city, it was responsible for 44.5 per cent of all the primary poverty. Rowntree also conducted a detailed investigation into the diets of unemployed families, and compared them with the diets of the population as a whole. His results suggested that unemployed people consumed a diet which was worse in all respects than the diets consumed by those in work.[5]

The revelation that so many unemployed people were living below the poverty line prompted an ongoing debate about the impact of unemployment on the nation's health. The government's Chief Medical Officer insisted that there was no clear evidence that unemployment had led to a deterioration in health standards, and that the health of the population as a whole had been well maintained. However many observers greeted these observations with profound disbelief. In 1936 Dr George M'Gonigle compared the death rates of two groups of employed and unemployed families in Stockton-on-Tees, and concluded that the death rates experienced by the unemployed families had been consistently higher over a four-year period. Other studies claimed that unemployment had led to a deterioration in the health of wives and mothers, and several observers claimed that there had been an increase in the incidence of children's diseases.[6]

The question of how far unemployment did lead to a deterioration in the health of unemployed people and their families has also generated a fierce debate among historians. In 1979 Jay Winter carried out a detailed study of changes in infant and maternal mortality rates, and concluded that 'it would be wrong to perpetuate the view that among the costs of the depression of the early 1930s was a deterioration in the health of women in childbirth and of their infants'. However this ostensibly 'optimistic' conclusion has been challenged on a number of occasions, and most recent studies have suggested that unemployment did have an adverse effect on health, even if this was not always reflected in the official statistics. In 1988 Bernard Harris suggested that unemployment may have had an adverse affect on children's growth rates, and Winter himself has argued that unemployment led to a reduction in the birth weights of the children and grandchildren of those who were born 'during the worst years of the depression'.[7]

In focus: Unemployment and Health: Child Health Statistics in the 1920s and 1930s

---

One of the most important of all aspects of the interwar unemployment debate concerned the impact of unemployment on the health of children.

Unemployment and Health: Child Health Statistics in the 1920s and 1930s (continued)

During the 1920s and 1930s the government used the statistics collected by School Medical Officers at their routine medical inspections to support the claim that the health and nutrition of the child population had been well maintained. However the government's opponents argued that these statistics were notoriously unreliable and that it was inconceivable that children could continue to flourish on an 'unemployment diet'. This controversy illustrates two issues which were central to the interwar unemployment debate: the limitations of scientific knowledge and the reluctance of central government to undertake the kind of research which might produce a more realistic assessment of child health.

The school medical service was established in England and Wales following the passage of the Education (Administrative Provisions) Act of 1907. The Act compelled local education authorities to make arrangements for the medical inspection of all elementary schoolchildren, and gave them the power to make arrangements for medical treatment. The government said that every child ought to be examined by a doctor on at least three occasions, and that the results should be published in the School Medical Officers' Annual Reports. By 1910 the vast majority of children were being examined at the ages of five and thirteen, and an increasing number were also being examined at the ages of seven or ten. In 1913 the government decided to amend the regulations and after the First World War all children were examined at the ages of five, eight and twelve.

Although the School Medical Officers were required to inspect for a wide range of medical conditions, the government attached particular importance to the assessment of nutrition. In 1911 the Chief Medical Officer of the Board of Education, Sir George Newman, declared in his *Annual Report* that 'defective nutrition stands in the forefront as the most important of all physical defects from which schoolchildren suffer', and these statistics played a vital role in the government's efforts to monitor the standard of child health during the 1920s and 1930s. In 1930 Newman wrote that the combined efforts of the state and voluntary agencies had 'more or less held in check any rapid deterioration in the physique of schoolchildren' in the most depressed areas, and that in the country as a whole 'the nutrition of schoolchildren appears to be on the upward grade'. In 1931 he concluded that 'the schoolchildren ... are better nourished than at any previous time of which we have record'. In 1932 he said that 'the depressed state of industry and the need for national economy [do] ... not appear to have exerted any measurable ... ill-effect upon the child population'. In 1933 he said that even though there had been a slight increase in the proportions of children who were recorded as suffering from malnutrition, 'these slight variations are not of significance[, and] they do not, in fact, imply any real increase in malnutrition'.

Unemployment and Health: Child Health Statistics in the 1920s and 1930s (continued)

The government's opponents made three major criticisms of the way in which the nutrition statistics were compiled and interpreted. In the first place, it was clear that many Medical Officers failed to use the standard classifications and that others interpreted the same categories in very different ways. For example, the School Medical Officers for Blackburn and Smethwick both classified children as either 'good', 'fairly good', or 'bad', but the School Medical Officer for Smethwick defined 'fairly good' as 'normal', and the School Medical Officer for Blackburn defined 'fairly good' as 'subnormal'. The second problem was that there was no obvious 'fit' between the classification of 'subnormal' and 'bad' nutrition and the identification of children who were suffering from malnutrition. In London, for example, 4.7 per cent of children were classified as having either 'subnormal' or 'bad' nutrition, but only 0.95 per cent were regarded as malnourished. The third problem was that the standards which were used to assess nutrition varied enormously from area to area. As Dr J.C. Spence observed in 1934:

> There are at present no definite standards or formulae by means of which the physique and state of nutrition can be estimated with mathematical accuracy. An expression of the incidence of poor physique must therefore be regarded as an opinion, the validity of which will vary with the experience of the observer and the methods which he uses.[8]

Many of the most serious defects in the school medical statistics were exposed by the wide variations which existed between the returns from different areas. It seemed common sense to expect that these returns should bear some relationship to the socio-economic characteristics of the areas in which the children lived, but many School Medical Officers reported that the incidence of malnutrition in apparently prosperous areas was greater than the incidence of malnutrition in much poorer areas. In 1931 the School Medical Officer for Bootle reported that the proportion of children suffering from 'malnutrition requiring treatment' was twelve times greater than the figure for Liverpool, and thirty times greater than the figure for Birkenhead. In comparable areas of Northumberland, the incidence of malnutrition varied from 0.54 per cent of the school population to 7.5 per cent, and the School Medical Officer for Twickenham reported that the incidence of malnutrition in his area was six times greater than the recorded incidence of malnutrition in Wigan. In 1933, 110 children were reported to be suffering from malnutrition in Cambridge, whereas the School Medical Officer for Gloucester reported a mere seventeen. The School Medical Officer for Ely reported that 6.03 per cent of children were suffering from malnutrition, whereas in Chesterfield only one child out of 8,988 was found to be malnourished.

Unemployment and Health: Child Health Statistics in the 1920s and 1930s (continued)

This brief examination of the history of the school nutrition statistics highlights one of the most important problems facing the student of interwar Britain. Throughout this period, the government assembled large amounts of data relating to mortality and, to a lesser extent, morbidity, but – as Richard Titmuss pointed out – these statistics revealed very little about the ordinary state of health of those who 'live[d] among these dying people'.[9] The most obvious source for this kind of information was the school medical service, but, as we have seen, the statistics collected by the school medical service were far too unreliable to provide more than the most general outline of the population's health and nutrition. By the end of the 1930s, even the Board of Education was forced to acknowledge the intrinsic defects of a system which it had spent more than thirty years trying to perfect. In 1940 the Board's Senior Medical Inspector, Dr J. Alison Glover, wrote:

> The [present] writer has tried to defend the method of clinical assessment on many occasions, and the obvious conclusion of this examination is painful to him, but it cannot be denied that a very large proportion of the [nutrition] returns are so unreliable as to be valueless for any purpose. 'A gem cannot be polished without friction, nor a method perfected without adversity.' Clinical assessment, however, as a method, has so many intrinsic flaws that with the friction of common use it flies to pieces.[10]

Unemployment and Mental Health

Although the main focus of debate has concentrated on the relationship between unemployment and physical health, contemporaries also expressed great concern over the relationship between unemployment and psychological health. In 1934 Maurice Robb argued that unemployment 'undermines the character of the affected individual, destroys the socialising influences of training, and alters his attitude to life', and James Halliday claimed that unemployment was directly associated with the onset of 'psychoneurotic' disease. Many interwar researchers believed that the psychological effects of unemployment could be described in terms of a 'transition' from optimism to pessimism to fatalism. In 1938 Philip Eisenberg and Paul Lazarsfeld wrote:

> We find that all writers who have described the course of unemployment seem to agree on the following points. First there is shock, which is followed by an active hunt for a job, during which the individual is still optimistic and unresigned; he still maintains an unbroken attitude. Second,

when all efforts fail, the individual becomes pessimistic, anxious, and suffers active distress; this is the most crucial state of all. And third, the individual becomes fatalistic and adapts himself to his new state but with a narrower scope. He now has a broken attitude.[11]

The 'stage theory' of unemployment has recently been criticized by Ross McKibbin on the grounds that it is excessively deterministic and takes insufficient account of individual circumstances, but there can be little doubt that unemployment was a powerful cause of psychological stress.[12] In addition to the strains which were directly associated with the loss of work, such as the destruction of an established time-structure and the loss of status and identity, unemployed people also had to cope with the problems caused by loss of income and the fear of the means test. So far as the majority of unemployed workers were concerned, it was perhaps the constant pressure of economic insecurity, rather than the loss of the 'satisfactions' associated with the loss of work, which was the most potent cause of mental anxiety. As one unemployed wood-carver wrote in 1934: 'The worry and misery of living on the dole make us low in spirits and depressed in health. We cannot shake off the general debility, the nervous irritation and bouts of indigestion and headaches, because the main cause – worry – cannot be removed'.[13]

Conclusion

The rise of mass unemployment after 1920 represented a profound challenge to Britain's established social and political order. The government responded to this challenge by introducing a number of major changes in social policy, of which the most important were the decisions to extend the unemployment insurance scheme and introduce new allowances for the relief of long-term unemployment and the unemployed worker's dependants. In addition to this, the government also encouraged voluntary organizations to launch charitable appeals and to establish a variety of social service schemes, including the occupational centre movement and the national allotments society. However, despite these efforts, it is difficult to reach any unequivocal conclusions about the impact of these measures on the welfare of unemployed people and their families. Stephen Constantine has argued that the unemployed workers of the 1920s and 1930s were better off than the unemployed (or even employed) workers of the 1870s and 1880s,[14] but they were less well off than the majority of employed workers, and their living standards fell well below the levels which had been promised to them at the end of the First World War.

From the point of view of many contemporary observers, as well as many historians, one of the most remarkable aspects of the interwar years was the fact that unemployment appeared to have so little impact on Britain's underlying political stability. In 1966 the sociologist W.G. Runciman sought to explain this development on the grounds that unemployed workers did not experience feelings of 'relative deprivation' when they compared their situation to that of their friends and neighbours.[15] However it is arguable that Runciman and his supporters may have overestimated the degree of stability and underestimated the part played by unemployed workers in determining benefit rates. In addition to organizing national protests, unemployed workers also campaigned on a local level to ensure that individual relief committees interpreted benefit regulations rather more flexibly than central government might have wished, and it was this, as much as anything else, which helped to protect the unemployed from the more extreme forms of hardship which they might otherwise have experienced.

Bibliographical Note

The rise of mass unemployment in interwar Britain has received a great deal of attention from historians and economists. The best general histories of the period are C.L. Mowat, *Britain between the Wars* (London, 1955); J. Stevenson and C. Cook, *The Slump: Society and Politics during the Depression* (London, 1977); and J. Stevenson, *British Society 1914–45* (Harmondsworth, 1984). There are useful overviews of the unemployment problem in S. Constantine, *Unemployment in Britain between the Wars* (London, 1980) and S. Glynn and A. Booth (eds), *The Road to Full Employment* (London, 1987). The history of social policy is discussed in M.A. Crowther, *British Social Policy 1914–39* (Basingstoke, 1988), and B. Gilbert, *British Social Policy 1914–39* (London, 1970). There is no full-length treatment of the role played by voluntary agencies, but the history of the National Unemployed Workers' Movement is examined in P. Kingsford, *The Hunger Marchers in Britain 1920–39* (London, 1982). The best starting-points for the debate over the social consequences of unemployment are J. Winter, 'Infant mortality, maternal mortality and public health in Britain in the 1930s', *Journal of European Economic History*, vol. 8 (1979), pp. 439–62, and C. Webster, 'Healthy or hungry 'thirties?'', *History Workshop Journal*, vol. 13 (1982), pp. 110–29. The interwar years also generated their own literature of social investigation. Two of the most famous studies of unemployment are Pilgrim Trust, *Men without Work* (Cambridge, 1938) and G. Orwell, *The Road to Wigan Pier* (London, 1937; repub. Harmondsworth, 1962). For fictional accounts of the impact of unemployment, see W. Greenwood, *Love on the Dole* (London, 1933; repub. Harmondsworth, 1969) and W. Brierley, *Means-test Man* (London, 1935; repub. London, 1983).

Notes

1. W. Beveridge, *Full Employment in a Free Society* (London, 1944) p. 64; N.F.R. Crafts, 'Long-term unemployment in Britain in the 1930s', *Economic History Review*, vol. 40 (1987), p. 420.

2. W. Hannington, *The Problem of the Distressed Areas* (London, 1937; repub. 1976) p. 197; G. Orwell, *The Road to Wigan Pier* (London, 1937; repub. 1962) p. 74; H.L. Beales and R.S. Lambert (eds), *Memoirs of the Unemployed* (London, 1934) p. 146.

3. P. Kingsford, *The Hunger Marchers in Britain 1920–39* (London, 1982) p. 7; W.G. Runciman, *Relative Deprivation and Social Justice: a Study of Attitudes to Social Inequality in Twentieth-Century England* (London, 1966); J. Stevenson and C. Cook, *The Slump: Society and Politics during the Depression* (London, 1977).

4. For contrasting views, see Stevenson and Cook, *The Slump,* pp. 145–94, and R. McKibbin, 'The social psychology of unemployment in interwar Britain', in R. McKibbin, *Ideologies of Class* (Oxford, 1991) pp. 228–58.

5. B.S. Rowntree, *Poverty and Progress: a Second Social Survey of York* (London 1941) pp. 110, 150, 182–5.

6. G.C.M. M'Gonigle and J. Kirby, *Poverty and Public Health* (London, 1936) pp. 264–75; B. Harris, 'Unemployment, insurance and health in interwar Britain', in B. Eichengreen and T. Hatton (eds), *Interwar Unemployment in International Perspective* (Dordrecht, 1988) pp. 149–83.

7. J. Winter, 'Infant mortality, maternal mortality and public health in Britain in the 1930s', *Journal of European Economic History,* vol. 8 (1979), p. 440; M. Mitchell, 'The effects of unemployment on the social conditions of women and children in the 1930s', *History Workshop Journal,* vol. 19 (1985), pp. 105–27; N. Whiteside, 'Counting the cost: sickness and disability among working people in an era of industrial recession 1920–39', *Economic History Review,* vol. 40 (1987), pp. 665–82; B. Harris, 'The height of schoolchildren in Britain 1900–50', in J. Komlos (ed.), *The Standard of Living and Economic Development: Essays in Anthropometric History* (Chicago, 1994); C. Webster, 'Healthy or hungry 'thirties?'', *History Workshop Journal,* vol. 13 (1982), p. 125; J. Winter, 'Unemployment, nutrition and infant mortality in Britain 1920–50', in J. Winter (ed.), *The Working Class in Modern British History: Essays in Honour of Henry Pelling* (Cambridge, 1983) p. 254.

8. J.C. Spence, *Investigation into the Health and Nutrition of Certain of the Children of Newcastle-upon-Tyne between the Ages of One and Four* (Newcastle-upon-Tyne, 1934) p. 16.

9. R.M. Titmuss, *Poverty and Population: a Factual Study of Contemporary Social Waste* (London, 1938) p. 309.

10. Public Record Office, ED50/204, *Nutrition: Improvement and Assessment.*

11. M. Robb, 'The psychology of the unemployed from the medical point of view', in Beales and Lambert (eds), *Memoirs of the Unemployed,* pp. 271–87; J.L. Halliday, 'Psychoneurosis as a cause of incapacity among insured persons', *Supplement to the British Medical Journal,* 9 March 1935, pp. 85–8 and 16 March 1935, pp. 99–102; P. Eisenberg and P. Lazarsfeld, 'The psychological effects of unemployment', *Psychological Bulletin,* vol. 35 (1938), p. 377.

12. R. McKibbin, 'The social psychology of unemployment'.

13. Beales and Lambert (eds), *Memoirs of the Unemployed,* p. 117. See also *ibid,* p. 141. For a thinly-disguised 'fictional' account, see W. Brierley, *Means-test Man* (London, 1935; repub. 1983).

14. S. Constantine, *Unemployment in Britain between the Wars* (London, 1980) p. 30.

15. Runciman, *Relative Deprivation and Social Justice,* pp. 55–77.

13 Attitudes to War: Pacifism and Collective Security

Martin Ceadel

Introduction

The British public first became seriously concerned about war prevention in the interwar period. During the 1920s it developed doubts about the methods and results of the First World War, became concerned that new technology (in the form of chemical warfare and military aviation) would make another such war even more destructive, and tried to convince itself that the League of Nations (the pioneering international organization created at the Paris Peace Conference of 1919) could resolve international disputes and bring about multilateral reduction of armaments. By the end of that decade the policy favoured by the government (as in most countries) of seeking to assure national security by maintaining strong armaments and possibly also alliances – 'defencism' as I shall call it[1] – was harder to justify than at any time in modern British history; and the peace movement – those people and organizations promoting alternatives to defencism – grew to an unprecedented size. During the 1930s, however, as the prospects for disarmament faded when Japan, Italy, and Germany demanded territorial and other concessions, the British public had to decide whether the interests of peace were better preserved by a policy of containment or by one of accommodation. The peace movement received even more attention than ever, but lost its fair-weather supporters, and, like public opinion generally, became divided on the merits of collective security. Most people initially favoured making some concessions to Hitler; but his demands were such that by September 1939 there was a widespread acceptance that despite the risks he had to be stopped by force.

Pre-1914

Before the First World War Britain's insular position and comparatively strong navy had given it a degree of security which enabled it largely to ignore

Continental Europe (other than the Channel ports). This security had enabled it to escape both attack on its home territory and compulsory military service ('conscription'), and to direct its modest military resources primarily to the defence or extension of its empire, where wars were fought far from public scrutiny. This security had also permitted a peace movement to emerge sooner and on a less insignificant scale than in any country other than the even more secure United States: this was because in a relatively secure country it was possible to preach peace without seeming disloyal or defeatist. The other major factor explaining the comparative strength of the peace movement in Britain (and also the United States) was the strength of liberalism and Protestant Christianity within the political culture: these encouraged respectively a belief in the harmony of interests among different countries and a belief that foreign policy should serve moral ends. But British political culture also had a strong conservative strand, which insisted that defence of crown, country, and empire was a patriotic duty. Defencism thus remained the dominant ideology of international relations. Moreover, since Britain had only intermittent worries concerning possible attack from the Continent, the peace movement, though stronger than in other countries, was small by comparison with movements interested in domestic reforms; and there was little public interest – even in the weeks leading up to the First World War – in international affairs.

The Impact of 1914–18

Attitudes to War and International Affairs

It is indicative of Britain's strategic detachment and liberal-Protestant culture that the British government justified its intervention in the First World War in terms more of its moral obligations (its pledge to Belgium and its duty to destroy Prussianism in a war to end war) than of its vital interests (the Channel ports). The cohesion of British society was revealed in the way it responded to the call to arms with what now seems an astonishing idealism and national unity, and in the way – despite a marked war weariness after 1917 which must raise doubts about how long the war could have been sustained politically had Germany not collapsed when it did – it retained its will to win. Yet the experience changed Britain's international outlook in two fundamental ways: it exposed a significant number of its citizens to the realities of war for the first time; and it discredited the belief that the country could wholly detach itself from European quarrels. Not only did a British army fight in Europe for the first time since the Crimean War of 1854–56; it did so for more than four years, and experienced a war of attrition which was impossible to romanticize in the traditional manner. Moreover conscription was introduced in 1916, and in all 5.2 million men served in the army. In addition British civilians suffered direct attack by airships and the first generation of military aeroplanes: though casualties were few, the psychological shock was considerable. In all approximately 700,000 British soldiers and civilians – double the total of the Second World War – were killed. Even though conscription was ended in 1919, there was no possibility of Britain retreating into its former semi-isolationism. For one thing, it was permanently vulnerable to air attack from the Continent. For another, it was committed to maintaining the European territorial settlement decided at the Paris Peace Conference, and had further responsibilities as a member of the League of Nations. In addition, its imperial responsibilities were extended by its acquisition (nominally as 'mandates' of the League of Nations) of certain former German and Ottoman colonies.

The Peace Movement

The war also transformed the peace movement. The long-established prewar peace societies (the oldest of which dated from 1816) became moribund; and the initiative passed to five new societies which, founded amid the patriotic hysteria of the early phase of the war, were made of sterner stuff.

Two, both founded in the last two months of 1914, were pacifist in the strict sense in which the word will be used in this chapter: they opposed military force unconditionally. (Members of the peace movement who did not take this absolutist position – for example, because they supported collective security or people's wars – will here be called *pacificists*, as first suggested by the historian A.J.P. Taylor.)[2] One, catering primarily for the socialists of the Independent Labour Party, was founded in November 1914: it rejected all wars, but concentrated on the more limited aim of opposing conscription, and called itself the No-Conscription Fellowship. The other, consisting of devout Christians was set up the following month. Though avowedly pacifist, it called itself the Fellowship of Reconciliation (FoR) and mostly adopted a quietist approach. The existence of a small but determined core of pacifists was further demonstrated by the 16,500 conscientious objectors to conscription. Though comprising only 0.33 per cent of the total of conscripts plus volunteers, they had a public impact out of all proportion to their numbers. Since women were excused military service and could not be accused of cowardice, they were more free to campaign against the war. The most striking peace initiative during the First World War was the international congress of women at The Hague in neutral Holland in April 1915 organized by leading suffragists in Europe and the United States. It led in October 1915 to the creation of the Women's International League (WIL), though this was to have little influence – in large part because its attempt to combine both pacifists and *pacificists* in one organization restricted its ability to formulate clear policies.

The most influential societies were overtly *pacificist*, and called for reforms in the way international relations were to be conducted once the war was won. In September 1914 the Union of Democratic Control (UDC) was founded by radicals and socialists (including Ramsay MacDonald) who had felt Britain's involvement in the war to be unnecessary but who now argued merely that the postwar settlement should take account of the wishes of the people affected. Its semi-isolationist approach was largely adopted after 1917 by an increasingly war-weary Labour Party since it could unite the pro-war majority and anti-war minority. In May 1915 a League of Nations Society was launched to focus the efforts of the liberal intellectuals who had been insisting since the outbreak of the war on the need for an international organization. Though at first disparaged as 'pacifist', the League of Nations became respectable once the United States entered the war in April 1917 under a president, Woodrow Wilson, committed to the idea. Indeed a second society, the League of Free Nations Association, was founded by government supporters who hoped that the League might be a way of maintaining the economic and even military cooperation against Germany which the allies had built up during the war. With the war about to end the two League organizations merged in October 1918 as the League of Nations Union (LNU).

The First World War had thus forged a new peace movement which was both toughened by adversity and divided into a pacifist and a *pacificist* wing. The former, though tiny and unpopular, had shown what was later to be widely accepted as courage and sincerity. The latter, though divided between the sceptical radicalism of the UDC and the optimistic moderation of the LNU, had already begun to influence public discussion of foreign policy. Although victory produced an upsurge of patriotism which caused the defeat in the December 1918 General Election of most candidates perceived as holding anti-war views, foundations had been laid for increased peace activism in the postwar period.

Postwar Disenchantment

In contrast to the considerable attention devoted to the soldier poets writing during the war itself, the reaction against the First World War which occurred during the 1920s has yet to be comprehensively studied, particularly from the perspective of the social or cultural historian. It will here be suggested that this reaction had two aspects, concerned respectively with the fighting itself and the fruits of victory.

Despite official censorship (which caused an early postwar novelist to complain that before the armistice the 'blue pencil of the censor was too busy to allow a realist ... a chance of exposing the Truth'),[3] the self-censorship of a press keen to project an idealized version of the war, and the difficulties faced by many soldiers in communicating their alienating experience to civilians, it was not possible to prevent knowledge of the true conditions at the Front being widely diffused during the war itself. Indeed as the right-wing critic Douglas Jerrold pointed out at the height of the war-books controversy in 1930, the idea that it was works like Erich Maria Remarque's *All Quiet on the*

Western Front (1929) which turned the public against the idea of war ignored the fact that millions of people had experienced the war personally and many more had been told about it by members of their family: 'and if their own experiences or the experience of their relatives did not "turn them" effectively against the "idea of war", Mr Remarque's book is unlikely to have done so'.[4] Moreover, the soldier poets produced what is now regarded as the definitive interpretation of the human experience of trench warfare, even if some of it was not yet published and what was reached only a small literary circle. Novels about the war were published in large numbers: seven in 1914, twenty-five in 1915, forty-three in 1916, forty-six in 1917, and fifty-one in 1918. Although most romanticized the war, not all did so: in particular, Henri Barbusse's *Under Fire* (1917), a translation of the novel published in Paris the previous year as *Le Feu*, was in many respects the prototype of the 'realistic' trench novel, even though the *Times Literary Supplement* (*TLS*) managed to make it sound like cheery propaganda. ('A very full, vivacious picture of the French soldier as he appears in his various types to one who associates intimately with him in his military service.') And, as the poet Edmund Blunden later noted, from 1917 there was a markedly more critical spirit in wartime literature.[5]

In the immediate postwar years the public was provided with many official reminders of the casualties the war had involved: a Peace Day was celebrated on 19 July 1919 at a temporary Cenotaph in Whitehall; Armistice Day with its emotive two-minute silence became an annual event from November 1919 onwards; the Unknown Soldier was entombed in the permanent Cenotaph in 1921; and war memorials listing the local dead were constructed all over the country. Numerous war books of all kinds were published: forty works of fiction appeared in 1919, which explains why a reviewer of A.P. Herbert's novel about Gallipoli and the Western Front, *The Secret Battle*, which appeared in April 1919, commented wearily on 'the stream of war chronicles that has been poured out during recent years'. Thereafter the number declined: thirteen novels appeared in 1920, and seven in 1921; and when Patrick Macgill's novel *Fear* (1921) was published, it was received with the comment that it 'comes a little late in the day. There have been so many war books'. As we shall see in our case study on war literature, these early novels sold badly enough to convince publishers that the war had become an unpopular subject. But, as the critic and historian Cyril Falls was to point out in 1924, this 'unpopularity does not, it would appear, extend to war-history'; and another of Douglas Jerrold's complaints about the claims made for the war books of the late 1920s was that they overlooked 'those scores and scores of earlier books of history, reminiscence and adventure which for the first eight years of peace followed each other in such an unending stream'.[6] Even allowing for a degree of sanitization in these accounts, it can be assumed that knowledge of the war's military realities was continuing to spread.

Yet it is clear that for the most part the British public did not yet wish to translate this knowledge into a moral or political judgement about the war,

Plate 13.1. Lutyens's temporary cenotaph. In 1919 many official memorials to the war dead were erected throughout the country, and Armistice Day became an occasion of national remembrance. It was not until the later 1920s that a more critical discussion of the purpose, conduct and outcome of the war gained public acceptance.

preferring in so far as it could to indulge the escapist pleasures for which the postwar years were to become known. As the critic Desmond MacCarthy later noted: 'men can only bear to examine painful events which have receded a little into the past, and there is a natural unwillingness to disparage military glory while bereavement is fresh'.[7] Jerrold believed that an additional factor was the 'silly illusion of inferiority' felt by those either too old or too young to have fought, which made them avoid the subject. What brought about disenchantment was thus not new knowledge about the way the war had been fought. Moreover, the passing of time was a necessary but not a sufficient condition, since there was to be no equivalent reaction a decade after the Second World War. The crucial factor was a loss of confidence in the war's promised benefits. The UDC and the Labour Party had insisted from the start that the international fruits of victory were being squandered: they criticized the Treaty of Versailles (the settlement imposed on Germany in 1919) as too punitive, the League of Nations as too much a league of victor governments as distinct from a league of all peoples, and France in particular as too vindictive towards Germany. Their semi-isolationist critique attracted more widespread support as economic depression began at home in 1921, undermining wartime promises of a land fit for heroes, and as a crisis arose in Europe as a result of Germany's reluctance to pay 'reparations' to its former enemies. The economist John Maynard Keynes, who had criticized the Treaty of Versailles in a controversial book, *The Economic Consequences of the Peace* (1919), noted in a sequel written late in 1921 an 'immense change in public sentiment over the past two years. The desire for a quiet life, for reduced commitments, for comfortable terms with our neighbours is now paramount'.[8] An early, though small symptom of this change of mood was the decision of the No-Conscription Fellowship, the one peace society to have wound itself up at the end of the war, to reconstitute itself in February 1921 under the name No More War Movement (NMWM). Another, more significant one was the moderate success in 1922 of C.E. Montague's *Disenchantment*, an elegant and restrained description of how the extraordinary idealism of the volunteers of 1914 had been undermined by the wartime deficiencies of their leaders and by the Treaty of Versailles, thanks to which 'the garland of the war was withered before it was gained'.

A further sign of diminished belief in the results of the war was that to have opposed it ceased from 1922 to be a political liability. The first former conscientious objector to win election to Parliament, Morgan Jones, did so at a by-election in August 1922; Ramsay MacDonald, who had been defeated by a war hero in a by-election only the previous year, not only returned to Parliament at the November 1922 Election but became leader of the Labour Party; and in January 1924, when MacDonald became the first Labour Prime Minister, nine UDC members sat in the Cabinet with a further six as junior ministers. In addition, the international tension of the early 1920s (and the fact that France began building a large air force) encouraged alarmist speculations about future war. In 1923, for example, a leading military writer,

Major-General J.F.C. Fuller, who believed that air power might humanize war by the use of non-lethal gas, could write in all apparent seriousness:

> I believe that, in future warfare, great cities such as London, will be attacked from the air, and that a fleet of 500 aeroplanes, each carrying 500 ten pound bombs of, let us suppose, mustard gas, might cause 200,000 minor casualties and throw the whole city into panic within half an hour of their arrival. Picture, if you can, what the result will be: London for several days will be one vast raving Bedlam, the hospitals will be stormed, the traffic will cease, the homeless will shriek for help, the city will be in pandaemonium. What of the government at Westminster? It will be swept away by an avalanche of terror. Then will the enemy dictate his terms, which will be grasped at like straw by a drowning man. Thus may the war be won in forty-eight hours and the losses on the winning side may be actually nil![9]

From the summer of 1924, however, when France had made a concession over reparations by agreeing to the Dawes Plan, the international situation seemed somewhat to improve. The Locarno Treaties were signed in 1925, inaugurating a period of seemingly better Franco-German relations; international trade grew; preparations began to be made for a World Disarmament Conference; and the signatories of the Kellogg-Briand Pact of August 1928 renounced aggressive war. These events raised public confidence in the League of Nations. Since the LNU's policy now seemed more constructive than that of the UDC, which went into rapid decline, it grew rapidly under the leadership of Viscount Cecil of Chelwood, who (as Lord Robert Cecil) had been one of the principal architects of the League's Covenant in 1919 and who resigned from the Conservative Cabinet in 1927 because it was insufficiently committed to disarmament. The Labour Party adapted to the new mood. Although at its 1926 conference it had, from a mixture of pacifist and anti-capitalist motives (the latter strengthened by that year's general strike), carried by acclamation a resolution rejecting all war (including one in support of the League), it was thereafter induced by Arthur Henderson to drop its former scepticism about the League and the attainability of disarmament. Indeed so popular had these causes become that by the time of the May 1929 General Election Conservative politicians found it prudent to conceal their own doubts regarding their prospects of success.

The apparent improvements in the international situation did not dissipate the mood of disenchantment, however. Indeed to some extent they made it worse. They raised hopes which were soon dashed, the contrast between the pretensions of the Kellogg-Briand Pact and the continuing reality of international politics giving particular scope for cynicism. And in one respect they raised the level of anxiety: in order to stimulate public support for the abolition of military aviation at the World Disarmament Conference peace campaigners painted alarmist pictures of aeroplanes wiping out whole populations with gas bombs which lent credence to the developing genre of popular fiction which dealt with this theme. In addition, international progress was not matched by equivalent improvements in domestic conditions where unemployment and industrial conflict persisted. The importance of domestic discontents should not be exaggerated, however: in particular it should be noted that the spate of war books began almost exactly a year in advance of the Wall Street Crash of November 1929.

In focus: The War Books of 1928–30

Most previous serious novels, diaries, and memoirs about the war had been commercial failures even when well reviewed: A.P Herbert later described the 1919 edition of *The Secret Battle* as a 'flop d'estime'; and Winston Churchill acknowledged in the preface to a more successful reissue in 1928 that it had been 'at that time a little swept aside by the revulsion of the public mind from anything to do with the awful period just ended'. By the standards of some later books these works were fairly restrained. The *TLS* noted approvingly that Herbert, whose hero cracks under the strain of prolonged war service and is shot for cowardice, 'expressly states that he is not attempting to indict a system', and that in *Fear* Patrick Macgill – whose publisher had boasted of the 'terrible picture' which it presented – 'does not seek the squalid for its own sake, nor is he too "powerful" '. Similarly Frank Gray's autobiographical *The Confessions of a Private* (1920), though denouncing the inefficiencies, squalor and inequalities of army life, lauded the ordinary soldier and never questioned the value of the war itself. Nonetheless such books may have been too unsettling for public taste since they did markedly less well than the former military padre Ernest Raymond's *Tell England: a Study in a Generation* (1922), which ran through twenty-two impressions in two years. Though its second half dealt with Gallipoli, its first half was a conventional public-school yarn; and it was marketed, appropriately, as 'A Great Romance of Glorious Youth'. Publishers steadily reduced their output of war novels: only six came out in 1922, three in 1923, and two in 1924.

The difficulties faced by serious writers in the mid 1920s can be illustrated by considering the efforts of the pacifist writer Max Plowman to publish a memoir of trench life. Douglas Jerrold later blamed 'the literary cliques who make the market in books' for the neglect of war literature at this time; and it is true that when Plowman first approached publishers in the spring of 1924 they had seemingly made their minds up in advance. Alec Waugh of Chapman and Hall replied that 'good though this is, I do not believe we could at this late day sell it ... I feel almost certain it would be a loss'. H.R. Wakefield of Collins reported that previous experience suggested that 'such books were no use for the big London book-shops and the libraries, and that its sale was almost entirely made by the private soldier, who was interested to

The War Books of 1928–30 (continued)

remember, while the officer was only interested in forgetting'. Jonathan Cape also turned it down, albeit with the prescient comment that he did not believe 'that War Books are finished with' and expected a 'big book about the war' to present itself 'maybe after ten years'. Plowman's text remained unpublished until the autumn of 1927 when J.M. Dent published it as *A Subaltern on the Somme* by 'Mark VII' – a pseudonym adopted to avoid libel.

Though its early sales were modest, the fact it had appeared at all was nonetheless an early sign of increasing interest in war literature. Plowman's publisher had commented on accepting his manuscript that he had simultaneously been offered a similar work and that this 'shows which way the wind blows'; and one of his reviewers noted: 'Books about the war are multiplying fast, and some of those recently published are exceedingly good'. The number of war novels published had increased to seven in each of 1925 and 1926 and to eight in 1927. There was also a sign that criticisms of the war were becoming more outspoken: for example, Hugh Quigley's *Passchendaele and the Somme*, published in February 1928 and purporting to be an essentially unaltered war diary composed in 1917, claimed bitterly that 'if every one could visualize always this horror and know its human application, war would absolutely cease, and our ruddy generals find a new occupation other than that of spreading an aureole round hell ... War remains at best a nauseating blasphemy'.[10]

In the autumn of 1928 war literature began to make a significant impact. The tenth anniversary of the armistice was an apt time for the war generation to take stock. And by then, as the trade journal *Publisher and Bookseller* also pointed out, there was a younger generation curious to learn about the war. The first of the successful war books was an elegantly understated memoir by Edmund Blunden, *Undertones of War*, which appeared in November 1928: written four years earlier, it had, as Blunden later recalled, been accepted by a publisher who

> ran into some trouble as he tried to get the book into circulation; but as it happened the period of unpopularity of books about World War 1 was ending – a period which has shed oblivion more or less over many admirable personal studies of experience such as the recent renewal of interest in that war may bring to light.[11]

December 1928 saw the first production of R.C. Sheriff's play *Journey's End* (with Laurence Olivier in the lead). Victor Gollancz at once snapped up the text for publication; and the following month the play moved to the Savoy Theatre where it ran for 594 consecutive performances. And – showing that the change in public taste was not confined to Britain – in January 1929 Erich Maria Remarque's *All Quiet on the Western Front* was published in book

The War Books of 1928–30 (continued)

form in Germany, having been serialized in a newspaper from 10 November to 9 December 1928: an English edition followed in March 1929.

These books sold well: the *Publisher and Bookseller* announced at the end of 1929 that 'Sheriff's *Journey's End* was easily the most popular book throughout the year'; and, despite a 'constant preoccupation with bodily functions' which according to the *TLS* distinguished it from its English equivalents, Remarque's English edition sold 300,000 copies in six months. These successes created a breakthrough which was soon exploited by a second wave of war books published in 1929–30: whereas ten novels had been published in 1928, twenty-five appeared in 1929, and thirty-six in 1930. A few of these second-wave works had been in the pipeline. Richard Aldington, who had made three abortive attempts – in 1919, 1925 and 1927 – to write *Death of a Hero* had begun his final and successful attempt in October 1928: he later admitted that it 'was lucky that I didn't get it done sooner, for the book eventually came out as the boom in war books was in full swing'.[12] Henry Williamson suspended the writing of *The Patriot's Progress* (1930) out of irritation at what he considered Remarque's undeserved success, and thus missed the height of the boom. Many, however, were specially written to meet the need, artlessly identified in an advertisement in the *Publisher and Bookseller* as early as 31 May 1929: 'Undoubtedly the best sellers of recent months have been books about the war: there is a public for them and the demand has not been satisfied'. Reviewers eventually complained of 'so many narratives hastily spewed up to the plaudits of their publishers'; and in a bibliography of the genre published in 1930 Cyril Falls repeated the 'common gossip that several writers sat down to produce one in the same vein after watching Herr Remarque's sales go soaring up into the hundred-thousands'.[13] Robert Graves admitted that money was a motive in writing *Goodbye To All That* in 1929; and 'Private 19022' (Frederic Manning) dedicated *Her Privates We* (1930) to his publisher 'who made me write it'. The genre started to become inbred: 'Ex-Private X' admitted in his memoir *War is War* (1930) to having seen *Journey's End* nine times; Evadne Price's *Not So Quiet: Stepdaughters of War* (1930), written under the name Helen Zenna Smith, was a feminist response to Remarque's novel; Charles Edmonds' *A Subaltern's War* (1929), based on drafts written in 1919–20, was a revisionist protest against the 'acidulated Radicals' who had produced much recent war literature; and in Noel Coward's play *Post-Mortem*, written late in 1930, war literature became part of the story: the hero, killed in action in 1917, returns as a ghost thirteen years later to test whether the war had secured the expected results and finds the war-books controversy, which a friend had predicted in 1917, in full swing. Other prominent books published in 1929–30 included Siegfried Sassoon's *Memoirs of an Infantry Officer*, R.C. Sheriff and Vernon Bartlett, *Journey's End: the Novel*, Brigadier-General F.P. Crozier's *A Brass Hat in No Man's Land*, and two American books: James B. Wharton's

The War Books of 1928–30 (continued)

Squad and Ernest Hemingway's *A Farewell to Arms.* This second wave also reached the cinema where its impact was increased by the introduction of sound: in 1930, films of *All Quiet on the Western Front* and *Journey's End* were released, as well as other realistic war films such as the German director G.W. Pabst's *Westfront 1918.* The cumulative effect of this output can best be judged from the description by the humourist A.G. Macdonell. Assuring his readers that his own volume *England, Their England* (1933) was – despite a first chapter set in the trenches – not a war book, he promised:

> From Chapter II to the end there will be no terrific description of the effect of a chlorine-gas cloud upon a party of nuns in a bombarded nunnery, or pages and pages about the torturing remorse of the sensitive young subaltern who has broken his word to his father, the grey-haired old vicar, by spending a night with a mademoiselle from Armentières. There will be no streams of consciousness, chapters long, in the best style of Bloomsbury, describing minutely the sensations of a man who has been caught in a heavy-howitzer barrage while taking a nap in the local mortuary. There are going to be no profound moralizings on the inscrutability of a Divine Omnipotence which creates the gillyflower and the saw-bayonet ... And, finally, there are going to be no long passages in exquisite cadences and rhythms, shoved in just to show that I am just as good as Ruskin or any of them, about the quietness of life in billets in comparison with life during a trench-mortar bombardment ....

By the spring of 1930, when the second wave began to saturate its market, war literature had become the subject of public controversy. Often the complaint was aesthetic, the genre's opponents questioning whether authenticity justified the detailed descriptions of the horrors and human frailties of trench life which many authors produced. *The Times* complained: 'All the ingredients go in – mud, oaths, explosions, blasphemy, injustice, cowardice, drink, physical horrors, sex, introspection, insanity'. And the *TLS* wondered: 'What great ideal is served by minute descriptions of latrines, the equivalents of which in peace-time conditions do not yet appear to have attracted the attentions of the strongest realists? Is there anything in them to make the world safe for peace and democracy? Is it probable that bad language will strengthen the League of Nations?'[14] Some reviewers suggested that the 'sensation and alleged indecencies' to be found in many war books were an essential part of their commercial appeal.

At other times the charge was of libelling the combatants of 1914–18. There was, however, less nationalist outrage than in Germany, where Nazi-inspired riots led to the temporary banning of the film of *All Quiet on the Western Front* in December 1930. The complaints made in Britain often

The War Books of 1928–30 (continued)

reflected the social anxieties of the upper and middle classes. The latter were reassured by, for example, Raymond Asquith's 1930 film version of *Tell England*: though more anti-war in tone than the novel on which it was based, its favourable presentation of the public-school heroes 'vindicated ... their dominant role in society', in the words of a film historian, and also portrayed the working classes as 'cheerful, illiterate, dialect-speaking cannon fodder'.[15] But they were particularly upset by the otherwise decorous *Journey's End*, as the correspondence columns of *The Times* revealed, because it imputed drunkenness to the officer class. And they often also disliked works emphasizing the unrespectable behaviour of some ordinary soldiers because it revealed an ambiguity in their own attitude to the working class. As the literary critic A.C. Ward described it:

> Bill Walker in May 1914 was a 'street-corner hooligan'; Bill Walker in December 1914 was a 'beloved Tommy'; Bill Walker in May 1919 was a 'loafer on the dole'. If in May 1929 a fellow-soldier wrote a novel in which Bill Walker appears as a liar, a thief, a boozer, a foul-mouthed adulterer, and yet also a brave fighter who never got cold feet, the novelist would be accused of libelling the British soldier.

The truth, Ward insisted, was that 'Bill Walker in the army was the same as Bill Walker out of the army, with such intensification or modification of his natural tendencies as the circumstances allowed or impelled', and that the war books merely recognized this.[16]

The most serious complaint against the genre was that, by concentrating on war from the perspective of the individual combatant, it ignored the overall geo-strategic picture. As *The Times* put it: 'the war books are not about the War. They are rather accounts of personal experience in the War and personal grievances against the War'. In the words of Douglas Jerrold: 'To the individual personally, all operations of war are meaningless and futile', because battles made sense only when considered as struggles between large units. Therefore: 'By the simple device of omitting from the book the relationship of the part to the whole, the writers of these books make *every* incident and *every* tragedy seem futile, purposeless and insignificant'. Jerrold denied that a war which had been unavoidable and had 'changed the course of history' could be so regarded, and insisted: 'Not only was the war neither futile nor avoidable, but it was not believed to be either by the men who fought'.[17] Yet some critics endorsed the war books. According to Ward, the very fact that such questions as 'Had the war, then, been fought in vain? Was the post-War world no different (except in poverty and pain) from the pre-War world?' could be asked at all 'was the worst shock that idealism had suffered since Wartime illusions shrivelled'. And he dismissed Jerrold's negative answer to these questions with the comment that

The War Books of 1928–30 (continued)

the only possible test of the futility or otherwise of the War is to inquire whether the War has increased the sum of human happiness, or if it seems likely to. Can we say to each bereaved woman, to each wounded soldier, to each workless ex-soldier, 'Because of your loss, the world is to-day (or will be tomorrow) a happier place'? If we cannot, then the majority will continue to think of the War as futile.[18]

The boom in war books was clearly over before the end of 1930: in 1931 the number of war novels dropped to ten. (It was to be thirteen in 1932 and only four in 1933, and remained in single figures thereafter.) It was not just that the public had become bored: it was also becoming more preoccupied with both a possible future conflict and the slump, as was shown by the increasing number of next-war novels and works dealing with domestic issues.

Polarization Begins 1931–35

The end of the 1920s and beginning of the 1930s represented the peak of anti-defencist feeling in Britain. One symptom was the remarkable size of the LNU: in 1931 it collected 406,868 annual subscriptions – an astonishing total for a peace organization. In contrast the UDC was moribund; and the pacifist societies, the NMWM and FoR, claimed only 3,000 to 3,500 members each – as did the WIL. The LNU was benefiting from an ideal combination of pessimism and optimism at this time. The former – disillusion with the last war and fear of another – was necessary to increase public interest in the peace issue. The latter – a growing confidence in the League of Nations and in the World Disarmament Conference which was at last scheduled to meet in Geneva in February 1932 under Arthur Henderson's presidency – was necessary to turn anti-war sentiment in an idealistic direction rather than towards merely prudential policies such as appeasement or defeatism. The LNU had, moreover, deliberately looked on the bright side: although it did not deny that the League of Nations could in the last resort employ military sanctions against an aggressor, its leading figures, by claiming that its 'normal sanction is the public opinion of the world'[19] and emphasizing the prospects of disarmament, implied that it would not in practice have to use force. Such optimism, however, proved impossible to sustain as the decade progressed. Just nine days after Viscount Cecil had, on 10 September 1931, told the League of Nations Assembly at Geneva 'There has scarcely ever been a period in the world's history when war seems less likely than it does at present', Japan launched its

Plate 13.2. 'The dear general will be **so** sorry he missed this': peace meeting in 1937. Italy's conquest of Abyssinia, Hitler's remilitarization of the Rhineland, and Franco's seizure of power in Spain together challenged the idea of collective security and led to the polarization of the peace movement. Pacifists, *pacificists* and supporters of 'peaceful change' embraced a spectrum of views from non-intervention through appeasement to rearmament.

conquest of the Chinese province of Manchuria; the first of the major acts of aggression that were – albeit more gradually than is sometimes remembered – to polarize both defencists and the peace movement. The former eventually split into advocates and opponents of appeasement, and the latter into advocates and opponents of collective security.

The Manchuria crisis, by showing that a warrior culture like Japan was willing to defy world public opinion, started the process whereby the LNU lost its fair-weather members who had assumed the League would prevail by moral authority alone. Some turned to pacifism, a viewpoint which had seemed unnecessarily extreme in the late 1920s when the more practical *pacificist* approach seemed to be achieving results: 800 volunteers responded to the call in 1932 for a pacifist 'Peace Army' to station itself between the Japanese and the Chinese, though in the event their services were not called upon. Other LNU members sought a more explicit commitment to military sanctions: a New Commonwealth Society was founded in 1932 to campaign for the creation of an international police force. Understandably, however, the LNU leadership sought to arrest its decline in membership by finding a compromise that would not only satisfy both pacifists and sanctionists but also avoid jeopardizing the prospects of the World Disarmament Conference. It therefore emphasized economic sanctions as an effective method of deterring or punishing aggression but one that did not use military force and thereby provide a justification for not disarming.

The polarizing process was continued by Hitler's accession to power on 30 January 1933, though, contrary to many subsequent claims, the short-term effect of this event was to revive memories of 1914 and stimulate demands that Britain should never again be drawn into Continental quarrels. On 9 February 1933, for example, the student debaters at the Oxford Union passed by 275 votes to 153 a pacifist motion, 'That this House will in no circumstances fight for its King and Country', which provoked widespread controversy in the press; on 4 October 1933 the Labour Party unanimously adopted a resolution 'to take no part in war'; and, especially after Hitler's withdrawal of Germany from both the League of Nations and the World Disarmament Conference on 14 October 1933, the right-wing *Daily Express* and *Daily Mail* called for Britain to stay out of what they saw as a developing Franco-German crisis, although unlike the peace movement they wanted Britain to rearm and strengthen its imperial ties as a deterrent. Not until 1934 did opinion turn in the direction of resistance to Germany. In July the government announced its first rearmament programme; and in October the Labour Party repudiated its no-war motion of the previous year and re-affirmed its commitment to what Henderson called 'the constructive and collective peace system' of the League of Nations. In reaction against such developments the fashionable Anglican clergyman, the Revd H.R.L. ('Dick') Sheppard wrote a letter to the press published on 16 October 1934 which called for postcard pledges of support for pacifism. But there were limits to this polarization of opinion: the Labour Party and LNU both opposed rearmament; and the 'collective security' which entered common usage in 1935 was understood less as a policy of containment than as a middle way between such a policy and pacifism.

In focus: The 'Peace Ballot', 1934–35

The best evidence for public understanding of this issue is provided by the National Declaration on the League of Nations and Armaments, generally known as the Peace Ballot; a private referendum carried out by the LNU at Viscount Cecil's insistence between November 1934 and June 1935. Cecil wished to demonstrate that public support for the League and disarmament was greater than the right-wing press, which had conducted some rather dubious small-scale polls of its own, had claimed; and the Ballot benefited greatly from pre-emptive criticisms of it by the government and Conservative Party which united the Opposition and the peace movement behind it. It turned into the most impressive operation ever mounted by a British 'cause' group: nearly half a million activists distributed and collected questionnaires;

The 'Peace Ballot', 1934–35 (continued)

and 11,640,066 adults – an estimated 38.2 per cent of the United Kingdom population aged over 18 – filled them in.[20] The results, which revealed minor but revealing variations over time and from region to region, were very much as the organizers hoped:

1. Should Great Britain remain a Member of the League of Nations?
    Yes: 95.9% No: 3.1% Doubtful: 0.1% No answer: 0.9%

2. Are you in favour of the all-round reduction of armaments by international agreement?
    Yes: 90.6% No: 7.5% Doubtful: 0.1% No answer: 1.8%

3. Are you in favour of the all-round abolition of national military and naval aircraft by international agreement?
    Yes: 82.5% No: 14.6% Doubtful: 0.1% No answer: 2.8%

4. Should the manufacture and sale of armaments for private profit be prohibited by international agreement?
    Yes: 90.1% No: 6.7% Doubtful: 0.1% No answer: 3.1%

5. Do you consider that, if a nation insists on attacking another, the other nations should combine to compel it to stop by
    (a) economic and non-military measures?
    Yes: 86.8% No: 5.5% Doubtful: 0.2% No answer: 7.4%
    (b) if necessary, military measures?
    Yes: 58.7% No: 20.3% Doubtful: 0.4% No answer: 20.4%

By the time the results were declared in June 1935 most attention focused on Question 5, since the prospects of disarmament had faded and in the last month of polling there was mounting concern about an Italian attack on Abyssinia. Although later represented by its detractors as pacifist – perhaps from confusion with Dick Sheppard's peace pledge – the 58.7 per cent approval to Question 5b disproves this. Nonetheless the significantly higher percentage of yes answers to Question 5a indicates that more than a quarter of all respondents supported economic sanctions only; and it is probable that a number of those supporting military sanctions believed that these might take the form of a naval blockade only. The Peace Ballot probably influenced Baldwin's decision, following Mussolini's attack on Abyssinia in October 1935 and the League's imposition of mild economic sanctions, to call a general election at a time when the government could present itself as supporting collective security (even though, as became apparent once the election was won, it was secretly working for a compromise with Italy).

After 1936: Polarization Completed

The League did not impose effective economic sanctions against Italy – largely because Mussolini threatened military retaliation, thereby making clear to the British public that there was no middle way and that collective security involved the risk of war. Combined with two other crises in 1936 – Hitler's remilitarization of the Rhineland, and Franco's rebellion in Spain – the Italian conquest of Abyssinia forced defencists and the peace movement to clarify their thinking. In a book written at this time a Conservative MP, Sir Edward Grigg, acknowledged that 'the nation is being torn by two powerful and conflicting currents of opinion' which he labelled respectively 'limited and unlimited liability in the matter of going to war'. Advocates of limited liability like himself wished to restrict Britain's commitments to the defence of its homeland and empire and 'a zone west of the eastern frontier of France, Belgium, and Holland', whereas those he pejoratively described as favouring unlimited liability believed that it was also necessary to stop Germany conquering eastern Europe.[21] The peace movement also polarized. The LNU continued to support collective security even though its risks had become apparent – a decision symbolized by inviting Winston Churchill to join its executive committee (though he chose to become president of the New Commonwealth Society instead) – and eventually accepted rearmament: this led to a further slide in its membership. Some former LNU members joined the Peace Pledge Union (PPU), which Dick Sheppard launched in May 1936 with the support of many prominent intellectuals such as Vera Brittain, Aldous Huxley, John Middleton Murry, and Bertrand Russell. This soon absorbed the ailing NMWM, and, peaking at 136,000 members in April 1940, became the largest pacifist society in history. (By contrast the FoR, though expanding rapidly in the late 1930s, had less than 10,000 members; and the WIL, paralysed by its attempt to appeal to *pacificists* as well as pacifists, remained at about 3,500 members.) Others stopped short of pacifism but supported 'peaceful change' – the calling of a new peace conference to revise in Germany's favour what remained of the 1919 settlement – which in 1937 supplanted collective security as the peace movement's principal slogan. Indeed by the end of that year the peaceful-change wing of the peace movement had become as embarrassingly supportive of Prime Minister Neville Chamberlain's accommodating brand of defencism as the collective-security wing had to Churchill's confrontational brand.

Although with polling in its infancy it is hard to assess public opinion, it seems that most people initially wished to give appeasement a chance before risking a war which, despite a slight moderation in expectations of destructiveness resulting from the sight of civilians stoically enduring air attack in Spain and China, was still expected to be awesomely destructive. This mood reached its climax with the welcome given to the Munich Conference in September 1938, which avoided war by pressuring Czechoslovakia to cede territory to Germany. Thereafter the balance of opinion began to change, in part because of guilt towards the Czechs. And when on 15 March 1939 Hitler occupied Prague, proving for the first time that his goals went beyond the incorporation of all Germans into the *Reich*, support for appeasement crumbled: even Chamberlain retreated from it by guaranteeing Poland on 31 March; and conscription was announced on 26 April. A majority of people seem from this point to have accepted war as almost inevitable. They realized that Hitler had been given every chance to show that his aims were limited but had instead shown himself to be an expansionist who would menace western Europe if given a free hand in the east.

When war came for Britain on 3 September 1939, there was a much better public understanding of its strategic justification than there had been in 1914, even though it came after a German attack on a more distant country, Poland, and even though the prospect of civilian casualties was much greater. There was consequently less need to present the war as a moral crusade or to feel ideologically threatened by a militarily insignificant minority which took a different moral view: the pacifists of the PPU and FoR and the 60,000 conscientious objectors were treated more tolerantly than their First World War equivalents despite being rather more numerous. And since there was also a realization that Hitler's regime was an unprecedentedly evil adversary, there was no need to idealize British society in order to point up the contrast: to 'defend the bad against the worse' was the justification which C. Day Lewis put forward in his 1942 poem 'Where are the war poets?'

Historiography

Soon after Churchill succeeded Chamberlain as prime minister in May 1940 it became convenient, particularly for those wishing to shift the blame away from the Conservative-dominated governments of 1931–40, to blame the peace movement for creating a public opinion in which politicians found appeasement so much easier an option politically than containment. This scapegoating of the peace movement necessitated a considerable exaggeration not only of the latter's influence but also of the pacifist content of LNU policy in the 1930s. And it led to a reaction whereby defenders of the peace movement went too far the other way – for example in seeking to deny the obvious affinities between the policy of peaceful change which many of them supported and that of appeasement. Recently more detached academic studies have started to appear, though most of these have been engaged in the primary historiographical task of establishing and interpreting the principal facts and concepts rather than in the secondary one of challenging or refining a received wisdom. More primary work is still needed – into perceptions of war, into grass-roots peace activism, and into the class and gender composition of the peace movement. There are many interesting school projects and undergraduate theses to be written on these and other topics using local newspapers and material in local record offices.

Bibliographical Note

There is as yet no authoritative major study of the British peace movement over the whole of this period. Martin Ceadel's 'The Peace movement between the wars: problem of definition' in Richard Taylor and Nigel Young (eds), *Campaigns for Peace: British Peace Movements in the Twentieth Century* (Manchester, 1987) is an overview based on original research which will eventually result in a full-length work. James Hinton's *Protests and Visions: Peace Politics in 20th Century Britain* (London, 1989) is an intelligent general survey from a left-wing perspective. Although Caroline Moorhead is a distinguished journalist, her *Troublesome People: Enemies of War 1916–1986* (London, 1987) is extremely disappointing. Substantial books have, however, appeared on particular strands of the peace movement, notably Jill Liddington's *The Long Road to Greenham: Feminism and Anti-Militarism in Britain since 1820* (London, 1989), Jill Wallis's *Valiant for Peace: a History of the Fellowship of Reconciliation 1914 to 1989* (London, 1991), Donald S. Birn's *The League of Nations Union 1918–1945* (Oxford, 1981), and Martin Ceadel's *Pacifism in Britain 1914–1945: the Defining of a Faith* (Oxford, 1980). There have been detailed studies of individual episodes, such as Martin Ceadel's 'The "King and Country" debate, 1933: student politics, pacifism and the dictators', *Historical Journal* vol. 22, 1979, and of individual peace campaigners, such as Elaine Kaye's *C.J. Cadoux: Theologian, Scholar and Pacifist* (Edinburgh, 1988).

There is no adequate general work on attitudes to war. There is some material on anticipations of the Second World War in Martin Ceadel's 'Popular fiction and the next war, 1918–1939' in Frank Gloversmith (ed.) *Class, Culture and Social Change: a New View of the 1930s* (Brighton, 1989). The reaction against the First World War has been much studied from a literary standpoint, notably in Paul Fussell's *The Great War and Modern Memory* (New York, 1975) and Samuel Hynes, *A War Imagined: the First World War and English Culture* (London, 2nd edn, 1992). I found John Onion's *English Literature and Drama of the Great War, 1918–1939* (London, 1990) particularly useful, but learned of Rosa Maria Bracco's *Merchants of Hope: British Middlebrow Writers and the First World War, 1919–1939* (New York, 1992) only after completing this chapter. For social historians, there is food for thought in the concluding sections of J.M. Winter's important study, *The Great War and the British People* (London, 1986).

Notes

1. For this term see Martin Ceadel, *Thinking about Peace and War* (Oxford, 1987) ch. 5.

2. A.J.P. Taylor, *The Trouble Makers* (London, 1957) p. 51n. See also Martin Ceadel, *Pacifism in Britain 1914–1945: the Defining of a Faith* (Oxford, 1980) pp. 3–6.

3. Patrick MacGill, *Fear!* (London, 1921), Preface.

4. D. Jerrold, *The Lie About The War* (Criterion Miscellany No. 9, London, 1930) p. 8.

5. Edmund Blunden, 'Introduction', in Edmund Blunden *et al.*, *The War 1914–1918: a Booklist* (London, 1930) p. 2. Figures for war novels in this chapter are arrived at by counting the adult novels published in Britain listed in Philip E. Hager and Desmond Taylor, *The Novels of World War I: An Annotated Bibliography* (New York, 1981).

6. *The Critic's Armoury* (1924) p. 216; Jerrold, *Lie About The War*, p. 11.

7. *Life and Letters* (Nov. 1929) p. 399.

8. J.M. Keynes, *The Revision of the Treaty* (London, 1922), republished in *The Collected Writings of J.M. Keynes*, vol. 3 (London, 1971) pp. 4–5.

9. J.F.C. Fuller, *The Reformation of War* (London, 1923) p. 150; see also pp. 130–1. For other views of this sort see Martin Ceadel, 'Popular fiction and the next war, 1918–1939' in Frank Gloversmith (ed.), *Class, Culture and Social Change: a New View of the 1930s* (Brighton, 1980).

10. H. Quigley, *Passchendaele and the Somme: A Diary of 1917* (London, 1928) p. 185.

11. Edmund Blunden, *Undertones of War* (London, 2nd edn, 1965) p. 5.

12. R. Aldington, *Life for Life's Sake: a Book of Reminiscences* (London, 1968) p. 301.

13. Cyril Falls, *War Books: A Critical Guide* (London, 1930) p. x.

14. *The Times* 10 Apr. 1930; *TLS* 12 June 1930 p. 486.

15. Jeffrey Richards, *The Age of the Dream Palace* (London, 1984) p. 291.

16. A.C. Ward, *The Nineteen-Twenties: Literature and Ideas in the Post-War Decade* (London, 1930).

17. *The Times* 10 Apr. 1930; Jerrold, *Lie About The War*, pp. 22–5.

18. Ward, *The Nineteen-Twenties*, pp. 10, 148.

19. Gilbert Murray, *The Ordeal of this Generation* (London, 1929) p. 131.

20. See Martin Ceadel, 'The first British referendum: the Peace Ballot, 1934–5', *English Historical Review*, vol. 95 (1980), pp. 810–39.

21. Sir Edward Grigg, *The Faith of an Englishman* (London, 1936) pp. 7, 99, 303.

14 The New Consumerism

Sue Bowden

Introduction: Patterns of Consumer Expenditure in the Interwar Period

Between the end of the First World War and the outbreak of the Second World War, there were important shifts in the levels and distribution patterns of consumer expenditure in the United Kingdom. In 1910–14, expenditure on durable goods, at £169.6 million, only accounted for 4.8 per cent of consumer expenditure. Throughout the interwar years, the level of expenditure on durable goods increased steadily, reaching £332.2 million in 1930–34 and £395.9 million in 1935–38 (all in constant 1938 prices). Although, as Table 14.1 demonstrates, expenditure on all types of goods grew, the rate of growth of expenditure on durable commodities far exceeded that for any other class of good, and durable goods came to assume a greater proportionate importance in the pattern of consumer expenditure. Meanwhile spending on perishables, semi-durables and rent accounted for a declining expenditure share. Perishables, for example, accounted for 52.3 per cent of consumer expenditure in 1910–14 but for 47.7 per cent by 1935–38. Durable goods, however, rose from 6.7 per cent of consumer expenditure in 1920–24, to 7.7 per cent in 1925–29, 8.4 per cent in 1930–34 and 9 per cent in 1935–38.

Measured in terms of the distribution of expenditure, the 'new consumerism' in the interwar years may be attributed to the growth of expenditure on three main items of household spending: fuel and light, durable household goods and transport and communications, all of which assumed greater importance in terms of increased levels of and shares in total consumer expenditure in these years (Table 14.2).

Table 14.1. Consumers' expenditure at constant (1938) prices classified by durability, UK, 1910–38 (£m)

	1910–14	1920–24	1925–29	1930–34	1935–38
Perishables	1791.1	1709.5	1834.3	1932.8	2086.2
Semi-durables	402.3	398.7	433.0	451.1	490.0
Durables	169.6	226.2	283.9	333.2	395.9
Rent	333.7	368.3	393.4	428.9	471.7
Other services	731.2	656.2	748.6	827.5	933.0
Total	3427.9	3358.9	3693.2	3973.5	4376.8

Note: Stone and Rowe defined perishable goods as those goods which last up to six months in use; semi-durable goods as those which last more than six months but less than three years and durable goods as those goods which last longer than three years. For example, perishables would include food, drink and tobacco, whilst clothing was classed as semi-durables and household furnishings and equipment were classed as durables.

Source: Richard Stone and D.A. Rowe, *The Measurement of Consumers' Expenditure and Behaviour in the United Kingdom, 1920–1938, Volume II* (Cambridge, 1966) Table 64, p. 135.

Table 14.2. Consumers' expenditure at constant (1938) prices, UK, 1910–38 (£m)

	1910–14	1920–24	1925–29	1930–34	1935–38
Food	981.9	1002.3	1116.7	1231.1	1285.9
Alcoholic Drink	502.5	351.8	320.5	264.6	286.4
Tobacco	84.0	113.0	123.6	137.8	163.3
Rents, rates and water charges	333.7	368.3	393.4	428.9	471.7
Fuel and light	137.3	138.7	155.0	163.7	182.7
Clothing	367.2	356.7	388.8	403.1	434.8
Durable household goods	134.7	176.9	218.0	258.5	289.4
Transport and communications	131.5	188.5	241.9	258.2	326.1
Other goods	164.1	204.3	219.9	243.6	293.4
Other services	591.0	458.5	515.4	584.0	643.4
Total	3427.9	3359.0	3693.2	3973.5	4377.1

Source: Stone and Rowe, *The Measurement of Consumers' Expenditure* Table 56, p. 125.

The first two categories, that is fuel and light and durable household goods, largely relate to what has become known as the 'electrification of the home' during the interwar years. It was in this period that the supply of electricity was extended and made available to the majority of households. Prior to this time, fuel and light were supplied by candles, gas, and solid fuel. In 1931, less than a third of all homes had electrical power. By 1935, more than half of all homes had electricity and, at the end of the period, nearly two-thirds enjoyed the benefits of electricity, the remaining third being largely confined to rural areas (Table 14.3).

The Growth in Ownership of Consumer Durables

Many of these 'wired' homes used electricity for lighting purposes only. In the 1930s, however, there was increasing growth in the use of electric appliances in the home. By the end of the period, lighting only accounted for about a quarter of all domestic electric power consumption. In 1933, the average annual consumption of electricity per domestic consumer was 468 kilowatt-hours. By 1939, it had grown to 610 kilowatt-hours. Not only were more people being connected to electricity supply in this period, but also each consumer was using increasing amounts of electricity.

Many of the 'new' consumer durables in the interwar years were domestic electric appliances designed to deal with specific housework tasks: cookers, fridges and water heaters for cooking; water and space heaters for heating; irons and wash boilers for laundry, vacuum cleaners for cleaning. The household appliances in question can be divided into two broad categories: the heavy power consuming equipment which had to be specially connected to electric power and was largely distributed by the power supply undertakings; and the lower power consuming equipment which required no special fitting and was acquired from a variety of retail outlets and electrical contractors. Cookers, water and space heaters and water boilers are examples of the former; vacuum cleaners and irons fell into the latter category. Prior to nationalization, electricity supply was operated by both private companies and local authorities. Both performed a dual role as distributors of electric power and suppliers of electrical appliances. Before the Second World War there were about 650 supply undertakings.

Ownership of electric appliances also fell into two groupings, with the heavy power consuming cookers, water and space heaters and water boilers all achieving low penetration levels and the lower power consuming vacuum cleaners and irons achieving high ownership levels (Table 14.3).

'New consumerism' in the interwar years was not confined to domestic electric technology used for housework. It equally applied to a growth of expenditure on domestic leisure and communication goods, notably the motor car, the radio and the telephone, all of which experienced substantial growth

Table 14.3. The growth of ownership of domestic electric appliances, 1931–38

	Percentage of homes wired for electricity	Percentage of wired homes with electric				
		Cookers	Irons	Water heaters	Wash boilers	Fridges
1931		4.0				
1932	31.84	4.9				
1933	49.15	6.1	56.4	1.2	0.9	
1934	49.33	9.3		1.9	1.4	
1935	54.54	11.3		3.1	2.0	
1936	57.75	13.4	70.9	3.8	2.4	2.3
1937	61.77	15.4		4.8	2.9	
1938	65.39	16.9		5.6	3.5	2.4

Source: Electrical Trading and Electrical Times, *Annual Marketing Surveys,* London 1933–38 inclusive.

rates in these decades. In 1924, there were only 579,800 motor cars in use, 238,000 private telephone rental services and 15.4 radios per thousand families. Ten years later, there were nearly one and a half million cars in use and over 660,000 private telephone rental services. At the end of the 1930s, there were 68.3 radios per thousand families, over two million cars in use and well over a million private rental telephone services (Table 14.4).

Ownership of Consumer Durables in the Interwar Period in the Context of Longer-run Trends in Consumer Expenditure

Superficially, the evidence would suggest major changes in the level and pattern of consumer expenditure, with an enhanced premium on spending on a range of consumer durables designed to accommodate housework, leisure and communication related activities. How does the pattern of expenditure in the interwar years fit in the context of long-term patterns of consumer expenditure?

The growth of the market for consumer durables is often described as a three-stage process. Initially, the goods are expensive, are perceived as luxuries and bought only by the most affluent. Supply side changes emanating from technological change lead to price reductions which shift ownership into the second, 'middle' stage. Since the goods are still relatively expensive and have some luxury connotations, ownership only spreads to the middle groups of society. Mass ownership follows from further technological changes which result in price reductions, thus making the goods affordable to the majority of the population.

Table 14.4. The growth of ownership of durable goods for leisure, transport and communication

	Number of radio licences per 1000 families	Motor cars in use	Rentals of telephone services for personal use
1922	5.8		176,000
1923	10.7		204,000
1924	15.4	579,800	238,000
1925	20.0	692,800	274,000
1926	21.7	800,300	321,000
1927	23.4	898,900	369,000
1928	26.0	997,900	419,000
1929	29.6	1,098,100	468,000
1930	37.1	1,177,900	514,000
1931	44.5	1,192,900	551,000
1932	50.0	1,236,000	580,000
1933	56.1	1,313,300	609,000
1934	60.7	1,420,500	667,000
1935	64.4	1,592,400	757,000
1936	68.3	1,726,000	882,000
1937		1,890,400	1,024,000
1938		2,045,400	1,143,000

Sources: Society of Motor Manufactures and Traders, *The Motor Industry of Great Britain* (London, 1924–39); British Broadcasting Association, *Annual Report* (London, 1938) p. 73; Stone and Rowe, *The Measurement of Consumers' Expenditure*, Table 31, p. 76.

In the UK the first, luxury stage of market development is associated with the period before the First World War, when consumer durables were expensive and ownership was limited to the wealthier members of society. The final, mass market stage can be dated from the late 1950s when ownership of most consumer durables began to diffuse throughout society. The interwar years represent the mid stage in which we can identify both the second and the transition to the third stage in the development of mass markets for consumer durables.

In the case of domestic electrical goods, the period witnessed the beginning but by no means the completion of the shift into mass ownership of domestic technology. Contemporaries in the electricity industry certainly believed that the market for its products was located in the middle classes and, from the mid 1930s, the Electrical Development Association and the Electrical Association for Women began to campaign for greater use of electrical appliances among the working classes. Despite the extension of electricity supply and the growth in usage of electrical appliances in the home, it was not until 1958 that 25 per cent of households in the UK owned a washing machine; 50 per cent ownership levels of this good were not achieved until 1964. Fridges did not achieve 25 per cent and 50 per cent household ownership levels until 1962 and 1968 respectively.[1] The interwar years were a period of transition, when ownership was spreading but had not become the norm among working-class households.

In sharp contrast, the motor vehicle market was firmly located in the second stage in the diffusion process in the interwar years. Although contemporary observers of this industry commented on the extension of car ownership among the middle classes, they equally assumed that the market for cars was essentially confined to the upper and middle income groups in society. Mass ownership of cars was essentially a postwar phenomenon, largely associated with the growth of hire purchase and the used car market. By 1956, 25 per cent of households owned a car; 50 per cent did so by 1965. The one durable which did achieve mass ownership in this period was the radio, which is discussed in Chapter 15. There are few memoirs of middle and working-class life in the period which do not mention the radio.[2]

Some caution is required therefore in speaking of the interwar years as representing 'new consumerism' defined in terms of the growth of mass markets for a range of consumer durables. With the exception of the radio, the iron and the vacuum cleaner most durables achieved low penetration levels. The interwar years do, however, constitute an important stage in the development of mass markets for consumer durables.

Class and Regional Patterns in Consumerism

The 'new consumerism' of the interwar years was largely a middle-class phenomenon. The key exceptions to this general rule were the radio, the vacuum cleaner and the iron. The other leisure and communication durables, namely the motor car and the telephone tended to be owned by the more affluent members of society. By the late 1930s, for example, the motor car had become a necessity among the professional middle classes, particularly in rural areas. The class dimension was repeated in the case of the more expensive, heavy power consuming domestic electric appliances designed to alleviate housework. Ownership of electric fridges, cookers, space and water heaters and washing machines tended to be limited to middle-class women.

Consumerism in this period also had an important regional dimension, with ownership being more heavily concentrated in the more affluent parts of the country, suggesting income and price constraints on ownership. In 1938, for example, average consumption of electricity per domestic consumer was highest in the South East (at 861 kilowatt-hours) and lowest in the North East (at 386.4 kilowatt-hours), whilst motor car ownership in that year varied from just under 20 per cent of all households in the South East to under 12 per cent in the North.

What then explains both the growth of expenditure and the constraints on the development of a mass market for consumer durables in the interwar period? The mass market for consumer durables was firmly established in the United States in the interwar years. In 1939, 60 per cent of American households had a washing machine, 33 per cent a dish washer, 56 per cent a refrigerator, 48 per cent a vacuum cleaner, over 80 per cent a radio and over 70 per cent a motor car. Why was there no mass market in the UK? Explanations for the causes and constraints are to be found in demand as well as supply side factors. As Chapter 11 has already indicated, the 1920s and 1930s witnessed the growth of the 'new industries'. Between 1920 and 1938, the annual percentage growth in output in the vehicle industry, at 6.6 per cent, was far in excess of any other industry at this time and well above the average for all manufacturing industry (2.6 per cent); output growth in electrical engineering, at 4.7 per cent, was equally impressive.

Supply Side Changes

New Technology and Increased Output

The introduction of new machinery and production processes together enabled manufacturers to increase output and, more importantly, to realize economies of scale. Such supply side changes led to cost reductions which, in turn, enabled manufacturers to cut purchase prices. The average price of a motor car, for example, fell from £388 in 1924 to £213 in 1938, whilst the General Electric Company was able to reduce the price of its electric washing machines by more than 50 per cent in the 1930s. In the case of the motor vehicle industry, manufacturers also adopted a deliberate production and marketing strategy of introducing, from 1924, smaller cars which were cheaper to buy and run than the more expensive large models. A typical small 7 to 8 horsepower model cost about £160 in 1938; an 11 to 16 horsepower car (in the medium size category) would have cost about £310 at that date.

As a result of the introduction of new technology and improvements in production processes, both the vehicle and the electrical engineering industries were able to achieve large increases in production. In 1924, for example, 116,600 motor cars were produced; by the end of the 1930s, the industry was producing over 340,000 motor cars a year – a performance which compared most favourably with that of the UK's major European competitors. In 1938, UK production of 341,000 motor cars was well in excess of that of France (199,800), Germany (276,600) and Italy (59,000). In 1907, the value of production in the electrical engineering industry was just under £14 million. By 1930, it had risen to just over £87 million; five years later the gross output of the industry was just under £107 million. Although electrical machinery and parts together with power and lighting equipment made up the bulk of output, accounting for 21.3 per cent and 13.5 per cent respectively of gross output (in value terms) in 1935, the growth in the importance of telephone and wireless equipment was particularly notable. In 1907 the radio industry was too insignificant to be recorded in the Census of Production and in 1924, the value of production was less than £1 million. By 1935, however, wireless production was valued at just under £6 million. The growth of production of telephone equipment was equally impressive – rising from just under £4 million in 1924 to over £5.5 million by 1935.

This, however, did not constitute mass production for the mass market. Mass market production of consumer durables is more correctly located in the 1960s when, for example, the motor vehicle industry was producing in excess of 1 million motor cars a year and average electricity consumption per domestic consumer was in excess of three million kilowatt-hours a year.

The Growth of Owner-Occupation and the Extension of Electric Power

An important factor in the growth of the market for consumer durables was the growth of owner occupation and the housing boom which took place in the interwar years. At the beginning of this period, the private landlord dominated the domestic property market, with less than one house in five being owner occupied. In 1914, private rented housing accounted for 80 per cent of the housing stock; council and owner occupied houses accounted for 1 per cent and 10 per cent respectively. The 1920s and 1930s witnessed a large-scale building programme and a significant change in the tenure of housing stock. Between 1919 and 1939 just under four million houses were built, of which over one million were constructed by local authorities. By 1939, private rented accommodation accounted for only 46 per cent of the total stock whereas council and owner occupied housing accounted for 14 per cent and 31 per cent respectively.[3]

The relationship between the 'new' industries and the housing sector was seen to be mutually beneficial by authors such as Richardson. Electricity supply and appliances were seen to be selling features of many new homes, whilst the building of houses meant an extension of electricity supply and wiring and new demands for domestic appliances.[4] Many of the new houses were built in suburbia, which stimulated the demand for motor cars. Not all houses were fully supplied with electricity however. For example, it was not policy for the local authorities to incorporate domestic electric cooking and heating in new council houses. The more usual policy was to fit gas and give tenants the option of installing electric appliances at their own cost. Private rented accommodation ranged from comparatively humble individuals to great property owners and the evidence would suggest that the latter were far more receptive to domestic electrification than the former. In London, for example, the most active private property companies in these terms were the Commissioners of Crown Lands and the Ecclesiastical Commissioners. In both cases new rented flats were supplied with electric cookers, water heaters and portable fires. However, by far the greatest demand for electricity derived from the private owner occupied sector, whilst motor car ownership tended to be associated with the professional middle classes in rural areas.

Running Costs and Consumer Credit

Reductions in purchase prices emanating from the realization of economies of scale in production do not provide the full supply side explanation for the growth of expenditure on consumer durables. Two further factors were instrumental: reductions in running costs and the increased availability of hire and hire purchase. Most of the 'new' goods involved running costs – be it electrical power for the domestic appliances or running and standing costs for the motor vehicle. In many respects, the growth of demand for consumer durables in this period depended more on the reductions in running costs than on decreases in purchase prices which, in turn, reflected both the attempts of manufacturers to improve the quality and reliability of their products and, in the case of electricity, the growth of supply, which in turn depended on the extension of the Electricity Grid and deliberate policies on the part of the supply undertakings to make power available to more consumers. These initiatives in turn created economies of scale and facilitated the reduction in electricity tariffs. In 1932, for example, the average marginal cost of cooking with electricity was 4.668d; by 1938 it had fallen to 3.404d. Reductions in purchase prices and running costs were not however the only supply side factors underpinning the growth in demand for consumer durables; a third factor, deferred payment, was also instrumental.

The prime concern of the electricity industry in the interwar period was to boost consumption of electricity in both the home and in industry. Increases in domestic consumption could only be achieved by persuading customers to extend their use of electricity away from lighting only, since this used minimal amounts of power, towards a range of domestic appliances, in particular heavy power consuming goods. There were, however, two major obstacles to the realization of this objective: the cost constraints experienced by many households in the period which precluded outright acquisition of many of the goods; and, secondly, what the industry considered to be inertia on the part of many potential consumers. The industry attributed this perceived inertia to both a reluctance on the part of consumers to change from gas to electricity and resistance to 'new' gadgets which, in turn, were believed to reflect both ignorance and an aversion to new technology. Electrical appliances were in most instances not new but replacement goods. To persuade consumers to switch from gas and/or solid fuel to electricity thus involved a learning process. The consumer, in other words, would have to be educated to use electricity.

To deal with these problems, the electrical appliance manufacturing industry and the supply undertakings adopted the marketing strategy of introducing a range of deferred payment schemes which, it was hoped, would allow consumers to acquire the new products without incurring heavy initial purchase costs and give them the opportunity to use the appliances, thus experiencing first hand the benefits they offered. The term 'deferred payment' was used to cover three main schemes: hire of electrical appliances, hire purchase of electrical wiring and hire purchase of electrical appliances. From the mid 1920s, supply undertakings began to offer both hire and hire purchase schemes for wiring and for the heavier power consuming appliances. By 1934, 68.5 per cent of the undertakings offered hire schemes and 77 per cent offered hire purchase schemes. Other electrical appliances were also sold on hire purchase terms direct by manufacturers and retailers, often via one of the new finance houses specialising in hire purchase schemes for consumer durables. Bowmaker, for example, specialized in hire purchase schemes for vacuum cleaners and radios.

But how important were these schemes in overcoming perceived cost constraints and consumer inertia? The evidence suggests that they were significant. By the end of the 1930s, over three-quarters of sales of radios and vacuum cleaners were on hire purchase terms. Hire purchase sales of vacuum cleaners and radios in that year were worth £2.6 million and £12 million or 1.7 per cent and 7.8 per cent of all expenditure on furniture, furnishings and household equipment respectively. The limited evidence available suggests that hire was equally important in stimulating use of heavy power consuming equipment. In Hull and Manchester, for example, over 80 per cent of the electric cookers in use in 1938 were hired. Assuming that consumers were paying 0.5 pence per unit for electricity, then revenue from hired cookers in the country as a whole in 1938 represented 5.2 per cent of total revenue from domestic lighting, heating and cooking in that year. It is doubtful, however, that the schemes would have met with such success had they not been supported by the growing relative cost advantage of electricity in these years. Consumers in the 1930s appear to have responded more to an increase in the price of gas than to a fall in electricity costs and to have based their decision-making on relative fuel costs as well as deferred payment facility availability.

Advertising

Marketing schemes promoting deferred payment facilities were accompanied by intense advertising which aimed to educate and persuade potential consumers in the potential benefits of electrical goods. In the case of domestic electrical goods, the potential consumers of the goods were the housewives who performed housework. In order to create a climate of consumption, to

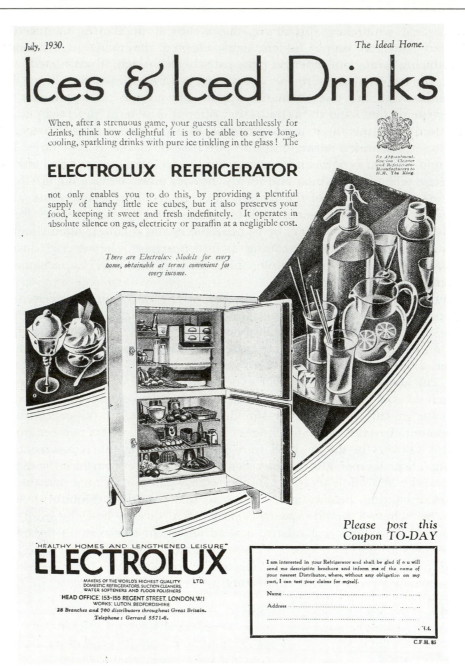

Plate 14.1. 'Ices and Iced Drinks' from the *Ideal Home*, 1930. Advertising for new consumer durables focused on middle-class aspirations – in this case the ability to serve iced drinks to guests. The advertisement discretely points out that consumer credit is available; refrigerators are 'obtainable at terms convenient for every income.'

change perceptions of electric appliances away from luxuries to necessities, and to persuade women of the advantages of ownership, the electricity industry embarked on advertising campaigns designed to educate women into the advantages of its products by emphasizing that its products helped the housewife become a better housewife. As far as the industry was concerned the implications and hence marketable features of electric technology were threefold: its potential to reduce the hard physical work involved in many areas of housework; to reallocate time to the 'caring' aspects of housewifery and raise standards of cleanliness; and finally its ability to reduce dependency on paid help in the home. Advertising was used to portray household technology as productivity enhancing and as easing the transition in the nature of domestic service away from the live-in to the daily help.

For most of the period press advertising was concentrated in local newspapers and middle-class women's magazines. The only national newspapers regularly used were the *Daily Mail*, the *Daily Express* and the *Financial Times* (winning over the male householder was obviously given high priority by the industry). Advertising by the late 1920s was not taken in the popular weeklies read by lower-class women. Influence in the media was achieved not only by the advertisements but also by exploiting the cooperation of local newspapers for the insertion of electrical news. What then were the effects of electrical appliances on the lives of women at this time?

In focus: Women and the 'New Consumerism'

There were two main ways in which the growth of the electricity industry might be expected to have impacted on women: in terms of employment possibilities in the industry and in terms of their domestic lives in relation to housework. The official evidence suggests that the 'new' industries had a marginal impact on female labour force participation at this time. The share of women in the 'new' industries was low and did not record any substantial increase. The electrical engineering industry was too small at the time to have any significant impact on women's labour force participation.

The limits to potential change in the domestic lives of women are indicated in the low permeation levels of most electrical appliances (Table 14.3). Most women could not afford to own and run electric appliances. Electric space and water heating appliances could have had a significant impact on the time and labour of the housewife, yet at the end of the 1930s less than 6 per cent of electrified homes owned such products. The consumer durable which had most impact on women's lives was undoubtedly the radio (see Chapter 15) which provided entertainment and information – thus perhaps making the hard physical work involved in housework and the constant demands of child care more tolerable.

Electrical appliances did however contribute to an increase in the time spent in housework by middle-class women since they were important in

Women and the New Consumerism (continued)

contributing to the transition away from full-time live-in servants to daily domestic help. By the 1930s constraints on both the supply of women willing to accept work as full-time domestic servants and on middle-class families living on fixed incomes meant that many households no longer employed domestic servants. Domestic technology eased the reallocation of housework away from the domestic servant to the middle-class housewife and her occasional daily help.

They also contributed to the reformation of domestic ideology in the interwar years with its emphasis on ever increasing standards of cleanliness, child care and nutrition. Domestic technology allowed women to perform specific tasks more often and 'better' and to spend more time looking after children (for example vacuuming a carpet every day instead of cleaning it with a broom once a week). Domestic technology thus added to the momentum of the interwar period which saw many middle-class women performing housework that their grandmothers would never have dreamed of doing.

The Motor Vehicle Industry and Consumer Credit

The motor vehicle industry also used hire purchase schemes to boost ownership levels, although in this case the prime motivation was to smooth seasonal fluctuations in purchases and the schemes were not operated directly by the manufacturers or retailers but by finance houses such as United Dominions Trust. Hire purchase in the motor vehicle industry is one example of cooperation between industry and the City, in which the impetus for such schemes emanated not from industry but from the finance houses.

Although the terms and conditions of hire purchase in the United Kingdom were among the best in Europe, the percentage of cars sold on hire purchase in this country (60 per cent) was lower than that in Germany (75 per cent), Italy (75 per cent) and the US (64 per cent). Only the French recorded lower levels (50 per cent). The explanation is rooted in qualitative and quantitative credit rationing imposed by the finance houses. They preferred, for example, customers who were householders, owned their own business, were married and had children, on the grounds that such individuals had a great incentive to maintain regular payments. Most people, moreover, would have found the costs prohibitive despite the favourable terms. The deposit on a medium size Morris Cowley car in the early 1930s was equal to about a quarter of the average income of a salaried householder; monthly payments spread over eighteen months would have amounted to over £9 a month. The costs of hire purchase were thus too high for the majority of householders in this period. Mass ownership of motor cars is associated with the 1960s and the increased availability and acceptability of used cars and widespread use of consumer credit.

The success of such campaigns has, in the final analysis, to be measured in terms of ownership levels. The limitations of the marketing and advertising schemes are reflected in the fact that the majority of the population did not own most of the 'new' consumer durables in the interwar years. What then were the constraints on the development of mass markets in this period?

Constraints on the 'New Consumerism'

Purchase Prices, Running Costs and Average Incomes

Despite the falls in purchase prices and running costs, most consumer durables in the interwar period were too expensive for the majority of the population. Despite the growth in real incomes in the period, average incomes were less than £100 a year. Even the cheapest car would therefore cost in excess of the average annual income of three-quarters of the population. The majority of households survived on an average weekly income of less than £5 (Table 14.5). Relatively low disposable income among the working class must be one explanation as to why this group did not become major consumers of either cars or heavy power consuming electric household appliances. In such cases, the bulk of expenditure went towards the basic necessities of life, namely food and housing. The Ministry of Labour Survey into the weekly expenditures of working class households in 1937–38 reported that the average weekly expenditure on fuel and light for an industrial working class family was £0.32, of which expenditure on coal amounted to £0.158. This means that the amount available for expenditure on electricity and/or gas for lighting and other domestic uses was £0.162.[5] Yet the total weekly electricity bill for a household having lighting on assisted wiring terms and hiring an electric appliance would have been £0.199. A major constraint on ownership of heavy power consuming electric durables was, therefore, the low incomes of the majority of the population.

It may be of course that additional factors were important in determining working-class attitudes to the 'new consumerism'. In many respects electric appliances were replacement rather than new products. There is good reason to believe that familiarity with gas and solid fuel (and the absence of any real motivation to switch) deterred many consumers. In addition, the patterns of 'new consumerism' may reflect priorities in the purchasing decision. The widespread ownership of the radio implies that working-class families set a higher premium on domestic leisure and communication for the family rather than on appliances for specific housework tasks.

Table 14.5. Average weekly wages in the UK, 1924–38 (£)

1924	2.80
1925	2.82
1926	2.79
1927	2.81
1928	2.79
1929	2.79
1930	2.79
1931	2.75
1932	2.70
1933	2.69
1934	2.72
1935	2.75
1936	2.81
1937	2.86
1938	2.95

Source: Barry Eichengreen, 'Unemployment in Inter-war Britain', *ReFRESH* no. 9 (1989), p. 4.

The Skewed Distribution of Income

The problem of low average incomes was compounded by the highly skewed distribution of income in the country. Before the Second World War, £250 was commonly regarded as the social dividing line marking off the working classes from the rest of society. Households in receipt of more than £250 a year constituted about a quarter of the population. The skewed distribution of income also explains the contrasts in regional patterns of ownership of consumer durables in the interwar years, since 37.7 per cent of middle-class families (income-based definition) lived in London and the South East. Only 3.8 per cent and 2.5 per cent of middle-class families lived in Northumberland and Durham and the northern rural belt respectively. The same regional pattern emerges if the definition of middle class is changed to professional and salaried households. In 1934, 50.5 per cent of professional households and 37.1 per cent of salaried households lived in London and the South East. Only 5.7 per cent of professional households and 9.1 per cent of salaried households lived in the North.[6]

It was this group of people who largely enjoyed the benefits of the 'new consumerism' of the interwar years. As Chapter 11 has indicated, it was this group who largely participated in private owner occupation in the 1930s. The same group extended consumerism to incorporate motoring, domestic leisure and communication (the radio and the telephone) and domestic technology. Households in receipt of £250–350 and £350–500 a year were spending between £8.7 and £12.3 a year on motoring (i.e. exclusive of purchase costs) and £9.4 and £13.6 on domestic help, licences (required for radios) and holidays; those in receipt of between £500 and £700 a year were spending £26.8 a year on motoring and £25.5 on domestic help, licences and holidays.[7] The 'new consumerism' of the interwar years, in terms of ownership of consumer durables, was class specific. For the majority of the population consumerism remained limited to expenditure on the basic necessities of life, eased for some by the acquisition of a radio and/or an iron.

Historical Interpretations: the Performance of the Motor Vehicle Industry

'New consumerism' in the interwar period, as the above analysis has shown, did not constitute mass production for mass markets in the case of the motor vehicle industry. At given levels of production, purchase prices were too high for the majority of the population to acquire cars. Even at the end of the 1930s, many middle-class households still did not own a car. Does this then imply some kind of failure on the part of the manufacturers? Should they have implemented mass production methods on the American Fordist lines? (that is, the manufacture of standardized products in huge volumes using special-purpose machinery and unskilled labour). In this section we review the evidence on the performance of the UK motor vehicle manufacturers, namely at this point in time Austin, Morris, Rootes, Singer, Standard, Ford and Vauxhall.

Three reasons have been given for the 'failure' to introduce mass production methods on the American model in the UK in the interwar period. The first, and most debated, is the Lewchuk thesis that the motor manufacturers opted not to introduce the new technology because they were afraid of provoking trade union resistance.[8] According to Lewchuk, managers veered away from the American system because they distrusted labour's ability to work at the required pace and because they believed Fordism would provoke non-cooperation, whereas labour feared that management would try to cut piece rates if increased work norms were introduced. The result was the so-called British system characterized by lack of standardization, lack of high throughput production processes involving high technological investment, and imperfect management control over shop floor practices (for the prewar antecedents of this system, see Chapter 3).

This theory, however, has been disputed by Bowden and Turner and by Tolliday on two grounds: firstly, that it exaggerates the extent of union power and management fear of union non-cooperation; and, secondly, that it underestimates the demand side requirements for mass production.[9] According to Tolliday, mass production on the Fordist model was only viable when there was a large, predictable and expanding market. Bowden and Turner have shown that demand was growing, but had not saturated among the middle classes in this period, and that short-term profitability was assured by a strategy which concentrated on extending demand in the existing, middle-class market. In the interwar period, when export markets were non-existent and when domestic incomes were both low and heavily skewed, the market was not conducive to mass production.

The second explanation relates the failure to invest in high technology to the financing policies of the manufacturers. Investment in new capacity was ceded to the higher claims of dividends. Church has shown that between 1922 and 1939, Austin paid out nearly 70 per cent of its profits on ordinary and preferred dividends and on interest on long-term loans, whilst, according to Overy, between 1927 and 1951 Morris earned nearly £55 million in pre-tax profit, but retained only 26 per cent in the firm.[10] The reasons for this strategy have been traced to the fear that dissatisfied investors would replace existing managers by mounting take-over bids.

The viability of this explanation depends, again, on the rationale for committing large investment funds to mass production technology. If there was no mass market for mass production motor cars, then investment in the required technology would have been at best a high risk strategy. It would only pay manufacturers to invest in the machinery and processes if the market existed. The evidence suggests otherwise in this period. Although capital/labour ratios were low in the British motor industry (throughout the 1930s Austin employed between £175 and £200 of fixed capital per employee, whereas at Ford in Detroit the amount of fixed capital per worker grew from $3,194 in 1914 to $5,544 in 1921), the major UK manufacturers, despite periods of financial difficulties, survived and ended the interwar years extremely profitable. In 1937, for example, Morris was recording annual pre-tax profits of just under £2 million. In the same year net trading profits at Austin were nearly £1.25 million.[11] There was then little immediate incentive to switch production methods; profitability was assured by retaining existing methods and existing markets.

The final explanation relates to the organization of the industry: notably the number of firms and the failure to effect vertical integration of production and distribution. Although the number of firms fell from 113 in 1914 to 33 by 1938, no single firm dominated the British market as Ford dominated the US market. Oligopoly and standardization of the production process in the United States was a reflection of the size and affluence of the American market. Mass production made sense only when a large volume of output enabled a firm to gain most of the economies of scale at each stage of production. Not only was total output in the UK too small to justify mass production, but the industry was too differentiated to achieve economies of scale from large volume output.

Plate 14.2 The 'Hillman Minx' from *The Motor,* 1933. Most advertising for cars was targeted at men, but advertisers were aware that women's views were also important. This advertisement makes an explicit appeal to female readers, emphasizing the beauty, range of colours and grace of the car, as well as its low price.

This problem was compounded by the product differentiation strategy adopted by contemporary manufacturers which culminated in each manufacturer making a range of models which, in turn, led to higher costs of production and hence higher unit costs.

The performance of the industry in the final analysis however, has to be judged in terms of the strategies adopted by the contemporary manufacturers. They believed that the 'new consumerism' was a middle-class phenomenon and that their production and marketing strategy should be based on the premise that demand was limited. The market in the interwar years was neither large nor predictable. In such circumstances mass production would have been a high risk strategy. The motor manufacturers, by choosing to avoid risk, ensured that 'new consumerism' in terms of the motor car remained a middle-class affair. As such, the contemporary manufacturers reflected a wider problem in British industry at this time: in opting for risk aversion they merely replicated the behaviour of manufacturers in most industries at this time.

Bibliographical Note

The key role of the 'new' industries and the development of consumerism in the interwar period were first advanced in a series of articles by Harry Richardson which are included in D.H. Aldcroft and H.W. Richardson, *The British Economy, 1870–1939* (London, 1969). Revisionist work since the 1960s has questioned the key role played by the 'new' industries and has instigated a series of important in-depth studies on individual industries. The best and most comprehensive survey of the electricity supply industry is L. Hannah, *Electricity Before Nationalisation* (London, 1978). Good surveys of the electrical engineering industry are to be found in Alfred D. Chandler, Jr., *Scale and Scope; The Dynamics of Industrial Capitalism,* (Cambridge, Mass., and London, 1990) and R.E. Catterall, 'Electrical engineering', in N.K. Buxton and D.H. Aldcroft (eds), *British Industry between the Wars* (London, 1979).

From the 1970s, the electrical industry has formed the focus of important research by feminists interested in the impact of technology in the home on the lives of women. M. Glucksmann, *Women Assemble; Women Workers and the New Industries in Inter-War Britain* (London, 1990) provides the essential feminist perspective on women and the electrical engineering industry in the interwar years. Other surveys of household work and the impact of technology include C. Hardyment, *From Mangle to Microwave* (Cambridge, 1988), and C. Davidson, *A Woman's Work is Never Done* (London, 1982). For women's own assessment of changes in their domestic life see E. Roberts, *A Woman's Place: an Oral History of Working-Class Women, 1890–1940* (Oxford, 1984).

R. Church, *Herbert Austin; The British Motor Industry to 1941* (London, 1979) and R.J. Overy, *William Morris, Viscount Nuffield* (London, 1976) are invaluable histories of the two key motor vehicle manufacturers in the interwar period. The best overviews of the industry are to be found in chapters by R. Church and M. Miller in B. Supple (ed.), *Essays in British Business History* (Oxford, 1977) and in Buxton and Aldcroft (eds), *British Industry between the Wars*. A recent revisionist view which argues against the performance of the motor vehicle manufacturers is W. Lewchuk, *American Technology and the British Vehicle Industry* (Cambridge, 1987). This has been countered by Steven Tolliday in two important pieces, 'Management and labour in Britain, 1896–1939' in

S. Tolliday and J. Zeitlin (eds), *The Automobile Industry and Its Workers; between Fordism and Flexibility* (Oxford, 1987) and 'The failure of mass production unionism in the motor industry 1914–1939' in C. Wrigley (ed.), *A History of British Industrial Relations, Volume III, 1914–1937* (Brighton, 1987), and by S. Bowden and P. Turner, 'Some cross-section evidence of the determinants of the diffusion of car ownership in the interwar UK economy', *Business History* vol. 35 (1993), pp. 55–69.

Interwar living standards and consumption patterns were analysed in a number of contemporary social surveys, notably H. Llewellyn Smith, *The New Survey of London Life and Labour* (9 vols, London, 1930–35) and B. Seebohm Rowntree, *Poverty and Progress* (London, 1941). For an evocative interpretation of changing middle-class lifestyles see A.A. Jackson, *The Middle Classes, 1900–1950* (Nairn, Scotland, 1991).

Notes

1. See S. Bowden and A. Offer, 'Household appliances and the use of time: the United States and Britain since the 1920s', *Economic History Review* (1994).

2. See, for example, Robert Graves and Alan Hodge, *The Long Weekend; A Social History of Great Britain, 1918–1939* (1940, London) pp. 171–90; Robert Roberts, *The Class Slum* (Manchester, 1971) p. 229; Margery Spring-Rice, *Working Class Wives* (London, 1939) p. 99.

3. Sean Glynn and John Oxborrow, *Interwar Britain; A Social and Economic History* (London, 1976) pp. 221, 227.

4. Harry Richardson, 'The basis of economic recovery in the nineteen-thirties; a review and a new interpretation', *Economic History Review* vol. 15 (1962), pp. 344–63.

5. Ministry of Labour, 'Weekly expenditure of working class households in the United Kingdom, 1937–1938', *Ministry of Labour Gazette* (London), December 1940, January 1941 and February 1941.

6. Estimated from G. Harrison and F.C. Mitchell, *The Home Market; a Handbook of Statistics* (London, 1936) pp. 60–1, and A.L. Chapman and R. Knight, *Wages and Salaries in the United Kingdom 1920–1938* (Cambridge, 1953).

7. Phillip Massey, 'The expenditure of 1360 British middle class households in 1938–1939', *Journal of the Royal Statistical Society* vol. 105, Part III (1942), pp. 159–85. See, in particular, Table XVIII, p. 177.

8. Wayne Lewchuk, *American Technology and the British Vehicle Industry* (Cambridge, 1987).

9. Steven Tolliday, 'Management and labour in Britain, 1896–1939' in S. Tolliday and J. Zeitlin (eds), *The Automobile Industry and Its Workers; between Fordism and Flexibility* (Oxford, 1987) pp. 29–56, and Steven Tolliday, 'The failure of mass production unionism in the motor industry 1914–1939' in C. Wrigley (ed.), *A History of British Industrial Relations, Volume III, 1914–1937* (Brighton, 1987); Sue Bowden, 'Demand and supply constraints in the Inter-War UK car industry: Did the manufacturers get it right?', *Business History* vol. 33 (1991), pp. 241–67; Sue Bowden and Paul Turner, 'Some cross-section evidence of the determinants of the diffusion of car ownership

in the interwar UK economy', *British History* vol. 35 (1993), pp. 55–69; Sue Bowden and Paul Turner, 'The UK consumer and the demand for consumer durables in the UK in the interwar Period', *Journal of Economic History* (1993).

10. R. Church, *Herbert Austin; The British Motor Industry to 1941* (London, 1979) pp. 214–15; R.J. Overy, *William Morris, Viscount Nuffield* (London, 1976) p. 129.

11. G. Maxcy and A. Silberston, *The Motor Industry* (London, 1959) p. 211; Lewchuk, *American Technology* p. 146; Overy, *William Morris*, Table 10, p. 51; Church, *Herbert Austin*, Table 6, p. 84.

15 Cinema and Broadcasting

Andrew Davies

The growth of the leisure industries was widely identified by contemporary commentators as one of the most profound social changes of the early twentieth century. Two of the most influential developments were the rise of the cinema and the advent of radio broadcasting, forms of mass entertainment which were in their infancy in the 1890s, yet occupied a central position in national life by the 1930s. These changes aroused a great deal of controversy. Some observers viewed the growth of leisure largely in terms of social progress. The cinema was widely seen as opening up a new world of romance and adventure, whilst radio was viewed as improving the quality of domestic life, providing news and information as well as entertainment. Others, however, warned that mass entertainment posed significant dangers. The cinema was seen by some conservative critics as undermining established social and moral values. Left-wing commentators, on the other hand, tended to argue that Hollywood films provided a new 'opiate' for the masses, promoting political apathy during periods of economic distress and high unemployment.

The growth of mass entertainment, already under way by 1914, was further stimulated by the restrictions imposed upon drinking during the First World War. The strength of beer was reduced, prices were increased through taxation and public house opening hours were shortened. These changes were maintained after the war, and although the pub retained a central role in working-class neighbourhood life, the extent of drinking (and drunkenness) declined as other forms of mass leisure grew during the interwar period. The commercial dance hall, for example, came to symbolize the increasing affluence and freedom of youth, and the early 1920s saw halls opening throughout urban Britain as new American styles of music and dancing were adopted by enthusiastic 'jazzers'. The holiday industry also grew substantially. Blackpool, Britain's most popular holiday resort, drew seven million visitors annually by the 1930s, and the first purpose-built holiday camp was opened by Butlin's at Skegness in 1937. Spectator sports flourished, with the total attendance at first division football league matches rising to fourteen million during the 1937–38 season, compared with six million in 1908–9. The popular passion for gambling was heightened, as betting on horse races was augmented by the introduction of commercial greyhound tracks during the 1920s; and by the spectacular growth of the football pools which developed a national framework during the interwar period, and attracted an estimated ten million regular punters by the late 1930s. While the growth of mass leisure attracted widespread interest among social commentators, the interwar period also saw significant developments in middle-class leisure patterns. Predominantly middle-class sports such as tennis and golf grew in popularity, and motoring provided new interests and opportunities for the middle classes. Private car ownership, which stood at 100,000 in 1919, reached two million by 1939, although the overwhelming majority of working-class families were excluded.

The Demand for Leisure

The growth of the leisure industries during the interwar period was stimulated by a reduction in the working week for those in full-time paid employment. In 1919 and 1920, approximately seven million workers gained reductions averaging over six hours a week, bringing the average working week down to forty-eight hours, compared with fifty-four hours before the First World War. Average weekly hours remained at the level of forty-eight during the 1920s and 1930s, and many social commentators and trade unionists saw the increase in leisure time as one of the major social gains of the period. The question of holidays with pay also became a prominent issue in the aftermath of the First World War. By the early 1920s, an estimated one million manual workers were covered by agreements for paid holidays, but following the onset of economic depression by 1921, employers tended to resist such demands on the grounds that they would increase labour costs. Significant progress was only made in the changing economic climate of the mid to late 1930s, when trade union campaigns to secure holidays with pay met with much greater success, and by 1938, 7.75 million workers out of a total occupied population of 18.5 million were in receipt of paid holidays.[1]

Expenditure on leisure increased markedly during the interwar period, due to rising real wages and a decline in family size. The social investigator Seebohm Rowntree, in a study of York during the mid 1930s, estimated that the increase in real wages amounted to an improvement in the standard of living for working-class families of around 30 per cent between 1899 and 1936. Moreover, the decline in family size meant that proportionately less of a family's income was devoted to basic necessities such as food. One of the major consequences, as Rowntree noted, was a significant widening of the opportunities for leisure.[2] In national terms, expenditure on entertainment and recreation rose from £195.1 million in 1920 to £262.5 million in 1938 (at 1938 prices). However, it is interesting to note that the amount spent on alcohol fell from £426.5 million to £306.4 million over the same period, which in part no doubt reflected a transfer of expenditure from drink towards activities such as cinema-going.

Despite these broad trends, it is important to recognize that access to leisure was structured by class, income, gender and age. Poverty and unemployment could dictate that men in working-class areas were unable to take part in the customary masculine pursuits of drinking, gambling and attending football matches. Participation in leisure was also structured by profound inequalities based on gender. Married women tended to have considerably less time and money for leisure than their husbands, and although working hours in industry declined after the First World War, women's domestic responsibilities could leave them with very little free time, especially if they were responsible for the care of young children. The lives of married women, especially among the working classes, contrasted sharply with the experiences of youths, who used their relative freedom from domestic responsibilities to take full advantage of the new opportunities provided by the growth of the cinema, dance hall and seaside holiday. Despite the growth of the leisure industries during the 1920s and 1930s, leisure therefore remained a sphere in which social inequalities were dramatically highlighted. This can be demonstrated with reference to the holiday industry. By 1937, for example, despite the growth of Britain's seaside resorts and the emergence of holiday camps, only around a third of Britain's population of forty-six million were taking a holiday away from home of a week or more.

The Advent of Radio Broadcasting

Radio broadcasting was first undertaken on a regular basis in Britain following the formation of the British Broadcasting Company (BBC) in 1922.[3] Although Marconi first experimented successfully with radio technology in 1896, the radio, or 'wireless' as it was popularly known, was used only by a small group of enthusiasts prior to 1914. The state assumed control of radio technology under the Wireless Telegraphy Act of 1904, which determined that all transmitters and receivers were to be licensed by the Post Office, but by 1914 there were only 2,150 licences in operation. With the outbreak of war, transmissions were forbidden and equipment impounded under the Defence of the Realm Act. However, the war proved to be a turning point in the history of radio, as the technology was substantially developed through extensive military use. The growth of broadcasting was restricted between 1918 and 1921, largely because radio technology was now considered to be vital for military purposes, but following extensive lobbying by radio manufacturers and amateur 'wireless' enthusiasts, restrictions were eventually lifted and by 1922 the Post Office had negotiated with the six largest manufacturers to form the BBC.

The BBC was established because the Post Office sought to avoid the chaos which had resulted from unrestrained broadcasting in the United States. Two of the central features of British broadcasting were established in 1922. Firstly, the BBC was to be a monopoly service, and thus free from commercial pressures. The wavebands were considered to be public property, and this paved the way for the emergence of the ethos of 'public service' broadcasting, which came to dominate BBC programming. Secondly, from 1922 the BBC was to be funded by a 10s licence fee, administered by the Post Office. This gave the government of the day a strong element of indirect control over broadcasting policy, as the BBC was ultimately responsible to a government minister, the Postmaster General. In 1925, the Crawford Committee was set up to examine the development of broadcasting in Britain. The Committee rejected the notion of broadcasting for profit, and also rejected the possibility of direct state control, advocating instead that the BBC should become a public corporation, acting in the national interest. The BBC duly became a corporation in 1927, with John Reith appointed as its first Director General.

Established as a service operating in the public interest, the BBC was driven from the beginning by a strong sense of moral purpose. Reith was adamant that radio should not be given over to entertainment alone, and saw the BBC's mission as improving cultural and educational standards among the listening public. Reith argued that it was the BBC's duty to educate public tastes. Early critics, however, argued that the Corporation's hierarchy was imposing its own values upon the listening public, and showing little regard for the varied tastes of its audience. The BBC was also alleged to be socially elitist. Most of its staff were drawn from public school and Oxbridge backgrounds, and their accents alone ensured that the BBC was perceived to be part of Britain's ruling establishment.

Reith's conception of public service broadcasting extended to a broad vision of radio's potential social and political functions. Broadcasting was seen as a means of bringing the different classes together and thus promoting social unity. Coverage of major national events and royal occasions was seen as providing the BBC with the role of 'making the nation as one man'. Reith also saw radio as having immense potential for contributing to the creation of an informed and enlightened democracy. In the age of the mass electorate, radio could highlight the range of arguments over the issues of the day. The question of political coverage, however, generated much bitterness. Accusations of bias, by politicians on both the right and the left, were widespread during the 1920s and 1930s, and the BBC largely bowed to government pressure through the Post Office not to deal with controversial political discussion. A proposed series of talks on 'A Citizen and his Government', for example, featuring Oswald Mosley and Harry Pollitt putting the cases for fascism and communism was dropped after discreet Cabinet intervention. As a result, the potential for the BBC to contribute to the formation of a more educated democracy was barely realized, and it was commonly alleged during the 1930s that the BBC was only able to broadcast talks which were acceptable in the most conservative circles.

The controversy over political coverage was brought to a head by the

General Strike in 1926. Reith resisted Churchill's proposal that the BBC should be commandeered for the purpose of government propaganda, yet the BBC clearly sided with the government against the strikers, even though coverage was much more moderate than Churchill demanded. Government ministers were able to appeal directly to the radio audience, a privilege denied to Labour Party and trade union leaders. The tenor of most news broadcasts showed clear support for the government, and tended to be uplifting in spirit, often focusing on events such as the arrival of food and fuel supplies which would boost the morale of the government and its supporters. This was bitterly resented by the strikers, some of whom began to refer disparagingly to the BBC as the 'British Falsehood Corporation', even though they still depended on the radio as their main source of information. With the press heavily hit by the strike, broadcasts made a dramatic impact. Radio was the main source of news in the country as a whole, and the maintenance of the BBC service served to provide an element of calm and normality at the peak of the strike.

Although furious allegations of bias were made by contemporary left-wing politicians, Paddy Scannell and David Cardiff have argued that the BBC had little choice other than to show support for the government. To have done otherwise would have jeopardized the licence fee, and possibly even the future of the BBC. Reith hoped that the Corporation's display of 'responsibility' during the strike would earn the right to deal more fully with controversial political issues in the future, but he was soon disappointed. According to the terms of the BBC's charter, drawn up in late 1926, controversial broadcasts were expressly forbidden at the insistence of the Postmaster General. The BBC's independence was therefore strictly partial. Governments rarely interfered directly in the day-to-day running of the Corporation, but broadcasters operated at all times in the knowledge that they could be brought to heel by direct or indirect pressures, including the threat to withhold the licence fee.[4]

The popularity of the radio grew steadily from 1922 onwards. In 1924, licences were held by 10 per cent of British households, rising to 30 per cent by 1930, 48 per cent by 1933, and 71 per cent by 1939. However, this still left an estimated 13.5 million people, mainly drawn from the poorer sections of the working class, without access to a radio at the outbreak of the Second World War. Oral evidence from the Lake Counties suggests that middle-class families tended to purchase radio sets before their working-class counterparts, and as late as 1934, it was reported that the 'wireless' was 'almost unknown' in the slum areas and among the poorer classes generally in Liverpool.[5] In terms of the cost of radio equipment, crystal sets were relatively inexpensive at around £1–2 during the 1920s, although mass-produced valve sets cost £5–6 by the mid 1930s, when average weekly wages for adult male manual workers stood at little over £3.

During the 1920s, listening to the radio was predominantly a male hobby, and an individual one. Radios could easily cause domestic strife, as reception was so faint that entire families had to sit in silence in order to allow a wireless enthusiast to 'listen in'. However, by the 1930s, as the higher quality valve sets provided much superior reception, the radio became a new focus for family entertainment in the home. In working-class districts, radio was an important incentive to domesticity, and tended to draw families into the home in areas where leisure time was otherwise largely spent in the streets. Jennings and Gill, who conducted a detailed study of the impact of broadcasting in a working-class area in Bristol during the mid 1930s, found that the radio was highly valued as a form of companionship, brightening time spent doing housework, for example, whilst it was generally agreed that the radio had widened the range of family conversation. In keeping with the ethos of public service broadcasting, the BBC sought to encourage a seriousness of purpose among the listening public. However, for the most part, audiences used the radio for relaxation and entertainment. A survey of a random sample of BBC listeners in 1939 revealed that the most popular programmes were those featuring variety and musical comedy, and music by theatre and cinema organists, military bands and dance bands.

Plate 15.1.   Listening to the funeral service of George V in an Essex farmhouse. By enabling people in all parts of the country to participate passively in national events, radio broadcasting enhanced a sense of national identity.

Mark Pegg has suggested that by 1939, the advent of broadcasting had led to a series of important social changes. Firstly, as Reith had anticipated, the BBC did contribute to an altered sense of national identity. Radio coverage brought a sense of 'participation in the spirit and emotion of national events', profoundly changing the relationship between the nation and the royal family, for example. Radio also served to broaden the interests and knowledge of the listening public, and by 1939 had gained ascendancy over the press as a means of spreading news and information. Thirdly, radio led to the increasing domestication of leisure, thus contributing to changes in the pattern of family life in many households. However, despite Reith's vision, the BBC did not provide a means of social engineering. Accents, for example, were largely unaffected by the advent of broadcasting. Jennings and Gill found that Bristol dialects were intact in 1939, despite the best efforts of the BBC to promote the use of 'educated Southern English'. Indeed, the accents of BBC announcers were highly resented in parts of northern England, Scotland and Wales.[6]

The Expansion of the Cinema Industry

The cinema grew very rapidly during the decade prior to the First World War, rising from a fairground novelty to become the most popular form of commercial entertainment in Britain. During the 1920s and 1930s, a host of social commentators remarked upon the immense popularity of film-going, especially in working-class areas, with the Report of the Conference on Christian Politics, Economics and Citizenship held in 1924 declaring that the 'pictures' were 'solidly established as the pastimes of millions'. Throughout Britain's towns and cities, the growth of the cinema was spectacular. Liverpool had 96 cinemas in 1939 compared with 32 in 1913, whilst Birmingham's cinemas grew in total from 57 to 110 over the same period. Nationally, there were already around 3,000 cinemas in Britain by 1914, rising to almost 5,000 during the 1930s, and by 1939 there were an estimated 23 million cinema admissions each week.

Prior to 1914, the majority of cinemas were either converted shops or small, purpose-built picture houses seating only 200 to 400. Most were owned by small-scale entrepreneurs with a record of involvement in the local entertainment industry. By the late 1920s, however, the structure of the industry was changing dramatically with the rise of the national cinema chains such as Odeon Theatres, and Gaumont British which owned over 300 cinemas by 1928. Following the formation of the national chains, the 1920s and 1930s saw the great age of cinema building in Britain. As Jeffrey Richards has commented: 'The buildings themselves became escapist fantasies, their decor and accoutrements – sweeping marble staircases, silvery fountains, uniformed staff and glittering chandeliers – providing a real-life extension of the dream world of the screen'.[7] Cinemas built in the form of Egyptian temples or

Spanish haciendas provided exotic settings in which to watch Hollywood adventures and romances, while the Odeon cinemas with their streamlined curves and Art Deco embellishments became a distinctive symbol of 1930s architecture. The cinemas of the late 1920s and 1930s, like the 'gin palaces' of the nineteenth century, were intended to provide an atmosphere of luxury and well-being which the majority of those in the audiences had hitherto barely imagined. Of course, these lavish 'super-cinemas', often seating audiences of 2,000 or more, contrasted sharply with picturehouses built prior to 1914, many of which were renowned by the 1920s as 'bug huts' or 'flea pits'.

The *Social Survey of Merseyside*, published in 1934, estimated that 40 per cent of the local population attended the cinema each week. As elsewhere, the cinema was most popular in working-class areas. Among adults, women tended to go more often than their husbands, and this finding was echoed by Rowntree, who found that 75 per cent of adult cinema-goers in York during the late 1930s were women. The Merseyside survey also noted that youths attended the cinema in greater numbers than the population as a whole. This was the case in all the major towns and cities. In Manchester, for example, it was common for working-class youths to attend the cinema two, three or even four times a week, and on certain nights audiences at cinemas in working-class districts could be composed entirely of young people.

During the 1930s, a number of social observers found that the cinema was highly popular among the unemployed. Surveys of South London, Cardiff, Liverpool and Glasgow all suggested that cinema-going was the single most important leisure activity among unemployed men and youths, although men without work tended to attend cheap matinée showings and were therefore segregated socially from those in full-time employment. However, going to the 'pictures' was never a universal pastime, even in the urban working-class areas where the cinema held its greatest appeal. Although youths of both sexes were regular film-goers, a significant number of older married men resisted the lure of the cinema in favour of the more traditional masculine pursuits of drinking, gambling and sport. Moreover, although married women tended to be more enthusiastic film-goers than their husbands, there remained a substantial minority of working-class women who could not find the time or the money to visit the cinema. Margery Spring Rice's survey of the lifestyles of working-class wives during 1939 included an account of: 'A woman in Sheffield who is very poor, lives in a slum house, and has four children, is in extremely bad health. She says she must rest sometimes during the day – and she sometimes plays cards or ludo "as that is cheaper than the pictures – I have no money for pictures" '.[8] Women in the poorest working-class households frequently enjoyed little or no access to mass entertainment.

Films only gradually acquired a substantial middle-class audience. Initially patronized by the urban working classes, cinema only gained widespread acceptance in middle-class circles during the late 1920s and 1930s. The transition from silent to 'talking' pictures from 1928 led to a renewed upsurge in cinema building, spreading to middle-class suburbs, and the Odeon chain, in particular, offered luxury and respectability to a growing middle-class clientele. In 1932, the Commission on Educational and Cultural Films declared: 'it is becoming distinctly rare to find an educated person who does not know something about the outstanding films of the last year or two ... The cinema is acquiring prestige'.[9]

The influence of Hollywood was clearly evident in the streets, shops, offices, cafes and dance halls of Britain's towns and cities throughout the 1920s and 1930s. Screen heroes and heroines inspired a heightened sense of fashion, especially among working-class youths, many of whom strove to emulate the appearances, mannerisms and speech of their favourite American stars. Journalists from London to Manchester bemoaned the tendency among youths to adopt both American accents and Hollywood slang. Nor was this alleged vice confined to the cities. As the Welsh writer H.W.J. Edwards commented on the Rhondda Valley in 1937: 'the delightful local accent is broken up by such words and phrases as "Attaboy!", "Oh Yeah!" and "Sez you"...'.[10]

Young men's fashions borrowed heavily from Hollywood. In particular, 'gangster' styles fitted the importance traditionally attached by youths to notions of masculine strength and aggression, and as a journalist reported from 'Islington's most notorious cafe' in 1934: 'Nearly every youth, with a very long overcoat and a round black hat on the rear of his head, was to himself a "Chicago nut" '. However, whereas male youths used ideas drawn from the cinema to reinforce established values, Hollywood popularized new images of femininity. For young working-class women, films held out a vision of a way of life which was vastly different from the poverty and strife of their mothers' lives. As Jerry White has commented: 'The emancipated woman or career girl was one of the dominant stereotypes of the 1920s and 1930s, with stars like Claudette Colbert and Joan Crawford making their own careers in the role'. They were widely copied, and thus as Sally Alexander has recently remarked, mimetic images of Harlow, Garbo and Crawford paraded Britain's high streets, as they glowed across the cinema screen. Some young women spent their weeks literally acting out what they had seen in the latest films. Adopting the smart clothes and the tilt of a hat favoured by a Hollywood actress gave a temporary illusion of glamour and wealth, of being like Greta Garbo or Ginger Rogers, and thus at least temporarily satisfied a yearning to escape the domestic treadmill which their mothers had suffered. J.B. Priestley commented that one of the most striking characteristics of the 'new post-war England' was the appearance of 'factory girls looking like actresses'. A new element of classlessness in fashion resulted, so that by the 1930s it was increasingly difficult to judge the social origins of a young woman by her appearance.[11]

In focus: Cinema-going in Bolton during the 1930s

Some of the most detailed surveys of leisure patterns in interwar Britain were carried out by Mass-Observation. Founded by the journalist Charles Madge and the anthropologist Tom Harrisson in 1937, Mass-Observation aimed to promote research into everyday life among the mass of industrial workers in Britain. During the late 1930s, much of their activity was based in Bolton, which they considered to be a representative industrial town, and Mass-Observation conducted detailed studies of cinema-going, pub culture and the seaside holiday as central features of local life.

In addition to interviewing cinema managers and observing audiences during films, Mass-Observation issued questionnaires at three cinemas in Bolton in order to gather information about the local impact of the growth of the film industry. As Jeffrey Richards and Dorothy Sheridan have pointed out, Mass-Observation's questionnaires are of great value because historians have little other contemporary evidence of the views of cinema-goers themselves on the key questions of why the cinema was so popular, and what audiences thought of the films of the day.[12] The questionnaires were distributed during March 1938, and 559 responses were received. The venues were chosen to reflect the range of Bolton's cinemas, and included the Palladium, described by Richards and Sheridan as a 'fleapit', which had opened in 1919 and drew most of its audience from the working-class area nearby. By contrast, the Odeon, which had opened in Bolton city centre in 1937, was chosen to represent the palatial 'super cinemas' of the 1930s. Complete with cafe and resident organist, the Odeon drew a socially-mixed clientele, including a relatively high proportion of middle-class customers.

Perhaps the most striking feature of the replies to the Mass-Observation questionnaire is the strength of the devotion to the cinema among this sample of Bolton's film-going public. Some went to see films that they particularly enjoyed two or even three times, and popular Hollywood romances, especially, were clearly a highlight of many people's lives. The intense popularity of the cinema was also highlighted by a cinema manager who pointed out that even during strikes at local mills or engineering works, when working people were unable to afford their customary evening trips to the cinema, takings rose at the cheaper afternoon showings as film fans were highly reluctant to miss out on the latest productions.

The replies to the Mass-Observation questionnaire show very clearly that the appeal of the cinema lay in its ability to provide both high quality entertainment and an opportunity for people to be 'taken out of themselves' and to forget their troubles. Mrs Lillie Williams, aged seventy-eight, who attended the Odeon 'super cinema' once a week, spoke for many when she remarked: 'I go to the films to be entertained, amused, to forget everyday worries'. Bolton's cinema-goers told how films could be uplifting, promoting a real sense of well-being, and providing a chance to laugh or cry and thus forget the anxieties of everyday life. The cinema could also provide a sharp

Cinema-going in Bolton during the 1930s (continued)

but welcome contrast with the world of work. Thomas Weatherall, one of the working-class youths who frequented the Palladium, declared:

> I like Western films, because there is plenty of excitement, action, killing. When you have spent a dull, dreary day in the spinning room you want to see some open air life as you usually get in Western films.

When prompted by Mass-Observation's questionnaire, however, film fans on the whole were adamant that religion and politics had little place on the screen. Entertainment, rather than instruction, was desired.

Bolton's film-goers were highly enthusiastic in their assessment of the value of the cinema in their everyday lives, yet they formed a critical, rather than passive, audience. As the manager of the Embassy cinema pointed out, his regulars were quick to inform him of their likes and dislikes, expressing their disapproval with comments such as 'How much did they pay you to put that rubbish on?' Moreover, the replies to the Mass-Observation questionnaire reveal a wide diversity of opinion among cinema audiences. War films, for example, were well received by some, yet regarded with horror by others who wanted no reminder of personal tragedies which had resulted from the First World War.

The most popular category of film among Mass-Observation's sample was the musical romance, followed by drama and tragedy, history and crime. Musical romances were by far the most popular films among all sections of Bolton's film-going public, with the notable exception of the male youths among the working-class audience at the Palladium who were devotees of crime films. Commenting on the broad preferences among women and men, Richards and Sheridan remarked that:

> In general, the women seem to have been drawn to films about sensitive, long-suffering, self-sacrificing women, often tied to ungrateful or unworthy husbands and children, and the men to films about tough *macho* he-men, who are good in a fight, stand up for what is right, and love their country. This tells us something about the self-image of men and women in 1930s Bolton.[13]

Of course, these self-images were deeply rooted in Bolton neighbourhoods prior to the emergence of the cinema. The most successful films were those which appealed to pre-existing popular values and beliefs. It is interesting to note that whereas the emancipated 'career girls' played by Claudette Colbert and Joan Crawford provided role models for the young and single, Bolton women still empathized with depictions of long-suffering wives and mothers, which reflected more directly the potential realities of women's experiences after marriage.

Cinema-going in Bolton during the 1930s (continued)

The Mass-Observation questionnaires highlighted the clear preference for American films among British cinema audiences: 63 per cent of those who replied stated that they preferred American films, with only 18 per cent opting for British and the remainder of the sample undecided. Hollywood productions were generally judged to be more polished, fast moving and spectacular than their British counterparts, and the quality of the acting in American films was widely considered to be superior. As James Walsh, a regular in the predominantly working-class audiences at the Palladium, explained:

> British films are tame, the actors self conscious and wooden, the settings easily recognized as the work of novices. Experience dating from the first showing of Al Jolson in *The Singing Fool* goes to show that the man in the street likes pictures which advertise an American cast. One knows it will be a good picture. One often hears the remark, 'It's a British Picture, let's go elsewhere.'

Certain categories of British film were well received by Bolton audiences, most notably the comedies of Gracie Fields and George Formby and historical epics such as *Victoria the Great*. The majority of British productions, however, with their upper-class 'society' settings and 'Oxford accents' held little appeal.

The Impact of Cinema upon Popular Attitudes

Throughout the 1920s and 1930s, it was widely believed that the cinema was highly influential in shaping attitudes and values, especially among the urban working classes who made up the bulk of the cinema audience. According to conservative social commentators, for example, the cinema posed a grave threat to social and moral values. American films, especially, were alleged to undermine respect for the family and the institution of marriage, while 'gangster' films were seen as glamorizing crime and thereby eroding respect for the law. As Jeffrey Richards has shown, the novelty and immense popularity of the cinema made it a convenient scapegoat for contemporary moralists, and the pernicious influence of films was widely condemned by a chorus of teachers, clergymen, magistrates and politicians. However, despite attempts to blame an apparent increase in juvenile delinquency upon the cinema, researchers failed to establish any clear links between cinema attendance and patterns of crime, and police opinion on the issue was divided. Some Chief Constables even argued that the cinema performed the valuable functions of reducing drunkenness, and keeping working-class youths off the streets and thus away from potential brushes with the law.

Fears surrounding the impact of films upon popular attitudes led to the adoption of censorship in Britain with the formation of the British Board of Film Censors (BBFC) in 1912. In the light of the prevailing belief that predominantly working-class audiences were heavily influenced by films, anxieties over social and moral values were allied to a concern that films might be used to inflame the working class during periods of economic and political unrest. The BBFC was established by the film industry in order to allay such fears, and operated independently of the government of the day. However, the censors tended to show strong respect for the perceived wishes of governments, and tended to adopt a highly conservative stance in their treatment of social, moral and political issues. A tight rein was kept on portrayals of sex and crime, whilst the censors banned the treatment of many political and religious themes, which were seen as unsuitable material for an entertainment industry. The BBFC argued that films about political controversies or industrial disputes might provoke disorder and unrest, whilst a focus on social problems could demoralize audiences. There were therefore very few realistic depictions of working-class life in films during the 1920s and 1930s.

In 1936, a proposal for a film version of Walter Greenwood's novel *Love on the Dole* was submitted to the BBFC. *Love on the Dole,* which dealt graphically with the impact of unemployment upon individual workers and their families, had been successfully converted into a stage play but the film proposal was flatly rejected by the BBFC. The censors considered the proposal to contain 'too much of the tragic and sordid side of poverty', whilst objections were raised to a number of specific scenes, including a depiction of a clash between unemployed demonstrators and the police. Similarly, *Blue Cafe,* a 1933 stage play which depicted a Soho underworld of prostitution and drug dealing, was rejected by the BBFC with the verdict: 'The whole story centres around the dope traffic. The language and morals are impossible. Under no circumstances could we pass a film based on this play'.[14]

The impact of censorship has been one of the central themes in recent historical studies of the cinema. Nicholas Pronay, for example, has argued strongly that censorship dictated that films did not carry political messages conflicting with those of the government. Instead, he suggests, films successfully fostered social harmony, faith in British institutions and hope of better days. Confirming this argument, Jeffrey Richards asserts that censorship amounted to a 'coherently organised form of social control' which provided powerfully for the maintenance of the status quo. The censors shielded the existing social and political orders from criticism, thus helping to preserve them. Certainly, censorship meant that some aspects of British society were not examined in any depth in British films. There were no realistic depictions of crime or the criminal underworld, or of strikes and industrial conflict.[15]

Taking this approach a stage further, Tony Aldgate and Jeffrey Richards have both suggested that the films of most popular British stars of the 1930s actively promoted social consensus. The films of Gracie Fields and George Formby, it is argued, advocated faith in the existing structure of society during periods of acute economic depression. Gracie Fields became a national symbol during the 1930s. Indeed, the resilient 'Lancashire lass' was so popular that in 1939, during a serious illness, she received 250,000 letters and telegrams wishing her well. Whereas the 'society' settings of the majority of British productions met with little popular approval, Fields played characters who were unashamedly working-class, and she was hugely popular among working-class audiences who could easily identify with her. However, she became a national symbol, rather than just a working-class heroine, from the mid 1930s, as her films saw the injection of an increasingly patriotic emphasis. She was also frequently romantically involved with upper-class, old Etonian type characters, leading Richards to suggest that her films promoted the ideals of class reconciliation and social consensus.

While *Love on the Dole* was never filmed during the 1930s, Gracie Fields made several films which touched on issues of mass unemployment in northern England, most famously *Sing as We Go*, which was released in 1934. At the beginning of the film, it is announced that the mill where Fields works is due to close. The film stresses that the management face unemployment along with the rest of the workforce, and Fields's response is that everyone must confront the closure with resilience and cheerfulness. Moreover, she declares, the works' musical should be kept going: 'If we can't spin, we can still sing'. For most of the film, the action switches to Blackpool where Fields takes a series of seasonal jobs, well away from grim reminders of life in a textile town decimated by unemployment. She returns at the end of the film, when a new production process is miraculously discovered, and the mill is able to reopen. She leads the workforce back to the sound of triumphant singing, and amid much waving of the Union Jack. The film's message was clear, stressing the need to show courage, humour and optimism in the face of hardship. Not surprisingly, Conservative politicians saw Fields as an ideal influence on working-class film-goers.[16]

Historians such as Pronay, Aldgate and Richards have tended to suggest that films were deliberately and successfully used to foster faith in the existing structure of society during the 1920s and 1930s. However, this view has been challenged by Stephen Jones, who argued that the cinema should not be seen as a 'cultural propaganda machine'. Film production was geared to the market, and therefore needed to appeal to the tastes of a predominantly working-class audience. Ultimately, films had to reflect, rather than attempt to remould, popular attitudes and ideas.[17] Moreover, if films were not allowed to address issues such as industrial conflict, or 'controversial' political topics, then the cinema may have had only a limited impact upon the formation of popular social and political values. Indeed, it might be argued that such attitudes were more profoundly shaped by other areas of people's lives, such as experiences of work and unemployment, or trade union membership. The

Plate 15.2. A triumphant Gracie Fields in *Sing As We Go*, 1934. The popularity of Gracie Fields rested on her characters exhibiting a combination of working-class grittiness and overt patriotism. Her films presented an image of British society in which class harmony was more important than class difference.

major difficulty facing historians here is that it is impossible to *measure* the impact of films upon their audiences, or to untangle the influence of the cinema from other influences which determined people's social and political attitudes.

During the 1920s and 1930s, left-wing commentators feared that films were providing a narcotic, a new 'opiate of the masses', and thus functioning as a kind of social safety valve during periods of widespread unemployment and poverty. The cinema was seen as providing a dream world which allowed people to forget their hardships. This view was most famously expressed by George Orwell, who listed films as one of the cheap luxuries which, he felt, had between them averted revolution in Britain by the mid 1930s. As Orwell put it:

> You may have three halfpence in your pocket and not a prospect in the world, and only the corner of a leaky bedroom to go home to; but in your new clothes you can stand on the street corner, indulging in a private daydream of yourself as Clark Gable or Greta Garbo, which compensates you for a great deal.[18]

Again, we should perhaps be cautious here. People certainly went to the cinema in order to forget about their troubles, and to add some romance and glamour to their lives. However, even two or three trips to the cinema a week were unlikely to make up entirely for the difficulties posed by inadequate housing, poverty, unemployment or poor medical provision. Whilst the cinema certainly improved the quality of life in urban working-class areas, including areas of high unemployment, the cinema alone did not transform working-class living standards, and broader political explanations are needed to explain the weaknesses of parties of the left in Britain during the 1930s.

Many social critics, on both the right and the left, tended to regard cinema audiences as passive, and to assume that people simply internalized the messages contained in films. However, audiences may have ignored these messages, or viewed them cynically. Significantly, a survey of cinema-going among working-class youths in Manchester during the early 1930s showed that they were very critical of the films that they saw, and did not always believe that depictions of the lives of other social classes in films were realistic.[19] Some caution is therefore needed in discussions of the impact of films on people's attitudes and values. Perhaps both right and left-wing anxieties regarding the cinema were largely unfounded. The rise of the cinema did not lead to a collapse of moral values, yet nor did films 'dope' the working-class.

Bibliographical Note

The most comprehensive national survey of leisure during the interwar period is Stephen Jones's *Workers at Play: a Social and Economic History of Leisure 1918–1939* (London, 1986) which usefully charts the growth and impact of the commercial leisure industries, including the cinema. By contrast, in a local study, A. Davies *Leisure, Gender and Poverty: Working-class Culture in Salford and Manchester, 1900–1939* (Buckingham, 1992) explores the impact of poverty as an everyday constraint upon the use of free time and stresses the depth of gender and generational divisions in leisure patterns.

In *Broadcasting and Society 1918–1939* (Beckenham, 1983), Mark Pegg argues that the growth of radio broadcasting generated profound social changes, helping to create a new sense of national identity, and prompting changes in family leisure patterns. Paddy Scannell and David Cardiff, in *A Social History of British Broadcasting. Volume One 1922–1939. Serving the Nation* (Oxford, 1991) provide a cogent and stimulating account of the formation of BBC programming strategies, showing how public service broadcasting developed within the constraints imposed by government pressures.

The essential work on the cinema in interwar Britain remains Jeffrey Richards's path-breaking study, *The Age of the Dream Palace: Cinema and Society in Britain 1930–1939* (London, 1984). Richards charts the mass appeal of the cinema and the intensity of the social anxieties it aroused, arguing that partly due to stringent censorship, films acted as a conservative social force during the 1930s. An alternative to Richards's approach is suggested by Stephen Jones, who argues in *Workers at Play* that film-makers needed to reflect rather than attempt to remould popular attitudes. *Mass-Observation at the Movies* (London 1987), edited by Jeffrey Richards and Dorothy Sheridan, provides the most detailed case-study of the culture of film-going during the interwar decades. The literature dealing with the cinema in Britain has recently been augmented by a useful comparative study, Peter Stead's *Film and the Working Class: the Feature Film in British and American Society* (London, 1989).

Notes

1. S.G. Jones, *Workers at Play: a Social and Economic History of Leisure 1918–1939* (London, 1986) pp. 15–20. I would like to thank Jon Lawrence and Steven Fielding for their comments on an earlier draft of this chapter.

2. B.S. Rowntree, *Poverty and Progress: a Second Social Survey of York* (London, 1941) p. 468.

3. The following account of radio broadcasting is largely based upon two recent studies: M. Pegg, *Broadcasting and Society 1918–1939* (Beckenham, 1983) and P. Scannell and D. Cardiff, *A Social History of British Broadcasting. Volume One 1922–1939. Serving the Nation* (Oxford, 1991).

4. P. Scannell and D. Cardiff, 'Serving the nation: public service broadcasting before the war' in B. Waites, T. Bennett and G. Martin (eds), *Popular Culture: Past and Present* (London, 1982) pp. 164–5.

5. L. Murfin, *Popular Leisure in the Lake Counties* (Manchester, 1990) p. 18; A. Davies, *Leisure, Gender and Poverty: Working-class Culture in Salford and Manchester, 1900–1939* (Buckingham, 1992) p. 40.

6. Pegg, *Broadcasting and Society*, pp. 218–19, 159–61.

7. J. Richards, *The Age of the Dream Palace: Cinema and Society in Britain 1930–1939* (London, 1984) p. 19. This assessment of the expansion of the cinema industry draws heavily upon Richards's account.

8. Cited in Davies, *Leisure, Gender and Poverty*, p. 75.

9. Richards, *Age of the Dream Palace*, pp. 15–16.

10. P. Stead, 'The people and the pictures: the British working class and film in the 1930s' in N. Pronay and D. Spring (eds), *Propaganda, Politics and Film, 1918–45* (London, 1982) p. 81.

11. J. White, *The Worst Street in North London: Campbell Bunk, Islington, between the Wars* (London, 1986) pp. 166, 193–4; S. Alexander, 'Becoming a woman in London in the 1920s and 1930s' in D. Feldman and G. Stedman Jones (eds), *Metropolis, London: Histories and Representations since 1800* (London, 1989) pp. 263–6.

12. J. Richards and D. Sheridan (eds), *Mass-Observation at the Movies* (London, 1987) p. 32. The following case-study is based upon Part 1 of this volume.

13. Richards and Sheridan (eds), *Mass-Observation at the Movies*, p. 40.

14. Richards, *Age of the Dream Palace*, pp. 119–20; R. Murphy, 'Riff-raff: British cinema and the underworld' in C. Barr (ed.), *All our Yesterdays: 90 years of British Cinema* (London, 1986) p. 286.

15. N. Pronay, 'The first reality: film censorship in liberal England', in K. Short (ed.), *Feature Films as History* (London, 1981) pp. 125, 135; Richards, *Age of the Dream Palace*, p. 107.

16. T. Aldgate, 'Comedy, class and containment: the British domestic cinema of the 1930s' in J. Curran and V. Porter (eds), *British Cinema History* (London, 1983) pp. 268–70; Richards, *Age of the Dream Palace*, ch. 10.

17. Jones, *Workers at Play*, pp. 84–5.

18. Stead, 'The people and the pictures', p. 80; G. Orwell, *The Road to Wigan Pier* (Harmondsworth, 1962) pp. 79–81. First published in 1937.

19. Davies, *Leisure, Gender and Poverty*, pp. 95–6.

PART THREE: 1939–1990s

16 The War Economy

Peter Howlett

An Overview of the Wartime Economy

The most significant feature of the British economy in the Second World War was that the market oriented economy of the interwar years was replaced by a centrally managed economy in which the state allocated the most important resources, decided what should be produced, and determined how much should be paid for it. How this transformation came about will be discussed in the subsequent sections whilst this section sets out the broad trends of the wartime economy.

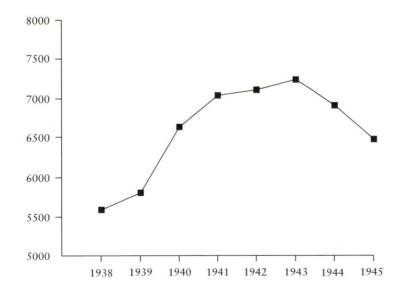

Figure 16.1. Gross domestic product, 1938–45 (£m, constant 1938 market prices). *Source:* C.H. Feinstein, *Statistical Tables of National Income, Expenditure and Output of the UK, 1855–1965* (Cambridge, 1972) T16.

The growth of the economy in real terms, at constant 1938 market prices, is shown in Figure 16.1. The onset of war in 1939 led to a sharp jump in Gross Domestic Product (GDP) and it continued to rise thereafter, reaching its wartime peak in 1943. By 1945 GDP had fallen below its 1940 level but it was still 16 per cent higher than it had been in 1938. Within this overall rise there was a marked change in the composition of GDP, as is shown in Table 16.1. The change in government expenditure is the most significant feature: its share of GDP rose from about one-twelfth in 1938 to half by 1943. This reflected the dominant position the state sector came to play in the war economy: the government had to pay for the greatly expanded numbers of troops in the armed forces and it had to buy the munitions and other goods needed to arm, feed, clothe and accommodate them. The relative and absolute increase in government expenditure was achieved at the expense of civilian consumption (whose share of GDP fell by over a third between 1938 and 1943 and whose absolute value fell by 15 per cent) and non-war related investment (such as housebuilding).

Table 16.1. The main components of GDP, 1938 and 1943 (as % of GDP)

	Consumption	Government	Investment	Net exports
1938	79	13	12	−4
1943	52	50	4	−6

After: C.H. Feinstein, *Statistical Tables of National Income, Expenditure and Output of the United Kingdom, 1855–1965* (Cambridge, 1972) T16.

Table 16.1 does not do justice to the disruption the war caused to trade. It cut Britain off from former trading partners, either because they were now military enemies or because they had been conquered by the enemy or because of military action by the enemy to deliberately disrupt trade. Thus, for example, imports from the major European countries had accounted for 20 per cent of total British imports by value in 1938 but accounted for only 0.2 per cent in 1941; and almost 11 million gross tons of British merchant shipping would be lost during the war to enemy action. The need to produce increased numbers of military ships also reduced the capacity available for building and maintaining the merchant marine and shipping capacity proved to be a major constraint on the British war economy. Finally, the need to produce munitions for the war effort led the government to deliberately curtail export efforts after 1940. The result was that the volume of both imports and exports fell: imports fell by 30 per cent between 1938 and 1942; exports decreased even more dramatically and by 1943 were only 29 per cent of their 1938 volume. Worldwide wartime inflation meant that in value terms the fall in export earnings was a little less steep than the decrease in export volume: export earnings halved between 1938 and 1943. Unfortunately for Britain import prices soared so that despite the fall in import volume their cost rose; for example, in 1945 Britain was importing only 62 per cent of the 1938 level of imports but they cost 23 per cent more than in 1938 (this also partly reflected the increased proportion of finished goods imported during the war).

The fall in export earnings and the rising cost of imports resulted in balance of payments difficulties. The cumulative current account deficit for the war period came to £10 billion. About 12 per cent of this deficit was met by the sale of overseas investments and a further 35 per cent by the accumulation of overseas debts; however, the most important source of financing (amounting to £5.4 billion) was provided by net grants from the US, and to a lesser extent Canada (see below).

The advent of war naturally meant that the armed forces had to be greatly expanded. This was achieved mainly through conscription, which eventually covered all men between the ages of eighteen and forty-five, although a 'ring fence' was placed around certain key occupations. Thus, the armed forces increased from 480,000 men in 1939 to 4.7 million men and 437,000 women by 1945, at which stage they accounted for almost a quarter of the working population. Where did the labour for the expansion of the armed forces, and of the munitions industries, come from? Two obvious sources were the unemployed (in early 1940 there were still more than one million people unemployed in Britain but by 1942 there were less than 100,000) and workers in other industries (for example, textile workers were drafted into the armed forces or were moved into the munitions industries). However, there was a third source: an increase in the size of the working population; that is, more people were attracted into the labour market by appeals to both their patriotism and their pockets (through the inducement of higher wartime wages). At its wartime peak the working population in Britain had increased by three million. A significant factor behind this increase was the number of women attracted into the labour market.

Manpower was viewed by the state as the ultimate constraint on the economy during the war and therefore it adopted measures to ensure that labour was directed to where it was most needed. To achieve this the state gave itself wide ranging powers to control the supply and movement of labour although it tried to use these powers as little as possible, fearing too much compulsion and state intervention might cause industrial unrest, and tried to alleviate their effects by supporting many improvements in working conditions and welfare and by using wage incentives. State wartime manpower planning recognized three categories of civilian employment: Group I industries were the munitions and related industries, such as metals, engineering, aircraft manufacture, motor vehicles, shipbuilding, and chemicals; Group II industries were 'other essential industries', such as agriculture, transportation and the utilities; Group III industries were 'less essential industries', such as textiles, building and services. The trends in civilian employment are shown in Figure

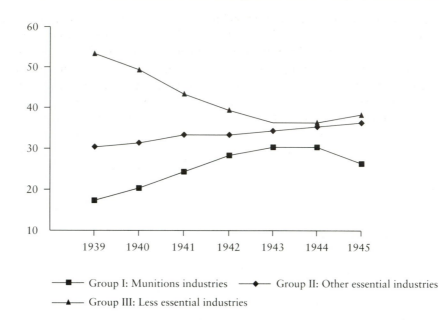

—■— Group I: Munitions industries   —◆— Group II: Other essential industries
—▲— Group III: Less essential industries

Figure 16.2. Civilian employment, 1939–45 (as % of total). *After.* Central Statistical Office, *Statistical Digest of the War* (London, 1951) p. 8.

16.2. The most noticeable feature is the decline of the Group III industries and the rise of the Group I industries: in 1939 their respective shares of civilian employment were 53 per cent and 17 per cent; by 1943 these shares had become 36 per cent and 30 per cent. This neatly illustrates the shift of the economy from peacetime production to wartime production and the transfer of workers from industries deemed less essential to the war effort to the munitions industries. However, two other features of Figure 16.2 are noteworthy: firstly, the importance of Group II industries is shown by their gradual rise from 30 per cent of civilian employment in 1939 to 36 per cent by 1945; and second, despite all these changes, throughout the war the ranking of the three industry groups in terms of employment size did not change. Group III was always the largest, followed by Group II and then Group I.

These changes in employment were reflected in changes in production and not surprisingly the war saw a marked change in industrial structure. Munitions production increased dramatically. To give just three examples: in 1938 Britain produced less than 3,000 aircraft but by 1943 the country was producing more than 26,000 aircraft annually; in the same period tank production increased from 419 to 7,476 and .38 inch pistol production rose from less than 4,000 to over 107,000. The corollary of this expansion of the munitions and related industries was the contraction of the consumer goods industries. Consumer goods production was deliberately restricted by the state (to release resources for munitions production, and for exports) through the Limitation of Supplies Orders. These required wholesalers to register with the

Board of Trade and restricted their sales to the domestic market to a fixed proportion of their prewar level. The first Order was applied to cotton cloth with a wartime ceiling of 75 per cent of prewar sales. In June 1940 it was extended to cover a wide range of goods. As the need to squeeze the Group III industries increased so the ceiling they operated under was gradually reduced. This in turn led to the state encouraging a concentration of production capacity in those industries, under a nucleus firm, which was to last for the duration of the war; the capacity and labour released by this concentration was to be transferred to Group I industries. The process was abetted by the 'utility scheme' in clothing and furniture whereby standardized designs were compulsorily introduced.

In focus: Women and the War

The wartime expansion of the armed forces meant that industry was denuded of men and they had to be replaced so that the economy could provide the soldiers with munitions, clothing and food. Once the well of unemployment had run dry society had to turn to women to meet the demands of industry. Indeed, this is what had happened in similar circumstances in the First World War (as shown in Chapter 9) and the expansion of female employment in both world wars was dramatic. In the Second World War the number of women in the working population increased by nearly 50 per cent, and of every five new workers attracted into the wartime labour market four were women. Women workers played a pivotal role in many important industries, accounting, for example, for a third of the nation's engineering workforce and over half of the chemical industry workforce. In some workplaces they encountered hostility as they were seen as a management 'Trojan Horse' that would be used to dilute skills (or, from the management perspective, to weaken restrictive trade practices and overmanning). Also, despite this impressive mobilization of female workers their average earnings still lagged behind those of male average earnings: a typical example was the chemical industry where in mid 1943 women on average earned 55 per cent of average male earnings.

The increased participation rate of women in the First World War did not extend into the interwar period, partly as a result of the postwar slump and resulting mass unemployment. The impact of the Second World War appears to have been more positive (although the complex interaction of the factors affecting the supply and demand of female labour makes it difficult to come to a firm conclusion). In the immediate postwar years the number of women in the labour force declined either because they were displaced from their jobs by men being demobilized from the armed forces or because they decided to withdraw from the labour force (for example, many young females had probably postponed marriage and having children during the war and thus withdrew from work in order to achieve those

Women and the War (continued)

goals). However, the war did seem to change many women's views towards the labour market, particularly that of younger women who had gained a considerable amount of economic freedom by working for high wages in the munitions factories; and there is evidence that the trend of female labour force participation was significantly higher in the 1950s compared to the interwar years, although this may also reflect the pressures of full employment on the postwar labour market.

Plate 16.1. Women bricklaying in 1941. The demands of wartime production meant that women were called on to take new jobs. Women accounted for four out of five new workers attracted into the wartime labour market, and made significant inroads into sectors such as engineering and construction hitherto dominated by men.

The Prelude to War

The deterioration in the international situation in the 1930s saw Britain gradually accelerate the build-up of its armed forces in the expectation that a major conflict was drawing closer. The rearmament programme started in earnest in 1935 (see Chapter 11). Drawing on the experience of the First World War, plans were laid to enable the country to move swiftly and smoothly to a war footing should it become necessary. The experience of the problems encountered in the First World War and the actions taken to solve them (see Chapter 9) were absorbed by planners in the interwar period and informed most of the plans for mobilization in the Second World War. The Ministry of Munitions, the key government department in the First World War, provided much of the inspiration for the planned administrative structure of wartime government in the 1930s and the system of raw material controls adopted at the outbreak of war in 1939 was modelled on its predecessors in the First World War. Manpower planning in the Second World War reflected many of the measures eventually adopted in the First World War, such as conscription, the protecting from the draft of workers in key industries and the creation of a ministry to coordinate manpower policy across both the armed forces and civilian employment. Other interwar preparations also reflected lessons learnt in that conflict: the stockpiling of strategic materials, such as non-ferrous metals, cotton, hemp, iron ore and rubber; a 'shadow factory' scheme was initiated to extend the capacity of the munitions industries (for example, in order to meet the increased demand for aircraft in a future war additional capacity was created in the aircraft industry and in selected motor vehicle firms); lists were compiled of firms which did or could produce wartime munitions; a system of food control and rationing was planned and ration books were printed.

Prewar rearmament was aided by a series of decisions: in March 1938 the government abandoned any 'business as usual' policy it may have had by announcing that the assumption that rearmament should not impede normal trade would be dropped; the Royal Air Force was also freed from normal Treasury financial limitations in 1938, to be followed by the navy and the army in 1939. The removal of financial restrictions did not mean, however, that there were no constraints on rearmament. The Treasury maintained some control because of worries about hard currency reserves. This acted as a fairly effective constraint on spending, and the armed forces and munitions industries were not freed from this constraint until the advent of the Churchill government in May 1940.

The Phoney War

August and September 1939 were months of great activity as wartime preparations were formalized. The most important piece of legislation in this period was the Emergency Powers (Defence) Act, passed on 24 August 1939, an enabling act that gave the government wideranging powers and was the bedrock of all future wartime legislation. Many new ministries were created to oversee the war economy that would emerge. These included Ministries of Supply, Food, Shipping, Economic Warfare, Home Security and Information; the Ministry of Labour was expanded to include National Service responsibilities. At the apex of the state the peacetime Cabinet was replaced by a smaller War Cabinet and there was a proliferation of War Cabinet committees that would form the backbone of the wartime administration. Certain habits proved hard to break, however, and financial planning still held sway (mainly because of the reserve constraint the economy was operating under in this period). Thus, Treasury men still played prominent roles on most of these new committees and the Chancellor of the Exchequer remained the most important minister after Prime Minister Chamberlain.

This initial activity was followed by a lull in the actual land campaigns and these months became known as the period of the Phoney War. The lull also seemed to affect the conversion process of the British economy to a full war footing. Average weekly government war expenditure, for example, rose relatively slowly from £20 million in September 1939 to £33 million by April 1940; once Churchill replaced Chamberlain in May, it rose more rapidly, reaching £52 million by June 1940 and over £70 million by the end of the year. The war was far from phoney at sea, however, as German U-boats and pocket battleships attempted to disrupt British trade and the British attempted to impose an economic blockade on Germany. The latter strategy was unsuccessful because the Russo-German pact, which had seen the carve up of Poland, gave Germany access to the markets of Eastern Europe in addition to its relatively good access to important neutral trading countries such as Sweden.

The most serious problem the British economy faced in this period was the deterioration in its reserve position. A major reason for this was that Britain was buying many vital stores in the US and the latter's neutrality position meant that these had to be paid for by cash. The situation was not helped by the rapid rise in import prices (between August 1939 and March 1940 they increased by 43 per cent, compared to a rise in export prices of only 14 per cent in the same period). It was made worse by the rapid increases in civilian employment and earnings and the slow adoption of rationing, which led to increased imports of food and raw materials to meet increased civilian demand. In order to finance all these purchases Britain had to maintain a strong export drive: in the last quarter of 1939 exports amounted to £103 million; by the second quarter of 1940 they were £130 million.

In focus: Rationing

One aspect of government wartime policy that affected every individual in the country was the rationing of basic foodstuffs, clothing and other consumer goods. Under rationing everybody was given a similar amount of ration coupons or points with which they could then get these basic, but scarce, goods. There were three main reasons why rationing was introduced: inflation, equality and nutrition. Firstly, in the absence of rationing it was likely that the prices of important basic goods would be bid up very quickly and this would stoke up general inflationary pressure in the economy (rationing in effect limited the ability of consumers to spend and forced them to save more). Also, if the prices of basic goods were bid up then the poorer members of society might not be able to afford them and it was seen as unjust that economic might should decide who in the economy would shoulder the burden of a war-induced problem; thus rationing helped to spread this burden more equitably (and would prevent profiteering). Finally, it was felt that rationing could be used to make more of limited food supplies and, through the types of rations made, could also be used to raise the basic nutritional level of the population (indeed, one fear behind prewar planning was that the war might result in malnutrition and starvation).

The first form of rationing introduced was a coupon system which allowed consumers to exchange coupons for a guaranteed ration. It was initially applied to petrol and basic foodstuffs (such as butter, meat, sugar and tea). In June 1941 a second scheme based on a points system was introduced; this allowed consumers to spend a specified number of coupon points within a certain time period on a range of goods (it was, in effect, an alternative system of money). Initially the points scheme covered clothes and footwear but it was later extended to other foodstuffs and consumer goods (including, from 1942, soap and sweets). The strength of the points system was its greater flexibility compared to the coupon system: it was much easier to extend the range of goods covered by the points system (since the government simply specified how many points were needed to purchase them and it did not have to print millions of new coupons specifically for each new good rationed); also, it was easier to differentiate between different types of any particular good to give a more equitable amount of purchasing power (for example, children's clothes had a lower points value than adult's clothes). For morale reasons certain goods were never rationed during the war, such as bread, potatoes, alcohol and tobacco (the latter two also provided the Exchequer with much needed tax revenues). Finally, the wartime rationing system was complemented by a massive subsidization of food prices by the government. Rationing was not perfect (there was a black market in rationed goods) but it was a great success: it was a valuable aid in the fight against inflation, it helped to persuade the population that the government was pursuing its economic war aims equitably, and it did help to improve the general nutritional level of the nation.

Rationing (continued)

Rationing did not end with the war but was continued in the postwar period, mainly to keep control of inflation and to increase forced savings that could then be channelled into much needed investment. Indeed it was even extended: bread was rationed for the first time in July 1946, and potatoes in November 1947. Britain, however, was not the only country to extend rationing into the postwar period; for example, sugar was still rationed in the US in 1947. The rationing of many goods (clothing, furniture, petrol, soap and certain foodstuffs) had ended by 1950 but the rationing of the main foodstuffs continued until the mid 1950s.

Plate 16.2. A clothes-remodelling service during the war. The rationing of clothes from 1941 forced consumers to 'make do and mend', but as this photograph shows, ingenious ways were found to keep clothes looking stylish.

The Churchill Government

On 10 May 1940 Winston Churchill became the new Prime Minister at the head of a National Coalition government. The Phoney War had ended and on the day Churchill took office German forces invaded Holland and Belgium; by mid June they had driven British forces from Europe at Dunkirk and gained control of France, leaving Britain to stand alone against the German aggressor. There then followed the aerial warfare of the Battle of Britain in which Britain repulsed the threat of German invasion. On the economic front the Churchill broom swept the country into proper and full war mobilization. One of the most important first actions taken by Churchill was to recognize the futility of trying to operate within normal peacetime financial considerations and to replace financial planning with physical planning (which included ending the export drive). Financial planning was based on pounds and pence, on the monetary resources available to the economy and to the state. Physical planning was based on the demand for and supply of physical resources. Thus, state planning moved from allocating money to government departments, to allocating labour, steel and factory space to them.

Under Churchill the Treasury lost its role as the key government department (the holder of the monetary purse) and this position passed to a series of War Cabinet committees concerned with the allocation of materials, labour and other physical resources. In this system government departments (like the newly created Ministry of Aircraft Production) made bids for physical resources to central committees, which in turn made allocations to the departments based on the strategic priority of their production programme. The departments could then issue licences to the firms working on their orders which would allow the firms to get the resources they needed. The wartime economy had become a centrally managed economy in which the market had been displaced by state-determined production plans. This, in turn, led to the state machinery for the first time absorbing large numbers of technical experts, principally economists and statisticians, to help provide the detailed advice now needed. Thus, for example, the Central Statistical Office and the Economic Section of the War Cabinet (the latter staffed by leading academic economists) were established and the most famous economist of the day, John Maynard Keynes, was drafted into the Treasury.

Keynes had argued that the government needed to adopt a radically new method of framing its budgetary policy and, in particular, it had to adopt measures to close the potential inflationary gap between aggregate demand and aggregate supply.[1] Figure 16.3 illustrates the problem the economy was facing according to Keynes: aggregate demand would rise (represented by the shift in the aggregate demand curve from D1 to D2) due to increased wartime wages; thus, a gap between it and aggregate supply (curve S1) would emerge (represented by the distance AB); normally this gap would be closed by an increase in prices (from P1 to P2) and by the economy moving to a new equilibrium at point C. Indeed, the situation was even more severe than Figure

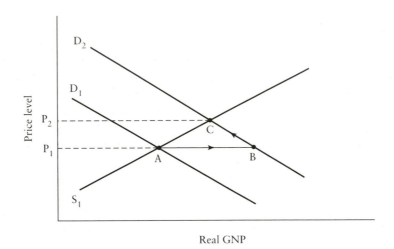

Figure 16.3. The inflationary gap

16.3 suggests because aggregate supply was also falling as the government deliberately contracted the consumer goods industries and this increased the inflationary pressure. The distance P1P2 was therefore the potential inflationary gap because if the government did nothing then prices would rise. To prevent this Keynes suggested that it should soak up the excess aggregate demand through taxation and other measures and this in turn required the government to first estimate what the potential inflationary gap was.

These ideas underpinned the April 1941 Budget. For the first time the budget became a comprehensive survey of the economy, and it attempted to calculate what level of taxation and forced saving was necessary to close the inflationary gap. Thus, it introduced a series of measures to increase savings (and hence reduce potential expenditure), and it increased all forms of taxation on individuals, on companies and on goods; it also introduced cost of living subsidies in the hope that these would help to moderate wage demands. The 1941 Budget was a success (although the manipulation of the cost of living index and the general control of prices by the government disguised inflation rather than erased it) and future wartime budgets refined the methods it set out; indeed, budgetary policy would never return to the prewar system. Another important feature of the 1941 Budget was that it was the first to be conceived of in National Income terms.

March 1941 had seen two other events that would have important implications for the economy: the initiation of Lend-Lease by the US which would remove the financial constraint of having to pay cash for American goods and the beginning of the Battle of the Atlantic. The latter threatened vital shipping supply lanes and posed a serious threat to the war effort. It lasted until March 1943 after which the advent of radar (an important wartime invention) helped to turn the tide against the U-boats.

To Victory, 1942–45

By the beginning of 1942 Britain had gained as allies the two nations that would emerge as the superpowers of the postwar era: the USSR (which had been invaded by Germany in June 1941) and the US (attacked by Japan in December 1941). Ironically, the first economic impact of their entry into the war was to increase the burden on Britain. In the US the need to build up its military strength meant that resources were diverted from supplying Lend-Lease aid to the British in order to provide munitions for its own armed forces; for example, aircraft deliveries from the US in the first two quarters of 1942 were less than they had been in the last quarter of 1941 although thereafter they (and American supplies in general) increased rapidly. Russia, on the other hand, had lost much of its productive capacity in the German invasion and it needed aid from both the US and Britain. By mid 1942 Britain had supplied Russia with significant quantities of munitions, materials and foodstuffs, including 1,800 aircraft and 2,250 tanks, and by mid 1943 the total value of its aid had amounted to almost £190 million.

Within Britain a new department, the Ministry of Production, was created to provide a single voice for all the war departments in discussions with the US and a series of joint US-UK committees was set up to coordinate what was now a joint war production effort. The Ministry of Production also became the focus of resource allocation and absorbed many of the Cabinet committees that had dealt with these issues previously.

The major problem the economy faced in this period was the manpower constraint: by the end of 1942 it was becoming obvious that the economy was not going to be able to expand its manpower pool much further. Thus, manpower budgeting became the chief tool of planning. Fortunately, the peak in the working population in 1943 coincided almost exactly with the peak in munitions production. The latter reflected the build-up to the D-Day invasion of Europe in June 1944 (the British and Americans took a deliberate decision to first concentrate their efforts on winning the war in Europe). The need for specialist orders for the D-Day operation (such as the Mulberry Harbour and large numbers of landing craft) placed a heavy new burden on the economy and it is a testimony to the success of the wartime planning machinery that it was able to meet these demands. Less than a year after the Normandy landings Germany had surrendered. The war with Japan, however, continued. As late as 1944 Allied planners had thought that this conflict would last for a further two years after the defeat of Germany. However, the planners had not taken into account the devastating impact of the most significant invention of the Second World War, the atomic bomb, and in the event Japan surrendered a mere three months after Germany, on 14 August 1945.

Historiographical Interpretations

The Importance of Lend-Lease Aid

How did the war affect the economic relationship between Britain and the US? Were the Americans altruistic in their relationship with Britain? Was Lend-Lease aid 'the most unsordid act in history' as Churchill claimed? Or did the Americans (as Keynes believed) act as far as possible in their own economic self-interest?

The US had adopted a neutral stance in the mid 1930s which meant that Britain could not expect effective American economic aid if it became embroiled in a war and that it could only obtain American resources on payment of cash. This meant that Britain had to maintain a large export flow in order to provide the finance for necessary American imports. The American stance merely reflected a strong political force in that country for a relatively isolationist policy and it would be wrong to criticize its population and political leaders for not following a policy that would be in the best interests of another country.

In February 1940 Britain and France decided to accelerate their dollar expenditure in the US. American industry, however, was not capable of producing munitions in the quantities desired and therefore much of the Allied cash went on expanding American munitions capacity. Thus, British finance was important in increasing American war potential and ensuring that when the US entered the war it did not do so from a cold start. Even where orders were placed there were often difficulties. One example of this was British orders for new ships to relieve an important bottleneck in the economy. Britain ordered 60 new ships and 100 second-hand ships from the US in 1940 (partly in exchange for leasing bases in Newfoundland and the West Indies). However, the first of the new ships was not delivered until the latter part of 1941 and many of the second-hand ships needed substantial, and costly, repair work before they were properly seaworthy. On the other hand, in this period President Roosevelt did try to provide help for Britain where he could and this was of some importance, although not decisive, in the crucial Middle East theatre.

Finally, in March 1941, the US came off the fence and passed the Lend-Lease Act. This allowed Britain, and other Allied countries, to buy goods in America on credit and not pay the bill until after the war. Lend-Lease aid made an important contribution to the British war effort, providing vital supplies of foodstuffs, aircraft, tanks and other materials and munitions, and net Lend-Lease aid eventually totalled $21 billion. However, it was far from altruistic: Britain was expected to pay a bill at the end of the war; critics, like Keynes, claim that Lend-Lease was only introduced when Britain was virtually bankrupt; and one condition of Lend-Lease was that Britain should withdraw from certain export markets where it was in competition with American firms. (This would have important repercussions, particularly in South America.)

Critics also point out that Lend-Lease was ended just one minute into the first day of official peace and the Americans demanded an immediate settlement of the bill which plunged Britain into a dollar crisis. This was in sharp contrast to Canada which had also provided vital aid to Britain during the war, totalling $1.2 billion, but did not ask for any repayment. In defence of the US, it had expended resources on Lend-Lease aid and the conditions of the arrangement had been clear; also, in its final settlement it did recognize the important role that Britain had played in the war and the constraints it had faced, and thus the final settlement it asked for was only $650 million, or just 3 per cent of the total aid provided.

The Impact of the War

Did the Second World War have any lasting impact on the British economy? Traditional views, dating from the 1950s and 1960s, that it did have important consequences have come increasingly under attack in the 1980s for either exaggerating its effects or for misinterpreting them.[2]

The first argument is that the influence and role of government was changed dramatically by the war: it came to play a much larger role in the economy, and adopted Keynesian economic policies, and its wartime taxation and related policies created a more equitable society. There is no dispute that in terms of the proportion of public expenditure in GDP the war led to a permanent expansion of the state sector. This has been called the 'displacement effect' because although the high levels of government expenditure that occurred during a war were not maintained after it, it did not fall back to the prewar level either. The question of when, if ever, the government adopted Keynesian policies is the subject of continuing debate: the current view would appear to be that the 'Keynesian Revolution' occurred in the immediate postwar years (see Chapter 17) and not during the war itself (which was managed on the basis of planning physical, not financial, resources). An alternative view is that Keynesianism was never embraced. Thus, until the 1970s short-term balance of payments considerations dominated economic policy and thereafter monetarism came to the fore, and in the earlier period the government generally ran a surplus on its current account (see Chapter 18).

There is little empirical support for the suggestion that the war witnessed a more equitable distribution of wealth and indeed the tax base was greatly widened during the war (and the majority of the population now had to pay income tax under the Pay-As-You-Earn scheme, introduced in 1943). The traditional reply to this would be that the war was instrumental in creating the welfare state and that this caused a major redistribution in the nation's resources towards the poorest members of society. However, this too lacks empirical support as studies of the impact of the welfare state suggest that it was the middle class which benefited most from it.[3]

Another argument has focused on the impact of the war on British industry.

Barnett has said that the British deluded themselves that the war had demonstrated the strength of British industry and the economy in general.[4] He argues that their victory was based on American and Commonwealth aid which helped to hide an underlying export weakness. Thus, in the postwar period Britain invested large amounts of scarce resources in building houses and erecting the welfare state rather than investing in new plant and machinery and research and development, and tackling important deficiencies in technical education and training. However, just as Barnett claims postwar leaders exaggerated the success of the war economy he in turn exaggerates its deficiencies. If the picture of British industry as weak, poorly managed (by both government and businessmen) and divisive were really true then at the outbreak of the war it must have resembled a house of cards and Hitler would merely have had to blow across the Channel to make it come tumbling down. This did not happen because although the British economy did face serious structural problems whose roots could be traced back to at least the end of the nineteenth century, it was still one of the leading industrial nations in the world and, indeed, in the postwar years it would experience its highest ever rates of growth. During the war British industry did perform extremely well under difficult circumstances and a long line of wartime inventions and innovations, including radar, penicillin and atomic energy, attested to a still deep well of research potential.

The argument about not investing in new plant and machinery echoes a traditional view that Germany and Japan were the postwar economic miracles precisely because they were defeated in the war and their economies were devastated. Thus, in the reconstruction period they had to invest heavily in new plant and machinery, embodying the latest technology, and this gave them an important competitive advantage over Britain. There are two weaknesses in this argument: firstly, there was no reason why in later years Britain could not redress the balance by replacing its old machines with new machines (which presumably would then give it a competitive advantage over Japan and Germany); second, it has been shown that it was not the age of industrial machinery that decided how efficient an economy was in this period but how (and how often) the machinery was used.

Bibliographical Note

The starting point for any review of the literature of this period must be the comprehensive series of officially commissioned volumes on the wartime economy, crowned by the books of W.K. Hancock and M.M. Gowing on *The British War Economy* (London, 1949) and M.M. Postan on the more specific topic of *British War Production* (London, 1952). Hancock and Gowing show how the general constraints on the economy, such as manpower and shipping capacity, were tackled and how important American aid was; they also argue that prewar planners underestimated the scale of the economic transformation necessary to fight the war. Postan's is a more readable book, with crisper judgements, and he lays more stress on resource, production and administrative bottlenecks within the economy. A neat summary of the official history viewpoint, supported by other and often more critical literature, is provided by the chapter on the Second World War in the textbook by Sidney Pollard, *The Development of the British Economy, 1914–1990* (London, 4th ed, 1992). 'The wartime economy, 1939–1945' by P. Howlett in R. Floud and D. McCloskey (eds), *The Economic History of Britain since 1700. Volume 3* (Cambridge, 1994) elaborates many of the themes touched upon in this chapter and also offers a rationale for the supplanting of the market by state direction in the war. It is complemented by the article by J. Harris, 'War and social history: Britain and the Home Front during the Second World War', *Contemporary European History* vol. 1 (1992), pp. 17–36, which provides a concise summary of the revisionist view of the period and the impact of the war. Finally, the performance of the British war economy is placed in a comparative perspective by Alan Milward, *The Economic Effects of the Two World Wars on Britain* (Basingstoke, 2nd ed, 1984), and by Mark Harrison, 'Resource mobilization for World War II: the USA, the UK, USSR and Germany, 1938–1945', *Economic History Review* vol. 41 (1988), pp. 171–92.

Notes

1. J.M. Keynes, *How to Pay for the War: a Radical Plan for the Chancellor of the Exchequer* (London, 1940).

2. See: S. Broadberry, 'The impact of the World Wars on the long run performance of the British economy', *Oxford Review of Economic Policy* vol. 4 (1988), pp. 23–37; J. Harris, 'War and social history: Britain and the Home Front during the Second World War', *Contemporary European History* vol. 1 (1992), pp. 17–36; P. Howlett, 'The wartime economy, 1939–1945', in R. Floud and D.N. McCloskey (eds), *The Economic History of Britain since 1700. Volume 3* (Cambridge, 1994); A.S. Milward, *The Economic Effects of the Two World Wars on Britain* (Basingstoke, 2nd edn, 1984).

3. J. Le Grand, *The Strategy of Equality* (London, 1982).

4. C. Barnett, *The Audit of War* (London, 1986).

17 Austerity and Boom

Catherine R. Schenk

At the end of the Second World War, the British economy was in a shambles. The transition from war to peace had begun before the actual end of hostilities with the scaling down of munitions production and redeployment of labour to exporting industries but the expected breathing space between victory in Europe and victory over Japan was cut short by the atomic bombs in Hiroshima and Nagasaki. When hostilities finally ceased in August 1945, a seemingly enormous task of reallocating resources, rebuilding industrial potential and restoring exports loomed in front of the first peacetime government.

In hindsight the recovery from war after an initial period of austerity appears dramatically successful. The decade after 1945 was one of rapid growth, low inflation and the achievement of full employment to which the British governments had committed themselves during the war. At the time, however, the prospects seemed less optimistic and fears of a boom and slump similar to that of 1919–21 ushered in a spirit of continued austerity. When that threat receded, recurrent balance of payments crises seemed to threaten the prospects for steady growth. With demand and employment pressing sustainable limits, inflationary pressure was seen as a constant threat to growth and the balance of payments.

Austerity, 1945–47

The economic situation certainly seemed dire for the Labour government elected in July 1945. The new Prime Minister Attlee warned that 'It is vital to realise that we have come through difficult years and we are going to face difficult years and to get through them will require no less effort, no less unselfishness and no less work than was needed to bring us through the war'.[1] In 1919 there had been a general wish to return to the policies of the pre-1914 era and the fundamental changes wrought by the war were ignored with serious consequences for the British economy. The intention after 1945 was to push forward onto a new path of policy and create an economic environment based on a welfare state and government direction of the economy. In the short term, however, the aim of the Labour government was to avoid the mistakes of 1919–20 which they believed had prompted a restocking boom and recession as a result of the premature abandonment of controls. A further motive for continued austerity was the need to contain domestic consumption in order to divert scarce resources towards production for export.

The war had left Britain's external position in an extremely precarious state. By 1945 foreign exchange reserves were at the low level of £491 million while external liabilities had accumulated to £3,567 million as a result of the war effort. Under agreements with the Commonwealth, British wartime expenditure on troops and munitions had been met by the transfer of British securities to her creditors rather than cash payment. Table 17.1 shows the amount of UK liabilities compared to the level of foreign exchange reserves.

Table 17.1. UK sterling liabilities, 1945–50

| | £ million | | | | | |
	1945	1946	1947	1948	1949	1950
(A) Sterling liabilities	3,567	3,636	3,856	3,497	3,669	3,989
(B) Reserves	491	603	501	398	482	1,036
Ratio of (A) to (B)	7.3	6.0	7.7	8.8	7.6	3.9

Sources: For liabilities, *Bank of England Statistical Abstract*, no. 1, 1970. For gold, dollar and convertible currency reserves, IMF, *International Financial Statistics*.

In order to repay these obligations and to finance the necessary imports for recovery, exports had to be increased quickly. This pressure was accentuated by the abrupt termination of the Lend-Lease arrangement with the US. Immediately after V-J Day, President Truman announced that all Lend-Lease material on the way to the UK and all future supplies from the US would have to be paid for in American dollars.

The task facing the first Labour government, therefore, required juggling internal and external economic targets. To increase domestic demand too quickly would threaten the export drive and absorb greater imports, putting the balance of payments at risk. The low level of reserves would thus not permit too rapid expansion at a fixed exchange rate. This environment was seen to be well-suited to the Labour ideology of increasing the role of government in the direction of the economy. Controls over production and supply had proven themselves in wartime and were to be continued in the postwar period, not only for ideological reasons but also to help resolve the obstacles to growth and full employment which were posed by the postwar disorder. The route chosen was a balance of direct controls to constrain demand, low interest rates to promote investment and government commitment to a welfare state to alleviate the burden of austerity on those who could least support it. Almost all of the controls imposed in wartime were initially maintained by the Labour government. These covered allocation of raw materials, rationing of consumer goods and food, and controls over the volume and direction of private investment and construction.

Direct Controls

Consumer rationing touched the British individual most closely and was especially focused on clothing, furniture, coal and food. Clothing rationing came to an end in 1949, food in 1954 and rationing on coal was maintained until July 1958. The amount of consumer expenditure subject to rationing rose from about 25 per cent in 1946 to 30 per cent in 1948 before dropping away to around 12 per cent in 1949 after clothing and furniture ceased to be rationed. This compares with about one-third of consumer expenditure in the final years of the war. Some items, such as bread and potatoes, which were not controlled during the war were put on ration in the postwar period. As shortages of supply receded, however, the controls were removed. Given the rapid dismantling of most of the schemes after 1948–49, the impact of consumer rationing was minimal by the 1950s.

At the end of the war, controls over allocation of raw materials were much more pervasive than consumer rationing. In 1945 fifteen major raw materials were subject to allocation, ranging from wool and cotton to leather and sulphuric acid. In 1948 these controlled materials still made up 94 per cent of all materials purchased by industry. This proportion was then gradually reduced until controls were reimposed in response to the Korean war in 1951. By 1954, however, only 26 per cent of industrial input was subject to allocation. Since most raw materials were imported the allocation schemes were relaxed as imports expanded and supply shortages were resolved. Domestic coal, however, continued to be subject to allocation until 1958. The effect of this category of controls is difficult to assess since the government was eager to supply all the raw materials at its disposal to industry. The impact was thus more on the targeting of specific sectors and restraining price increases due to shortages in the early years after the war.

As the 1940s drew to a close direct controls appeared to be a decreasingly effective instrument with which to direct the national economy. Controls were periodically tightened, for example in the crisis of 1947, but their failure to deliver the instant results expected pushed them into disrepute.

One category of direct controls which has not yet been addressed is controls on imports. Tariffs and quotas were used in conjunction with domestic rationing and allocation of raw materials to contain demand and to protect the balance of payments. Import policy was enacted in concert with the rest of the sterling area group of countries after 1945. The sterling area comprised the Colonies and Commonwealth except for Canada (which attached itself to the dollar area) and various other small countries such as Burma, Iceland, Iraq and Persian Gulf States. Members pooled their foreign exchange earnings in London and so operated a common policy to conserve them, especially through controls on American dollar expenditure. In 1947 and 1948 the UK and the rest of the sterling area agreed to restrict imports to 75 per cent of their 1946 level.

Employment

Along with price stability, the Labour government was committed to full employment. This was another hangover from the disastrous interwar period

"The switch-over from war-production was rather sudden."

Plate 17.1. 'The switch-over from war production was rather sudden'. The abrupt end of 'lend-lease' at the end of the war forced the government to maximize export earnings. Physical controls of raw materials were continued as the government instructed businesses to shift rapidly from munitions to the production of goods for the overseas market.

when the experience of mass unemployment had shocked the British public and policy makers. For employment policy, the main task in 1945 was to secure an orderly demobilization and to direct labour into key sectors for recovery of domestic production and exports. The government was particularly concerned about the apparent labour shortage in agriculture, coal mining and textiles.

In the first year after the war, the timetable of returning to the prewar level of armed forces was cautious due to the continued unsettled state of overseas affairs. Thus by June 1946 the armed forces still stood at over two million people compared with 480,000 in June 1939. After 1947, with the independence of India and the dramatic manifestation of labour shortage at home in the form of the Fuel Crisis, demobilization was accelerated so that by the end of 1948 only 810,000 people were engaged by the armed forces.

Offsetting the increase in civil employment due to demobilization was the withdrawal of some workers from the labour market. From the end of 1945 to 1948, the labour force fell by 6 per cent or 1.33 million people. This was especially due to the withdrawal of women from paid work. Nevertheless, by 1948 labour had ceased to be a constraint that preoccupied the government and its attention turned to shortages elsewhere that might threaten their commitment to full employment and the achievement of external balance.

In focus: The Fuel Crisis of 1947

The winter of 1947 marked a major retreat along the path of reconstruction and recovery. The coal shortage of that year struck at both households and industry and seemed to represent a failure of the Labour government's strategy of postwar planning. Despite the tight hold the government had over allocation of resources and production, it was unable to avoid a shortage of one of the most fundamental factors of production. The causes of the Fuel Crisis of 1947 reveal some of the weaknesses of planning.

The supply of adequate coal was considered to be fragile from the end of 1945 and by 1946 ministers and officials were forecasting a shortage. Table 17.2 shows the total output, consumption and distributed stocks of coal from 1945 to 1947. After the war, output had fallen significantly from the prewar levels. While production did start to recover, consumption increased faster so that stocks were run down through the second half of 1946.

The major constraint on production of coal was a shortage of labour due to enlistment during the war and unwillingness of people to return to the pits given the plentiful vacancies in other sectors after the war. Table 17.3 shows that not only were there fewer miners but they were less productive than before the war.

The Fuel Crisis of 1947 (continued)

Table 17.2. Coal production, consumption (weekly averages) and stocks (end of period)

Period		Output	000 Tons Consumption	Distributed Stocks
1938		4,353	4,353	–
1945		3,506	3,597	12,442
1946	August	3,065	3,144	9,343
	Sept	3,759	3,492	10,320
	Oct	3,891	3,690	10,878
	Nov	3,896	3,984	10,397
	Dec	3,629	4,069	8,466
1947	Jan	3,714	4,159	6,700
	Feb	3,784	4,053	5,519
	March	3,852	3,905	5,477
	April	3,677	3,553	6,056
	May	3,800	3,446	8,007
	June	3,856	3,324	10,638
	July	3,333	3,095	12,122
	Dec	3,792	4,048	16,149

Source. A.J. Robertson, *The Bleak Midwinter 1947* (Manchester, 1987) p. 181.

Table 17.3. Labour and productivity in coal mining (weekly averages)

	Wage-earners (000)	Output per worker's shift (tons)
1938	782	1.14
1945	709	1.00
1946	697	1.03
1947	712	1.07

Source. Robertson, *The Bleak Midwinter 1947*, p. 181.

The Fuel Crisis of 1947 (continued)

The effort by Shinwell, Minister of Fuel and Power, to recruit more labour to the mines has been criticized as inadequate. Labour exchanges, for example, were not told to give recruiting miners priority above other sectors of industry. The National Union of Miners also played a part. It was uncooperative, for example, about hiring foreign labour to fill the vacancies until finally this was accepted in January 1947. The delay meant many did not reach the pits until the summer of 1947, well after the crisis had passed. Shinwell, however, was the major obstacle to taking serious measures to stave off the impending crisis. As late as September 1946 he was still denying that there was a shortage of miners and in October he denied the need for mandatory cuts in coal consumption despite recommendations from officials.

Transport problems also contributed to the crisis by impeding the distribution of coal to those industries and regions that needed it most. Bad weather and a shortage of railway waggons were the main culprits. Freezing temperatures, snow and gales inhibited coastal shipping and kept miners from work. The cold weather which began at the end of January 1947 had the added impact of increasing demand for fuel for heating.

Even before the emergency was formally declared in Parliament, the coal shortage and bad weather had forced short weeks and factory closures. The result was the first postwar taste of unemployment as automobile, paper and rubber factories announced closures at the end of January. At Austin Motors alone, 17,000 workers were faced with indefinite lay-offs. Unemployment increased to 1.75 million in February 1947 from 400,000 a month before. The failure to ensure supplies of a fundamental raw material for industry and the renewed prospect of unemployment threatened the government's credibility. These concerns were highlighted by the fact that the coal industry was in the process of nationalization at the height of the crisis.

Finally, on 7 February Shinwell was forced to announce that all electricity was to be completely cut off for industry in the South East, Midlands and North West and domestic supplies were cut for three hours in the morning and another two hours in the afternoon. These cuts were continued for three weeks. In addition, a coordinated effort was finally introduced to improve distribution by using army lorries and navy ships and by targeting the use of the railways for coal transport. A reduction in the standard working week for miners from six days to five was finally approved in April and in February houses for miners were sanctioned by the government to improve the prospects of recruiting to the industry.

Mistakes were undoubtedly made which compounded the unavoidable impact of the bad winter of 1947. As seen above, the Minister of Fuel and Power was slow to grapple with the problem, especially the need to recruit more actively. Once he did act, however, it is possible that the response was overenthusiastic. Through February and March stocks of coal at power stations were built up to two weeks' supply at the expense of industrial

The Fuel Crisis of 1947 (continued)

demand. During the cuts, 5 per cent of coal output was merely added to stocks instead of being used for industrial production. The result was a loss of industrial production and exports which set back the recovery and the export drive by six to nine months. Manufacturing production fell by 25 per cent in February from the already low level of January. The cost in terms of exports was estimated at the time to be £200 million although a more realistic estimate would be closer to £100 million. Given the reserves crisis of later in the year this amount may have significantly worsened the balance of payments.

The Fuel Crisis reveals some of the problems of planning. Some events cannot be anticipated but this, arguably, was not the case here since the crisis was predicted from 1945. A danger of planning is that the results are only as good as those who apply them. In a crisis, policy may tend to extremism and mistakes may be made when ministers are under pressure. As Alec Cairncross has noted, 'planning has its technical side: but it is also a political art and one in which on this occasion the Labour government fell down badly'.[2] Much of the blame must fall on the shoulders of the Minister of Fuel and Power and those who appointed him.

The Balance of Payments

Underlying all these domestic policies was the preoccupation of the Labour government with the balance of payments problem. As noted above, the most pressing postwar problem was the need to restore Britain's export power. Given the need for imports for reconstruction and the need to provide a cushion of foreign exchange reserves against the claims posed by outstanding sterling liabilities, it was not going to be enough to restore exports to their prewar level. The target was set at a 50–70 per cent increase on the 1939 level of exports.

At the end of the war, British exports were only at a third of their 1939 level. Invisible earnings were also reduced due to the liquidation of £1,000 million of overseas assets during the war and the interruption of merchant shipping. The problem was exacerbated by the concentration of international supplies in the US which meant that exports to America were the most important to finance imports. The US, however, was self-sufficient to a greater extent than elsewhere and Britain faced competition from other recovering countries penetrating the US market in the scramble for dollars.

Table 17.4 shows the British balance of trade in the postwar years. In the first two years after the war, the push for exports was somewhat disappointing. The volume of exports accelerated in 1948, however, and by the end of the year had increased by 75 per cent above the 1946 level while the value of imports had increased only 65 per cent in the same period.

Table 17.4. British balance of trade, 1946–54

					£ million				
	1946	**1947**	**1948**	**1949**	**1950**	**1951**	**1952**	**1953**	**1954**
Exports	920	1146	1604	1847	2254	2752	2831	2677	2825
Imports	1082	1560	1794	1978	2390	3501	2959	2896	3020
Balance	−162	−414	−190	−131	−136	−749	−128	−219	−195

Note: All values f.o.b. at current prices.

Source: HMSO, *UK Balance of Payments 1947–57* (London, 1959).

In addition to trade policy, the dollar deficit was met by negotiated loans from the US and Canada. After the abrupt end of Lend-Lease in August 1945, the British quickly organized a mission to negotiate a dollar loan to cover necessary supplies. The result of two-and-a-half months of hard bargaining was the Anglo-American Financial Agreement of 1946. Under its terms a line of credit of $3.75 billion plus $650 million to pay for Lend-Lease goods was made available on the understanding that the UK would come to an arrangement with its creditors to fund, write off or repay the sterling liabilities shown in Table 17.1. These debts were viewed by the US as a major obstacle to Britain dispensing with exchange controls and achieving convertibility. With so much unstable sterling in foreign hands, Britain could not afford to make it convertible because of the low level of reserves. On the assumption that these liabilities could be excluded, the UK was also obliged to make sterling convertible one year after the Agreement was signed. Accommodation on the sterling balances proved to be impossible and the second requirement proved a monumental catastrophe. In the end, convertibility was to be sustained for six weeks from 15 July to 20 August 1947 at the expense of most of the American loan.

Britain's external economic problems were part of the more general realignment of the international monetary system after the war. In 1944 the countries of the United Nations had come together in Bretton Woods, New Hampshire to design a coordinated programme for international monetary relations to be enforced and facilitated by the International Monetary Fund and the International Bank for Reconstruction and Development. The goal was to introduce a managed international economy which would avoid the destructive, uncoordinated policies of the 1930s. This was to be achieved by multilateral trade and payments and the removal of trade barriers. Fixed exchange rates were to be supported by short-term lending from the International Monetary Fund.

In the event, however, the system which emerged was much circumscribed by the inability of most of the countries to allow their currencies to be convertible until their foreign exchange reserves had increased. In the interim, multilateral systems emerged on a regional rather than a global scale. In 1950, the European Payments Union was formed to allow multilateral trade among Western European countries including the UK. In addition, the sterling area mentioned above allowed multilateral trade and payments among its members. The external policy of the UK was therefore centred around a fixed exchange rate for an unconvertible pound within multilateral payments systems with Western Europe and the sterling area.

In international trade, the price of British exports had to be in line with those overseas to be competitive. If British prices were too high, this could be offset by a decrease in the value of the pound. In a regime of fixed exchange rates, however, increases in domestic price levels would be translated into a loss of export competitiveness instead of a devaluation of the pound. This meant that there was continual pressure to contain domestic demand and therefore prices during the postwar period.

The End of Austerity, 1947–52

The year 1947 can be seen in hindsight as a turning point both for the Labour government and for the British economy. The internal and external crises of that year demonstrated by the coal shortage and the shortlived attempt at convertibility were a low point in the postwar recovery. This was the first year that GDP growth faltered. It also marked the end of the fear of a postwar slump as inflationary pressure mounted despite the gradual balancing of the fiscal budget. After 1948, with the help of $2.7 million of Marshall Aid from the US and the dismantling of controls, the economy began to turn the corner from austerity to growth.

In February 1948 Harold Wilson, then President of the Board of Trade, announced a 'Bonfire of Controls' for the following November. In the intervening months rationing, allocation and other direct controls on production were removed. At the same time, however, price controls were introduced to restrain inflation. Not all of the controls were removed successfully. The attempt to de-ration sweets and chocolate in April 1949, for example, merely resulted in their disappearance under the counter and the rise of a black market. The government was forced to reintroduce rationing of sweets in August the same year.

Experiments were also made with more traditional peacetime policy instruments. Considerable debate surrounds the timing of the full adoption of Keynesian policy (see Chapter 16) but a consensus has emerged that November 1947 was the first peacetime budget which fully employed the Keynesian demand management techniques that had been instigated during the war. In the atmosphere of the convertibility crisis and fears of inflationary pressure, a strictly deflationary budget was proposed for the autumn to contain aggregate demand and close the inflationary gap (see Figure 16.3). The Treasury was particularly concerned at the rising cost of food subsidies and the possible inflationary impact this was having through encouraging increases in demand for food. Chancellor Dalton resisted cuts in food subsidies but removed subsidies on clothing and footwear, raised company profits tax and indirect taxes on consumption, especially of alcohol, which combined to raise the tax yield by £197 million. The inflationary pressure subsequently eased.

Nationalization

After 1947, the government also found time to implement its programme of nationalization of industry which was a major feature of Labour's political agenda. Table 17.5 shows the dates of nationalization and the size of the industry by number of workers in 1950. Nationalization meant bringing industry into public ownership to be run and controlled by the government. The goal was to ensure that industry worked in the interests of the country as a whole rather than for the profit of individuals. Although this doctrine was closely connected with the Labour Party it was not strongly contested by the Conservative opposition. Utilities and fuel were the most obvious sectors for public ownership given their propensity for natural monopoly and the perceived potential for economies of scale, while other sectors such as iron and steel were more controversial both within the Labour Party as well as amongst the Conservative opposition. Nationalization was achieved through purchase of the shares and assets of private companies and appointing new boards of management. Altogether, the compensation paid by the government amounted to £2,639 million and brought some two million workers into the public sector.

Table 17.5. Nationalized industry

	Date	Number of Workers in 1950
Bank of England	1/3/1946	6,700[a]
National Coal Board	1/1/1947	730,000
Cable and Wireless	1/1/1947	9,500[a]
British Transport Commission[b]	1/1/1948	890,000
British Electrical Authority and Area Electricity Boards	1/4/1948	170,000
British Gas Council and Area Gas Boards	1/5/1949	140,000
Iron and Steel Corporation	15/2/1951	235,000

Note: [a]Numbers employed in 1951. [b] British Transport Commission included rail and road transport.

Sources: H.A.Clegg, 'Nationalized industry' in G.D.N. Worswick and P. Ady (eds), *The British Economy 1945–51* (Oxford, 1952) p. 425; A.K. Cairncross, *Years of Recovery* (London, 1985) p. 466.

The impact of public ownership on efficiency is the subject of ongoing debate. Nationalization often meant the combination of a large number of individual firms under one administration. With such large scale enterprises it was possible to have diseconomies of scale as well as increased efficiency. The reduction in competition might also affect efficiency. The changes wrought by nationalization, however, should not be overestimated. In practice, there was considerable continuity in personalities heading the industries since the Board of Managers almost always included the old owners and managers because their expertise was required. The difference was that they were now accountable to Parliament instead of private shareholders.

Devaluation, 1949

Despite the progress made in the domestic economy, the external balance continued to pose a threat to stability. At the end of the war, Britain had returned to a parity of $4.03 to the pound despite the dramatic changes in the competitive power of the British economy over the course of the war. Although devaluation was not discussed in the first postwar years, in early 1948 rumours began to spread that the exchange rate of the pound was unsustainable. Pressure mounted as the US suffered a mild recession which adversely affected UK and sterling area exports. As the Labour government hesitated, speculators sold sterling, putting strain on the central reserves. In the first quarter of 1949 the reserves fell by £82 million and this accelerated to £157 million in the second quarter.

The Labour government was unwilling to reintroduce austerity measures to curtail demand through cuts in expenditure just when recovery seemed to be achieved. It was believed by officials in the Bank of England and the Treasury, however, that devaluation alone would not solve the underlying imbalance between the UK and the rest of the world and that any positive short-term effects on competitiveness might merely be absorbed in inflation unless strong deflationary measures accompanied devaluation.

In the end, the Chancellor and Prime Minister were convinced that devaluation could no longer be avoided. The pound was finally devalued 30 per cent to $2.80 to the pound on 19 September 1949. Accompanying domestic measures, however, were delayed for a further month except for an increase of 5 per cent in the profits tax. In the end the piecemeal cuts in government expenditure did little to support the devaluation but the actual impact is difficult to assess because of the disruption to prices and production which accompanied the Korean War in the next year.

The Korean War and Rearmament

Just when the period of austerity seemed to have ended, events in the Far East produced another obstacle to achieving a 'normal' economic climate in which to pursue growth and full employment. In June 1950 the dispute between North and South Korea erupted into an international conflict which involved the armed forces of members of the United Nations and NATO. The UK was required to rearm and engage in another major military conflict just five years after the end of the Second World War. Domestically the conflict prompted a step backwards to the austerity of the postwar period, seen for example in the reimposition of rationing of some goods and central allocation of raw materials. In the external economic situation, however, the Korean War can be seen to have set the seal on the postwar period and marked a new departure for the British economy.

In April 1951, the government proposed to double defence expenditure within two years. The UK expected to be helped in this effort by the United States in the spirit of the common effort against Communism, especially to fund imports of necessary supplies from the US. In the end £3,879 million was spent in the three years 1950/51 to 1953/54 and the American contribution was much below the level expected.

The burden of rearmament fell most heavily on the metal and engineering industries where resources had to be diverted to munitions production. Shortages reappeared in key materials such as steel, sulphur and cotton which restrained the growth in productivity. Yet productivity growth was essential to maintain the level of civilian production when additional resources were being directed to the rearmament campaign. The diversion of resources to military production also threatened the export drive which became more important as import prices rose due to rearmament in the US and elsewhere.

The actual burden posed by the Korean War on the economy is open to some dispute. The impact on industrial investment and on the export drive is seen by some as having long-term consequences for the performance of the British economy. These years also witnessed a sharp increase in inflation due mainly to increases in the price of imports. As Alec Cairncross has pointed out, however, defence never absorbed more than 12 per cent of the output of metals and engineering industries. He concludes that 'rearmament in Britain probably did less harm to the economy, in the short run at least, than the rise in import prices that resulted from rearmament elsewhere'. The economic impact of the Korean War should therefore be judged in an international context.

The winter of 1951 marked the third balance of payments crisis since the war. It seemed to contemporary observers that odd numbered years were blighted after the crises of 1947 and 1949. The problem in 1951 was the dramatic increase in the price of raw material imports. Over the course of 1951, the impact of these increases on the foreign exchange reserves was softened by surpluses earned by sterling area countries. Since many members of the sterling area were raw material producers, they benefited from the increased demand for their exports and earned substantial foreign exchange which was deposited in London. By the end of 1951, however, the price boom had ended and the overseas sterling area began to run deficits thus withdrawing their previous earnings which put extra strain on the central reserves. The response was to tighten import controls both in the UK and in the rest of the sterling area until balance was achieved by the end of 1952.

The last year of the Labour government reflects poorly on the successes they had achieved during their period in office. The transition from wartime to peacetime production and distribution had been accomplished within a short period and the seemingly insurmountable problems posed by the war were overcome. The Conservative government elected in 1951 had much to be thankful for in that it came to power after the most painful elements of reconstruction had been completed.

In focus: Robot 1952

In the midst of the balance of payments crisis of the winter of 1951, the election of a Conservative government encouraged some officials to hope for a radical change in policy that might relax the external constraint on growth. In January 1952 Leslie Rowan (Treasury Second Secretary), George Bolton (Deputy Governor of the Bank of England) and R.W.B. (Otto) Clarke in the Treasury devised a proposal to abandon the fixed exchange rate of sterling and allow a depreciation of the pound to ease the pressure on the balance of payments. This top secret plan took on the codename ROBOT from the combination of their names. This has been seen by some economic historians as a lost opportunity to turn the British economy onto a new path which would have allowed faster growth by relieving balance of payments problems. With the release of secret government documents relating to the rejection of ROBOT, historians have better evidence with which to judge the reasons for this decision. This evidence gives insight into how the Cabinet weighed up external and internal goals.

The ROBOT plan in its final form prescribed convertibility of sterling at a floating exchange rate combined with blocking 80 per cent of outstanding liabilities to the sterling area. Letting the exchange rate float down would ease the pressure on the reserves since the government would not be obliged to use them to support the value of the pound. Speculators would supposedly ease off their sales of sterling as the exchange rate fell. The plan had an advantage over a devaluation to another fixed rate in that speculators would not be able to exhaust the exchange reserves in a future crisis. The government could, therefore, pursue domestic expansion and full employment without considering the level of reserves since the exchange rate would bear the burden of the impact of domestic policy on the balance of payments. It was anticipated that while the pound would sink initially, it

Robot 1952 (continued)

would eventually float to its equilibrium level. In the short term a depreciation would discourage imports and cheapen exports, thus solving the balance of payments crisis.

The plan was supported by the Bank of England, officials in the Treasury and by the new Chancellor R.A. Butler and was presented to the Cabinet at the end of February 1952 in preparation for the March Budget. The opposition was led by Churchill's adviser Lord Cherwell, who argued that a floating rate would not solve the balance of payments problem because depreciation would lead to an inflationary spiral when import prices rose. In his view, the balance of trade deficit was not a question of price competitiveness but of supply which could not be solved through exchange rate policy. Indeed a dramatic increase in costs through higher prices for imported raw materials would threaten production and employment. Relaxing the external constraint did not guarantee the domestic goals of growth, full employment and price stability.

For Prime Minister Churchill, the threat to domestic goals was considered the most important obstacle to ROBOT and, given the failure of the Cabinet to come to a consensus, the plan was rejected. In the short term, Churchill's decision was vindicated by the recovery of confidence in sterling from March 1952 after the budget, a rise in Bank Rate to 4 per cent and renewed import controls. In the longer term, however, the shallow reserves continued to be an important constraint on the pursuit of domestic growth and full employment throughout the 1950s. What the discussion on ROBOT reveals is that there was not a clear choice between external and internal goals since they were interdependent.

Prosperity at Last, 1952–55

The striking aspect of the transfer of economic policy-making from the Labour Party to the Conservatives was the remarkable continuity of policy. This came to be characterized by the combination of the names of the outgoing Chancellor Gaitskell with his replacement Rab Butler in 'Butskellism'. Keynesian management of the economy was continued as were many of the direct controls that had survived the 'Bonfire' of 1948. Food subsidies were cut in the first Conservative budget but the foundations of the welfare state remained untouched. Only iron and steel and road haulage among the new nationalized industries were returned to private ownership.

The Conservative government came to power in the midst of the worst balance of payments crisis since the war but found few new approaches to the conflict between external balance and internal growth. The only revolutionary proposal which was to float the sterling exchange rate was, as we have seen, rejected. Monetary policy was redeployed to contract domestic demand and one of the first acts of the new government was to raise Bank Rate from 2 per cent to 2.5 per cent in November 1951 and then to 4 per cent the following March. Bank Rate was changed six times between 1951 and 1955 whereas it had remained constant at 2 per cent since the end of 1940. The emphasis of policy, however, continued to be laid on the government budget.

In the end, the crisis of 1951–52 essentially solved itself as import prices fell and the rearmament effort receded. The crisis, however, did have a lasting psychological impact as the external constraint in the form of recurring balance of payments problems seemed to challenge the objectives of full employment and growth. Given the small margin of external reserves any relaxation in the vigilance of the campaign against domestic inflation appeared to lead directly to external crisis. On the other hand, high interest rates and capital controls ran counter to the government's domestic goals for growth. What resulted was a pattern of alternative restraint and expansion which became known as the 'Stop-Go Cycle' (see Chapter 18).

In the immediate years after 1952, though, the external constraint was relaxed and policy returned to expansion. In 1953 income tax was reduced by sixpence on the pound from 9s6d to 9s and purchase tax on consumer durables was cut from 66.6 per cent to 50 per cent while tax allowances for investment were restored to encourage capital formation. Harold Macmillan, as Minister of Housing, launched an ambitious programme of housing construction, aiming at 300,000 houses per year, a target he reached by the end of 1953 and repeated in every year to 1957.

Table 17.6. The British economy, 1951–57

	1951	1952	1953	1954	1955	1956	1957
Percentage change from previous year							
GDP	2.5	0.0	4.0	4.0	3.0	2.0	1.5
Industrial production	3.5	−3.0	6.0	7.0	5.0	0.5	1.7
Retail prices (inflation)	11.9	6.7	1.4	3.4	5.9	3.3	4.4
Changes in expenditure (£m 1954 prices)							
Fixed investment	0	0	225	200	125	150	125
Consumer durables	0	−25	150	150	100	−125	100
Other consumption	−150	−25	325	400	350	250	200
Percentage unemployed	1.2	2.0	1.6	1.3	1.1	1.2	1.4

Source: J.C.R. Dow, *The Management of the British Economy, 1945–60* (Cambridge, 1964) pp. 74, 93.

Table 17.6 shows changes in the economy between 1951 and 1957. Industrial production increased dramatically from 1953 to 1955 as did GDP, ensuring that the full employment target was met. A striking aspect of Table 17.6 is the dramatic increase in expenditure on consumer durables and other consumption in the boom years of 1953–55. The British people finally seemed to be rewarded for their earlier sacrifice as the era of mass consumption arrived. Table 17.7 shows some components of consumption of consumer durables. New items such as television sets were to transform the quality of life of the average British household.

Table 17.7. Consumption of selected consumer durables (monthly averages) 1949–57

	New car registrations (thousands)	TV sets (thousands)	Refrigerators (£000)
1949	12.8	17.4	384
1950	11.1	42.4	445
1951	11.4	57.6	455
1952	15.7	65.3	231
1953	24.7	95.4	343
1954	32.7	104.2	515
1955	41.9	140.5	666
1956	33.4	119.4	538
1957	35.5	151.3	779

Source: M. Hall, 'The consumer sector' in Worswick and Ady (eds), The British Economy, p. 432.

Chancellor Butler reigned over a period of expansion from 1951–55 that, while not free from external crisis, did much to dispel the memories of wartime austerity. Under his successors, however, growth rates slowed down as inflation was contained through demand management. In 1955 inflation associated with the boom prompted a loss of confidence in the exchange rate of sterling which was met with a harsh autumn budget and a rise in the Bank Rate from 3 per cent to 4.5 per cent. In 1956 the Suez Crisis caused a short-term crisis and contractionary policy was continued, but by 1957 fixed investment and consumption were recovering. By July 1957, the new Prime Minister Harold Macmillan was able to assert:

> most of our people have never had it so good. Go around the country, go to the industrial towns, go to the farms, and you will see a state of prosperity such as we have never had in my lifetime – nor indeed ever in the history of this country.[3]

Historical Interpretation: Was the Commonwealth an Economic Burden in the 1950s?

A common claim about the 1950s, as about the late nineteenth century, was that Britain's overseas interests were excessive and posed a drain on the economy which could have been avoided. The criticisms focus on the expense of keeping a military force abroad, excessive investment overseas and the costs of maintaining the parity of sterling. The result was a fragile balance of payments that inhibited growth of the economy.

This view of British postwar policy was promoted by a group of financial journalists who wrote influential books in the 1950s and 1960s. Andrew Shonfield, Norman Macrae and Susan Strange all criticized the role of the Commonwealth in British policy. In emotive terms Shonfield claimed 'that the British economy is robbed of necessary nourishment, that its growth is stunted, as a result of this too vigourous pursuit of overseas investment'.[4] Strange asserted as part of her thesis that the support of sterling as an international currency had been too costly for the British economy, that 'the Commonwealth idea in British politics ... provided one powerful rationalization for a do-nothing strategy for sterling'.[5] Macrae agreed that maintaining the fixed exchange rate of sterling had generated speculative capital flows which sparked domestic retrenchment, damaging Britain's economic performance.[6] The condemnation of external economic policy in the 1950s is echoed in a myriad of contemporary and more recent literature such as that by Sidney Pollard.[7]

The central plank in these criticisms is the gap between finance, which appeared to be focused on overseas projects, and industry which was apparently seeking investment capital without success. The other major contention is that a floating exchange rate would have been beneficial but that policy-makers were inhibited from choosing this option because of their commitments to sterling's role in the international economy.

While intuitively compelling, these arguments are more difficult to prove empirically. Part of the problem is wrapped up with assumptions of what British policy would have been instead of the alignment to the sterling area and Commonwealth. This is especially true for predicting the impact of a floating exchange rate on British economic performance. Despite the longevity of this debate, no systematic assessment of the possible impact has supported either argument. However, in a period when inflationary pressure was strong, such as in the later 1950s, it must be supposed that a devaluation could not guarantee an improvement in the competitiveness of British exports.

A more substantial obstacle for the argument about capital flows is the paucity of reliable information about how big these flows were and what impact capital formation has on economic growth. Since statistics on overseas investment were not collected, researchers must rely on rough estimates. The evidence suggests however that, unlike the similar assertions about the end of the nineteenth century, capital flows were small relative to domestic capital formation. This implies that even had this capital been diverted to domestic use it would not have made much of a contribution to UK investment. Furthermore, when comparing the UK with other Western European countries in the 1950s, it is productivity that seems to account for most of Britain's relatively poor performance rather than the volume of investment. The problem then becomes a question of quality rather than quantity of investment which would probably not have been solved by imposing controls on overseas investment.

This issue in Britain's postwar economic policy raises some popular difficulties in economic history. The first is the temptation to apply conclusions about one period to apparently similar problems of a later period. Historians tend to look for patterns or similarities over time and so have a predilection for continuity. In this case, the debate about British overseas investment before the First World War has influenced historians trying to explain British economic performance eighty years later.

The second feature is that assumptions must be supported by evidence and theory. In this case, the theoretical link between the volume of investment and growth is very tenuous. Moreover, the evidence that is available (while not complete) contradicts the conclusion that overseas investment was 'excessive'. Finally, there is the question of causation. Perhaps the flow of investment overseas was the result of a lack of profitable opportunities at home. In this case, the overseas investment was a symptom not a cause of Britain's relatively poor industrial performance. No thorough study has been made to determine the causes of overseas investment after 1945 so this central issue has yet to be determined.

The impact of the Commonwealth on British policy and the performance of the British economy is, therefore, an ongoing focus for research. After forty years of investigation, the suspicion that the impact was negative has still to be proved.

Bibliographical Note

Many books have been written about the Labour government's economic policies from 1945 to 1951 and the transition to peace. The most authoritative is Sir A.K. Cairncross, *Years of Recovery: British Economic Policy 1945–51* (London, 1985). This includes useful chapters on international as well as domestic policy and gives some insight into the bureaucratic process of policy-making. The theoretical underpinning of policy is addressed in Alan Booth, *British Economic Policy 1931–49: Was there a Keynesian Revolution?* (London, 1989). An entertaining account of the political environment of the Labour government is P. Hennessy, *Never Again: Britain 1945–51* (London, 1992). Among older texts, the most reliable is G.D.N. Worswick and P. Ady (eds), *The British Economy 1945–50* (Oxford, 1952) which has chapters on a wider range of domestic topics than Cairncross. Their follow-up volume *The British Economy in the Nineteen-fifties* (Oxford, 1962) is also useful.

For the 1950s, the classic text is J.C.R. Dow's masterful account of postwar economic policy in *The Management of the British Economy 1945–60* (Cambridge, 1964). Unfortunately a more modern equivalent has yet to be written and the reader is directed to general texts on postwar economic policy such as J. Tomlinson, *British Macro-economic Policy since 1940* (London, 1985). Samuel Brittan's *Steering the Economy: the Role of the Treasury* (Harmondsworth, 1971) also gives a good summary account of the formulation of the economic policies of the Conservative governments.

Notes

1. J.E.D. Hall, *Labour's First Year* (London, 1947) p. 13.

2. Sir A.K. Cairncross, *Years of Recovery: British Economic Policy 1945–51* (London, 1985) p. 383.

3. Quoted in D. Childs, *Britain since 1945: a Political History* (London, 1979) p. 106.

4. A. Shonfield, *British Economic Policy since the War* (London, 2nd edn, 1959) p. 108.

5. S. Strange, *Sterling and British Policy* (London, 1971) p. 323.

6. N. Macrae, *Sunshades in October: an Analysis of the Main Mistakes in British Economic Policy since the mid Nineteen-fifties* (London, 1963) p. 125.

7. S. Pollard, *The Wasting of the British Economy: British Economic Policy 1945 to the Present* (London, 1982) p. 88.

18 The 'Golden Age', 1955–1973

Peter Howlett

The 'Golden Age': an Overview

The period 1950–73 is viewed by some historians as the 'Golden Age' of the international economy, although in Britain the economy may have glittered a little less brightly than in other countries. This was a period of high growth rates, low unemployment and low inflation. It was achieved against the backdrop of the Bretton Woods fixed exchange rate system and in a world in which many policy-makers and economists believed that Keynesian demand management had given them the tools to properly regulate economic fluctuations. It stands out as a period of great success, especially when contrasted with the maladjustments and disequilibrium normally associated with the interwar years and the years after 1973.

Between 1951 and 1973 the British economy, in terms of Gross Domestic Product, grew at a rate of 2.8 per cent per annum which exceeded the long-run growth rates experienced both before the First World War and in the interwar years (indeed, on an annualized basis the rate of growth between 1951 and 1973 was 40 per cent higher than that between 1924 and 1937). This performance is even more impressive when population growth is taken into account: in terms of GDP per head the annualized growth rate between 1951 and 1973 of 2.4 per cent was a third higher than the interwar rate and double that of the pre-1914 rate.

Another impressive feature of this period was the low rate of unemployment, which contrasts starkly with the high levels of unemployment experienced in other periods. In the 1930s the unemployment rate had averaged 12.7 per cent but between 1951 and 1973 it averaged a mere 2 per cent; in terms of numbers, in the interwar period unemployment never fell below one million whereas the average level of unemployment in the 1950s was 338,000 and in the 1960s 459,000. During the 1970s the average level of unemployment reached 973,000, with the one million barrier being breached again in 1976 and below which unemployment has never looked like falling since. It should also be noted that even in the 'Golden Age' differences in regional unemployment rates (reflecting uneven regional economic development or structural economic problems) remained marked: for example, in 1965, when the unemployment rate for Britain was a mere 1.4 per cent, regional rates of unemployment varied from 2.8 per cent in Scotland, 2.6 per cent in Wales and 2.5 per cent in the North to less than 1 per cent in the Midlands and the South East (and in Northern Ireland unemployment was 6 per cent).

Finally, policy-makers in the 'Golden Age' managed to combine high growth and low unemployment with low inflation. Before 1950, except in times of war, inflation was relatively subdued (indeed, the interwar period was characterized by deflation) but it was to become a serious problem in the postwar era. The contrast is therefore between the inflation rate before 1973 and the inflation rate after 1973. From 1950 until 1967 the average annual rate of inflation was 3.8 per cent but it crept up to an average of 7.5 per cent per annum between 1968 and 1973 before exploding after the oil price shock of 1973; in 1973 the retail price index increased by 16 per cent and indeed this was the average annual rate of inflation between 1974 and 1980.[1]

The macro-economic performance was matched by improvements in living standards: infant mortality, often taken as one of the most sensitive measures of living standards, almost halved between 1950 and 1973, falling from 31.2 per thousand live births to 17.2; life expectancy also rose from 66.4 years to 69.2 years for men and from 71.5 years to 75.6 years for women. In more conventional terms the rise in the standard of living can be seen by the rise in average weekly earnings: the average male employed in manufacturing industry saw his weekly earnings rise from £7.83 in 1950 to £41.52 in 1973 and at the same time the average amount of hours he worked per week had fallen from 47.5 hours to 44.7 hours (in real terms this represented a doubling of his average earnings per hour worked). Female workers also saw their average earnings increase and their average hours of work decrease but on the debit side they failed to see an erosion of the differential between their average earnings and that of their male counterparts, indeed it widened: in 1950, female workers in manufacturing industry earned, on average, 53.1 per cent of male workers' wages but by 1970 this figure had fallen to 50.9 per cent.

The most obvious signs of this increased affluence were in the ownership of homes and consumer durables. In 1950 less than three in ten households owned their own home but by 1973 more than half did and car ownership had risen dramatically from 46 cars per thousand head of population to 247. Within the home the ownership of a whole range of domestic appliances increased in this period: the percentage of households owning washing machines increased from 7.5 per cent to 66.9 per cent; the percentage owning refrigerators increased from 3.2 per cent to 68 per cent; in 1950 only about

Plate 18.1. A typical kitchen in *c.* 1950. The continuation of rationing into the 1950s prevented consumers from using their rising incomes to purchase consumer goods.

one household in every fifty owned a television but by 1973 more than 90 per cent had one. These changes in the ownership of consumer goods understate the improvement in living standards because the quality of the goods had also increased; to give just one example, the public transmission of colour television only began in 1968 and already by 1973 one in five households had colour television licences.

Britain was not the only country to experience a 'Golden Age' in this period: the US, Japan, West Germany and indeed most of the developed world

Plate 18.2.   A modernized kitchen in *c.* 1970. The consumer boom of the 1960s
transformed the interior of houses. Kitchens had to expand in size to accommodate the
multitude of new durable goods, and to adapt to new patterns of domestic life.

saw high growth rates, low unemployment and low inflation. It was the
experience of these other countries that takes the shine off Britain's 'Golden
Age' because despite its historically good record its major competitors did
better. Table 18.1 demonstrates the relative failure of British growth compared
to its three major competitors (the US, West Germany and Japan), or rather
compared to two of them. Of these four economies British nominal GDP grew
the least rapidly between 1950 and 1973 and the Japanese economy grew most
rapidly. When the nominal GDP figures are adjusted to take account of price

Table 18.1. The relative performance of Britain, 1950–73: economic growth (average annual % growth)

	UK	US	West Germany	Japan
GDP	3.0	3.7	5.9	9.4
Real GDP per head	2.9	2.1	4.7	7.8
Real GDP per hour worked	3.1	2.4	5.7	7.4

After. A. Maddison, 'Growth and slowdown in advanced capitalist economies: techniques of quantitative measurement', *Journal of Economic Literature* vol. 24 (1987)

changes (which gives real GDP) and of either the changing population or the amount of hours worked by the labour force in the economy (the second and third rows in Table 18.1), the British performance still looks weak compared to both West Germany and Japan although it is stronger than the American performance. Britain also performed poorly when measured in these terms against all the other major developed nations. The causes of this relative failure will be discussed in Chapter 19.

A major cause of the growth in the world economy in this period was the thawing of international trade barriers. Nationally and internationally the decade witnessed the gradual dismantling of controls and a move towards greater economic freedom. This was the result of a concerted international attack, led by the Americans, on all forms of barriers to international trade. It took its most obvious form in the General Agreement on Tariffs and Trade (GATT) which was initiated in 1947 with the aim of reducing trade barriers, tariffs and all forms of trade discrimination in the belief that this would encourage world economic growth. This international movement was bolstered by intra-national developments, particularly in Europe, which also helped to reduce trade barriers and encourage growth. The most obvious examples of this were the European Economic Community (EEC), founded in 1957 and of which initially Britain was not a member, and the European Free Trade Association (EFTA), which Britain helped to found in 1959. The overall results of all these changes were reductions across the international economy in import controls and tariff levels.

Such developments were only possible because of the stability of the international monetary system which was itself the result of cooperation between the leading developed nations. The basis of this cooperation stemmed, to a large degree, from the Bretton Woods Conference of July 1944. This laid the basis for three important postwar institutions: the Bretton Woods system itself, the International Bank for Reconstruction and Development, and the International Monetary Fund (IMF). (See Chapter 17). Further, just as the nineteenth century was dominated by Britain and the pound, so this period was dominated by the US and the dollar. Both were periods of stability and recognized international leadership in the world economy, especially when compared to the rudderless interwar years. When apparent structural problems emerged within the American economy after 1973 and when both West Germany and Japan started to challenge American hegemony, the result was that the 'Golden Age' gave way to an age of relative confusion.

The growth of international trade did stimulate British exports: between

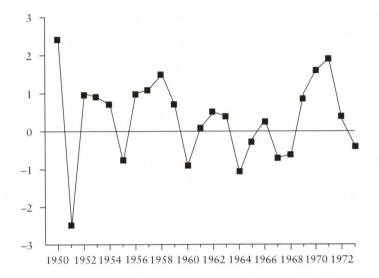

Figure 18.1. Balance of payment current account, 1950–73 (as % of GDP). *After:* N.F.R. Crafts and N. Woodward (eds), *The British Economy since 1945* (Oxford, 1991) p. 9.

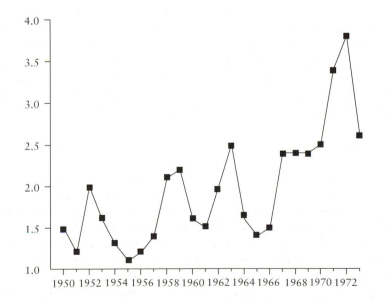

Figure 18.2. Rate of unemployment, GB, 1950–73 (in %). *Sources: British Labour Statistics, Historical Abstract,* pp. 316–17; *Annual Abstract of Statistics* (1973) pp. 202–3.

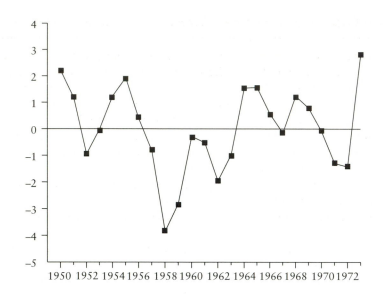

Figure 18.3. Real GDP (% deviation from trend) 1950–73 (at 1985 factor cost). *After*: *Economic Trends* (1993) p. 10.

1950 and 1963 the volume of exports increased by 25 per cent, and it increased by a further 40 per cent between 1963 and 1970. However, export growth was more rapid in other developed countries. This mainly reflected the fact that British exports were oriented to markets 'that either had below average growth rates or [were adopting] import-substitution policies'.[2] It also reflected a growing lack of price competitiveness: throughout the period French and German manufactured export prices were less than British prices and by the mid 1960s American prices were also more competitive than British prices. The result was a dramatic decline in the British share of world exports: in 1950 Britain accounted for about a quarter of all world manufactured exports, by 1960 this share had fallen to 16.5 per cent and by 1975 it was less than 10 per cent. At the same time the lifting of import and current account controls in Britain at the end of the 1950s and the general liberalization of world trade resulted in a rapid increase in imports: in 1950 exports and imports were roughly in balance but by 1970 whereas exports were equivalent to 10 per cent of GDP, imports accounted for 18 per cent of GDP. This in turn caused balance of payments problems for the British economy. The situation is illustrated in Figure 18.1 which shows the current account balance as a percentage of GDP. It clearly shows how the ending of import controls in the late 1950s had an adverse effect. Figure 18.1 also reflects the difficulties policy-makers had in reconciling the political need for internal balance and the economic need (imposed by the fixed exchange rate system) for external balance.

In focus: Britain and the European Economic Community (EEC)

The EEC was founded in 1957 with the signing of the Treaty of Rome by West Germany, France, Italy and the Benelux countries. It was primarily a customs union: that is, within the EEC there was to be free trade whilst around the union would be placed a tariff barrier. However, the EEC also had longer-term political and economic goals that called for greater integration and greater harmonization between member countries (involving free movement of capital and labour, harmonization of laws and equality of fiscal practice). Britain favoured the idea of free trade but was less willing to accept the proposed economic and political integration. This was one reason why Britain did not join the EEC when it was first created.

Another reason related to the economic costs and benefits of joining. A customs union involves both trade-creation (the reduction of internal barriers stimulates trade and hence economic growth) and trade-diversion (the customs union tariff barrier reduces trade with non-member countries). Thus, a country should only join a customs union if the potential trade-creation is greater than the potential trade-diversion. For the original members of the EEC their trade was dominated by trade with the other members and therefore trade-creation would almost certainly be greater than trade-diversion. (It has been estimated that by 1970 the excess amounted to $9 billion, or 2 per cent of the EEC's GDP.) Britain, however, traded primarily with the countries associated with the sterling area, and Western Europe only accounted for about a quarter of British trade. Thus, it was likely that for Britain trade-diversion would be greater than trade-creation.

By 1970 this situation had changed: Western Europe now accounted for half of all British exports whilst the sterling area only accounted for a quarter. It was also felt that Britain's lower growth rate compared to the EEC countries since 1957 reflected the benefits of the customs union. (Between 1960 and 1973 British output per hour worked had increased at 4.1 per cent per annum, compared to 5.5 per cent for West Germany and 6.4 per cent for France.) The creation of the EEC had caused a widening of markets in Europe which, in turn, created greater opportunities for specialization and economies of scale for member countries (particularly since the original members were relatively complementary economies in that they produced and consumed similar sorts of goods). Another incentive for joining the EEC in the early 1970s was that Britain had a traditional trade orientation towards countries that produced primary products but in the postwar period world trade in manufactured goods (produced by developed economies such as those of the EEC) was increasing more rapidly than world trade in primary goods. Therefore unless Britain increased its trade with Europe it might lose an important opportunity to expand.

Britain made two unsuccessful attempts to join the EEC in the 1960s (both were blocked by France) but was finally successful in 1973.

The 'Stop-Go Cycle' and the Radcliffe Report, 1955–64

The 1950s saw the emergence of the 'Stop-Go Cycle'. In the 'Go' phase of the cycle the domestic economy would expand, pushing down unemployment and pushing up spending. The increased spending would suck in imports, putting pressure on the balance of payments, and fuel inflation. This would prompt the government to bring in a package of tax increases and credit restrictions in order to choke off demand. The economy would then move into the 'Stop' phase of the cycle whereby demand would fall, economic growth would slow down and unemployment would rise. The operation of the cycle can be clearly seen in Figures 18.1, 18.2 and 18.3: Figure 18.2 shows the percentage rate of unemployment for Britain between 1950 and 1973, with low levels of unemployment being associated with boom, or 'Go', years and high levels with 'Stop' years; Figure 18.3 shows the percentage deviation of the rate of growth of real GDP from its trend rate of growth between 1950 and 1973. Thus, 1955 was a trough year in unemployment terms (Figure 18.2) and a peak year in terms of real GDP growth (Figure 18.3) reflecting the 1955 boom. This boom led in turn to a balance of payments deficit (Figure 18.1) as imports increased, and was followed by accelerating wages and prices which forced the Chancellor to introduce a deflationary package of measures in 1956 (as a result of the Suez Crisis these measures also included petrol rationing); and so the economy entered a 'Stop' phase and unemployment rose and the rate of growth declined. Sometimes, as in 1959, the government deliberately engineered a 'Go' phase to coincide with an election.

The 'Stop-Go Cycle' continued into the 1960s. Thus, the July 1961 Budget was a 'Stop' budget which involved increased taxes, new controls on overseas investment and a 'pay pause' for the public sector. By 1963, with an election looming, the government attempted to boost the economy but the Conservatives still lost power to Harold Wilson. Wilson had launched a fierce attack on 'Stop-Go', which he believed was detrimental to long-term growth, but his government would itself adopt many of the measures associated with the classic 'Stop-Go' policies. The impact of 'Stop-Go' is considered more fully below.

One of the most striking features of economic policy in this period was the relatively unimportant role allotted by policy-makers to the control of the money supply. It could be argued that this, at least initially, reflected the fact that inflation was not a serious problem in the period. However, it also reflected a deliberate policy choice that was crystallized by the Radcliffe Committee on the Working of the Monetary System, commissioned in 1957 by Thorneycroft, the then Chancellor of the Exchequer. He set up the Committee because of fears about the persistence of inflation. Thorneycroft believed that this was strongly linked to the control of bank credit and the money supply. In effect, Thorneycroft wanted the Committee to recommend that the control of the money supply be upgraded as a policy instrument. He was to be disappointed. The Radcliffe Report, when it finally appeared in 1959, rejected the idea that the money supply was a sufficient instrument to influence the course of the economy and argued that the liquidity of the economy (the ease of obtaining money) was what mattered. Its practical effect was to confine the control of the money supply to the dustbin of economic policy instruments (putting the emphasis on interest rate manipulation), where it would remain until it was retrieved by a Labour chancellor (Healey) under pressure from the IMF, in the mid 1970s.

Growth, demand management and intervention, 1964–70

The Wilson government (1964–70) adopted a more interventionist approach to the economy and demand management gave way to experiments with economic planning (including prices and incomes policies and regional policies). It was a period that started with high hopes but which was to end in disappointment. The hopes that economic planning would stimulate stable long-term growth were thwarted by the resilience of the Treasury and the 'Stop-Go Cycle'; attempts to evolve a workable prices and incomes policy to combat creeping inflation were not very successful; relations with Europe were strained as a second attempt to join the EEC was rebuffed by another French veto; and hopes of re-establishing sterling as a, if not the, leading international currency fell on stony ground partly as a result of its overvaluation against the other major currencies. The devaluation of sterling in 1967 was typical of British policy during this period in being probably too little, too late. On the brighter side, unemployment never crept above 2.5 per cent and London was restored as an international banking centre (partly due to the development of the Euro-dollar market).

Despite the high growth rate Britain had enjoyed in the 1950s there was concern in the early 1960s about the persistence of balance of payments problems, particularly in the current account (see Figure 18.1), and about the poor performance of the country relative to other developed nations. This led to much talk about indicative planning. This was used by the French with apparent great success. Indicative planning involved the government consulting with employers and workers to compile a series of target growth rates for the coming period. There would be a target for the growth of the overall economy and for things like investment and exports, and each industrial sector would also be given a target. The philosophy behind indicative planning was that it would create stability by, among other things, letting businessmen know what the government hoped to achieve (and presumably would direct its policies towards) and therefore enabled them to invest with greater confidence.

In Britain the first step towards such a system came under the Conservative government with the creation, in 1962, of the National Economic Development Council (NEDC). The NEDC was a tripartite organization (consisting of representatives from the trade unions, employers and the government) which was given responsibility for coordinating the planning apparatus. It did, in fact, produce an indicative economic plan but this was a rather vague document that suggested a higher growth rate was more desirable in the long run but which made no firm suggestions as to how to achieve this goal in the short run. However, economic growth and economic planning were now on the political agenda and when the Labour Party was returned to power it was committed to both.

In 1964 the Labour government created the Department of Economic Affairs (DEA). It was responsible for coordinating planning and for policy on prices and incomes (and the NEDC in effect became an advisory body to the DEA). The DEA quickly set about its task and, in September 1965, published the National Plan. In order to produce and carry out the National Plan the DEA had also created a regional network (primarily to improve the flow of information on which to base the plan) and, in early 1965, the National Board for Prices and Incomes (which was to suggest a norm for price and wage increases and to investigate increases that exceeded this norm). The Plan itself called for a 25 per cent increase in output over the period 1964–70 (an annualized rate of 3.8 per cent, well above the rates achieved before 1965). Within this broad figure it was intended that investment and exports should rise more quickly than consumption.

Unfortunately the National Plan and formalized economic planning were to have a short life, primarily because of the undiminished power of the Treasury. When the DEA was created the idea was to reduce the influence of the Treasury. It was thought to be too conservative and to have contributed to 'Stop-Go' and thus sacrificed long-term growth for short-term demand management considerations. Thus, under the new scheme the Treasury was supposed to concentrate on short-term financial and monetary matters while the DEA was to be responsible for long-term management of real resources. However, the Treasury retained all its important powers (its responsibilities for public expenditure, monetary policy and the exchange rate) whilst the DEA failed to establish an equivalent strong base. At the first sign of economic difficulty the Treasury asserted itself and blew down the house of cards upon which the National Plan rested: in July 1966 a typical balance of payments crisis emerged, the Treasury argued for and got a typical 'Stop' reaction and the National Plan was abandoned. The DEA limped on before final abolition in 1969. Its planning responsibilities passed to the Treasury whilst the Department of Employment and Productivity inherited price and incomes policy.

The Labour government also adopted a more interventionist stance with industry but it is doubtful whether its strategy could be called an industrial policy. Wilson had successfully campaigned on a slogan based on 'the white heat of technology' which argued that Britain could achieve better economic growth by harnessing its technological capabilities more fully. This found its expression in his creation of the Ministry of Technology whose aim was to disseminate new technical and other information to the leading edge industries such as aircraft, nuclear power, computing and high-grade engineering. In fact, this department was an amalgam of many smaller departments and specialist bodies, and internal friction and a lack of a clear policy direction meant that it never fulfilled its potential. On the issue of market structure the Wilson government found itself facing in two different directions: on the one hand, the Monopolies and Mergers Act of 1965 seemed to strike a blow against increased market concentration in making all mergers that were worth more than £5 million or that would account for more than one-third of the market the subject of statutory investigation; on the other hand, the Industrial Reorganisation Corporation (IRC) was created in 1966 partly to encourage mergers in the belief that the large corporations prevalent in the American and German economies were to some extent responsible for their success. The IRC was involved in fifty mergers in its lifetime (it was abolished in 1971), including the creation of British Leyland, although this accounted for only a small fraction of the total mergers during that period.

In focus: Professor Phillips – his Machine and his Curve

Professor A.W.H. Phillips (1914–75) is famous in economics for two things: his machine and his curve. Postwar economics in Britain was dominated by Keynesian economic theory and the Phillips Machine was a hydraulic representation of the economy as seen through Keynesian eyes (see Figure 18.4). At the bottom of the machine was a tank of coloured water representing national income; this water would then flow round the machine (representing the circular flow of income in the economy) and at various stages it would experience leakages (in the form of taxes, savings and imports) and injections (in the form of government spending, investment and exports) before returning to the national income tank. It thus showed quite clearly the relationship between stocks and flows in the economy. The operator of the machine could vary such things as the level of taxation, the propensity to save and the rate of interest (but not the exchange rate since this was a world of fixed exchange rates) and could demonstrate quite sophisticated interactions within the economy. The Phillips Machine is an apt metaphor for the belief in the 1950s and 1960s that Keynesian economics had cracked the macroeconomic nut and that government policy could be used to fine tune the economy in order to avoid any serious macro-economic problem.

The Phillips Curve first appeared in a 1958 article in which Phillips drew a series of curves based on historical data that suggested that there was a stable and inverse relationship between unemployment and inflation. Thus, high levels of inflation were associated with low levels of unemployment and vice versa. The Phillips Curve represented this as a downward sloping curve on a diagram with the rate of inflation on the vertical axis and the rate of unemployment on the horizontal axis.

Professor Phillips – his Machine and his Curve (continued)

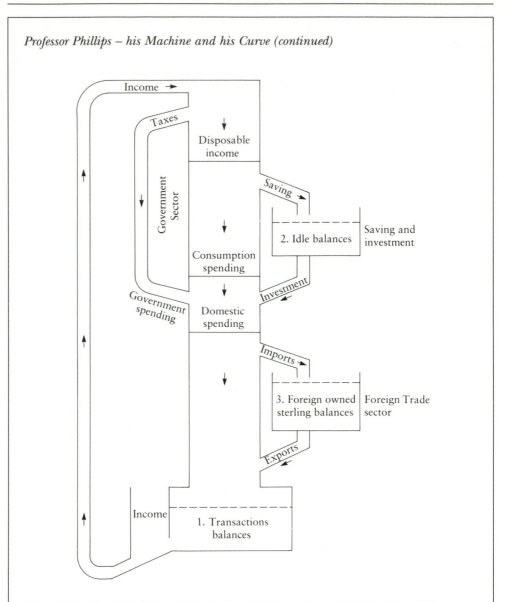

Figure 18.4. Simplified view of the Phillips Machine. *Source:* Nicholas Barr, 'The Phillips Machine', *LSE Quarterly* vol. 4 (1988) p. 321.

Phillips only presented a statistical relationship in his article and did not offer a theoretical explanation but every subsequent article on the relationship between unemployment and inflation referred to the Phillips Curve and discussed what its shape was, how it could be moved and the optimal position for an economy to be at on the curve. It appeared to have important policy implications too as it suggested that policy-makers could choose how much extra inflation they would tolerate in order to achieve lower rates of unemployment.

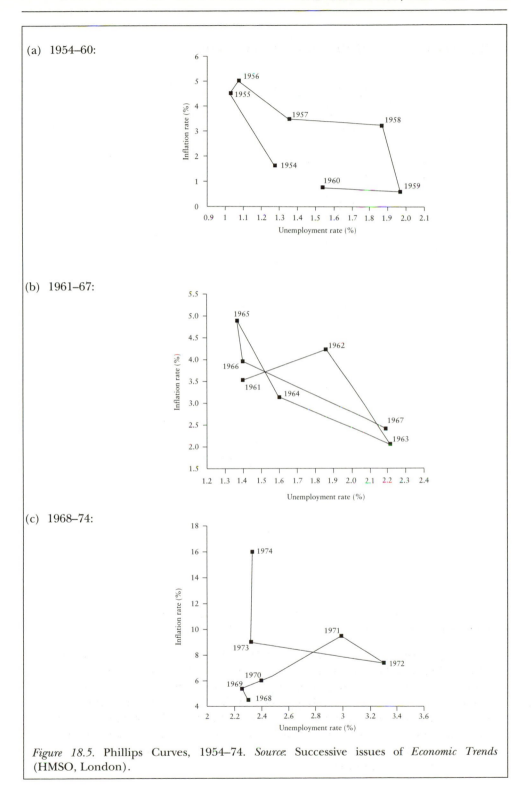

(a) 1954–60:

(b) 1961–67:

(c) 1968–74:

Figure 18.5. Phillips Curves, 1954–74. *Source:* Successive issues of *Economic Trends* (HMSO, London).

Professor Phillips – his Machine and his Curve (continued)

Did the British economy in this period mirror the Phillips Curve? Figure 18.5 shows the relationship between the rates of unemployment and inflation between 1954 and 1974. The first two periods do indeed seem to offer clear support for the Phillips Curve as they strongly suggest you could draw a downward sloping curve to represent the relationship. The story breaks down, however, after 1968. Economists reconciled such diagrams by arguing that the relatively simple view of the trade-off between unemployment and inflation ignored the fact that certain combinations could not be maintained indefinitely (since they would imply either excess demand or excess supply in the economy, a situation that normal economic forces would make unsustainable) and because it ignored the role of expectations. Most economic textbooks now teach that the downward sloping Phillips Curve only holds in the short run and that in the long run the Phillips Curve is vertical at the natural rate of unemployment.

The Path to Devaluation

In 1964 the Wilson government had inherited a Conservative-manufactured boom and thus its first move was to apply the 'Stop' brake; in particular, a 15 per cent surcharge on manufactured imports was introduced (much to the ire of Britain's partners in EFTA). However, other measures (such as increased pensions, the abolition of prescription charges, and the introduction of capital gains tax) alarmed the financial world and led to a run on sterling. This set the pattern for the next few years: the Spring Budget would either itself set off a run on sterling or would be followed by some other event which did so (in 1966, for example, it was French comments about the need for sterling devaluation if Britain were to join the EEC) and a more restrictive budget would be introduced in the summer. Indeed, as the 1960s progressed the overvaluation of sterling became more and more apparent: between 1960 and 1968 the annual average UK current account balance of payments was $0.38 billion in the red which compared to an average surplus of $3.66 billion in the US, $0.1 billion surplus in Japan, and $0.6 billion surplus in West Germany. It was not therefore surprising that devaluation finally came in November 1967: sterling was devalued from $2.80 to $2.40 (or 14.3 per cent). Figure 18.1 shows how the devaluation helped to cure, at least temporarily, the persistent balance of payments problems that had plagued the country during the 1960s.

The collapse of national and international consensus, 1970–73

The reprieve was short lived and the story of the 1970s for the British economy was one of external shocks and the gradual internal erosion of consensus policies. In 1971 the Bretton Woods system collapsed, giving way eventually to an international system of freely floating exchange rates. Sterling was allowed to float in June 1972 and this effectively ended the operation of the sterling area. The result was that the value of sterling against the dollar fell until 1977, when it hit $1.75, before staging a temporary recovery; its fall against the yen and the mark was even more dramatic. There was also a sharp deterioration in the balance of trade: between 1946 and 1969 the largest deficit was £712 million in 1968; by 1972 it was £2,586 million and the following year £5,351 million, indeed between 1972 and 1980 the smallest deficit was £1,542 million in 1978.

The erosion of internal consensus was best seen in the labour market where the postwar pledge to full employment was starting to fray at the edges. This was partly blamed on cost-push inflation which was itself the result of the failure to evolve a proper incomes policy and rising trade union power. The aim of incomes policies was to combat wage inflation and protect the balance of payments while not sacrificing growth. However, the Labour government, despite its apparently good relations with the trade unions, had been unable to develop a stable or successful incomes policy. The Heath government (1970–74) at first abandoned incomes policy but its desire to control the upward spiral of inflation led it to impose a statutory incomes policy in September 1972. This worked well until a series of events, capped by the oil price shock of 1973, led the coalminers to rebel. Their strike led to the introduction of a state of emergency and a three-day week (a similar situation had occurred in 1972 when the Heath government had tried to restrict the wage increases of public sector employees), and it caused the eventual fall of the Heath government.

Historiographical Interpretations

How Harmful was the 'Stop-Go Cycle' to the British Economy?

The period from 1951 to 1967 is associated with the economic policy regime known as 'Stop-Go' whereby the government acted against imbalances in the economy (typically a balance of payments problem) to either expand or contract the economy. It used both fiscal and monetary policies to 'fine tune' the economy. Fiscal policies typically entailed changes in the tax rate (of both income tax and expenditure taxes) and in government expenditure to either increase effective demand in the economy (thus initiating a 'Go' phase) or to reduce effective demand (thus initiating a 'Stop' phase). These fiscal policies were bolstered by a range of monetary policies; for example, in order to contract the economy the government could raise the rate of interest, increase the amount of money clearing banks had to keep in reserve (which would effectively reduce their ability to lend money), restrict new capital issues or building society lending or introduce new hire purchase controls (the latter was a popular tool because it directly affected consumption, and the finance of small firms, but did no long-term damage to the economy). The impact of 'Stop-Go' on the British economy has been the subject of much debate. In particular it is claimed that it created an unstable environment that was detrimental to the long-term growth of the economy (although it should be noted that until at least 1964 contemporaries rarely criticized the underlying ethos of the policy but were more concerned about the size and timing of measures adopted).

The problem of timing is best summarized by Michael Surrey: 'policymakers based their decisions (via currently available indicators) on what had already happened to the economy rather than on what was likely to be happening in future when policy changes had their effects.'[3] It was therefore quite likely that the economy was naturally adjusting to, say, overexpansion and that the effect of a deflationary budget in this case merely exaggerated the downturn. This is a problem policy-makers in all economies face at all times: the information they have will always be about the past and their skill comes in judging to what extent that information reflects the current and future economic state. It therefore seems unfair to single out the 'Stop-Go' policy-makers on these grounds.

The argument that 'Stop-Go' was a policy dominated by short-term considerations whose cumulative affect was to greatly harm most long-term objectives (such as full employment, growth and structural changes in the economy) was put forward by Harold Wilson in the 1964 Election and it was a theme subsequently taken up by several economists and historians. A good synthesis of this argument is provided by Sidney Pollard[4] who argues that the 'Stop-Go Cycle' helped to exacerbate the export problem facing the British economy and ignored its import problem and thus created a downward spiral that made Britain's continued relative decline inevitable. This cycle may not have been initially caused by the government but its policies strongly influenced it. In terms of exports the key problem was the effect of 'Stop-Go' on investment: the continual expansion and contraction sapped the confidence of businessmen and made them wary of undertaking new investment projects; also, the 'Stop' policies deliberately attempted to restrict investment in order to reduce effective demand. The lack of new investment reduced the scope for productivity gains through new technology which in turn resulted in a deterioration in British price competitiveness and hence a fall in exports. Since the 'Stop' phase was often initiated because of a balance of payments problem the reduction in exports merely started off the whole cycle again, thus: 'failure in productivity led to losses in exports; these led to balance of payments difficulties, and these, in turn, led to government short-term measures which were certain, in the long-term, to make the productivity failures worse and start the cycle up again, in less favourable circumstances, as soon as the restrictions were taken off'.[5] As to imports, the striking feature of import growth in this period was that those imports which grew most rapidly, such as machinery and steel, were goods also produced in Britain which suggested that the economy was facing a capacity constraint.

The counter-argument to this is best put by Surrey.[6] He first points out that it has been argued that rather than weakening business confidence the 'Stop-Go' regime increased it by providing a stable policy framework; in particular, it was made clear that the government was committed in the medium run to full employment, a stable exchange rate and, in the later stages, growth. Indeed, the data on investment in this period would seem to support this view as it was high compared to the pre-1939 levels. The response to this would be that in the absence of 'Stop-Go' investment could have been even higher (and could have helped to relieve the capacity constraint).

The second string to the Surrey bow is less easily attacked. If 'Stop-Go' induced economic fluctuations that were destabilizing to the British economy then other economies that faced similar fluctuations must also have fared badly. In fact, evidence from European economies in this period suggests they suffered even greater fluctuations but also managed to achieve higher growth rates over the long run. If the British experience of 'Stop-Go' was not unusual then the cause of British relative decline must be found elsewhere and it is hard to disagree with the conclusion by Alford: 'comparisons with other economies suggest that stop/go was not the problem rather it was the weakness of the underlying trend of growth which exaggerated the effect of stop/go phases.'[7]

The Decline of the Manufacturing Sector

In 1955 industrial employment as a share of total civilian employment reached 48 per cent (with manufacturing accounting for 36 per cent). These figures were unparalleled in British history and indeed remain almost without equal in the experience of other capitalist economies. This high relative level was partly the result of distortions caused by the wartime economy and the export drive of the immediate postwar years. Although the number of workers employed in the manufacturing sector continued to grow until 1966 its relative share declined as it grew less rapidly than the overall labour force. Thereafter employment in manufacturing declined and by 1973 it accounted for only 32 per cent of the workforce. In this period the agricultural sector also declined in relative terms (it accounted for 6 per cent of the civilian labour force in 1950 but only 3 per cent in 1973). The beneficiary of these falls was the service sector: by 1966 it already accounted for more than half the civilian labour force and by 1973 its share had risen to almost 55 per cent.

These changes led to many heated debates. It was argued, particularly by the Cambridge economist Nicholas Kaldor, that manufacturing was capable of higher rates of growth of productivity than services and therefore a shift towards services would reduce the productivity growth of the economy. Kaldor had the ear of the Labour government and in September 1966 it introduced the Selective Employment Tax (SET) to try and encourage the movement of labour from services to manufacturing. It was a 15 per cent payroll tax but public sector employees got a 100 per cent refund and manufacturing employees got a 130 per cent refund. The SET faced theoretical and practical difficulties. Kaldor's argument, for example, glossed over the enormous difficulties of measuring productivity in the service sector and his empirical evidence came under attack (mainly because it was claimed he demonstrated a correlation but not causation). Also, in 1968 the government abandoned the Kaldor line by effectively extending the SET to all industries (it thus became a tax to encourage labour-saving investment). The rising level of unemployment sounded the death knell for the SET and it was abandoned in 1973.

Another argument was that the public sector, which was included in the service sector, was largely unproductive, particularly when compared to more market-oriented sectors, and its growth had a damaging effect on the economy. Finally the de-industrialization thesis (which can, in part be traced to the original Kaldor thesis) argued that the shift towards services was eroding the ability of the country to meet its balance of payments commitments (an argument that has more weight in the post-1973 era). However, both of these arguments also suffered from a definitional vagueness and lacked comparative empirical support (for example government sector employment in Britain was not an obvious outlier when compared to its major competitors; and the decline of manufacturing employment and the rise of service sector employment is a feature common to all developed economies). Most of these arguments also ignore two things: first, that the share of the manufacturing sector in the early to mid 1950s was unusually high; second, that the sector enjoyed fairly rapid and increasing rates of productivity growth throughout this period.

Bibliographical Note

This period lacks a definitive economic history and economic historians have as yet written surprisingly little about it even in article form. J.C.R. Dow, *The Management of the British Economy 1945–69* (Cambridge, 1964) and W. Beckerman (ed.), *The Labour Government's Economic Record, 1964–70* (London, 1972) provide a useful contrast as Dow takes a relatively sceptical line on the role of the government in the 1950s whilst the Beckerman collection is generally enthusiastic about the more interventionist Labour government. Sidney Pollard's Keynesian flavoured textbook, *The Development of the British Economy, 1914–1990* (London, 4th edn, 1992) is still the best written about the experience of the British economy since 1914 and the chapters on the period after 1950 are packed full of detailed information and intelligent discussions of the literature and debates. The pamphlet by B.W.E. Alford, *British Economic Performance 1945–1975* (London, 1988) is arranged by theme and provides a succinct appraisal of the main debates in each topic. (It also provides a very useful briefly annotated bibliography.) The collection edited by Charles Feinstein, *The Managed Economy* (Oxford, 1983) reproduces several key articles (by Matthews, Paish, Opie and Kaldor) which tackle the major themes of the period; Feinstein also provides an informative introductory paper. The volume edited by N.F.R. Crafts and N. Woodward, *The British Economy since 1945* (Oxford, 1991) attempts to bring together the most recent views of economic historians on the postwar period and of particular interest are the papers on budgetary policy, trade, inflation, unemployment, economic growth, and regional policy; and again there is a good introductory paper by the editors. Some of these papers provide a revisionist slant to material presented in the other works cited. Finally, the volume edited by Andrea Boltho, *The European Economy: Growth and Crisis* (Oxford, 1982) gives an excellent view of Britain as part of a wider European experience, with papers on individual countries (including Surrey on the UK) backed up by a series of thematic papers (which at times present strongly opposing views) on topics such as growth, inflation and the impact of the EEC.

Notes

1. N.W.C. Woodward 'Inflation', in N.F.R. Crafts and N. Woodward (eds), *The British Economy since 1945* (Oxford, 1991) p. 189.

2. J. Foreman-Peck, 'Trade and the balance of payments', in Crafts and Woodward (eds), *The British Economy*, p. 146.

3. Michael Surrey, 'United Kingdom', in Andrea Boltho (ed.), *The European Economy: Growth and Crisis* (Oxford, 1982) p. 536.

4. Sidney Pollard, *The Development of the British Economy* (London, 3rd edn, 1983) pp. 419–30.

5. Pollard, *British Economy*, p. 421.

6. Surrey, 'United Kingdom', pp. 528–53.

7. B.W.E. Alford, *British Economic Performance 1945–1975* (London, 1988) p. 87.

19 Crisis and Turnaround? 1973–1993

Leslie Hannah

Government Policies and the World Economic Slowdown

In the world economic boom, which began with reconstruction after the Second World War and ended with the oil crisis of 1973–74, Britons generally bemoaned their position at the bottom of the international growth league tables and the depressing Stop-Go cycle of government macro-policy. Nonetheless, Chapter 18 has shown that in this 'Golden Age' they satisfyingly raised their living standards faster than in the past. In the 1970s and the 1980s, Britain's growth performance rarely equalled the achievements of these postwar boom years. Yet, with a general world economic slowdown, its economic performance was now more kindly judged by economic analysts. Political judgements, too, were highly coloured by the changing economic context, as policy changes and Stop-Go cycles became more extreme than in earlier decades. In assessing this most recent period, we do not yet have the benefit of a long historical perspective to help evaluate the permanent significance of the changes we are still going through. The issues raised by the move to more market-oriented policies, encapsulated in the tag 'Thatcherism', which characterized 1980s policy, remain highly controversial.

One area in which broad, bipartisan agreement emerged from former heated controversy was in Britain's commitment to the European Common Market. After British entry to the Community on 1 January 1973, the referendum called in 1975 by Harold Wilson showed a decisive majority of the electorate were in favour of confirming Britain's membership and this quelled Labour Party doubters. Later controversies, though corrosive, were not about the principle of membership of the customs union but about the speed of development implied by the Single European Act and the Maastricht Treaty: that is, about the form of further integration. Entry to the Community precipitated a substantial shift in Britain's trade pattern: between 1972 and 1993 the proportion of Britain's trade with Common Market partners rose from under a third to more than half. Britain – with its transatlantic and imperial links now taking a back seat – was becoming more closely integrated with its European neighbours and competitors.

The broader international environment also changed. In 1972, with the Bretton Woods system of fixed international exchange rates ended, sterling was allowed to float. This compounded the disorder created by rising oil prices. Crude oil prices were tripled in 1973–74 by OPEC (the Organisation of Petroleum Exporting Countries). This created new problems of economic cooperation between the governments of the leading industrial countries and of recycling surpluses, but Britain was itself soon a net exporter of oil as the North Sea fields were developed. With a strong balance of payments, Britain in 1979 abandoned controls on capital exports, which had first been imposed in the 1930s, thus accelerating the integration of global capital markets and intensifying financial market pressures for convergence of British and overseas government policies (e.g. on interest rates) and of economic performance. The paths of adjustment of governments, firms and consumers to these changes were not easy: while freely floating exchange rates made for greater freedoms for them in some ways, they also created greater uncertainties and new policy dilemmas.

Such new political and economic pressures encouraged governments worldwide to reconsider their support of the vested interests of domestic pressure groups; these pressures were nowhere more effective than in Britain. The turbulent 1970s saw two governments – one Conservative, one Labour – defeated at the polls, having unsuccessfully wrestled with 'stagflation' (as the combination of rising inflation and rising unemployment was called), with sterling crises and – the most immediate cause of both governments' downfalls – with striking workers. Edward Heath's Conservative government of 1970 abandoned an initial free market approach for a more interventionist line, but still clashed with the miners, newly emboldened by rising oil prices to strike for higher pay in February 1974. The Conservatives lost the ensuing election to the Labour Party. The new Labour government failed either to control the boom in public expenditure or to establish a credible relationship with the trade unions (optimistically labelled a 'social contract') to restrain rapidly accelerating inflation. The party secured a clear parliamentary majority only from the second election of October 1974 to March 1977, but stayed in government for another two years with minority party support. While the leadership engaged in rather sterile debate with its own strengthened left wing on issues like Europe, industrial policy and incomes policy, urgent real policy issues of industrial restructuring, retraining and educational reform were largely unaddressed, while wasteful subsidies to declining and inefficient industries increased. The International Monetary Fund intervened with a standby loan in the sterling crisis of 1976, during which the pound depreciated from above $2.00 in March to $1.60 in October (more than the 1967 devaluation). That and the move to the right in the party leadership under James Callaghan (prime minister from 1976) constrained the subsidies to unsustainable firms. However, the government was unable to create a consensus for its pay policy to restrain inflation in the 'winter of discontent' of

Plate 19.1. 'Labour isn't working': a Saatchi & Saatchi Conservative campaign poster from the 1979 election. Under Labour unemployment had risen to over one million; the Conservative party promised sound finance and economic stability. Yet by 1980 a Conservative government had seen unemployment rise to two million and it was to reach three million by 1982.

public sector strikes in 1978–79. Labour lost the 1979 Election to Mrs Thatcher, the second government of the decade to be defeated at the polls amid stridently alarmist assertions of the ungovernability of Britain in the face of trade union strife.

Mrs Thatcher had the advantage of a working parliamentary majority, confirmed in the Elections of 1983 and 1987 and in the 1991 Election victory of her successor as Conservative Prime Minister, John Major: the first time since the 1832 Reform Act that any party had won four elections in a row. With the defection of the centrist Social Democrats from Labour in 1981 and the Labour Party internally in disarray, Britain had an unusually long period of (effectively) one-party government, with an impotent and divided Opposition. The postwar consensus of 'Butskellism' (see Chapter 17) was decisively broken and an initially hesitant Conservative government adopted increasingly radical, free-market policies to change the direction of the British economy. 'Supply-side' policies to improve micro-economic performance ranged from the sale of council houses to their tenants and the privatization of a wide range of nationalized industries to further cutbacks in industrial subsidies and attacks on the trade unions' legal immunities.

The political stability of Conservative rule was not paralleled by economic stability: indeed the peaks and troughs of the business cycle (see Figure 19.1) became even more marked. With the control of inflation given priority over other macro-economic objectives, a determined monetary squeeze accentuated the contraction of 1979–81. Confidence in the low rates of inflation then

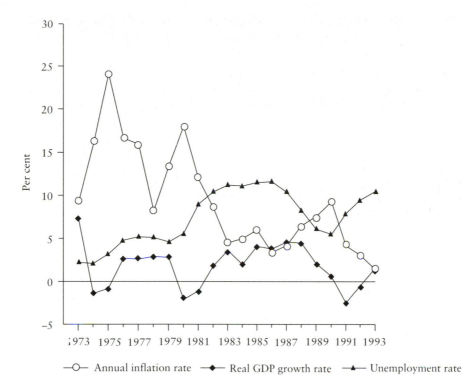

Figure 19.1. Inflation, unemployment and real GDP growth (1973–93). Sources: Retail price inflation from annual issues of *Economic Trends* (HMSO, London); GDP growth rate (compromise estimate) from annual issues of *Economic Trends;* and unemployment rate from annual issues of OECD, *Labour Force Statistics* (Paris).

achieved and in the long sustained recovery of the mid 1980s, led to an overoptimistic misreading of the indicators and the effective abandonment of monetary targets in the Thatcher-Lawson boom of 1988–89. The following slump – the worst postwar, with more than 3 million unemployed and negative GDP growth in 1990 and 1991 – lasted until the autumn of 1992, when the signs of recovery began to reappear. The slump was prolonged by a mistaken and doomed attempt to tie sterling to the European exchange rate mechanism, resulting in excessively high interest rates until speculators, seeing the unsustainability of the government's position, fortunately forced the abandonment of this policy in 1992.

The Overall Performance Record: 1970s Crisis, 1980s Turnaround?

In the heyday of the 1980s, large claims were made for the achievements of the government's alleged full-hearted commitment to monetarism; in fact, its commitment proved shallow and its macro-economic achievements in stabilization policy were abysmal. Claims of economic turnaround in the 1980s must, then, centre rather on the productivity growth performance and the government's micro-economic policy changes. Table 19.1 shows the rate of productivity growth in the major industrial economies since 1960. The periods chosen span years of business cycle peaks for the industrial world (1960, 1973, 1979 and 1989) to ensure reasonable comparison of underlying trends (comparison between troughs, e.g. between 1981 and 1992, would show similar trends). The latter two periods also happen to correspond broadly to the period of Labour government (1974–79) and Thatcher government (1979–90). Insofar as government influenced the conditions for growth instantaneously (rather a large assumption), they may thus be taken as a measure of the success of Labour and Conservative economic stewardship. The business sector only is measured, since productivity in the government sector is less reliably reported (though casual evidence does not suggest it was improving any less fast in Britain than in other major OECD countries). Finally this is a measure of total factor productivity, that is a weighted measure of the efficiency with which both capital and labour are being used.

Table 19.1. Total factor productivity growth in the business sector in the major industrial economies, 1960–89

	1960–73	1973–79	1979–89
OECD overall	2.8	0.5	0.9
US	1.6	−0.4	0.4
Japan	5.9	1.4	2.0
Germany	2.8	1.8	0.8
France	4.0	1.7	1.7
Italy	4.6	2.2	1.3
UK	2.3	0.6	1.5
Canada	2.0	0.8	0.4

Note. The G7 countries (the seven largest industrialized economies in the world) are ranked in declining order of GNP in 1989.

Source. OECD statistics, tabulated in Crafts, *Can De-industrialisation ....?*, p.40.

The first column of Table 19.1 shows the situation familiar from earlier chapters: Britain in the 1960s and early 1970s (as for much of the last hundred years) lagged significantly behind the productivity growth of her industrial rivals (with the notable exception of the US which had already achieved productivity levels more than double Britain's and Europe's by the mid twentieth century). In 1973–79 (column 2) all countries suffered a substantial slowdown of productivity growth following the oil crisis, though Britain continued to perform significantly worse than her major European rivals and Japan. Yet, in the 1980s, the situation changed radically: though now growing more slowly than in the 1960s, for a decade British productivity grew nearly 50 per cent faster than the average OECD country, putting it much nearer the leaders of the growth league in that period, like Japan. The gap which had opened up in the 1960s and 1970s with Britain's leading manufacturing competitor in Europe – Germany – was substantially closed in the 1980s: in 1977 German manufacturing productivity was 49 per cent above the UK's, by 1989 it was only 15 per cent above.[1]

This was a remarkable performance, but it will not be clear how sustainable it is for some years. Doubts increasingly surfaced in the slump of 1989–92 about the improvement in the underlying capacity for growth. Is Britain's manufacturing core – within which productivity growth has in the past been concentrated – now too small? Manufacturing *productivity* grew even faster in 1979–89 than the overall figures in Table 19.1 but manufacturing *output* grew at less than 1 per cent per annum. Nearly all the increase in investment in the later 1980s went into services, not manufacturing, and half of it went into the City of London, much of it wasted, for example on unoccupied property developments, just as poor manufacturing investments in unsustainable firms in the 1970s had been wasted. The share of manufacturing in gross domestic product fell from 27 per cent in 1973 to 26 per cent in 1979 and only 20 per cent in 1990; the fall in manufacturing employment was even steeper. This present level of commitment of resources to manufacturing is not, however, unusually low among OECD economies, particularly in view of the new status gained by Britain as the only major industrial country self sufficient in oil (thus requiring fewer manufacturing exports than formerly to break even on trade account). Britain has maintained its position in the high-tech industries, but a substantial balance of payments deficit nonetheless again emerged, peaking at 5 per cent of GDP in the boom year of 1989. The glaring gaps in Britain's trade performance were in medium-tech consumer durables, notably in cars and consumer electronics, where imports (and latterly the output of foreign-owned domestic producers) came completely to dominate the British market. It thus remained a moot point whether the underlying investments in capital equipment throughout industry and services, or in more intangible assets such as the skills of the workforce or research and development, were sufficient to sustain appropriate levels of manufacturing output. Britain was by the early 1990s only the sixth largest of OECD industrial powers behind America, Japan, Germany, France and (arguably, though not certainly) Italy. On many indicators of long-run competitive capability Britain now ranks behind the richer industrial leaders like Germany and Japan, but it still compares favourably with other rivals with similarly modest living standards and labour costs, such as Italy.

The clearest indicator to ordinary people of the 1980s productivity increase was the rapid and sustained rise in earnings of those in work. Indeed the rise in real earnings (see Table 19.2) was the most rapid on record. Consumption increased even more rapidly, as easy credit in the 1980s boom, rising imports and declining inflationary expectations permitted a spending spree which peaked in the artificial and unsustainable boom of the late 1980s. With the employed workforce rising from 22.5 millions in 1979 to 26.9 millions at the peak in 1989[2] (the bulk of the increase being among women and in the service industries), more people were becoming better-off faster than in any previous decade in British history.

The performance on productivity and earnings growth thus showed a marked improvement in the 1980s over the 1970s, but other indicators of economic performance were more equivocal. Many more people became unemployed than had been considered tolerable by governments before 1973: with an increase in the numbers of unemployed from 1 million in 1979 to 3 million (11.1 per cent of the labour force) by 1986, and only a brief recovery to 1.7 million (6.5 per cent of the workforce) in 1989, before a further deterioration by 1993 to 3.2 million (11.5 per cent of the workforce). The latter figure was almost as many as in the depth of the world depression of 1932, though it was a smaller proportion of the enlarged 1993 population.[3]

The view that recent governments have given greater priority to controlling inflation, after a close shave with damaging levels of inflation (inflation averaged 16 per cent between 1973 and 1980 and peaked at 18 per cent in 1980) is confirmed by Table 19.2. Despite a blip as a result of the Lawson boom (inflation rose again to 9.3 per cent in 1990), inflation fell to below 2 per cent by 1993, the level considered the norm in the 1960s. The trend to controlling inflation while permitting rising unemployment was common to most industrial countries, but Britain's record on unemployment deteriorated more rapidly than the OECD average. Its record on inflation, on the other hand, improved faster than that in other OECD countries in the 1980s and early 1990s. Yet this improvement remained a Pyrrhic victory. Since the main gains are from a low *and stable* rate of inflation, the policy gyrations, particularly between 1986 and 1992, simply increased the cost of *any* macro-economic policy pursued by Britain, by creating distrust in the international money markets. It also increased uncertainty and thus discouraged domestic investment, while arbitrarily redistributing income, as many of those who had borrowed money at high rates in the expectation of continuing house price rises found to their cost.

The Supply Side: Industrial Policy and Human Resources

In the early 1980s the government explicitly stated that it wished to address the issue of inflation by a monetarist macro-economic policy (a quest in which,

Table 19.2. Indicators of economic performance, 1960–89 (%)

	1960–73	1973–79	1979–89
Real earnings increase (average growth p.a.)	2.1	0.5	2.8
Inflation (retail price index average annual increase)	4.8	14.7	8.0
Unemployment rate (percentage of labour force unemployed, average)	1.9	3.4	9.1

Source. Author's calculations derived from successive editions of *New Earnings Survey* (HMSO, London), *Economic Trends* (HMSO) and OECD, *Labour Force Statistics* (Paris).

we have seen, it was only partly successful) but wished to refocus its growth policy on the 'supply-side'. Of course, all governments pursue supply-side policies, whether consciously or not, in that they set the rules of the game under which economic enterprise in a capitalist or mixed economy operates. Politicians typically exaggerate the extent to which they can affect the process, however, and often misinterpret both the areas where their intervention can have most effect and the timescale over which government policies can operate effectively. A comparison of the British automobile and pharmaceutical industries presented below shows the complexity of the process by which industrial policy interacts with international markets and with the creation within companies of organizational and technological capabilities. Twenty-five years ago the British car industry, dominated by British Leyland, with half of UK production, was inefficient and found it increasingly difficult to export. In subsequent decades British Leyland declined and several British car firms, despite extensive government aid, neared collapse, causing extensive foreign imports. In pharmaceuticals, two British firms emerged from a position as modest participants, behind the Swiss, American and German leaders, to rank among the world's largest and most successful pharmaceutical multi-nationals.

The difficulty of 'picking winners', that is of generalizing such industrial success by specific industrial interventions, led many to believe that the efforts of the state should be focused on correcting market failure in the infrastructure of industrial success, where a modest state role could be most effective. Industrial subsidies declined markedly in the 1980s, while government expenditure on training increased considerably, principally in response to the greater needs of the unemployed. There was also a considerable expansion of higher education and attempts to establish higher standards in primary and secondary education. The results were not, however, impressive. British universities were highly elitist, in the sense that a smaller proportion of school-leavers went to university than was common in other advanced countries, but they were more generously subsidized by the state for doing so (see Chapter 21). Only slow progress was made in persuading the middle classes (who formed the bulk of students) to pay more of the costs of their educational privileges; so most expansion of higher education came from lowering quality.

International tests of, for example, mathematical ability, showed Britain slipping behind other countries in the general quality of the formal educational attainments of her teenagers leaving school. Careful comparisons of training on the job, apprenticeships and the acquisition of work skills revealed that the unusually large proportion of British youngsters who left school aged sixteen were also very poorly served by the mix of private and public provision which Britain had evolved. The inadequate investment in human capital in Britain was particularly tragic for the inner-city, undereducated and unemployed working class. The large, evident gap between an egalitarian, education-conscious society like Japan and the unfitness of many British workers for competition in the modern industrial world propelled education and training into party political manifestos. Yet this was not sufficient to overcome the deeply entrenched vested interests of teachers, trainers, and the educationally privileged in the present system; and neither left nor right in Britain seemed to mobilize effective concern (glimpsed, for example, in the US, which faced similar problems in its inner cities) for change. What was necessary was to initiate business-government-education-community partnerships to change the attitudes of its growing urban lumpen-proletariat and their opportunities in education and training: in the long run only this could credibly offer them economic hope.

The worsening educational plight of the underprivileged was paralleled by a deterioration in their relative economic status, as inequality increased in the 1980s. While this was a worldwide phenomenon, as wages responded to an increase in the relative demand for educated manpower, the tax and benefit policies of the Thatcher years meant that British trends to greater inequality were extreme. The poorest 20 per cent of households hardly shared in the general prosperity of these years and, relatively, they became significantly worse off.[4] While tax and benefit changes were claimed to improve incentives, convincing measurement of these alleged effects proved elusive. Moreover, there remained many perverse incentives in the benefit system (in which implicit tax rates of around 100 per cent were faced by many poor people). The reduction between 1979 and 1988 of the top tax rate on earned income from 83 per cent to 40 per cent and of the standard rate from 33 per cent to 25 per cent (with compensating increases in VAT) did, it is true, reduce incentives for avoidance and evasion by the better-off and produced a more workable tax system.

However, contrary to the political image successfully promoted by Mrs

Thatcher it did not reduce overall taxation. This rose from 38.5 per cent of GDP in 1979–80 to 40.75 per cent of GDP in 1989–90; both above OECD averages. The Thatcher governments did succeed in reducing public *spending* as a share of GDP: from 43.5 per cent in 1979–80 to 38.75 per cent in 1989–90. The difference between the two (government spending minus taxes) is, of course, public borrowing. A high public sector borrowing requirement of 5 per cent of GDP in 1979–80 was – with the benefit of North Sea oil revenues and proceeds from the privatization programme – transformed into a public sector debt *repayment* by 1989–90. The costs of increased unemployment benefits and other spending increases in 1989–92, however, recreated a large public sector deficit, which exceeded 6 per cent of GDP in 1993. A politically difficult combination of intensified 'Thatcherite' spending *cuts* with tax increases was then again considered essential by informed commentators.

In focus: Industrial Policy and Performance in Automobiles and Pharmaceuticals

---

The weakness of the British car industry was evident when the major British-owned producers, controlling half of all British car production, merged to form British Leyland in 1967–68, creating the fifth largest car manufacturer in the world after the US 'Big Three' and Volkswagen. As the company's market share fell and the financial situation deteriorated, the state took over ownership, but it was for some years unable to agree a viable strategy with the BL management and workers. Eventually the decision was made drastically to slim down the operation, introduce new technology licensed from Japan (with a 20 per cent shareholding by Honda) and radically reform work practices. The Rover Group (as the newly renamed operation is now called) had a UK market share in 1993 of only 13 per cent. The foreign-owned sections of the domestic car industry – the French-owned Peugeot-Talbot (formerly Chrysler/Rootes) and American-owned Ford and Vauxhall (General Motors) – fared somewhat better, but no British producer performed as well as the French, German and Italian carmakers, and more than half of the cars sold in Britain were imported by the early 1990s. Hopes for closing that trade gap then principally rested on firms like Toyota and Nissan, which had started manufacturing cars in Britain in greenfield sites in Derbyshire and the North East. They achieved high levels of productivity and a strong export performance in Europe. Examples of ineffective government intervention in industries like cars – which had high costs both in direct subsidies by the state to British Leyland and other domestic producers and in high car prices paid by British consumers – made governments increasingly cautious about subsidizing inefficient firms. The traditional economists' emphasis on the possible need for state intervention to correct 'market failure' was, understandably, increasingly tempered by a practical realization that 'state failure' could also occur: pressure from

Industrial Policy and Performance in Automobiles and Pharmaceuticals (continued)

interest groups in the car industry had made effective state intervention extremely difficult and often counterproductive to the aim of establishing an internationally competitive industry.

The policy of government towards the pharmaceutical industry looks at first sight very different. Indeed, when three firms – Glaxo, Beechams and Boots – argued that there should be mergers to create a British pharmaceutical company to compete on equal terms with the American, German and Swiss giants of the industry, the government had agreed with the Monopolies Commission in rejecting the request in 1972. At that time, the largest British firm, Glaxo, ranked sixteenth in the world pharmaceutical sales league and the other British pharmaceutical manufacturers were ranked below fortieth. Yet by 1993, Glaxo ranked first and Beechams (which had taken over the American firm Smith Kline) ranked fourth in the world sales league. It is tempting to see in this a parable of the virtues of the competitive free market, and that element is certainly present. The Monopolies Commission had correctly seen the limits to economies of scale in pharmaceutical research and development. Glaxo had been extraordinarily lucky with the development of its ulcer drug, Zantac, which accounted for half its sales though its success went deeper than that: it had developed its US marketing, for example, rather than merely acquiring such skills by buying Beecham. Beecham, in turn, had developed the research and development capabilities which it had been banned from acquiring through the rejected merger with Glaxo. It is too simplistic, however to suggest that the two world-beating British pharmaceutical firms were merely pursuing the logic of the market system. The success of these pharmaceutical multinationals was also based on decades of government investment in British biological and medical research, not to speak of a very well-balanced National Health Service drug purchasing policy, which did not featherbed them (like the German system) but at the same time did not squeeze their profits so hard they could not afford R & D (like the French system). The lessons to be drawn from their successes were, therefore, more deep-rooted and complex than a simple Thatcherite free marketeer might suppose. But that they had done better than the Rover Group, with much less direct government input, was plain to see.

The Supply Side: Industrial Relations and Privatization

Two supply-side policies of the 1980s – the reform of trade union law and the privatization programme – were distinguished both by being unlikely to have been undertaken by an alternative government of the left and by being broadly successful. The Labour government's failure to reform acknowledged problems in British trade unions in the 1960s led Edward Heath's government of the early 1970s to attempt trade union reform, but unsuccessfully. On the other hand, the later reforms of Mrs Thatcher's governments proved (against most expert advice) to be both legally enforceable and effective. The major changes were outlawing the closed shop and secondary picketing, strengthening union members' voting control over union officials and strike decisions, and stripping the trade unions of most of their legal immunities and powers to discipline blacklegs. These changes were pushed through partly by determined policing and precautionary coal-stocking measures at key points such as power stations, and partly because the unions could only weakly resist in the conditions of rising unemployment in which the key changes were initiated. Trade union membership, which had risen to an all-time high of 53 per cent of the labour force by 1979, fell below 40 per cent in the 1990s. The unions of course remained major participants in wage negotiations, particularly in the public sector and manufacturing, but their negotiating stance now reflected their weaker position; strikes became distinctly less frequent. The reforms brought British trade union law nearer to that of other advanced industrial countries, creating more democratic unions though with fewer positive rights than many trade unions abroad.

British unions could now more effectively be faced by managements with the key issues of work discipline, productivity increases and pay, and British labour markets became more flexible. While the precise impact remains the subject of debate among industrial relations specialists, a significant number even of left-inclined specialists acknowledge that the sustained labour productivity achievements noted above in the 1980s partly derived from trade union reforms and the shock effect of the recession which accompanied them. The effects were particularly noticeable in the manufacturing sector (in which the trade unions had traditionally been strongest) and in the public utilities (where privatization and deregulation provided an added impetus to change).

The privatization programme was one which was distinctively Thatcherite, though it was not wholeheartedly adopted until after her second election victory, when both its feasibility and popularity were evident. The problems of the nationalized industries dated back to unsatisfactory attempts in the 1950s and 1960s to resolve the complex issues of devising appropriate management, pricing and investment policies for public corporations. The nationalized industries' difficulties had intensified in the 1970s, as pressure groups within the industries (and particularly trade unions) had gained concessions from their state owners, while governments had imposed price controls on them as a means of controlling inflation. The result was a combination of very poor levels of profitability with extensive overmanning by the end of the 1970s. The high levels of state subsidy to support the production of many uneconomic goods and services – from high-tech nuclear power to inefficiently labour-intensive steel or coal production – were rarely openly agreed and itemized in return for public benefits (except in a few cases such as subsidized local rail services). Rather they were absorbed in general nationalized corporation losses funded by Treasury payments, in a way which discouraged both managers and politicians from accepting responsibility for the abysmal performance of industries employing 12 per cent of the population. Where there was foreign competition, bad public sector stewardship severely compromised the long-run ability of the nationalized companies to survive; in the case of utilities and other protected industries it raised the cost of services to taxpayers and consumers, thus reducing the living standards of the bulk of the population not employed in them.

Initially Mrs Thatcher and her advisers considered privatization desirable but politically quite impossible, and concentrated on re-establishing financial controls. These measures were successful: the efficiency gains which followed give Mrs Thatcher claim to a title – the best manager the nationalized industries ever had – which she would not have wished to make herself. British Steel, which (under both private and public ownership) had for decades had levels of productivity inferior to US and German competitors, achieved in the 1980s the highest steel productivity levels of any advanced industrial country. British Telecom, which (when in state hands in the 1970s) had persistently failed to meet the Treasury's target of 5 per cent per annum productivity increase, easily exceeded the softer, post-privatization, regulatory target of 4 per cent so the target was progressively increased. By the 1990s BT was more ambitiously aiming to exceed the 7 per cent per annum productivity increase which new labour practices and new technology made possible.

There were, of course, some criticisms of the privatized industries. Facts which politicians and managers had earlier conspired to conceal from the public – like the excessive cost to taxpayers of subsidies for both British nuclear power and British coal – were more transparently embarrassing under a regime of privatization. The rebalancing of retail tariffs in more competitive, privatized industries also resulted in real price increases for small consumers, but more economically rational pricing overall. There were thus economic gains and political losses, though the latter were offset by popular discounted share offers and tax reductions. More seriously, many of the industries were privatized without adequate attention to splitting up monopolies and establishing competitive conditions, creating unnecessary difficulties for regulators who nevertheless made the best of a difficult job. In a few cases – notably buses – price and quality of service deteriorated. It was striking, however, that the option of renationalizing the industries was no longer a serious element on the Labour Party's agenda, as the general success and popularity of the policy changes became evident. Serious debate on the public utilities came to focus on the best form of regulation and the degree of competition rather than on the sterile issue of ownership which had for too long preoccupied British politicians.

Conflicting Interpretations of the Performance of Thatcherism

Many of the key facts of economic change in the two decades covered by this chapter are not the subject of great controversy, but the interpretation to be placed on them is: indeed the emphasis of the preceding paragraphs is hotly disputed by many participants in today's political debates. Contemporary history is inextricably intertwined with current debate on desirable policies for the future, though in the last two decades political debate has perhaps become less stereotyped by inherited political and economic dogma. For example, it became plausible to suggest in the heyday of 1980s 'Thatcherism' that the Conservative Party was the true radical party, while it was the Labour Party which reacted to preserve many aspects of the status quo, for instance in the public sector and trade unions. Party loyalties were overturned: Mrs Thatcher saw no need to defend her Conservative predecessors before 1979 and indeed accused them of perpetrating many of the same mistakes as Labour; while in the Labour Party the government of Mr Wilson and Mr Callaghan (1974–79) had few defenders, being generally considered one of the weakest ever Labour administrations. Newspapers also became less stereotyped in their interpretations: in the 1992 Election the businessmen's paper, the *Financial Times*, advocated voting Labour, while left-leaning critics became more willing to admit the possibility of state failure as well as market failure, and to attack vested interests which had previously been sacrosanct.

A central reason for disagreement about whether the Thatcherite experiment of the 1980s heralded a fundamental turnaround in Britain's economic performance was not only that commentators differ in the yardsticks by which they evaluate performance – that is true of any period – but that the yardsticks gave remarkably inconsistent results for this period of rapid and uneven change. Because the period was one of unusual instability, for example, careful choice of dates between which growth rates are calculated (or inflation rates are reported) can produce figures suggesting success or failure. The growth rate from the slump of 1981 through the long boom to 1989 was extremely high, but measured only from the peak to the related trough (1979–81 and 1989–92) growth was low. While partisan commentators have thus had a field day, it is clearly preferable to use an underlying trend rate of growth for a lengthy period, or to calculate growth from peak to peak (e.g. 1979–89) – or trough to trough (1981–92) – as we have done in Tables 19.1 and 19.2.

As these tables show, however, the choice of yardstick, even with sensibly chosen growth indicators, offers opportunities to both sides in the debate. Detractors of Thatcherism tend to compare Britain's 1980s productivity growth with that of Britain *in the 1960s*; supporters, on the other hand, insist that Britain's performance in the 1980s *relative to other countries at the same time* was impressive. Which is the right comparison? That depends on the question. Implicit in much of the debate is an attempt to assess what happened under Thatcherism compared with what would have happened without. The question thus becomes which comparator is a reasonable approximation to such a 'counterfactual' world. Would the hypothetical 'non-Thatcher' government have been more like British governments of the 1960s or like overseas governments of the 1980s? The answer is not easy, but may well be: 'a bit of both', for the Opposition had inherited many of the characteristics of the 1964–70 Labour government but, like left-inclined parties in power in other countries in the 1980s, had also learnt a lot from recent experiences. Then there is the question of whether the background conditions of the 1980s were more or less favourable to growth than the 1960s. Again reasonable observers can give different answers. All OECD countries tended to experience slower growth after 1973 than before, but explanations of this differ: rising energy costs after the OPEC oil price increases and the breakdown of international macro-economic coordination (with the shift from fixed to fluctuating exchange rates) have been adduced as causes. Whatever the cause, if we see the boom in world growth and trade of the 1960s as offering greater opportunities than the more constrained world of the 1980s, other countries in the 1980s seem the most appropriate yardstick. But, if we see the potential for growth as being determined principally by the extent that a country has fallen behind the industrial leaders – as in the 'catch-up' hypothesis – then Britain was well placed to grow rapidly in the 1980s relatively to others. The right comparator in this case would not be either of those typically chosen, but rather an industrial laggard in a comparable period. The problem of the appropriate comparator is thus not easily soluble. Indeed, it is arguably because economists have not solved the general question of why growth rates differ over time and across nations that we have no clear guidelines on the appropriate yardsticks to use in this particular case.

Similar problems are encountered in interpreting the trade-offs between performance on growth and in other variables – such as inflation and unemployment – shown in Table 19.2. Would growth have been higher if more of the workforce had been employed? Would inflation have been higher, too? How do we weight the value of one percentage point off the inflation rate against a similar shift in the growth rate? or in the unemployment rate? or in other indicators of economic welfare that are not shown, such as inequality? or the value of increased leisure? or the problems caused by increased crime? Even if we dislike the increased inequality, did it enable Britain to achieve lower unemployment rates for the unskilled? Does the example of America (where the wages of the low-paid stagnated as in Britain) and Germany and France (where the low-paid increased their real earnings faster than the better-paid) support the case that greater inequality helped employment in a society with low educational attainment? If the skill level of the British workforce had been improved, could this trade-off between earnings and employment have been changed? These are all questions on which reasonable men and women can differ, but honest participants in such debates should try to spell out the assumptions implicit in the comparisons they are making, rather than naively asserting that 'the statistics speak for themselves'.

Bibliographical Note

The performance of the economy since 1973 is set in a longer postwar context in N.F.R. Crafts and N. Woodward (eds), *The British Economy since 1945* (Oxford, 1991), and in the final four chapters of Sidney Pollard, *The Development of the British Economy 1914–1990* (London, 4th edn, 1992). The generally poor record of the Labour government from 1974 to 1979 is defended in Michael Artis and David Cobham (eds), *Labour's Economic Policies* (Manchester, 1991), while the effect of Conservative economic policies is considered in Jonathan Michie (ed.), *The Economic Legacy 1979–1992* (London, 1992). Nicholas Crafts presents a careful assessment of the achievements of supply-side economics and places the performance of Britain in comparative perspective in *Can De-Industrialisation Seriously Damage Your Wealth? A Review of Why Growth Rates Differ and How to Improve Economic Performance* (London, 1993). The successes and failures of the privatization programme are weighed-up in Matthew Bishop and John Kay, *Does Privatization Work? Lessons from the UK* (London, 1988). Dennis Kavanagh and Anthony Seldon provide a broader social and political assessment of the 1980s in *The Thatcher Effect: A Decade of Change* (Oxford, 1989). There are useful overviews of many current issues in the *Oxford Review of Economic Policy*; see, for example, vol. 4, no. 1, Spring 1988 (*Long Run Economic Performance in the UK*) and vol. 7, no. 3, Autumn 1991 (*Economic Policy in the 1980s*).

Notes

1. S.R. Broadberry, quoted in N. Crafts, *Can De-Industrialisation Seriously Damage Your Wealth?* (London, 1993), p. 7.

2. It fell to 25 million in 1992.

3. In 1932 unemployment reached 3.4 million or 15.6 per cent of the smaller 1932 workforce.

4. S.P. Jenkins, 'Income inequality and living standards: changes in the 1970s and 1980s', *Fiscal Studies* vol. 12 (1992), pp. 1–25. See also P. Johnson and S. Webb, 'Explaining the growth in UK income inequality: 1979–1988', *Economic Journal* vol. 103 (1993), pp. 429–35.

20 Postwar Welfare

Rodney Lowe

On 5 July 1948, Attlee's Labour government placed an announcement in the press proclaiming 'this day makes history'. It was the Appointed Day upon which many long-planned reforms, including the National Health Service (NHS), National Insurance and National Assistance, were finally to be implemented. Significantly, however, the term 'welfare state' was not mentioned. Indeed, if it was widely used at all in 1948, it was in the US as a term of abuse by opponents of President Truman's proposals to extend the New Deal. This absence of any collective term for Labour's legislative initiatives reflected a lack of unity, even within Cabinet, over the precise scope and underlying purpose of government intervention.

If the creators of what was later to be known as the welfare state were themselves disunited, how much more so have been their successors. The traditional ideological divide between individualism and collectivism remains. In a complex modern society, is individual welfare best advanced through the market with the role of government restricted to the correction of proven market failings (as broadly advocated by the Conservative Party)? Or is it maximized by a greater degree of state intervention designed to engineer a more 'equal' society (as advocated by the Labour Party)? Such questions cannot be resolved by detached technical calculations because the costs and benefits of welfare policy, in aggregate and individually, cannot be measured accurately. To justify aggregate expenditure, for example, what value can be placed upon one of the major advances in postwar welfare – the peace of mind guaranteed by services such as social security and the NHS to those whose lives had earlier been haunted by the ever-present threat of absolute poverty or lack of access to adequate health care? Conversely, with what confidence can improvements in individual welfare be attributed to increased expenditure on the relevant government service? Infant mortality is, for example, one of the most sensitive indicators of welfare and between 1940 and 1985 it decreased in England and Wales from 56 deaths per thousand live births to 9. Was such an improvement due, however, to increased expenditure on the NHS, on other welfare services (such as housing or child benefit) or on changes not directly associated with government (the discovery of new drugs or changed lifestyles)? There is, in short, a major difference between 'policy outputs', which are the direct result of specific government policies, and 'welfare outcomes', which are the consequence of a range of government and non-government influences.

The study of postwar welfare, therefore, goes to the heart of political controversy and raises technical questions of great, and perhaps unanswerable, complexity. To provide a brief guide, this chapter will summarize the evolution of the welfare state and the simultaneous improvements in individual welfare. It will then examine the political and interrelated historiographical controversy surrounding these developments.

The Evolution of the Welfare State

The history of the welfare state may be divided into two. The first 'classic' phase lasted from 1948 to the mid 1970s. Dominated by memories of mass unemployment and poverty in the 1930s, the prevailing assumption was that government intervention in economic and social policy was in both the individual's and the national interest. It alone could guarantee 'full' employment, a minimum income for all and the universal provision of other services (such as health care and education) to the highest possible standard. This consensus finally broke in the mid 1970s. The key event was a speech by the Labour prime minister, James Callaghan, to his party conference in September 1976 in which the abandonment was announced of the postwar commitment to maintain a 'high and stable level of employment'. Not only did this dramatically narrow the concept of the welfare state. Thereafter the term was used as a synonym for a core of social services – social security, the NHS, education, housing and the personal social services – rather than a broad set of economic and social measures designed to maximize welfare through the labour market as much as through state-provided services. It also, as Beveridge had predicted in December 1942, placed all social expenditure under intense financial pressure.

The Beveridge Report, with its detailed proposals for a system of social security based on three preconditions or 'assumptions' (family allowances, a comprehensive NHS and the maintenance of a high level of employment), has often been described as the blueprint for the welfare state. Its importance, however, should not be exaggerated. There are three main reasons for this. First, as the Report itself admitted, by 1939 Britain enjoyed a range of welfare services 'on a scale not surpassed and hardly rivalled in any other country in the world'.[1] Wartime innovations, such as the universal provision of school meals and milk, strengthened it still further. Secondly, the Report's detailed proposals for social insurance were either not implemented or else hastily abandoned. Finally, and perhaps most importantly, Beveridge as a traditional liberal had a very restricted view about the role of government – which Conservative ministers in the 1980s were gleefully to rediscover. In guaranteeing to all a minimum income, he insisted, government must ensure that it neither eroded individual responsibility nor redistributed wealth between classes. Hence his insistence on an insurance rather than a tax-based system (so that recipients 'earned' their right to relief) and the provision of flat rate benefits based on a very low estimate of subsistence need – whereas most other countries provided earnings-related benefits. If individuals wanted to ensure their accustomed standard of living, they should take out private insurance. 'To give by compulsory insurance', Beveridge reasoned, 'more than is needed for subsistence is an unnecessary interference with individual responsibilities'.[2]

The Report, nevertheless, had an inspirational effect both at home and abroad. Above all, it appeared to provide what the poor had long wanted – freedom from fear of poverty as of right without a means test. This was to be achieved by the implementation of a system of social insurance, based on two crucial principles: comprehensiveness and universalism. In return for a single weekly contribution, all risks to an individual's or a family's income would be covered (in comparison with the incomplete patchwork of interwar schemes). Social *security* would thereby be achieved. Moreover everyone was to be included in the scheme so that no stigma would fall on claimants and a measure of communal solidarity, as experienced in the war, could be retained. The Report was also inspirational in a second sense: its promise of a concerted attack on the five giants of Want, Disease, Ignorance, Squalor and Idleness. The most important giant was undoubtedly Idleness because, as Beveridge argued, economic and social policy should not be antagonistic – as they had been in the 1930s and were to become again after 1976 – but complementary.

Plate 20.1. A *Daily Herald* cartoon depicting the five evils which Beveridge saw as threatening society. Idleness was the most important of the five evils identified by Beveridge in his 1942 Report, because full employment was the most effective way of promoting individual welfare for the majority of the population.

Full employment, or the guarantee of a rewarding job, was far more important to individual welfare than any state handout. By maximizing tax revenue and minimizing claimants it was also crucial to the adequate funding of welfare policy. Equally, social policy – if properly targeted – was an essential prerequisite and not an impediment to economic growth. International competitiveness was dependent on a healthy, well-trained, mobile workforce and thus on effective health, educational and housing policies.

The Report provoked Churchill's Coalition government, against the wishes of the Prime Minister and the Treasury, into the serious planning of postwar reconstruction. Before VE Day, two of Beveridge's assumptions were realized. The 1944 *Employment Policy* white paper committed postwar government to the maintenance of a 'high and stable level of employment'. Between the resignation of Labour and the 1945 election, the Caretaker Conservative government also passed the Family Allowance Act which provided mothers with a weekly payment, admittedly below subsistence level, for all children after their first. Then, as has been seen, the third assumption was fulfilled in 1948 with the inauguration of the NHS. At the same time four other reforms were implemented: the National Insurance Act; the National Assistance Act, formally ending the Poor Law and providing means-tested benefits for the few who remained uninsured; the Children Act, with its insistence that care should be based on the proper development of each child's 'character and abilities'; and the Town and Country Planning Act, extending planning controls to all future development in order to protect the environment. It was to this series of reforms, together with the 1944 Education Act (see Chapter 21), that the collective term 'welfare state' was commonly applied by 1951.

Under the succeeding thirteen years of Conservative rule (1951–1964) the welfare state was not disbanded as many had predicted. There was a continuing battle within Cabinet over the extent to which welfare should be provided by the market and the state or, more specifically, over the balance to be struck between the level of taxation (which was held to impair economic performance) and welfare expenditure. It was lost by the economic liberals, as was demonstrated by the resignation in January 1958 of the Chancellor of the Exchequer, Thorneycroft, over 'excessive' welfare expenditure. In the wake of a sterling crisis, he had sought a £76 million package of cuts, including the withdrawal of family allowances from the second child; but this was rejected because, in the words of Prime Minister Macmillan, modern governments had 'an inescapable obligation to large sections of the community, the evasion of which would be both inequitable and unacceptable to public opinion'.[3] Such an appeal to the principle of equity and to electoral expediency exemplified the nature of postwar welfare consensus. The Conservatives did, however, start to change the nature of state welfare. They sought to transform the 'welfare' state into an 'opportunity' state by using government policy to reward initiative. Hence the greater use of tax relief to encourage owner-occupation and the take-up of private occupational pensions. In the wake of the 1961 Plowden Report, *The Control of Public Expenditure*, they also sought the coordinated planning of welfare expenditure. Hence the establishment of the Public Expenditure Survey Committee with its five-year programme of public expenditure tied to future forecasts of economic growth.

Nevertheless in the 1960s welfare expenditure continued to grow and, in common with most other countries, it exploded in the early 1970s (see Table 20.1). This was the consequence of rising expectation among both the consumers and producers of welfare. Powerful pressure groups such as the Child Poverty Action Group, founded in 1965, gave greater articulacy to those in need. Increased professionalism also meant major administrative reforms (such as the establishment of social service departments in all local authorities in 1971 and the reorganization of the NHS in 1974) which were extremely expensive, as well as greater militancy at all levels within public employment (which was ultimately to lead to the 'winter of discontent' in 1979). Renewed emphasis was also placed by successive Labour governments on the redistributive nature of welfare even when, owing to scarce resources, this meant increased means-testing. This emphasis was especially pronounced after the 1974 election when, under the 'social contract' with the trade unions, improvements in the 'social wage' were used to counter demands for higher industrial wages.

Plate 20.2. 'This is the road to *both* tax cuts and the welfare state'. This cartoon of 1950 depicts Churchill steering the 'ship' of state in the opposite direction to that favoured by R.A. Butler, the moderniser of the Conservative party. In the 1950s Conservative governments remained internally divided over the issue of whether to cut taxes or cut welfare spending. In 1958 the Chancellor of the Exchequer, Thorneycroft, resigned after failing to persuade the cabinet to reduce welfare spending.

Table 20.1. Relative cost of individual welfare services, 1951–88

	1951–52	1961–62	1971–72	1976–77	1981–82	1987–78
% of total welfare expenditure						
Social Security	33	38	39	37	43	45
Education	20	24	26	24	22	22
Health	23	21	21	20	21	21
Housing	20	13	12	16	10	8
Personal Social Services	2	2	3	4	4	4
Welfare expenditure as % of public expenditure	43	41	47	55	52	56
Welfare expenditure as % of GDP	16	16	20	26	24	23

After: R. Lowe, *The Welfare State in Britain since 1945* (Basingstoke, 1993), appendix; J. Hills (ed.), *The State of Welfare* (Oxford, 1990) pp. 361–2.

With a decline in economic growth (and thus government revenue) after the 1973 oil crisis, the bubble ultimately burst in 1975. Cash limits were imposed on each service and welfare expenditure was actually cut in real terms by almost 5 per cent in 1977/78. Thereafter, however, it resumed its inexorable rise despite the election in 1979 of the Conservatives under Mrs Thatcher, committed to the ending of the postwar 'dependency culture' and to the 'rolling back of the state'. Throughout the 1980s it increased annually in real terms, by up to 4 per cent in election years, whilst its consumption of GDP remained stable at 23–24 per cent. There were several reasons for this unexpected feature of Thatcherism. There was a steady increase in elderly (and very old) people requiring pensions and health care. High unemployment was, as predicted by Beveridge, extremely expensive to relieve. Labour-intensive social services could not match the productivity gains in other areas of employment and so grew relatively more expensive (the 'relative price effect'). The principal reasons, however, were the popularity of state welfare and the lack of any viable alternative. Universal services, such as pensions and the NHS, remained popular not least amongst the government's own supporters – as did the increasingly expensive tax concessions, such as mortgage interest relief. Moreover the market, and especially private insurance companies, remained distinctly cool towards radical proposals such as those advanced in 1982 and 1986 respectively to replace the NHS with a system of private insurance and to end state earnings-related pensions.

Consequently in the early 1980s, welfare cuts – with the exception of housing – were limited. Although painful to individuals, they were largely marginal (such as the freezing, rather than the cancellation, of child benefit) or targeted on 'undeserving' minorities (as with the tightening-up of the qualification for unemployment benefit). It was not until the Conservatives' third election victory in 1987, that 'the dog finally barked' and the assumptions and structures of postwar welfare policy came under direct attack. In order to counter the 'dependency culture', Supplementary Benefit was transformed into Income Support and its 'additional payments', designed to meet exceptional need, into the Social Fund – to which claimants were expected to repay 70 per cent of their grants. To roll back the state, the powers of local government were greatly eroded and responsibility given to smaller accountable bodies such as school governors, housing associations, hospital trusts and budget-holding GPs. Whether the government's broader aims were thereby achieved, however, is debatable. Its own supporters, for example, remained as dependent as ever on tax relief for their standard of housing, higher education and occupational pensions. Public expenditure on welfare did not decrease in real terms. Moreover, the erosion of local democracy significantly increased the power of central government both as a regulator and a paymaster.

In focus: Universalism versus Selectivity

The battle since 1942 over whether services, such as family allowances/child benefit, should be universal or selective highlights the administrative, political and historical tensions which have characterized postwar welfare policy. Beveridge advocated universalism since it would end the hated means test. Help would reach those in need since benefit was automatic and bore no stigma. The quality of service would remain high since all had an interest in it. Moreover, amongst left-wing groups such as the Fabians, it was hoped that universalism would preserve the communal solidarity experienced in war and even effect a greater redistribution of wealth.

Beveridge was vigorously opposed by the Treasury in 1942 and the Fabians by the right-wing Institute of Economic Affairs in the 1960s. Universalism, to them, was wasteful since it required a vast bureaucracy to tax and then make payments to those who were not in need. It also failed to help those in genuine need because scarce resources were spread too thinly. It was far better to target those in need and make them adequate payments, whilst reducing the overall cost of welfare and allowing taxpayers to spend more of their own money. The duty of government was to maximize freedom by guaranteeing to all a minimum income but then by allowing everyone to make their own spending decisions.

Neither party felt able to implement its principles fully. The Conservatives sought greater selectivity but feared the electoral consequences of reintroducing the means test (in the 1950s) and of withdrawing universal benefits from their own supporters (in the 1980s). Labour in the 1960s sought greater universalism but, acknowledging the scarcity of resources, resorted to greater means-testing. This dilemma was peculiarly British because the legacy of the Poor Law had made means-testing so unpopular. In other countries, such as Norway, it was natural for the Labour Party to advocate means-testing to target the needy whilst the Conservatives sought universal provision which would benefit their own supporters.

Social Security and Poverty

The extent to which legislative change affected individual welfare can best be judged in relation to the evolution of individual services. Employment and education policy are covered in Chapters 16–19 and 21; the NHS is treated below as a case study. Of the remaining policies, social security was by far the most expensive and in the mid 1960s succeeded defence as the most expensive item of public expenditure (see Table 20.1). Beveridge's vision had been simple but its implementation was far from simple. Everyone was to be guaranteed as of right a subsistence-level benefit in return for a weekly insurance contribution. Given regional variations in the cost of living, however, a flat rate benefit could not guarantee subsistence everywhere. From the start, therefore, it was 'inadequate' in high cost areas; and it became universally inadequate as upratings failed to match inflation and as public perceptions of an acceptable 'poverty line' rose. Moreover many risks proved to be uninsurable. Many disabled people and the rising numbers of single mothers, for example, could not undertake waged work and therefore could not make their qualifying contributions. As a result, means-tested benefit – which Beveridge had hoped would wither away – expanded both to 'top up' inadequate insurance benefits and to support the uninsured. By the mid 1970s there were in addition to National Assistance (renamed Supplementary Benefit in 1966) forty-five different means tests and the system had become as complex as interwar provision. Beveridge's vision was further spurned when pensions in 1959 and then most insurance benefits in 1966 were placed on an earnings-related basis. Increased contributions swelled government revenue and increased payments were intended to 'float' claimants off means-tested benefit. This brought Britain into line with Continental practice but it directly contradicted Beveridge's vision of a limited role for government.

The effectiveness of policy may be judged by the number of people recorded as being in poverty. This is no easy task because the definition of poverty changed in the 1950s from the absolute concept favoured by Beveridge (the minimum income needed to meet certain basic needs) to a relative one (a level of income rising in line with average wages or lifestyles). What precise monetary figure could be placed on relative poverty, so that the poor might be counted? The conventional solution is to use the current level of National Assistance/Supplementary Benefit/Income Support which since 1959 has been broadly based on the relative concept. The most famous measure was 140 per cent of the standard rate of National Assistance plus rent (40 per cent being added to cover the income claimants might have disregarded, such as war pensions, and the one-off payments for exceptional needs, such as furniture, to which they were entitled). By this measure Townsend and Abel-Smith in 1965 'rediscovered poverty', which the welfare state was assumed to have eradicated, by calculating that 7.8 per cent of the population (4 million people) were in poverty in 1953/54 and 14.2 per cent (7.5 million) in 1960. By 1985 the number had doubled to 15 million.

Alternatively, by the standard rate alone, it has been calculated that between 1.3 and 2.6 million were in poverty by the early 1970s. By 1985 this had risen to 2.4 million people below and 7 million people on the poverty line.[4] The chief victims were the old, who were either unaware of or ashamed to claim means-tested benefit; young children in large families, because of the falling real value of Family Allowance/Child Benefit; and the low paid who were disqualified both from claiming Supplementary Benefit when employed and, until 1976, from receiving the full amount when unemployed if it exceeded their previous income (the 'wage stop').

These figures do not mean that the poor were living in physical conditions equivalent to those before 1945 or in contemporary undeveloped countries. Even in the 1980s the real income of most claimants increased in real terms. They do mean, however, that help was not getting through to all who were entitled to it and that, in a period of general affluence, an increasing number of people were falling significantly below average living standards. Moreover the social security system on occasion actually compounded the problem by creating a poverty trap: as the income of the poor rose, so they lost the right to certain means-tested benefits whilst becoming liable to tax. In extreme cases their real income actually decreased. By 1988, it has been calculated, half a million claimants were caught in this trap.

Housing

Housing was potentially the most divisive social policy because it involved the rights of private property. For Conservatives these rights were traditionally the keystone of a free society whilst for Labour they were a historic source of exploitation. Despite the ideological conflict (which flared up in the 1951 and 1964 elections) progress was nevertheless made towards the realization of agreed objectives: the provision, within a well-planned environment, of a sufficient number of houses of adequate quality and at a reasonable price. The 1947 Town and Country Planning Act gave local authorities the power to control all development, even if this was not always wisely used. At least prewar urban sprawl was restricted and, with the creation of national parks in the 1940s and conservation areas in the 1960s, some positive measures were taken to protect the environment. Equally, the 'crude' housing shortage of 729,000 dwellings in 1951 was eradicated by the late 1960s. Because of the inappropriate location of some dwellings and such factors as 'second' homes, this did not mean that the 'actual' housing shortage was resolved, although this was itself calculated to have been reduced from 1.5 million to 0.5 million dwellings between 1971 and 1986. However, the increasing number of officially homeless families (40,000 by 1989) and of people sleeping rough in city centres were a clear cause for continuing concern. So too might have been the quality of housing since the housing shortage in the early 1960s had largely been resolved by the building of prefabricated tower blocks which themselves, in social and material terms, soon became ripe for demolition. The overall number of dwellings adjudged unfit, however, fell by one-fifth to just over one million between 1971 and 1986. This was, in part, a triumph for a switch in emphasis from the demolition of 'slums' to the more cost-effective policy of renovation after 1968.

Was this increased supply of higher-quality housing available at a reasonable price? Undoubtedly the cost of housing in Britain became relatively high, because of the failure to address successfully the fundamental issue of a scarce supply of land. Labour's attempts to nationalize either development land or the profits to be made from it were half-hearted and were quickly reversed by the Conservatives. However, as in all European countries, the immediate cost to households was held down by government subsidy. The major beneficiaries were increasingly owner-occupiers with the cost of tax relief on mortgage interest repayments, at £5.2 billion by 1988–89, equalling the cost of all other direct government expenditure on housing. Simultaneously council house tenants were charged proportionately higher rents, although a variety of means-tested benefits (consolidated into housing benefit in 1986) was available to those in need. The one sector of the housing market not to be subsidized was the privately rented sector in which, ironically, the poorest tenants often lived. The Conservatives sought to make this sector more profitable for landlords by removing rent controls (most notably in the 1957 Rent Act) whilst Labour sought to assist tenants by increasing security of tenure and imposing 'fair' rents. It was the lack of subsidy, however, which meant that this sector went into sharp decline (see Table 20.2). It was replaced by owner-occupation, which was to be particularly boosted in the 1980s with the regular annual sale of over 100,000 council houses under the Conservatives' 'right to buy' policy. This predominance of owner-occupation was unique in Europe, although it was a trend other countries gradually followed.

Table 20.2. Housing tenure in Britain, 1945–88

	% of total			
	Owner occupied	Public rented	Private rented	Other
1945	26	12	54	8
1976	53	32	15	–
1988	66	23	12	–

Sources: Lowe, *The Welfare State*, p. 251; HMSO, *Social Trends 21* (London, 1991), p. 146.

The Personal Social Services

The personal social services affect most directly the welfare of those in greatest need. They have, however, traditionally been the Cinderella of welfare services (see Table 20.1) and were the last to be professionally coordinated. Only after the 1969 Seebohm Report on Local Authority and Allied Personal Social Services were social workers brought together into a single social service department within the relevant tier of local government. Even then their role remained uncertain. Were they to anticipate or to react to problems? The issue was at its most acute in child abuse cases, where they were alternately criticized for respecting and interfering with parental responsibility. Even more fundamentally, were they to supplant or supplement other carers – most notably families and long-established charities (such as the NSPCC which had effective responsibility for the prevention of child neglect after 1945)? Given the lack of resources, supplementation came to be recognized as the only practical policy. This was confirmed by the 1990 National Health Service and Community Care Act which encouraged social workers to oversee but not to provide services. Thus community care has come to mean not care *by* the community in small local authority run institutions, as it was defined in the 1970s, but as care *in* the community by families and charitable bodies (subsidized where necessary by government) and by commercial ventures (such as private nursing homes).

Both parties saw community care, however defined, as a cost-effective and humane alternative to traditional institutional care. Care for the elderly in hospitals, for example, was expensive and destroyed old people's dignity and independence (although the corresponding cost in terms of the independence, and thus the welfare, of informal carers was often overlooked). The Conservatives in particular welcomed a decline in the 'dependency culture'. In the late 1960s and 1970s, the increased resources devoted to the personal social services brought the often appalling conditions of groups, such as the elderly and the mentally ill, up to a reasonable standard. Thereafter irregular increases in real expenditure could do little but match increasing demand.

The Redistribution of Income and Wealth

Taxation is the final way in which government can influence individual welfare because the way in which money is raised is often as important as the way in which it is spent. Over time the postwar tax system became more regressive. There were three main reasons. The burden of direct taxation fell less on corporations and the comparatively rich, but more on those on or below average incomes. This was mainly because the higher rates of taxation were reduced and, as an unplanned consequence of inflation, the effective income threshold at which tax became payable fell. In the mid 1970s the absurdity was reached that a married worker with two children became liable to tax when his earnings were still below the poverty line. Secondly, an increased proportion of government revenue (especially in the 1980s) was raised by flat rate indirect taxes which disproportionately hit the poor. Rises in VAT and, in particular, the community charge (poll tax) were prime examples of this shift. Finally tax relief for companies and individuals ('occupational' and 'fiscal' welfare) grew, to the advantage of the better-off. Managers rather than workers enjoyed subsidized company perks, such as cars; they could also afford more expensive tax-deductible assets, such as mortgages. Tax relief, moreover, eroded the tax-base from which government had to finance increased expenditure and thus required heavier rates of direct and indirect taxation on the less well-off.

Contrary to contemporary opinion, therefore, the tax system did not significantly redistribute income and wealth. Calculations are fraught with technical difficulties (and monetary assets should never be taken as a simple proxy for welfare, which includes non-monetary assets). Official estimates, however, are provided in Tables 20.3 and 20.4. In relation to income, the relative share of the top 10 per cent did decline but only until the 1980s; and even then it was largely redistributed within the next 40 per cent, whose share surprisingly increased after taxation. With personal wealth, the share of the top 1 per cent equally declined but it was redistributed among the top 50 per cent whose share increased in the 1980s. Even allowing for pension rights, the share of the bottom 50 per cent in 1990 was only 16 per cent of total wealth.

Table 20.3. Distribution of personal income in the UK

Per cent	Percentage of total income received by each group before and after direct tax		
	1949	1975–76	1984–85
Top 1	11.2 (6.4)	5.6 (3.6)	6.4 (4.9)
Top 10	33.2 (27.1)	25.8 (22.3)	29.4 (26.5)
Next 40	43.1 (46.4)	49.9 (50.3)	48.3 (48.6)
Bottom 50	23.7 (26.5)	24.3 (27.4)	22.2 (24.9)

Note: Figures in brackets are for income after taxation. Information was presented in a different format after 1984/85.

Sources: A.H. Halsey, *British Social Trends since 1900* (Basingstoke, 1988) p. 152; HMSO, *Social Trends 18* (London, 1988).

Table 20.4. Distribution of wealth in the UK

Per cent	Percentage of total wealth held by each group				
	1950	1976		1990	
Top 1	47.2	21	(12)	18	(11)
Top 10	74.3	50	(34)	51	(37)
Top 25	–	71	(55)	72	(60)
Top 50	–	92	(80)	93	(84)

Note: 1950 figures are for England and Wales only. Figures in brackets include estimated pension wealth as well as marketable wealth.

Source: Cmnd 7595 (1979) Table 4.5; HMSO, *Social Trends 23* (London, 1993) Table 5.20.

Increasingly sophisticated attempts have been made to calculate the combined effect of welfare policy and taxation on individual income. A household's original income is calculated; then its disposable income (with the addition of cash benefits and the subtraction of direct taxes); and then its final income (with the addition of benefits in kind and the subtraction of indirect taxes). The calculations for 1989 are summarized in Table 20.5. The final income of the bottom 40 per cent may be seen to have increased considerably, that of the top 20 per cent to have declined sharply. Large differences remain, however, because of the widening divergence of original income and the disproportionate take-up by the better-off of more expensive benefits in kind such as subsidized higher education. As a result, many have concluded that the greatest redistribution of income is within an individual's lifetime rather than between different income groups.

Table 20.5. Redistribution of income through taxes and benefits in the UK, 1989 (£)

Income	% of all households				
	Bottom 20	Next 20	Middle 20	Next 20	Top 20
Original	1280	4760	11,580	17,850	30,050
Disposable	3960	6550	10,730	14,980	23,970
Final	5200	7210	10,340	13,740	21,400

Source: HMSO, *Social Trends 23*, Table 5.14.

In focus: The National Health Service

The NHS and the welfare state have become so closely identified that they are commonly regarded as synonymous. To many, the NHS represents the highest ideals and achievements of state welfare. In terms of social justice and equality, it provides everyone with access to an *optimum* level of care as of right – whereas social security, for example, only offers a *minimum* income to those who have 'earned' their right through insurance contributions. In terms of efficiency, it makes good certain proven market weaknesses such as the imperfect knowledge of consumers. Public provision of health care also ensures fuller coverage and lower administrative costs than either social insurance (as practised in interwar Britain) or private insurance (as still practised in the US). Moreover, in terms of results, postwar health standards have risen appreciably. Average life expectancy at birth, for example, rose between 1950/52 and 1983/85 by between five and six years as a result of the decline in infant mortality already noted and in deaths from infectious disease.

Such general approval for the ideal of the NHS, however, has coexisted uneasily with increasing concern about its efficiency as a practical deliverer of health care. Bureaucracy and waiting lists have appeared excessive; morale has remained low throughout the service; and it has been deemed necessary to effect three major reorganizations (in 1974, 1982 and 1988). Improvements in health standards, it can also be argued, were merely the continuation of prewar trends and were more pronounced in other countries. Clearly all has not been well with the NHS and over time Bevan's legacy – the creation of an elitist service committed to 'universalizing of the best' – has come under attack. Public expectations and possibilities of medical science are boundless whilst economic resources are scarce. The fundamental challenge for the NHS, therefore, has been to devise a method of allocation which rationally defines and then delivers the best practical, not an ideal, level of health care. A service dominated by hospital consultants was not well suited to this task. Inevitably curative medicine took precedence over preventive with the result that a national *sickness* rather than a national *health* service was created. Which represents the optimum use of scarce resources: the provision of a network of readily accessible health centres, designed to raise the average health standards of all (as proposed in the 1940s); or the provision of a network of technically advanced but remote district general hospitals, catering for exceptional individual need (as built in the 1960s)? Low morale in a profession which, by historic standards, was enjoying good conditions and rates of pay may also be attributed to the disappointment of unrealistic hopes raised by the promise of 'universalizing the best'.

The importance and practical shortcomings of the NHS have made it a particular target for radical criticism. Marxists have noted that doctors, by concentrating on the biological causes of illness (the 'medical model' of

The National Health Service (continued)

health care), have enabled private enterprise to pass on to the general taxpayer the cost of ill-health arising from more general causes such as industrial pollution. By creating a healthy workforce and fostering a sense of equality, the NHS has also increased productivity (and hence profitability) and reinforced the legitimacy of capitalism. Feminists attack on two main fronts. Disease is defined by doctors who are predominantly male with the result that specifically female illnesses and needs are marginalized. With a predominance of men in positions of power and of women in subordinate positions (such as nurses and ancillary workers), the NHS as an employer has also reinforced the unequal sexual division of labour. The New Right, in contrast, is concerned with the monopoly position – and thus the vested interest and public unresponsiveness – of the medical profession. Their preferred solution is health vouchers, which would give consumers the financial power to select their own mix of treatment. This has been adjudged impractical. Instead, since 1988, an attempt has been made to increase efficiency and accountability by the creation – in experiments such as hospital trusts – of internal or 'quasi' markets. Finally, historians have scrutinized the continuing popularity of the NHS and thereby highlighted its advantages for the middle classes. They were the main beneficiaries in 1948 because previously they had had to pay the full, and rapidly escalating, cost of health care. They would also appear to have enjoyed a disproportionate share of the more expensive facilities. Therefore whilst, in the 1950s and after 1976 especially, inequalities between regions and social classes were undoubtedly reduced, the NHS contains structural impediments to the achievement of even greater equality.

The Historiographical Debate

There were three main driving forces behind the creation of the welfare state. The first was the need for a greater standardization of publicly financed services, the uneven implementation of which had been exposed by evacuation. This for most civil servants was the principal justification for greater centralization. The second was the desire, after the mass unemployment and poverty of the 1930s, for the more efficient use of resources. Economists have since provided theoretical explanations for the greater potential efficiency of state welfare. Markets may misallocate resources because of the absence, in the real world, of perfect knowledge and perfect competition (the assumptions upon which their theoretical efficiency depends). Moreover markets may underprovide services which are in the common, as opposed to private, interest because they cannot accurately measure externalities (the incidental benefit or cost to others of an individual's private choices). The third driving force was the desire for greater equality. This variously meant equality of treatment by government (as implicit in Beveridge's proposals for universal flat rate insurance), equality of opportunity (as sought by the 1944 Education Act) or equality of outcome. It was the latter, especially when advocated in the 1960s by those who wanted to engineer a greater redistribution of income, that was by far the most controversial.

Most commentaries on postwar welfare policy have been written not by historians but by those concerned with current policy. Until the 1970s most assumed the relative efficiency of state intervention and supported the principle of redistribution, although individual policies and the general direction of welfare policy were often severely criticized. Within this tradition falls the classic official history of wartime social policy, R.M. Titmuss, *Problems of Social Policy* (London, 1950) and the equally classic text written by a fellow professor at the London School of Economics, T.H. Marshall, *Social Policy* (London, 5th edn, 1985). However, with the perceived crisis of the welfare state in the mid 1970s three more critical perspectives were adopted.

Marxists questioned the ulterior motives of state welfare if not its efficiency. It was designed, so they argued, not to foster equality and justice but to reinforce capitalism. It might therefore be seen either as social capital (assisting profitability by providing assets such as a healthy, well-trained workforce which industry could not provide for itself) or as social expenses (legitimizing capitalism by removing some of its worst iniquities). The most quoted example of this approach is I. Gough, *The Political Economy of the Welfare State* (London, 1977) although a more accessible introduction is J. Dearlove and P. Saunders, *Introduction to British Politics* (Cambridge, 2nd edn, 1991). A corollary to this attack was a fierce debate, not least within the Labour Party itself, over the record of the Attlee government. Did its welfare reforms advance or betray its supporters' interests? The standard defence is K.O. Morgan, *Labour in Power* (Oxford, 1984).

At the other extreme the New Right questioned both the efficiency and the objectives of state welfare. In both economic and social policy, so it argued, the market alone had the ability over time to respond to changing needs and to satisfy them in the most cost-effective way. State welfare typically expands to satisfy the needs not of consumers but of producers (politicians seeking votes and civil servants seeking enhanced careers). It also limits choice with serious consequences for the maintenance of political freedom. This critique took its initial inspiration from F.A. Hayek, *The Road to Serfdom* (London, 1943); and its most effective embodiment, which greatly influenced Conservative ministers in the 1980s, is C. Barnett, *The Audit of War* (London, 1986). Its peroration ends with an attack on the 'segregated, subliterate, unskilled, unhealthy and institutionalised proletariat hanging on the nipple of state maternalism'.[5]

The third radical critique is that mounted by feminists. They accept the material gains enjoyed by women after 1948 but argue that they have been achieved at an unacceptable price. Reforms such as social security are seen subtly to reinforce the economic dependence of women on men (because the right to social security for non-working married women depends on their husbands' contributions and is therefore lost, for example, on divorce). Equally, other policies such as community care and family allowances are seen to reinforce women's traditional role as unpaid carers and mothers. The pioneering work here was E. Wilson, *Women and the Welfare State* (London, 1977), whilst a balanced review of recent literature is provided in J. Lewis, *Women in Britain since 1945* (Oxford, 1992).

Two more specific controversies have recently arisen. The first concerns the postwar consensus on welfare. Was it a myth or reality? The classic case for its wartime creation is P. Addison, *The Road to 1945* (London, 1975) which is most fully challenged in K. Jefferys, *The Churchill Coalition and Wartime Politics* (Manchester, 1991).[6] The essential point would seem to be that, whilst ideological differences and party conflicts should not be minimized, neither should the agreed constraints (such as the commitment to 'full' employment) within which all governments worked until 1975. Related to this debate is the question of why state welfare was so quickly transformed in the 1940s from a demeaning concession to a social right. P. Baldwin in *The Politics of Social Solidarity* (Cambridge, 1990) has argued that it was because increased longevity and higher expectations had raised the cost of health care, pensions and education beyond that which previously self-reliant groups felt they could afford. They therefore sought the security of state collectivism. This argument links closely with the burgeoning literature on the redistributive impact of state welfare. Are the middle or the working class its major beneficiaries? This issue is particularly well examined in relation to the 1970s by J. Le Grand in *The Strategy of Equality* (London, 1982). Baldwin's work also underlines the importance of comparative history in defining the agenda for analysis and in identifying what was unique about the British welfare state. The best introduction to comparative analysis is perhaps G. Esping-Andersen, *The Three Worlds of Welfare Capitalism* (Cambridge, 1990).

Bibliographical Note

The fiftieth anniversary of the Beveridge Report saw the publication of two general texts on postwar welfare by M. Hill, *The Welfare State in Britain: a Political History since 1945* (Aldershot, 1993) and by R. Lowe, *The Welfare State in Britain since 1945* (Basingstoke, 1993). For the period since the mid-1970s these should be supplemented by J. Hills (ed.), *The State of Welfare: the Welfare State in Britain since 1974* (Oxford, 1990). This is a more technical analysis but each chapter contains a non-technical summary. All three books contain full bibliographies covering general and theoretical work as well as histories of individual policies. R. Klein, *The Politics of the National Health Service* (London, 2nd edn, 1989) is an exceptional book on an exceptional area of policy.

The wartime influence on postwar welfare developments is sympathetically discussed by P. Addison in *The Road to 1945: British Politics and the Second World War* (London, 1975), and critically assessed in C. Barnett's *The Audit of War: The Illusion and Reality of*

Britain as a Great Nation (Basingstoke, 1986). For an introduction to welfare rather than to welfare policy, the relevant statistics and a commentary on the complexity of their interpretations are provided by A. H. Halsey, *British Social Trends since 1900* (Basingstoke, 2nd edn, 1988). This may be supplemented by the Annual government publication, *Social Trends.*

Notes

1. Cmd 6404, para. 3.

2. Cmd 6404, para. 294.

3. Public Record Office, CAB 130/139 GEN 625.

4. The assumptions on which these calculations are based are discussed in R. Lowe, *The Welfare State in Britain since 1945* (Basingstoke, 1993) ch. 6.2 and J. Hills (ed.), *The State of Welfare: the Welfare State in Britain since 1974* (Oxford, 1990) ch. 7.

5. An essential critique of Barnett's thesis is provided by José Harris in 'Enterprise and welfare states' published in T. Gourvish and A. O'Day, *Britain since 1945* (Basingstoke, 1991). She is also the author of the classic biography, *William Beveridge* (Oxford, 1977).

6. A summary of the debate is R. Lowe, 'The Second World War, consensus and the foundation of the welfare state', *Twentieth Century British History* vol. 1 (1990), pp. 152–82.

21 Education and Social Mobility

Michael Sanderson

From Butler to Baker

The postwar years opened in a mood of high idealism in education. R.A. Butler's Education Act of 1944 raised the school leaving age to 15 and created the Ministry of Education. More important it required that pupils be given an education appropriate to their 'age, abilities and aptitudes' but did not specify what form this should take. The chief types of schools were three, the grammar, the secondary technical and secondary modern – the so called tripartite structure. These were not created by Butler but inherited from the system created in the 1900s by Sir Robert Morant, the then chief civil servant of the Board of Education, the Ministry's predecessor. The 1944 Act accordingly perpetuated an Edwardian system of schooling and retained some of its social class assumptions.

Apart from this three ambiguities lay at the heart of the thinking behind the Act. Firstly there was a belief that it would bring about 'equality of opportunity', a very popular slogan and aspiration of the early 1940s. Yet was this equality to be brought about by all pupils receiving the same education (irrespective of different abilities and aptitudes)? Or going to the same school (as advocates of early comprehensives hoped)? Or was it simply to be the equal right to take a selection examination which would prove just how unequal children's abilities were? Or was it merely to be a hope that the different types of school in the tripartite structure would be regarded as equal by being given 'parity of esteem', in another phrase of the time? In practice the interpretation of 'equality of opportunity' came to rest heavily on the last two. Second there was a conflict inherent in this neat phrase 'ability and aptitude'. A child might show high academic abilities at age 10/11 without having any marked aptitudes. Conversely a child might have aptitudes (a handiness with a saw or a sewing machine) without a high intellectual ability. The danger was that lack of academic ability was taken to imply the possession of technical *aptitude*; unsuitability for the grammar school to imply suitability for the technical school. This problem was compounded since educational psychologists of the time believed that they could detect and measure *ability* at 10/11 but not *aptitude* until much later. Third, disregarding the above, Butler was influenced by the commonsense psychological assumptions of Sir Cyril Norwood expressed in a report of 1943. This was that minds were of three types – abstract, mechanical and concrete. There was no evidence that this was so at the age of 10/11, Norwood was a headmaster not a psychologist. But this analysis neatly fitted the existing structure and its class assumption: abstract, grammar school, professions; mechanical, technical school, crafts; concrete, modern school, lowly skilled. It mirrored not only the Edwardian occupational structure but the military view of society – officer, NCO, other ranks – familiar to wartime and National Service Britain of the 1940s and 1950s. Perpetuation rather than radical change was the dominant ethos.

The major achievement of the Act was the abolition of fee paying in grammar schools. In the interwar years about 60 per cent of places in such schools were taken by middle-class fee payers whether they were suitable for an academic education or not. The exclusion of this category after 1945 would, it was hoped, free places for more intelligent children of poorer means and bring about a truer alignment of types of intelligence with the three types of secondary school.

Local Education Authorities (LEAs) set out to implement the Act. They drew up their plans providing 56 per cent of their schools as Modern Schools, 15 per cent as grammar and 7 per cent as technical schools. This ratio of 8:2.5:1 was hardly a balanced tripartite system. As a sign of future times 5.5 per cent of schools were designed to be comprehensives. Whereas the grammar and technical schools were justified by their 'academic' and 'mechanical' purpose, there was no clear thinking on the purpose of the secondary modern schools. Attempts to justify them did so in terms of how they overlapped the functions of technical schools. In practice they were residual schools for the 75 per cent of children who 'failed' the 11+ examination. This was the examination taken by children between the ages of 10 years 6 months and 11 years 5 months for entry to secondary education. The most successful were allocated to grammar schools, those below them to secondary technical schools where available and the 'failures' to the secondary modern schools. The education system of the 1940s and 1950s was underlaid by the uneasy assumption that three quarters of its children were already failures at the age of eleven. Between 1945 and 1956, 536 new secondary modern schools were built but this was only a small proportion of the 5,000 secondary modern buildings most of which were old higher elementary, central, 1930s modern schools which carried the resonances of pseudo-secondary education for the working classes which had dogged their origins. In the 1950s, 87 per cent of their intake came from skilled and unskilled manual workers.

A lively debate (see below) led to demands for the replacing of the post-1945 structure with the comprehensive school. This form was being pioneered in Windermere (1945) and Anglesey (1949), with Kidbrooke in London as the first purpose-built comprehensive in 1954. Anthony Crosland,

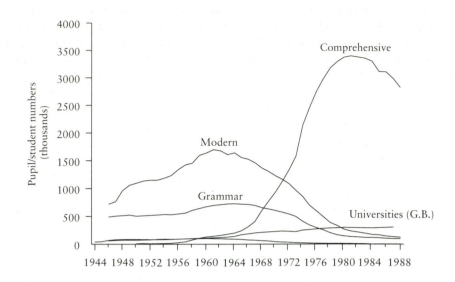

Figure 21.1. Pupils and students (schools and universities, England and Wales). *After:* Brian Simon, *Education and the Social Order 1940–1990* (London, 1991) pp. 583–5, 597–8.

the chief theoretician of the Left had published his influential *Future of Socialism* in 1956 advocating greater social equality through the comprehensive school. His American wife was familiar with them in the US and Crosland felt strongly on the matter: 'if it is the last thing I do, I'm going to close every grammar school in England'. With the return of a Labour government in 1964 Crosland became Secretary of State for Education and issued his circular 10/65 (12 July 1965) requiring LEAs to draw up plans for going comprehensive. The 11+ was to be abolished as was the tripartite system for which it selected. All were now to go to the same school. The number of pupils at comprehensives soared from 128,835 pupils in 1960 to over a million by 1971. In spite of the return of the Conservatives in 1970 and Margaret Thatcher's reversal of the Crosland circular with her own 10/70 in 1970, the number of pupils in comprehensives continued to rise to over two million by 1974 when Labour returned. By 1979 comprehensives contained over three million pupils and by the end of the 1980s they educated 88 per cent of pupils.

If comprehensivization was one major revolution in schooling in the postwar years, the other was the Thatcherite revolution of the 1980s. The most important element was Kenneth Baker's Education Act of 1988. This required schools to produce curricula statements to meet the requirements of the national curriculum. There was to be assessment of pupils at 7, 11, 14 and 16 with the results of the last three being made public. Parents could choose schools and thus set up competition between them for pupils with the prospect that, owing to falling rolls, the less successful would close. Teachers were to be subject to annual appraisal and lost the right to negotiate pay as they used to do through the now abolished Burnham Committee. Schools with over 200 pupils could opt out of LEA control and manage their own finances.

Secondly, the General Certificate of Secondary Education (GCSE) replaced the GCE which had started in the early 1950s and the CSE which catered for pupils of a much lower standard, usually in secondary modern schools. The conflation of both into the GCSE was intended to provide an examination for a wider range of ability than either. Linked with this move, the Conservatives introduced a national curriculum devised by subject committees under a National Curriculum Council. The British government had traditionally played no part in laying down a required curriculum in schools (save for the period of the Codes for elementary schools from 1862 to 1891). What schools taught had been left to headmasters to decide, shaped by the examination demands of university examining boards. The concern to get more technology into schools and ensure appropriately patriotic history teaching and grammatical English made a more *dirigiste* approach necessary.

Thirdly, the Conservative revolution brought new astringent values to education, partly under the influence of Sir Keith Joseph. These have included a concern to inject market competition into schools with league tables of results. The Conservatives have been deeply suspicious of the educational 'establishment' and have sought to undermine it. There has been a degradation of the 'professional' pretensions of schoolteachers with an invoking of parental (consumer) power against them. The state curricular control has removed areas of discretion from them as they have lost bargaining rights. LEA officials have similarly lost power as the opted-out schools left their control. The monopoly of schools inspection by Her Majesty's Inspectors (HMIs) is being broken by teams of contractors from outside the system who will be hired in by schools. University Departments of Education are playing a diminishing role in the training of teachers, who spend more time in selected schools. This 'establishment' from which power is being removed is held responsible for creating and running a defective educational system which has failed to prevent Britain's decline in industrial status. Finally, there has been a healthy concern to introduce into schools the values of technology and wealth creation to break down the snobbery associated with an arts-dominated liberal education.

Technical Education

As regards technical education various things have gone wrong since 1945. The root problem has been the failure to develop the prewar Junior Technical School into the Secondary Technical School as part of the tripartite system. These schools were to be selective, usually taking the second cut of 11+ selection and so reinforcing the inferior status of technical compared to academic abilities. There were 319 technical schools in 1948 but these had declined to 266 by 1960. Thereafter they rapidly vanished, their 72,449 pupils of 1950 dwindling to 2,502 by 1985. Various reasons lay behind this. LEAs did not envisage technical schools as an important part of their plans to implement the 1944 Act. Parents as ratepayers preferred their councils to build grammar schools to increase their children's chances of entering higher education and the professions. Since technical schools were also expensive, councils preferred to build large, cheap secondary modern schools for the mass of children. Technical schools combined the dual disadvantage of lower prestige and high cost. Secondly, an important policy decision was taken in 1955 by the Minister of Education, Sir David Eccles, not to develop technical schools. His view was that able scientists should be in grammar schools and technicians in secondary moderns and that there was little justification for a third type of school. Thirdly, the technical schools were initially absorbed into bilateral grammar schools and then devastatingly eliminated by being swallowed up by comprehensives. In 1955 technical school pupils accounted

Plate 21.1. An engineering laboratory at a seconday technical school. In the tri-partite system of secondary education established by the 1944 Education Act, seven per cent of schools were supposed to be technical schools, but by the 1980s these specialist schools had virtually disappeared, and technical education in Britain was recognized as being woefully inadequate.

for 4.6 per cent of secondary school pupils and comprehensive schools accounted for a mere 0.8 per cent. By 1985 the proportions were 0.06 per cent and 85 per cent respectively. The supersession of technical schools by comprehensives came about between 1959 and 1960.

This is probably the most important error in education since 1945. The assumption was that technology could be catered for adequately in other secondary schools. This hope has proved unfounded. In the 1960s a bitter division arose between the Nuffield Foundation Science Teaching Project and the Schools Council project in Technology. The former emphasized grammar school academic science; the latter applied crafts and technology. The tensions between the groups and personalities betrayed the nation as did the Department of Education and Science which remained aloof. Nothing effective was devised to replace the vanished Secondary Technical School and the optimistic urgency about technology in schools had dwindled by the 1970s. Reports in the early 1990s castigate the inadequacy of technology teaching in secondary schools.

This has had damaging knock-on effects. There were encouraging developments at the higher end of technical education. In 1956 several leading technical colleges were designated as Colleges of Advanced Technology (CATs) to undertake advanced work. In 1966–67 these were elevated to technological universities. Behind them a further group of technical colleges, originally twenty-seven and subsequently thirty-two were upgraded to polytechnics to provide degree work validated by the Council for National Academic Awards. These in turn have been upgraded to universities in 1992. Yet the lack of technically-qualified students from schools has undermined these developments. To compensate for this lack the technological universities, CATs and polytechnics have engaged in a 'policy drift' to build up their activities in the humanities and social studies. The CATs (the future technological universities of the 1960s) told Robbins that they intended to have 80 per cent of their students in science and technology and 20 per cent in the arts and social studies. But by 1974 the actual spread was 67.6 per cent and 32.4 per cent respectively. Likewise the polytechnics in 1965 had 57.9 per cent of the students in science and technology and 28.2 per cent in arts and social studies. By 1978 their proportions had reversed to 33.9 per cent and 50.4 per cent respectively.

Various recent devices are trying to fill the gap. The Youth Opportunities Programme was introduced in 1978 to give jobless school leavers work experience through tuition and work studies. This was replaced in 1983 by the Youth Training Scheme but also at a low level. This in turn gave way to Youth Training in 1990 but dealing with only 2 per cent of the labour market. More organizations overlay these. In 1986 the National Council for Vocational Qualifications (NCVQ) was to rationalize and evaluate the plethora of courses and qualifications while the Training and Enterprise Councils (TECs) from 1990 were employer-led bodies to assess local training needs. Yet in spite of this shoal of initiatives no comprehensive and coherent programme of technical training has emerged.

There are two developments in which hope may be put for the revival of technical education. In 1983 the Technical and Vocational Initiative (TVEI) was started with the aim of offering pupils aged fourteen to eighteen a more vocationally oriented curriculum. It provides funds for projects in schools in technology, information technology and crafts like catering and horticulture. It is an area of hope. The nearest the system has come in recent years to replacing the old technical school has been the creation of the City Technology College in 1988. These are to offer a curriculum with a strong emphasis on technological, scientific and practical work, business studies and design. It was originally intended that they would be financed by private-sector firms but this has not materialized. The government wanted twenty CTCs by 1990 but by 1992 only thirteen existed. This is nothing compared with the 324 technical schools at their peak in 1946.

Universities

The expansion of secondary education had inevitable knock-on effects for higher education. In the 1930s only 1.7 per cent of eighteen year olds went to university. The war itself had drawn attention to the importance of war science – radar and the atomic bomb notably. Immediately after the war the Percy Report (1945) and the Barlow Report (1946) called for an expansion of university education to increase the supply of scientists needed in peacetime industry no less than in war. Percy wanted a quadrupling of engineers and Barlow a doubling of scientists, an expansion of all universities and the creation of a new one.

Various factors made these calls for expansion undeniable. Firstly, returning servicemen already expanded the university population to 68,400 by 1946–47 compared with the prewar 50,000. Secondly, a trend of staying on in the sixth form became evident in the 1940s and 1950s. It was encouraged by the full employment of the postwar years and the removal of paying for fees and the cost of books and stationery by the 1944 Act. The exclusion of 11+ failures from the grammar school must also have raised the academic quality of the schools and hence the potential catchment for the swelling sixth forms. The extension of compulsory education to the age of fifteen also drew more children nearer to sixth form entry. The high quality of teachers attracted to grammar school teaching in the depressed 1930s were now the sixth form subject specialists of the 1940s and 1950s. Accordingly boys and girls in sixth forms rose from 32,000 in 1947 to 53,000 by 1958, an increase of 66 per cent. It is remarkable that this increase had been achieved with a generation born in the 1930s when the birth rate was actually falling and then static. Thirdly, the ending of the war brought a rise in the birth rate – the 'bulge'. This generation of young people would reach university age in the early 1960s with the number of eighteen year olds rising from 533,000 in 1959 to a peak of 812,000 in 1965. Had nothing been done to respond to the 'trend' and the 'bulge' then by the late 1960s some 25,000 young people a year would have been denied a higher education they merited.

Furthermore, there was unease about the social exclusiveness of the universities. A third of children born to higher professional parents in 1940 went on to higher education (in the late 1950s), but only 1 per cent of children of semi and unskilled workers did so. It seemed questionable that more opportunities had been opened up to enable the working classes to enter grammar schools yet this had had so little effect on higher education. In 1962 a cumbersome system of supposedly competitive local and state scholarships was replaced with a simple mandatory obligation on LEAs to finance any student accepted at university. Finally, there was an awareness that Britain had fallen behind her industrial competitors in the provision of higher education by the late 1950s. At that time 4 per cent of British young people went to university compared with 20 per cent in the US, 10 per cent in Sweden, 11 per cent in Belgium, 8 per cent in Holland and 7 per cent in France. It was not unreasonable to raise British levels to those of France. Nor was it unreasonable, since most of these countries had faster rates of economic growth than Britain, to hope that improving our higher education would raise our growth levels also. There had already been a postwar expansion of students from 68,452 in 1946/47 to 107,699 by 1960/61. The Victorian civic universities had expanded and several new institutions were granted charters as independent universities: Nottingham (1948), Southampton (1952), Hull (1954), Exeter (1955), Leicester (1957), Keele (opened 1950, chartered 1962). Yet the Robbins Report of 1963 called for a further expansion to 197,000 places by 1967/68. Accordingly 'new' 1960s universities were created at Sussex (1961), York and East Anglia (1963), Lancaster, Strathclyde and Essex (1964), Warwick and Kent (1965). These were planned before the publication of the Robbins Report but Stirling (1967) followed its recommendations. In addition, in 1966/67 nine CATS were elevated to technological universities. With the Robbins expansion student numbers nearly doubled to 200,121 by 1967/68; that was 6.3 per cent of eighteen year olds.

In spite of these expansive trends the expectation that university expansion would lead to a great increase in working-class participation have been disappointed. In the late 1950s only 3 per cent of working-class adolescents went to university. A.H. Halsey has shown that although students in higher education have quadrupled since 1963 to over a million, the proportion entering from the manual working class has scarcely changed since 1961–70 when it was only 3.1 per cent.

There have been social gainers. The number of mature students has increased massively in the 1980s from 134,000 to 237,000. In the older (non-polytechnic) sector they make up 14.5 per cent of students compared with 10 per cent in 1985. They are older people whose academic potential was unrecognized in secondary modern schools, married women taking the opportunity to increase their qualifications after the independence of their children, and increasingly, the redundant seeking a fresh start. There has also been an increase in women going to university from the early 1960s when they made up about a quarter of university students to 1990 when they were 45 per cent of new entrants. There was a more than four-fold increase in women going to university between the early 1960s and the late 1980s. Yet since there was only a 10 per cent increase of girls in public schools over this time it suggests that the state sector of comprehensive and grammar schools was largely responsible for the raised standards and expectations among girls which made this possible. Overall the achievement has been remarkable. Students have risen from 200,000 in 1967 at the end of the immediate Robbins expansion to one million by 1992. The effect of releasing five times as many graduates into the labour market as the 1960s, twenty times as many as the 1930s, has been an inevitable lowering of the expectations of graduates who are no longer the elite they once were. Indeed many arts graduates would have been better employed gaining skills as mechanics, caterers and construction workers. The awareness of this may be an element in the resistance of working-class children to enter a higher education which yields diminishing rewards.

Social Mobility

Educational opportunity has undoubtedly expanded but has social mobility and is there any connection between the two? The four surveys of social mobility taken between the 1940s and 1960s found an increasing tendency for sons of manual workers to rise to non-manual work and a diminishing tendency for sons of non-manual workers to fall to manual work.[1]

Table 21.1. Social mobility, 1940s–60s

Would be 11+ in	Survey	Manual rise to non-manual	Non-manual fall to manual
1940	1949	15.6	15.7
1942	1951	17.9	10.2
1953	1962	18.8	7.8
1954	1963	18.8	10.8

Source: A.H. Halsey (ed.), *Trends in British Society* (London, 1972), pp. 146–7.

These survey results show gradual changes in social mobility over a relatively short period which covers two generations, the first of which was educated before the 1944 Act (the first two surveys), while the later generation were beneficiaries of the Act (the last two surveys). The absorption of working-class children upwards into the professional, managerial and clerical classes of the postwar years has led to the so called embourgeoisement of the affluent worker – his adoption of middle-class elements of lifestyle and attitudes. This is reflected in changing aspirations. W.G. Runciman found that in 1962, 82 per cent of manual workers wanted their children to go to university, which was very similar to middle-class expectations of 88 per cent.[2]

That education has been a powerful engine in social mobility has been demonstrated by A.H. Halsey in 1978. He finds Britain a quite fluid society with a substantial minority of men changing from their fathers' social class (Table 21.1). It is the working class which is the most self perpetuating and the middle class the most open to educated newcomers. Halsey shows the educational experience of the stable middle class and those moving upwards to the middle class in 1972 in percentages.

Table 21.2. Educational experience of middle and working-class children, 1972

	Private primary schooling	Selective secondary schooling	University degree
Stable middle class	32.0	88.4	29.8
Lower middle rising to middle class	11.7	67.9	13.5
Working class rising to middle class	1.6	63.1	12.8
Middle falling to working class	3.8	33.5	0.5
Lower middle falling to working class	3.0	21.9	0.1
Stable working class	0.6	14.7	0.1

Source: A.H. Halsey, *Change in British Society* (Oxford, 1978).

Similarly these quite high percentages may be contrasted with the much lower ones for the downwardly mobile to the working class and the stable working class itself. At all points of comparison, the downwardly mobile and lower classes were vastly lower in educational experience and achievement than the upwardly mobile and middle classes.

Goldthorpe and others have also shown the different paths of children of different social classes through different educational experiences and to different levels of future occupation (Table 21.2).

The strong self perpetuating bias is evident, but that 37 per cent of children of manual parents rose and 28 per cent of white collar children fell indicates a healthy element of fluidity.

Table 21.3. Educational and occupational mobility

	Children of manual parents		Children of whitecollar parents	
Education	9% to grammar schools	77% to non selective schools	33% to grammar schools	53% to non selective schools
Employment	37% to white collar jobs	51% to manual jobs	57% to white collar jobs	28% to manual jobs

Source: J.H. Goldthorpe *et al.*, *The Affluent Worker in the Class Structure* (Cambridge, 1971), p. 135.

In focus: The Public School Revolution

Whatever the problems of the state system of education one undoubted success of the postwar years was the public or independent schools. They entered the postwar years apprehensively. They had been damaged by the economic depression of the interwar years when the falling birth rate and constrained middle-class incomes restricted their market. In 1944 Lord Fleming, a Scottish judge, reported his proposals to widen access to the public schools. He recommended that pupils could be sent to public schools paid for by their LEA or by the Ministry of Education. Yet no 'revolution' followed from this. Many schools were keen on the scheme; they had nothing to lose and it brought them more income. Yet LEAs were generally suspicious of it. They saw it as a device to use public money to subsidize the private sector of schooling and help it recover from its financial problems of the 1930s. It also became evident that Ministry money would not be forthcoming and the whole burden of cost would fall on the LEA. Most importantly LEAs rightly took the view that they should be spending their ratepayers' money improving the state system for the benefit of all children, not in providing extra special privileges for one or two. Moreover the more they spent on improving their own grammar schools the less manifestly superior would the public schools be; the less purpose would be served by diverting children from the state to the private sector. In any case by the 1950s the public schools themselves were in a buoyant condition and had no need of subsidized local authority children bringing social dissonances to their controlled communities.

The public school revolution came not from Fleming but from other factors. From 1964 the Labour government, concerned about the divisive and elitist nature of the public schools, determined to abolish their independent status and integrate them into the state system. A Public Schools Commission was appointed in 1965 to consider this. Many Labour MPs wanted not merely integration but abolition.

The Public School Revolution (continued)

The public schools responded with what has been called the 'public schools revolution'. Firstly they expanded their numbers. The pupils in schools belonging to the Headmasters' Conference (the best definition of a public school) increased from 96,539 in 1961 to 119,002 by 1988, a 23.3 per cent increase. The proportion of the male school-age population attending public school rose from 4 to 5 per cent in the interwar years to 7 per cent. To a lesser extent this was also the case in the girls' public school sector. The total number of pupils in 123 schools of the Girls' Schools Association (the girls equivalent of the Headmasters' Conference) rose by 10.5 per cent between 1961 and 1988. This was encouraged by various factors. The 1944 Education Act had excluded 11+ failures. Many middle-class parents whose offspring would have gone to grammar schools as fee payers now had no alternative but to seek places in the independent sector. The absorption of grammar schools into the comprehensive sector and the abolition of the direct grant grammar school in 1975 reinforced this trend.

*"Trouble is, the bulk of the Labour hierarchy are dead against Public Schools because they **didn't** go, and the rest because they **did**."*

Plate 21.2. *Punch*'s comment on public schools in 1964. The public schools had too many friends in high places, including the cabinet, for Labour to be able to carry out its threat to abolish the public school system.

The Public School Revolution (continued)

Secondly, the schools became more attractive in that they began to pay more attention to the sciences. In 1955 an Industrial Fund for the Advancement of Scientific Education was established. Over £3 million was subscribed by 141 companies for scientific laboratories and education in the public schools. By 1980 over half of public school boys going to university were studying science, engineering or medicine. The old liberal education, classics, arts bias of the public schools was being broken down and the schools reoriented to a modern scientific business world.

Thirdly this trend was doubtless encouraged by the new predominance of parents coming from the business classes. At Eton in the 1960s, 39 per cent of parents were businessmen and 25 per cent were professionals. Financially declining professions like the clergy and schoolmasters were ceasing to be able to send their children to public schools. Lawyers, doctors and senior civil servants could still do so but successful businessmen were best placed. The reason for this was the inflation of public school fees. Between 1961 and 1988 the average fees of five leading public schools (Eton, Winchester, Rugby, Charterhouse, Harrow) rose almost fifteen-fold (from £456.80 to £6,813) while overall inflation rose by a factor of just over ten. That fees rose more than inflation while numbers continued to rise gave an advantage to the wealthy. Businessmen had the means and were attracted by a more relevant curriculum.

Fourthly, the schools were paying more attention to academic standards generally. There was less concern about sporting 'blues' among the staff and more about 'firsts' and PhDs. By 1979 independent schools won 64 per cent of open awards to Oxford and Cambridge. The leading handful (Dulwich, Winchester, Westminster, Eton, St Pauls) regularly won fifty places a year each at the ancient universities. Academic excellence came to be prized as much as social cachet.

The power of the public schools in the creation of elites in Britain remains undiminished. In the 1960s over 80 per cent of judges, QCs, directors of prominent firms, directors of the Bank of England and Church of England bishops were ex-public school boys. It is also remarkable how little has changed in the last twenty years. A survey of 'top people' made by *The Economist*[3] in 1972 found that 67 per cent had been to public schools and this was still 66 per cent in 1992. The perception of the sustained role of the public schools but the increased need for wealth to enter them lay behind the Assisted Places scheme created by the Education Act of 1980. This enables poorer children of high ability to attend fee paying schools at the taxpayers' expense. Some 4,000 places a year are taken up and this may help to leaven the lump of this most flexibly adaptable sector.

Historical Interpretations: Comprehensive Schools

Perhaps the most important debate in education since the Second World War has been that about the reshaping of the tripartite structure into the comprehensive school. The idea of the multilateral school, as it was then called, emerged in the interwar years and was espoused by left-wing educational groups. The Spens Report in 1938 suggested that LEAs still reorganizing their secondary education should consider this multilateral form. What was envisaged was a school with academic, technical and other buildings grouped round some central feature like playing fields. The pupils, whatever their abilities and aptitudes, would belong to the same school. This would obviate the social distinctions of the tripartite system, the snobbery of the grammar school and the second rate status of the technical.

The arguments in favour of the comprehensive school emerged out of dissatisfaction with the operation of the tripartite system and selection. In the early 1950s the work of Floud, Halsey and Martin showed how little the 1944 Education Act had increased working-class chances of going to a grammar school.[4] In a famous passage they observed that 'the likelihood that a working class boy will reach a grammar school is not notably greater today despite all the changes than it was before 1945. Rather less than 10 per cent of working class boys reaching the age of 11 in the years 1931–41 entered selective secondary schools. In 1953 in South West Hertfordshire the proportion was 15.5 per cent and in Middlesbrough 12 per cent'. The class differential remained wide. In Hertfordshire 59 per cent of the children of professional, business and managerial fathers went to grammar schools and in Middlesbrough 69 per cent. In both places only 9 per cent of children of unskilled manual workers enjoyed such success.

The work of J.W.B. Douglas in the 1960s threw light on why the situation had changed so little and why such disparities persisted.[5] The selection system was fundamentally unfair and wasteful of ability. Whether a child achieved a grammar school place depended too much on the lottery of the regional provision of grammar schools. In 1959 a child living in south west England stood a 35 per cent chance of going to a grammar school, and in Wales a 33 per cent chance. If on the other hand the child lived in the central South, the chances were reduced to 19 per cent and in the North East to 22 per cent. A situation in which a child could nearly double or halve its chances of going to a grammar school by a slight change of residence was unacceptable to critics of selection.

Secondly, performance in the 11+ test depended on the social class of the candidate. Douglas demonstrates that whereas 41 per cent of upper middle-class mothers had a high interest in the school progress of their children, only 5 per cent of lower working-class mothers did so. Whereas three-quarters of the former wanted their children to go to a grammar school only a half of the latter had this aspiration. The great enthusiasm for secondary education evinced by the higher classes and the apathy of the lower transmitted itself to their offspring between the ages of eight and eleven and influenced their performance in the test. Regional inequalities were compounded by those of the social class of the child's family.

Thirdly, the 11+ test itself was held to be a fraud. It usually consisted of an intelligence test (well developed since the 1920s), a test in arithmetic and in English. It was the latter which aroused most suspicion since a child's range of vocabulary and fluency of articulation owed more to his family background than his schooling. The social class of the child was being subtly tested yet again. Moreover the use made of the test results was a fraud. The impression was given that the test was a high jump whereby some fixed standard had to be reached and if it were then the candidate would be awarded a place. Yet it was remarkable that in every grammar school in every town in every year there were just enough desks and chairs awaiting those who cleared the standard. The grammar school merely creamed off enough to fill its places however large or small. This further undermined the pretensions to national fairness in selecting an elite of high academic ability.

Fourthly, the 11+ had adverse effects on primary schools. The urgent need to pass the examination, to achieve success for the pupils and status for the schools prompted streaming from the age of seven. Seven year olds were grouped into classes likely to pass the 11+ and those not; accordingly a self fulfilling prophecy became built in as the 11+ became the 7+. If there was unease that ability was being excluded from the grammar school so there was a complementary concern that others were being misselected for an academic secondary education for which they were unsuitable. The Early Leaving Report in 1954 found that 14.5 per cent of boys and 17.6 per cent of girls left grammar school in 1949 under the age of sixteen.

The comprehensive school would obviate all these difficulties and bring positive benefits. It would ease transition between the different academic and technical levels of the school as teenagers' aptitudes developed. This was especially important since even psychologists who believed that intelligence was detectable at the age of ten or eleven did not believe that distinctive aptitudes showed themselves until about the age of thirteen. Such transference under the tripartite system was difficult and comparatively infrequent. Furthermore, the comprehensive schools would have to be large and this would bring economies of scale of central facilities – assembly halls with large stages for theatrical presentations, craft workshops and so forth. Moreover it would provide high salaried posts for headmasters of large schools which would attract people of calibre into the teaching profession. This argument appealed to R.A. Butler.

On the other side were counter arguments of the defenders of the status quo who were sceptical of the comprehensive school. Sir Cyril Burt, the leading educational psychologist of the day, remained convinced of the existence and measurability of 'g' (general intelligence). He believed that it was found in large populations in a normal distribution and that it remained constant through life and was detectable at the age of ten or eleven. He remained confident in the validity of grammar school selection. Secondly, the *Black Papers* deplored the way that comprehensives destroyed the competitive elitism of the grammar school in the pursuit of egalitarianism.[6] It was healthy that the 11+ examination taught even young children that success and failure resulted from endeavour or the lack of it. The selective test also recognized the reality that not all, of any age, have the same levels of ability. Indeed a perverse and tyrannical form of inequality was being perpetrated by the comprehensive school, namely the equal treatment of unequal talents. An institution designed for mixed ability merely hobbled the hare in the interests of the tortoise. Standards would be levelled down to uniform mediocrity. To defenders of the grammar school this was a serious betrayal of the rights of the working class to rise. From Morant to the Labour Ministers of Education in the 1940s, the grammar school was seen as a vehicle of social mobility for the most able of the working class. To abolish it and replace it with the comprehensive school was to kick down the ladder.

Moreover the distinctive part-public school ethos of the grammar school would be lost in the comprehensive. The rugger, military cadet corps, prefects, masters in gowns called 'Sir', the easy assumption of preparation for authority risked being tainted with the ethos of the secondary modern whose numbers would predominate. There was the lurking fear that the potential 'nobs' would become the veritable 'yobs'. Paradoxically the converse argument was also used against the comprehensive schools. Julienne Ford found many of the hopes for these schools unfounded.[7] Children in comprehensives had friendships largely with their own social class. They did not widen cross-class relationships as much as grammar schools did. Nor did the working-class child do as well in academic streams in comprehensives as they did in grammar schools.

The debate is far from over. In 1993 the Secretary of State for Education, John Patten, declared himself to be in favour of schools opting out and reconverting to selective grammar schools where appropriate. It is still a live issue.

Conclusion

In some respects the postwar record of education has been creditable. The school-leaving age has been raised twice, to fifteen in 1945 and sixteen in 1972. Educational expenditure as a percentage of GDP has risen from 3 per cent in the 1950s to 6 per cent in the 1970s before falling back to 5 per cent in the 1980s. Educational expenditure actually overtook that of defence from 1969 and has remained ahead. We have seen the expansion of opportunities in higher education and even the public schools. Yet the system has failed to keep Britain competitive with its industrial neighbours. Some key indicators in Table 21.3 suggest this.[8]

Table 21.4. Comparative educational performance, 1991

| | **1991 percentages** | | |
	a) 16 year olds reaching the equivalent of GCSE grades A–C	b) Young people obtaining upper secondary school qualifications 18+	c) Young people 16–19 in full and part time education and training
Germany	62	68	79
France	66	48	76
Japan	50	80	94
England	27	29	56

Source: A. Green and H. Steedman, *Educational Provision, Educational Attainment and the Needs of Industry* (London, 1993) pp. 7, 8, 16.

The English system has been too much designed to select and reward high achievement rather than encourage the broad majority. It has been poor in forming the less academic youngsters into a technically efficient manual workforce for manufacturing industry. Moreover in Germany (after the Napoleonic Wars), in France (after the Revolution) and in Japan (after the Meiji Restoration) education has been seen as a vital element in nation building. These countries accordingly retain a greater respect for the importance of education than is traditionally the case in England. It can be argued that too much effort has been devoted to widening social opportunities and not enough to the content of education to make it industrially relevant. The abandoning of the technical school, the failure of school technology, the policy drift in polytechnics and technological universities have been part of that. We are now a poorer country than our major competitors and have less resources to improve our education. But we need to raise expectations and for the future we need a shift of emphasis to create a population perhaps less educated and more trained, less cultivated and more skilled.

Bibliographical Note

The literature is vast. The fullest authoritative survey is Brian Simon, *Education and the Social Order 1940–1990* (London, 1991) and a useful treatment up to the 1960s is Roy Lowe, *Education in the Postwar Years, a Social History* (London, 1988). Michael Sanderson, *Educational Opportunity and Social Change in England 1900–1980s* (London, 1987) is a shorter synopsis for the general reader.

The supersession of tripartism by the comprehensive schools is recounted in David

Rubinstein and Brian Simon, *The Evolution of the Comprehensive School 1926–1972* (London, 1973) and J.G.K. Fenwick, *The Comprehensive School 1944–1970* (London, 1976). The secondary modern school is dealt with in William Taylor, *The Secondary Modern School* (London, 1963) and the technical school in Gary McCulloch, *The Secondary Technical School, a Usable Past* (London, 1989) and Michael Sanderson, *The Missing Stratum, the Technical School in England* (London, 1994).

The public school revolution is analysed in John Rae, *The Public School Revolution* (London, 1981) and other aspects in G. Walford, *British Public Schools, Policy and Practice* (London, 1984). On higher education W.A.C. Stewart, *Higher Education in Postwar Britain* (Lewes, 1989) surveys the whole field. D. Kavanagh and A. Seldon, *The Thatcher Effect* (London, 1989) chs 14–15 are good on the 1980s reforms.

On social mobility see A.H. Halsey, *Trends in British Society since 1900* (London, 1972) ch. 5 and *Change in British Society* (Oxford, 1978, 1986) ch. 6.

The best treatment relating postwar education to Britain's economic decline is D.H. Aldcroft, *Education, Training and Economic Performance 1944 to 1990* (Manchester, 1992) while Michael Sanderson, 'Social equity and industrial need: a dilemma of English education since 1945' in T.R. Gourvish and A. O'Day, *Britain since 1945* (London, 1991) is also suggestive on this theme.

Notes

1.   A.H. Halsey, *Trends in British Society since 1900* (London, 1972) ch. 5.

2.   W.G. Runciman, *Relative Deprivation and Social Justice* (London, 1966).

3.   *The Economist*, 15/25 December 1992.

4.   J. Floud, A.H. Halsey, and F. Martin, *Social Class and Educational Opportunity* (London, 1956).

5.   J.W.B. Douglas, *The Home and the School* (London, 1964).

6.   C.B. Cox and A.E. Dyson, *The Black Papers on Education* (London, 1971).

7.   Julienne Ford, *Social Class and the Comprehensive School* (London, 1969).

8.   A. Green and H. Steedman, *Educational Provision, Educational Attainment and the Needs of Industry* (London, 1993) is but the latest of several reports by the National Institute of Economic and Social Research to this effect.

22 Women since 1945

Pat Thane

The Family

The trends established at the beginning of the century towards smaller family size continued. Indeed the birth rate reached such an exceptionally low level in the early 1930s that there was some panic that the British population was dwindling excessively. However the war years saw a rise which reached a peak of 20.7 births per thousand of population in 1947. The birth rate fell again in the 1950s, though not to the levels of the 1930s, rose to close to the postwar peak in the middle 1960s, then fell from 18.8 births per thousand of the UK population in 1964 to 16.2 in 1971. Thereafter to the mid 1980s it averaged 12.8 since when it has remained stable.

The latter fall coincided with the introduction and spread of the use of the contraceptive pill. This was a dramatic breakthrough in birth control technique, but it cannot unambiguously explain the decline in births since the birth rate had fallen to lower levels in the 1930s when birth control techniques were more cumbersome and, so far as we are aware, less widely available and understood. The influence of the pill was almost certainly greater upon sexual attitudes and practices among at least a minority of the population, until the health hazards of long-term use became clearer in the 1970s and AIDS emerged in the later 1980s. Abortion also became more readily available following the Abortion Act of 1967, but in view of our ignorance of preceding levels of illegal abortion we cannot assess its impact upon the birth rate, though it is likely to have been small.

The two-child norm was firmly established by the postwar years as was the practice of marriage. In the nineteenth century a high proportion of men and women did not marry and this remained true of 14 per cent of women through the first third of the twentieth century. Females remained a majority of the population though the gap was narrowing (20,819.4 females to 19,133.0 males in 1931; 22,742.2 females to 21,015.6 males in 1951). The trend towards almost universal marriage began in the 1920s until by the 1970s nearly every adult female married at least once. In the 1980s however, despite much public discussion of the importance of marriage and the family, marriage and remarriage rates fell. By 1993 almost one third of registered births were to parents who were not formally married, although more than half of these parents were residing at the same address. For reasons that are so far obscure there appears to have been a shift among a significant section of the population from formal marriage to stable cohabitation.

This followed a period in which not only had marriage become more popular but its likely duration lengthened. Falling adult mortality rates reduced the incidence of widowhood. Of marriages contracted in the 1880s, 13 per cent would have been broken by death within ten years, 37 per cent within twenty-five. Of marriages undertaken in the later 1930s, 79 per cent survived for twenty-five years. Thereafter divorce rather than death became the great disrupter of marriages, producing in the 1980s disruption rates very similar to those caused by death in the early nineteenth century.[1] The widowed single mother, a familiar nineteenth-century figure, has been replaced by the divorced, separated or never-married single mother. The postwar growth of divorce should be seen against this background. In 1968, 3.7 per thousand of the UK married population divorced; in 1970, 4.7; and in 1971, 6.0. The divorce rate peaked in 1985 following a change in the law in 1984 which allowed divorce after one year of marriage rather than after three.

Work

Census statistics provide a somewhat more reliable guide to numbers of women in paid employment than earlier in the century, though comparisons with other statistical sources, such as National Insurance records, suggest that there is still a tendency to undercount.[2] All sources undercount women in casual jobs such as domestic cleaning; in addition, there are members of the 'hidden workforce' who are employed in various forms of 'outwork' by manufacturers in their own homes, or by kin in small family businesses such as shops. Since the 1950s many female members of the growing ethnic minority populations have joined these categories.

Table 22.1. Women in the labour force, 1951–81

	1951	1961	1971	1981
As % of total labour force	31	33	37	40
As % of women aged 20–64	36	42	52	61
Part-time as % of total labour force	12	26	35	42
% all married women aged 15–59 in labour force	26	35	49	62

Source: Jane Lewis, *Women in Britain since 1945* (Oxford, 1992) p. 65.

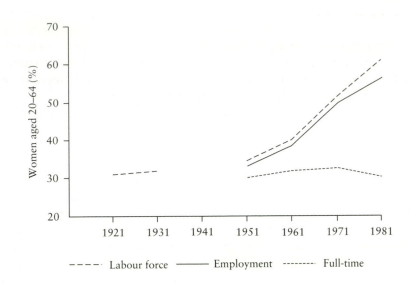

Figure 22.1. The trend in female economic activity rates among women aged 20–64, GB, 1921–81. *Source:* H. Joshi (ed.), *The Changing Population of Britain* (Oxford, 1989).

The data in Table 22.1 indicate the continuing importance of paid work for women and the importance of part-time work. In fact as Figure 22.1 shows, all of the increase in rates of female employment since 1945 is accounted for by part-time employment.

Women were encouraged to enter the labour market during the war and 7.75 million of them were in paid work in June 1943 (see Chapter 16). From 1943 the government had been aware of the likelihood of a postwar labour shortage and started to plan to keep as many women as possible in the labour force. However when the war ended more women returned to the home than had been hoped. The numbers in paid work fell to six million in June 1947 and from 1947 to 1949 the Ministry of Labour campaigned to persuade women to return to the labour market.

Rather than being pushed from the postwar labour market many women left voluntarily to start families having delayed marriage or childbirth due to the war; hence the postwar baby boom described above. It does not appear to be the case, as is often asserted, that such women were forced to give up work by the closure of the day nurseries which had been opened during the war. Rather, the closures mainly came later, as a result of government cuts in the early 1950s. The chief targets of government propaganda for women to remain in the workforce were older women who had completed their families and the pattern of employment immediately after the war was that such older women remained in the labour force whilst others re-entered it who had spent the war years at home caring for children.

Paid Employment

The total numbers of women in the British paid labour force grew by 300,000 in each of the three years following 1947; by 1961 the total was 8.4 million; by 1981, 8.7 million. Given the inadequacy of statistics for previous periods it is unwise to argue, as is often done, that this represents an historic rise in women's paid employment. It may be that it has simply become more visible in official statistics; the truth is that we do not know.

What clearly was established after the war was a new life-cycle pattern for women which remained into the 1990s. In the interwar years middle-class women entered the labour market for the years between education and marriage and then overwhelmingly left it permanently. Working-class women tended to take paid work after marriage whenever household finances required it and to withdraw when children became old enough to contribute to the household income. In the 1930s fewer such women were in paid work due to the combined effects of unemployment in the depressed areas and increased affluence elsewhere. From the late 1940s the numbers of women aged over thirty-five returning to paid work after a period of childbearing climbed, increasingly by the 1960s also among the middle class, while most mothers took some years out of the labour market to care for children. A two-phase work pattern was established as the norm for most women.

Though the government was anxious to keep women in the labour market after the war, it showed little inclination to extend their opportunities; women were expected to take up the jobs they had traditionally filled. They did not always accept this willingly. In May 1945, 400 women made 'strong protests' when they were ordered to leave an electrical engineering factory for the textile mills, where wages and conditions were inferior. It proved difficult to coax women back into this most traditional of female occupations.

Most women however remained concentrated in lower status, poorly paid white collar, service and industrial occupations. Their pattern of employment was also regionally uneven. The proportions in paid work were highest in the affluent South and East, low in Wales. The numbers in professional jobs rose only slowly. By 1961 there were still only 8,340 female medical practitioners (15 per cent of the profession) and 1,031 women in the whole legal profession (3.5 per cent); 1,580 were surveyors and architects (2.3 per cent) and there were 25 women MPs. Women were 47.5 per cent of 'social welfare and related workers'.

Government social surveys in 1943 and 1947 indicated that 58 per cent of women believed that married women (with or without children) should not 'go out to work'. But this sentiment was weaker among younger women and surveys through to the 1970s showed its continuous decline. In 1947 marriage rather than childbirth was the chief determinant of withdrawal from the labour market. That also was to change.

Plate 22.1.   A *Woman's Own* cover from 1949. Women's magazines in postwar Britain presented a cosy image of marriage and domesticity.

Equal Pay?

Women's pay in most occupations remained as unequal as their opportunities. This was reviewed by the Royal Commission on Equal Pay, which reported in 1946. The Commission was a product of demands from women which had been simmering, especially in white blouse public service occupations such as teaching and the civil service, since the 1930s.

The Royal Commission provided a comprehensive description of the grossly unequal position of women in the labour market. It acknowledged that the problem of defining 'equal pay' was that in a gender-divided labour force men and women rarely did precisely equal work. The problem therefore was to establish whether *comparable* work was unequally remunerated. Inequality was most strongly evident in the public sector. In the civil service, teaching and local government men and women evidently did identical work, pay scales were clearly laid down and equally clearly disadvantaged women. Generally in the public sector differentials averaged 50 per cent at the lower levels; the few women at the top fell only 10 per cent behind their male equivalents. The problem was not only of pay but of unequal promotion. In a number of professional occupations – such as university teaching, the BBC, architecture, medicine and as MPs – women formally had equal pay, but as we have seen, their numbers were few.

Most women in paid work were in the private sector divided in roughly equal proportions among secretarial and clerical work, retailing and similar services, and manufacturing. The strict gender division of labour, the small scale of many operations and the complex and often individual forms of pay negotiations, systems of payment and gradings, especially in industry, made the precise position difficult to assess and even more difficult to change. According to the Ministry of Labour in January 1945 the average earnings of women in industry were 53 per cent of those of men. Women in the private sector were also less organized and vocal on the issue. In the white blouse public sector women were strongly unionized and their unions mostly supported equal pay even when, as in the case of the civil service unions, they had a majority male membership.

The Royal Commission's careful enquiry found that women's lower earnings were influenced by the lower average age of female workers and disguised a great variety of earnings even among women working at similar tasks in the same industry. They concluded that in most cases the pay differentials could not be explained in rational economic terms, i.e. as a reliable measure of higher male productivity. Rather they were believed to be products of the influence of what the Commission called 'assumptions drawn from the sociological background' combined with both the effects of oversupply of female labour in the restricted range of occupations open to them and with the relative youth and inexperience of most female workers. The Commission concluded that the argument that men deserved a higher 'family wage' to provide for their dependants had ceased to play a significant role in wage determination.

The Commissioners put forward a strong argument in principle for equal pay for comparable work, but they concluded that implementation in the near future would be harmful to the economy. They found 'no doubt in our minds about the extent and intensity of the present discontent' among women on the question. The evidence did not suggest to them that most men would resent equal pay. Three of the four female members signed a minority report dissenting from this unwillingness to make more positive recommendations.

The Labour government shared the Commission's view that implementation of equal pay would wreck their economic strategy, as did the Conservatives when they took office in 1951. Women and trade unions in the public sector continued to campaign on the issue, though this was muted until the early 1950s probably due in part to a real desire to assist Labour to build a full employment welfare state. From 1952 they began to protest more vigorously until in 1955 the government at last announced that equal pay would be introduced into the civil service, local government and teaching, gradually over six years. There were occasional strikes over equal pay in the private sector, e.g. at the Hillingdon engineering works near Glasgow in 1955, but no equivalent campaign to that in the white collar public sector emerged.

Unpaid Work

Women in the home came under conflicting pressures. Mothering became a more exacting task as psychoanalytic theories of and studies of the psychological ill-effects of maternal deprivation in early childhood were widely disseminated.[3] Although their prescriptions were derived from studies of the unusual condition of total maternal deprivation (e.g. of orphans living in institutions), they generated a climate of belief that well-adjusted people needed to spend the bulk of their first five years in the company of their natural mothers. Historically this was a new requirement. Mothers who could afford it had not previously hesitated to leave their children with nurses, and poor women could rarely provide full-time mothering. Exacting standards were demanded of mothers.

Women's magazines were another source of encouragement to women to give prominence to their domestic roles, though they also encouraged attention to personal appearance and to fashion and very little, before the 1970s, to careers or paid employment. New magazines such as *Woman* and *Woman's Own*, focusing on beauty and domesticity, were launched during the 1930s though it was after the war that their sales rocketed from about 3.1 million per week in 1946 to 7.7 million in 1950 and an all-time high of 11–12 million in the later 1950s. In the mid 1950s, 58 per cent of women read weekly magazines, which were most popular among lower-middle and working-class women, while just over a third read monthly magazines, such as *Vogue*, which were directed mainly at the middle class.

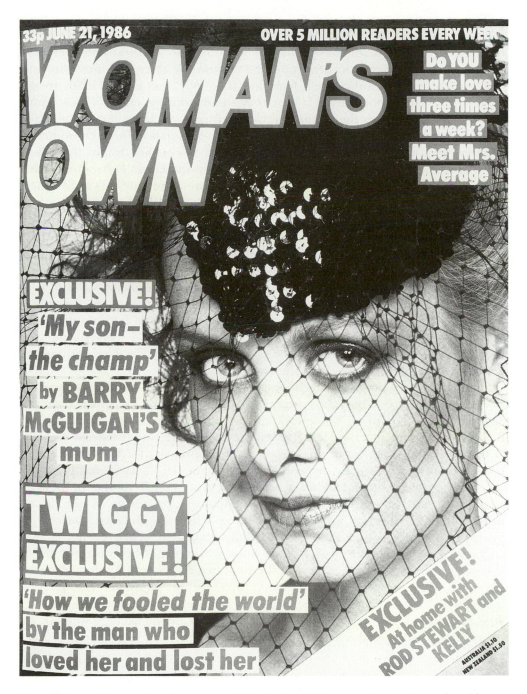

Plate 22.2. A *Woman's Own* cover from 1986. By the 1980s women's magazines placed less emphasis on domestic bliss and more on the joy of sex.

The magazines encouraged the desire of many women for comfort and glamour following the privations of war. There was high female demand for furnishings and household goods as well as for clothes and personal possessions, though this was frustrated by continuing shortages, austerity and government disapproval of such feminine frivolity.[4] Also in the 1950s media reports of isolated housewives in new towns and housing estates ('New Town Blues') conflicted with their other prevailing image of contented domesticity. Magazines must have provided some escape and consolation for such women.

Enjoyment of women's magazines does not necessarily imply that their readers became solely domestically-oriented fashion slaves. Full employment enabled more unmarried and older married women to buy things for their homes and for themselves, to improve their self-image and their environment, especially as austerity eased in the 1950s. Many women still carried the double burden of domestic and paid work and partly in consequence opted for part-time paid work. This was somewhat eased by improvements in housing, in the range of domestic technology available – the electric replacing the steam iron, more slowly the washing machine dispelling the heavy labour that washing had been for women throughout time – and at least as important, improvement in women's health. Working-class women had had more limited access than their menfolk to health care before the war and surveys suggested the appalling health conditions many of them suffered.[5] The National Health Service was an especial benefit to such women.

Improved conditions and technology raised expectations of standards of domestic labour, but they gave women a greater degree of choice over the amount of time spent on housework and for those who historically had been heaviest burdened this time fell. Table 22.2 shows that on average in the UK, as in the US, the amount of time taken up by housework for women changed little, indeed tended to rise, between the 1930s and 1970s. However when the UK data is disaggregated by class we find a distinct fall in the housework burden of working-class housewives, accompanied by a rise in the hours worked by middle-class women (coinciding with the decisive decline in living-in servant-keeping) until in the 1960s that also began to fall. These reductions in time spent by women on housework cannot be explained by an increase in male domestic labour. As the final two columns of Table 22.2 show, although the average man did indeed increase his domestic labour time between the 1960s and 1990 – from about 16 minutes per day to a little over 40 – this was still only one-ninth of the time spent by the average woman! Of course these averages also mask individual variations.

Table 22.2. Average number of minutes per day devoted to housework by men and women

	US 'Homemakers'	UK 'Housewives'	UK female working class	UK female middle class	US males	UK males
1928	440	–	–	–	–	–
1930	450	–	–	–	–	–
1937	445	405	480	235	–	–
1950	–	–	500	–	–	–
1952	450	–	–	–	–	–
1961	–	440	440	440	21	19
1965	470	–	–	–	–	–
1972	–	–	–	–	26	16
1975	–	355	345	370	–	–
1983	–	–	–	–	50	42

After. A figure supplied by Professor Jonathan Gershuny, University of Essex.

In focus: Surveys of Women and Paid Work

A succession of surveys suggested how strong were the barriers against equal employment opportunities for women. Viola Klein in a survey of *Britain's Married Women Workers* tried in 1957 to discover 'how ordinary men and women feel' on the question. By this time birth of the first child had become the normal occasion for women to give up work. Greater affluence and the accessibility of higher living standards meant that couples opted for a period of accumulation before the birth of children. When women returned to work in later life the reason they most often gave was raising the family standard of living. Klein concluded:

> The outstanding impression gained from this survey is that women's lives, today as much as ever, are dominated by their role – actual or expected – as wives and mothers ... there is no trace of feminist egalitarianism ... nor even is it implicitly assumed that women have the 'right to work' ... the isolated references to the 'equality of the sexes' were made by men ... Men appear on the whole to be less conservative in their outlook in these matters than they are usually assumed to be ....

Surveys of Women and Paid Work (continued)

However about a third of the men interviewed disapproved of married women working outside the home and most disapproved of mothers of young children taking paid work. Klein also questioned employers and discovered an extreme unwillingness to adapt to the needs of married women.

Similar findings came from a 1959 survey by the Ministry of Labour of 50 per cent of all women who had graduated in science and engineering in Britain in 1954 and 1956 (only 708 in all) and a sample of employers in relevant industries. Three-quarters of the graduates were employed in teaching at various levels or in the public service. The minority working in industry felt undervalued and felt that they had more limited prospects than men. The employers' responses indicated that they were right. Though many considered woman scientists 'particularly good at detailed work', 60 per cent paid higher rates to men on the grounds that men had a longer-term career commitment (not born out by the women's responses) and had dependants to support. A quarter of employers allowed women no opportunities for promotion and others limited the level to which they could rise in view of the presumed difficulties of allowing women to hold authority over men. Only 28 per cent of managers were wholly in favour of employing women.

A study carried out by Nancy Seear and colleagues three years later was undertaken at the request of a group of industrialists who feared a coming shortage of people trained in science and technology and that an opportunity would be lost if women were not trained in these fields. The team surveyed older girls in seventeen schools and found that a substantial minority were interested in training, but it was difficult for them to obtain information and they encountered serious discouragement on all sides. They did not want to have to struggle against prejudice and so were opting for teaching as a career because it was socially acceptable and could be combined with domestic roles.

Employers and teachers expressed conviction that women could not perform well in the sciences and employers were convinced that they did not make good managers – 'Women have emotional crises and can't take being kicked' stated one. Interviews with women in industry showed that they were planning their careers on a lifetime basis but felt that they would find it difficult to obtain retraining on returning after childrearing. In general they felt that their talents and skills were under-used. Seear concluded:

> The question is not whether women should be allowed better opportunities, but rather whether as a community we can afford to continue to waste their trained powers ... of course there are difficulties (such as women's family responsibilities) ... but these are not the fundamental difficulties. From this survey the basic problem seems to be prejudice.

Surveys of Women and Paid Work (continued)

A much larger survey carried out in 1965 for the Ministry of Labour confirmed these findings.

Hannah Gavron's study of north London housewives in the early 1960s (published as *The Captive Wife*, Harmondsworth, 1966) suggested that life was not substantially better in the home: 35 per cent of the working-class wives and 21 per cent of the middle-class ones felt that they had married too young. They claimed that they had done so primarily to escape from their families and, in the case of working-class girls, from monotonous low-paid work. They 'were now full of regrets for the things they had not done' primarily in respect of training and work.

Most felt that their marriages were more egalitarian than those of their parents, though 62 per cent of the working-class wives (only 1 per cent from the middle class) did not know their husband's earnings. Gavron was struck by the similarity of attitudes between the classes and by the fact that few of the women 'saw their lives dominated by the role of wife and mother'. She concluded that the worlds of education and work were too exclusively geared to the male life-cycle. School should prepare women for the life pattern that was becoming normal for most of them; above all they should have access to training and education in later life.

The theme of the inadequacy of female education and training and the resulting deleterious effects on the economy was also trenchantly put by the Report of the, all male, (Donovan) Royal Commission on Trade Unions and Employers Associations of 1968. On the basis of interviews with managers and trade unionists and the findings of another survey by Nancy Seear the Commission concluded:

> Lack of skilled labour has constantly applied a brake to our economic expansion since the war and yet the capacity of women to do skilled work has been neglected ... Women provide the only substantial new source from which extra labour and especially skilled labour can be drawn ... Many of the attitudes which support the present system of craft training and discrimination against women are common to both employers and trade unionists and deeply engrained in the life of the country. Prejudice against women is manifest at all levels of management as well as on the shop-floor.

Seear commented that: 'Even the most ardent feminist will agree that there is no great upsurge of protest by women against the existing situation'. However this did not necessarily mean that women approved of it: 'Human beings are remarkably adaptable and most people once they have recognized a brick wall for what it is decide not to bang their heads against it'. The biggest obstacle was that 'in subtle and not so subtle ways an atmosphere is created which still makes it appear peculiar or comical for women to be both feminine and using their capacities to the full'.

The Women's Movement

An active women's movement was less evident between the end of the war and the 1960s than at the beginning of the century, or in the interwar years when winning the vote gave women's activism greater vigour than is generally recognized, or from the later 1960s. Yet we have seen women protesting against unequal pay. The Conservative government clearly took the influence of female white collar workers seriously enough to give way on equal pay, in the face of the strong lobby in their party which was hostile to any but a domestic role for women.[6]

Women asserted themselves in other ways. They insisted upon wearing the 'New Look', the flowing, feminine style of dress which was such a welcome contrast to the severe square shoulders and short skirts of wartime when it was launched by Christian Dior in 1947, despite clothes rationing and solemn government disapproval of garments which required so much cloth in the most troubled year of the immediate postwar economy.

Women resisted this prolongation of austerity by making and adapting their own versions of the new style.[7] This did not necessarily imply opposition to Labour rationing and austerity policies as a whole. It is generally assumed by political sociologists that women have a natural inclination to vote Conservative, though there is little hard evidence for this. In particular it has been assumed that women reacted especially strongly against the postwar Labour government and that this was a major reason why Labour lost the 1951 Election. Much has been made of the role of the noisy but probably marginal Housewives League as the voice of female protest against Labour and austerity.

A majority of women voters voted Labour in 1945.[8] Opinion poll evidence indicates that despite some volatility in 1946–47 working-class female voters supported Labour more strongly up at least to 1950 than did working-class men, though middle-class women swung strongly to the Conservatives.[9] Working-class women may have been weary of austerity, but many of them had long known austere lives and they had reason to be grateful for the health and welfare services initiated by Labour.

Female voting has not been systematically studied in the following decades, though it is clear that in the 1980s British women exhibited an anti-Conservative, though not necessarily pro-Labour, bias which paralleled the movement of women in a number of western countries away from conservatism towards progressive and green causes. Such gender differences in voting suggest that on occasion at least, even in the 1940s, many women perceived their interests differently from many men. However, the class differences in female political allegiance serves to warn us of the danger of generalizing too readily about 'women'.

Alongside more indirect forms of female dissidence, a thin thread of overt protest about gender inequality survived through the 1950s. In 1956 Alva Myrdal and Viola Klein's *Woman's Two Roles. Home and Work* proposed means to achieve a 'fairer distribution of work and leisure between the sexes' and also enhanced social value and status for women's role inside as well as outside the home:

> All their productive efforts whether paid or unpaid, whether inside or outside their homes, should be taken into account; whether they educate children or spin cotton is of minor concern in this connection.

The volume appeared in an influential sociology series and remained in print until its second edition in 1968. Simone de Beauvoir's *The Second Sex* was translated into English in 1953 and had an immense impact upon individual women; as had the feminism of Doris Lessing's *Golden Notebooks* (1962). Similarly, small but persistent numbers of women in Parliament in all parties, in academic and literary life, in trade unions and in surviving women's organizations kept alive a certain discontent about gender inequalities.

There were signs of a stronger stirring of the women's movement in the mid 1960s. Two successor organizations to the suffrage campaigns, the Six Point Group and the Fawcett Society, initiated alliances among other groups concerned about women's rights, such as the National Council of Women, the National Council for Civil Liberties and women's professional and employment associations. They aimed at constitutional pressure for equal opportunities, equal pay, equal taxation and improved treatment of single mothers. They encouraged women to join trade unions and supported a flurry of strikes for equal pay in the private sector in the mid 1960s, most famously that of women machinists at Ford's at Dagenham. Simultaneously women in mixed sex organizations, in particular the TUC and the Labour Party, were increasingly active on issues of gender inequality. Labour won a firm majority in 1966, supported by a higher proportion of eligible female voters than they had obtained in any postwar election (in 1964 they had won their lowest postwar proportion). In 1967 Labour set up a committee to investigate discrimination against women, which reported in 1969 and 1972.

From 1968 a more radical strand of feminism emerged out of the Campaign for Nuclear Disarmament and other radical groups, often in reaction against the male domination of such groups. It was also inspired by the growing civil rights and women's movement in the United States. It became active in a variety of fields: welfare rights, organization of low paid women, improved nursery care. The women involved were more self-consciously radical in their forms of organization than were the older groups and concentrated more on issues concerning sexuality, control over reproduction, gay rights, violence against women and less on matters of work and training. They tended to be critical of orthodox political groupings, anti-institutional and sceptical of the possibilities of legislation as a vehicle for change (see Chapter 25).

Though there was cooperation between the two wings of the movement, there was also tension, similar to that between militant and moderate suffrage campaigners before 1914; and as with their predecessors, commentators have tended to credit the more public and militant strand with both such change

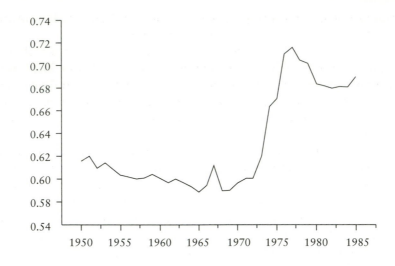

Figure 22.2. Women's wages relative to men's, hourly earnings, full-time manual jobs.
Source: Department of Employment October enquiry, all industries.

and such regression as occurred. In both periods, however, it is probably more useful to see the two strands as complementary. Between them they raised a wide range of issues and a widespread awareness of gender inequalities which have not since vanished from the public scene, even though visible feminist activism (especially of the more radical kind) declined in the 1980s. It also seems that the more radical wing, rather than being the sole or chief originator of the 'second wave' of feminism, was itself a product and part of a wider movement detectable from the mid 1960s and with longer, if slender, roots in the movements of the earlier part of the century.

The later 1960s, in fact, saw legislative changes which developed alongside rather than clearly grew out of the revival of the women's movement, since they predate its most active phase, notably the Abortion Reform Act, 1967, which attracted a wide range of support among women. In 1970 the Equal Pay Act followed the breakdown of a Labour-initiated attempt to bring about a way forward negotiated between employers and trade unions as well as pressure from women.

The Act established equal rates of pay for the same work, or work that had been rated as equivalent under a job evaluation scheme. It was designed to remove only that element in pay differentials that was judged to be due to direct gender discrimination, not that due to the younger age, lesser training or experience of females, though these may indirectly derive from discrimination. Compliance was to be voluntary until 1975. Barbara Castle, who as Minister of Labour was largely responsible for the Act, was well aware of its inadequacies and the potential for evasion. But she argued that 'legislation cannot cover every possible development' and it was essential for government to give a moral lead on this as on other issues.

The Act was followed by an increase in women's relative hourly earnings which is unlikely to have been coincidental (see Figure 22.2). There remained however a gap between the pay of men and women of comparable age and experience which cannot be explained in conventional economic terms.[10] In a number of cases women have been able to achieve equal pay only by appeal to the European Court.

The Act left untouched the processes that impeded women from advancing to higher earning occupations. A succession of anti-discrimination bills were brought before Parliament in the early 1970s, one of them drafted by Nancy Seear, now a Liberal Baroness. This bill gave rise to a House of Lords Select Committee in 1972. This drew on a range of research, including some from the Department of Employment, which demonstrated statistically, yet again, the concentration of women in low paid, low skilled jobs. The research organization Political and Economic Planning had investigated women in top jobs and concluded that discrimination was difficult to prove, yet the statistical disparity between the numbers of women at the lower levels of most professions and at the top left discrimination, often unconscious, as the only likely explanation. The Sex Discrimination Act of 1975 attempted to deal with this difficult area and established the Equal Opportunities Commission to administer and monitor it.

Again, the outcome is difficult to measure. In the 1980s significantly more women than before entered certain business and professional occupations. In 1988, 50 per cent of entrants to the law were female. Women made up 21 per cent of all solicitors and barristers and 22 per cent of GPs. Yet only 3.2 per cent of surgeons and 0.5 per cent of engineers were female. In 1984 fewer than 3 per cent of university professors were women and a similar proportion of MPs. Among less well trained women, government policies encouraged expansion of the low paid, low skilled jobs which have long been the preserve of most women and their employment protection was weakened. At the 1981 census three-quarters of all female workers were in just four of the sixteen occupational categories of the census: personal services (i.e. cleaners, hairdressers); clerical; professional workers in health, education and welfare; and selling (mainly shop assistants), and there was little sign of change through the 1980s. It remains true in the 1990s that 'women' live through greatly differing experiences.

Debates and Interpretations

Many of the issues raised by this chapter are similar to those which emerged in Chapter 6, in particular the tension between observable continuities in the relative situations of men and women and observable diminutions in gender inequality; and the problems of interpreting and explaining both 'hard facts' and the more elusive sources (magazines for example) which we must use if we are to understand the modern world. An important contrast which emerges in this chapter is between the strong continuities in gender inequality in the workplace and in other 'public' roles (numbers of representatives in Parliament, for example); and striking discontinuities in aspects of behaviour normally defined as 'private', concerning in particular marriage and the family, such as the rising divorce and more recent falling marriage but rising cohabitation rates. All of these, it should be said, have not been peculiar to Britain but were international phenomena in developed countries. We obviously have to ask not only how to explain continuity in the concentration of females in poorer paid, lower status, less skilled occupations with poor career prospects but also why this has persisted in the face of equal continuity in the volume of clear, publicly available evidence (often from government or government-appointed bodies) that this was the case and was harmful to the economy? Is it in any sense an outcome of rational economic choices by individual employers and/or by women? Of a bias against women among both employers and the makers of government policy so deep as to override suggestions that such behaviour is economically irrational? Or do men and women have different aspirations from one another which are rational in other than economic terms?

Of course this chapter also shows a significant improvement in female access to certain professional occupations during the 1980s. This also requires explanation, and only time will tell whether such access is accompanied by equal access to promotion and top salaries. In part it is an outcome of increased access of females to higher education and, it seems, of changed aspirations on the part of middle-class families for their daughters. By the 1980s they were less likely than in the 1950s to give daughters markedly inferior education compared with their sons and to have markedly lesser career aspirations. But these are changes which also require explanation. The feminist movement since the 1960s may have played a role in increasing both mothers' aspirations for their daughters and the daughters' own aspirations. And/or the clue may lie in middle-class insecurity and consequent preference for two incomes, or to recognition that the high divorce rate implies that females may need to be self-supporting in middle life.

Equally mysterious is the recent change in partnership practices. The rise in divorce can be explained in part by legal, in part by demographic change. The sharp increase in divorce followed legislation which made it easier to obtain. However the change in the law was in part a response to demand, which suggests the existence of considerable discontent within marriage. The demographic explanation is that greater longevity meant that most marriages contracted in early life were potentially of historically unprecedented length. Unhappy marriages previously broken by death had now to survive or be terminated by some other means. Quite possibly the recent turn away from marriage is a response to the rising divorce rate: people are perhaps becoming cautious about entering into marriage until they feel some confidence about its staying power. It may be a significant comment on the supposedly extensive power of the state over individual action that this change has happened despite an explicit commitment on the part of the government of the 1980s and early 1990s to the preservation of the 'traditional' family.

Much of the above is speculation and it is important to be aware how limited is our understanding of important changes and continuities in contemporary life. It is equally difficult to explain the upsurge of the organized women's movement in the 1960s. It followed no evident improvement or deterioration in gender inequalities. It is sometimes interpreted as a conscious revolt by young women against the lives their mothers led in the 1940s and 1950s, which are portrayed as narrowly domestic and bounded by consumerism. Yet we have seen how many women re-entered the paid workforce after raising young families from the end of the war onwards and the spread of this practice through the social classes by the early 1960s. A belief that women were deliberately excluded from the paid workforce after the war, as a matter of government policy, is deeply embedded in folk myth yet it was clearly not the case. The government was actively campaigning from before the end of the war for women to remain in paid work, though not for the improvement of their prospects therein. Government propaganda made a clear distinction between mothers of young children, whom it did not encourage to work outside the home, and older women whom it did. And women responded. This raises a question about the role of history in everyday discourse: why do some quite inaccurate images of the past come to be so widely believed?

Further apparent evidence of the narrowly domestic horizons of postwar women has been derived from studies of magazines and other sources (such as advertisements) which stressed fashion, beauty and consumerism. Yet such texts are far from easy to interpret if we are using them as a source for exploring women's expectations and motivation. It can be argued that the possibility of dressing well and looking good which opened up for many more women after the war than before, as family incomes rose and many more mass produced consumer goods were available, strengthened the confidence of many women, gave them a greater sense of control over their own lives, which they passed on to their daughters who perhaps took this sense of control and independence in different directions. The point of this is to indicate the variety of plausible interpretations which can be placed upon apparently straightforward sources and the need for some subtlety in interpretation.

It is also important to be aware that misapprehensions are embedded in scholarly as well as popular discussion. The notion that women are less likely than men to be politically active and, if they are, are more likely than men to be Conservative is a trusted standby of Politics texts. However, it has been clearly shown, for instance in J. Siltanen and M. Stanworth, *Women and the Public Sphere* (London, 1984), that remarkably little evidence relating to these propositions exists, and that where it does it contradicts them.

Bibliographical Note

There are very few surveys available of this recent period, on which research is only now beginning; Jane Lewis, *Women in Britain since 1945* (London, 1992) provides an introduction. The essay by Pat Thane, 'Towards equal opportunities? Women in Britain since 1945' in T. Gourvish and A. O'Day (eds), *Britain since 1945* (London, 1991) focuses upon the issue of equal pay and equal opportunities, but tries, inevitably briefly, to sketch in the wider context. In *Women's Rights at Work* (London, 1985), Elizabeth Meehan covers the equal pay and opportunities ground more fully and in comparison with the United States. Shirley Dex, *The Sexual Division of Work* (Brighton, 1985) surveys the gender division of labour very thoroughly, and Penny Summerfield's *Women Workers in the Second World War* (London, 1984) surveys the war and immediate postwar situation in which many women sought to combine home and work in difficult circumstances. The essay by Michael Anderson, 'The social implications of demographic change' in F.M.L. Thompson, *The Cambridge Social History of Britain 1750–1950, Volume 2* (Cambridge, 1990) surveys the demographic background for the earlier part of the period, and the essay by Heather Joshi referred to in Note 10 is helpful on the later period.

Notes

1. M. Anderson, 'The social implications of demographic change' in F.M.L. Thompson (ed.), *The Cambridge Social History of Britain 1750–1950, Volume 2* (Cambridge, 1990) pp. 29–30.

2. Pat Thane, 'Towards equal opportunities? Women in Britain since 1945' in T. Gourvish and A. O'Day (eds), *Britain since 1945* (London, 1991) pp. 193–5.

3. Notably John Bowlby, *Child Care and the Growth of Love* (London, 1953).

4. I am indebted to the work of Dr Ina Zweiniger-Bargielowska, University of Wales, Aberystwyth, for the content of the two preceding paragraphs.

5. Margery Spring Rice, *Working Class Wives. Their Health and Conditions* (1939, reprinted London, 1981) provides an especially vivid, and harrowing, description.

6. Harold L. Smith, 'The Politics of Conservative reform: the equal pay for equal work issue, 1945–55', *Historical Journal* vol. 35 (1992) pp. 401–15.

7. This I also owe to Dr Zweiniger-Bargielowska.

8. Monica Charlot, 'Women and elections in Britain' in H.R. Penniman (ed.), *Britain at the Polls, 1979* (Washington and London, 1981) p. 244.

9. James Hinton, 'Women and the Labour vote, 1945–50', *Labour History Review* (Winter 1992) pp. 59–71.

10. H. Joshi, 'The changing forms of women's economic dependency' in H. Joshi (ed.), *The Changing Population of Britain* (Oxford, 1989) pp. 165–9.

23 Immigration and 'Race Relations' in Postwar British Society

Tony Kushner

In 1925 the Conservative Home Secretary, William Joynson-Hicks, told a Jewish delegation that 'the entry of aliens to this country was not a right, it was a privilege'. Indeed, the number of aliens allowed to settle in Britain during the 1920s can be numbered in the hundreds – a result of the draconian restrictions of the Aliens Act of 1919 aimed particularly at Jews, Chinese and other 'undesirable' foreigners. Such exclusionism stands in stark contrast to the situation in the mid Victorian period when, as Bernard Porter suggests, 'her policy of asylum remained an inviolate feature of Britain's national life'.[1] The absence of controls until 1905 enabled British society to share in the mass immigration of people from eastern and southern Europe, even if this was not on the same massive scale as the USA. The situation since 1945 differs from the interwar period most obviously in the return of mass immigration leading to a society which is blatantly multi-cultural and multi-racial. By 1990 there were at least 2.5 million non-white people in Britain representing 5 per cent of the total population. Nevertheless, as the century draws to a close, parallels can be drawn with the interwar years. Fierce immigration controls exist, aimed particularly at those from the New Commonwealth. Moreover, life for many ethnic minorities is difficult, especially in an atmosphere of exclusive 'Englishness' which tends to marginalize and pressurize those deemed to be 'different'. This chapter will chart the changes and continuities since 1945 that have seen Britain move reluctantly to a country of mass immigration yet finish with the most restrictive immigration/refugee policy within the European Community.

European Immigrants

Textbook accounts of modern British history tend to provide a standard chronology of postwar race relations. We first hear of the arrival in 1948 of the ship *Empire Windrush* with its 492 West Indians on board. The next reference is normally to the Notting Hill race riots of 1958 closely followed by the 1962 Commonwealth Immigrants Act. The final mention tends to be that of the inner-city riots of the 1980s highlighting the involvement of black youths in the disturbances. More up-to-date accounts might also include the 'Rushdie Affair' from 1988 onwards. There is a grave danger in such approaches, especially in the possibility of providing a 'pathological' view of black people in Britain. Black people arrive, create a 'race problem', are opposed by public and then by state and finally rebel on the streets. Much is excluded, including the complex realities of both the black experience and white responses in Britain. Black people are represented only as rioters or book burners and, in the process, we lose sight of the rich, if sometimes problematic, legacy of mass immigration in modern British society.

One of the factors that is often forgotten (especially by those calling for immigration controls) is that the largest postwar group coming to Britain are the Irish. In fact, Afro-Caribbeans did not arrive in any great number until the early 1950s and those from Asia later that decade. By the time of the Notting Hill riots the combined non-white population of Britain was less than 200,000 (including 125,000 West Indians and 55,000 Indians and Pakistanis) whereas the Irish-born population was nearer 900,000. Moreover, in the period from 1945 to 1950, when the British government was most active in recruiting foreign workers, up to 200,000 came from Europe and only a few thousand from the 'non-white' Commonwealth. It needs to be stressed that much of the debate about minority groups in immediate postwar Britain continued to concentrate on the Jews rather than black groups. For example, in the history of collective British racist violence, the widespread antisemitic riots of August 1947 have been almost totally forgotten both in terms of popular memory and 'mainstream' historiography.

Why did Britain move away from its interwar restrictionism and why did it take so long for debate to start to focus on those of colour? The impact of the Second World War lies at the heart of the answer to both questions. On the one hand, as a report published in 1945 put it: 'The experience gained during the present war, when large numbers of soldiers, sailors, airmen and civilians belonging to the United Nations have been welcomed to this country, offers a favourable opportunity for developing a new attitude [towards immigration].'[2] On the other, the refusal of the British government to challenge the American army's policy of segregation with regard to the 170,000 Black GIs present on British soil (as well as its fears of racial mixing between black soldiers and white women) also pointed to the future. Britain's small black port communities in the interwar period had been viewed and treated in a pathological manner by the local state in cities such as Cardiff and Liverpool. Attempts were made through Alien Seamen Orders in 1920 and 1925 to remove the black presence altogether. The war against Hitler had done little to dispel the idea of black people as essentially problematic and the state was anxious not to start a further 'colour problem' after 1945.

Another immediate impact of the war was an intense labour shortage after

1945 as attempts at reconstruction began. Fears about the falling birth rate and the ageing nature of the British population had been limited to a few activists in the interwar period. After the war, however, the crisis in labour supply brought such concerns into the mainstream of British politics. A Royal Commission on Population was established in 1944 and delivered its report in 1949. Two years earlier the government's *Economic Survey for 1947* stated clearly that 'foreign labour can make a useful contribution to our needs ... This need to increase the working population is not temporary; it is a permanent feature of our national life.' Some of the gaps in the labour market, particularly in coalmining, agriculture, textiles and the provision of domestic labour, were thus filled through the Polish Resettlement Corps and the various headings under the European Volunteer Workers (EVWs) scheme. Although many thousands came to Britain in the immediate postwar years under these projects, the selection of these individuals was far from random. In the report of the Royal Commission on Population, the question of migration came under Part 2: 'Population and the National Interest'. Tellingly, the section on inflows was entitled 'Problems of Immigration'. It suggested that 'Immigration on a large scale into a fully established society like ours could only be welcomed without reserve if the immigrants were of good human stock and were not prevented by their religion or race from intermarrying with the host population and becoming merged in it.'[3]

Most of the EVWs were deemed to meet these criteria, but black people (and, as will emerge, Jews) certainly were not. But another factor in the recruitment of white European workers was at play – these men and women from countries such as Poland, the Ukraine and Italy were aliens and therefore had few rights in British society. They could be employed as a reserve labour force and, if necessary, be dispensed with later. In contrast, black workers from the Commonwealth had British citizenship – rights confirmed in the British Nationality Act of 1948. The restrictions placed on the EVWs at the behest of British labour created distinct problems for these newcomers. The EVWs should not be employed if British labour was available and were the first to be laid off if a downturn in the economy occurred. As one Pole remembers: 'I really felt a second class citizen'. Many of the east European groups who came to Britain after the war now see themselves as well-established and are often held up to be excellent examples of integrated immigrants (in implied criticism of later, coloured arrivals). Even Salman Rushdie in his vicious attack on the many forms of British racism in *The Satanic Verses* points to 'the existence in a South London borough of a pub in which no language but Ukrainian could be heard' to indicate that British hospitality is not yet dead.[4] This perspective is important but should not disguise the strong economic and cultural opposition to the EVWs in the late 1940s and beyond which forced many to seek opportunities elsewhere. The EVWs, like the Huguenots before them, have become an idealized immigrant group and in the process hostility to them when they first arrived has been conveniently forgotten. American society was the beneficiary of both groups as a result of British intolerance.

New Commonwealth Immigrants

Although attention was still focused on white immigrants after 1945, the issue of black minorities very slowly became one of governmental and local concern. Newsreels of the arrival of the *Empire Windrush* are now frequently shown to illustrate the official welcoming of these Jamaicans who had served in the British forces or war factories. As early as 1948, however, efforts were made by the British government to discourage such movements. The official policy was not totally negative – black students, who would play an important later role in colonial government, were encouraged and efforts were made to make sure they did not encounter any discrimination in Britain.

In contrast, a mass movement of black people was seen as strictly undesirable as it would create popular disquiet, and Afro-Caribbeans and Asians were not regarded as suitable workers. In 1949 the Labour Cabinet first discussed the possibility of instituting control of coloured immigration and a committee was formed leading to a report two years later. Several important themes emerge from these interdepartmental discussions involving the Home Office, Colonial Office and Ministry of Labour. First, black people were deemed to be a problem even though they numbered only 20,000–30,000 in 1950. Second, there was a desire to avoid any impression of state racism which might alienate the colonial national movements, especially 'at the present stage of Commonwealth development'. The solution, which operated throughout the 1950s without much success, was to agree informal measures of control with the colonial governments as these emerged 'to reduce the flow at the source'.[5] Third, although the problem of discrimination was recognized, only informal, voluntary measures to combat it were proposed. It should be emphasized that although the issue of coloured immigration had been raised, it was not a major one at the national level at this early stage. It is significant, however, that the solutions considered to this 'problem' were to stop black immigration rather than to combat white racism. Only concern about black colonial opinion stopped the extension of the aliens legislation to encompass non-white Commonwealth citizens. State policy in the 1950s was marked by a neglect of domestic issues of racism, and by informal measures of control agreed with the New Commonwealth governments (the Conservative Cabinet also rejecting blatant exclusion based on grounds of colour in 1955 and 1956). But the decade also saw limited recruitment schemes for West Indian workers (such as those of the London Transport Executive and the Regional Hospital Boards) to carry out jobs no British workers would fill. These schemes also reflected the fact that the source of postwar continental labour through displaced persons and ex-prisoners of war was now no longer available.

Nevertheless, the vast majority of West Indians, Indians and Pakistanis arriving in the 1950s came independently. The climate and general greyness of Britain came as a shock to many, as did the popular hostility that awaited them. The 'Mother Country' turned out to be far less welcoming than their English-centred education had led them to believe. It would be misleading, however, to portray the new immigrants as naive. Most came to 'better themselves' away from their devastated domestic economies and there was, certainly in the case of the West Indians, a close correlation between the state of Britain's Stop-Go economy in the 1950s and the level of immigration. Indeed, it was only after the McCarren-Walter Act of 1952 restricted West Indian immigration to the United States that Britain became a major area of settlement. It should also be remembered that West Indians as well as Indians and Pakistanis harboured great desires to return. Ironically it was the pressures caused by widespread discrimination that stopped this occurring. Rather than returning 'home' with a surplus, all energies were spent on economic survival in Britain. Only when the threat of controls seemed imminent in 1960 and 1961 did the economic rationale for immigration break down to be replaced by a frantic struggle to 'beat the ban'.

Patterns of Settlement

Even in a peak year of West Indian settlement, 1956, just 30,000 arrived (Irish immigration was running at roughly double this rate). Even so, the nature of black communities in Britain was fundamentally changing. Before 1939, black communities were traditionally linked to the ports such as Liverpool, Glasgow and Cardiff. The war opened up opportunities and there was a move 'inland' which intensified after 1945. Slowly the port communities gave way in significance to settlements in the industrial conurbations in the North and Midlands. The capital continued to be a major centre of concentration but it extended beyond the classic area of immigrant concentration, the East End of London. Southall became a focus of Asian settlement and Lambeth, Camden and North Kensington were particularly important centres of Afro-Caribbean settlement. North Kensington was the location for the notorious Notting Hill riots of 1958 and it is worthy of further consideration.

The impact of the racist riots of 1958 on the black minority should not be minimized. Frank Springer, a Barbadian, recalls that 'Those years were painful, it was a terrifying ride to the edge of darkness, having to endure all the friction'.[6] Violence and the fear of violence were very real. The year after the riots a black youth, Kelso Cochrane, was brutally murdered in the area. The riots for the first time helped to ease the divisions between Jamaicans, Trinidadians, Barbadians and others and allow organizations such as the West Indian Standing Conference (1958) to come into being. Links between Afro-Caribbeans and Asians were also strengthened.

Racism and discrimination were everyday features in the lives of many Afro-Caribbean and Asian immigrants in the 1950s. The settlement of so many West Indians in the appallingly overcrowded houses of North Kensington itself reflected the unavailability of accommodation in other parts of London and the desire to find security in numbers. There was, however, another side to

Plate 23.1.   Children in Notting Hill in the 1960s. Although Notting Hill was the scene of a notorious race riot in 1958, in the 1960s it developed as a vibrant multi-cultural community, and the Notting Hill carnival is now the largest street festival in Europe.

this experience. Close and lasting friendships developed between black and white people in the area and many were offered protection by neighbours in the tense weeks of August 1958. Building on this parallel tradition of tolerance and goodwill, the Notting Hill carnival emerged in the 1960s and is now the largest street festival in Europe. The carnival also reflected the cultural vitality of North Kensington. The area, through its nightlife, developed during the 1950s its own dynamism and excitement which offered a marked contrast to the drab conformism of Britain during the 1950s. As one West Indian pensioner recalls: 'We done a lot for Britain. We bring life to them, no matter what they say ... We give all our energy and our strength and all the riches that we can get ... We give them another culture and background that they didn't have before'. Such a perspective was sadly missing from government considerations when the issue of controls was again raised at the end of the 1950s.[7]

The Control of Immigration

The connection between the Notting Hill riots and the Commonwealth Immigrants Act of 1962 has been overdrawn. The most obvious point in this respect is the four-year gap between the two. Furthermore, as late as 1960 the Conservative Home Secretary, R.A. Butler, commented that it was 'very unlikely that this country will turn away from her traditional policy of free entry'. After the riots, the Prime Minister, Harold Macmillan, wrote that 'we can, I hope, reduce the rate of immigration *without* legislation. At least, we must give this a trial.'[8] In short, the solution preferred throughout the 1950s – that of informal controls – was proposed. There was still no desire to alienate the Commonwealth unnecessarily, especially at a time when state racism in South Africa and the southern states of the US was international news and there was an intense fear of Soviet influence extending. But the continued refusal to make a public commitment to black settlers proved to be the undoing of this strategy of informal measures and general low key approaches. Immigration increased dramatically and the climate within Parliament changed. Cyril Osborne, who had campaigned to keep Britain white throughout the 1950s, was joined in the Commons after the 1959 election by a new group of Conservative MPs from the West Midlands who were strident in their demands for coloured immigration control (encouraged by pressure groups such as the Birmingham Immigration Control Association formed in 1960). In addition, and of crucial importance, was the downplaying of Commonwealth in government considerations and, as a substitute, an increasing interest in the EEC. The restraining factor of Commonwealth opinion was now removed and in 1962 the Conservatives passed the Commonwealth Immigrants Act which set up categories of entries and the use of employment vouchers. The Labour Party under the leadership of Hugh Gaitskell objected on ideological grounds to what it saw as discriminatory legislation (made blatant by the refusal to include the Irish under its terms). Nevertheless, Harold Wilson, the new Labour leader after the death of Gaitskell, first accepted the need for immigration control in 1963 and then tightened the labour permit requirements of the 1962 Act through a White Paper in 1965. It was also the Labour Party that was responsible for the Second Commonwealth Immigrants Act of 1968 aimed at excluding Kenyan Asians – British passport holders escaping from a brutal Africanization programme. The 'redefinition' of British passport holders was to be repeated in 1990 when all but a wealthy minority of Hong Kong Chinese were effectively barred from coming to Britain.

Legislation was consolidated and strengthened through the 1971 Immigration Act which brought together all the twentieth-century control measures. Through a patriarchy clause, primary immigration of non-white people was effectively ended. Ten years later another Conservative government produced a new Nationality Act which for the first time removed the principle of *Civis Britannicus Sum*. The 1988 Immigration Act further strengthened

Plate 23.2.   A 'West Indian, English, Asian Food Store'. Multi-culturalism is evident in every British high street, where food shops and restaurants established by members of ethnic minority groups have transformed tastes.

government controls and powers of deportation. It should not be assumed, however, that the domination of the Conservatives in the passing of this legislation has meant that there has been no consensus between the two major parties on issues of race and immigration. There was a tacit agreement not to raise immigration in the 1970s (both Conservatives and Labour were in favour of firm controls and wanted to avoid the racial populist/neo-Nazi National Front becoming an electoral threat) and the 1981 Nationality Act was based on a Labour Party Green Paper of 1977. In 1976 the previously weak anti-racist legislation of 1965–68 (and the quangos that went with it) were replaced by the third Race Relations Act which created the Commission for Racial Equality. The new Act outlawed both direct and indirect discrimination and is still the most powerful piece of legislation of its type in Europe. The Race Relations Bill was not opposed by the Conservatives, again stressing the consensus of the 1970s. Whether that consensus has subsequently broken down will be addressed below.

Race Relations and Discrimination

Race relations legislation has often accompanied (and acted as a sop to the critics of) immigration control based on colour discrimination. In Roy Hattersley's famous dictum in 1965, the year of the first Race Relations Act and Labour's White paper: 'Without integration limitation is inexcusable: without limitation integration is impossible.'[9] Many have suggested an alternative interpretation to that offered by Hattersley: the practice of racism by the state in keeping out black people has only served to legitimize racism in society as a whole. The existence of potentially powerful anti-discrimination legislation has been hindered by both the lack of political will to implement it and the countervailing justification of racism by the state's example. Governments since the 1960s have continued to label black people, rather than racism, as a problem. As the fiftieth anniversary of the defeat of Nazism beckons, it has been estimated by a Home Office minister that up to 330,000 incidents of racial harassment occur each year. One in ten London Asian or Afro-Caribbean households has suffered racial harassment in or near its home and one in three feels threatened by its existence. Figures for 1988–90 suggest that black ethnic minorities in Britain face an unemployment rate of 13 per cent (although West Indians, Pakistanis and Bengalis suffer far greater than Indians and African Asians) compared to 7 per cent for white people. Detailed reports of the organization PEP (Political and Economic Planning) and its successor PSI (Policy Studies Institute) on the position of black ethnic minorities in Britain from the 1960s to the early 1990s paint a gloomy picture. Although there are variations from group to group, the most obvious feature of these surveys is the depressing lack of change reported in them.[10] Black people in Britain suffer from more unemployment, poorer housing, education and health care and have little mobility within the employment market. Taken as a whole, the life chances of black people are greatly diminished compared to the white majority.

These stark facts in conjunction with the endemic nature of racial harassment make it no exaggeration, in the words of Salman Rushdie, to suggest that black people inhabit 'different worlds' in Britain.[11] Racism and discrimination still represent a hidden tradition in a country that has swallowed wholesale its own myths of decency and fair play. Yet if there is a tendency to ignore this grim reality of contemporary Britain, there is an equal danger in portraying black people simply as victims. The contribution of Britain's immigrants since 1945 and their offspring across all aspects of society has been immense. Modern youth culture, to give a popular example, displays in its music, fashion and street life a fusion of inputs from many ethnic groups. Britain, like it or not, is now blatantly a multi-cultural society – we have moved a long way from the 1950s when half the population had never seen a black person and many West Indian immigrants were touched 'for luck'. The clear diversity of modern Britain has enriched the possibilities available to enjoy life in the 1990s.

Yet it would be foolish to see multi-culturalism as straightforward and unchallenging. Rather than the superficial appreciation of the 'three S's – saris, samosas and steel bands' – there will be real dilemmas in the future as the Rushdie affair has graphically illustrated. The controversy over *The Satanic Verses* involved critical matters such as the conflict between liberal individualism and ethnic particularity; freedom of expression and the sensitivities of members of a much-abused ethnic minority religion; the idea of Christian Britain with its established church and the concept of a religiously plural society. There are not and will not be easy answers to these problems and pain and suffering have been caused on all 'sides' of the Rushdie Affair. Historians have been slow to accept that questions of ethnicity, race and immigration have played an important part in the British past before the Second World War. Since 1945 these issues have intensified in importance – to ignore them as the century comes to a close is to bury one's head in the sand and to hark back to a mythical mono-cultural past society that in reality never existed.

In focus: Holocaust Survivors in Postwar Britain

The choosing of a group who numbered, at most, several thousand, may seem unusual as a case study in a country that has seen the immigration of literally millions of individuals. There are, however, several important reasons for this focus. First, immigration to Britain since 1945 has been assumed to have consisted of those of colour. Second, government opposition to their arrival in any large numbers reveals the continuity of forms of anti-alienism which emerged in the late nineteenth century. Third, their popular treatment in Britain indicates that the Holocaust, far from making racism unrespectable in postwar Britain, was in fact little understood for many years after 1945.

Of the refugees in the displaced persons camps in postwar Europe, roughly a quarter were Jewish survivors of the Holocaust. These camps provided many of the people recruited for the EVW schemes yet perhaps less than 1 per cent of those who came to Britain from 1945 to 1950 were Jewish. This discrepancy can partly be explained by the desire of many Jews to emigrate to the United States and Palestine but other factors were at work. As David Cesarani has illustrated, Jews were still viewed as problematic immigrants. This was partly because it was assumed, according to one senior Foreign Office official, that there would be 'opposition from public opinion at home' if Jewish displaced persons were recruited. It was also felt that East European Jews were untrustworthy and would make poor workers. Such views had wide currency in the British labour movement. When approached by Jewish trade unionists to help their co-religionists 'languishing in the most dire conditions' in the displaced persons camp, the TUC responded that the idea that these survivors could help the British economy was 'wide of the mark'.[12]

Holocaust Survivors in Postwar Britain (continued)

Ernest Bevin, the Foreign Secretary, was particularly hostile to the few Jewish survivors who reached Britain after 1945. He told the Home Secretary late in 1945 that he was 'anxious to avoid the concentration of large numbers of refugees from Europe, especially Jewish refugees, in the towns'. Bevin also thought the Jewish displaced persons 'might be steered into agriculture or any other sphere where they would be most useful'. Jews, like the blacks, were seen as undesirable immigrants because they would not assimilate and were of inferior stock. Their general exclusion from postwar Britain indicates the racialization of immigration policy and the continuation of state policies dating from the Aliens Act of 1905.

The treatment of the few survivors reaching Britain is also revealing. Kitty Hart, a Polish Jew who was sent to Auschwitz as a fifteen year old, came to Birmingham after the war from a Quaker relief camp. She recalls that 'everybody in England would be talking about personal war experiences for months, even years, after hostilities had ceased. But we, who had been pursued over Europe by a mutual enemy, and come close to extermination at the hands of that enemy, were not supposed to embarrass people by saying a word.' Another young Jew who had survived Westerbork and Belsen had similar experiences in London: 'I found it better not to talk about the concentration camps, and not to do or say anything that would make me appear different from anyone else. People simply didn't understand what we'd been through, and they didn't make allowances for anything ... From the time I left the camp I was shunted about, and there was nothing solid, nothing firm in my life; and I am angry when I look back and consider how we were treated when we came to England'.[13]

There were a small minority of people – Jewish and non- Jewish – who *did* appreciate what the young survivors had been through and made great efforts to help them come to terms with what had happened as well as rebuilding their lives in Britain. Most survivors kept quiet and only now are facing up to their past in a British culture that has only recently attempted to confront the horrors of the Jewish catastrophe during the war. That some survivors have experienced success and contributed greatly to their adopted homeland is a tribute to their fortitude. The overall treatment of Holocaust survivors, however, indicates both the difficulties which British society has had in dealing with the needs and requirements of vulnerable ethnic minorities since the war and the desire of the state to allow entry only to the 'right kind' of immigrant.

Interpretations: Is Contemporary Britain Racist?

Are issues of race and immigration of only minor significance in contemporary Britain or are they central to questions of national identity underlying all political questions? A case for the former can be made by indicating the 'failure' of racist politics in Britain. Whilst *Le Front National* can command the support of between 10 and 20 per cent of the French electorate, the combined might of the National Front and the British National Party in the 1992 General Election received a grand total of 11,821 votes. Not one parliamentary seat has been won by the National Front since its formation in 1967. The electoral support for right-wing extremism has been so minimal in postwar Britain that not even the most generous system of proportional representation would have changed their abject failure at the ballot box.

Further support for the marginalization of race/immigration issues could be marshalled through the case of Enoch Powell. Powell, in his famous 'Rivers of Blood' speech in Birmingham in April 1968, predicted racial violence and the ultimate destruction of Britain if coloured immigration were not stopped. Later that year at Eastbourne, he added his mystical vision of the nature of English national identity: 'the West Indian does not by being born in England, become an Englishman. In law, he becomes a United Kingdom citizen by birth [changed later with the Nationality Act of 1981]; in fact he is a West Indian or Asian still'. Powell had his parliamentary and public supporters in 1968, but reassurance has been found with regard to the unrespectability of racism in Britain because after his speech he was immediately dismissed from the Shadow Cabinet by Edward Heath.[14] Powell could therefore be seen as a test case – public comments deemed to be racist are beyond the pale of respectability, even if they carry popular approval. Politicians since Powell have learnt the lesson. Such issues are not on the agenda and only Conservative eccentrics such as Sir Nicholas Fairbairn (April 1992) or Winston Churchill (May 1993) have been stupid enough to try to resurrect Powellism. Black ethnic minorities support all three major parties and since 1987 (four members in that year, six in 1992) have had a sizeable presence in Parliament. Zig Layton-Henry provides an optimistic scenario suggesting that issues of immigration were given little prominence in the 1992 campaign and that the 'results of the election seemed to indicate that black candidates were more widely accepted by the electorate than ever before'. Layton-Henry even downplays the role of racism in the defeat of the black Conservative candidate, John Taylor, at Cheltenham (arguing it was part of a natural, regional swing to the Liberal Democrats).[15]

An alternative scenario has been offered by those who have stressed the cultural roots of British racism and the crucial importance of race in the formation of an exclusive, nationalist ideology of 'Englishness'. Rather than dying with Powell in 1968, it is argued that much of his vision came to fruition with the prime ministership of Margaret Thatcher from 1979. Thatcher had broken the tacit silence on issues of race and immigration at the start of 1978 with her infamous remarks that the British were 'really rather afraid that this country might be swamped by people with a different culture'.[16] Thatcher had no need to explain to the electorate who these people were – immigration debates since the 1960s had focused almost exclusively on those of colour.

Some have credited Thatcher with the effective destruction of the National Front as a credible force in the 1979 election. Moreover, it is argued, firm immigration control has subsequently stopped the growth of far right groupings in contrast to the rest of Europe. There are, however, problems with this analysis. First, far right groups in Britain since 1945 have always been hindered by their connection to the Nazis. The Second World War has an enormously important place in British popular memory and anything that is construed as an attempt to revive Nazism is doomed to failure. Second, talk of a far right revival in western Europe has been overblown. The one major exception is France, but elsewhere neo-fascist groups are receiving only 3 or 4 per cent support in opinion polls. Third, the Conservatives under Margaret Thatcher did not desire to tighten immigration and nationality laws simply in order to limit the success of the National Front. They did so because such policies, including the Nationality Act of 1981, were part of their political and cultural vision. Indeed, their legislation throughout the 1980s, which gave Britain the most restrictive immigration and asylum laws within the European Community, were passed at a point when the National Front was almost defunct.

The further critique of the Thatcher years is that the progress made in the area of multi-culturalism has been reversed and replaced with an insular English nationalism. This is particularly clear in the important sphere of education where the new National Curriculum in subjects such as History, English and Music has concentrated on a mono-cultural interpretation and downplayed a pluralistic approach. Ethnic minorities are being pushed to conform but at the same time they are still viewed as an alien, un-English presence. This was particularly emphasized in the inner-city disturbances of the 1980s where black youths – rather than issues of poverty, appalling housing conditions and unemployment – were seen to be the problem. Paul Gilroy and others have argued that the high level of white involvement in the disturbances was conveniently ignored in the attempt, particularly by the popular media, to criminalize and pathologize black youth. The British state, argue some cultural critics, having effectively sealed itself off from a black flood from the outside, was now beginning to engage in internal colonialization with the police playing a major role in the process. It is argued that there is now no need to actually mention black people explicitly – code words such as the importance of maintaining law and order are all that is necessary to tap into a populist, racist sentiment. Robert Miles and Annie Phizacklea go even further and predict that now the reserve army of black labour is no longer required, a policy of mass 'repatriation' is the next step for the government to take. Such a deterministic Marxist analysis is open to major criticism. There is a downplaying of ideological constraints involved in what would be openly racist state policies against largely British citizens. Nevertheless, up to a third of those asked in opinion polls have said they would support some measures of 'repatriation'.[17]

Dealing with the place of racism in British society is always a difficult problem. Britain's reputation is at stake and there has been a tendency to deny that any problem exists. Britain is not Nazi Germany but it does not follow from this that it is therefore immune to intolerance. Since 1945 expressions of racism on biological grounds have become unrespectable but new expressions of hostility have emerged based on cultural rather than 'scientific' grounds. In Britain, however, cultural objections to immigrant and minority groups such as Jews have a long history – hence the ease with which prewar policies continued after 1945 in the selection of newcomers. Since 1945 an almost totally hegemonic anti-Nazism has not precluded the existence of violent racism and discrimination which has now reached endemic proportions. There is a need to move beyond the complacent belief that Britain is 'different' and away from the xenophobic assumption that racism is only a problem on the Continent.

Bibliographical Note

After the Second World War, social anthropologists dominated the study of racial minorities in Britain. This led to works such as Kenneth Little, *Negroes in Britain* (London, 1948) and Michael Banton, *The Coloured Quarter* (London, 1955). Sociologists were increasingly drawn to the question of 'race relations' from the 1950s and works such as Ruth Glass, *Newcomers* (London, 1960) and Sheila Patterson, *Dark Strangers* (London, 1963) were important liberal-inspired accounts of postwar West Indian arrivals in Britain. It was not until the 1970s that historians became involved in the subject, led by Colin Holmes at the University of Sheffield. The historical journal *Immigrants and Minorities* was started in 1982 and contains a host of valuable articles relating to the post-1945 period. Colin Holmes, *John Bull's Island: Immigration and British Society, 1871–1971* (London, 1988) is the most comprehensive history of the subject. Extremely valuable textbook accounts that take the story up to the present include John Solomos, *Race and Racism in Contemporary Britain* (London, 2nd edn, 1993) and Zig Layton-Henry, *The Politics of Immigration: Immigration, 'Race' and 'Race' Relations in Post-war Britain* (London, 1992). Important histories of individual minority communities include Terri Colpi, *The Italian Factor: the Italian Community in Great Britain* (Edinburgh, 1991); Geoffrey Alderman, *Modern British Jewry* (Oxford, 1992); Muhammad Anwar, *The Myth of Return: Pakistanis in Britain* (London, 1979) and John Western, *A Passage to England: Barbadian Londoners Speak of Home* (London, 1992). A complex intellectual history of British race thinking is provided by Paul Rich, *Race and Empire in British Politics* (Cambridge, 1986).

Those involved in cultural studies, especially in Birmingham at the Centre for Contemporary Cultural Studies, produced important works on race from the late 1970s – see especially Paul Gilroy, *There Ain't No Black in the Union Jack: the Cultural Politics of Race and Nation* (London, 1987). James Donald and Ali Rattansi (eds), *Race, Culture and Difference* (London, 1992) and Peter Braham, Alli Rattansi and Richard Skellington (eds), *Racism and Antiracism: Inequalities, Opportunities and Policies* (London, 1992) provide key essays reflecting the cross-disciplinary and sophisticated approach that now represents the latest work in the area.

Notes

1. Joynson-Hicks, 6 February 1925 in Board of Deputies of British Jews archive, E3/78, Greater London Record Office; Bernard Porter, *The Refugee Question in Mid-Victorian Politics* (Cambridge, 1979) p. 2.

2. Fabian Society, *Population and the People: A National Policy* (London, 1945) p. 49.

3. *Economic Survey for 1947* (Cmd 7046, 1947) p. 28; *Royal Commission on Population: Report* (Cmd 7695) p. 124.

4. Polish Reminiscence Group, *Passport to Exile: The Polish Way to London* (London, 1988) p. 15; Salman Rushdie, *The Satanic Verses* (New York, 1992; orig. 1988) p. 398.

5. See Public Record Office CO 537/2572 and 2573; CAB 129/28,17,41 and 44 all reproduced in Ronald Hyam (ed.), *The Labour Government and the End of Empire 1945–1951* Part 4 *Race Relations and the Commonwealth* (London, 1992) pp. 13–47.

6. John Western, *A Passage to England: Barbadian Londoners Speak of Home* (London, 1992) p. 65.

7. Pam Schweitzer (ed.), *A Place to Stay: Memories of Pensioners from Many Lands* (London, 1984) p. 35.

8. Paul Foot, *Immigration and Race in British Politics* (Harmondsworth, 1965) p. 134; Harold Macmillan, *At the End of the Day, 1961–1963* (London, 1973) p. 75.

9. E.J.B. Rose (ed.), *Colour and Citizenship: A Report on British Race Relations* (London, 1969) p. 229.

10. Many of the PEP/PSI findings and latest findings are reported in Trevor Jones, *Britain's Ethnic Minorities: an Analysis of the Labour Force Survey* (London, 1993).

11. Salman Rushdie, 'The new empire within Britain' in his *Imaginary Homelands: Essays and Criticism 1981–1991* (London, 1991) pp. 129–38.

12. David Cesarani, *Justice Delayed: How Britain Became a Refuge for Nazi War Criminals* (London, 1992) p. 79; TUC archives, Box 324, Modern Record Centre, University of Warwick.

13. Chuter Ede to Dennys, 19 November 1945 and Bevin to Isaacs, 21 February 1946 in PRO LAB 8/99; Kitty Hart, *Return to Auschwitz* (New York, 1985) pp. 11–12; Anton Gill, *The Journey Back From Hell* (London, 1988) pp. 152–4.

14. B. Smithies and P. Fiddick (eds), *Enoch Powell on Immigration* (London, 1969).

15. Zig Layton-Henry, *The Politics of Immigration: Immigration, 'Race' and 'Race' Relations in Post-war Britain* (Oxford, 1992) p. 120. There was significant local Conservative opposition to the appointment of Taylor at Cheltenham and the defeated candidate reluctantly acknowledged that racism (in spite of his impeccably 'English' behaviour) was a major factor in his defeat.

16. Thatcher on *World in Action*, ITV, 30 January 1978.

17. Paul Gilroy, *There Ain't No Black in the Union Jack: The Cultural Politics of Race and Nation* (London, 1987); Centre for Contemporary Cultural Studies (eds), *The Empire Strikes Back* (London, 1982); A. Sivanandan, *A Different Hunger* (London, 1982); Annie Phizacklea and Robert Miles, *White Man's Country: Racism in British Politics* (London, 1984).

24 Religion and 'Secularization'

John Wolffe

Shortly after the end of the Second World War, Mass-Observation conducted a study of popular attitudes to religion in an unspecified London borough. It was concluded that:

> Not more than one person in ten ... is at all closely associated with any of the churches, and about two-thirds never or practically never go to Church. The majority, however – four out of five women and two out of three men – give at least verbal assent to the possibility of there being a God, and most of the rest express doubt rather than disbelief. Uncompromising disbelievers in a Deity amount to about one in twenty.[1]

The somewhat negative tone with which this quotation opens illustrates the widespread perception of the twentieth century as a period in which religion became marginal to everyday life. However almost any other activity that attracted the committed involvement of up to a tenth of the population, the passive sympathy of two-thirds to four-fifths of a sample, and was totally rejected by only one-twentieth of respondents, would be regarded as a successful and influential historical force. Thus we confront immediately the problem of how to interpret the evidence regarding the place of religion in the life of the people of Britain during the decades after 1939: should we dwell on how far the 'tide of faith' had gone out, or concentrate our attention rather on how much water remained in the sea?

The view of the twentieth century as an era of decline in organized religion is one that can superficially be supported by sequences of statistics such as those in Table 24.1. During the first half of the century near stability in absolute numbers in the Church of England and the Methodist Churches masked significant decline in their proportional support in the population. From the 1960s falls in both absolute and relative terms were steep and unmistakable. The sequence for the Church of Scotland, however, indicates the danger of overgeneralization: here there was a modest advance in numbers in the first quarter of the century, and even in the 1950s the pattern was stability rather than decline. Other regional and national contrasts were very marked: in Northern Ireland in 1971 more than 90 per cent of the population identified with a particular denominational group.[2] There were also significant gender differences: around 1980 female churchgoers were 55 per cent of the total in England, 62 per cent in Scotland and 63 per cent in Wales. We shall explore further below the difficulty of interpreting such statistics, but for the moment they represent an important caution against viewing trends in religious commitment in a uniform fashion.

Table 24.1. Membership of selected religious denominations, 1900–80 (in m with % of total population in brackets)

	Church of England		Church of Scotland		Methodist	
1900	2.90	(8.9)	1.15	(25.7)	0.77	(2.1)
1924	3.54	(9.3)	1.30	(26.6)	0.83	(1.9)
1939	3.39	(8.2)	1.29	(26.2)	0.80	(1.7)
1950	2.96	(6.7)	1.27	(24.9)	0.74	(1.5)
1960	2.86	(6.2)	1.30	(25.1)	0.73	(1.4)
1970	2.56	(5.6)	1.15	(22.0)	0.62	(1.1)
1980	1.82	(3.7)	0.96	(18.7)	0.49	(0.9)

Notes: (a) The figures for the Church of England are calculated as a percentage of the population of England and Wales, but do not include the Church in Wales. They are electoral roll numbers, which first became available in 1924: the figure for 1900 is an estimate for comparison extrapolated from the Easter Day communicant figures for that year. Figures for the Church of Scotland are given as a percentage of the population of Scotland; those for Methodists relate to the whole of Great Britain.

(b) Calculations are based on the nearest available census data; that for 1939 is extrapolated from the 1931 and 1951 censuses.

(c) Figures for the Church of Scotland and the Methodists include all the bodies amalgamated to form these churches as constituted at the present time.

The Early Twentieth Century

Nevertheless these figures indicate that for some important religious groups the period between 1900 and 1939 was a watershed. The Victorian era had seen a great flowering of religious energies, still apparent today in its massive legacy of church buildings. This did not produce anything approaching universal churchgoing, but in the face of the challenges of industrialization, urbanization, and rapid population growth, the proportion of commitment and observance remained approximately constant at least until the 1880s.

Thereafter, especially among Nonconformists, relative decline set in, but the Church of England proved to be initially more resilient, and it was not until after the turn of the century that absolute numbers declined.

Explanations of the loss of Victorian momentum are numerous and can only be noted briefly here. It is frequently argued that the cultural impact of Darwinian ideas of human origins, and historical and moral criticism of the Bible progressively undermined the ideological credibility of Christianity. From the perspective of social history the relative success of the churches in the nineteenth century has been attributed to their importance as 'midwives' of the transition to an industrialized, class-based society, and their subsequent decline to social redundancy once that process was complete. A related argument is to point to the growing importance of the state in taking over administrative, educational, and social welfare functions previously exercised by religious organizations. Explanation is also couched in terms of a crisis of morale within organized Christianity itself, with theological uncertainty and institutional ossification feeding off each other.

On the other hand, especially outside England, significant signs of religious vitality remained. The continuing loyalty of around a quarter of the Scottish population to the Church of Scotland was probably assisted by the completion in 1929 of a process of Presbyterian reunification which facilitated the identification of church and nation. Similarly the disestablishment of the (Anglican) Church in Wales in 1920 freed it from the appearance of being an alien English institution and its communicant numbers had increased by more than 20 per cent by 1939. The Roman Catholic Church also benefited from an enduring sense of community identity among the Irish population in Britain: as late as the 1960s total Mass attendances in England and Wales were more than two million. In a more diffuse and limited fashion the Church of England was also shielded somewhat from decline by the patriotic loyalties it inspired as a national church.

The impact of the two world wars on religious life was an ambivalent one. To a limited extent a sense of spiritual crusade rekindled a form of Christian devotion in both 1914 and 1939–40. The observances of Armistice Day and Remembrance Sunday were to provide an enduring link between the churches and the wider community. The Second World War also gave a prophetic status and national prominence to Christian leaders such as William Temple, briefly Archbishop of Canterbury from 1942 to 1944 and George Bell, Bishop of Chichester, a vigorous opponent of the bombing of German cities by the Royal Air Force. On the other hand not only did the wars disrupt the normal habits of Christian practice, but for many they challenged conventional theological assumptions. Experience of the Western Front in the First World War tested to the limit belief in the providence and care of God; the horror of the Nazi concentration camps in the Second World War again led many to doubt either God's omnipotence or His goodness. It is certainly observable that the 1940s saw rather sharper falls in denominational memberships than the interwar period had done, although the situation stabilized again in the 1950s.

The Limitations of Statistics

How much do the dry bones of the figures for membership really tell us about the religious life of the British people since 1939? Certainly they indicate significant trends over time, but the information that, say, 6.7 per cent of the population of England and Wales in 1950 had their names on the electoral roll of a Church of England parish tells us little if it is taken in isolation from other evidence. On the one hand people could identify themselves with a Christian denomination for social rather than spiritual reasons (although this is in itself an interesting phenomenon for the historian); on the other the widespread perception that 'You do not need to go to church to be a Christian' suggests that membership statistics may significantly understate popular religious belief. Certainly such figures routinely excluded one very significant group: children judged too young to make a formal profession of faith or undertake the responsibilities of church membership. Their attendance at religious worship was often involuntary and frequently ceased in the mid to late teens, but not before it had left them with a certain deposit of diffuse Christian ideas.

Influence of this kind helps to explain the high proportion of vaguely theistic belief noted by the Mass-Observation researchers in 1947, and also evident in the opinion poll and survey evidence summarized in Table 24.2. This has to be regarded with caution because a great deal depends on the phrasing of questions, which differed slightly between the sources used in the table. The general impression is of downward drift in the extent of belief, especially in the perception regarding the nature of Jesus that defines a broadly orthodox Christian. Even in the 1980s, however, the extent of belief in some kind of God had not changed radically from that prevalent in the late 1940s.

Table 24.2. Opinion poll and survey returns on religious belief (%)

	God	Belief in Jesus as Son of God	Life after death
1947	84		49
1957	78	71	54
1963	71	60	53
1973	74		37
1982	73	43	40

Sources: George H. Gallup, *The Gallup International Public Opinion Polls: Great Britain 1937–1975* (2 vols, New York, Random House, 1976), I, pp. 166, 405, 682; II, pp. 1250–1; Helen Krarup, *Conventional Religion and Common Religion in Leeds, Interview Schedule: Basic Frequencies by Question* (Leeds, University of Leeds [Department of Sociology], Religious Research Papers, 12 [1982]), pp. 46, 48–9.

Quantitative evidence is helpful in pointing up both significant changes and notable continuities in the history of religion in Britain since the Second World War. Even more than in other fields of social history, however, it is ultimately something of a blunt and potentially treacherous instrument. It accordingly needs to be complemented by a brief survey of other major developments.

The 1950s and 1960s

As the figures in the tables indicate, the 1950s were indeed a period of near stability in religious life. Geoffrey Fisher, Archbishop of Canterbury from 1945 to 1961, was distinguished more by administrative acumen than prophetic vision, a make-up shared by his Roman Catholic counterparts, Cardinals Griffin and Godfrey. Such leaders generally seemed well-suited to their times. The machinery of institutional Christianity was kept in fairly good order, and, even if there was little sign that past decline was being reversed, the loyalty of the faithful was nourished and retained. The Billy Graham crusades in the middle of the decade were a serious attempt to evangelize the unchurched, but their most enduring result was probably a reawakening of spiritual fervour among existing congregations. Meanwhile Christianity seemed assured of a prominent place in national and cultural life: in 1953 Elizabeth II was crowned queen amidst the glories of Anglican ceremonial; the novels and theological writings of C.S. Lewis enjoyed great popularity; while the building of a new Coventry cathedral, consecrated in 1962, became a potent symbol of reconstruction after the horrors of war.

Before the end of the decade, however, signs of change were in the air. In January 1959 the recently-elected Pope John XXIII announced the summoning of a general council of the Roman Catholic Church, which eventually convened in Rome in October 1962, and lasted until the end of 1965. The Council transformed the nature of Roman Catholic liturgy and in 1967 Pope Paul VI authorized the saying of Mass in the vernacular. There was a general softening of the Roman Catholic Church's authoritarian ethos, and a reformulation of doctrine in terms that drew closer to other Christians and hence stimulated ecumenical activity. In 1968, however, the publication of Paul VI's encyclical *Humanae Vitae*, condemning artificial methods of contraception, indicated that the process of reform had its limits and gave rise to widespread conflict and demoralization in the Roman Catholic Church. In the meantime controversy of a rather different kind had been stirred by the publication in 1963 of a short book by the Anglican Bishop of Woolwich, John Robinson, entitled *Honest to God*. Faced with the secularity of South London, Robinson argued for a new theological language that would make sense for men and women outside the churches and implied a fundamental rethinking of traditional images of God and the supernatural. Moreover such change and controversy in the religious world both reflected and contributed to the general social and cultural climate of radical questioning and reform characteristic of the 1960s. In particular the arguments over *Humanae Vitae* related to a much more widespread secular climate of change in sexual mores, in which relationships outside marriage lost much of their social stigma, and abortion and homosexual relations between consenting adults were legalized. In this environment even more liberal Christians struggled not to seem out of touch.

Britain's final retreat from empire in the 1960s also had important implications for religious consciousness. During the late nineteenth and early twentieth centuries a sense of imperial civilizing mission had combined potently with Christian evangelistic zeal to give ideological legitimation to British control over non-European territories. In 1947 the granting of independence to India and Pakistan had removed a key support of this structure of cultural assumptions; in the 1960s the 'wind of change' in Africa took this process much further. Britain was left less sure of herself, her identity and her role in the world, and, given the extent to which religion had earlier been bound up with patriotism, national uncertainty contributed to the climate of religious questioning. Meanwhile ever-increasing facility of travel and communication heightened awareness of religions other than Christianity in Britain, as in the West generally. Buddhism, in particular, gained a following among the indigenous population of the United Kingdom.

Religious Minorities and Christian Reassertion

Moreover, one important legacy of empire remained to challenge traditional assumptions at home. Up to the 1950s Britain had been a 'Christian' country in the sense that for the vast majority of the population Christianity was the only obvious organized religious option. True, there was a long-standing Jewish community, numbering about 300,000 in 1920 and rising to about 450,000 by the 1960s, but this was religiously self-contained and did not expect or seek converts from the majority population. By the mid 1960s, however, substantial numbers of Hindus, Muslims and Sikhs had arrived in Britain, mainly from the Indian subcontinent and East Africa (see Chapter 23). Initially at least these groups resembled the Jews in their relative isolation from 'mainstream' religion and culture, but gradually their presence began to diversify the range of religious options apparent to the people of Britain. Table 24.3 indicates the approximate size of these communities, whose total numbers by the 1980s were approaching two million, a comparable figure to the number of active Anglicans in England. It should be borne in mind, however, that table 24.3 identifies ethnic communities rather than those actively practising their religion, who were likely to be significantly less numerous. Thus an assertion such as the claim that 'there are more Muslims than Methodists' is only a half-truth because it does not necessarily compare like with like. Moreover, the extent of the impact of ethnic minority religions varied substantially over the country in reflection of the geography of settlement itself, concentrated in London and the other major cities, notably Birmingham, Bradford and Leicester. In rural and small town Britain, it remained possible, even in the late 1980s, for people to live their daily lives without ever encountering an adherent of a religion other than Christianity.

Table 24.3. Estimates of minority religious populations in Britain *c.*1988

Ba'hais	5,000+
Hare Krishna	10,000+
Hindus	300,000+
Jains	20,000
Jews	350,000
Muslims-South Asians	700,000
Muslims-Middle Eastern/African	200,000
Sikhs	300,000
Unification Church	1,400
Zoroastrians	5,000

Sources: Kim Knott, 'Other major religious traditions' and 'New religious movements', in Terence Thomas (ed.), *The British: their Religious Beliefs and Practices 1800–1986* (London, 1988); G. Parsons (ed.), *The Growth of Religious Diversity: Britain from 1945, Volume I Traditions* (London, 1993).

The legacy of the 1960s proved to be an ambivalent one. Although, as we have seen, statistical measures of the extent of religious commitment and practice were set firmly on a downward trend, there were three important contrary tendencies. Firstly, among those still identifying with organized religion levels of commitment tended to increase. In particular among Christians there was a resurgence of evangelical forms of belief and practice, characterized by strong emphasis on the authority of the Bible, and a stress on personal conversion and commitment. During the 1970s evangelicalism gained further stimulus from the charismatic movement which claimed the direct inspiration and prompting of the Holy Spirit, and contributed to a wider trend to freer and more culturally 'relevant' forms of worship. Thus, while overall church membership declined, support for evangelical and charismatic churches grew substantially, masking an even steeper falling off in numbers affiliated to 'Catholic' and 'liberal' churches. The overall strength of Christianity was also reinforced by the relatively high levels of commitment

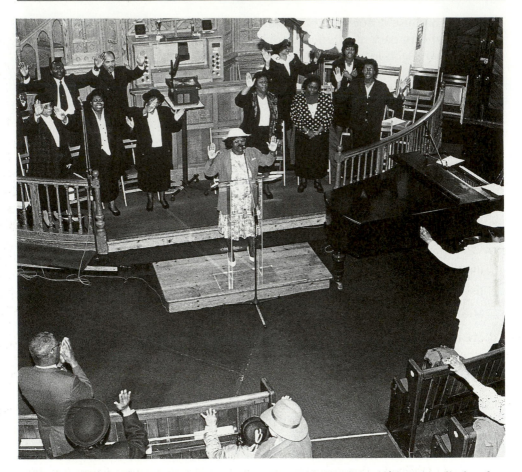

Plate 24.1. The Tooting New Testament Assembly, 1993. Since the 1970s evangelical and charismatic churches have bucked the declining trend in Christian worship. Afro-Caribbean immigrants have been particularly influential in establishing new charismatic churches

among Afro-Caribbean settlers in Britain. These often felt themselves 'frozen out' of existing 'white' churches, but developed their own forms of vigorous religious expression, predominantly, but not exclusively, charismatic in character. Parallel developments were evident among Muslims (see below), Hindus, Sikhs, Jains and others, who during the 1970s and 1980s increasingly developed formal religious organizations, publications and buildings. These helped to stimulate and sustain higher levels of practice and commitment.

Secondly, the period after 1970 was one of considerable religious innovation. Within Christianity the trends noted in the previous paragraph gave rise to what was, in effect, a new denomination, the independent or house churches. There were also numerous New Religious Movements: 450 or so have been traced during the period since the Second World War,[3] but these became much more diverse and prominent in the last two decades of the period. The adherents of organizations such as the Unification Church ('Moonies') and the Hare Krishna movement were widely in evidence witnessing on the streets. Considerable controversy followed, partly because of various well-publicized cases of alleged 'brain-washing' of recruits, but also because the absolute claims to the loyalty of their devotees made by such bodies were an implicit challenge to the secularity and conventional Christianity of the majority of the population. In the 1980s religious innovation took a further turn with the emergence of the loose network of spiritualities and worldviews collectively known as the New Age.

Thirdly, in the 1980s religion gained increasing prominence in public life. In 1982 Pope John Paul II made a high-profile visit to Britain which attracted considerable interest from the media. In 1984 widespread controversy was stirred when David Jenkins, the bishop-designate of Durham, publicly expressed doubts regarding the Virgin birth and bodily resurrection of Christ. The drama was heightened when a major fire broke out at York Minster during a thunderstorm shortly after Jenkins's consecration in the building, provoking not altogether flippant suggestions that divine wrath was being manifested. The interesting feature of the Jenkins affair was not that a bishop was rethinking central Christian doctrines – Bishop Robinson had said more radical things two decades before – but that the media and its audience still seemed to find such episcopal utterances to be worthy of note. Similarly, discussions over the role of women in religious organizations, above all the controversy over their ordination to the Anglican priesthood, attracted widespread public interest. Religion also acquired greater prominence in political life, notably in disagreements between church leaders and supporters of the Conservative government over the most appropriate means of marking victory in the Falklands War of 1982, and over the relative merits of schemes to regenerate the inner cities. In 1988 Margaret Thatcher took a step without obvious precedent among postwar prime ministers in setting out the religious basis of her approach to politics in a speech to the General Assembly of the Church of Scotland. Finally, in 1989, hostile Muslim reaction to Salman Rushdie's novel *The Satanic Verses* stirred a controversy which raised profound questions about the nature of British culture, the place of minority groups within it, the role of religion in the contemporary world, and the standing of Britain abroad.

In focus: Muslims in Britain

As the largest single religious minority in postwar Britain, Muslims serve as a particularly good example of the social and historiographical issues raised by the presence of substantial non-Christian groups in Britain. It should be noted that a Muslim presence in this country can be traced back to the late nineteenth century: a mosque was built in Woking in 1889 and communities

Plate 24.2. Inside the Bristol Jamia mosque. Mosque registration figures (p. 437) almost certainly understate actual numbers, given the likely existence of numerous unofficial house mosques. By the 1980s more purpose built mosques were appearing, an indication of the increasing stability of muslim communities and of their growing economic resources.

Muslims in Britain (continued)

developed in several ports as a result of the settlement of seamen from the Middle East and India. Postwar immigration massively increased Muslim numbers. Estimates of the total size of the population have varied enormously, a reflection of the difficulty of obtaining reliable figures in the absence of any census question on religious affiliation and a lack of the kind of membership figures for mosques that exist for Christian denominations. Calculations are normally based on the numbers born in such predominantly Muslim countries as Pakistan, a basis that becomes less reliable with the passing years, as a second and third generation have been born in Britain. Furthermore such estimates cannot measure actual religious practice, although inferences can be drawn from samples such as that of Muslim householders in Handsworth (Birmingham) in 1981, 45 per cent of whom attended public worship at least once a week,[4] a substantially higher proportion than for any major Christian group outside Northern Ireland.

Muslims arrived in Britain with a legacy of historic division among themselves, partly from the traditional divergences of Islam, between Sunni and Shi'a, Sufi and legalist; partly from the range of movements that developed in the Indian subcontinent during the nineteenth century aiming to preserve the faith intact in the face of British rule; partly from the linguistic and cultural variations among those coming from different parts of the world, and different regions of India, Pakistan, and Bangladesh. Faced with the fragmented nature of a religion whose adherents made a great virtue of their professed solidarity, Muslim leaders – often self-appointed – took a number of initiatives designed to develop some united organization. Such attempts, however, often compounded the problem that they were designed to solve, as organizations like the Union of Muslim Organizations, the Islamic Foundation, and the Muslim Institute were unable to gain anything approaching universal support.

The growth of mosque registrations is a good indicator not so much of the numbers of nominal Muslims as of the extent of organized religious activity. Up to 1965 there had only been thirteen mosque registrations in Britain, but by 1985 this total had swelled to 338; 239 of which had occurred in the decade since 1976.[5] The typical mosque was not purpose-built, but was rather a converted terrace house, hall or warehouse. By the 1980s larger traditionally Islamic mosques began to be built, giving enhanced dignity and stability to the community, but in some cases, such as the Regent's Park Mosque in London (1978), these were somewhat remote from the lives of ordinary Muslims.

For Muslims, as for other recently-settled religious groups, the surrounding society and culture presented serious challenges. Were they to isolate themselves indefinitely from a Britain that increasingly looked like a permanent home, or to run the risk of their religion being eroded by assimilation to Christianity or secularity? The issues were complicated by the

Muslims in Britain (continued)

difficulty of distinguishing clearly between Muslim religious teaching and cultural practice, a confusion which was most apparent in relation to the emotive interlocked issues of the regulation of sexuality and the status of women. Education too became a controversial matter, as children of different religions went to school alongside each other and Muslim parents grew more articulate in their demands for distinctively Islamic instruction.

By the 1980s Muslims had become a major force in the religious life of Britain, but *The Satanic Verses* affair was to underscore their own sense of insecurity, and conversely, the feeling of the rest of the population that Islam had become a 'threat'. This latter perception was a revealing one because it points up the extent to which a predominantly secular society still felt itself challenged by religion.

Historical Interpretations: Has Britain been Secularized?

The concept of secularization has been advanced by sociologists and, less frequently, historians as a general model for explaining and describing what is portrayed as the gradual marginalization of religion in 'modern' society. The aim is to provide a wider context for immediately obvious processes such as declining church attendance and membership. Secularization, it is suggested, is inherent in the long-term reorganization of society and culture consequent upon the 'enlightenment' and the 'industrial revolution'. Eighteenth and nineteenth-century intellectuals dethroned theology from her position as 'queen of the sciences' and developed modes of understanding the world that did not need resort to supernatural agency. Meanwhile industrialization and urbanization were removing the great majority of the population from an environment subject to the vagaries of nature, and substituting the artificial rhythms and rationality of the factory and the office. Even though death remained ultimately inescapable, medical advance meant that it was for most people postponed until remote old age and removed from the family circle into the clinical environment of hospitals. The twentieth century saw the mushrooming of alternative forms of leisure – the cinema, professional sport, the motor car, television – that distracted people from church attendance on Sundays and filled their consciousness to the exclusion of spiritual concerns. All these factors meant that for the majority of the population religious ideas and activities became much less prominent. Moreover, the argument runs, even the church itself became secularized, in that it came to accept the values of the surrounding culture and adjusted its teaching to suit its audience. Where there was continuing religious vitality and activity this was only a subcultural phenomenon, sustained by those who had opted out of the mainstream of society in order to continue a supernaturalist view of the world whose credibility could not be supported by any other means.

At first sight the argument is a persuasive commonsense one, which provides a satisfactory general framework for understanding the decline of organized religion in modern Britain. Doubts begin to arise, however, when the case is pushed further and it is proposed that there is an inherent contradiction between 'modernity' and religion, which has condemned the latter to marginalization in the contemporary world, whereas it had been central to life in a 'pre-modern' culture. Broader chronological and geographical perspectives render such an hypothesis questionable. The medieval and early modern eras cannot be simplistically described as a golden age of faith; while in the Victorian period organized religion initially flourished during the transition to an industrial economy. The secularization hypothesis is also – at least in its crude form – inadequate for explaining the case of the United States where, in one of the most developed and technologically advanced societies in the world, organized religion remained in the second half of the twentieth century substantially stronger than in Britain.

Even in a specifically British context it is unsatisfactory simply to regard signs of continuing religious vitality as isolationist exceptions that prove the rule. The growing charismatic churches of the 1970s and 1980s in important respects – such as their use of music – reflected the surrounding culture rather than rejecting it; ethnic minority groups became more loyal to their religions even as in other respects they became more integrated into British life. Even among those who did not regularly practise any religion rates of nominal identification remained high: in 1974, 41.6 per cent of an English sample considered themselves to be 'Church of England'; in 1988 more than two-thirds of first marriages were still being celebrated in church.[6] Nearly all deaths were still followed by some kind of religious ceremony. Opinion polls might detect a drift away from the boundaries of Christian orthodoxy, but by the 1980s there were signs that the movement was towards Eastern and New Age religious ideas as well as towards secularity.

Moreover, the historian of postwar Britain should not ignore the case of Northern Ireland where, in a 1973 sample, 92 per cent of Roman Catholics and 34 per cent of Protestants claimed to attend church at least once a week.[7] The province is often dismissed as a somewhat embarrassing anomaly, but in terms of the history of religion, it may well better be regarded as an indication of potentialities that remained on the mainland. Although Northern Ireland has been economically and socially one of the less well developed parts of the United Kingdom, its degree of 'backwardness' was insufficient to explain its continuing religiosity on the basis of the secularization hypothesis. It represented rather an extreme case of a situation where culture and a history combined to support religion as an important part of personal and community identities in an essentially 'modern' society. A similar tendency can be observed in ethnic minority religions and theologically conservative Christian groups on the mainland. For a significant minority of the British people the contemporary secular world seemed not so much secure and rational as unstable and irrational. Accordingly religious structures of meaning – whether in charismatic Christianity, resurgent Islam, or the New Age – continued to provide a satisfying basis on which to find and develop an identity. At a more diffuse level religious rituals continued to appeal as a means of marking the passing of time, and the joys and griefs of personal and national life, and thereby providing some overall framework for human experience. A rounded account of the history of religion in Britain between 1939 and 1990 therefore needs to balance the language of decline and secularization with an awareness of continuity, adaptation and new beginnings. These processes have considerable relevance to an understanding of the wider course of social and cultural history.

Bibliographical Note

Statistical data on organized religious activity has been derived (unless otherwise indicated in footnotes) from Robert Currie, Alan Gilbert and Lee Horsley, *Churches and Churchgoers: Patterns of Church Growth in the British Isles since 1700* (Oxford, 1977) and Peter Brierley, *'Christian' England: What the 1989 English Church Census Reveals* (London, 1991).

Study of religion in postwar Britain has been somewhat fragmentary, with the historian's interest in change over time often overshadowed by the contemporary preoccupations of sociologists of religion. One might for example contrast the historical approach of P.A. Welsby, *A History of the Church of England 1945–1980* (Oxford, 1984) with the more sociological emphasis of Steve Bruce, *God Save Ulster: The Religion and Politics of Paisleyism* (Oxford, 1986) or M.P. Hornsby-Smith, *Roman Catholics in England: Studies in Social Structure since the Second World War* (Cambridge, 1987). Two important local studies by historically literate sociologists are David Clark, *Between Pulpit and Pew: Folk Religion in a North Yorkshire Fishing Village* (Cambridge, 1982) and R. Williams, *A Protestant Legacy: Attitudes to Death and Illness among Older Aberdonians* (Oxford, 1990).

Minority religions have attracted an increasing body of scholarship, to be found in the publications of organizations such as the Commission for Racial Equality, the Centre for Research in Ethnic Relations (University of Warwick), the Centre for the Study of Islam and Muslim-Christian Relations (Selly Oak Colleges), and the Community Religions Project (University of Leeds). Similarly, however, this primarily reflects the preoccupations of sociologists and religious studies specialists, whose work has not yet led to the publication of much systematic historical analysis.

The closest approaches to an historical synthesis from single authors are Alan D. Gilbert, *The Making of Post-Christian Britain* (London, 1980), Adrian Hastings, *A History of English Christianity 1920–1990* (London, 1991) and D.W. Bebbington, *Evangelicalism in Modern Britain: a History from the 1730s to the 1980s* (London, 1989). None of these, however, considers religions other than Christianity. For wider perspectives it is necessary to consult a number of multi-authored works: Paul Badham (ed.), *Religion, State, and Society in Modern Britain* (Lampeter, 1989); Gerald Parsons (ed.), *The Growth of Religious Diversity: Britain from 1945: Vol. I, Traditions; Vol. II, Issues* (London, 1993); Terence Thomas (ed.), *The British: Their Religious Beliefs and Practices 1800–1986* (London, 1988); and an anthology of sources and comment edited by John Wolffe, *The Growth of Religious Diversity in Britain from 1945: A Reader* (London, 1993). Gilbert's *Making of Post-Christian Britain* is also the best introduction for historians to the secularization debate, although for more current perspectives it might be supplemented by Steve Bruce (ed.), *Religion and Modernization: Sociologists and Historians Debate the Secularization Thesis* (Oxford, 1992).

Notes

1. Mass-Observation, *Puzzled People: A Study in Popular Attitudes to Religion, Ethics, Progress and Politics in a London Borough* (London, 1947) p. 156.

2. John Fulton, *The Tragedy of Belief: Division, Politics and Religion in Ireland* (Oxford, 1991) p. 14.

3. Kim Knott, 'New religious movements', in Terence Thomas (ed.), *The British: Their Religious Beliefs and Practices 1800–1986* (London, 1988) p. 161.

4. P. Ratcliffe, *Racism and Reaction: A Profile of Handsworth* (London, 1981) p. 86.

5. J. Nielsen, 'Muslims in Britain: searching for an identity?', *New Community* vol. 13 (1987), p. 387.

6. K. Medhurst and G. Moyser, *Church and Politics in a Secular Age* (Oxford, 1988) p. 142; Tom Griffin (ed.), *Social Trends* vol. 20 (London, HMSO, 1990), p. 166.

7. Ian McAllister, 'The Devil, miracles and the afterlife: the political sociology of religion in Northern Ireland', *British Journal of Sociology* vol. 33 (1982), p. 335.

25 Pressure Groups and Popular Campaigns

Paul Byrne

None may doubt that the postwar years have seen major changes in Britain's status and role in the world. Economic decline, the loss of Empire, and the search for a new European identity have all been important themes since 1945. One might expect such changes (and, it must be said, relatively poor record of performance) to have led to significant changes in Britain's political system, and yet this is not the case. Parliamentary and party politics in the 1990s are little different from those of the late 1940s and 1950s. The two-party system, buttressed by an electoral system which exaggerates the success of those two parties, is still dominant. In comparison with our Continental or transatlantic counterparts, British government is still centralized, secretive and working through much the same institutions and procedures as in 1945. At first sight, this may seem odd; after all, Britain's political system is legendary for its flexibility. Unencumbered by a written Constitution, a formal Bill of Rights and some form of Supreme Court, each government has the ability to make drastic reforms in the way in which politics and government are conducted, provided it can maintain the support of its majority in the House of Commons. Why, then, has there been so little change?

Political Culture

For many commentators, the answer lies in the nature of Britain's political culture – that is to say, those values and beliefs on the part of both politicians and public, about not only what should be done but also how it should be done. It is commonplace to refer to Britain having a consensual political culture – meaning that there is widespread agreement upon the rules of the political game, how politics should be conducted and what sort of issues should be addressed. A classic text on the differences in political culture across the developed world at the beginning of the 1960s[1] characterized Britain as having an unusually deferential culture which produced a high level of regime support – in other words, most of the British people were, for most of the time, content to limit their participation in politics to the 'normal' channels of elections and mainstream political parties, and to leave the details of politics in the hands of established politicians. Analyses of events in the 1970s and early 1980s have drawn attention to sporadic outbursts of less conventional political behaviour – for example unrest in inner city areas, or associated with industrial action on the part of miners or other public sector workers – but generally conclude that these are the exceptions which prove the rule of stability and a readiness to channel political demands, support and opposition through the officially recognized channels of parliamentary and local politics. There are two flaws in this assumption; one which is increasingly recognized by academic observers, and one which is more often than not overlooked.

The first is that there are definite signs of change in Britain's political culture. The two party system may still rule in Parliamentary terms, but many more people are prepared to vote for other parties. Perhaps more significantly, research on the strength of loyalty and attachment people feel towards either of the main parties shows a marked decline since the 1970s. The 'average' British voter is now much more prepared to switch loyalties, or not to bother voting at all – participation in local elections remains low. Membership of the mainstream political parties, at its height in the 1950s, has fallen significantly, as has that of traditional pressure groups like trade unions. The actions of particular governments have had an effect upon this, of course; the trade unions would not be in their present parlous condition were it not for a combination of unemployment and a government's reluctance to talk to them during the 1980s. Nevertheless, most commentators in the 1990s acknowledge that disenchantment and apathy are becoming as notable characteristics of the political culture as deference and support for the existing system.

The second is that, despite the conventional wisdom that the British people prefer to participate only through legitimate and 'respectable' channels, there has always been a minority prepared to act more unconventionally and – perhaps more surprisingly – a majority prepared to approve of this whilst not actually joining in.[2] Some argue that this is a reflection of changes occurring throughout the Western world. The best known proponent of such an argument is Inglehart, who has developed the concept of post-materialism.[3] His proposition, based upon a survey across nine European countries in the early 1970s, is that the postwar generation has different values to those of the preceding generation. He argues that the relative prosperity of Europe after 1950 has meant that people are less concerned with material goals (employment, housing, consumer goods, and so on) and more concerned with 'higher order needs' – emphasizing personal growth and development, and rejecting formal hierarchies in favour of participation at all levels of decision-making. He supports this idea by pointing to the outbreak of unconventional protest activity throughout the West since the 1960s – movements centred on students, civil rights (especially in America), women, the environment and peace. It is on the experience of such movements in the British context that this chapter will concentrate.

Social Movements

As one might expect, the new ideas expressed by such movements have been reflected in the forms of organization chosen to advance them. One of the problems of studying such movements is their nebulous nature. Almost by definition, they lack a formal structure, clearly identifiable leaders or formal statements of their aims and objectives. This can best be understood by comparing them with more traditional groupings. They are different from political parties because, with a few isolated exceptions, they do not put forward candidates in elections; nor are they formally organized into hierarchical structures. They differ from protectional interest groups (for example, trade unions) because they are not based upon advancing the interests of just one functional or professional grouping in society. They have some features in common with promotional interest groups, in that they seek to advance some cause; they do so, however, without resorting to the formal structure evident in most promotional interest groups and, more importantly, because they are prepared to use much more unconventional tactics than promotional groups. Hence the tendency to describe such movements as 'social movements'. Lacking a formal structure, their supporters are bound together by a shared ideology or view of the world, a desire to achieve much more radical and fundamental changes in society than more conventional pressure groups, a readiness to use both conventional (lobbying, petitioning) and unconventional (marches, civil disobedience) tactics, and an emphasis upon combining social change with personal change – that is to say, 'living out' the cause both in public and in private.

It is as well to clarify from the outset that there is no question of such activity replacing more traditional forms of political participation; it is more a case of new forms of political activity supplementing conventional participation. As we shall see, the majority of those attracted to these new forms of political expression come from just one part of society, the educated middle class, many of them having remained active within traditional political activity as well. Nevertheless, the ideologies of mainstream parties and interest groups have changed over the last thirty years, incorporating many of the arguments espoused by such movements, so a serious assessment of their role and impact is clearly justified.

Drawing a clear boundary between social movements and more conventional political groupings is not easy, as movements can grow out of more conventional group activity. The 1984 Miners' Strike, for example, started as conventional (if unusually widespread) industrial action, but spawned a wider movement centred upon miners' wives and other action groups. Whilst this displayed most of the organization features associated with social movements (being based upon networking), it was directed towards a specific issue – pit closures – and therefore did not have the wider goals associated with social movements. Another related example is the anti-apartheid movement. This came to prominence in the 1970s, again because of a specific issue (UK tours by South African sporting teams, especially rugby); it has outlived the resolution of that particular issue, but has not been able to retain anywhere near the level of support it enjoyed at its height. When activities such as these are centred upon a particular event or issue, it is difficult to retain the support and enthusiasm of supporters over time. Miners' support groups, for example, fell into abeyance when it was perceived that the battle over pit closures was lost; the anti-apartheid movement, once it lost the specific impetus of protests against particular events, went the same way. Without broad aims (as in the environmental movement) or an emphasis upon the importance of personal change (as in the women's movement), it can be hard to maintain momentum. It serves to remind us that social movements, even when they are in broad agreement with each other, are effectively also in competition. There is not an inexhaustible supply of people willing to devote their time and energy to such movements; if one movement appears to have less relevance for such people at any time, they will often switch their commitment to a related movement.

Our task is not made easier by the fact that movements tend to ebb and flow over time; the effect on some is to change them from loose movements into more structured organizations akin to conventional groups or parties. Most of the movements which came to prominence during the postwar period demonstrate this. For example, two distinct phases can be discerned in the history of Britain's major peace movement, the Campaign for Nuclear Disarmament (CND). Formed and enjoying its first phase of public prominence in the late 1950s and early 1960s it dwindled almost to the point of extinction in the 1970s, and re-emerged in the 1980s. Similarly, the women's movement which arose in the 1970s was preceded by a first wave of feminism between 1900 and 1920. The ecological movement attempted to transform itself into a national political party, although as we shall see, this has met with mixed success. In what follows, we shall concentrate upon these three movements.

One way of distinguishing both between social movements and more conventional groups, and between different social movements themselves, is to consider the relationship between structure and aims. Figure 25.1 expresses this for some of the more important movements in Britain since 1945, and demonstrates the difference between them and mainstream parties and groups.

Some movements have both loose structures and wideranging aims; others may lack a formal structure but be preoccupied with a single aim. Some movements have been so loosely structured and have had such wideranging aims that they can barely be considered a coherent movement at all. The

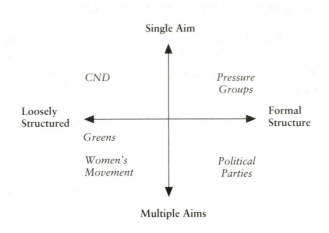

Figure 25.1. Comparison of social movements and mainstream parties/groups.

student movement which came to prominence in both Europe and America during the late 1960s is one such example. A wave of protest swept through Western universities at this time, achieving great prominence in some countries (notably France, Germany and America) where students were directly confronted by the governments of the time, and a less obvious but equally pervasive impact in countries such as Britain which sought to ignore rather than tackle such problems head-on. The student movement in Britain was characterized by shared ideas and ideals rather than any formal structure. Supporters of the movement were motivated in part by specific political issues (the Vietnam War and British involvement in the conflict between Nigeria and Biafra were particularly important), but also by a belief in the development of a new 'lifestyle' – one that centred upon the explosion of pop and rock music (fuelled by relative affluence), sexual freedom (fuelled by new developments in contraception such as the birth control pill), an espousal of revolutionary and feminist thinking and the beginnings of a concern with environmental issues, and a rejection of hierarchy in favour of much more extensive participation at all levels of decision-making. Communication was via networks (that is, overlapping and interlocking informal and personal contacts) rather than structures, and the role of the media was very important in making this possible. The rapid expansion of television, pirate and new youth oriented radio stations, and the growth of an 'underground' press made possible by technological innovation – all contributed to a climate in which both national and international communication between like-minded individuals became much easier.

The Women's and Environmental Movements

It can be argued that the student movement in Britain was a relatively short-lived phenomenon, confined to the late 1960s, but its lasting influence cannot be doubted. It served to socialize many young people, not only into radical aims, but also into new ways of seeking to achieve those aims. The women's movement, for example, grew out of the student movement of the 1960s. 'Second wave' feminism, which most agree started around 1970, drew many of its supporters from radicalized students. Its revival centred initially around the Women's Liberation Movement (WLM), which organized a national conference in 1970 at which four basic demands were agreed – equal pay, equal education and opportunity, extensive nursery provision, and free contraception and abortion on demand (see Chapter 22). Two further aims were added in 1974 – financial and legal independence for women, and no discrimination against lesbians – and a seventh aim in 1978 – freedom from intimidation by threat or use of violence or sexual coercion.

The WLM was essentially a forum for diverse women's groups, the women's movement not having a membership or formal structure. Many small, localized groups were formed, some based on race or sexual orientation, others simply on locality, but all stressing the importance of politicizing what had previously been seen as personal – both sexual (contraception, abortion, sexual preference) and inter-personal (gender relations generally). Many of the women involved were active in other political spheres (a feature common to most social movement supporters). This, together with differences over aims and priorities, led to different factions emerging with the women's movement. Two, at least, could be identified by the beginning of the eighties – Radical feminists (who argued that gender was the main factor in the distribution of power in society) and Socialist feminists (who contended that, although gender was an important factor, it was overshadowed by class as a source of division in society). If the WLM had possessed a formal structure, no doubt such internal frictions would have led to overt internal conflict. As the movement was based largely on informal networking, however, it could absorb such disagreements quite easily. Recurring specific events – the periodic attempts to change the law on abortion being a good example – also served to bring the movement together. The tremendous exposure the issue of feminism received in the media, moreover, meant that the movement's message was being communicated almost regardless of what the activists were doing.

This was an important factor in the 1980s as more and more 'traditional' women's organizations (the Women's Institute, for example) reflected the changing attitudes of their membership by campaigning on 'feminist' issues. This, combined with a Labour Party and trade union movement under attack and consequently more receptive to potential recruits, saw all wings of the movement coming together to enter a new phase of mobilization. The 1980s were a decade in which the women's movement decided to stop spending its time on internal argument and concentrate energies outside the movement. Women's participation and influence increased significantly in the Labour Party and the trade unions, and also to a lesser extent in the other parties; by the beginning of the 1990s both had introduced new procedures to increase the representation and power of women within their organizations. The success of the women's movement was even more striking in electoral terms, as all the parties moved quickly to respond. By the 1992 General Election, all the major parties promised to meet at least some of the objectives pursued by the women's movement – for example, equal pay, child benefits, equal rights in the workplace, maternity rights and so on. Labour, the Green Party and the Scottish National Party also committed themselves to creating a Ministry of Women if elected.

The environmental movement has also seen some of its aims adopted by mainstream parties. This is perhaps surprising as, unlike the women's movement, it has sought to compete on equal terms with the established parties by forming its own political party – but this has had a dismal electoral record. Founded in 1973,[4] the Green Party has never achieved more than 1 or 2 per cent of the vote in general elections; it did achieve some 15 per cent of the vote in the European Parliament elections in 1989, but fell back to its normally low level in the General Election three years later. The paradox is partly explained by the fact that the Green Party is only one of the organizations within the environmental movement; there are, in addition, a large number of pressure groups concerned with the environment (ranging from traditional organizations like the Council for the Protection of Rural England to the militant Greenpeace). Indeed, Britain is reputed to have more people involved in such groups than any other European country, most estimates putting the total at some two million. This has been one of the major problems facing the Green Party – few of these groups are willing to overtly ally themselves with the Green Party for fear that other mainstream parties would then ignore them. It means that the Green Party is effectively in competition with these groups for potential supporters' time, energy and commitment; given the Green Party's lack of electoral success, many such supporters prefer to devote their energies to single-issue (often local) groups, where there is more chance of some concrete success.

This raises the question of whether the Green Party should be seen as part of a wider social movement, given its status as a national political party. The answer lies partly in its ideology, but more in its organization. The ideology is radical and wideranging – it incorporates everything from the predictable (opposition to nuclear energy and weaponry, a commitment to renewable energy and conservation) to the more unusual (a radical restructuring of the economy into much smaller, largely self-sufficient units, based partly upon barter and direct exchange of goods and services, and a long-term aim of reducing the population from 56 million to around 40 million). It is in its organization, however, that the Green Party most closely resembles a social movement. Although it has a national framework, the party is highly

Plate 25.1.   Greenpeace: 'No Legal Pollution'. The militant actions of Greenpeace campaigners – here seen attempting to block the effluent discharge pipe of a chemical factory – has raised the public profile of the environmental movement, and has helped to put environmentalism on the agenda of all major political parties.

decentralized, with local party organizations having much more autonomy than their counterparts in the other parties; national officers are often unaware of what is happening at the local level, let alone controlling it. This reflects the party's strong ideological belief in the importance of decentralization, and has led to an enduring and bitter internal dispute on the question of national leadership. The Green Party has always resisted the idea of a single national leader, insisting instead that it should be guided by a collective leadership (usually two or three individuals). This has led to the formation of two broad factions – those who believe the commitment to decentralization is more important than any electoral benefits which might accrue from the electorate being able to identify a national leader, and those who think that if the party is to compete in the national political arena, it must have more centralized decision-making and a single leader. It is indicative of the party membership's strong ideological beliefs that, despite losing some of its best-known figures who have become impatient with such attitudes, the Green Party has still resisted a move towards centralization.

Despite this, the Green Party and the wider environmental movement can take satisfaction from the 'greening' of national politics, as the mainstream parties have moved quickly to avert its possible threat by introducing environmental policies into their own manifestos. Perhaps the greatest success has been in the sphere of education, as schools and colleges have incorporated a green perspective into their curricula on a wide scale. This has not been the result of any deliberate campaign by the environmental movement, but is more a reflection of the attitudes of many of the well-educated middle class who form the teaching profession.

If the women's and environmental movements can claim some success, the same cannot be said of the other main social movement in postwar British politics, the peace movement. Like the environmental movement, the peace movement also has a 'peak' organization – the Campaign for Nuclear Disarmament (CND). Unlike the Green Party, however, CND can claim to be the real centre of the wider movement, not least because it includes about half the membership of the wider peace movement within its own ranks, and is the only national organization within the movement. It is to CND's experiences since the 1950s that we now turn.

In focus: The Campaign for Nuclear Disarmament

We must start by acknowledging a paradox. CND is the best known protest movement in postwar British politics. Although there had been mass support for individual initiatives centred upon pacifism during the interwar years (the Peace Ballot being a notable example – see Chapter 13), it was the postwar era which saw such sentiments organized into a recognizable movement. CND has been in existence for longer than other major protest

The Campaign for Nuclear Disarmament (continued)

movements – it started in the 1950s whereas the postwar women's and environmental movements did not get off the ground until the late 1960s at the earliest. Its symbol (or logo) is far better known than that of any other movement; it has been able to mobilize up to a quarter of a million people to support its protests – far more than either the women's or the environmental movements have ever been able to manage. It has great symbolic importance in the British political culture – if the media wish to produce a stereotype of 'well-meaning' protest, it is to CND that they invariably turn. The paradox arises when one considers results. Governmental policy from the 1970s has increasingly reflected the concerns of both the women's and environmental movements; by the 1990s, all the major political parties were concerned to demonstrate their commitment (at least in theory) to the causes of sexual equality and ecological awareness. Unilateral nuclear disarmament, however, has been spurned by all parties when in government; admittedly it has been adopted as policy by the Labour Party more than once since the 1950s, but each time it has caused near fatal dissent within the party, usually resulting in Labour withdrawing its commitment. Only once (in 1983) has a Labour General Election manifesto included a promise to pursue the issue, and even that commitment was renounced by leading members of the party at the time. In short, the most popular movement in postwar British politics is the one that has achieved the least in terms of concrete changes in public policy. This is something which requires explanation.

One reason lies in the nature of the issue which CND addresses. Most social movements tend to pursue more than one goal – the women's movement, for example, is concerned with issues ranging from sexual identity to equality in the workplace, and the environmental movement tackles a wide variety of both economic and social issues. CND, however, has remained committed to one single overriding goal, the adoption of unilateral nuclear disarmament. Nothing less than a British government renouncing the possession of nuclear weapons, regardless of what other governments are doing, would satisfy CND.

There are two important dimensions to this. Firstly, CND is fundamentally a moral campaign; it does not offer its members any particular benefits (as do protectional groups like trade unions), but can only inspire them by the force of its moral and intellectual arguments. This means it tends to attract supporters who feel very strongly about the issue, but are also very reluctant to see any change of tack in the movement's approach. Their principles tend to be 'non-negotiable' – in other words, whilst it might seem sensible to moderate certain stances (e.g., the insistence upon unilateral rather than multilateral action; the anti-NATO position) to try and make governments more willing to listen, or to graft on additional causes (e.g., opposition to nuclear energy) in order to attract more supporters, any such moves are

Plate 25.2. Aldermaston March, 1958. 'Ban the bomb' marchers and CND members, like the majority of pressure group activists, have been drawn predominantly from the middle class.

The Campaign for Nuclear Disarmament (continued)

vetoed by various groups of supporters within the movement. Secondly, CND is addressing an issue which is at the very heart of central government. Defence generally is an area in which governments are accustomed to making their own decisions without much input from Parliament or interest groups (unless one includes the armed forces under this heading), and the role of nuclear weapons within this defence policy is seen as even more of an issue for governments alone to decide. Nowhere is the traditional obsession with secrecy in government more apparent than in the area of nuclear weapons. Far from encouraging public debate, fundamental decisions on nuclear weapons are taken behind closed doors. The decisions to first build nuclear weapons in 1947 and to update the nuclear deterrent in the 1970s, for example, were both taken by small groups of ministers who did not even consult the full Cabinet, let alone Parliament or any groups outside government. Indeed, for lengthy periods since 1945, the issue of nuclear weapons has not even been on the political agenda – that is to say, all the major parties were in agreement, and the issue was simply not discussed. In short, there must have been times when the leading figures of CND felt themselves to be between a rock and a hard place – mobilizing supporters who would not countenance any change of direction or purpose against governments who felt no obligation to listen. It is in this context that we must assess the varied experiences of CND over the last forty years.

CND grew out of two smaller groups, each of which was formed in 1957 to protest against the testing of nuclear weapons which took place in the 1950s – the National Committee for the Abolition of Nuclear Weapon Tests (NCAWT) and the Emergency Committee for Direct Action against Nuclear War (DAC). The cause was taken up by leading intellectual figures on the left, leading to the creation of CND in January 1958. From the outset, there were disagreements about how the Campaign should work; most of the leading intellectual figures favoured a strategy of persuading politicians by reasoned argument; others, however, especially those who had already engaged in civil disobedience (Non-Violent Direct Action – NVDA) with the DAC, preferred more direct tactics such as mass protest marches. Indicative of this internal disagreement was the first London to Aldermaston march; although endorsed by CND, it was organized by activists in the DAC. It was only when the march was a success (attracting some 10,000 people) that CND bowed to the inevitable and agreed to organize subsequent marches. During the early 1960s these attracted between 50,000 and 150,000 supporters, and put CND on the political map. But this was at the expense of an internal rift – NVDA activists formed the Committee of 100, which not only took a leading role in mass demonstrations but also organized other forms of NVDA (e.g., 'sit-down' protests in public places).

The Campaign for Nuclear Disarmament (continued)

Whatever the internal arguments over tactics, these were soon submerged as the issue of nuclear disarmament was taken up by a Labour Party in the throes of one of its periodic factional struggles. Labour, having lost three elections running (1951, 1955, 1959), was led by Hugh Gaitskell, perceived to be on the right of the party. In an attempt to revive its electoral fortunes, he was attempting to persuade the party to drop its explicit commitment to nationalization (the Clause 4 debate). This was strenuously resisted by those on the left of the party, who not only generally favoured unilateral nuclear disarmament, but saw it as a useful issue on which to base their more general disagreement with Gaitskell, a known anti-unilateralist. The Left secured a famous victory at the party's 1960 Annual Conference, when a unilateralist policy was adopted. Gaitskell turned the issue into one of loyalty to the party, by openly rejecting the Conference decision, and pledging to seek its reversal. Labour members had to choose between unilateralism and loyalty to their leader; support for the former would split the party. Trade union leaders in particular, realizing that the issue had effectively become a vote of confidence in the leadership, fell into line, and the policy was duly reversed at the 1961 Conference. The death of Gaitskell in 1963 and Wilson's accession to the leadership (coming from the left of the party) raised hopes that the party would swing back to the unilateralist cause, but Wilson quickly made it clear that he had other priorities; the left were sufficiently trusting of his leadership, and distracted by Wilson's emphasis upon economic and technological issues, that they largely lost interest in unilateralism – after all, they no longer needed a stick with which to beat their own leadership. Events in the international sphere also had an impact; a multilateral agreement banning nuclear tests in the atmosphere was concluded in 1963, and the Cuban missile crisis of 1962, whilst underlining the dangers of nuclear weapons, had – by its eventual resolution – also suggested that the nuclear superpowers could be relied upon to back off before the point of no return. CND went into rapid decline after these events and the election of a Labour government in 1964. Its membership shrank to a few thousand, and the young people who had been its most active supporters turned their attention elsewhere – to the student movement and the Vietnam War in particular.

CND was not rejected so much as ignored, but it managed to just survive. Its impact on popular culture was such that, despite a very small number of active supporters, it was still widely perceived as an established protest group on the left of British politics. It may only have succeeded in attracting support from the better off and better educated in society – the classic study of CND's 'first wave' of protest summarized its membership in the 1960s as being predominantly the educated middle class[5] – but for many on the left 'the bomb' had become a powerful symbol of all that was wrong with capitalism and right- wing politics. From the mid 1960s to the end of the

The Campaign for Nuclear Disarmament (continued)

1970s whilst Labour was in power most of the time, the issue remained in the background. At the beginning of the 1980s however, political and technological changes combined to bring it into the forefront once more – and the bare bones of CND remained to have new life breathed into them.

The issue of nuclear weaponry and disarmament would arguably have become controversial in the early 1980s regardless of which party was in power in Britain, because of both national and international developments. In 1979, NATO took the decision to introduce Cruise and Pershing missiles in Europe. These both offered the possibility of highly accurate targeting and different launching options (Pershing was ground-based, Cruise could be launched from ground, sea or air) but, because of their short range, had to be situated in close proximity to those targets. This, more than any other single decision, sparked off protest across Europe, as some perceived this to be an escalation of the arms race. Meanwhile, the British government decided to replace the ageing Polaris with the new Trident missile system from America. Dubbed the 'Rolls Royce' of intercontinental missiles, Trident represented the state-of-the-art in long-range, submarine-based nuclear weaponry. As such decisions on the 'core' of Britain's independent nuclear deterrent are only made every twenty years or so, this inevitably had a high political profile. It is hard to imagine, however, that such events taking place under a Labour government would have sparked quite the scale of response that they did under Thatcher. The Labour governments of the 1960s and 1970s, after all, had kept Britain's nuclear deterrent and updated it (all at considerable cost), and remained firmly committed members of NATO without inspiring much in the way of protest. In the early 1980s, however, these developments were taking place in a political context where Labour and its strongest power-bases were under fierce attack from a Conservative government determined to alter British society. The trade unions, local authorities, the public sector – all were on the receiving end of successive Thatcher administrations intent upon reducing their power and influence. In such an environment, support for CND was a highly attractive option for those who wished to register their protest against Thatcherism.

There was a massive influx of supporters to CND in the early 1980s, membership of national CND growing from a few thousand to around 85,000 by the mid 1980s, with a further estimated minimum 100,000 belonging to local CND or Peace groups. Mass demonstrations attracted between 100,000 and 400,000 participants.[6] Survey evidence of the national membership suggests that, while the Campaign was attracting far more adherents than in the 1960s, support was still coming disproportionately from the educated middle class, many working in the public sector, and most identifying themselves as Labour supporters. There were those who did not fit this mould, of course – CND had internal specialist sections covering Liberals, Trade Unionists, Christians and Youth as well as Labour – but their

The Campaign for Nuclear Disarmament (continued)

core support was still to be found among the teachers and 'caring' professions, with as many female as male supporters and most being aged under forty, whose counterparts had rallied to the cause twenty years earlier.

In contrast to the 1960s, CND in the 1980s put much more effort into 'conventional' ways of bringing pressure to bear. Parliamentary lobbying, doorstep canvassing and glossy publications were all seen as important. There was no question of renouncing more unconventional protest, however; even if the leadership had wished it, parts of the membership were insistent that it should continue. NVDA and other civil disobedience continued throughout the 1980s, either organized (or at least condoned) by national CND, or within local groups even if the centre disapproved. The best known example was the Greenham Women's Peace Camp, established outside a Cruise missile base in 1981. This was not a CND initiative, the idea coming from the women themselves, and CND maintained an uneasy relationship with the women thereafter. The women's separatist stance (men were not encouraged to participate) was one which CND found hard to swallow, but there was no doubt about the high regard in which the women were held by CND's membership – whenever the Camp was discussed at CND Annual Conferences during the early 1980s, for example, representatives from Greenham invariably received an ecstatic reception from delegates. There were many other instances from within the Campaign of activists engaging in civil disobedience despite misgivings on the part of the leadership about the effect this was having on CND's public image. Perhaps they should not have been so concerned; public opinion polls in the early 1980s saw up to a third agreeing with unilateral nuclear disarmament, although a substantial minority agreed with the aims but not all the tactics of the Campaign.[7]

The real problem for CND was not the variety of protest events its supporters mounted, but the escalation of unilateralism to a major issue in party politics, especially during the 1983 General Election. Labour passed motions in favour of unilateral nuclear disarmament at its Annual Conferences in both 1980 and 1981; this, together with the European Community, being the main reasons behind the breakaway of the Social Democrats in 1981, something which only further convinced those on the left of the party that unilateralism was the right way forward. In 1982, unilateralism finally received the two-thirds Conference majority that ensured it would be part of Labour's overall programme; Labour went into the 1983 Election with a manifesto promising cancellation of Trident, opposition to the deployment of Cruise, and the removal of all nuclear bases (i.e., British and American) within five years. The Conservatives, fresh from a successful Falklands Campaign, sensed electoral blood, and pulled out all the stops to claim that Labour was intent upon leaving Britain 'defenceless'.[8] They were helped by the fact that senior figures within the Labour Party

The Campaign for Nuclear Disarmament (continued)

(e.g., Callaghan and Healey) were openly critical of their own party's stance. The effect was clear and marked; as Crewe noted, the 1983 Election decisively shifted opinion away from the unilateralist cause – among Labour as well as Conservative and Alliance supporters.[9] Labour under Kinnock moved swiftly to moderate the party's stance. Although the party went into the 1987 Election still maintaining a commitment to cancel Trident and remove American nuclear weapons from Britain, Labour's campaigning on the issue was deliberately low-key. As in 1983, post-election analysis strongly suggested that defence had been a vote-losing issue for Labour. By the time of the 1992 Election, Labour had moved back to a clear commitment to multilateral rather than unilateral disarmament. By then, of course, events on the international stage had changed dramatically; Gorbachev and the Reagan/Bush administrations had agreed to remove intermediate nuclear weapons like Cruise from Europe, the Soviet Union had disintegrated, and the threat of nuclear superpower confrontation had virtually disappeared. The effect upon CND has been marked: membership in the 1990s has halved, and media coverage has been virtually non-existent. It enjoyed a brief resurgence during the Gulf War, but has dropped back again since. It can, however, take some consolation from the fact that – even at this level – it is still holding on to many more of its members than it did during its earlier period of decline in the 1960s.

CND and other European peace movements claimed some credit for the burst of nuclear disarmament in the late 1980s and early 1990s, arguing that it was their determined opposition and wide popular support which motivated such changes; Thatcher and her allies, on the other hand, argued that it was their determination to deploy Cruise and modernize Britain's deterrent which brought the Soviets to the negotiating table. There is no way to prove either of these claims (although the electoral unpopularity of unilateralism undermines CND's claims). Where CND's success cannot be denied is in simply getting the issue talked about, getting it onto the political agenda. In the 1970s, as in the 1990s, nuclear defence was a political issue on which discussion was effectively restricted to the governmental and military elite; in the 1960s and 1980s, it was a matter for popular and widespread discussion. The electorate's verdict may well have been negative in the final analysis, but CND's achievement in making the political elite openly discuss matters that they would have preferred to keep behind closed doors was of considerable significance.

Interpretations

Given the lack of formal organizations and membership which typifies social movements, it is hard to estimate the number of people who have actively participated in them since 1945. Bearing in mind that all the survey evidence suggests a considerable degree of overlapping membership (it is by no means uncommon to find individuals who are active in all three of the movements we have considered here), the number of people active in these movements is almost certainly less than a million, and may well be around half a million. Even this latter figure, however, is arguably impressive, as one must remember that none of these movements offers the direct and material benefits associated with more conventional groups. With the possible exception of the women's movement (because of its emphasis upon personal change and liberation), social movements are appealing to what have been termed 'conscience constituents' – that is to say, supporters who do not stand to benefit directly or exclusively from a social movement achieving its goals.

Britain has not been unique in seeing the mobilization of such philanthropic movements, of course; a similar postwar trend can be seen in most European countries and the US. This has led some commentators to talk of a 'new politics' arising – one which is less materialistic, less formal and more participatory than mainstream parties and groups. It is hard to assess this claim in relation to the women's movement, as so little is known about its supporters. As far as the peace and environmental movements are concerned, however, the evidence suggests that such claims must be treated with a degree of scepticism. The support they have attracted has come largely from the well-educated middle class, more often than not working in the public sector. Such people have not turned their backs upon more conventional political participation (most of the individual membership of the contemporary Labour Party, for example, comes from such a background), but have supported social movements as well as mainstream organizations. It is true that the postwar period has seen changes in Britain's political culture; declining party memberships and loyalties, an increase in negative voting as people vote against the party they dislike rather than because of some positive feeling about the alternatives, and a generally much less deferential culture. Whilst there is some evidence to suggest that at least some of the educated middle class have been inspired to supplement their attachment to 'old' conventional politics with support for the protest activities of social movements, there is very little evidence to suggest that the less well-off in British society have been motivated to follow their example. If the political attitudes of some of the middle class have become 'post-materialist', the evidence of postwar protest in Britain suggests that those of the working class could better be described as 'apathetic' rather than 'alternative'.

Bibliographical Note

The relationship between conventional pressure groups and more unconventional protest movements is covered briefly in most of the textbooks on contemporary British politics – for example, P. Dunleavy *et al.*, *Developments in British Politics 3* (London, 1990) and B. Coxall and L. Robins, *Contemporary British Politics* (London, 1991). Texts on CND include F. Parkin, *Middle Class Radicalism* (Manchester, 1968); R. Taylor and C. Pritchard, *The Protest Makers* (Oxford, 1988); J. Mattausch, *A Commitment to Campaign* (Manchester, 1989); and P. Byrne, *The Campaign for Nuclear Disarmament* (London, 1988). A good account of the early years of the women's movement can be found in E. Wilson, *Only Halfway to Paradise* (London, 1980); more recent developments are analysed in J. Lovenduski and V. Randall, *Contemporary Feminist Politics* (Oxford, 1993). Green parties across Europe are covered in F. Müller-Rommel (ed.), *New Politics in Western Europe* (Boulder, Colorado, 1989). The classic text on post-materialism is R. Inglehart, *The Silent Revolution* (Princeton, 1977), but a more accessible account of the theory as applied to the UK is A. Marsh, *Protest and Political Consciousness* (London, 1977).

Notes

1. G.A. Almond and S. Verba, *The Civic Culture* (Princeton, 1963).

2. A. Marsh, *Protest and Political Consciousness* (London, 1977) uses survey evidence to argue that over half of his respondents approved of the use of unconventional and extra-Parliamentary protest actions. In a study of the number of major political demonstrations across 136 states, Britain was ranked tenth.

3. R. Inglehart, *The Silent Revolution* (Princeton, 1977).

4. The Green Party had its origins in the People Party (a local initiative in Coventry in 1973), changed its name to the Ecology Party in 1975, and finally became the Green Party in 1985; see P. Byrne, 'Great Britain: the Green Party', in F. Müller-Rommel (ed.), *New Politics in Western Europe* (Boulder, Colorado, 1989).

5. F. Parkin, *Middle Class Radicalism* (Manchester, 1968).

6. P. Byrne, *The Campaign for Nuclear Disarmament* (London, 1988) pp. 151–3.

7. *Ibid*, pp. 211–15.

8. There was also evidence to suggest that the Conservative Government used the security services to monitor CND's activities at the time. *Ibid*, pp. 182–90.

9. I. Crewe, 'Britain: Two and a half cheers for the Atlantic Alliance', in G. Flynn and H. Rattinger (eds), *The Public and Atlantic Defense* (London, 1985).

26 Youth Culture

John Street

'You've got to wear their sorts of clothes, not funny ones but like mods, straight trousers, shorts and stuff like that. Else they won't hang around with you.'[1]

'By the time they are my age – 14 – most normal kids have formed into groups which are almost totally music-orientated ... New groups and slang are emerging all the time ... At our school the main groups are Ravers, Metallers, Fashion Victims and, of course, Trev and Sharons, which even adults have heard about.'[2]

Introduction: the Moment of Conception

A make of jeans or the label on trainers, the right image or the right expression, shared tastes in music or films; all are components of youth culture, and together these apparently trivial choices help to forge a sense of identity and a way of life, which in turn influence the wider culture and history of a country.

The twentieth century has witnessed many extraordinary, transforming inventions, things that have altered the way we have thought and acted. One of the most important – but most easily overlooked – is 'youth culture'. This may seem a strange claim. 'Youth', it might be supposed, is a fact of life, a part of our physiology; just as youth culture is the inevitable companion to life changes – a modern equivalent to traditional rites of passage. But it is, of course, not this simple. Age, like culture, owes as much to perceptions and understandings as it does to biology. 'Youth' and 'youth culture' are *creations* of particular times and places, the product of particular institutions and processes. We need only to think of child labour to recall a quite different view of what it meant to be young. This chapter is, therefore, an account of one period in the invention of youth – from the Second World War until the present, a period which saw the industrialization and commercialization of youth culture (and subsequently its globalization). It was a time when youth culture, you might say, came of age.

While many of the things which have been associated with youth – the leisure and lack of responsibility, the cults and moral panics – are not exclusive to the postwar world, they took on a special form then. They were integrated into the emerging economic order, and became the vehicle for any number of market enterprises and cultural expectations. In many ways, youth represented both the hopes and fears of the new order. Just as they continue to do so in the 1990s when the brutal murder of a two year old boy by two ten year olds, a terrible combination of evil and innocence, provoked a moment of national anxiety and self-doubt. This one incident stood as a kind of answer to the question, 'What have we become?' This is just another twist in a familiar saga. The press has long treated young people as the symbols and signs of social change, with young people's language, habits and pleasures marking the passage of time.

This social and psychological use of youth could not occur without its commercialization. The postwar world saw the emergence of youth as a vital market, a new and expanding source of revenue. It was this that prompted the dramatic changes in all forms of media, peopled by new generations of film stars (James Dean and Marlon Brando) and music stars (first Elvis Presley and then the Beatles), and out of them the new fashions and cults – the teddy boys, hippies, punks and Acid House ravers – that fuelled the moral panics. But while it is important to notice the huge economic, social and psychological investment made in youth, and in the way youth behaviour is stigmatized or celebrated, we have also to keep a sense of proportion.

Youth Culture's Family Background

Before discussing the proximate causes for the rise and form of postwar youth culture, it is worth reflecting briefly on the longer-term trends at work. John Davis, for example, argues that, while we can see forms of youth subculture in Britain from the Middle Ages onwards, our current notion of youth derives from the mid nineteenth century. In part, of course, this is a feature of increasing life expectancy. But it also owes something to changes in education policy, in legislation (most obviously as it applied to child labour), and in developments in psychology. It was only through the latter, and its identification of adolescence as a stage in human development, that the idea of 'youth' made sense. In setting the scene for the postwar blooming of youth culture, Davis writes:

By the Second World War the stage had been set. Within the range of variation by social class the years of adolescence – and in some cases youth – had been universalized as a transitional but nonetheless distinct age grade between childhood and adulthood. Professional and scientific theories had been developed to account for the special nature of this time of life and to define its psycho-social characteristics, and these had furthermore come to be appropriated by the general 'common sense' of our culture.[3]

It was only in such circumstances, with this notion of youth in existence, that the postwar explosion of youth culture could occur.

But just as youth culture needs a prehistory, it also needs a set of key actors – individuals and institutions who help to give that youth culture its particular shape. There are four such actors in this story. There are young people, who, it is important to note, do not form a single undifferentiated group, but are – like the rest of society – divided along class, gender and ethnic cleavages. Then there are the manufacturers of the products around which youth culture is organized – the fashion, film, music and broadcasting industries. These industries are intent upon creating a market for their products. Mediating between them and the consumers are the artists, the people who help create the industry's products and shape its market. The fourth and final set of actors are the regulatory institutions which, like the stars, try to impose a meaning and value on cultural activity. These include such people as politicians, priests, journalists and broadcasters, often described loosely as 'the Establishment'.

Between them, these four, with their different interests and ambitions, shape youth culture in their struggle for control over its form and direction (and its profits). Youth culture, despite the claims of some commentators, is never purely the product of a cynically exploitative industry, nor is it simply the result of populist desires or artistic creativity.

The Birth of Youth Culture

Youth culture announced itself most noisily with the advent of rock 'n' roll. For British youth, the music was represented by the relatively tame form of Bill Haley and his Comets. Haley's music had featured on the soundtrack of *Blackboard Jungle* (1955, but released in Britain in 1956). It drew enthusiastic fans, who on occasion expressed their enthusiasm in small riots in and around the cinemas.

Accompanying these activities was the youth cult forged by the teddy boys, with their drainpipe trousers, Edwardian jackets and quiffed hair. In contrast to many of the later waves of youth culture, the teddy boys were a largely working-class phenomenon. Their outbursts of delinquency (or the perceived threat of delinquency) elicited a horrified response from some guardians of public morality. Politicians and church leaders were quick to denounce the rioting and the culture that was alleged to have prompted it.

For those who condemned it, the youths' behaviour represented a profound moral decline, aggravated by the combined effect of American culture and commercial exploitation. The story is, of course, more complicated than this. Certainly, rock 'n' roll did constitute an important new addition to youth entertainment, and youthful behaviour did become more visible and did seem at odds with prewar patterns, but its form, as well as its causes and effects, need to be seen as part of a wider set of changes.

After the war, the experience of growing up was changed substantially by several factors: demography, education, the economy and National Service. First there was the 'baby boom' that expanded the size of the youth population (the number of fifteen to nineteen year olds rose from 3,174,000 in 1951 to 4,282,000 in 1965). This was compounded by the 1944 Butler Education Act which extended the period spent at school by raising the school-leaving age. In 1947, there were 32,000 sixth formers; by 1958, there were 53,000. The number of people aged fifteen or older in school in England and Wales doubled between 1955 (329,174) and 1965 (785,021). This meant that the transition to adulthood was delayed; it also meant that school now provided a focus and forum for these older children. Such changes to the pattern of adolescent development became allied, for boys at least, to National Service. The conscripts did not join up until they were eighteen, so the period between school and the forces offered a state of limbo, a freedom from formal responsibilities. As Bill Osgerby comments: 'National Service acted in tandem with developments in the State's provision for young people to identify formally the late teenage years as a distinct stage of life associated with particular demands and social problems.'[4]

But to enjoy this new found freedom, it was necessary to have the means to make use of it. There could be no leisure without money; and in an important sense there was no culture without consumption; as Simon Frith remarks, 'A teenager is the conspicuous consumer par excellence'.[5] The restarting of the British economy did, however, create opportunities for unskilled or semi-skilled youth to earn a significant wage. Without the burdens of a family or home to support, this disposable income allowed for new leisure pursuits: 'I mean a pound would buy a bloody good night out. You could probably have eight or nine pints and twenty fags and a couple of tanners for the juke box.'[6]

In themselves, however, money and free time do not create leisure opportunities. These depended on the actions of others. The government, conscious of the need to find ways to manage youthful energy, established the Youth Service which led to the proliferation of youth clubs, important proving grounds for budding musicians. The entertainment and manufacturing industries became aware of a new consumer. Market research surveys revealed a burgeoning new market. The films which symbolized the birth of youth culture were themselves examples of this phenomenon. *Blackboard Jungle*, and then movies like *Rebel Without a Cause* and *The Wild One*, were labelled 'teen-pics' because of their very deliberate audience targeting. These US imports were also to have an impact on the British film industry.

The music industry followed a similar route. A new audience for a new music (or a clever mixture of existing musical forms) allowed for a blossoming of record companies in the US and a wealth of new stars. But where in the US a network of small record labels emerged, in Britain the industry was dominated by Decca and EMI. Between them these two companies signed up the British answers to Elvis Presley: Tommy Steele and Cliff Richard.

These artists and their products had to be marketed and sold. This, like everything else in youth culture, did not simply 'happen'. It depended on broadcasters and others to disseminate them. BBC radio was slow to adapt to the new music, although television, driven by the competition posed by the launch of commercial TV in 1955, proved more hospitable. The BBC introduced *Six-Five Special* in 1957, and the following year ITV offered *Oh Boy!* Both were targeted directly at a youth audience, and each offered a mixture of pop, dance and fashion. For radio listeners, the main sources of the new music were the American Forces Network and Radio Luxembourg.

Together with the shift in the entertainments industry, there emerged a fashion industry, geared to supplying clothes which emulated the stars' and also created an impression of youthfulness. Clothes shops became an ever more prominent feature in British high streets.

Just as the music and the films, like the audience, were partly the product of a deliberate process, so too were the stars. British pop singers, for instance, were not simply clones of their American equivalents. Cliff Richard and Tommy Steele might have copied Presley, Eddie Cochrane and others, but their imitations were also the product of distinctive local traditions, most notably those of the music hall and British light entertainment as supplied by the BBC.

Finally, in trying to understand the emergence and character of 1950s youth culture, we cannot overlook its *meaning*. The music, films and clothes were not simply consumed. They were ways of establishing an identity. This identity was organized around a notion of youth, which in turn described itself through 'freedom'. Partly, this was the freedom of not being responsible (of not being your parents), but also it was the freedom to consume. America was a key component of this image. Both as a place and as a culture, the US symbolized what it meant to be young and free.

Youth Culture Cuts its Teeth

Similar forces to those which had helped to construct 1950s youth culture were also responsible for the changes within it. Throughout the late 1950s and early 1960s, British popular culture developed a certain distinctiveness; it was not just a plagiarized American culture.

Gradually, BBC radio acknowledged that the public service ethos did not require the complete marginalization of pop, and in 1962 it launched the show *Pick of the Pops*. This initiative was in part forced upon it by the emergence of the British beat boom (led by the Beatles and the Rolling

Stones), and in part by the evident success of its rival broadcasters. The competition represented by Radio Luxembourg was intensified by the arrival in 1964 of the pirate stations (Radio Caroline and Radio London), broadcasting outside British jurisdiction but penetrating teenage bedrooms up and down the country. Their eventual outlawing marked the point when the BBC finally embraced pop fully with the creation of Radio 1 in 1967.

The same period also saw the accompanying growth of the record, fashion and film industries. The explosion of the fashion industry was marked by the changing shop-fronts on London's King's Road and Carnaby Street, and by the new style pioneered by the founding of the clothing and design store Biba's in 1964 (later to be the target of the anarchist Angry Brigade bomb campaign in 1971, when radical politics were more fashionable). Biba, through the skill of its owner Barbara Hulanicki, was a success because 'it linked the highly and transiently fashionable to the alternative culture'.[7]

The British film industry marked its entry into the world of youth culture first through northern working-class dramas like *Room at the Top* (1959) and *Saturday Night and Sunday Morning* (1960), before venturing – via *Billy Liar* – into the 'swinging London' of 1963. Meanwhile the pop industry was also diversifying and expanding. The EMI-Decca duopoly was being eroded slowly, with the emergence of companies like Phillips, although between them the two giants they retained control over the groups that in their different ways symbolized 1960s youth culture: the Beatles (EMI) and the Rolling Stones (Decca).

The changes in the industry were manifested in the artists. They now saw themselves as self-conscious representatives of their audience; they were no longer just 'entertainers'. As representatives, they played out the emerging conventions of the 'generation gap', itself an idea that became central to the rhetoric of youth culture.

The explanation for all this does not lie solely with the audience, but there was a connection. Just as the 1944 Education Act altered the experience of working-class youth in the 1950s, so the expansion of higher education in the 1960s created a new middle-class youth. Where the 1950s cults were largely a working-class phenomenon, the 1960s ones were based on middle-class, suburban experience. This was especially true of the hippies of the mid- to late-1960s. With their drugs and their exotically-coloured clothes, with their magazines like *Oz* and *International Times*, with films like *Blow Up* and groups like Pink Floyd, youth culture came to be defined in terms of the desires and anxieties of a young people's world. Although not everyone saw it this way; as in the 1950s, the Establishment was quick to condemn. One *News of the World* story in 1969 about London hippies began: 'Drug taking, couples making love while others look on, a heavy mob armed with iron bars, filth and stench, foul language, that is the scene inside the hippies' fortress in London's Piccadilly.'[8]

If 1950s youth culture traded on the new consumerism made possible by capitalism, then its 1960s equivalent dwelt upon the limits of consumption, questioning its instrumental, privatized materialism. The hippies were a product of the politics of plenty. It was a version of bohemianism which drew on the politics of a vague communitarianism and on the anti-materialism of Eastern religions.

It was not all peace and love, though. Youth culture in the 1960s evolved two political styles. There were the hedonists with their 'happenings', and there were the radicals with their protests. For the latter, the music was a soundtrack to the campaigns against the war in Vietnam and the student-worker uprisings on the streets of Paris and elsewhere in 1968.

These two styles became linked together, however, in the label 'the counter-culture'. Its political possibilities and achievements have been extensively celebrated (not least because key figures in the media and political worlds had their formative experiences at this time), but they can be seen as part of an entirely predictable form of social change. For Bernice Martin, the counter-culture was another example of the attempt made by all societies to

Plate 26.1. Flower power at Woburn Abbey, 1967. Despite their unconventional dalliance with hallucinatory drugs and free love, most 1960s hippies came from, and returned to, conventional middle-class environments.

adjust to the increasing dominance of instrumental values and the marginalization of Romantic values. The key medium for such values are those in, or with aspirations towards, 'the expressive professions – the arts, education (particularly higher education), the mass media and the caring professions and semi-professions'.[9]

But youth culture was neither exclusively nor solely the province of the middle class. There was also a working-class youth culture which sometimes overlapped with and at other times clashed with the more publicized form. This division became more pronounced in the 1970s, but it was apparent long before. For all the attention given to hippie culture, the pop charts contained evidence of quite different tastes and cultures at play. One of the biggest selling records of the period was the soundtrack to *The Sound of Music.*

In focus: Creating Pop History: the Beatles

It is not hard to find extravagant claims for the importance of the Beatles. 'Nothing has changed ... the music culture of the twentieth century more fundamentally than the meteoric rise to fame of the Beatles', writes Peter Wicke.[10] *The Faber Companion to 20th Century Popular Music* describes the Beatles as 'the greatest popular musicians of the century'.[11] The Beatles are such a familiar feature of British youth culture – their story has been told so often, their contribution has been so widely acknowledged – that it is easy to take them for granted. But just as we need to chart the history of youth culture generally, so we need to *explain* the Beatles, to ask where they came from and why they succeeded. And to do this, we need to look to the city that shaped them, the culture they borrowed from, the opportunities they enjoyed, the audience that responded to them and the industry that packaged and marketed them.

The four Liverpudlians (John Lennon, Paul McCartney, George Harrison and Ringo Starr) who were eventually to form the Beatles brought together a particular set of musical experiences. They drew from the music hall tradition that their families (particularly McCartney's) had enjoyed and played. They had access to the latest American sounds, particularly the more sophisticated pop that was emerging from Detroit's Tamla Motown label and the witty self-penned songs of Chuck Berry. The Beatles' distinctive harmonies owed much to their love of US vocal groups like the Miracles and the Marvelettes, and their songwriting skills were indebted to Berry.

But two other ingredients were important in establishing the special talents of the Beatles. First there was the incentive to form a group. This was driven by the example of the 1950s skiffle boom and the success of Lonnie Donnegan ('It was after seeing Lonnie Donnegan that Paul began clamouring for a guitar'[12]). Skiffle was a derivative of traditional jazz and jug-band music. With cheap instruments (guitar, washboard and string bass), it was possible to make a sound that had pop credibility. The second

Creating Pop History: the Beatles (continued)

important ingredient was the confidence to write songs, rather than to confine themselves to cover versions. Such an idea did not occur to the earlier generation of pop performers. 'It was skiffle,' observes Simon Frith, 'that gave young British musicians the chance to develop their own ideas ... outside the framework of the industry: skiffle gave them the folk confidence to play without polish, without showbusiness, without advice, without capital. The most immediately noticeable thing about the Beatles ... was their detachment from Tin Pan Alley – they wrote their own songs.'[13]

These skills were overlaid by an equally crucial sense of style. This gave the Beatles the sense of what they were doing and why. They were not just making music, they were making art, albeit art not sanctioned by any formal authority. This was the ingredient brought by John and his art school background. The art school provided a framework through which a rudimentary musical talent, teenage rebelliousness and a vague artistic sensibility were to blossom into the Beatles' sound and image.

Two other individuals were crucial to the Beatles' success: their manager Brian Epstein and their record producer George Martin. Epstein had watched the early success of the Beatles from the vantage of the family music business in Liverpool. But it was not just his ability to spot the trend, it was his talent in fashioning it that was to make the difference. Epstein was vital to the process by which the Beatles were turned into a 'marketable product'. And it was Martin – until then a producer of novelty/comedy records for the Parlophone label, a subsidiary of EMI – who was given the freedom to shape the group's sound and then to translate the Beatles' more adventurous later experiments into a recordable reality.

The impact of these individuals was, though, crucially dependent upon the way the industry had become receptive to the ideas and ambitions of Epstein and Martin. The Beatles marked the point when the record industry began to take pop seriously as a long-term commercial property. Until then it had been widely believed that pop was a novelty whose day would soon pass. The change of attitude resulted in the development of more sophisticated marketing techniques. At the same time, EMI relaxed its highly paternalist, ruthless control over its pop performers. The Beatles, Martin and Epstein – partly because they lived on the fringes of the EMI establishment in the Parlophone subsidiary – were allowed greater autonomy.

The BBC was then to play an important part in allowing the Beatles to develop their skills. As Frith points out, 'Rather than simply imitating the style of American Top 40 Radio, British youth club shows such as "Saturday Club" promoted local enterprise. Skiffle is a case in point. They also gave groups such as the Beatles a chance to develop a relationship with their radio audience that was not just a sales pitch.'[14] This context allowed the Beatles to develop their style and their skills. They could practise and experiment in public; such opportunities were largely denied to their

Creating Pop History: the Beatles (continued)

American counterparts, who worked in a world where the advertiser was monarch.

Finally, there was a growing market for what the Beatles had to offer. Not only were there young people with the money and opportunity to enjoy pop, but they also had the incentive. The Beatles represented a way of making sense of their world and their place in it. As Charlie Gillett wrote:

> The Beatles unwittingly exploded the image of working-class youth ... Their social message was rarely expressed, but hung about their heads as an aura of impatience with convention and evident satisfaction with wealth and fame, and was expressed in the carefully chosen styles of bizarre clothes.[15]

It was important too that the Beatles appeal acknowledged women as fans, in ways that rock 'n' roll had not, or at least not to the same extent.

There has always been a temptation to treat the Beatles as a unique pop phenomenon, one that secured success by virtue of talent alone. To look more closely at their story is to reveal other influential interests and actors. The Beatles, no more than youth culture generally, did not just 'happen'. They had to be packaged, marketed and sold; they had, too, to mean something to their consumers. It should be clear that to explore the history of the Beatles is not to deny their importance or their genius.

Youth Culture – Those Difficult Years

While the rhetoric of 1960s youth culture was often anti-materialist, and although the period has been celebrated as a moment of popular revolt, it was in fact the time when the cultural industries became most firmly ensconsed. The commercialization of youth culture was now a fact of life. The record industry expanded through countless new labels (albeit licensed to a relatively small number of major companies). The market in magazines and posters, and a whole range of other sundry items, blossomed. The media which had been slow to embrace the emergent youth culture of the 1950s, save as a threat to moral propriety, were now much more willing to indulge it. On television, programmes aimed at youth became more frequent. Radio 1 became an increasingly established youth institution.

But if the 1960s spawned a political revolt against the complacency that capitalism's apparent success engendered, then the 1970s saw a politics which challenged the viability of capitalism. Within the world of youth culture, these doubts were experienced in two ways. First, there was the gradual increase in unemployment, a trend to which the young were especially vulnerable at a time when there was no accompanying expansion of higher education to compensate. Secondly, the plight of the economy was felt acutely by a record industry that had grown substantially in the late 1960s. The industry's overstretch was symbolized by the bloated ambitions of the new breed of rock stars, with their extravagant costumes, their pantechnicons full of equipment, and their pompous attempts to fuse classical and rock genres.

This was the world into which punk burst. Affecting fashion, design, film and music, punk announced itself as an angry, loud and deliberately shocking cultural form. It embodied a DIY ethos, a questioning of hi-tech and big business style. It was as much an attitude as a set of identifiable products. It allowed – albeit briefly – consumers and creators to question old assumptions about how culture should work. Perhaps most importantly, punk provided a forum for women. Where previous cults had tended to marginalize women or render them passive, punk provided powerful female models in bands like the Slits and performers like Poly Styrene and Siousie Sioux.

Punk, though, was not an inevitable consequence of its wider context. It, like the cultures that both preceded and succeeded it, was a deliberate creation. Its leading lights, its most articulate representatives, were sharp, alienated products of art schools, art schools which themselves had broadened their curriculum to accommodate the burgeoning of popular culture. And while the record companies, and other commercial purveyors of youth artifacts, were outmanoeuvred by the new breed of punk entrepreneurs, they were soon to catch up. Indeed, without their involvement there would have been no punk culture.

Youth Culture Comes of Age

It may seem paradoxical but the iconoclasm of punk heralded the integration of youth culture into a wider culture. Punk prompted a revival of the flagging record industry, it also breathed life into publishing and fashion industries. And riding on this change of fortune were a number of creative talents: pop entrepreneur Malcolm McLaren, fashion designer Vivienne Westwood, film maker Derek Jarman, and design artists Neville Brody and Jamie Reid, who were to become part of a culture that was no longer exclusive to youth. It is a path that can be traced in the trajectory of publishing that runs from the punk fanzines to *The Face*, *GQ* and *Arena*. It can also be detected in events like Live Aid, Comic Relief and other such charity enterprises. What these occasions borrowed were the populist politics that were part of punk's rhetoric, but deprived of its anarchic entrepreneurism.

The pop stars who organized Live Aid in 1985 (Bob Geldof of the Boomtown Rats and Midge Ure of Ultravox) did not present themselves as spokesmen for (disaffected, rebellious) youth. Instead they saw themselves as speaking for the population at large (as their US counterparts announced 'We

Plate 26.2. A punk wedding in Southampton. Although punk appeared to many observers to represent an anarchic and spontaneous outpouring of youth rage, it was consciously created and manipulated by a new breed of punk entrepreneurs.

are the World'). This change could also be detected in the way the tabloid and broadsheet press came to treat pop culture as part of the mainstream. In *The Times* and *Daily Telegraph*, rock reviews appeared next to opera reviews; in the tabloids, the gossip columns treated pop stars as equivalents of Hollywood film stars and TV entertainers. By the 1980s the audience for the traditional forms of youth culture now extended across several generations. Those over thirty-five were as much part of the 'youth market' as were the fifteen year olds. Indeed, while those between fifteen and nineteen were still the main purchasers of singles, the group buying the most albums were aged twenty-five to thirty-four. It was this older audience who were targeted in the promotion of the compact disc (CD), and the recycling of past successes that this involved. The CD, in fact, performed a similar function to punk in keeping the record industry afloat.

A Second Childhood?

Technology has always played a central part in the history of youth culture. The sound of rock 'n' roll depended on the technologies of amplification and the microphone; its dissemination depended on the vinyl disc, transistor radios and cheap record players. Increasingly sophisticated recording technology allowed the Beatles to experiment; and cheap recording technology allowed punk to flourish. So it was with more recent cultural changes. The current sound of 1990s mainstream rock owes much to the development and marketing of the CD; just as the sound of modern dance music has derived from sampling and other such technologies. In the film and television worlds, the video recorder has had similarly dramatic consequences. But without doubt the single most important technology for the youth culture of the 1990s has been the computer game. The outcry that emerged in the 1990s over Acid House parties, rave culture, the drug Ecstasy, and New Age travellers repeat familiar patterns of moral panic, whilst also revealing interesting nuances in the form and meaning of youth culture. But they do not signify any new paradigm. The computer game is much less easily accommodated. Nintendo and Sega games may now fill the rack space in record shops once occupied by vinyl albums; this does not, however, represent a straight swap. The computer game is one stage in the development of a technology which allows individual consumers high degrees of control. They are a prominent part of the era of interactive culture.

It is too early to say what this new technology signifies for youth culture, except that its accompanying panic is almost inevitably as misplaced as it is predictable. Suffice to say that were this chapter to be written ten years from now, computer games would warrant more than a passing paragraph. But then ten years from now, dwelling upon youth culture may, in any case, make little sense – not just because of its complete integration into mainstream culture. If the late twentieth century has been a time for youth, then it may be that the twenty-first century will be the one of the third (old) age.

Understanding Youth Culture

For the historian, one of the problems of studying youth culture is the material. In one sense, there is too much of it, and in another, too little. Few social phenomena can have produced so many artifacts, nor so many people with vivid memories of the experience. The trouble, though, is sorting through this material, knowing what is important or significant. In the choice of key artifacts there is inevitably a set of contentious judgements deployed. This is very apparent in writing about the history of popular music, where highly selective hindsight is at play. Commercial pop tends to be ignored in favour of rock, which is then seen as part of a tradition (on the lines of a literary tradition); certain kinds of music become part of the heritage, while others get written out. These judgements both shape and are shaped by the memories which historians may also solicit. It used to be said that 'If you remember the 60s, you weren't really there'. Certainly, oral history, particularly of a period that has been extensively mythologized, has to be treated with immense caution.

But the problem of detail is not just one of too much material, it is also one of too little. Because modern 'youth culture' has been treated dismissively for much of the time, official records and academic study have been underdeveloped. There are clear signs that this is changing. The last ten years has seen the emergence of institutions like London's Museum of the Moving Image and Bradford's Museum of Photography, Film and Television; the British Library's National Sound Archive has jazz and pop archivists. Slowly, too, higher education has granted academic status to the study of popular culture, in sociology, literature, film and music departments.

The fact that youth culture has been recognized in this way does not mean that there is agreement about *how* it should be studied. The history of the study of youth culture has passed through many phases, followed many avenues and relied on many disciplines. In the late 1950s and early 1960s, youth culture, appearing in the guise of popular culture, began to feature in the discussion of English literature. It did not always receive an enthusiastic embrace. Writers like Denys Thompson, inheritors of the Leavisite approach, were intent upon establishing principles for 'discriminating' in judgement of culture.[16] The point was to preserve the Great Tradition from mass barbarism, where the 'mass' was often a code for the 'working class'. And even those, like Richard Hoggart, who were sympathetic to working-class culture still worried about the damaging effect of commercial culture.[17] An important exception to these two streams in literary studies was Raymond Williams. His writings, although deriving from the study of literature, rejected the idea of 'art' as a disembodied entity.[18] His analysis was informed by a marxism which drew attention to the means by which culture was produced and consumed. Williams was to be the inspiration behind the development of cultural studies generally. Another important influence was the historical work of E.P. Thompson who, in *The Making of the English Working Class*, emphasized the role of culture in the creation of class identity.[19]

Their approaches both meshed with and provided guidance to the way sociologists were approaching youth culture. Sociology had, of course, devoted considerable attention to 'youth'. Sociologists were contributors to the debate about the behaviour of the young in the 1950s, out of which emerged a substantial literature on 'delinquency'. This representation of youth behaviour as somehow problematic provoked a reaction from other sociologists who argued that the phenomenon was greatly exaggerated, and that, more importantly, to see it as a 'problem' was to beg the question: a problem for whom? The focus of study shifted to understanding youth behaviour from within, to make cults and youth culture intelligible from the perspective of the participants. This approach found its fullest expression in the Centre for Contemporary Cultural Studies (under the successive leadership of Richard Hoggart, Stuart Hall and Richard Johnson) at the University of Birmingham. New insights were brought to the way that youth cults were forged as a way of resisting the impact of capitalism on young people's lives.

The CCCS approach held sway not only in sociology but in cultural studies generally. But it was not without its critics, writers often themselves from the Centre. Feminists drew attention to the way that women were marginalized from the focus on cult activity. In a similar vein, others were critical of the *sub*cultural focus which tended to look only at minority or highly visible forms of youth cultural activity.

These challenges from within cultural studies have been accompanied by critiques derived from other disciplines or approaches. Cultural studies lacked any very conscious historical sense. Historians argued that the signs of youth culture were part of a larger and yet familiar pattern of social adjustment.

Another external critique has come from those who argue that the cultural studies approach pays too little attention to the content and the production of culture. It says nothing about how and why a record, for example, acquires meaning. Such questions have – slowly – come to be addressed within musicology, which for a long time resisted the thought that pop music was a relevant part of its discipline. Attached to the emphasis on the meaning of youth culture is the concern to account for its production. Here the task is to explain youth culture through the way the industry, the mass media and the artists work to *construct* an audience and a meaning for what is consumed.

Bibliographical Note

For details of youth culture in the period, see the books by Robert Hewison *In Anger: Culture in the Cold War 1945–60* (London, 1981) and *Too Much: Art and Society in the Sixties 1960–75* (London, 1986) for a view from a distance; see George Melly's *Revolt into Style* (London, 1971) and Jeff Nuttal's *Bomb Culture* (London, 1969) for a view from within. For a history of cultural change with a strong theoretical element (drawn from cultural studies), see Iain Chambers' *Popular Culture: The Metropolitan Experience* (London, 1986) and also J. McGuigan, *Cultural Populism* (London, 1992). For an oral history of the 1960s, see Jonathon Green's *Days in the Life* (London, 1988). Two different sociological perspectives on cultural change can be found in Bernice Martin's long cycle view, *A Sociology of Contemporary Cultural Change* (Oxford, 1981), or Mike Brake's subcultural account, *The Sociology of Youth Culture and Youth Subcultures* (London, 1980). For the arguments about interpreting youth culture, see Simon Frith and Andrew Goodwin (eds), *On Record* (London, 1991); and Angela McRobbie, *Feminism and Youth Culture* (London, 1992). On the impact of pop music and the media see Simon Frith, *Sound Effects* (London, 1983), and D. Strinati and S. Wagg (eds), *Come on Down? Popular Media Culture in Post-war Britain* (London, 1992).

Notes

1. Quoted in Department of Education and Science, *Young People in the 1980s* (London, 1983) p. 11.

2. Anon., 'The happiest days of my life', *The Guardian*, 24 May 1993.

3. J. Davis, *Youth and the Condition of Britain* (London, 1990) p. 84; see also pp. 25–41.

4. B. Osgerby, ' "Well, It's Saturday Night an' I Just Got Paid": youth, consumerism and hegemony in post-war Britain', *Contemporary Record* vol. 6 (1992), p. 291.

5. S. Frith, *Sound Effects* (London, 1983) p. 183.

6. Quoted in Osgerby, ' "Well, It's Saturday Night ...', p. 294.

7. E. Wilson, *Adorned in Dreams* (London, 1985) p. 193.

8. Quoted in M. Brake, *The Sociology of Youth Culture and Youth Subcultures* (London, 1980) p. 95.

9. B. Martin, *A Sociology of Contemporary Cultural Change* (Oxford, 1983) p. 21.

10. P. Wicke, *Rock Music: Culture, Aesthetics and Sociology* (Cambridge, 1990) p. viii.

11. P. Hardy and D. Laing, *The Faber Companion to 20th Century Popular Music* (London, 1990) p. 48.

12. P. Norman, *Shout! The True Story of The Beatles* (London, 1981) p. 28.

13. Frith, *Sound Effects*, p. 96.

14. S. Frith, *Music For Pleasure* (Oxford, 1988) p. 3.

15. C. Gillett, *The Sound of the City* (London, 1983) p. 265.

16. D. Thompson (ed.), *Discrimination and Popular Culture* (London, 1964).

17. R. Hoggart, *The Uses of Literacy* (London, 1957).

18. See, for example, R. Williams, *Culture and Society* (London, 1958).

19. E.P. Thompson, *The Making of the English Working Class* (London, 1963).

27 The Role of the State in Twentieth-Century Britain

Paul Johnson

What have been the most significant developments in British economic, social and cultural life over the course of the twentieth century, and what accounts for them? This is a little like asking about beauty, wisdom or goodness; opinions will vary widely and will fluctuate over time. Individual responses may conflate the personal experience of maturation and ageing with secular changes in economic and social conditions. Since personal physical well-being and relative income tend to decline in old age, it is perhaps not surprising that some older people look back to events in the past with fonder sentiments than those with which they view the present, even though the *average* health status of seventy year olds and their absolute and relative economic position has improved markedly throughout the century.

Other, sometimes more fanciful, attempts at stylizing and summarizing twentieth-century development may make inapposite comparisons. In a classic BBC television series of the 1960s, *Adam Adamant*, an Edwardian gentleman detective re-emerged into swinging London from six decades of slumber in a block of ice. He was bedazzled by the bright lights of Piccadilly Circus, the escalators on the Underground, and the fact that breakfast consisted of cereals delivered from a cardboard box rather than kedgeree from a silver serving dish. But as well as travelling in time, Adam Adamant had travelled across the social spectrum from gentleman's club to single person's bedsit. Comparison of this sort made between the former lifestyle of an elite and the current lifestyle of the majority will inevitably underestimate the extent of material improvement. It is a tendency deeply rooted in our patterns and processes of cultural inheritance. The buildings and artifacts of the Edwardian period that are still in use (or preserved in museums) today, together with the works of literature and of art, are primarily the relics of upper and middle-class society. The mean streets of the poor have long since been swept away by slum clearance schemes, their ornaments broken-up or consigned to junk shops, their pulp novels of romance, mystery and murder relegated to some remote shelf in the British Library.

As well as recognizing the highly partial nature of our physical inheritance from the past, we also need to be aware of the selective and distorting nature of popular memory. A nation that can elevate the rout and evacuation of its army at Dunkirk into a point of national pride clearly has a profound ability to reinvent its past. Recollections of imperial greatness that linger in the tawdry bombast of songs like 'Rule Britannia' – and in parts of the school curriculum in history advocated by the Secretary of State for Education, Kenneth Baker, in 1988 – reflect an unwillingness to come to terms with the reality of relative economic and military decline. But the distortions of popular memory are not the preserve of patriots; the labour movement has created its own mythology of solidarity which belies the reality of factionalism.

Despite these problems inherent in any assessment of the historical record, it is nevertheless possible to discern one unambiguous aspect of twentieth-century development which has profoundly affected economic and social life – the increasing role of the state. Agencies and instruments of the state at both local and national levels have had a growing influence on people's lives, both through direct contact and indirectly through the moulding of social attitudes and organizations. During the boom years of the 1950s and 1960s public policy and state organizations were frequently lauded as progenitors of prosperity, but economic slowdown and the rise of 'new right' ideology meant that by the mid 1980s the state was more often vilified for its inefficiency, waste and subversion of personal economic and social incentives. But the passion of recent arguments about the role of the public sector in social and economic life has tended to obscure the fact that debate over the legitimate role of government has been a recurrent theme of political discourse throughout the twentieth century. In order to trace some of these historical threads, this chapter will examine developments in two key instruments of the state – public bureaucracy and the civil law – and in two key outcomes – the provision of economic security and the development of social stability.

Public Bureaucracy

A crude indicator of the growing role of the state is the rise in the relative share of the workforce directly employed in public administration. Figure 27.1 shows that over the course of the twentieth century civil servants have multiplied from less than 2 to more than 6 per cent of the workforce. This increase is a function of two distinct trends – of a gradual but sustained expansion of local government employment, and of much more erratic fluctuations in central government employment, with sharp increases associated with both world wars followed by clear but less pronounced decreases in the postwar decades. Central government's rising share of total employment reflects a similar pattern in the share of public expenditure in GDP, which has grown rapidly during war and fallen back in peacetime, but never to the prewar level. Peacock and Wiseman have labelled this the

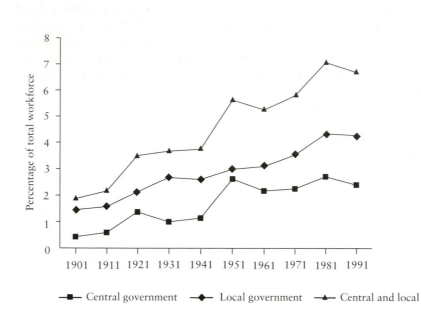

Figure 27.1.   Share of total workforce employed in central and local government.

'displacement effect' – the way in which full-scale war seems to have displaced public expenditure onto a permanently higher trajectory.[1] Quite why war has had this effect on the size of the public sector is a matter of some dispute, but it is clear that one effect of the world wars has been to bring ordinary citizens into a permanently closer relationship with paid officers of the state.

Figure 27.1 shows only the growing relative size of the workforce *directly* employed by central and local government. The size of the overall public sector workforce has increased much more rapidly, particularly after the Second World War as most health workers moved into the public sector with the establishment of the National Health Service, as the education system expanded and as more than two million workers were affected by the Labour government's nationalization programme (see Table 17.5). In the early 1990s, even after a spate of privatization, public sector workers accounted for around a quarter of the total British workforce, with the National Health Service being the largest single employer in Western Europe.

This expansion of public bureaucracy and service provision has made the state much more central to the economic and social life of the majority of Britons. In 1900 contact for most people with paid agents of the state was still relatively infrequent, although there had been a marked development of state regulation and activity since the mid nineteenth century. By the end of Victoria's reign local government had begun to encroach on the lives of ordinary citizens through the public provision of education by School Boards, through the regulation of housing and sanitary conditions by public health inspectors, and in many places through the municipal control of transport systems and gas and water supplies. The idea of public intervention was increasingly supported by socialists who saw the state as the means for the redistribution of wealth, and by progressive liberals who saw state agencies as a mechanism for limiting (or compensating for) the deleterious consequences of market competition. The course of local government intervention was, however, driven as much by the practicalities of governance in expanding and increasingly complex urban environments as by ideology.

Whether the intervention was welcomed by the majority of working-class people is unclear. Henry Pelling has suggested that public intervention often involved real costs for working-class households – through required improvements in sanitation, reduction in overcrowding, or restriction on child employment – and so was more often opposed, ignored or avoided than acclaimed.[2] Irrespective of how public intervention was greeted, it is clear that it was strictly circumscribed and that direct contact with agencies of the state was rare. In 1900 only paupers were in immediate receipt of public munificence, and only schoolchildren in regular contact with public sector employees – their teachers. Furthermore, most people had no overt economic relationship with the state, at either local or national level. Thresholds for the payment of income tax and death duties were set at levels well above working-class financial capacities, and local taxes (rates on property) were compounded in the rental payment made to landlords. Workers did bear their share of indirect customs and excise duties, but they were not personally liable for tax, and could live their adult lives with virtually no direct financial association with agents or instruments of the local or central state.

Seventy years on, individual links with the state were very different. By the 1970s all people were tied into a direct, lifelong economic relationship with the central state through the tax and benefit system. This began with the introduction of contributory national health and unemployment insurance in 1911, was extended by the inclusion of most manual workers in the income tax system during the Second World War, and culminated with the establishment of the postwar welfare state. The means-tested nature of many welfare benefits has resulted in a growing number of households being subject to direct economic investigation by civil servants who, from 1948, have been employees of a centralized bureaucracy rather than a locally-controlled relief agency. In 1900 barely 2 per cent of the population was in receipt of poor relief and so subject to assessment by Poor Law relieving officers. Despite the intention of Beveridge to use the National Insurance system to whittle away means-tested benefit, both the number of different means-tests and of people affected has risen inexorably. In 1951 more than 4 per cent of the population was supported by a means-tested income supplement. By 1970 this had risen to almost 8 per cent, and taking account of other income-related assistance such as housing benefit, 12 per cent of the population was subject to a government means-test by 1982.

Public bureaucracy has extended well beyond the financial sphere of the tax and benefit systems. The potential abuse of new technologies has been seen as a reasonable ground for regulation, particularly when the new activities they make possible have wide popular appeal. Cinema censorship from 1912, and the regulation in the 1980s of the content of videotapes, follow in the footsteps of the prohibition of off-course street betting from 1906 to 1961, and the restriction of opening hours of licensed premises since 1914, as examples of the twentieth-century state actively interfering in the leisure activities of ordinary people. The licensing of radio and TV receivers, and of cars and drivers, have linked this regulation with an effective mechanism for raising government revenue.

Other parts of the state bureaucratic apparatus have been established or expanded to regulate institutions and organizations in the belief that this would either directly protect individual welfare or correct undesired consequences of market competition. An example of the former is the regulation of the purity of foodstuffs, now the responsibility of local trading standards officers but begun in the mid Victorian period by medical officers of health; while the establishment of the Monopolies Commission in 1948 is a case of the latter. Behind most sales and purchases today – whether of goods, services or labour – there is some element of regulation and control of standards by local or national civil servants. In the 1980s the Conservative government identified the pervasive nature of bureaucratic regulation as a stultifying influence on economic activity, and began a conscious policy of decontrol. The most celebrated case was in October 1986 when dealing in the City of London was deregulated in a 'Big Bang', but similar relaxation of control has covered a broad range of activities including the inspection of schools, the setting of minimum employment conditions, and the sale of non-dangerous drugs. The presumption behind these reforms is that people no longer need the hidden bureaucratic hand of the nanny state to tell them what they can or cannot do; in a mature industrial society adults should be allowed to exercise judgement in their own best interests in a free market. Yet despite this deliberate government design to reverse a twentieth-century trend towards increasing levels of bureaucratic interference, fears have been raised that the central state has become more rather than less authoritarian in recent years through an accretion of new legal powers.

The Role of the Civil Law

The expansion of twentieth-century public bureaucracy has been underpinned by legislation. Governments of all political colours have repeatedly used the civil law to grant themselves new powers. The most dramatic examples of this were the Defence of the Realm Act of August 1914 and the Emergency Powers (Defence) Act of August 1939. Total war demanded extensive control of civilian economic and social life, and this was achieved through a large-scale wartime increase in the number of civil servants and in the state's legal powers. Government interference in civilian life in the First World War was perhaps the more significant because it represented more of a discontinuity with the prewar traditions than was the case in 1939. Victorian voluntarism, so deeply entrenched in nineteenth-century church and charitable activities and in friendly society and trade union self-help, managed to sustain the military effort until the beginning of 1916, but there was a limit to the willingness to give lives. Conscription, the ultimate legal imposition on the individual by the state, deeply troubled many non-pacifist liberals, as did the direction of civilian manpower and the subjection of the market mechanism to overt government control. But the primacy of the war effort, particularly after Lloyd George became premier at the end of 1916, marks this period, in the view of José Harris, 'as a crucial turning point in the evolution of modern politics and the modern British state'.[3] At the outbreak of the Second World War conscription, rationing, the requisition of supplies and the direction of labour came much more rapidly and with much less heart-searching and disagreement. In 1939, unlike 1914, there was little disagreement that the citizen was beholden to the state.

The authoritarian wartime legislation is the most acute example of government using the civil law directly to regulate economic and social life, but there are many more enduring peacetime examples. Two that have been consistently newsworthy have been the laws relating to trade unions and to property. From the Trades Disputes Act of 1906 which relieved unions from liability for civil damages incurred by an employer as a result of strike action, to the series of Employment Acts of the 1980s which prohibited secondary picketing and abolished the closed shop, there has been a see-saw of legislation. Governments have used the law to change the legal status of trade unions and collective bargaining, sometimes to reward unions, sometimes to cajole them and sometimes to punish them, though not with any simple party-political predictability.

In the property market repeated legislative intervention has ensured that investment in real estate has never been 'as safe as houses'. The introduction of rent control in 1915, and its continuation ever since with varying degrees of comprehensiveness and intensity, has amounted to a direct appropriation of the personal wealth of rental property-owners by the state. Although rent control has been more favoured by Labour than Conservative governments, the Conservative Party has been less than forthright in its defence of this element of private property. Indeed it is a Conservative government in the 1990s that has pressed ahead with reform of leasehold law, favouring the interests of long-term tenants above those of freehold owners. The sanctity of private property emerges not as a fundamental principle of government but as a legal contrivance that can be repeatedly revised to suit changing economic, social and political circumstances.

This malleability of the civil law, particularly in the absence of a British Bill of Rights, has allowed governments to fundamentally alter or abrogate the rights of citizens, even in peacetime. The Prevention of Terrorism Act, first passed in 1974 and constantly renewed ever since, has removed basic legal rights from people suspected of terrorist activity, and the series of immigration and nationality acts passed by both Labour and Conservative governments since 1962 have redefined and narrowed rights of settlement and citizenship. Other legislative changes of the 1980s appear to have strengthened the power of central government over subsidiary administrative bodies. The establishment by the 1988 Education Act of a National Curriculum reverses a century of local teacher determination of the school syllabus, and increased powers of control from Westminster of local authority expenditure have severely circumscribed the decision-making autonomy of local councils. It should be noted, however, that the principle of central government interference with the education system or local authority finances is long established. Labour and Conservative administrations in the 1960s played political football with the concept of the comprehensive school (see Chapter 21), and local authorities have been dependent on central government financial assistance since the introduction of rate support grants in 1888. Complaints by civil liberty groups that the authoritarian power of the central state has undergone unprecedented expansion since the early 1980s seem premature, but so too do claims that the frontiers of the state have been rolled back, that people have been freed of unnecessary bureaucratic and legislative constraint.

In focus: The Standardization of the Life Course

In Edwardian Britain people could live their lives with little interference from public authorities, and in particular with little formal structuring of their life course – that is, of being told what could (or could not) be done at any particular age. In 1900 it was only relatively young children who were regulated or categorized according to age. Those aged under seven were deemed not to be responsible for any criminal acts they might commit, and since 1880 children between the ages of five and ten had been compelled to attend full-time schooling, with half-time attendance permitted for eleven year olds who had reached defined attainment targets. Attendance was regulated by school attendance officers who kept records of children living in their locality and pursued truants and their parents. In addition, a series of factory acts had, by 1891, established a minimum working age of eleven in factories, and allowed eleven to fourteen year olds to work no more than half time. This legislation was, of course, largely dependent on enforcement by employers who relied on sometimes dubious declarations of age provided by children or their parents. Finally, the age of consent for sexual relations had been set at sixteen in 1885. Beyond sixteen the only significant age restriction related to men – they had to be eighteen to join the regular army, and twenty-one to vote. Women were allowed to do neither.

The Standardization of the Life Course (continued)

Over the course of the century many of the age thresholds relating to children have been raised. In 1901 the minimum working age was raised to twelve, in 1919 the minimum school-leaving age was set at fourteen, and by 1973 it had been raised to sixteen, with added restrictions introduced on the maximum working week for young persons under eighteen. In 1908 the imprisonment of children under fourteen was prohibited, and the death sentence was abolished for people under seventeen. Since that date the treatment of children by the criminal law has been repeatedly revised and liberalized.

More significant, however, has been the way in which new age thresholds have been introduced for adults. One of the most important has been the pension age. In 1900 old age had physical but not official meaning. Although many older people were in receipt of poor law relief, they qualified because of need, not because of age. In 1908 the qualifying age for receipt of a state pension was set at seventy, though receipt of this pension was conditional on a means test (see Chapter 5). From 1928 contributory pensions were paid to people from the age of sixty-five, subject only to their having paid a sufficient number of National Insurance contributions. In 1940 the age threshold for women was reduced to sixty, and from 1948 these thresholds of sixty-five for men and sixty for women effectively became the standard retirement age, since receipt of a public pension was now made conditional upon having permanently left the labour market. Subsequently small pension supplements have been introduced for persons reaching the age thresholds of seventy-five and eighty. In addition, from 1988 contributors to personal pension schemes have been allowed to make use of favourable tax concessions in drawing their pension from any age above fifty-four. Over time, therefore, particularly with the expansion of the social security system, the later part of the life course has become increasingly structured by state regulation.

The same is true of entry to adulthood. The age of legal majority was reduced from twenty-one to eighteen in 1970 (the voting age had been lowered the previous year), but there are many other legal age thresholds which have been created in the twentieth century. Reaching the age of sixteen bestows on people the right to ride a moped, have heterosexual intercourse, buy cigarettes and get married. One year on and they can drive a car, a further year and they can buy a drink, place a bet, and watch an adult film. At the age of nineteen children are deemed by the rules of the social security system no longer to be dependants, though they continue to have entitlement for student grants assessed on the basis of parental income. By the age of twenty-one they can drive a heavy goods vehicle and men can have homosexual intercourse. But up to the age of twenty-four claimants of means-tested cash benefits receive a lower rate because they are not deemed to be living in independent households.

The Standardization of the Life Course (continued)

As a by-product of other subject-specific legislation, the state has come to define a multitude of age-specific stepping-stones through life that were quite unknown at the end of the Victorian period. In an important sense, therefore, twentieth-century governments have standardized the passage of individuals through their life course.

The Provision of Economic Security

One of the most significant outcomes of state activity in twentieth-century Britain has been a long-run enhancement in the degree of economic security enjoyed by individuals. This has been the result of deliberate economic and social policy which, for most of the time, has been unambiguously popular. Yet it has also been a contentious achievement, regarded by some as a primary cause of both the deteriorating relative performance of the British economy and the growing dissonance of modern social relationships.

As already noted, in 1900 individuals had to cope with the inevitable unpredictability of economic life by whatever means they could. Mutual unemployment insurance through trade unions, mutual sickness insurance through friendly societies, life insurance with companies such as the Prudential, savings in the Post Office, accumulation of the 'divi' at the Co-operative store, money stacked up on the mantelpiece or under the mattress, the sharing of resources with neighbours, relatives and friends, raising a loan from the pawnbroker or borrowing from the local loan shark – these were the everyday economic strategies of working-class life. They were made necessary not only by the fluctuating financial needs of expanding and contracting families, but also by the precarious nature of wage income. Most manual workers had no job security and could be dismissed or laid-off at short notice according to the cycle of trade or seasons. The millions of members of mutual insurance and self-help organizations in Edwardian Britain are proof of the enormity of effort made to achieve some higher level of economic security in a changeable world. Those who failed ended up reliant on the Poor Law.

Much of the social legislation enacted by twentieth-century governments, from the Old Age Pension Act in 1908 and the 1911 National Insurance scheme to the postwar Labour government's 'welfare state' and its more recent extensions, has been directed towards enhancing economic security, towards constructing a social safety net that stretches from the cradle to the grave. Not only has a guaranteed income been provided to individuals during periods of sickness, unemployment, disability and old age, but the costs of health care have, since 1948, been largely assumed by the state, as have the full cost of secondary schooling (since 1944) and university education (since 1962).

REPORT TO THE NATION   No. 20

July 5

THIS DAY MAKES HISTORY

Insurance and assistance to help in all the changes and chances of life, a free national health service for all—these are the great landmarks in British social progress which we have reached this month.

Who will pay for them? We must pay for them ourselves. Into the national insurance fund will flow contributions paid by those who are employed, by their employers, by those who are on their own, and sums of money paid by the Government out of the taxes collected from all of us. Out of it will flow the unemployment, sickness, widowhood and maternity benefits, and retirement pensions. The health service will be paid for almost entirely out of taxes. Taxation pays completely for national assistance and family allowances.

How will we pay for them? We must pay for them out of production. The cash benefits drawn by the unemployed, the ill and injured, and the old, are their claims on a part of the nation's production, even though they cannot add to that production themselves. When we put resources into the health service—doctors and nurses, bricks and mortar and power—it means we can't use them to increase output of goods.

So if we are to have these new benefits and all the goods we want, too—well, then we've got to make more goods. And we ought to find that the freedom from anxiety that insurance will give and the better health resulting from the health service will help us to answer the call for

MORE AND MORE PRODUCTION

How the two schemes work

National Health Service	**National Insurance Scheme**
Provides all forms of medical advice and care, hospital and specialist services, medicines, drugs and appliances, as well as a family doctor.	Provides cash benefits during sickness, injury, unemployment and widowhood; payments at childbirth and at death, and pensions for the industrially disabled and on retirement.
Is available to everybody, whether insured or not, and there are no fees to pay.	These benefits are available only to contributors and their families.
You can use any part of it, or all of it, as you wish.	Contributions are compulsory for most people, and cards must be stamped from July 5th on.
If you have not yet chosen your doctor, do so now; get an application form E.C.1 for each member of the family from Post Office or Public Library.	If you (or your employer for you) have not got a card yet, apply by filling in the form C.F.6 available at all Post Offices.

— *Issued by His Majesty's Government* —

Plate 27.1. The 'appointed day' in 1948 when the NHS and National Insurance systems began operation. The beneficent arm of the state was most evident in the introduction of a comprehensive system of social protection after the Second World War. This public information advertisement points out that welfare benefits are paid for out of current production.

Housing costs have been lowered for purchasers by the allowance of tax relief on mortgages, and for renters by the provision of public housing at below-market rents. Since 1945 parents have been assisted with child-rearing costs through the payment of family allowances (Child Benefit from 1975).

In addition many strands of macro-economic policy have also served to enhance individual economic security. Nationalization of coal, transport, gas, electricity and iron and steel after the Second World War gave workers in these industries new levels of job security, since the state was prepared to underwrite financial losses. The National Economic Development Council, established in 1962, was one of several institutional mechanisms designed to assist government plans to coordinate economic activity, maximize growth and attain the goal of full employment established by the 1944 white paper. How far such policies were responsible for the economic achievements of the postwar period is unclear, but there can be little doubt that the combined effects of social policy, economic policy and world trading conditions gave people in the quarter century from 1950 a degree of personal economic security and prosperity never previously experienced.

Although protection for all citizens from Beveridge's five 'giant evils' of Want, Sickness, Squalor, Ignorance and Idleness has never been complete, the extension of new levels of economic and social security to the majority of the population can be seen as a major achievement of twentieth-century public policy (see Chapter 20). However, the provision by the state of these new social rights inevitably involved the placing on individuals of new obligations to the state, most obviously in terms of taxation. The enormous scale of health, unemployment and pension provision, particularly after the Second World War when the system was extended from manual workers to all categories and classes of the population, meant that social expenditure came to dominate government accounts (see Table 20.1). National Insurance contributions were increased and the income tax net widened by the quite conscious decision not to uprate tax thresholds in line with inflation. All adults became tied into a reciprocal financial relationship with the state (and so with their fellow taxpayers), making net contributions for most of the time from the age of sixteen until pension age, and making net withdrawals during retirement.

The extension of public involvement in personal economic affairs was never accepted as desirable in all political quarters. Before the First World War proponents of individualism argued that the provision of public funds to the poor as a matter of right through the payment of pensions would demoralize the recipients by devaluing their own efforts at self-help. During the Second World War the refugee Austrian economist F.A. Hayek published a comprehensive critique of state intervention, *The Road to Serfdom*, but at the time it was the ideas of Beveridge that commanded majority support. But with the conjunction of rising inflation, unemployment and industrial unrest in the 1970s there arose in conservative circles a trenchant critique of public provision of economic security which extended well beyond a concern with the classic welfare state. The social safety net failed the poor, it was argued, because instead of bouncing them back into active economic participation it entrapped them in a dependency culture. For low-income households additional income resulted in the loss of means-tested benefits on almost a pound-for-pound basis, so there was little incentive to work. More affluent households had little need of a social safety net, but they made use of burgeoning public sector employment opportunities and 'middle-class' parts of the welfare state such as university education as a kind of social deck chair, providing a comfortable, stress-free life untouched by the pressures of market competition. Meanwhile taxes on the wealth creators – entrepreneurs, industrialists, financiers – were excessive and capricious, inducing them to take their expertise and dynamism overseas.

This analysis offered a profound challenge to twentieth-century traditions of expanding public provision of economic security. It did not deny that security was both popular and desirable, but it suggested that economic security freely given undermined incentives to work, earn, accumulate, innovate and improve. The state had a responsibility to protect the weak, but not to coddle the majority. The safety net should be set at an adequate but low level and everyone should have to face the pressures and uncertainties of market competition. In Edwardian Britain the quest for economic improvement and 'national efficiency' had encouraged the government to raise the level of economic and social protection, but in the 1980s similar goals, changed circumstances and a radically different analysis has led to a deliberate reduction in personal economic and social security.

What effect this reversal of a twentieth-century trend towards the greater public provision of personal economic security will have on macro-economic performance, on personal economic behaviour and on social cohesion remains to be seen.

The Development of Social Stability

As well as changing personal economic conditions, state activity has affected the nature of social cohesion and behaviour in both destructive and constructive ways. The destructive aspects are much as early twentieth-century critics of state intervention predicted. By assuming the economic functions of voluntary organizations such as friendly societies and voluntary hospitals, public welfare provision has supplanted the extensive network of mutual assistance that existed at the end of Victoria's reign. By relaxing divorce laws and by assuming some of the costs of family dissolution, the state has weakened family structures. Through insensitive and inappropriate public housing policy and design, local authorities have displaced and destroyed traditional community structures. These are some of the oft-cited, though not always fully-documented, detrimental consequences of ill-directed or excessive public sector intervention.

Yet it can equally well be argued that state action has promoted social stability and cohesion in direct and indirect ways. The establishment in the mid 1970s of the Equal Opportunities Commission and the Commission for Racial Equality are examples of direct attempts to prevent discriminatory forms of social exclusion. In the interwar period the BBC, under its director John Reith, consciously attempted to use broadcasting as an indirect means of promoting social unity and a common culture (see Chapter 15). The state education system and the established church arguably attempt to do much the same. At the local level the mid Victorian flowering of civic pride led to the construction by local authorities of thousands of public parks and gardens, which in the twentieth century have been supplemented by playgrounds, village halls, community centres, youth and pensioner clubs, swimming pools and sports centres. These are often taken for granted as community resources, yet they are the outcome of deliberate public sector activity. But perhaps the most important mechanism for the promotion of social stability and cohesion has been the broad array of economic and social policies which, by providing guaranteed minimum incomes and by maintaining a high level of employment, have managed to prevent the complete social exclusion of disadvantaged groups that has occurred, for instance, in some US cities. Whether the high unemployment rates, rising inequality and greater exposure to economic uncertainty experienced in Britain since the early 1980s will create a large-scale problem of social exclusion is a pressing question for the 1990s.

Interpretations

What should we make of these twentieth-century changes in the role of the state? Has the free-born Briton of some (imagined) former age become the regulated subject of a public bureaucracy which is itself increasingly under the authoritarian control of central government? This is how the blatantly political use of the police and security forces to coerce and control mineworkers during their strike of 1984–85 appeared to some observers. But the potency of the example does not prove the case. Coercion and control of strikers and protesters has a long history. For example, in the years immediately before and after the First World War troops were used on a number of occasions against strikers, leading to the deaths of two men in Liverpool in 1911 and the placing of tanks on the streets of Glasgow in 1919. And during the mass protests and hunger marches of the 1930s, the secret service infiltrated the National Unemployed Workers' Movement.

Has public provision of personal economic security, particularly since 1945, so diminished work incentives that the long-term capacity of the economy to compete in world markets has been fatally undermined? This case has been vigorously advanced by Barnett who has argued that politicians squandered the resources of the country at the end of the Second World War by spending on

Plate 27.2 Troops and police on the streets of Liverpool during a transport strike in 1911. The authoritarian arm of the British state has been used repeatedly in the twentieth century against organized labour – particularly during the 1911–14 strike wave, the 1926 General Strike, and the 1984–85 miners strike.

welfare services when they should have been investing in physical and human capital. As the economy faltered in the 1970s others suggested that excessive welfare spending and public sector employment was the root cause of stagnation.[4] But once set in a comparative perspective this case appears fragile – over the period 1960–75, for instance, both the rate of growth of social expenditure *and* the overall rate of economic growth was higher in Germany, France and Japan than it was in Britain.

Has the accumulation of power by central government and the replacement of voluntary associations by public welfare services removed from people both the opportunity and the need to combine and collaborate? There has been a clear shift in the balance of administrative and legal authority across the course of the century from local to national government, but this does not mean that pluralism has been replaced by authoritarianism. Chapter 25 demonstrates that pressure group activity is vibrant, and as Mrs Thatcher learned to her cost, the will of central government can be bent or broken on issues, such as the Poll Tax, which mobilize widespread popular opposition.

Has the comprehensive involvement of the state in the economic and social life of individuals produced a less cohesive, less caring society? Rising rates of divorce, crime, and public disorder can be pointed to as evidence of a social malaise, but it is not obvious how far these trends can be attributed to state action (or inaction) rather than more diffuse social developments. An alternative view might emphasize the continuity of reciprocal care and support exchanged within families and between neighbours, the thousands of people regularly involved in charitable and voluntary activity, the millions who gave to Live Aid and Comic Relief. Despite the extensive economic, social and cultural change that has occurred since 1900, Britain remains a largely peaceful, tolerant, and pluralistic society, and the state can claim some, at least, of the credit for this achievement.

Bibliographical Note

Accessible and stimulating surveys of the role of government in British society are provided by Pat Thane, 'Government and society in England and Wales, 1750–1914', and José Harris, 'Society and the state in twentieth-century Britain', both in F.M.L. Thompson (ed.), *The Cambridge Social History of Britain 1750–1950, Volume 3* (Cambridge, 1990). Two good collections of essays on the importance of war as a catalyst for social and governmental change are K. Burk (ed.), *War and the State: The Transformation of British Government 1914–1919* (London, 1982), and H.L. Smith (ed.), *War and Social Change: British Society in the Second World War* (Manchester, 1986). The argument that the government overestimated the economic strength of the nation and overcommitted itself to welfare expenditure after the Second World War is vigorously presented in Corelli Barnett, *The Audit of War* (London, 1986) and vigorously challenged by José Harris in 'Enterprise and welfare states: a comparative perspective', *Transactions of the Royal Historical Society* 5th ser., vol. 40 (1990). An overview of economic and social policy throughout the century can be found in G. Peden, *British*

Economic and Social Policy: Lloyd George to Margaret Thatcher (Hemel Hempstead, 2nd edn, 1990) and a survey and assessment of postwar governments can be found in P. Hennessey and A. Seldon (eds), *Ruling Performance: British Governments from Attlee to Thatcher* (Oxford, 1987).

Notes

1.   A.T. Peacock and J. Wiseman, *The Growth of Public Expenditure in the United Kingdom* (London, 2nd edn, 1967).

2.   H. Pelling, 'The working class and the welfare state' in H. Pelling, *Popular Politics and Society in Late Victorian Britain* (London, 1968).

3.   José Harris, 'Society and the state in twentieth-century Britain' in F.M.L. Thompson (ed.), *The Cambridge Social History of Britain 1750–1950, Volume 3* (Cambridge, 1990), p. 71.

4.   C. Barnett, *The Audit of War* (London, 1986); R. Bacon and W. Eltis, *Britain's Economic Problem: Too Few Producers* (London, 1976); OECD, *The Welfare State in Crisis* (Paris, 1981).

Key Dates and Events

1900   Labour Representation Committee formed.
British garrison under siege from Boer forces at Mafeking is relieved; widespread popular celebration in Britain.
Conservative government re-elected.

1901   Death of Queen Victoria, accession of Edward VII.
Taff Value Judgment makes trade unions liable for damages sustained by employers against whom strike action has been taken.
First football crowd exceeding 100,000 in Britain.
Publication of Seebohm Rowntree's *Poverty, A Study of Town Life*.

1902   Boer War ends.
Education Act abolishes school boards in England and Wales and establishes new local education authorities which create rate supported grammar schools.
Midwives Act licenses and improves standards in midwifery.

1903   Joseph Chamberlain launches Tariff Reform Campaign.
Formation of Women's Social and Political Union (the Suffragettes).

1904   Formation of Fédération International de Football Associations (FIFA).
Empire, Ardwick Green, Manchester becomes the first large music hall to be converted into a cinema.
Report of Inter-departmental Committee on Physical Deterioration.

1905   Unemployed Workmen Act – allows local authorities to use limited public funds to provide work for the unemployed.
Aliens Act restricts settlement of foreign immigrants.
Formation of Sinn Fein and of Ulster Unionist Council.

1906   Liberal government elected.
29 Labour Representation Committee MPs elected; they change name to the Labour Party.

Parliament passes Street Betting Act to outlaw cash betting other than at race courses.
Trade Disputes Act reverses Taff Value Judgment.
Education (Provision of Meals) Act allows subsidized school meals for children of the poor.

1907   Education (Administrative Provisions) Act introduces medical inspection of school children.
Women allowed to become local and county councillors.
Boy Scouts founded by Baden-Powell.

1908   Old Age Pensions Act passed, coming into effect in 1909.
Ford Motor Company sell first 'Model T' in Britain, imported from US.

1909   Labour Exchanges Act establishes register of vacant jobs.
Lloyd George's 'People's Budget' rejected by House of Lords.
Trade Boards Act sets minimum wages in 'sweated industries'.
Osborne Judgment prevents trade unions from using funds for political purposes.

1910   Liberal minority government elected in two general elections in January–February and in December.
Death of Edward VII, accession of George V.
Suffragette campaign includes arson; suffragette prisoners mount hunger strikes.
London Palladium opened.

1911   National Insurance Act introduces contributory health insurance for most manual workers, and contributory unemployment insurance for workers in 'precarious' trades.
Parliament Act removes power of veto from House of Lords.
Payment of MPs introduced.
Two strikers shot dead by troops in Liverpool during protests in support of dock and railway strikes.

1912   First Music Hall Royal Command Performance.
British Board of Film Censors established.
Irish Home Rule Bill introduced; opposition to home rule mobilized in Ulster.

1913   Trade Union Act reverses Osborne Judgment, thereby allowing trade unions to use their funds for political purposes.

1914   'Curragh mutiny' of army officers in support of Ulster unionists.
Suffragette riots in London.
Anglican church in Wales disestablished.
Britain declares war on Germany, 4 August.
Defence of the Realm Act gives government wide-ranging emergency powers.

1915   Government negotiates 'Treasury Agreement' with trade unions over dilution of skilled labour.
Creation of Ministry of Munitions headed by Lloyd George.
Women's international peace conference at The Hague.
Introduction of rent control on working-class housing.

1916   Conscription introduced for unmarried men aged 18–41 in January; extended to married men 18–41 in May.
Easter rising in Dublin suppressed.
Battle of the Somme – over 620,000 Allied casualties (1 July – 19 Nov.).
Lloyd George replaces Asquith as Prime Minister.

1917   United States enters war on side of Britain and her Allies.
Russian revolution.
Significant industrial unrest, especially in engineering trades (the 'May strikes').

1918   Representation of the People Act gives vote to all men over 21 and to women over 30 who are ratepayers or wives of ratepayers. Women entitled to become MPs.
Rationing of meat, butter and margarine introduced in February.
Armistice Day – 11 November.
Government introduces Out-of-Work Donation to support unemployed during demobilization period.
Education Act raises school leaving age to 14.
Maternity and Child Welfare Act extends maternity and child welfare services.
General election returns conservative-dominated coalition with Lloyd George as Prime Minister.

1919   Government unpegs Sterling–Dollar exchange rate and leaves Gold Standard.
League of Nations created at Paris Peace Conference.
Germany signs peace treaty with Allies at Versailles.
National memorial to the war dead, the Cenotaph, unveiled in Whitehall.
Housing and Town Planning Act (Addison Act) gives subsidies to local authorities and private builders for construction of dwellings.
Sex Disqualification Removal Act opens all professions, except the Church, to women.
Aliens Act restricts immigration of Jews, Chinese and other 'undesirable' foreigners.
Ministry of Health established.

1920   Rent Act extends scope of rent control.
Unemployment Insurance Act extends unemployment insurance to all manual workers outside railways, agriculture and government service.

Government of Ireland Act partitions Ireland into Ulster and the South, each with its own parliament.

1921 End of postwar boom. Committee under Sir Eric Geddes appointed to examine scope for public expenditure cuts.
British Legion organizes first national Poppy Day (11 Nov.).
Expansion of unemployment insurance scheme to include dependants' allowances.

1922 Implementation of so-called 'Geddes Axe' programme of public expenditure cuts.
Conservatives win majority in November general election.
Formation of British Broadcasting Company (to become the British Broadcasting Corporation in 1927).
Irish Free State comes into formal existence.

1923 German hyperinflation.
Women allowed to obtain divorce on same grounds as men, including adultery.
December general election: Conservatives lose overall majority but as largest party remain in office until new parliament convenes.

1924 Conservative government defeated when parliament meets in January.
First (minority) Labour government takes office with Ramsay MacDonald as Prime Minister.
Housing Act (Wheatley Act) increases public subsidy for houses built for rent at controlled levels.
Conservatives win October general election.

1925 Return to the Gold Standard at £1 = $4.86.

1926 General Strike lasts for 9 days. 4,000 strikers prosecuted, 1,000 imprisoned.

1927 Trade Disputes Act makes general strike illegal; restricts trade union political levy to workers who 'contract-in'.

1928 Payment of contributory pensions to widows and elderly people over 65.
Voting age for women reduced from 30 to 21.
First showing in British cinemas of 'talking pictures'.

1929 Local Government Act abolishes Poor Law Guardians and transfers their functions to local authorities.
General election gives Labour most seats; they form a minority government.
Wall Street Crash; beginning of depression in Britain.
Publication of Erich Maria Remarque's *All Quiet on the Western Front*.

1930 Poor Law renamed Public Assistance.
US Hawley-Smoot tariff initiates international trade war.

1931   Kreditanstalt collapses.
Financial and political crisis in Britain; Labour government breaks up;
three-party National Government formed.
Britain leaves Gold Standard.
Unemployment rises above three million.
National Government wins election, with a mainly Conservative majority.
Unemployment benefit cut by 10 per cent; long-term unemployed
subject to household means test. Widespread protest at these measures.

1932   Import duties introduced.
Britain begins to recover from depression.
Ottawa Conference agrees limited scheme of imperial preference with
dominions.
National Unemployed Workers' Movement (NUWM) organizes hunger
march to London.

1933   Hitler becomes German Chancellor.
'New Deal' begins in USA.

1934   NUWM hunger march to London followed by mass lobby of parliament.
Government restores unemployment benefit rates to 1931 level.
Special Areas Act introduces first regional economic policy.

1935   Results of Peace Ballot show substantial support for 'collective security'
through League of Nations.

1936   Death of George V; Edward VIII accedes to throne, but abdicates after
ten months; accession of George VI.
'Jarrow March' of unemployed to London.
Publication of J.M. Keynes's *The General Theory of Employment, Interest and
Money.*
Regular TV broadcasts begin from Alexandra Palace.
Hitler remilitarizes Rhineland; Franco leads right-wing rebellion in
Spain.
Foundation of pacifist Peace Pledge Union.

1937   First purpose-built holiday camp opened by Butlin's at Skegness.

1938   Munich agreement on Czechoslovakia signed with Hitler.

1939   Compulsory military service introduced in June. War against Germany
declared 3 September.

1940   Chamberlain resigns; coalition government formed under Churchill.
British troops evacuated from Dunkirk.
Purchase tax introduced to reduce demand for luxury goods.
'Battle of Britain' for control of air supremacy (July–Sept.).
London 'blitz' (Sept.–Oct.).

1941   'Lend-Lease agreement with US.

German invasion of Russia (June) brings Soviet Union into war on side of Allies.
Japanese attack on Pearl Harbour (Dec.) brings USA into war.
Determination of Needs Act ends household means test.
Discovery of penicillin.

1942　Beveridge Report published.

1943　USA, UK and USSR agree to found United Nations.
Income tax extended to include most workers; pay-as-you-earn scheme of direct deduction of tax from wages is introduced.

1944　'D-Day' landings in Normandy.
R.A. Butler's Education Act establishes basis for tri-partite division of secondary education, with selection based on the '11 plus' exam.
White papers on *Employment Policy, A National Health Service* and *Social Insurance* published.
Bretton Woods agreement setting up International Monetary Fund (IMF).
First operational use of a jet engine.

1945　War with Germany ends (7 May).
Family Allowance Act introduces cash payments to parents.
Labour government elected in July, Attlee PM.
War with Japan ends (15 Aug.).
End of Lend-Lease.

1946　National Insurance Act, National Health Service Act and National Assistance Act legislate for a 'cradle to the grave' welfare state.
New Towns Act establishes development corporations for new towns.
Bread rationing introduced in July.

1947　Nationalization of coal industry comes into effect.
Fuel crisis and power cuts (Feb.–March).
Anti-semitic riots in Britain.
School leaving age raised to 15.
Convertibility of sterling resumes at £1 = \$4.03 on 15 July and suspended on 20 August after massive loss of foreign currency reserves.
Britain signs General Agreement on Tariffs and Trade (GATT) to lower tariffs and trade restrictions.
India granted independence.

1948　'Bonfire of Control' announced (Feb.).
British Nationality Act.
'Appointed day': NHS, National Insurance, National Assistance implemented.
End of bread rationing.
Olympic games held in London.

1949   Devaluation of £ from $4.03 to $2.80.
       Formation of North Atlantic Treaty Organization (NATO).

1950   Labour government re-elected in February.
       Korean war begins.
       Formation of European Payments Union to allow multi-lateral trade
       among West European countries.

1951   Re-armament programme announced.
       Iron and steel industry nationalized.
       Bevan resigns from Labour cabinet over imposition of charges in NHS.
       Conservative government elected in October; Churchill Prime Minister.
       Festival of Britain celebrates postwar recovery.

1952   Death of George VI; accession of Elizabeth II.
       Last great London smog kills 4,000.
       Britain explodes its first atomic bomb.

1953   Iron and steel denationalized.
       Korean war ends.

1954   Food rationing ends.
       Opening of Kidbrooke, the first purpose-built comprehensive school.

1955   Eden replaces Churchill as Prime Minister; Conservatives win general
       election.
       ITV, the second (and commercial) television channel begins
       broadcasting.
       London declared a smokeless zone.

1956   Suez crisis.
       Creation of Colleges of Advanced Technology.
       Clean Air Act intensifies control of air pollution.
       First nuclear power station commissioned at Calder Hall.
       John Osborne's *Look Back in Anger* starts attack by angry young men on
       the 'establishment'.

1957   Macmillan replaces Eden as Prime Minister.
       Rent Act removes or loosens control of rents on over five million
       houses.
       European Economic Community (EEC) founded.

1958   Treasury ministers resign from government in belief that welfare
       expenditure is excessive.
       Coal rationing ends.
       Racist riots in Notting Hill.
       CND founded; first Aldermaston March.
       First eight-mile stretch of motorway opened.

1959   Conservative government re-elected.

National Insurance Act introduces earnings-related principle for contributions and some benefits.

Foundation of European Free Trade Association (EFTA) by Britain and other non-EEC nations.

1960   Compulsory military service discontinued.

Invention of contraceptive pill; in widespread use by 1963.

1961   Britain begins to negotiate for membership of EEC.

Committee of 100 organizes 'sit-down' demonstrations against nuclear weapons in London.

Staging of *Beyond the Fringe* and publication of *Private Eye* introduce satire movement.

1962   Commonwealth Immigrants Act introduces entry voucher scheme.

Local education authority mandatory grants for university students replace competitive examination for LEA scholarships.

Establishment of National Economic Development Council to facilitate economic cooperation between government, business and unions.

That Was the Week That Was extends satire to the BBC.

1963   Britain's entry to EEC refused.

The Beatles have three number one records.

Foundation of the National Theatre.

Robbins Report advocates the expansion of higher education.

1964   Labour government elected, Wilson Prime Minister.

Second public TV channel, BBC 2, begins transmission.

The mini-skirt arrives.

1965   Government announces a five-year National Plan for economic growth and creates Department of Economic Affairs.

Establishment of Prices and Incomes Board to regulate wage and price increases.

First Race Relations Act and formation of Race Relations Board.

Circular 10/65 requiring local education authorities to reorganize on comprehensive lines.

'Rediscovery' of poverty; foundation of Child Poverty Action Group.

Rent Act reintroduces rent control.

Prime Minister Harold Wilson nominates the Beatles for MBEs.

Metropolitan Police establishes 'Special Patrol Group' trained for riot control and gun use.

Abolition of death penalty.

1966   Labour win general election with increased majority.

National Assistance renamed Supplementary Benefit.

Colour TV introduced.

England win the football World Cup.

1967   Second application made to join EEC; again vetoed by France.
Devaluation of £ from $2.80 to $2.40.
Radio One is launched.
Students occupy London School of Economics.
Abortion Act allows legal termination of pregnancy. Family Planning
Act allows local health authorities to provide a family planning service.
Legalization of private homosexuality between consenting males over
21.
National Front formed from a number of extreme-right, anti-
immigration parties.

1968   Public expenditure cuts; NHS prescription charges re-imposed.
Commonwealth Immigrants Act aimed at excluding Kenyan asians.
Enoch Powell's 'Rivers of Blood' speech.
Seebohm Report published on re-organization of personal social
services.
Fulton Report calls for radical overhaul of civil service.
Collapse of Ronan Point tower block prompts re-evaluation of high-rise
housing policy.
Widespread student unrest; large anti-Vietnam war demonstration in
Grosvenor Square, outside US embassy.
Nudity on stage with the opening of the musical 'Hair' after abolition
of Lord Chamberlain's powers of theatre censorship.
Pope Paul VI issues encyclical *Humanae Vitae* condemning artificial
contraception.

1969   Voting age lowered from 21 to 18.
British troops sent to Northern Ireland on active service.
First polytechnics designated: Hatfield, Sheffield, Sunderland (30 were
designated between 1969–73). Open University established.
Divorce law liberalized by allowing 'irretrievable breakdown' in a
marriage as grounds for divorce.

1970   Equal Pay Act to prevent discrimination in pay between men and
women; implementation on a voluntary basis until 1975.
Conservatives win general election; Heath Prime Minister. Third British
attempt to join EEC begins.
Thatcher circular 10/70 intended to reverse 1965 policy on
comprehensivization of secondary education.
Expenditure on education exceeds that on defence for the first time.
First national conference of Women's Liberation Movement.

1971   Immigration Act introduces patriality condition which effectively ends
primary non-white immigration.
Industrial Relations Act gives government broad powers of intervention
in industrial disputes; widely opposed by trade unions.
Abolition of free milk for schoolchildren.

Collapse of Bretton Woods system of fixed exchange rates.
Decimalization of currency: £ s. d. replaced by £ p.

1972   Miners' strike leads to State of Emergency with large-scale power cuts.
Imposition of a statutory incomes policy.
Sterling 'floats' against other currencies.
British troops shoot dead civilians in Londonderry on 'Bloody Sunday'.
Abolition of Stormont government in Northern Ireland.
Major reform of structure of local government.
First publication of *Cosmopolitan* and *Spare Rib*.

1973   Britain becomes member of EEC.
School leaving age raised to 16.
First commercial radio stations begin broadcasting.
Foundation of Green Party (called People's Party to 1975, Ecology Party
to 1985).
Purchase tax replaced by value added tax (VAT).
OPEC raises price of oil.
Miners, power workers and railmen ban overtime. Three day-working
week introduced from end of December in face of power shortages.

1974   Heath calls February general election; miners' strike begins. No overall
majority at election. Labour form minority government; Wilson Prime
Minister.
Miners' strike and three-day week end in March.
Police national computer becomes operational, providing direct
information links to all police stations.
October general election sees Labour win majority.
Demonstration in Red Lion Square (London); clashes between
National Front and anti-fascist groups leaves one man dead.
First flight of Anglo-French supersonic passenger aircraft, Concorde.
Financial aid from government used to prop-up British Leyland.

1975   Referendum gives clear majority for staying in EEC.
Equal Pay Acts come into force; Sex Discrimination Act establishes
Equal Opportunities Commission.

1976   Wilson resigns; Callaghan becomes Prime Minister.
Third Race Relations Act establishes Commission for Racial Equality.
Police Complaints Board established.
Speech by Callaghan abandoning 'full employment' as a primary goal
of government policy.
Sterling crisis; Britain negotiates loan from IMF.
Introduction of cash limits on public expenditure programmes.

1977   Celebration of Queen's Silver Jubilee. BBC bans the Sex Pistols 'God
Save the Queen'. It reaches number two in the charts.
Fireman strike; troops called in to provide alternative service.

1978   Government imposes 5 per cent wage norm which is rejected by many unions.

'Winter of Discontent': industrial action in many sectors including hospital, municipal and water workers.

Proposals for devolution of government in Wales and Scotland fail to win necessary majority in referendum.

1979   Conservatives win general election; Thatcher Prime Minister.

1980   Riots in St Paul's district of Bristol.

Unemployment rises above two million for first time since 1938.

Education Act removes obligation on local education authorities to provide school meals and milk.

Housing Act gives council tenants the right to buy their homes.

Abolition of controls on international capital movements.

1981   Nationality Act.

Employment Act outlaws secondary picketing of industrial disputes.

Riots in Brixton (London), Toxteth (Liverpool) and Moss Side (Manchester).

Four leading Labour MPs form breakaway Social Democratic Party which forms electoral alliance with Liberal party.

Establishment of women's Peace Camp outside cruise missile base at Greenham Common.

1982   Unemployment rises above three million for first time since 1933.

Second commercial TV channel, Channel 4, begins broadcasting.

Falklands War.

Massive demonstration at Greenham Common against siting of cruise missiles.

Pope John Paul II visits Britain.

1983   Conservatives re-elected with increased majority: Thatcher Prime Minister.

Establishment of Youth Training Scheme (YTS).

Kinnock becomes leader of Labour party.

1984   Pit closures announced; miners announce all-out strike. Serious violence between police and miners at mass pickets. Largest-ever peace-time mobilization of police in mining areas. Over 12,000 miners arrested during the course of the strike.

Government begins major privatization programme with sale of 51 per cent of British Telecom to the public.

Divorce allowed after one year of marriage rather than three.

1985   Miners' strike finally collapses; miners decisively defeated.

Fowler review of social security proposes abolition of state earnings-related pension scheme and extension of private provision.

Riots in Handsworth (Birmingham), and on the Broadwater Farm Estate at Tottenham (London) during which a policeman is stabbed to death. Government abolishes the (Labour dominated) Greater London Council; most functions transferred to London boroughs. London becomes the only major city in Europe without a unitary governing authority.
Report by Church of England on 'Faith in the City' criticized by the government for its interpretation of the problems of inner city areas.
Live Aid concert for famine relief.

1986 'Big Bang' deregulation of City institutions.
British Gas privatized; the largest privatization of the decade.
Serious riots outside Wapping (London) printworks of Rupert Murdoch's News International after over 5,000 workers are dismissed for taking strike action.
UK records first ever peacetime deficit in balance of trade in manufactures.

1987 Conservatives re-elected; Thatcher Prime Minister. Four black MPs elected to new Parliament.
Government plans to replace local rating system with a flat-rate Community Charge ('Poll Tax') in Scotland from 1989 and in England and Wales from 1990.

1988 Immigration Act further restricts rights of relatives and dependents to settle in Britain.
Income Support and Social Fund replace Supplementary Benefit for low income households.
Education Act introduces a national curriculum, budgetary control by schools and opting-out of local education authority control.
Satanic Verses controversy.

1989 Economy overheats in boom engineered by Lawson, Chancellor of the Exchequer.

1990 British Nationality (Hong Kong) Act prevents all but a small (and wealthy) minority of Hong Kong Chinese holders of British passports from settling in Britain.
NHS and Community Care Act: hospital trusts and budgetary holding GPs encouraged.
Large riot in London, and disturbances throughout country, in opposition to Poll Tax.
Margaret Thatcher ousted from premiership by rebellion of senior ministers and conservative backbenchers; John Major replaces her as Prime Minister.

1991 Electricity industry privatized; coal, railways and post office remain the only major nationalized industries.

1992   Conservatives re-elected with reduced majority: Major Prime Minister.
Sterling forced out of European exchange rate mechanism by
speculative pressure on foreign exchanges.

1993   Poll Tax replaced by a new local tax on property (council tax).
Britain ratifies Maastricht Treaty, excluding the EC Social Charter.
30 new universities created, chiefly from former polytechnics.

Notes on Contributors

Paul Johnson is Reader in Social History at the London School of Economics. His publications include *Saving and Spending: the Working-Class Economy in Britain 1870–1939* (1985) and, with Jane Falkingham, *Ageing and Economic Welfare* (1992).

Maurice Kirby is Reader in Economic History at the University of Lancaster. He has published widely on themes of British economic and business history. His most recent book, *The Origins of Railway Enterprise: the Stockton and Darlington Railway, 1821–1863*, was published by Cambridge University Press in 1993.

Clive H. Lee is Professor of Historical Economics at the University of Aberdeen. His publications include *The Quantitative Approach to Economic History* (1977) and *The British Economy since 1700: A Macroeconomic Perspective* (1986). His latest book, *Scotland and the United Kingdom: The Economics of the Union,* will be published in 1994. His principal research interests lie in twentieth-century economic growth and the history of economic thought.

Peter Wardley has taught at the universities of Aberdeen, Durham, Hull, Leicester, Nottingham and Swansea and is Senior Lecturer in Modern Economic and Business History at the University of the West of England, Bristol. Dr Wardley's publications include a number of articles on twentieth-century economic history and the development of historical computing. He is joint editor of the annual review of information technology which appears in the *Economic History Review.*

E.P. Hennock is Emeritus Professor of Modern History at the University of Liverpool. His publications include *British Social Reform and German Precedents. The Case of Social Insurance 1880–1914* (1987) and 'Concepts of poverty in the British social surveys' in M. Bulmer, K. Bales and K.K. Sklar (eds), *The Social Survey in Historical Perspective 1880–1940* (1991). He is working on a comparative history of social policy in Britain and Germany from 1850 to *c.* 1970.

Pat Thane is Professor of Contemporary History at the University of Sussex. She is author of *The Foundations of the Welfare State* (1982), co-editor (with Professor Gisela Bock) of *Maternity and Gender Policies. Women and the Rise of the European Welfare States, 1880s–1950s* (1991). She has written numerous articles on the history of social welfare, of women and of Labour in modern Britain.

Tony Mason is Reader in Social History, at the University of Warwick. His books include *The General Strike in the North East* (1970), *Sport in Britain* (1988) and *Only a Game? Sport in the Modern World* (1993). He is working on a book about football in Latin America.

David Feldman is Lecturer in History at Birkbeck College, University of London. He is the author of *Englishmen and Jews: Social Relations and Political Culture* (1994).

Jon Lawrence has held posts at University College London and the University of Cambridge, and is now Lecturer in Modern History at the University of Liverpool. He has written on many aspects of modern British history, and is currently completing a book for Cambridge University Press on *Parties, Language and the People: Beyond the 'Rise of Class Politics', 1868–1918.*

Dudley Baines is Reader in Economic History at the London School of Economics. He previously taught at the University of Liverpool and has held visiting appointments at the Universities of Monash, Melbourne and the University of California, Berkeley. His publications include *Migration in a Mature Economy* (1986) and *Emigration from Europe, 1815–1930* (1991).

Bernard Harris is Lecturer in Social Policy in the Department of Sociology and Social Policy at Southampton University. He has written a number of articles on the social consequences of unemployment and the history of child health. He is currently writing a book on the history of the school medical service in England and Wales between 1908 and 1974, to be published by the Open University Press in 1995.

Martin Ceadel is a Fellow of New College, Oxford, and a Lecturer in Politics at the University of Oxford, having previously held university lectureships at first Sussex then Imperial College, London. He is the author of *Pacifism in Britain 1914–1945: the Defining of a Faith* and *Thinking about Peace and War*, as well as of a number of articles and essays, and is currently writing a two-volume study of the British peace movement since its origins.

Sue Bowden is Lecturer in Economic History at the University of Leeds. She has written articles on the electrical and motor vehicle industry in the interwar period.

Andrew Davies is Lecturer in Economic and Social History at the University of Liverpool. His publications include *Leisure, Gender and Poverty: Working-class Culture in Salford and Manchester, 1900–1939* (1992) and, co-edited with Steven Fielding, *Workers' Worlds: Cultures and Communities in Manchester and Salford, 1880–1939* (1992).

Peter Howlett is Lecturer in Economic History at the London School of Economics. He has published several articles on the British economy in the Second World War and is currently working on a book on the long term impact of the war.

Catherine R. Schenk is Lecturer in International Economic History at Royal Holloway and Bedford New College, University of London. She completed her BA and MA at the University of Toronto and was granted her Ph.D. from the LSE. She has published several works on British external economic policy after 1945.

Leslie Hannah is Professor of Business History at the London School of Economics. He has published extensively on twentieth-century business, and is currently working on British postwar economic development in international perspective.

Rodney Lowe is Reader in Economic and Social History at the University of Bristol. He is the author of many articles and books on twentieth-century Britain, including *Adjusting to Democracy* (1986) and *The Welfare State in Britain since 1945* (1993).

Michael Sanderson is Reader in Economic and Social History at the University of East Anglia, Norwich. His recent publications include *Education, Economic Change and Society in England 1780–1870* (1983, 1991), *From Irving to Olivier: a Social History of the Acting Profession in England 1880–1983* (1984), *Educational Opportunity and Social Change in England 1900–1980s* (1987), *The Missing Stratum, Technical School Education in England 1900–1990s* (1994). He is editor of the Economic History Society's Studies in Economic and Social History.

Tony Kushner is Marcus Sieff Lecturer in the History Department, University of Southampton. He has published *The Persistence of Prejudice: Antisemitism in Britain During the Second World War* (1989), *The Holocaust and the Liberal Imagination: a Social and Cultural History* (1994) and edited four books on racism and minorities in British history.

John Wolffe is Lecturer in Religious Studies at The Open University, and formerly taught history at the University of York. He is author of *The Protestant Crusade in Great Britain 1829–1860* (1991) and *God and Greater Britain: Religion and National Life in Britain and Ireland 1843–1945* (1994).

Paul Byrne is Head of the Department of European Studies at Loughborough University. He is the author of *The Campaign for Nuclear Disarmament* (1988) and a number of articles on Social Movements in Britain.

John Street is Lecturer in Politics at the University of East Anglia, Norwich. His publications include: *Rebel Rock: the Politics of Popular Music* (1986), *Politics and Technology* (1992) and (with John Greenaway and Steve Smith) *Deciding Factors in British Politics* (1991).

Index